Envision in Depth

READING, WRITING, AND RESEARCHING ARGUMENTS

THIRD EDITION

Christine L. Alfano and Alyssa J. O'Brien
Stanford University

PEARSON

Boston Columbus Indianapolis New York San Francisco Upper Saddle River
Amsterdam Cape Town Dubai London Madrid Milan Munich Paris Montreal Toronto
Delhi Mexico City Sáo Paulo Sydney Hong Kong Seoul Singapore Taipei Tokyo

Senior Acquisitions Editor: Brad Potthoff
Senior Development Editor: David B. Kear
Senior Supplements Editor: Donna Campion
Executive Marketing Manager: Roxanne McCarley
Executive Digital Producer: Stefanie Snajder
Digital Editor: Sara Gordus
Media Project Manager: Jessica Kajkowski
Production Manager: S.A. Kulig
Project Coordination, Text Design, and Electronic Page Makeup: PreMediaGlobal
Cover Designer/Manager: Wendy Ann Fredericks
Cover Art: © Ric Feld/Associated Press
Senior Manufacturing Buyer: Roy L. Pickering, Jr.
Printer/Binder: R.R. Donnelley/Crawfordsville
Cover Printer: Lehigh-Phoenix Color

Credits and acknowledgments borrowed from other sources and reproduced, with permission, in this textbook appear on the appropriate page within text [or on page 586].

Library of Congress Cataloging-in-Publication Data

Library of Congress Control Number: Cataloging in Publishing Data is on record at the Library of Congress.

10 9 8 7 6 5 4 3 2 —DOC—18 17 16 15 14

PEARSON

www.pearsonhighered.com

Student ISBN 10: 0-321-89996-2
Student ISBN 13: 978-0-321-89996-5
A la Carte ISBN 10: 0-321-89548-7
A la Carte ISBN 13: 978-0-321-89548-6

CONTENTS

PART II: RESEARCH ARGUMENTS 115

Chapter 4 Planning and Proposing Research Arguments 116

Chapter 5 Finding and Evaluating Research Sources 142

Chapter 15 Claiming Citizenship 546

PREFACE

The Story of this Book

Several years ago, we (the authors) met as colleagues in the Program in Writing and Rhetoric at Stanford University. Our shared focus on teaching writing through attention to both written and multimedia texts led us to look for materials we could use in the classroom that would provide both excellence in pedagogical instruction—attending to such essentials as thesis statements, style, integrating sources, and avoiding plagiarism—along with cutting edge and even *fun* examples that offer sound rhetorical models for analysis. While we were able to gather materials from a variety of sources, our students wanted a book rather than a collection of handouts, and they offered to read our drafts in progress and submit their own writing as examples we could incorporate into our writing textbook. The result was *Envision,* an argument and research guide that walks students through the processes of analysis, argument, source evaluation, and research-based essay writing while keeping the examples fresh and relevant to student lives. Students learn to analyze written texts and a range of visual texts, from cartoons and ads to websites and film, while working through the nuts of bolts of writing thesis statements, titles, introductions, conclusions, in-text citations, and MLA-style bibliographies. Additional writing lessons focus on diverse modes of argument, plagiarism, academic document design, multimodal production, and presentations.

After the release of *Envision*, we learned that writing instructors at colleges and universities around the country faced a predicament similar to ours, but that many had the additional challenge of needing a collection of substantive, timely, and interesting readings on a range of subjects that would interest students. In response, we created *Envision in Depth*, which contains the same material as the original *Envision*, but also includes Part IV, a section that offers a rich array of written articles, visual texts, and instructional guidance on how to wrestle with issues, respond in writing to key controversies, and develop research projects from source materials.

Each of these later chapters opens with an overview, asking pressing questions and presenting diverse perspectives to consider. We then provide a range of readings, visual texts, interviews, competing articles, and media excerpts on the topic, along with thorough pedagogical guidelines to help students engage critically with the material. Headnotes frame each piece and offer essential context. "Reflect and Write" questions follow each text to provide opportunities for class discussion, written assignments, and even research projects on related materials. The prompts for collaborative writing enable in-class group work or simply ideas for additional assignments. Finally, each chapter concludes with a robust series of questions: both "Analyzing Perspectives on the Issue" and "From Reading to Research Assignments" prompt students to put readings in conversation, consider multiple interpretations at once, or conduct independent research and writing to advance their skills and expertise in meeting key composition outcomes.

As we now finalize the third edition of *Envision in Depth*, our continued hope is that this textbook might help students develop the skills, confidence, and enthusiasm for writing, researching, and communicating effectively about issues that matter to them.

What's New in this Edition

Based on extremely helpful, detailed, and insightful feedback from reviewers, instructors, and hundreds of students who have used the book, we have made significant revisions for this edition. With regard to Chapters 1 through 9, these changes enable students and teachers to:

- **Focus on the Writing Process**: This brand new edition prioritizes process by including exercises in every chapter called "Writer's Practice" that instruct students in a variety of writing skills, including how to compose a thesis statement, develop effective introductions and conclusions, evaluate sources, integrate quotations in a research essay, format a bibliography in MLA style, experiment with gestures in a presentation, or use the rhetorical appeals in spoken, written, or multimedia communication.
- **Learn from Model Writing:** New and updated annotated articles and student writing show readers exactly how to move from title to thesis, demonstrate methods for including direct quotations from sources, and compare various approaches to argumentation. This edition features written examples in every chapter, so that students can master writing about verbal—as well as visual—texts.

- **Explore Controversial Issues:** Chosen to speak to student interests, the new articles and sample student writing in this edition focus on gun metaphors in political discourse, genetically modified food, the Dove campaign for real beauty, American attitudes towards charity and international aid, research archives in Nazi propaganda, online gaming communities, and TED talks as a form of activism.
- **Examine Modes of Argument:** Now featuring three modes of argument instruction, this revised edition covers classical rhetoric, Toulmin, and Rogerian approaches to establishing claims and relying on evidence; an annotated reading demonstrates and compares these strategies of argument.
- **Understand Advanced Concepts in Rhetoric:** This edition's more detailed instruction in rhetoric takes students beyond a focus on audience and persona—and deeper than the appeals of *ethos*, *pathos*, and *logos*—to consider *kairos* and *doxa*, as well as *exigency* and *motive*. In addition, this edition features an expanded coverage and discussion of rhetorical fallacies. When focusing on the canons of rhetoric and the branches of oratory, contemporary examples illustrate these classical concepts and make the material come alive for student readers. Innovative end of chapter questions challenge students to complete writing assignments that engage these terms as sophisticated tools of analysis and argument.
- **Engage Deeply with the Research Process:** The expanded section on annotated bibliographies asks students to practice skills of summary and analysis when dealing with their sources. In addition, more detailed guidelines for conducting surveys and interviews helps prepare students for their own fieldwork for their research projects.
- **Acquire and Retain Writing Lessons:** The "Writer's Process" feature at the end of every chapter helps students put together all the lessons of the chapter in order to get started on the assignments, while the "Pre-Writing Checklist" in the first assignment provides summary and reinforcement, enabling retention.

With regard to the changes in **Part IV**—where students can explore topics in rich complexity through engaging with a range of interrelated texts—our reviewers and our students wanted us to focus our chapters down to one key theme, but also to explore that theme in greater depth and diversity. We listened and revised each multi-part chapter to center on one core topic that would capture and sustain student interest through analysis of contemporary examples across a range of media. In addition, we designed the following new features:

- **Engaging Readings:** This third edition of *Envision in Depth* now provides streamlined chapters that will interest students across the spectrum, through a focus on food politics, life online, body image, media and sports culture, situations of conflict and resilience, and issues of cultural identity, citizenship, and rights.
- **Purposeful Pedagogy:** *Envision in Depth* now delivers instruction geared towards writers working together, including a new chapter prompt, "Writing Collaboratively," that can be used for immediate in-class work as well as for homework projects. We also modified the analytical questions, writing assignments, and research projects to connect more clearly with the previous nine chapters. "Seeing Connections" notes in the margins point students back to lessons learned previously. Synthesizing prompts at the end of each chapter challenge students to put the readings in conversation or direct students towards specific research sources in order to develop their own research arguments.
- **Critical Literacy of a Range of Texts:** After carefully defining and demonstrating the concept of the "text" and how writing today spans a wide range of media—from traditional essays to tweets, from analytical articles to advertisements and editorial cartoons, from scripts to be read out loud to multimodal arguments that run on their own—this new edition offers both instruction in and examples of such multimedia "writing." Each newly focused chapter of *Envision in Depth* provides a range of texts for analysis and then asks students to reflect and write about each one, building their critical literacy and their academic competencies as writers.

The Substance at a Glance

From the very beginning, our philosophy in *Envision in Depth* has been to teach students about writing, rhetoric, and research by considering the different modes of argument that operate in our culture every day. Each chapter uses interactive and engaging lessons, and focuses both on analyzing and producing words (print materials, articles, blog posts, and even tweets) as well as on writing *about* images and other contemporary media (cartoons, ads, photographs, films, video games, and websites, to name a few). In this way, the book teaches *critical literacy* about all kinds of texts. Moreover, we provide numerous student writing examples and professional, published readings—both with annotations—in order to reinforce the writing lessons in each chapter and to demonstrate how students might successfully implement such strategies in their own texts. Our aim is to help students accomplish specific writing tasks for your courses as they encounter, analyze, research, and produce a range of compositions.

We have designed *Envision in Depth* to be flexible enough to adjust to different curricula or teaching styles. You can either follow the chronological sequence of chapters—moving from analysis to argument, bringing in research, then considering design and presentations—or you can consult the chapters and assignments in any order that meets the needs of your course and curriculum. More specifically, we have organized *Envision in Depth* into four parts:

Part I: Analysis and Argument

Chapters 1 through 3 encourage students to become proficient, careful readers of rhetorical texts and to learn practical strategies for crafting thesis statements, rhetorical analysis essays, and synthesis essays incorporating various perspectives. Students learn how to analyze the forms of persuasion in verbal and visual texts—from short articles and essays to political cartoons, ads, and photos—with an emphasis on rhetorical conventions. At the same time, we teach students key rhetorical concepts for effective communication, such as attending to audience, understanding rhetorical appeals and fallacies, and attending to exigency and motive.

Part II: Research Arguments

Chapters 4 through 7 focus on strategies of research argument for sustained writing projects. The lessons in this section of the book take students through key writing practices: writing a research proposal; keeping a research log; locating sources; integrating visuals; outlining, drafting, and revising; integrating sources in writing; and understanding the complexities of evaluating and documenting sources. Students have sample proposals, outlines, and drafts to consult as well as articles, propaganda posters, and film trailers to analyze. They learn how to identify, assess, and incorporate research into their own arguments while avoiding plagiarism and accomplishing successful documentation of sources. A newly revised chapter on MLA style offers visual modes for understanding documentation logic and an extensive array of examples to follow.

Part III: Design and Delivery

Chapters 8 and 9 teach students how to format and present their writing effectively. Students learn about document design—both for academic papers and for visual arguments—as well as how to translate written work into effective presentations. Students receive guidance on how to compose an abstract and bio as well as how to design op-ads, photo essays, websites, and multimodal arguments. They also gain important skills in practicing the canons of rhetoric and differentiating among levels of decorum.

Part IV: Readings

The last six chapters expand the scope of the book through readings, writing activities, and research prompts on clusters of topics. Our revised selections for the third edition focus on today's most engaging topics, which we hope will interest both students and teachers. These topics include debates over the food industry, competing perspectives on body image, explorations of new writing and social media technologies, challenges to contemporary sports culture, and current controversies regarding citizenship.

Online Resources

The Instructor's Manual

The Instructor's Manual for *Envision in Depth* provides teachers with pedagogical advice for each chapter, including conceptual overviews, teaching tips for working with the main concepts and reading selections in the chapter, and suggestions for classroom exercises and writing assignments. The Instructor's Manual also offers sample syllabi and ideas for organizing the reading and exercises according to days of the week. For access to the Instructor's Manual, please contact your Pearson representative.

MyWritingLab: Now Available for Composition

MyWritingLab is an online homework, tutorial, and assessment program that provides engaging experiences for today's instructors and students. MyWritingLab's hallmark features are now combined with new features designed specifically for composition instructors and their course needs: New Writing Assignments, including a composing space for students and customizable Rubrics for assessing and grading student writing; multimedia instruction on all aspects of composition—not just grammar; and, Item Analysis of class performance through advanced reporting. For students who enter the course under-prepared, MyWritingLab offers pre-assessments and personalized remediation so they see measurable outcomes and instructors spend less time in class reviewing the basics. Rich multimedia resources are built in to engage students and support faculty throughout the course. Visit www.mywritinglab.com for more information.

Meeting WPA Outcomes for Writers

Each chapter offers specific activities and assignments designed to help students meet the WPA Outcomes for First-Year Composition. The following table indicates the chapter's specific learning goals as they are aligned with the WPA outcomes statement, the major assignments offered in each chapter, and the media focus.

MAJOR ASSIGNMENTS AND LEARNING OBJECTIVES

CHAPTER TITLE	WPA OBJECTIVES MET BY THIS CHAPTER	MAJOR ASSIGNMENTS	MEDIA FOCUS
1: Analyzing Texts and Writing Thesis Statements	■ Understanding the rhetorical situation ■ Considering relationships among audience, text, and purpose ■ Textual analysis ■ Developing thesis statements	■ Personal narrative essay ■ Rhetorical analysis essay	Cartoons, comic strips, and editorial articles
2: Understanding Strategies of Persuasion	■ Strategies of argumentation ■ Understanding rhetorical appeals: *logos, pathos, ethos* ■ Fallacies or exaggerated uses of rhetorical appeals ■ Importance of *kairos* and *doxa*	■ Contextual analysis essay ■ Analysis of rhetorical appeals and fallacies ■ Comparison/contrast essay	Advertisements and written analysis of ads
3: Composing Arguments	■ Introductions and conclusions ■ Arrangement and structure of argument ■ Considering various modes of argument: Toulmin, Rogerian ■ Developing persona and rhetorical stance ■ Addressing opposing opinion in an argument ■ Writing with style	■ Position paper ■ Classical argument assignment ■ Toulmin and Rogerian argument analysis ■ Synthesis essay	Photographs, newspaper articles and images, opinion pieces, visual analysis essays
4: Planning and Proposing Research Arguments	■ Generating and narrowing research topics ■ Prewriting strategies ■ Developing a research plan ■ Drafting a formal proposal	■ Visual brainstorm ■ Research log ■ Informal research plan ■ Research proposal	Propaganda posters, historical images, rhetorical analysis essay
5: Finding and Evaluating Research Sources	■ Research strategies ■ Evaluating sources ■ Distinguishing between primary and secondary sources ■ Locating sources ■ Conducting field research, interviews, and surveys ■ Best practices for note taking	■ Critical evaluation of sources ■ Annotated bibliography ■ Field research ■ Dialogue of sources	Magazine and journal covers, websites, and annotated biliographies

CHAPTER TITLE	WPA OBJECTIVES MET BY THIS CHAPTER	MAJOR ASSIGNMENTS	MEDIA FOCUS
6: Organizing and Writing Research Arguments	■ Organizing and outlining arguments ■ Multiple drafts and revision ■ Integrating research sources: summary, paraphrase, and quotations ■ Writing and peer review	■ Formal outline ■ Peer review and response ■ Integrating sources ■ Writing the research argument	Film and movie trailers, film review and critique, drafts and revisions
7: Avoiding Plagiarism and Documenting Sources	■ Understanding intellectual property ■ Best practices in documenting sources: in-text citation and notes ■ MLA style rules and examples	■ Working with multimedia sources ■ Ethical note-taking ■ Citation practice ■ Producing a Works Cited list	Documentation examples; MLA style essay
8: Designing Arguments	■ Understanding the conventions of academic writing ■ Writing an abstract and bio ■ Decorum: appropriate voice and tone ■ Relationship between rhetorical situation and types of argument ■ Formatting and genre considerations	■ Writing an abstract ■ Constructing a bio ■ Integrating images in academic writing ■ Creating electronic arguments using multimedia (audio and visual)	Academic design examples, abstracts, bios, op-ads, photo essays, Websites, and multiple media
9: Delivering Presentations	■ Transforming written arguments into visual or spoken texts ■ Strategies of design and delivery ■ Writing a script: strategies of slideware ■ Using technology to address a range of audiences	■ Converting written to oral discourse ■ Writing a script ■ Developing a multimedia presentation ■ Learning delivery techniques	Presentations, poster sessions, PowerPoint and other slide software, multimedia writing

Acknowledgments

We'd like to offer our deep thanks to all those who helped us with the book over the years, and in the revision of this edition in particular. We are grateful to the reviewers whose comments informed our decisions about this revision: John Aramini, Erie Community College; Shannon Blair, Central Piedmont Community College; Ron Brooks, Oklahoma State University; Michael J. Compton, The University of Memphis; Linsey Cuti, Kankakee Community College; Trevor Dodge, Clackamas Community College; Susanna Kelly Engbers, Kendall College of Art & Design; Nicole P. Fisk, University of South Carolina-Columbia; Brittany Hall, Columbia State Community College; Susan Hanson, Texas State University; Liz Holtzinger-Jennings, Penn State University; Bethany Lee, Purdue University North Central; Chad Eric Littleton, University of Tennessee at Chattanooga; Vincent Piturro, Metro State College of Denver; Glenda E. Potts, J. Sargeant Reynolds Community College; Jenny Rice, University of Kentucky; Andrew Scott, Ball State University; Tracey Sherard, College of the Canyons; Suba Subbarao, Oakland Community College.

We extend our thanks to our colleagues at Stanford who have supported our revisions to *Envision in Depth*, particularly Paul Bator, Marvin Diogenes, Patti Hanlon-Baker, Chris Kamrath, Andrea A. Lunsford, Kelly Myers, and Zach Waggoner, whose advice, scholarship, and inspiring pedagogy helped enrich our work in this text.

We thank our expert team at Pearson, the dedicated drivers of the *Envision* series: Joe Opiela, Brad Potthoff, and David Kear; Kristy Zamagni and her staff at PreMedia Global; our contract support Jim Miller and Craig Leonard, as well as our first editor, Lynn Huddon, who from the start believed in this textbook.

We are grateful to all our students, both those whose enthusiasm for learning continues to challenge us to become better teachers, and especially those whose work appears in this edition: Dexian Cai, James Caputo, Vincent Chen, Molly Cunningham, Bries Deerrose, Natalie Farrell, Molly Fehr, Lindsay Funk, Tanner Gardner, Wendy Hagenmaier, Conor Hendriksen, Aaron Johnson, Amanda Johnson, Liz Kreiner, Hailey Larkin, Alina Lanesberg, Max Oswald, Jake Palinksy, Wan Jin Park, Stephanie Parker, Michael Rothenberg, Sophie Shank, Stella Hayoung Shin, Miranda Alfano-Smith, Nicholas Spears, Morgan Springer, Zachary Templeton, Tommy Tsai, Carrie Tsosie, and Michael Zeligs.

Finally, we extend our greatest appreciation to those who have rallied us all the way through: our friends and families. Thank you.

Christine L. Alfano and Alyssa J. O'Brien

Part I

ANALYSIS AND ARGUMENT

CHAPTER 1
Analyzing Texts and Writing Thesis Statements

CHAPTER 2
Understanding Strategies of Persuasion

CHAPTER 3
Composing Arguments and Position Papers

CHAPTER 1

Analyzing Texts and Writing Thesis Statements

Chapter Preview Questions

1.1 How do we read and analyze texts rhetorically?

1.2 What are effective strategies for analyzing rhetorical texts?

1.3 How does writing change across diverse media?

1.4 How should I brainstorm parts of an essay, including the thesis statement?

Words and images everywhere try to persuade us to think about the world in certain ways. We can see this persuasive power at every turn: from Facebook status posts with article links, to tweets 140 characters long with photos attached, colorful iPad ads, political campaign posters and cartoons, blog posts, and even video footage circulated online. In each case, these texts try to move us, convince us to buy something, shape our opinions, or make us laugh. By **texts**, we mean what people write in words (verbal rhetoric), what people say (oral rhetoric), and multimedia texts made up of both words and images (visual and multimodal rhetoric).

FIGURE 1.1 Mike Luckovich's political cartoon demonstrates through words and images how people commonly view "rhetoric" as a negative and dangerous form of communication.

Consider the text in Figure 1.1 by Mike Luckovich, a Pulitzer Prize winning cartoonist who publishes in the *Atlanta Journal Constitution*. Luckovich created this cartoon after the assassination attempt on Representative Gabrielle Giffords outside a Safeway store in Tucson, Arizona. Six people were killed, including a nine-year-old girl. Giffords herself was critically injured, along with 12 other people. The incident raised concerns over political speeches and website images that had used gun metaphors to target Democrats such as Giffords in upcoming elections. Some feared that such language and imagery might have contributed to the attack. In response to the controversy, Luckovich composed a cartoon as a persuasive text indicating his view. How does his text use both words and images to persuade audiences to think a certain way about the top term: "Violent Rhetoric"? Look at the hierarchy of values, beginning with "happy talk" at the bottom, moving through "warm conversation" and "friendly debate" to a more vigorous "spirited discussion." Notice how the words then become more negative, including "angry discourse" and "hateful speech." While we usually consider "hateful speech" to be the worst form of communication, Luckovich places "violent rhetoric" above it, as the very apex of dangerous discourse. The cartoon is ironic since when most people think of "rhetoric," they often think of "political rhetoric," which they perceive as either "empty" and meaningless (all talk, no action) or worse, as negative: harmful to the reputation of others, fear-mongering, and even hateful. The cartoon emphasizes this common view of rhetoric by placing the words "violent rhetoric" at the top.

But understanding this cartoon depends not just on analyzing the words. The location of words in particular places within the visual—and the visual elements themselves—also contribute in crucial ways to the meaning of the text. The lowered flag, for instance, might indicate that Giffords nearly died from her critical injuries, and indeed six people did die. The purposeful lowering of the flag to half-mast is itself a form of visual communication, well understood across America; it represents the nation's act of honoring a deceased person. The dome of the Capital Building in the background suggests that the government has lowered the flag and wants people to move from "violent rhetoric" to "spirited debate." In this way, the cartoon combines words and visual details to suggest both a tribute to Giffords and the need for calmer, gentler political communication. That is our understanding of the cartoon's argument when we **analyze the text rhetorically**. As you develop your skills of critical thinking and rhetorical analysis, you will also learn how to interpret and write your own arguments about such texts.

At the same time, you will learn how to apply your skills of analysis across a range of media, including printed or spoken words. With regard to the assassination attempt, many writers commented on the event through newspaper articles, on blogs, via email, and on Facebook or Twitter. In a blog post, for example, Barbara Morrill used the term *rhetoric* right in her title: "Violent Rhetoric and the Attempted Assassination of Gabrielle Giffords." While the title seems objective in tone, the writer then turns to very strong language in the opening paragraph in order to connect the two parts of the title:

> In the two days since the attempted assassination of Rep. Gabrielle Giffords, the debate has been raging over the culpability of the violent rhetoric that is so commonplace in today's political climate. Which of course has led to the rapid-fire peddling of false equivalencies by the right, where now, saying a congressional district is being targeted is the same as actually putting crosshairs on a district and saying it's time to "RELOAD."

By accusing the right of "rapid-fire peddling," the author frames words through a gun metaphor in a way that creates a vivid image in the reader's mind. She also refers to the metaphoric language that politicians had used—targeting a district, crosshairs, and "reload"—as evidence for her claim. The details of her written text parallel the elements of the cartoon (Figure 1.1). As you develop your skills of analysis about texts, keep in mind that you can understand them better if you look closely at all the specific elements, whether verbal or visual. To grasp this concept, let's follow one hypothetical student—we'll call her Alex—as she walks across campus with her newly acquired analysis skills.

1.1 How do we read and understand texts rhetorically?

UNDERSTANDING TEXTS RHETORICALLY

By shadowing Alex and noticing what she notices, you can construct her **personal narrative**, or written account of her journey, about the rhetorical texts she sees along the way. Everything from a poster in the dorm to a Tumblr page on a roommate's laptop—these are all rhetorical texts. Once you recognize how these texts try to influence your perspective about the world, then you can decide whether or not to agree with the many messages you encounter on a regular basis.

Let's begin in Alex's dorm room, just an average institutional room, which Alex and her roommate have decorated with Altoids ads they've ripped from magazines (see Figure 1.2). Preparing to leave, Alex glances at the image of the nurse stands above the written words, "Now this won't hurt a bit." The clichéd expression makes the ad humorous, since the nurse is holding not a needle, but rather the "curiously strong" Altoids, and through this humor it persuades consumers to buy the mints. There's also a large poster for the women's basketball team on one wall, and a small Snoopy comic about school prayer taped above the computer screen. Each text uses both words and images to persuade viewers, whether that be to support a sports team or think about a social issue in a new way.

FIGURE 1.2 The sarcastic Altoid ad from Alex's room.

As Alex walks down the hall, past the rooms of other students, she scans the photos and magazine clippings on their doors (all of which are rhetorical texts), and she pauses in the lounge where several of her friends are gathered around a large flat-screen TV watching a rerun of *The Colbert Report*. She considers Colbert's strategic use of patriotic symbols, such as a star on a blue background and a bald eagle (see Figure 1.3), as an argument for his status as a leader of American news and popular opinion. She watches until the show breaks for a commercial for Nike shoes, then she continues, down a stairwell decorated with student event flyers—a charity dance for the victims of a recent earthquake, a rally against immigration laws, a dorm meeting to plan the ski trip—and she pushes her way out into the cool autumn air.

FIGURE 1.3 Alex's glimpse of Colbert on TV.

Outside, Alex looks down at her smartphone and scrolls through recent Instagram posts as she walks along. She sees one friend's updated profile photo, another's pictures from a recent trip to New York City, and a third's reposting of a popular meme about studying. Putting away the phone, she notices the student newspaper on a bench and glances at the cover, where she sees a cartoon designed to grab her attention and raise her awareness

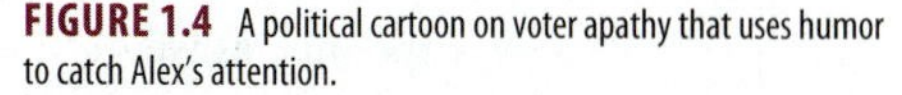

FIGURE 1.4 A political cartoon on voter apathy that uses humor to catch Alex's attention.

Source: © Tribune Media Services, Inc. All Rights Reserved. Reprinted with permission

FIGURE 1.5 A hand drawn student poster for an activist event.

about student apathy in political elections (see Figure 1.4). By analyzing the cartoon, she finds herself persuaded by its argument that students prefer popular culture (such as *American Idol*) over politics (such as governmental elections), and she decides to share the newspaper with her professor.

Now Alex has only two minutes to get to class, so she walks briskly past the student union with its bulletin boards covered with notices of upcoming events, such as one for the "Students for a More Just Society," which uses words in an eye-catching design in order to announce its brown bag activist event (see Figure 1.5). Passing the administration building, Alex observes students waving signs that protest the conditions of janitorial workers. She then weaves alongside a cluster of gleaming steel buildings that constitute the engineering quad and pauses at a thin metal sculpture called *Knowledge* guarding the entrance to the library. Finally, she reaches her destination: her 101 Law and Society course on Contemporary Legal Issues. But she's late. The professor has started already, and Alex watches as a slide consisting of words and clip art takes up the large screen at the front of the hall. The purpose of that text, she knows, is to educate her and challenge her to think carefully about free speech and gun control. The course TA gives Alex a handout, and she sits down in the back row, opening her laptop with the intention of taking notes. She's immediately distracted by the pages of Facebook, Twitter, Tumblr, and other sites that call for her attention. Closing those windows, she opens a blank word processing document instead, and then turns to examine the handout, which includes an excerpt from a Bloomberg news article on the use of gun metaphors in political campaigns.

With Alex safely at her seat, think about how many texts you noticed along her journey. Flyers, ads, posters, cartoons, videos, websites, newspapers, television shows, photographs, memes, statues, signs, PowerPoint slides, even architectural design: each is an example of rhetoric. Why? Because each text offers a specific message to a particular audience. Each one is a persuasive act. Once you begin to look at the world rhetorically, you'll see that just about everywhere you are being persuaded to agree, act, buy, attend, or accept an argument: rhetoric permeates our cultural landscape. Just as we did for Alex, you might pay attention to the *rhetoric* that you find on your way to class and then construct your own personal narrative consisting of words and images.

STRATEGIES FOR ANALYZING RHETORICAL TEXTS

1.2 What are effective strategies for analyzing rhetorical texts?

Offering one of the earliest definitions, the ancient Greek philosopher Aristotle characterized **rhetoric** as *the ability to see the available means of persuasion in any given situation*. While Aristotle's lessons in rhetoric emerged in the fourth century BCE as a form of instruction for oral communication—specifically, to help free men represent themselves in court—today, the term *rhetoric* has expanded to include any verbal, visual, or multimedia text that aims to persuade a specific audience in a certain place and time. To understand how such texts work, you need to analyze how each one targets a specific **audience**, how each has been composed by a specific **author**, and how each conveys a particular **argument**. This dynamic relationship is called the **rhetorical situation**, and we have represented it with a triangle in Figure 1.6.

As a writer, when you compose persuasive texts, you need to determine which strategies will work to convince your audience in a particular situation. There are many different choices to consider, and that is why rhetoric is both a dynamic and a practical art. Imagine, for instance, that you are involved in the following rhetorical situations and have to decide which writing, speaking, or multimedia communication strategies would be most persuasive for each case.

- **Attend to *audience*.** As a politician who has to *write an op-ed* for a newspaper or *speak at an interview* on CNN about your definition of marriage, you would use strikingly different metaphors and statistics depending on which constituency (or *audience*) you are addressing.
- **Attend to *author*.** As a common citizen, whether a student, parent, educator, or police officer, who wants to publicize a message against drug use to local middle school students, you might compose *speeches, emails, or posters with*

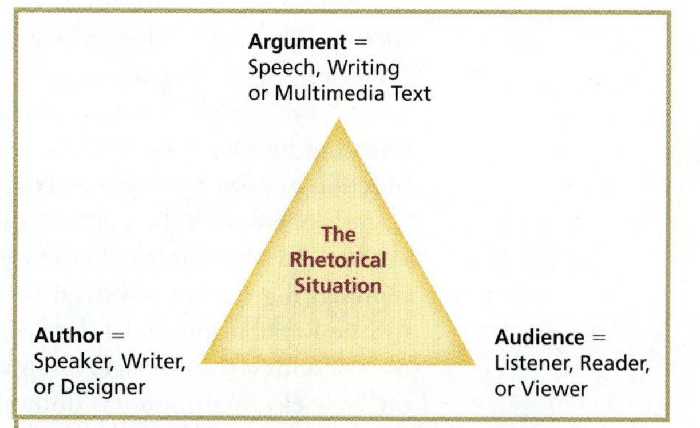

FIGURE 1.6 The rhetorical situation is dynamic and governs all communication, whether oral, written, or multimedia.

information graphics, and each one would be designed based on your position (as *author*)—teacher or police? student or parent?—while trying to reach the middle school audience.

- **Attend to *argument*.** In your first job as a fashion industry retailer who needs to adapt the company's marketing campaign to suit a range of media, you would revise the text (or *argument*) of the advertisements to fit the media, whether it was *Internet videos*, *TV spots*, or *print magazines*.

What these examples reveal is that rhetoric since Aristotle has been linked to *action*. It is far from "empty" but rather can motivate audiences to produce particular outcomes. As rhetoric scholar Lloyd Bitzer, who famously wrote about the rhetorical situation shown in Figure 1.6, argued: "Rhetoric is a mode of altering reality [...] by the creation of discourse which *changes reality* through the mediation of thought and action." More generally, you can understand rhetoric as any form of communication, for as Stanford Professor Andrea A. Lunsford explains, "Rhetoric is the art, practice, and study of human communication."

Understanding Visual Rhetoric

When persuasion—discourse or communication intended to change—happens through visual means, we call it **visual rhetoric** or "writing" with images. Since you are already familiar with the way that ads, movie trailers, posters, comics—and even memes and gifs—try to make you view an issue in a particular way, we will begin by focusing on *visual rhetoric*. Then, we will *transfer* what you have learned to *written rhetoric*. Moreover, as you begin to approach visual and verbal texts with a more critical eye, you will develop **critical literacy**—a life skill that entails knowing how to read, analyze, understand, and even create texts that function as powerful arguments about culture and the world around us.

Let's begin with the political cartoon in Figure 1.7 by Dan Reynolds. Produced during the 2012 elections, the cartoon uses well-known images representing the two political parties in the United States: an elephant for the Republicans and a donkey for the Democrats. But then, the cartoonist adds a third image: a hippopotamus. Notice that instead of stars on its back, the hippo has dollar signs. The word next to the image—"Hippocrit"—makes a play on words, suggesting that today's politicians are "hypocrites." But in what way are politicians false or pretending to have virtue that they lack? The visual element of the dollar signs persuades us to see that it is through their financial dishonesty that they deceive the public. Reynolds' criticism of today's political parties occurs primarily through *visual rhetoric*, or the elements within the third image in this cartoon. The *argument* of the text depends on the *audience* viewing the contrast between the stars and the dollar signs and understanding the nature of the hypocrisy.

FIGURE 1.7 The details of this cartoon makes a primarily visual argument about political parties in the United States today.

The comic strip in Figure 1.8. depends even more on visual elements to make its argument. Clay Bennett published this cartoon in the *Chattanooga Times Free Press* as a visual commentary on the state of the economy. Indeed, only the word "Economy" appears in the comic strip, suggesting the subject of the image. As you follow the red line from frame to frame, what interpretation do you begin to make? What point comes to mind when you see the red line end up, literally, in the toilet? In fact, the combination of the dark red line (resembling a stock market chart), the man's business attire, and his puzzled expression, all work together to make a powerful statement about the economic downturn in the United States and even globally. Thus while comic strips, political cartoons, animations, and other visual texts may seem merely informative about current events—or just plain funny—they do serve as an important mode of communicating ideas and making statements about social issues.

FIGURE 1.8 Bennett's series of images in this comic strip offer a logical visual argument about the state of the economy in the US.

One way to develop your critical literacy is to understand how cartoonists "write" with certain tools. The comic strip in Figure 1.9 offers a rare look at the research and writing process of a famous cartoonist, Marisa Acocella Marchetto, whose work has appeared in the *New Yorker*, *Glamour*, and the *New York Times*. The comic strip, from Marchetto's 2006 graphic novel memoir, *Cancer Vixen: A True Story*, presents a tremendous amount of information in a seemingly simple visual-verbal text.

In the second frame of the comic (see Figure 1.9), we see an image of Marchetto's hand using a pen to sketch out the drawing itself. In the bubble above the hand, Marchetto explains her writing process:

> "Cartoonists don't just sit there and draw out of their heads. Some of us are reporters. I go out on assignments like a regular reporter, except I write and draw my stories in comic strip form, which is called *reportage.*"

In the next frame, she builds her credibility as a reporter by stating her experience: "I was the *New York Times'* first cartoonist ever with 'the strip,' which ran every other Sunday in 'Styles.'" The subsequent frame of the comic displays her many press passes, and she again mentions the authority of her first job placement: "When people I'd worked for 'the paper of

FIGURE 1.9 Marchetto's "writing tools" include pens, sketch books, an audio recorder and even a camera.

record,' that calmed them down somewhat." With these two frames, Marchetto exposes the prejudice she faced as a writer of comic strips and visual media. People she interviewed during her research as a reporter did not take her seriously at first because she worked in a visual medium: the cartoon. But the images and words of this comic defuse that stereotype by presenting her work as legitimate and valuable in society. Her comic then educates us, as readers, by depicting the "tools of the trade" she uses in her *reportage.*

As Marchetto's comic reveals, "writing" also includes producing audio recordings, drawing cartoons, and composing graphic novels: these are actually valid forms of researching and writing arguments about the world. In fact, such multimodal texts can sometimes be even more powerful than words alone in reaching audiences.

This is the argument made by Scott McCloud in his groundbreaking book, *Understanding Comics*, one of the first texts to use visual rhetoric in order to help readers understand visual rhetoric:

> When pictures are more abstracted from "reality," they require greater levels of perception, more like words. When words are bolder, more direct, they require lower levels of perception and are received faster, more like pictures.

McCloud tells us we need to develop "greater levels of perception," or critical literacy, in order to read with greater levels of perception. In fact, we can look to the brief passage quoted here as an example of persuasive written rhetoric, in which McCloud makes very deliberate choices to strengthen his point. Notice how his words use comparison-contrast (pictures versus words), qualified language ("reality"), and parallel structure (both sentences move from "When" to a final phrase beginning with "more like") in order to convince his audience that images and words operate in similar ways. Such attention to detail is the first step in *rhetorical analysis*—looking at the way the writer chooses the most effective means of persuasion to make a point.

What is interesting about McCloud's rhetoric, though, is that he relies not just on written strategies of persuasion, but also on a combination of words and images to make his point. To fully appreciate McCloud's rhetorical decisions, we need to consider the passage in its original context. As you can see in Figure 1.10, McCloud amplifies his argument about comics by using the form of the graphic novel itself, creating a persuasive text that employs a strategic combination of words and images.

This complex diagram relies on the visual-verbal relationship itself to map out the complicated nature of how we understand both written text and images. The repetition and echoes that we found in the quoted passage are graphically represented in Figure 1.10; in fact, translated into comic book form, the division between word and image becomes a visual continuum that strongly suggests McCloud's vision of the interrelationship between these rhetorical elements. The power of this argument comes from McCloud's strategic assessment of the rhetorical situation: he, the *author*, recognizes that his *audience* (people interested in visual media) would find an *argument* that relies on both visual and verbal elements to be highly persuasive.

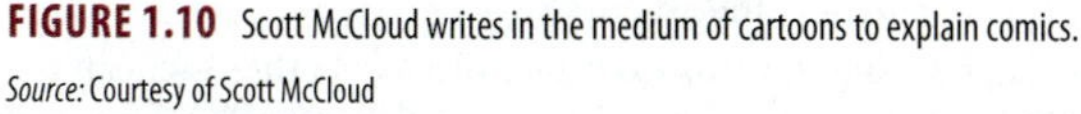

FIGURE 1.10 Scott McCloud writes in the medium of cartoons to explain comics.

Source: Courtesy of Scott McCloud

McCloud's example is also instructive for demonstrating the way in which word and image can collaborate in modern arguments. Today more than ever, rhetoric operates not just through word choice but also through choice of multimedia elements—images in a TV commercial, the audio of a viral ad on the Internet, the design choices of a website or flyer, even the layout strategies of your textbook. Therefore, we need to develop skills of analysis for all rhetorical texts. We need to understand argument *as writing across diverse media* and we need, therefore, to develop **multimedia literacy**, or a careful way of reading, analyzing, and understanding media (visual, verbal, and other rhetorical texts).

McCloud's persuasive writing strategies thus span both visual and verbal media. Understanding how both work as arguments will give you the ability and confidence to analyze and produce texts of your own. That is, these skills of analysis will help you approach other kinds of texts rhetorically: political speeches, scholarly articles, letters to the editor about timely issues, instant messaging and—as writing continues to evolve into new forms—blog posts, memes, mash-ups, and more.

Understanding Written Rhetoric

To understand how rhetoric works in written texts, you can examine any current newspaper article, blog, or even tweet. You might, for instance, do a Google search on the assassination attempt on Gabrielle Gifford and include the word "rhetoric" in your search. Then, you will find a contentious debate in writing about whether words themselves contributed to the use of gun violence. Let's examine another excerpt from the blog post by Barbara Morrill:

> And while there are many examples of the violent language employed by the right: "Second Amendment remedies," "resorting to the bullet box," calls to be "armed and dangerous," to name just a few, it's more than that. [...] Because since the election of Barack Obama, the right, both elected Republicans and their minions in the media, have pounded the non-stop drumbeat that Obama/Democrats/liberals want to destroy the country, they want to kill your grandmother, they're shredding the Constitution, they're terrorist sympathizers, they're going to take away your guns, that they're enemies of humanity, that the government is the enemy ...
>
> And that, as much as the obvious examples of violent rhetoric, can appeal to the extremist, the mentally unstable, or the "lone nut," to act. And last Saturday, one of them did.

In this written passage, Morrill repeats the word "And" at the beginning of each paragraph in a strategy that rhetoric scholars call *anaphora*. This creates a powerful rhythm and builds emotional energy. She then directly quotes words employed during the congressional election, and her strategy of listing them generates intensity and a hierarchy the way the words on the flagpole did for Figure 1.1. Switching to a different set of images, the author then attacks the character of elected Republicans through criticizing their "minions in the media" and asserting that they have "pounded the non-stop drumbeat" as if at war with Democrats. This condemning language produces a strong animosity in the writing that might sway a reader towards also condemning the Republicans. The next part of the sentence then offers another list, again using an exaggerated tone: "destroy the country, they want to kill your grandmother, they're shredding the Constitution, they're terrorist sympathizers, they're going to take away your guns, that they're enemies of humanity, that the government is the enemy." Morrill here spells out what she claims the Republicans tend to suggest in their media statements. She concludes by suggesting that such words function "as much as the obvious examples of violent rhetoric" to incite action by extremists such as the gunman who shot Gabby Giffords.

As you can see, these details can deeply move an audience. What we learn from reading this written text rhetorically is that when you analyze such texts, you can transfer what you know from reading visual texts: look for the vivid details, which in the case of language might include repetition, concrete metaphors, emotional phrases, and characterization of others that together act as what Aristotle would call "available means of persuasion" in writing. In this way, such written rhetoric, even while it disparages "violent language," is actually also forceful, even violent in its emphasis. It, too, is a form of communication that seeks to persuade audiences.

As you develop your analytical skills with regard to written rhetoric, you might find encouragement in Scott McCloud's point from *Understanding Comics* that "Writing is *perceived* information. It takes time and specialized knowledge to decode the abstract symbols of language." The purpose of this book is to help you develop the tools and acquire the knowledge to understand—or decode—the symbols we use to communicate with each other, including visual images but also written rhetoric in all its complexity. Let's take time now to consider a longer passage of writing. Remember Alex and her walk across campus? When she arrived at her 101 class on "Law and Society," her TA gave her a handout with an excerpt of a news article by Heidi Przybyla posted on *Bloomberg News*. As Alex reads, she uses her pen to write **annotations**, or brief points of analysis or observation, in the margins that indicate what strategies of persuasion are at work in each part of the article; As you read the article and Alex's accompanying *annotations*, add your own marks on points that you find provocative or interesting.

GIFFORDS SHOOTING IN ARIZONA MAY COOL U.S. POLITICAL RHETORIC, HURT PALIN

Heidi Przybyla

The shooting rampage in Tucson, Arizona, that killed six people and left U.S. Representative Gabrielle Giffords in critical condition is contributing at least momentarily to a cooling of U.S. political rhetoric.

Very loaded and emotional language stereotypical reference to rhetoric as something inflammatory (or "hot") and even dangerous.

The incident on Jan. 8, coming after the Jan. 5 opening of a new Congress in which Republicans took control of the U.S. House, led the House to postpone legislative business for the coming week as both parties rushed to condemn the attack.

More objective tone in this paragraph: use of dates and historical account of specific events.

Cites an authority (Baker) to make a point about the impact of the shooting on Palin's image.

It is also likely to hurt the image of former Alaska Governor Sarah Palin, said Ross Baker, a congressional scholar at Rutgers University in New Brunswick, New Jersey.

Mentions visual rhetoric used by Palin in election politics: note vivid descriptions. Possible essay topic: how the writer creates imagery with words.

The former Republican vice presidential candidate has posted on the Internet a map of the U.S. with the cross-hair symbols for a rifle scope dotting the home states of lawmakers, including Giffords, whom she was targeting for defeat in the 2010 congressional election.

Key quote-launches main points of article:
1. politicians need to stop partisan fighting;
2. Palin needs to change her "brand" (her image or persona).

The tragedy "will take some of the edge off of the polarization" and "will be used by lots of people as an exhortation for people to be kinder to each other," said Baker. At the same time, Palin's brand of "female macho," he said, "is not going to wear very well after this."

Counter-argument in this paragraph (alternate reasons for the shooting than the ones Przybyla mentions above). Quote from this paragraph in my essay to give a balanced perspective.

Lawmakers were careful to stress that the suspected shooter, identified as 22-year-old Jared Loughner, has a troubled past and appears mentally unstable. Regardless of whether it is determined that Loughner also had political motivations, members of both parties said politicians and the media play a role in setting an example of civility.

Subhead sets up argument for next section

Toxic Atmosphere

Author quotes politicians from CBS + NBC interviews.

"We are in a dark place in this country right now; the atmospheric condition is toxic," Representative Emanuel Cleaver, a Missouri Democrat, said yesterday on NBC's "Meet the Press" program. "Much of it originates here in Washington D.C., and we export it around the country."

Pattern of very strong emotional descriptions:

- toxic
- concerned
- angrier
- confrontational
- consequences

Again-possible paper topic: How these speakers, as well as Przybyla herself, creates strong imagery and emotion w/words.

"My colleagues are very concerned about the environment in which they are operating," House Minority Whip Steny Hoyer said on CBS's "Face the Nation." The Maryland Democrat termed the political climate in recent years an "angrier, confrontational environment," and cautioned that "what we say can, in fact, have consequences."

Republicans also said it's time for members of both parties to come together.

By writing her *annotations* in the margins, Alex begins to identify which aspects of the article's written rhetoric interest her most. She can then use those points in order to make her own argument for the essay assignment. What she has observed are the ways in which each speaker, as well as the article's author, uses strong emotional language to present a perspective on the *political rhetoric* (words and images) circulating prior to the assassination attempt. She will ultimately argue that such language is itself a powerful tool to sway public opinion as to the way that politicians should communicate with voters. Thus, Alex's analysis evokes the *rhetorical situation* (see Figure 1.6): she analyzes the way the writer (or *author*) uses language (or *argument*) to persuade the reader (or *audience*) of the newspaper article (or *text*).

As you develop your own skills of analyzing written rhetoric, you can also use *annotations* to help you identify and track your observations on how rhetoric works; these notes, gathered together, will enable you to generate your own interpretation and eventual argument. In fact, Sir Francis Bacon, the great philosopher, politician, and scientist from the Age of Enlightenment, developed a system of logical "inductive" reasoning based on the very practice of gathering observations and using them to construct knowledge, a new conclusion, or an argument. Echoing the position of Aristotle, he also saw rhetoric as that which moves others. Bacon asserted: "The duty and office of rhetoric is to apply reason to imagination for the better moving of the will." If we consider the words of Steny Hoyer quoted in the *Bloomberg* article, namely that "what we say can, in fact, have consequences," then we are on our way to understanding the power of rhetoric.

While rhetoric suffered slight marginalization in the nineteenth and early twentieth centuries, it has since made a strong return, with schools across both America and the world making what is called "the rhetorical turn" to see how writing of all kinds can communicate ideas and persuade audiences. When we make arguments about a text—in writing or in speech or with visual compositions—we are in fact using rhetoric as a practical art.

WRITER'S PRACTICE

Either in class with a partner, or on your own for homework, work on the scenarios below in order to understand the power of rhetoric as a persuasive act. In each case, first write down your ideas. Then, following the directions, write, speak, design, or present your own rhetoric to the class. Realize that the success of your argument will depend on your choice of media (verbal plea, written email, cover letter, visual poster, etc.) in relation to the specific *audience* you are addressing (coach, professor, potential employer, or peers).

- **Practice Oral Rhetoric:** Imagine that you have a big exam or a date to attend. Compose an oral argument that persuades your coach to let practice out early. After you draft your ideas, make your case face-to-face through in-class role-playing.
- **Practice Written Rhetoric:** When you realize that you will never finish an essay on time because of your heavy work schedule, you decide to ask for an extension on the paper's deadline. Craft an argument that would appeal to the personality of your teacher; after drafting it, type it out your plea to send it by email.
- **Practice Visual-Verbal Rhetoric:** When applying for a summer internship, you are asked to submit an online portfolio of work. Brainstorm ideas for the webpage, including well-selected images, words, colors, font, and possible links. Be sure to include links to your formal résumé in order to indicate your qualifications for the position. After completing your design, present your ideas to the class on your computer.
- **Practice Multimodal Rhetoric:** As Social Chair for your Greek House, you need to advertise an upcoming party: create a visually appealing multimedia ad, with animated gifs and all the contact information. Be as creative as possible, then make an event on Facebook that features your work in order to use multiple modes to persuade people to attend your function.

1.3 How does writing change across diverse media?

WRITING ACROSS DIVERSE MEDIA

As we begin to turn from analyzing texts to writing arguments of your own, we want to introduce you to a few more rhetorical terms that will help as you develop your critical literacy about how writing works across diverse media. One such term concerns the *urgent demand* that writers feel to respond to a situation. Have you ever seen a news article or heard about an event on campus that prompted you to respond strongly? When this happens, in rhetoric, we call this the **exigencies of a situation**, or the demands put upon a writer to respond immediately and urgently in the attempt to take action or raise a concern about a specific problem or issue.

Think about tweets sent out in response to a sports team winning a championship, a flash of celebrity gossip, or a crisis on campus. When the 2012 Presidential debates occurred, millions of tweets appeared as responses to words the candidates said or situations the candidates discussed. These are all contemporary instances of *exigency*. The scholar who gave us the rhetorical situation shown in Figure 1.6, Lloyd Bitzer, emphasized that *exigency* happens when change is possible: "An exigence is rhetorical when it is capable of positive modification and when positive modification *requires* discourse or can be *assisted* by discourse." That is, policies governing car parking on campus can potentially be modified through discourse, or language, but winter and death cannot.

FIGURE 1.11 Nate Beeler's cartoon uses humor in response to Disney's purchase of Star Wars.

Let's look at a more contemporary example. When Disney announced its acquisition of the Star Wars enterprise from George Lucas, people were shocked and even outraged. Many felt the need to respond through **discourse** (or forms of communication)—by tweeting, writing blog posts, composing articles in popular online magazines, and even drawing cartoons. In each case, the author felt prompted to respond urgently and immediately to what was widely viewed as a problem situation. In responding, these writers conducted another rhetorical act, one worth naming here in Chapter 1. That is, they all responded with a specific **motive**, or **purpose**. Whether that be internal and emotional, or objective—seeking to affirm or reaffirm the status quo—*motive* shapes the way authors write texts across media.

Consider the cartoon in Figure 1.11 by Nate Beeler, an award-winning editorial cartoonist for the *Columbus Dispatch*. Beeler created this text on October 31, 2012 in response to the merger. Entitled, "Disney Acquires 'Star Wars,'" the cartoon demonstrates the exigency that caused so many Americans to speak out or write about this surprising amalgamation between two enormous entertainment companies.

The giant head of Mickey Mouse, floating in space towards the galactic fleet, has an ominous look to it. The design of the image moving closer creates a sense of foreboding, and it suggests the *motive* of the cartoonist might have been to criticize this acquisition. Indeed, Mickey's head has been transformed into a version of the iconic Death Star, threatening to supplant the original space station/super weapon, which seems small and less imposing by comparison. Beeler is clearly presenting Mickey (and, by association, Disney) as the new "bad guy" of the Star Wars universe.

Moreover, the ironic words emerging from the space station, "I sense a great disturbance in the force," echo Obi-Wan Kenobi's classic line from *Star Wars Episode IV*; while in the original context Obi-Wan refers to the destruction of an entire planet and the death of its inhabitants, here the fleet makes a similarly ominous pronouncement about the impact of the Disney acquisition on the Star Wars franchise. Putting the visual and the verbal together, we perceive that Beeler exploits the imagery and lexicon of Star Wars fans themselves to convey his argument about the negative implications of the Disney's acquisition of Star Wars. It is a comic argument, to be sure, but it is an important position that arises from the exigencies of the situation.

Using a different form of media, many tweets also appeared in the wake of the acquisition as well. As urgent responses to the deal, the tweets (140 characters of writing) demonstrate how authors react in an attempt to use *discourse* to voice a personal position or in the hopes of modifying the situation. Most tweets use words alone. But they are creative in the small space of the tweet so that it becomes a digitally-mediated argument. For instance, in a tweet by the writer Andrés de Rojas, who goes by the Twitter handle @aderojas, the author plays on the well-known phrase from Star Wars, "May the Force be with you," and then adds ellipses to suggest a pause and switches "you" for "Mickey Mouse" so that his commentary looks like this: "May the Force be with… Mickey Mouse?" His strategically capitalized "Force" evokes Star Wars, while his careful punctuation indicates a pause and gives the punch line a humorous tone. In this way, the small medium of the tweet offers a powerful response. Moreover, the question mark at the end indicates his uncertainty over the acquisition, signaling his immediate discomfort with the situation. Notice how similar the pause is to the image of the back of Mickey's giant head floating towards the space station. As you start to recognize the commonality between the visual and the verbal, then you can begin to see how your strategies of critical literacy can transfer across diverse forms of "writing."

Another author named Raymond Kemp also used written discourse in a tweet to provide a critical stance on the merger. He wrote: "There was a disturbance in the force like the voices of a million nerds were silenced." Kemp also plays with the terms "disturbance" and "the force"—words we found in Nate Beeler's cartoon—but the ending of Kemp's sentence suggests a more critical perspective. That is, he makes a point that "the voices of a million nerds were silenced," indicating his motive, or purpose, includes an outcry against the potential way in which the "nerdy" series of Star Wars might change under the ownership of the more popular culture oriented vision of Disney.

Using both words and images, a third author created a tweet in response to the exigency of the news of the Disney-Star Wars merger through both verbal and visual rhetoric. Eric Alper's tweet begins with words that sound matter-of-fact, as if offering an objective response to the situation: "Disney buys Lucasfilm, the company behind Star Wars films, which can only mean one thing." His writing has the tone of a news report, and it is more informative than the previous tweets we examined. He does not even use the familiar phrase, "the Force," suggesting neutrality and a lack of insider knowledge. But then, he attaches a mash-up photo. In this image, he suggests how both Disney characters and Princes Leia from Star Wars might change as a consequence of the merger. Specifically, the image shows an animated drawing of the well-known Disney princesses, including Snow White, Cinderella, Ariel, Jasmine, Pocahontas, Mulan, and Rapunzel. But then positioned in the center is a cartoon version of Princes Leia from Star Wars, and she is wielding her blaster rifle. The image makes a pointed argument about how the gendered behavior among Disney females is sure to change, perhaps becoming more aggressive, and by doing so, Alper uses both humor and comparison-contrast in his hybrid text.

The tweet itself is easy to find with a Google search and was re-tweeted over 200 times by new authors to ever-broader circles of audiences. It eventually appeared in a *Time* entertainment article by Lily Rothman, who commented: "There are lots of princess-themed *Star Wars* tweets out there, but this one gets points for the visual aid." In her article, Rothman also inserted a title above the tweet that read, "A New Disney Princess." With these words, Rothman emphasizes the way in which the character (or onscreen *persona*) of Leia might change in becoming part of the Disney cast of romanticized female heroines. Rothman thus offers yet another perspective: while Alper suggests that Leia might inspire other Disney females toward battle, Rothman's title indicates that Leia might actually "soften" into more of a storybook princess in future appearances. Rothman's commentary on the tweet as *commentary* shows the power of writing across diverse media:

FIGURE 1.12 Mike Thompson's playful cartoon evokes many common symbols known to Americans in order to make a comic statement about the new resolve of the Republican Party.

using both words and images to respond to a situation and make an argument, writers contribute to an ongoing and dynamic public conversation on issues that matter in society today.

Analyzing Published Writing

In Nate Beeler's cartoon about Disney's acquisition of Star Wars, the argument is suggested; the position of the author is implied but not explicit. Now let's analyze a more politically charged example. Consider the powerful cartoon created by Mike Thompson, a three-time Pulitzer Prize finalist who publishes his work in the *Detroit Free Press* (see Figure 1.12).

The particular figure taking up most of the space on the left is recognizable to most twenty-first-century readers: the green skin, mechanical bolts in the neck, and stitched up forehead and wrists identify this character almost immediately as the monster Frankenstein. However, through one strategic addition, Thompson transforms this image from illustration into commentary; he places a pink sweater on the giant's body and the logo of the Republican party on his chest. Thompson's Frankenstein thus becomes a more feminized version of the monster, and the party logo demonstrates his membership in the Republican Party. In this way, Thompson uses visual elements in his cartoon to critique the strategies through which the Republican Party sought to change its image in the wake of losing the 2012 election.

The words voiced by the two human figures in the cartoon add to the argument. The supposed Dr. Frankenstein explains, "A Mr. Rogers Sweater!" evoking the popular children's TV program featuring a grandfatherly figure who always wore a soft-knit sweater and spoke to children softly and gently. The bent-over figure exclaims, "White House, Here we Come!" suggesting that with this new "image," the Republican Party will be more likely to win votes. Thompson's cartoon thus practices both visual and verbal means of persuasion, both of which are important to consider when we are analyzing and writing about a text. Through this combination, the cartoon becomes a springboard for lampooning cultural attitudes and political practices.

The words of the title, "A Republican National Committee Report Says the Party Must Improve Its Marketing," echoes the news of the day, when Republican leaders began communicating their plans for an image makeover in the face of electoral defeat. This cartoon thereby reflects real conversations and situations. But consider how insulting this cartoon might have seemed to Republicans who could have felt mocked by the pink sweater, the green monster representation of their party, and the gleefully optimistic words of the doddering human characters.

In fact, the cartoon generated quite a bit of controversy, including a lively debate in comments below the image, a place where writers today make their voices heard in response to situations that they feel demand attention. One such commenter, Craig Schulz, indicated his disappointment and disapproval with the argument he felt Thompson was making about the Republican Party. He wrote:

> Mike Thompson, what's the point? Another jab in the back to people with conservative ideals and values? Does your disrespect have any limits? The Freep is just another faction of the Democratic Party. The media today is low, lacks integrity, has little class. Mr. Thompson you belong to a propaganda machine. You can't read or watch anything that isn't spun one way or another, right or left. You are all a despicable lot!

Responding less than an hour later, the cartoonist replied:

> In your world, is everyone who disagrees with you on the issues automatically "despicable" [sic] lacking in integrity and of little class—or is it just me?

Thompson's reply emphasizes the point that we often react strongly against those who hold different views or perspectives than our own. This is especially true for political or editorial cartoonists, who, throughout the centuries, have offered a sharp commentary on current issues and public figures. From the densely symbolic eighteenth-century plates of William Hogarth, to the biting social satire of *Punch*'s illustrators, to the edgy work of political cartoonists such as Ann Telnaes, Mike Luckovich, and Daryl Cagle, the editorial cartoon has emerged as a succinct, powerful tool for writers to contribute to public dialogue on contemporary issues.

Addressing this issue that cartoons as written texts can often offend readers, Pulitzer-Prize winning cartoonist Doug Marlette once asserted in an interview that "the objective of political cartooning 'is not to soothe and tend sensitive psyches, but to **jab** and poke in an attempt to get at deeper truths, popular or otherwise'" (qtd. in Moore, emphasis added). Marlette's words reveal that cartoons are not just humorous texts but rather, as we have seen, they are rhetorical—they intend to persuade. Think back to the words of the angry commenter, who complained to Mike Thompson: "Another *jab* in the back to people with conservative ideals and values?"

Unfortunately for the viewer, it seems that such incitement is in fact the cartoonist's very purpose when he or she writes about current issues. Indeed, Marlette further argued in an article he wrote that "Political cartoonists daily push the limits of free speech. They were once the embodiment of journalism's independent voice. Today they are as endangered a species as bald eagles" (Tool). Such "speech" communicated through visual rhetoric thus provides an important democratic function, by letting a range of voices and perspectives on an issue emerge. As scholar Matthew Diamond wrote in an article called "No Laughing Matter," cartoonists "provide alternative perspectives at a glance because they are visual and vivid and often seem to communicate a clear or obvious message" (270).

What we can learn from this examination of rhetoric as writing across diverse media is that the relationship between interpretation and argument is a complex one. Although the author might intend to produce a certain argument, at times the audience may read it very differently. Not only is this true for political cartoons, but it is also true for political writing. Consider the following op-ed, published by Karl Rove in the *Wall Street Journal* just a few days before Obama's second Presidential Inauguration and concerning the same issue as Thompson's political cartoon. Entitled "After Four Bleak Obama Years, an Opportunity," the article seized upon the occasion to respond urgently to the situation faced by the Republicans—namely, that they had lost the 2012 election and needed to reconsider their image in light of how they related to voters. The article's author, Karl Rove, was a former deputy chief of staff to the president before Obama, George W. Bush. Rove organized the political action committee American Crossroads, and, after the election, put his reflections in writing this op-ed.

As you read this article, use the strategies of *critical literacy* that we've been developing throughout this chapter. Who is the main *audience*? How does Rove position himself as *author*? What is the author's *purpose* or *motive* in response to the *exigency* of the situation? Where and what is his *argument*? Which parts of the writing are most persuasive? What visual images does he convey with words? What is your response to the text? How does the argument of the op-ed compare to that of the cartoon?

AFTER FOUR BLEAK OBAMA YEARS, AN OPPORTUNITY

Karl Rove

Rove crafts his title to capture readers' attention.

As President Obama prepares to be sworn in a second time, it's a good moment to consider the state of the union during his era.

He opens his article by naming the *exigency*: the situation of Obama's re-election calls for a response to Obama's record.

As of his first inaugural, 134.379 million Americans were working and unemployment was 7.3%. Four years later, 134.021 million are working and unemployment is 7.8%.

In January 2009, 32.2 million people were on food stamps and 13.2% of Americans lived in poverty. Now, 47.5 million receive food stamps and the poverty rate is up to 15%.

Throughout the article, Rove then lists lots of facts and statistics. His tone seems almost objective, with only a few words such as "exhausted" [emphasis added] revealing that this article is in fact critical of Obama.

When Mr. Obama first took office, Social Security's trustees forecast it would go broke in 2041. Now the forecast date is 2037. Medicare's hospital trust fund will be **exhausted** by 2024, if not earlier.

On Jan. 20, 2009, the national debt stood at $10.627 trillion—or $34,782 for every man, woman and child. As of Tuesday, it had reached $16.435 trillion, or $52,139 for every American. The public debt was equal to 40.8% of gross domestic product on Jan. 20, 2009. By the end of last year, it had reached 72.8% of GDP and is forecast by the nonpartisan Congressional Budget Office to hit 76.1% this year.

The strong reliance on data offers Rove a compelling way to make his argument.

When Mr. Obama assumed office, median household income was $51,190. In 2011 (the last year for which data is available), median household income was $50,054. Household income declined more during the recovery, which began when the recession officially ended in June 2009, than it did during the recession, a first for America.

Last year, an average of 153,000 nonfarm jobs were created each month. At that rate, it will take 26 more months to get back to the number of jobs America had when the recession started in December 2007. Meanwhile, the workforce will have expanded by at least 8.6 million new people for whom there are no jobs.

However, when the phrase "it's worse" appears [emphasis added] the reader can see this as a *textual clue* that the writer strongly objects to Obama and sees his re-election as a problem to be addressed.

It's worse for manufacturing. Last year, an average of 15,000 manufacturing jobs were created each month. At that rate, it will take nearly 10 years to reach the number (13,743,000) of such jobs America had when the recession started.

Since the recession ended three and half years ago, the economy has grown an average of 0.4% a year. That compares to 1.6% growth per year for the previous decade (which covered two recessions, including the "great" one), 2.6% growth per year for the previous 20 years, and 3.2% on average since World War II.

To create jobs and growth, Mr. Obama asserts that the federal government has only a revenue problem, not a spending one. But in the last fiscal year before he took office (2008), revenues were $2.524 trillion and outlays $2.983 trillion. This fiscal year, revenues are expected to reach $2.913 trillion—but outlays have jumped to $3.554 trillion.

Here, the author uses the strategy of comparison-contrast to make his point.

It's those last data points in particular—outlays and spending—that present both challenges and opportunities for Republicans. Why? Because spending cuts in general and the abstract are **popular**, while spending cuts in the specific and concrete often are not.

Note his use of colorful language, such as "wearing green eyeshades."

To avoid coming off as just old-fashioned accountants wearing green eyeshades, Republicans will have to make a concerted effort to connect fiscal policy to economic growth and opportunity.

> Reductions in spending are a means to an end. Too often, Republicans speak as if they're the end in themselves.
>
> Fortunately some party leaders understand this. For example, Rep. Paul Ryan recently spoke of "a vision for bringing opportunity into every life—one that promotes strong families, secure livelihoods, and an equal chance for every American." He credited free enterprise for doing more than anything else "to lift people everywhere out of poverty." And Sen. Marco Rubio has marveled that, as a son of a hotel bartender, he could aspire to serve in Congress and argued that "only economic growth and a reform of entitlement programs will help control the debt" that threatens the country's future.
>
> GOP governors have added their voices to this line of argument. For example, Louisiana's Bobby Jindal wrote last month that "America is forever young because America is forever growing, leading the world. . . . All actions taken by Washington should be seen through this simple prism—will this help grow our economy?"
>
> Facts matter, but they're not enough. It's life stories and narratives that capture the public's imagination. That's something every Republican must internalize in the spending wars ahead. We need to move not simply minds but also hearts, to show what the "right to rise" means for every American. There are powerful stories to be told. Republicans better learn how to tell them, passionately and effectively.

Rove also quotes Paul Ryan, the vice presidential candidate, as well as other key party figures. This broadens his position statement from a scrutiny of Obama to a questioning of the words of Republicans.

Rove's closing paragraph offers a solution: don't just rely on numbers, but also tell stories and connect with voters on a heart-level.

The switch from objective language to directive language in the final paragraph reveals a sharper position, and indeed that is where Rove conveys his main point, or argument, in response to the 2012 election that saw the Republicans defeated by Obama's re-election. In his concluding sentence, he repeats the idea of "life stories and narratives," asserting that "Republicans better learn how to tell them, passionately and effectively." Using your own skills of *critical literacy*, you can select elements from the text—in this case, words and phrases—that would support your interpretation of this op-ed as an emotional response to the political situation facing the nation in January of 2013.

The varied ways that you and your classmates might read and respond to this op-ed depend on both *audience* and *context*, bringing to light again the importance of the *rhetorical situation*. Differences in your interpretation also reveal the importance of learning effective means of persuading others to see the text through a certain lens or way of reading and analyzing the text. That is, your task as a reader and a writer is both to study a text carefully and to learn how to persuade others to see the text as you see it. In order to learn how to do so, we will turn next to the key elements in writing an argumentative essay about your interpretation of a text—whether that text be written, visual, oral, or multimedia.

1.4 How should I brainstorm parts of the essay, including the thesis statement?

BRAINSTORMING PARTS OF AN ESSAY

We've learned that rhetoric works as a means of persuading an audience to accept the argument of the author. This is also true for the argument you make about a text. When you **write an analysis** in the form of an essay for class, you are crafting a rhetorical text in order to persuade your readers (the instructor and your peers) to accept your interpretation. Let's work through this process by brainstorming parts of an essay using the political cartoon by John Cole in Figure 1.13.

FIGURE 1.13 Cole's cartoon makes a powerful statement on contemporary events, spanning sports and politics.

- What elements stand out that you might analyze in your essay?
- What do you know about the author or the intended audience?
- What do you know about the timing or context of this text?
- What is your interpretation of the meaning or message of this text?

As you work through the questions above, you can see that your task as a writer is to argue convincingly for your audience to see the text the way you see it. In the case of Figure 1.13, what is the connection between the infamous case of Manti Te'o's fake or dead girlfriend and the Left (as a political party) in terms of their view of President Obama? What specific elements of the image can you discuss in presenting your argument about what kind of statement this cartoon makes?

Your challenge as a student of writing and rhetoric is not only to identify the argument contained by a text but also to *craft your own interpretation of that text*. This involves careful assessment of the ways in which the elements of the rhetorical situation work together to produce meaning in a text. In many cases, your analysis also must consider the interplay of words and images. While your analysis can take many forms—including a written essay, an oral report, a visual argument, or a combination of these—we recommend *writing out your answers* to the questions above when brainstorming the parts of an essay in order to generate all the material you will need to complete your assignment.

Developing a Thesis Statement

In brainstorming parts of an essay, you need to determine your interpretation of the meaning or message of a specific text (whether written, visual, or a combination of the two). In writing studies, we call this interpretation your **thesis**, or *the concise statement of your interpretation about a particular text, issue, or event*. A *thesis* should be more than a statement of observation or a fact. It should also be more than merely your opinion. It needs to combine **observation + evidence** (based in the elements of the text).

FIGURE 1.14 This cartoon by Daryl Cagle uses engaging visuals and well-chosen words to make an argument.

Source: Daryl Cagle, Cagle Cartoons, Inc.

FIGURE 1.15 Michael Ramirez's cartoon shows a static scene but also combines images and words.

Source: Michael Ramirez and Copley News Service

To understand how to generate a *thesis statement* using your skills of critical analysis, let's work through an example. Imagine that you want to write an argument about the cartoons in Figure 1.14 and Figure 1.15. Both comment on recent debates about immigration policy. How might you develop a thesis statement that persuasively conveys your interpretation of how these cartoons contribute to the debate surrounding the status of undocumented immigrants?

Start by jotting down what you see; make *close observations* about these cartoons. Then use questions to bring your argument into focus and to make a specific claim about the images. The end product will be a *working thesis.* The process of developing your thesis might look like this:

1. **Write down your observations.**

   Close observations: Both pictures focus, literally or symbolically, on the border between the United States and Mexico and on the way that we set up fences (or vault doors) to keep illegal immigrants out. Both also show holes in those barriers: one focuses on people running through a hole in the fence; the other shows a small door in the vault that looks as if it's been propped open from the inside. The words are interesting, too. In the Cagle cartoon, the big sign says "Keep out," while the smaller signs are designed to draw people in (see Figure 1.14). In the Ramirez cartoon, the small sign says "Cheap labor welcome," contradicting the message of the large, high-security door that blocks access to the United States (see Figure 1.15).

2. **Work with your observations to construct a preliminary thesis statement.**

   First statement: Both cartoons focus on the contradiction in American border policy.

3. **Refine your argument by asking questions that make your statement less general.**

   Ask yourself: How? What contradictions? To what effect? How do I know this?

4. **Revise your preliminary thesis statement to be more specific; perhaps include specific evidence that drives your claim.**

   Revised statement: The cartoons in Figure 1.14 and Figure 1.15 focus on the contradictions in American border policy by showing that on the one hand, the American government wants to keep illegal immigrants out, but on the other hand, economic forces encourage them to enter the United States illegally.

5. **Further polish your thesis by refining your language and asking questions about the implications of your working thesis statement.**

   Ask yourself: What do you find interesting about this observation? How does it tap into larger social or cultural issues?

6. **Revise your working thesis to include the implications or significance of your claim. Sometimes we call this the "*So What?*" point.**

   Working Thesis: The political cartoons in Figure 1.14 and Figure 1.15 offer a sharp commentary on the recent immigration debate, suggesting that official government policies against illegal immigration are undermined by economic forces that tolerate, if not welcome, the entry of undocumented workers into the United States. Yet the hole in the fence and the small door in the vault also suggest that such entry comes at great cost to immigrants who enter illegally.

In the working thesis, the significance appears as the final point about "great cost"—that is, the cartoons indicate that current immigration policies have serious consequences for undocumented laborers entering the United States. From this example, you can tell that a strong argumentative thesis does more than state a topic: it makes a claim about that topic that you will develop in the rest of your paper.

Let's look at one more example to further consider ways to produce sharp, clear, and persuasive thesis statements. The following thesis statements offer diverse interpretations of John Cole's cartoon (see Figure 1.16), published in 2012 in response to the popularity of the book and film, *The Hunger Games.*

FIGURE 1.16 John Cole's cartoon, "The Never-Ending Game," offers an international perspective on the popular American film.

Thesis 1: John Cole's cartoon on *The Hunger Games* offers a powerful perspective.

Assessment: *This thesis statement relies too heavily on subjective opinion: the author offers no criteria for evaluating the cartoon. What does it mean to be "powerful"? Moreover, the author does not include any elements of analysis or use evidence.*

Thesis 2: John Cole's drawing demonstrates his opinion about *The Hunger Games*.

Assessment: *This thesis statement is too much of a broad generalization and offers no critical interpretation of the meaning of the text. It does not make a claim as to what Cole's opinion is, and it relies too heavily on vague language.*

Thesis 3: According to my analysis, John Cole's cartoon shows a refugee's shock in reading about the income generated by the movie.

Assessment: *While this thesis is promising in that it offers some context, it nevertheless only describes the picture rather than offering a focused interpretation of the cartoon, despite the writer's claim to be making an argument.*

Thesis 4: In response to criticism about the film *The Hunger Games*, John Cole's 2012 cartoon, "The Never-Ending Game," shows a refugee's shock in reading about the income generated by the movie. By contrasting the media attention garnered by the movie to the stories about "war, poverty, and genocide" that appear inside the newspaper, Cole's text suggests that viewers take fictional tales such as *The Hunger Games* too seriously, at the expense of paying attention to those who suffer in real life situations across the globe.

AT A GLANCE

Testing Your Thesis

- Do you have a specific and interesting angle on your topic?
- Does it offer a statement of significance about your topic?
- Is the thesis sharp enough (not too obvious)?
- Could someone argue against it (or is it just an observation)?
- Is it not too dense (trying to compact the entire paper) or too simplistic (not developing your point thoroughly)?

Assessment: *While a bit long, this thesis statement does combine observation and significance. Of the four examples, it provides the most specific and argumentative articulation of the writer's interpretation of the cartoon.*

As the examples above demonstrate, a strong thesis is characterized by a specific and contestable claim. This central claim in turn functions as the heart and driver of a successful rhetorical analysis essay.

Analyzing Student Writing

Let's look at how one student, Sophie Shank, combines effective strategies of analysis with a carefully crafted thesis statement to compose her own rhetorical analysis of a recent editorial cartoon.

Sophie Shank
Rhetorical Analysis Essay
Prof. Chandra Shekhar

Better Watch Out: "Monsanto Claus" is Coming to Town A political cartoon warns of the destruction wreaked by GM corporation Monsanto in Vietnam

Sophie's title refers to the image she has chosen and hints at her thesis.

Come Christmastime, malls, houses and public areas across the U.S. will be plastered Santa Clauses, put up to evoke an emotional reaction from the viewer. Political cartoonist Khalil Bendib also uses this classic character to evoke emotion, but in this case, jolly old St. Nick is not so jolly. Everyone's favorite Santa has been replaced: out from under the Santa hat, the grim reaper sinisterly smiles down at two children. The figure is labeled "Monsanto Claus" to represent the genetic engineering corporation Monsanto and its destruction of

The essay begins by setting the context: describing Christmas in the US and then stating that the political cartoonist seizes upon this moment to make a strong social criticism.

Her writing is vivid and creative. Yet she also makes sharp points of observation about the cartoon's visual elements.

Near the end of the introduction, Sophie states her thesis: a strong statement of argument about her interpretation of the cartoon.

Notice that Sophie inserts the cartoon right into her essay (rather than at the end), so that her readers can pause and study its elements as they consider her thesis.

Vietnam, represented by the children, through Agent Orange and genetically modified organisms (GMOs). The disturbing image of "Monsanto Claus" looming over his innocent victim and offering poisonous-looking bottles evokes discomfort and fear in the audience (see Figure 1). Despite this overwhelming and seemingly complex image, in reality the author oversimplified the issue to remove personal ties between the largely American audience and the "villain" to convince the audience to condemn Monsanto without acknowledging their own role in the destruction.

Figure 1. Khalil Bendib's Cartoon criticizes Monsanto.

Sophie then analyzes the rhetoric of the cartoon in great detail, providing her interpretation of all the elements in the image.

The portrayal of Monsanto as the grim reaper instantly tags Monsanto as the villain in this situation, and sets a serious tone in the cartoon. A rosy-cheeked Santa face has been swapped for a skull, smiling menacingly and shocking the viewer. Accompanying the skull, a scythe protrudes from behind Santa's knee. This scythe indicates that beneath the Santa suit this figure is really the grim reaper, the personification of death. The idea of the grim reaper is scary in and of itself, but the audience is further unnerved by the grim reaper's disguise as one of society's most beloved figures. In this costume, the grim reaper can deceive innocent children.

The grim reaper also dwarfs the children, indicating that Vietnam is powerless next to Monsanto, thereby evoking fear, as well as a parental instinct to protect these kids.

Though we are first struck by these superficial differences between the portrayals of Monsanto and Vietnam, looking further into the cartoon reveals the historic context for their relationship. Monsanto products are utilized in many countries, but Vietnam is featured in order to highlight two historical events, the use of Monsanto product Agent Orange in the Vietnam War and the introduction of Monsanto-patented genetically modified seeds. Agent Orange killed vegetation in rural Vietnam in the 1960s and 1970s to drive guerillas out of hiding and force rural farmers to migrate to the U.S.-dominated cities. As it killed trees it also harmed civilians and raised the toxins level in the soil up to thirteen times the concentration recommended by the USDA. Likewise, Monsanto's genetically modified foods have not been proven entirely safe for consumption and have encouraged dangerous amounts of pesticide use.

Her essay then tackles the historical context for the elements in the cartoon, providing background knowledge that she gained through basic research, as shown in her works cited list at the end of the essay.

In the cartoon, Agent Orange and GMOs loom over the children as huge gifts in Monsanto's hands. The contrast in size between these large bottles and the tiny children emphasizes the imposing power of Monsanto's products. The gas snaking out of Agent Orange and the skull and crossbones add to the image's foreboding tone. This leaking gas also taps into our culture's stereotypical image of a "mad scientist." Popular

Returning to the cartoon and to her thesis, Sophie uses powerful language to persuade her reader to view the text through her interpretative lens.

She evokes common knowledge as well.

science fiction stories portray "mad scientists" conducting dangerous experiments, so this image alarms the audience and prevents them from trusting Monsanto engineers.

Using a strong transition, her argument builds from paragraph to paragraph.

This sense of danger is amplified through the exaggerated use of black, red, and grey, colors traditionally associated with injury and death. Splashes of green dot the bottles' bows to indicate that Monsanto products are disguised as innocent presents, but the vast majority of the figures associated with Monsanto's destruction are colored black, grey, and red. On the other hand, the children and the bird have a pastel color pallet to indicate their innocence. This use of color furthers the contrast between the villain and the victims, the bird, representing nature, and Vietnam. The bird has been placed in the "innocent" category because the bird is a bystander with no voice in the situation. Nonetheless, the bird's placement under the scythe suggests that the grim reaper is more powerful than the bird, and therefore that nature will face the consequences of Monsanto's actions.

She even attends to the colors of the cartoon and their symbolic values, as well as to the location of specific elements in the text.

From the bird in the bottom left corner to text scribbled across the top right, figures fill the majority of the frame, creating chaos and leaving the reader overwhelmed. The written speech bubbles and captions help the audience decode the messages within the chaotic frame. The text reveals what each figure symbolizes. However, the writing in isolation does not add much new information. Instead, the text follows the same rhetorical strategies that the visual elements employ. For

As her essay continues, Sophie analyzes the written words, demonstrating how skills of analysis transfer from one medium to another—from visual to verbal.

example, the phrase "4 million victims" is scrawled across the Agent Orange bottle to shock and evoke fear. Though this text appears to add facts and a rational perspective to the image, in fact the cartoonist does not have accurate information. The Vietnamese government and Red Cross of Vietnam report that four hundred thousand people were killed and up to one million have health problems due to Agent Orange. The number of people actually harmed by Agent Orange is less than half the amount reported in the cartoon. This misrepresentation of data prevents the author from using logic and reason to convince the reader and undermines his credibility.

By considering the counter-argument, she makes her own case stronger.

The author further undermines his credibility by oversimplifying the issue. By presenting the corporation as the grim reaper, he argues that the corporation's main goal is to kill. He disregards all other perspectives. For example, the author ignores the idea that Monsanto's products may increase agricultural yields and thereby save starving children. Though the author sacrificed his credibility, he was still able to use oversimplification as a strategy to ensure that the reader does not focus on the multiple sides to the story.

The omission of information about others responsible for spreading Agent Orange and GMOs further oversimplifies the issue. Agent Orange would not have damaged Vietnam if the U.S. military had not sprayed it. If the U.N. or the U.S. demanded stricter regulation of genetically modified crops, then the food would be safer to eat. Instead, U.S. FDA reports

Sophie's argument takes a surprising turn, claiming that the US military—and not Monsanto—are to blame for the death and destruction in Vietnam. She then extends this responsibility to food production.

As she builds the final points of her argument, she brings in strong consideration of the audience of the cartoon and the importance of the rhetorical situation.

on the potential danger of GMOs have been ignored. The image does not explain this; it only evokes fear of Monsanto itself. The cartoon does not point fingers at others involved in this situation because the audience—mainly U.S. citizens—will connect more easily to the image of a gigantic corporation as the villain, rather than acknowledging that their own government spread this destruction.

Similarly, the cartoon disregards the connection between Monsanto and the charities that have funded it, like the Bill and Melinda Gates Foundation. Much of the American public admires the Gates Foundation's work in the developing world, so Monsanto's association with this charity could cause second thoughts for the audience on the condemnation of Monsanto. The cartoon intentionally ignores the role of charities in the spread of Monsanto products so that the audience will immediately deplore Monsanto instead of considering multiple sides to the issue.

Her conclusion summarizes her main points in the essay and offers a memorable statement about the motive behind the text.

Through this oversimplification, the cartoon removes personal ties between the audience and the "villain," allowing the reader to condemn Monsanto without considering their own role in the issue. Despite the oversimplification of the issue, the overall metaphor in the image, combined with the jarring portrayal of the gigantic Santa grinning down at two vulnerable children, is very powerful. In the end, image is very effective at its goal: to instill a sense of fear in the audience and sway the public against Monsanto.

Works Cited

"Agent Orange." *Wikipedia*. N.p., 1 Oct. 2012. Web. 2 Oct. 2012. <http://en.wikipedia.org/wiki/Agent_Orange>.

Bendib, Khalil. Cartoon. *CorpWatch*. N.p., 4 Nov. 2004. Web. 2 Oct. 2012. <http://www.corpwatch.org/article.php?id=11638>.

"Genetically Modified Food Controversies." *Wikipedia*. N.p., 12 Oct. 2012. Web. <http://en.wikipedia.org/wiki/Genetically_modified_food_controversies>.

Herbert, Martha. "What is Genetically Modified Food (And Why Should You Care)?" *Brown University*. N.p., Spring 2002. Web. 19 May 2012. <http://www.earthsave.org/lifestyle/genfood2.htm>.

Sophie responsibly lists all the sources she consulted in working on this essay, including the cartoon itself.

She uses MLA documentation style, which we explain in Chapter 7.

THE WRITER'S PROCESS

As you turn now to write your own rhetorical analysis of a text, you'll be putting into practice all the skills you've learned in this chapter. You'll need to write down your observations of the text, spend time analyzing them in detail, and use these points of analysis as *evidence* to make an argument that will persuade others to see the text the way you see it. In other words, when composing your own rhetorical analysis, you need to use the same process we have worked through when analyzing different texts in this chapter:

- First, look carefully at all the elements in the text. Create a list of your observations or use the prewriting checklist in the first Writing Assignment to help you analyze the text more closely.

- Then, consider the argument of each element. How does it contribute to the text as a whole?
- Next, complete the rhetorical triangle (see Figure 1.6) for the text, identifying the author, the intended audience, and the argument, based on your observations of the details.
- Finally, put all these elements together and develop your thesis statement about the argument and significance of the text.

It's crucial to remember that when you write a rhetorical analysis, you perform a rhetorical act of persuasion yourself. Accordingly, you need to include the key elements of analytical writing: (1) have a point of interpretation to share with your readers, (2) take time to walk readers through concrete details to prove your point, and (3) lead your readers through the essay in an engaging and convincing way. But of all these, the most important is your argument, your interpretation of or position on the text—your *thesis*.

AT A GLANCE

Composing Rhetorical Analysis Essays

- Do you have a sharp point of interpretation, or *thesis*, to make about the text?
- Have you selected key elements or details to analyze in support of your thesis?
- Do you lead readers through your interpretation of the text by discussing important aspects in sequence? These might include:
  - Verbal elements in the text (words, font, quotes, dates)
  - Visual composition, layout, and images
  - Framing words for the text (article title, cartoon caption)
  - Color, arrangement, and meaning of items
- Can you include information about the author, intended audience, or context?
- Have you drafted a title for your own essay?
- Does your introduction name the author, date, and rhetorical situation for your text?
- Do your paragraphs build and progress through the essay using transitions?
- Have you offered a summary and a larger point or implication in the conclusion?
- Can you insert the image right into the essay and label it?

Spend some time working on your thesis before composing the entire draft. Make sure your angle is sharp and your interpretation takes into account audience, author, and argument as well as concrete points of visual and verbal composition.

Moreover, keep in mind the need to begin with observations, but avoid simply describing the elements you notice. Instead, zoom in on specific details and think hard about their meaning. Make a persuasive argument by using *specific* evidence to support your analysis of how the text succeeds at convincing an audience to perceive an issue in a particular way. These writing strategies will enable you to craft a persuasive and effective rhetorical analysis essay.

Seeing Connections
See Chapter 7 for more instructions on integrating images in your writing and referring to them correctly.

WRITING ASSIGNMENTS

1. **Written Analysis of a Cartoon or Comic:** Pick a cartoon or comic to examine from a news magazine such as *Time*, a newspaper, a webcomic collection such as xkcd or Penny Arcade, or an online archive such as Daryl Cagle's Political Cartoon website. Using the skills of analysis you have learned in this chapter, work through the questions in the checklist below and write out your answers. When you are done, go through the steps outlined in this chapter on how to generate an effective thesis statement. Share your work with a partner in class for feedback.

   ❑ **Topic:** What key issue is the comic or cartoon addressing?

   ❑ **Story:** On the most basic level, what is happening in the cartoon?

   ❑ **Audience:** In what country and in what historical moment was the cartoon produced? In what type of text did it first appear? A journal? A newspaper? Online? Was this text conservative? liberal? How does it speak to this audience?

   ❑ **Author:** What do you know about the artist? What kinds of cartoons does he or she regularly produce? Where does he or she live and publish? What kinds of other writing does this person do?

   ❑ **Argument:** What is the cartoon's argument about the issue? Is there irony involved (does the cartoon advocate one point of view, but the cartoonist wants you to take the opposite view)?

- ❑ **Composition:** Is this political cartoon a single frame or a series of sequential frames? If the latter, how does the argument evolve over the series?
- ❑ **Word and image:** Does the cartoon rely exclusively on the visual? Or are word and image both used? What is the relationship between the two? Is one given priority over the other? How does this influence the cartoon's overall persuasiveness?
- ❑ **Imagery:** What choices of imagery and content does the artist make? Are the drawings realistic? Do they rely on caricatures? Does the artist include allusions or references to past or present events or ideas?
- ❑ **Tone:** Is the cartoon primarily comic or serious in tone? How does this choice of tone create a powerful rhetorical impact on readers?
- ❑ **Character and setting:** What components are featured by the cartoon? A person? An object? A scene? Think about how character and setting are portrayed. What are the ethnicity, age, socioeconomic class, and gender of the characters? Do they represent actual people? Are they fictional creations? How are these choices rhetorical strategies designed to tailor the cartoon and its argument to its intended audience?
- ❑ **Cultural resonance:** Does the cartoon implicitly or explicitly refer to any actual people, events, or pop culture icons? What sort of symbolism is used in the cartoon? Would the symbols speak to a broad or narrow audience? How does the cultural resonance function as a rhetorical strategy in making the argument?

2. **Personal Narrative Essay:** Recall Alex's observations of rhetoric on her way to class; conduct a similar study of the rhetoric in your world. Write your reflections into a *personal narrative essay.* Discuss which types of visual, verbal, bodily, or architectural rhetoric were most evident, which were most subtle, and which you found the most persuasive. Conclude with a statement or argument about these texts—what do they collectively say about your community or culture? How do these texts try to shape the views of audiences through specific messages or arguments?

3. **Rhetorical Analysis:** Develop the analysis brainstorm that you completed for Assignment #1 above into a full *rhetorical analysis*, complete with a persuasive thesis statement. If you choose to analyze more than one cartoon on the same issue, introduce all your texts in the opening paragraph, and spend some time analyzing each one in detail. Make sure that your writing supports a thesis about elements and messages of all the texts you are analyzing.

4. **Comparative Rhetorical Analysis of Text and Image:** After you've begun Assignment #3, search through recent newspapers, newsmagazines, or a library news database like LexisNexis to find an article that addresses the same issue. Write a *comparative analysis of the text and the political cartoon*. What rhetorical strategies does each one use to make an argument? If you take a historical approach to this assignment, choose both a cartoon and an article that span the historical spectrum but focus on one issue, such as racial profiling, immigrant workers, or what's "hip" in the entertainment industry. Include specific details about each text, shape your observations into a thesis, and don't forget a title for your essay that previews your argument about these texts.

CHAPTER 2

Understanding Strategies of Persuasion

Chapter Preview Questions

2.1 What specific strategies of argument can I use to write persuasively?

2.2 What role do the rhetorical appeals of *pathos, logos,* and *ethos* play in persuasion?

2.3 How can I shape my argument based on time, place, and shared values?

FIGURE 2.1 This advertisement makes its pitch for the MacBook Pro using Apple's typical marketing approach: emphasizing simplicity and aesthetics rather than technical information.

What convinced you to buy that new smartphone, to try that new sports drink—or even to decide which college to attend? Chances are that some combination of words and images—a printed ad, TV commercial, flyer, brochure, or even a billboard—influenced your decision. Considered in this context, we can see that advertisers are rhetoricians, careful to attend to the *rhetorical situation* and to craft arguments designed to persuade their target audiences. By analyzing advertisements, we can discern specific strategies of argumentation that you can use to convince others in your own persuasive writing.

For instance, while walking across campus, you might come across a sandwich-board ad such as the one in Figure 2.1, positioned strategically outside the campus bookstore. Look carefully at its design: what strategies of persuasion does the MacBook Pro ad use to try to stop the passerby in her tracks and entice her to buy a new laptop? To what extent does the ad make a logical appeal, emphasizing the technical features of the laptop? How much does it rely on Apple's reputation to market this device? How does it appeal to a certain type of user experience by its use of vivid colors and simple, symmetrical design? As you can see, even a seemingly basic advertisement like this one is a carefully composed text, constructed to make a particular argument about a product.

Think of how other ads you've seen make you pause and pay attention. Ads in fashion or sports magazines often feature a photo of a celebrity or an attractive person to try to get their readers to connect emotionally with their products. TV commercials often use compelling stories or memorable examples to hook their audiences. Brochures tend to incorporate impressive statistics or factual evidence to support their claims. Pop-up ads on your computer use flashy animations and interactive games to encourage you to click through to their messages. In fact, often, it is not one but a combination of factors that we find persuasive—and many times these factors are so subtle that we hardly recognize them. Such techniques that are used to move and convince an audience are called **rhetorical strategies**.

Ads offer us a productive means of analyzing rhetorical strategies because they represent arguments in compact forms. An ad has to be quite efficient in its persuasion; it has to convey its message persuasively before its audience flips the page, fast forwards, hits mute, or closes the pop-up window. Ads also provide us with a particularly effective example of contemporary argument through their sheer ubiquity. Consider all the places ads appear nowadays: not just in magazines or on the television or radio, but also on billboards, the sides of buses, trains, and buildings; in sports stadiums and movie theaters; on T-shirts and baseball hats; as banners on webpages and sidebars on social media sites; even spray-painted on sidewalks or integrated into video games.

By analyzing advertisements, we can detect the rhetorical strategies writers select to make their points and convince their audiences. More importantly, by using advertising as a way to understand persuasion, we can take away lessons that apply to the composition of all sorts of texts, including those that you will produce in academic situations. In this way, you'll gain a working vocabulary and learn specific principles that you can use both to become a savvy reader of advertisements and also to produce your own persuasive written texts.

2.1 What specific strategies of argument can I use to write persuasively?

IDENTIFYING STRATEGIES OF ARGUMENTATION

Like more traditional writing, advertising often deploys **strategies of argumentation** to persuade. These can be used effectively to structure either a small unit (in an essay, a paragraph or section of the argument; in an ad, a small subset of the text) or a larger one (the argument as a whole). Let's look at how such strategies might operate in both advertising and academic texts:

- **Narration:** Using a story to draw in the audience

  How advertisers use this strategy: The Budweiser commercial, "Brotherhood" (see Figure 2.2) centers on the story of a man who raises a foal, sells it so it can become one of the Budweiser Clydesdales, and then is unexpectedly reunited with it after a city parade.

  How you might use this strategy in your own writing: You might hook your readers by telling a story that illustrates a key point of your argument or predisposes them to your line of thinking. For example, in an essay on fast-food marketing, you might open with the story of how a young child watches a McDonalds's commercial, is drawn in by its cheerful music, appealing colors, and product information, and then begs his mother for a Happy Meal for lunch.

FIGURE 2.2 The Budweiser "Brotherhood" commercial relies on narration to hook its audience, using the reunion of the man and his horse as the emotional climax of the story.

- **Comparison-Contrast:** Making a point through showing the similarities or differences between two or more items

  How advertisers use this strategy: Soap manufacturer Olay ran a comparison-contrast ad campaign arguing that its soap contained more moisturizer than its competitor Dove; it juxtaposed a picture of Dove soap next to a measuring cup marked "1/4 moisture" with a picture of Olay soap next to a measuring cup "1/3 moisture" to support this claim.

  How you might use this strategy in your own writing: You might show how advertisers have adjusted their marketing strategies over time by comparing, for instance, how Apple's commercials have changed from its iconic "1984" commercial, to its dancing silhouette iPod spots from the early 2000s, to today's iPad ads.

FIGURE 2.3 This Lego Friends ad centers on an example of their target audience and the types of creations that can be made with their product.

- **Example/Illustration:** Focusing on a specific, representative example to persuade your reader

  How advertisers use this strategy: The Lego ad in Figure 2.3 spotlights a smiling girl, holding her Lego creation, as an example of who might use the new Lego Friends products and what she might build.

  How you might use this strategy in your own writing: You might help your reader understand a larger issue (such as nationalism in advertising) by exploring a selection of examples (such as commercials with a patriotic theme that were broadcast during the 2002 Superbowl, shortly after the 9/11 terrorist attacks).

- **Cause and Effect:** Structuring an argument around the causal relationship between two elements, considering why something occurred or happened

  How advertisers use this strategy: Weight loss programs such as Jenny Craig are famous for cause-and-effect arguments, organizing their commercials around the idea that following their diet (cause) helps their customers lose weight (effect).

  How you might use this strategy in your own writing: You might write an essay about how the rise of DVR, TiVo, and other digital recording devices for your TV (cause) has changed the marketing strategies and design of television commercials (effect).

- **Definition:** Defining a term, concept, or theoretical premise for your reader

  How advertisers use this strategy: To promote its search engine, in 2009 Bing launched a series of commercials that defined "Search Overload Syndrome," which it claimed was the tendency of Google users to succumb to spontaneous verbal outbursts of unrelated information as a result of their unfocused Internet searches.

  How you might use this strategy in your own writing: In an essay on emergent forms of online advertising, you might devote a paragraph to defining the term "advergaming" before moving on to examine examples of this new genre of interactive games designed to promote a product or company.

- **Analogy:** Using a simpler or more familiar concept or metaphor to help an audience understand a complicated idea

  How advertisers use this strategy: Snickers uses analogy in its "You're Not You When You're Hungry" commercials; in one ad, a pair of young women chat with two men at a party, one of whom is played by actor Joe Pesci (a actor known for his portrayal of hostile, sometimes violent characters). In response to a harmless remark, Pesci becomes overtly enraged. His friend hands him a Snickers, saying, "You get a little angry when you're hungry." The conflict is resolved as Pesci taking a bite of the candy is transformed into a completely different actor with a friendly smile. The analogy becomes clear: the friendly man acts like – or, in this case, "becomes" — Joe Pesci when he is hungry, and Snickers fixes this problem.

  How you might use this strategy in your own writing: In an essay analyzing social media marketing, you might use a David and Goliath analogy throughout the paper to persuade your reader that the seemingly weaker force of Twitter advertising can pose a real threat to traditional corporate marketing.

- **Process:** Persuading through showing a series of sequential steps

  How advertisers use this strategy: The ad in Figure 2.4 relies on a process-based argument; it argues that Merrill's IRA is easy to use by showing the simple a-b-c steps the woman follows to invest her money.

  How you might use this strategy in your own writing: You might structure your argument around process in an essay about unrealistic images in fashion ads, demonstrating to your reader the process by which an average woman is transformed into a sexy fashion model through steps of applying makeup, setting her hairstyle, posing her body a certain way, selecting the lighting for the ad, and then the photoshopping the final image itself.

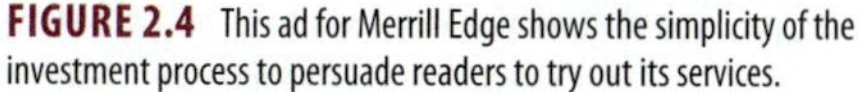

FIGURE 2.4 This ad for Merrill Edge shows the simplicity of the investment process to persuade readers to try out its services.

- **Description:** Describing an element, event, or idea in detail so as to set up background or create an impression on your reader

  How advertisers use this strategy: Advertisements for resorts and tropical getaways often paint a picture of the destination they are promoting, using vivid, descriptive language and beautiful images to motivate audiences to choose that locale for their next vacation.

  How you might use this strategy in your own writing: In your own ad analysis, you would include descriptive language to help your readers "see" the advertisement under consideration in detail so they would be more persuaded by your claims.

- **Classification and Division:** Helping the reader understand either how individual elements fit into a larger category or set of ideas, or how a larger category breaks down into component parts.

  How advertisers use this strategy: Car manufacturers like Honda and Toyota often run ads that promote their entire product line—from SUVs to compact cars—to show the variety of models they produce and invite their audience to select the one that best suits their needs.

  How you might use this strategy in your own writing: When writing about celebrity endorsements, you might formulate categories to help your reader understand the different ways such ads operate: for instance, expert-ads (ads based on the expertise of the celebrity); reputation-ads (ads that draw on the celebrity's overall public status, not necessarily related to the product); and parody-ads (ads that mock the celebrity's character or actions as a selling point).

When we turn to a more extended analysis of a written text, we will see the way in which you can combine multiple strategies of argumentation to make your own writing more persuasive. Consider, for instance, this excerpt from Ian Bogost's discussion of advertising in his book *Persuasive Games*, in which he sets up a theoretical foundation that he will later use in his discussion of "persuasion games" (short interactive games designed to advertise a product). As you read this selection, look carefully for the strategies Bogost uses to support his analysis.

PERSUASIVE GAMES

Ian Bogost

Here Bogost uses **classification/division** to taxonomize different types of advertising: he takes a larger category (advertising) and breaks it into component parts.

There are three important types of advertising that can participate in such persuasion games: *demonstrative, illustrative,* and *associative* advertising.

Having established the different parts, he now moves to **definition**.

Demonstrative advertising provides direct information. These ads communicate tangibles about the nature of a product. This type of advertising is closely related to the product as commodity; demonstrative ads focus on the functional utility of products and services. Among this category of advertisements, one might think of the "sponsor messages" of the golden age of television, ads that featured live demonstrations of detergent or "miracle" appliances. Also among this category are the copy-heavy print ads of the 1960s–1980s (examples abound in back issues of magazines like *National Geographic*), as well as modern-day television infomercials.

Ads like these focus on communicating the features and function of products or services. Consider [a] magazine ad for a Datsun hatchback [from the 1970s]. In the aftermath of the oil crisis of the 1970s, the ad foregrounds the car's focus on fuel economy, a tangible benefit, with the large headline "Nifty Fifty." Additional copy at the bottom of the ad further rationalizes and defends this position, citing a five-speed transmission with overdrive as a contributor to the car's increased fuel economy.

Illustrative advertising communicates indirect information. Illustrative ads can communicate both tangibles and intangibles about a product, with a focus on the marginal utility, or the incremental benefit of buying this product over another, or over not buying at all. These ads often contextualize a product or service differently than demonstrative ads, focusing more on social and cultural context. Consider another automobile ad, this one for a Saab sedan [...]. Unlike the Datsun ad, which depicts the vehicle in an empty space, the Saab ad places the car on a road and uses photographic panning to telegraph motion. No additional copy accompanies the ad, but the vehicle in motion serves to illustrate speed. The ad makes a case for the liveliness of the vehicle despite its "practical" four-door sedan frame, which is clearly visible in the center of the image.

To clarify his definition of demonstrative advertising, Bogost gives a brief list of **examples**.

He follows up with a more detailed **example** that relies on more detailed **description** to help the reader understand his point.

As he moves to the second category of advertising that he has identified above, he once again leads with **definition** and follows up with **example** and **description**.

Notice the use of **comparison-contrast** here to promote dialogue between the different terms and help his reader better understand how each of these types of advertising works.

In the paragraph that follows in the original chapter, Bogost proceeds to use the same structure to explore the concept of associative advertising.

UNDERSTANDING THE RHETORICAL APPEALS

2.2 What role do the rhetorical appeals of *pathos*, *logos*, and *ethos* play in persuasion?

The rhetorical strategies we've examined so far can be filtered through the lens of classical modes of persuasion dating back to 500 BCE. In writing about persuasion, Aristotle differentiated between **inartistic** and

artistic proofs. He defined *inartistic proofs* to be elements available to the writer, but not created by the writer. Statistics, laws, quotations from others, facts: these all fall under the category of inartistic proofs. *Artistic proofs*, conversely, comprise arguments that the speaker constructs through rhetorical strategies. The strategies and structures of argumentation analyzed above are examples of artistic proofs; they might leverage facts or external evidence, but the arguments themselves are designed by the author. For the rest of this chapter, we'll focus our attention on artistic proofs and how you can learn to wield such strategies of argument effectively in composing your own persuasive texts.

From Aristotle's perspective, artistic proofs were derived from one of three rhetorical appeals: the formal terms are ***pathos***, ***logos***, and ***ethos***. You might recognize them more readily by how they work: *pathos* operates through developing an emotional connection with the audience; *logos* persuades through facts and reasoning; *ethos* functions as an appeal to the authority or credibility of a person's character.

Each type of rhetorical appeal represents a mode of persuasion that can be used by itself or in combination, depending on an understanding of the rhetorical situation. As you might imagine, a text may employ a combined mode of persuasion, such as "passionate logic" (a rational argument written with highly charged prose), "good-willed *pathos*" (an emotional statement that relies on the character of the speaker to be believed), or "logical *ethos*" (a strong line of reasoning employed by a speaker to build authority). Since they appear so frequently in combination, you might find that conceptualizing *pathos, logos,* and *ethos* through a visual representation helps you to understand how they relate to one another (see Figure 2.5).

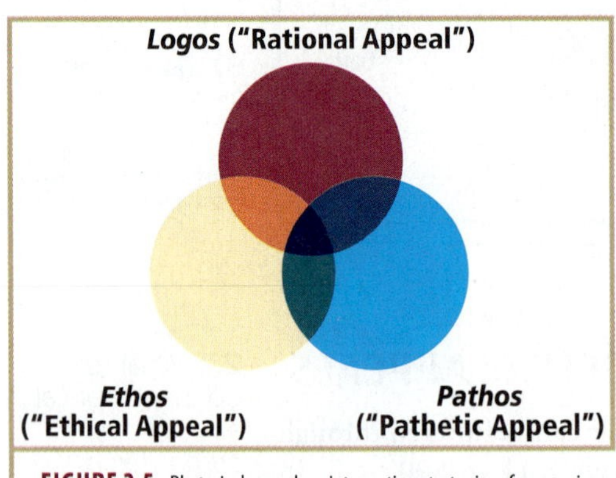

FIGURE 2.5 Rhetorical appeals as intersecting strategies of persuasion.

Since, as we discussed in Chapter 1, rhetoric involves careful and strategic assessment of the rhetorical situation in constructing persuasive arguments, let's look carefully at each of the appeals in turn to help you understand how you might use them in your own writing.

AT A GLANCE

Rhetorical Appeals

- ***Pathos,*** or "the pathetic appeal," refers to an appeal to the emotions: the speaker attempts to put the audience into a particular emotional state so that they will be more receptive to the speaker's message. Inflammatory language, sad stories, appeals to nationalist sentiments, and jokes are all examples of *pathos.*
- ***Logos*** entails rational argument: it appeals to reason and persuades the audience through clear reasoning and philosophy. Statistics, facts, definitions, and formal proofs, as well as interpretations such as syllogisms or deductively reasoned arguments, are all examples of "the logical appeal."
- ***Ethos*** is an appeal to authority or character; according to Aristotle, *ethos* means the character or goodwill of the speaker. Today we also consider the speaker's reliance on authority, credibility, or benevolence when discussing strategies of *ethos.* Although we call this third mode of persuasion the "ethical appeal," it does not strictly mean the use of ethics or ethical reasoning. Rather, *ethos* is the deliberate use of the *speaker's character* as a mode of persuasion.

Appeals to Emotion: *Pathos*

Roughly defined as "suffering" or "feeling" in its original Greek, the term *pathos* actually means to put the audience in a particular mood or frame of mind. Modern derivations of the word *pathos* include *pathology* and *pathetic,* and indeed we speak of *pathos* as "the pathetic appeal." But *pathos* is more a technique than a state: writers use it as a tool of persuasion to establish an intimate connection with the audience by soliciting powerful emotions.

We encounter ads that rely on *pathos* all the time, and, indeed, the composition of an ad often taps our emotions in ways that we barely recognize. Many use description or an analogy to set the mood, such as displaying an idyllic landscape scene to serve as the backdrop for a commercial for engagement rings or retirement funds or choosing a color scheme (bright primary colors or muted pastels) to create a specific effect. The music in the commercials, whether on television or radio, also produces a *pathos*-effect on the audience, from the catchy, up-beat jingles that create a positive association with a product to well-known songs that are repurposed to appeal to a particular generation, demographic, or type of consumer. When Hyundai filmed a commercial for its Sonata model car using Mozart's playful Piano Sonata #11 as the score, their message was clear: this car is sophisticated, classic, and yet still embodies a sense of lively fun.

Even more blatant examples of *pathos* in advertising abound: from an Iams dog food commercial showing an Irish Wolfhound exuberantly greeting his owner just home from a military tour abroad; to a Subaru commercial where a father looks into his car and sees not his teenager, but a 5-year-old version of her, getting ready to drive off in the car by herself for the first time; to the previously mentioned Budweiser "Brotherhood" example (Figure 2.2), where a man is reunited with a horse he had sold. In each case, the advertisement relies on creating an emotionally laden narrative to sell its product. The power of such stories is perhaps no better utilized than in commercials that sell life insurance or property insurance. The formulaic, yet powerful template for these types of *pathos*-infused ads are no doubt familiar to you: show images of devastated homes and families, especially small children; lead the audience step by step through the story of destruction or death; offer up the product (insurance) as a way to mitigate the depicted tragedy.

However, *pathos* does not only operate through triggering the highs and lows of sentiment in audiences. Sometimes the *pathos* appeal is more subtle, through evoking deep feelings such as patriotism, indignation, even hope or fantasy. Consider the Porsche commercial showing a sleek red car speeding along a windy mountain road, the Ford Escape TV spot featuring the rugged SUV plowing through a muddy off-road trail, or the Volkswagen ad playing on the car's unique, quirky design. Each of these ads uses *pathos* to produce a specific feeling in viewers: I want to drive fast, wind in my hair; I want to get off the beaten path, forge a new frontier; I want to stand out in a crowd and have fun.

You are probably even more familiar with another type of *pathos* appeal—the appeal to sexuality. Clearly, "sex sells." Look at Victoria's Secret models posed in near nudity or at Abercrombie & Fitch poster displays featuring models more likely to show off their toned abs than a pair of jeans (see Figure 2.6), and you can see how advertisers tend to appeal more to non-rational impulses than to our powers of reasoning. Perfume and cologne advertisers in particular often use the rhetoric of sexuality to sell their products, whether it be Calvin Klein's Eternity Aqua, Ralph Lauren's Polo Black, or even Axe's cologne ads, which demonstrate the "Axe effect" by showing cologne-wearers being mobbed by bikini-clad women. Such ads work cleverly to sell fragrance, not on the merits of the scent or on its chemical composition, but through the visual rhetoric of sexuality and our emotional responses to it.

Yet there is an even more powerful *pathos* appeal: what some students have named *humos*. Humor remains one of the most effective forms of

FIGURE 2.6 The photo display in a California Abercrombie & Fitch store window tries to draw consumers in by marketing sexuality as well as clothing.

persuasion; against our more rational impulses, the ads that make us laugh are usually the ones we remember. To prove this point, you need only think back to last year's Superbowl ads: Which ads do you remember? Which ads did you talk over with your friends during and after the game? Probably most of those memorable commercials relied on humor. The arguments these ads make may not always be the most logically sound, but the way they foster a connection with the audience makes them persuasive nonetheless.

Many of these same strategies can be used in academic writing to foster a connection with your audience. You might use the **first-person perspective** to invite your readers into your point of view or use **second-person direct address** to speak to them directly. You might include vivid **description**, **narration**, or **example** to draw them in, supplemented with careful attention to powerful **word choice** and **figurative language** (such as using metaphor, analogy, or personification). Depending on your rhetorical situation and purpose, you might even experiment with **tone** and **humor** as a way to get your readers to engage with your argument.

Consider, for instance, the way in which pop culture critic Doug Barry increases the persuasiveness of his analysis by using *pathos* to connect with his audience in his analysis of a Tide laundry detergent commercial below:

> Ah, the American father—that beer-guzzling, football-watching, hamburger-grilling lump of a human who so often prostrates himself on the family couch before his stupefied children like a sedated gorilla has been soundly mocked as a hapless oaf since, well, General Yepanchin in *The Idiot*. Then, of course, there's *every sitcom father ever*, even lumpy dinosaur Earl Sinclair, whose mere presence in the sitcom-dad pantheon suggests that working and middle class fathers have been supreme idiots since human fathers even existed.
>
> It's refreshing, then, to see a dad not play the dumb-dad clown every now and then. When Stereotypical American Clown Father appears in a commercial for some housekeeping chemical, it's usually to demonstrate his utter incompetence (dads don't clean, silly! they spill rib juice all over the couch as they slip into a meat stupor over the course of a lazy Sunday afternoon) and promptly exit stage right, a freshly chastised goon. A (relatively) new Tide commercial, however, doesn't rely on goon-father to hawk its detergent—Tide Dad is just a normal parent having a blast playing-pretend with his daughter. And what do they play in this blissful domestic imaginarium? Everything from fairy tale princess to wild west sheriff (hint: dad has to stay in a jail made of chairs until his power-drunk daughter decides to free him).

Many authors use narrative as a *pathos* device since readers tend to react powerfully to storytelling; however, here we see Barry relying on alternative methods to produce a similar effect. He uses rich imagery and word choice to paint a engaging description of the American father's typical pop culture incarnation: notice how he employs unusual and catchy modifiers ("beer-guzzling," "football-watching," "hamburger-grilling"); how he integrates striking imagery ("sedated gorilla," "hapless oaf," "dumb-dad clown"); how his allusions anchor his description in other cultural texts (General Yepanchin, Earl Sinclair). Even his strategies of emphasis—from italics for highlighting a point to rhetorical questions and his comical parenthetical asides—foster his connection with the reader by capturing his voice vividly. In its original online version, Barry's analysis was accompanied by a link to the commercial itself, which offered yet another mode of engaging the audience on an emotional level. In your own writing, you might similarly use *pathos*-driven language and images to solidify your argument and persuade your reader.

Exaggerated Uses of Pathos. Although writers often use *pathos* to move their audiences, sometimes they exaggerate the appeal to emotion for dramatic effect. While the intention might be to enhance persuasion, this misuse of pathos can significantly undermine an argument's effectiveness. Let's look at some of the most typical *emotional fallacies*:

- **Scare tactic:** In this case, *pathos* capitalizes on the audience's fears, sometimes unreasonably, to make a point. For instance, Allstate Insurance's recent Mayhem commercials—with actor Dean Winter personifying different types of "mayhem" (from heavy snow that collapses your garage roof, to a screaming toddler in the backseat, to a raccoon in your attic)—employ this sort of tactic to prompt viewers to update their insurance coverage.
- **Slippery slope:** This variation of the *scare tactic* suggests that one act will lead to a chain of events that results in an unforeseen, inevitable, and (usually) undesirable conclusion, without providing any evidence to support the claim. An AT&T smartphone commercial put a positive spin on this fallacy, demonstrating how the simple act of being able to check a train schedule on his smartphone led a man to meet his future wife, then experience a series of positive life events that culminated in his son becoming the President of the United States.
- **Over-sentimentalization:** The overabundant use of *pathos* can outweigh a focus on relevant issues. Occasionally, for instance, organizations like PETA overreach in their emotional appeals, showing the results of the abuse in such graphic detail that audiences actually tune out in horror rather than take action.
- **Bandwagon appeal:** Sometimes called the *ad populum* argument, this emotional fallacy hinges on the premise that since everyone else is doing something, you should too. Pepsi's campaign "The Choice of a New Generation" utilized the bandwagon appeal to argue that if you wanted to be identified with part of the new, hip generation, you needed to drink Pepsi.

- **False need:** In this fallacy, the author amplifies a perceived need or creates a completely new one. Companies market their products based on false needs all the time: think of the commercials you've seen advertising men's or women's razors, transparent Band-Aids, cinch-tie garbage bags, 'Smart' water, or lash-curling mascara. How many of those products reflect actual *needs*, and how many rely on a false need that has been constructed by the company or advertiser?

WRITER'S PRACTICE

Consider the following transcript from a 2012 DIRECTV commercial. Which emotional fallacy does this commercial rely upon in making its argument? Does this diminish its effectiveness as an advertisement?

> When your cable company keeps you on hold, you get angry. When you get angry, you go blow off steam. When you go blow off steam, accidents happen. When accidents happen, you get an eye patch. When you get an eye patch, people think you're tough. When people think you're tough, people want to see *how* tough. And, when people want to see how tough, you wake up in a roadside ditch. Don't wake up in a roadside ditch. Get rid of cable, and upgrade to DIRECTV.

Write a paragraph called "Why You Should Change to DIRECTV," arguing for the use of the product based on a *pathos* appeal, but avoid *exaggerated uses of pathos*. Experiment with deliberate word choice, tone, and strategies including narration and example to provoke an emotional response in your reader.

Appeals to Reason: *Logos*

Although some call *logos* the "logical appeal," it pertains to more than just formal logic. While *pathos* moves an audience on a non-rational level, *logos* engages our critical reasoning faculties to make a point. As a writer, you use *logos* when you construct an essay around facts and reason; in general, an argument based on *logos* will favor the use of logic, statistical evidence, empirical quotations from authorities, data, and proven facts.

We can get a broad sense of how *logos* works by turning our attention once again to advertising. In that medium, the mode of persuasion we call *logos* often operates through the written text; significantly, the Greek word *logos* can be translated as "word," indicating the way in which we, culturally, often look to words as repositories of fact and reason. However, in advertising, just

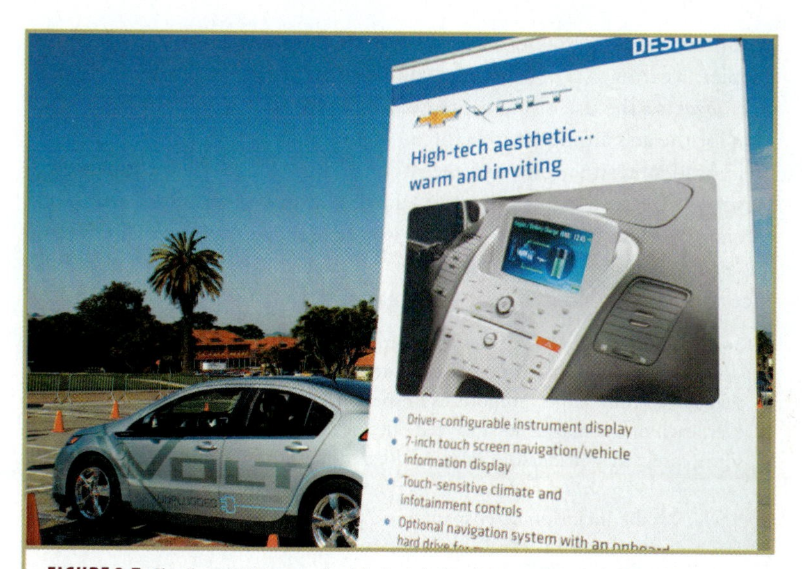

FIGURE 2.7 This Chevrolet Volt promotional display is designed to persuade its reader through *logos* by listing the car's various features.

as in academic writing, *logos* also emerges through the use of quantifiable data, statistics, and facts. The type of *logos*-based reasoning found in the Chevrolet Volt marketing display in Figure 2.7 appears in many ads that you may also be familiar with: think, for instance, of a computer ad that juxtaposes a striking photo of a laptop with a chart detailing its processor type, memory capacity, screen size, and graphics features; a commercial for a bank that features a smiling agent listing the reasons to open a checking account at that branch; the smartphone commercial that rattles off facts about its data plan, wireless coverage, and contracts terms. In each case, the advertisement drives its point through facts, evidence, and reason.

Some might even argue that *logos* as an appeal underlies almost all advertising, specifically because most advertising uses an implicit *causal argument:* if you buy this product, then you or your life will be like the one featured in the ad. Often the associations are explicit: if you use Pantene shampoo, then your hair will be shinier; if you buy Tide detergent, then your clothes will be cleaner; if you buy a Subaru, then your family will be safer driving on the road. Sometimes the *cause-and-effect* argument is more subtle: buying Sure deodorant will make you more confident; drinking Coke will make you happier; wearing Nikes will make you perform better on the court. In each case, *logos*, or the use of logical reasoning, is the tool of persuasion responsible for the ad's argumentative force.

In academic situations, writers often privilege a *logos*-based approach to persuasion because many scholarly claims draw on evidence from research to substantiate assertions. Consider the way Laurence Bowen and Jill Schmid use *logos* as a strategy of argumentation in this passage from "Minority Presence and Portrayal in Mainstream Magazine Advertising: An Update":

> Some might argue that the small number of minorities featured in mainstream magazine advertising may be due to a very deliberate media strategy that successfully targets minorities in specialized and minority media. However, each of the magazines analyzed does have a minority readership and, in some cases, that readership is quite substantial. For example, according to *Simmons 1993 Study of Media and Markets,* the Hispanic readership of *Life* is 9.9%, yet the inclusion of Hispanics in *Life*'s advertisements was only .8%. *Cosmopolitan* has a 11.3% Black readership, yet only 4.3% of the advertisements included Blacks; 13.3% of the magazines' readership is Hispanic and only .5% of the advertisements use Hispanics.

Notice how the authors drive their point home through reference to their research with mainstream magazines as well as to statistical data that they have both uncovered and analyzed. Their use of such concrete information and examples makes their argument much more convincing than had they provided a more general rebuttal to the statement that begins their paragraph. In this way, appeals to logic can take on many forms, including interpretations of "hard evidence," such as found in syllogisms (formal, structured arguments), reasoned arguments, closing statements in law, inferences in the form of statistical models, and appeals to "common sense" or cultural assumptions.

Logical Fallacies. As with *pathos*, *logos* can be susceptible to misuse. Such mistaken or misleading uses of *logos*, commonly called **logical fallacies**, often involve faulty reasoning that undermines the validity of an argument.

- **Post hoc ergo propter hoc fallacy:** This fallacy confuses *cause* and *effect*, namely, the idea that because something happened first (showering with an aloe-enhanced body gel), it causes something that happened afterward (getting a person you like to ask you out on a date).

- **Cum hoc ergo propter hoc fallacy:** A variation of the *post hoc fallacy*, this type of argument is often called a *correlation-causation fallacy* because it suggests that since two unrelated events happen at the same time (are correlated), they should thus be interpreted as *cause* and *effect*. For instance, the following syllogism is an example of a *cum hoc fallacy*: (1) a teenager plays his varsity basketball game wearing his new Air Jordans; (2) the teenager makes many key rebounds and jump shots while playing the game; (3) the Air Jordans caused his success in the game.
- **The hasty generalization:** Writers who use *hasty generalizations* draw conclusions too quickly without providing enough supporting evidence or considering all the nuances of the issue. A comic example of this type of argument can be found in a commercial for the Taco Bell bacon club chalupa taco: a young woman confides to her friend that she's carrying a chalupa tucked in her purse because "guys love bacon," a generalization the ad attempts to substantiate by showing her, moments later, surrounded by men who had been drawn to the woman by the "intoxicating" smell.
- **The either-or argument:** This fallacy involves the oversimplification of a complicated issue, reducing it to a choice between two diametrically opposed choices that ignore other possible scenarios. We see this fallacy often in commercials that compare a pair of competing products (iPhone vs. Android, Coke vs. Pepsi, Verizon vs. AT&T) without taking into consideration the other alternatives available to the consumer.
- **Stacking the evidence:** An argument that *stacks the evidence* presents only one side of an issue. Political candidates frequently use this strategy in their campaign ads by stating facts and data that support only their policy platform, without presenting an issue in its full complexity.
- **Begging the question:** This form of *circular logic* uses an argument as evidence for itself, thereby evading the issue at hand. A Statefarm ad provides a clear example of *begging the question*:

  Woman: I thought Statefarm didn't have all those apps.

  Man: Where'd you hear that?

Woman: The Internet.

Man: And you believed it?

Woman: Yeah; they can't put anything on the Internet that isn't true.

Man: Where'd you hear that?

Woman: The Internet.

In this quick exchange, the woman "begs the question" by using a claim from the Internet to argue that all claims found on the Internet are true.

- **The red herring or non sequitor:** Some arguments employ unrelated information or a *non sequitor* (in Latin, literally meaning "does not follow") in order to distract the audience's attention from the issue at hand. A sudden shift of topic or focus in an ad can function as a *red herring*. Dow Chemical's ad "The Human Element" shows a plethora of artistic and ecofriendly scenes that make the logical argument that the company relates to human connection and nature, but in fact serve as a red herring to distract the viewer from Dow's massive industrial production of oil, gas, and electronic products.
- **Straw man argument:** The visual metaphor of the *straw man* effectively represents this fallacy; the writer sets up a fake or distorted representation of a counterargument so as to have something to easily argue against and to present the writer's own position in a more favorable light. Here's one example: during the 2012 presidential campaign, vice presidential candidate Paul Ryan accused President Obama of using *straw man* tactics, citing the way the president characterized Republicans as anti-government and pessimistic about the country in his speeches. According to Ryan, in doing so, Obama was misrepresenting the opposing party's stance so as to ingratiate himself with the American people.
- **Equivocation:** Arguments that fall prey to this fallacy use ambiguous terminology that misleads the audience or confuses the issue. For instance, a 2008 commercial for California's Proposition 8 undermined its argument for marriage equality by using the term "rights" indiscriminately to refer to both legal rights and moral rights.
- **False analogy:** While an *analogy* can be a powerful strategy of argumentation, a *false analogy* claims that two things resemble each other

when they actually do not. For instance, a Mercedes-Benz commercial suggests that refraining from eating ice cream is like refraining from buying one of their cars, when in fact there is very little connection between the two actions.

Appeals to Character and Authority: *Ethos*

The last of the three classical appeals that we'll learn in this chapter is *ethos*—literally, "character." Perhaps you have used *ethos* in other disciplines to mean an argument based on ethical principles. But the *rhetorical* meaning of the term is slightly different: according to Aristotle, *ethos* works as a rhetorical strategy by establishing the goodwill or credibility of the writer or speaker. In a sense, almost more than with any other appeal, *ethos* involves a critical awareness of audience. It is the audience who evaluates your credibility as a writer and, therefore, the persuasiveness of the argument.

WRITER'S PRACTICE

Look carefully at the hypothetical advertising pitches below, each one of which represents a flawed use of *logos* as a marketing strategy. For each one, identify which type of logical fallacy it contains: *post hoc ergo propter hoc*; *cum hoc ergo propter hoc*; hasty generalization; either/or; stacking the evidence; begging the question; red herring; straw man; equivocation; or false analogy. Then, consider ways in which the pitch might be revised so as to make a more solid *logos*-based argument.

- Buy American because our products are made right here in the United States!
- In these increasingly complex financial times, if you try to manage your finances without a trained professional advisor, you could well find your life savings wiped out. Protect your savings: contact your local GoodCents agent today for a full portfolio review.
- Corey uses Sparkle Fresh mouthwash every morning and recently received a promotion at work. If you start using Sparkle Fresh, your career will take off too!
- Other paper towel companies don't care about global warming or climate change. Use Greener World paper towels: there's always 100% recycled paper on every roll.
- Buying the right car is like choosing the right spouse: you need to find one perfect for you. So choose a What-a-Catch-Car: it's dependable, affordable, and built to last.

In this way, *ethos* can be a very powerful tool for establishing trust and facilitating the persuasiveness of an argument. Based on the Aristotelian model, we can distinguish between three different operations of *ethos*:

1. *Ethos* based on practical skills and wisdom
2. *Ethos* based on virtue and goodness
3. *Ethos* based on goodwill toward the audience

As a writer you use *ethos* every time you pick up a pen or proofread your essay—that is, when you write, you construct your *ethos* through your word choice, your tone, your grammar and punctuation. However, you can establish *ethos* in other ways as well. By establishing *your authority* in relation to the topic—whether because of your depth of knowledge or your close engagement with the subject—you help your readers trust your claims. By constructing a sense of **common ground** with your audience, you can invoke shared values to draw more of a connection with your audience. By using **credible sources** in your research, you attest to the quality of your argument and analytic methodology. Likewise, by respectfully acknowledging **other arguments**, you establish yourself as fair-minded and well-informed on your topic; whether you ultimately concede a point or refute the counterargument, your willingness to entertain alternative positions increases your *ethos*.

The example that follows demonstrates how one writer uses *ethos* to set up the foundations for a complex argument. In this excerpt from her famous piece, "Sex, Lies, and Advertising," Gloria Steinem, founding editor of the feminist magazine *Ms.*, deliberately builds her *ethos* through an opening narrative. Her decision is strategic: she anticipates that the issue itself—the constraints that advertisers put on the content of women's magazines—might produce a skeptical reaction from her readers. Accordingly, she devotes her opening paragraphs to establishing both the validity of the problem and her own qualifications in terms of addressing it.

> About three years ago, as *glasnost* was beginning and *Ms.* seemed to be ending, I was invited to a press lunch for a Soviet official. He entertained us with anecdotes about new problems of democracy in his country. Local Communist leaders were being criticized in their media for the first time, he explained, and they were angry.

"So I'll have to ask my American friends," he finished pointedly, "how more subtly to control the press." In the silence that followed, I said, "Advertising."

The reporters laughed, but later, one of them took me aside: How dare I suggest that freedom of the press was limited? How dare I imply that his newsweekly could be influenced by ads?

I explained that I was thinking of advertising's media-wide influence on most of what we read. Even newsmagazines use "soft" cover stories to sell ads, confuse readers with "advertorials," and occasionally self-censor on subjects known to be a problem with big advertisers.

But I also explained, I was thinking especially of women's magazines. There, it isn't just a little content that's devoted to attracting ads, it's almost all of it. That's why advertisers—not readers—have always been the problem for *Ms.* As the only women's magazine that didn't supply what the ad world euphemistically describes as "supportive editorial atmosphere" or "complementary copy" (for instance, articles that praise food/fashion/beauty subjects to "support" and "complement" food/fashion/beauty ads), *Ms.* could never attract enough advertising to break even.

"Oh, *women's* magazines," the journalist said with contempt. "Everybody knows they're catalogs—but who cares? They have nothing to do with journalism."

I can't tell you how many times I've had this argument in 25 years of working for many kinds of publications. Except as moneymaking machines—"cash cows" as they are so elegantly called in the trade—women's magazines are rarely taken seriously. Though changes being made by women have been called more far-reaching than the industrial revolution—and though many editors try hard to reflect some of them in the few pages left to them after all the ad-related subjects have been covered—the magazines serving the female half of the country are still far below the journalistic and ethical strands of news and general interest publications. Most depressing of all, this doesn't even rate an exposé.

While the writing does use *pathos*, it also, more significantly, serves to enhance Steinem's credibility. Notice the way she builds her authority, or *ethos*:

1. First, she mentions that she was invited to a lunch with a political figure, indicating her importance in journalistic circles.
2. Next, after humorously introducing her main argument (that freedom of the press is curtailed by advertising), she demonstrates how she gracefully addresses counterarguments.
3. Then, she utilizes the discourse of magazine publishing ("supportive editorial atmosphere" and "complementary copy") to remind her audience of her *insider status* in the industry.
4. Lastly, she informs the reader directly about her long professional history working in media ("...in 25 years of working for many kinds of publications"). In this move, she situates her *ethos* not only in the current moment of her opening narrative but also in her continued involvement in the publishing field.

Having established her *ethos* in this opening section, Steinem can then move forward with her argument, which is driven largely by an accumulation of examples designed to further underscore her expertise and authority. Thus, *ethos* is a driving force in the persuasiveness of her writing.

To continue our exploration of the complexities of *ethos*, let's look to advertising once again and see how companies have long recognized the persuasive power of *ethos*. In fact, a brand logo is in essence *ethos* distilled into a single symbol: it transmits in a single icon the entire reputation of a company, organization, or brand identity. From the Nike swoosh to McDonald's golden arches or the Apple computer apple, symbols serve to mark (or brand) products with *ethos*.

Yet the power of the brand logo as a seat of *ethos* relies on the company's overall reputation with the consumer—a reputation that the company carefully cultivates through advertising campaigns. Many companies, for instance, trade on *ethos* by using spokespeople in their advertising campaigns. You've probably seen ads that invoke the practical skills or knowledge of the celebrity to sell a product: basketball superstar LeBron James selling basketball shoes or Martha Stewart selling linens, towels, and dishware. Sometimes companies even rely on this strategy when using a less famous spokesperson; for instance, we trust Flo from the Progressive Commercials or the Geico's talking gecko lizard because of both their clear goodwill toward the audience and the expertise and information they share during their commercials.

FIGURE 2.8 A Citibank billboard in New York City leverages Olympian Cullen Jones's *ethos* to draw in new customers.

However, many campaigns rely not only on the spokesperson's expertise, but also on the person's star appeal, character, and virtue. Consider the power of the billboard shown in Figure 2.8. On display during the summer of 2012, this billboard used Gold-medalist Cullen Jones's fame to vouch for Citibank's reputation and quality of services. We might not believe that Jones knows much about banking, but we trust him as a recognizable and admirable public figure. We find his argument persuasive because of our "knowledge" of his character and his willingness to put his reputation on the line to promote a product. Of course, ad campaigns based upon celebrity endorsements—specifically those based on Aristotle's categories of virtue and goodness—can backfire. Lance Armstrong's 2012 confession about his steroid use left advertisers from Nike to Giro and Radioshack scrambling to distance themselves from their endorsement deals with the world-class cyclist.

Clearly, *ethos* matters to companies because so much of their business relies on their reputation. For this reason, we often come across ads that market not a product but a corporate *ethos* intended to establish that company's credibility. One recurrent example of this appears in various oil company ads that have emerged over the last few years. Battling the perception that Big Oil, heedless of its role in global warming, is motivated only by ever-increasing profits, these ads inform us endlessly of each company's "green" policies and efforts to give back to the earth. In addition, *ethos* can be used as a tool in attack ads. Often, companies deliberately attempt to undermine the *ethos* of their competition as a way of promoting their own products. You probably have seen ads of this sort: Coke vs. Pepsi; DIRECTV vs. cable; Burger King vs. McDonalds. Samsung in particular has made a practice of targeting Apple in their smartphone commercials, from spots that mock iPhone users, standing in endless lines for the newest product release, to commercials that demonstrate how the Samsung features easily trump the capabilities of its Apple-brand competitor. In each case, the deliberate *comparison-contrast* builds up one company's *ethos* at another's expense.

Misuses of Ethos. Since *ethos* derives from credibility or trustworthiness, *misuses of ethos* tend to involve a breach of trust between the author and the audience. For this reason, you should take special care as a writer not to abuse this ethical contract with your reader. What follows are some of the most common misuses of *ethos*:

- ***Ad hominem:*** This strategy attempts to persuade by reducing the credibility of opposing positions through attacks on a person's character. Rather than focus on the argument itself, *ad hominem* criticizes the speaker or writer who makes the argument. We see *ad hominem* at work most often in political campaign advertisements, where candidates focus less on the issues at hand and instead emphasize their opponents' weaknesses. This *misuse of ethos* also happens in commercials where companies attack each other for the way they run their businesses rather than the quality of their products.
- ***Argument from authority:*** This type of argument involves a misrepresentation of skills and wisdom; the writer contends to be an authority—or holds another up to be an authority—based on an overinflated or fallacious suggestion of expertise. For instance, Oprah Winfrey came under fire in 2012 for tweeting an endorsement for the Windows Surface from her iPad; her credibility as a Surface user was immediately called into question.
- ***Association fallacies:*** This fallacy often takes the form of "guilt by association," where an argument is dismissed because it is associated with an undesirable person or position. Conversely, this fallacy can also unfairly promote or advocate an argument based on unrelated positive associations. We can find prominent examples of this technique at work in the political advertising during the 2008 presidential campaign: both Barack Obama and John McCain released commercials that used *guilt by association* to denigrate each other's characters.
- ***Appeal to anonymous authority:*** This type argument references broad, unspecified groups as its authority. For instance, while the

taglines "Four out of five dentists surveyed..." or "Studies indicate..." lend some credibility to advertising campaigns, unless the ads provide tangible references to *which* dentists, *which* studies, and *what* context, the argument is ultimately empty and unsupported.

- ***Authority over evidence:*** This mode of argument involves the practice of overemphasizing authority or *ethos* rather than focusing on the merits of the evidence itself. Celebrity endorsements based on goodwill can verge on this fallacy.

CONSIDERING CONTEXT AND VALUES: *KAIROS* AND *DOXA*

2.3 How can I shape my argument based on time, place, and shared values?

As you can tell from examining ads in this chapter, a successful argument must take into account not only the *rhetorical situation* but also the context—or right time and place—as well as the values of an audience. That is why the Citibank billboard of Cullen Jones shown in Figure 2.8 had tremendous resonance when first displayed right after the London Olympics in 2012, but was pasted over in favor of a more timely ad once "Olympics fever" had died down. In ancient Greece rhetoricians called this aspect of the rhetorical situation ***kairos***—namely, attention to the right time and place for an argument.

In your own writing, you should consider *kairos* along with the other aspects of the rhetorical situation: audience, text, and writer. It is important to recognize the *kairos*—the opportune historical, ideological, or cultural moment—of a text when analyzing its rhetorical force. You undoubtedly already consider the context for persuasive communication in your everyday life. For instance, whether you are asking a friend to dinner or a professor for a recommendation, your assessment of the timeliness and the appropriate strategies for that time probably determines the shape your argument takes. In essence, by picking the right moment and place to make your case, you are in fact paying attention to the *kairos* of your argument.

Consider Coca-Cola's ad campaigns. Coke has exerted a powerful presence in the beverage industry for many years, in part because of its strategic advertising. During World War II, Coke ran a series of ads featuring servicemen and showing inspiring slices of Americana that built its campaign around the nationalistic sentiment of a specific cultural moment. Look at Figure 2.9, an advertisement for Coke from the 1940s. This picture uses *pathos* to appeal to the audience's sense of patriotism by featuring a row of

FIGURE 2.9 This Coca-Cola ad used *kairos* to create a powerful argument for its World War II audience.

seemingly carefree servicemen, leaning from the windows of a military bus, the refreshing Cokes in their hands producing smiles even far away from home. The picture draws in the audience by reassuring them on two fronts:

- It builds on the nationalistic pride in the young, handsome servicemen who so happily serve their country.
- It is designed to appease fears about the hostile climate abroad: as both the picture and the accompanying text assure us, Coca-Cola (and the servicemen) "goes along" and "gets a hearty welcome."

The power of this message relates directly to *kairos*. An ad such as this one, premised on patriotism and pride in military service, would be most persuasive during wartime when many more people tend to support the spirit of nationalism and therefore would be moved by the image of the young serviceman shipping off to war. It is through understanding the *kairos* of this advertisement that you can appreciate the strength of the ad's rhetorical appeal.

An awareness of *kairos* likewise helps us see how a more current coke commercial is tailored to today's culture, speaking directly to contemporary concerns. The still frames in Figures 2.10, 2.11, and 2.12 represent three moments from Coke's recent "Coming Together" commercial. The ad begins by evoking a sense of history and *kairos*, with the female narrator asserting, "For over a hundred and twenty-five years, we've been bringing people together. Today, we'd like people to come together on something that concerns all of us: obesity. The long-term health of our families and the country is at stake. And as the nation's leading beverage company, we can play an important role." The message—that the Coca-Cola corporation fights obesity—is specifically designed to resonate with a twenty-first century audience concerned with health as well as national unity. The accompanying images reinforce this message, such as a close-up of a woman weighing herself

(Figure 2.10), a graphic presenting the number of low calorie choices Coca-Cola provides (see Figure 2.11), and a shot featuring the Coca-Cola mini to demonstrate the introduction of smaller serving sizes (see Figure 2.12). Watching this commercial, it becomes clear that Coca Cola is appealing to a world very different from the one experienced by the soldiers on the train in the earlier Coke ad.

Our examples also call attention to the way in which ads appeal to an audience's values, or ***doxa***. A crucial concept to the ancient Greeks, *doxa* means "popular opinion" or "belief"—a learned value system—since it refers to those values or beliefs that are deeply held by a particular community at a particular place and moment in time. The term is related to a concept you may know, *dogma*—or unchanging doctrine—but importantly, *doxa* can and does change over time. When an author considers *doxa* while crafting a persuasive text, she constructs an argument based on her understanding of the values held in common by a group of people. For instance, in the "Coming Together" commercial, Coca-Cola uses *doxa* when tapping into the audience's commitment to healthy living; while such a worldview might be spreading, it was not always the case (think of smoking ads in the past that glamourized such behavior). Moreover, while the appeal to national health works for an ad in the U.S. today, a contemporary Coca-Cola ad in Lebanon, by contrast, appeals to the culture's celebration of voluptuous singing

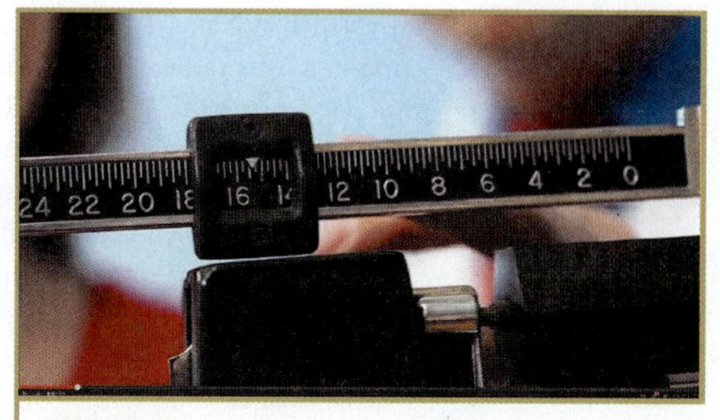

FIGURE 2.10

FIGURE 2.11

FIGURE 2.12 Stills from Coca-Cola's "Coming Together" campaign show a new focus on helping consumers make healthy choices.

divas, such as Nancy Ajram, and therefore presents a video focused on romance among adults rather than nutrition and children. By invoking the cultural values of each location, Coca-Cola deliberately uses *doxa* as a rhetorical strategy. You can probably think of many other examples of how attention to *doxa* works in arguments aimed at a specific demographic, even within the United States (for instance, Diet Mountain Dew ads that target Nascar lovers versus Honest Tea ads targeting bicycling enthusiasts). Consider also how political ads appeal to popular opinion or deeply held values of a specific community (such as a depressed region needing manufacturing jobs, an urban center supporting marriage equality, or a rural constituency opposed to gun control).

Attending to *kairos* and *doxa* in these ways enables us to understand differences in context and values, to see how persuasion makes powerful use of the present place and moment, and finally, to learn how we can implement these rhetorical strategies when composing our own arguments.

READING AN AD ANALYSIS

Now that we've seen how strategies of argumentation and the rhetorical appeals operate in advertising, let's look at how they come together in a written analysis. As you read David Zweig's *Slate* article about the 2013 Dove sketch artist ad campaign, consider not only whether you find his analysis persuasive, but also how he leverages different rhetorical strategies to make a compelling argument to his audience.

WHAT EVERYONE IS MISSING ABOUT THE LAUDED NEW DOVE AD CAMPAIGN

David Zweig

The very first sentence relies on *logos* (an impressive statistic) and *kairos* (reference to the article's timeliness) to call attention to the relevance of the commercial and the author's argument.

The flagship video for the Dove ad campaign "Real Beauty Sketches" has generated over seven million views since its debut less than a week ago. The video documents an experiment Dove conducted where several women, each sitting alone, describe themselves to a forensic artist behind a curtain as he sketches them. Then, in phase two, strangers whom the women had met briefly earlier also describe them to the artist. Afterward each woman is shown the two illustrations side by side—the one based on her description and the one based on the description by the stranger. The women are shocked, some tearing up, as they look at the two pictures. In all of the pairings the sketches based on the strangers' descriptions are far more attractive. Tagline: "You are more beautiful than you think."

The immediate press for the campaign has been glowing. A HuffPo piece wrote "despite the obvious commercial intentions behind this campaign, the message rings true." Babble's lead called it "powerful and poignant."

They're both right. And yet the point of the campaign is neutered at best, and more likely distorted by the fact that in the experiment all of the women are fashionable and reasonably attractive. What happens in the experiment if they were to use "regular" women who are poor, not stylish, unattractive? While the campaign's point that many women have uncharitable perceptions of their looks is well-taken, Dove's casting choice is disingenuous and ultimately harmful. This ad is the latest in Dove's long-running campaign of using a faux representation of "real" women.

The charade of keepin' it real is particularly egregious in this latest spot. Melinda, the slim brunette in skinny jeans with Zooey Deschanel bangs, and Olivia, with the piercing blue eyes and long golden hair, are two of the younger standouts. The more middle aged women all have a sophisticated urbane look about them, with contemporary hairstyles and makeup so tasteful it looks as if a Bobbi Brown stylist applied it (perhaps one did).

Watching the ad, I kept picturing all of the women I see on the subway, at highway rest stops, in suburban malls. Yes, some of them look like the women in the ad, but most of them don't. Imperfect dye jobs, baggy jeans, acne scars, and faces that could not be termed "thin so you could see her cheekbones," as Florence, one of the subjects in the ad, was described by the stranger. What are they to make of the ad? In a way this ad campaign is even worse for them than conventional

The article opens with a **description** of the commercial to provide a foundation for the analysis to follow. The description draws on a **narrative** structure to engage the reader.

Zweig now increases the *ethos* of his argument by including reviews of the commercial from the *Huffington Post* and the Disney-sponsored website, *Babble*.

The use of rhetorical question here points to the turn in his piece from description to analysis.

Here Zweig announces his **thesis statement**, establishing the direct for the rest of his argument.

Once again Zweig uses **description**, enriched by **vivid word choice**, to help his audience "see" the commercial he's discussing.

His use of first person here on the one hand creates a *pathos* connection with the reader, and on the other suggests his own *ethos* by grounding his analysis in his own observations and experience.

At this point, Zweig relies upon **comparison-contrast** to help us understand "what everyone is missing."

Zweig employs **definition** here parenthetically, anticipating his expanded use of this strategy in the subsequent paragraph.

ads because it has the pretense of representing them, and yet they still must notice they fall far short of "real" (real being defined in this context as average). At least every woman *expects* to not look like the models and actresses in standard beauty advertising.

In this paragraph, Zweig takes issue with the **definition** of beauty that Dove presents, clarifying how this concept is actually defined within the context of the commercial.

A separate, yet also important manipulation in the ad is the deliberate misuse of the word "beautiful." When they say, "You are more beautiful than you think," what they really mean is, "You are more attractive than you think." By distorting the definition of beautiful, they devalue the word's real meaning by perpetuating both the notion that everyone is beautiful, and even that beauty, as the most exceptional form of attractiveness, is something we all should strive for to begin with.

In the final line, Zweig makes clear that he is in fact analyzing a misuse of *pathos* in the ad and the way that it misleads the commercial's audience.

While the spot is moving, and has an ostensibly valuable message, in the end, it can only let real women down. In fact, its "poignancy" is what makes it so dangerous. Our emotional response clouds our ability to see it for what it really is—another cynical ad campaign.

THE WRITER'S PROCESS

As you turn to write up your analysis of advertisements in the way that David Zweig did for Dove ads, consider the ways in which your own writing can "sell" your argument to the reader. What is the rhetorical situation of your writing assignment? What *strategies of argumentation* and *rhetorical appeals* would be most effective in reaching your target audience? Do you want to use narration, a humorous analogy, or a stirring example to forge a connection with your readers based on *pathos*? Or is your written analysis better suited to *logos*, following the step-by-step process of reading an ad, drawing on empirical evidence, or looking at cause and effect? Perhaps you will decide to enrich your discussion through cultivating your *ethos* as a writer, establishing your own authority on a subject or citing reputable work done by other scholars. Finally, how can you make use of *kairos* and *doxa* as persuasive tools by evoking something from today's culture in your writing or appealing to the beliefs of your reader? In your essay, you certainly will use many of these strategies and a combination of rhetorical appeals; as we saw in the examples from this chapter, a successful argument uses various techniques to persuade its audience.

WRITING ASSIGNMENTS

1. **Written Analysis of an Advertisement.** Select a commercial or a print ad to analyze. You might choose a Superbowl commercial archived online, a print ad from your favorite fashion or newsmagazine, or even a classic advertisement from a different historical period (a 1960s Coke Ad? A Legos ad from the 1970s? A soap ad from the late 19th century?) archived online or in your local library. Having selected your advertisement, use the methods you practiced in this chapter to analyze which strategies it uses to persuade its audience. Refer to the checklist below to help you focus your analysis.

   - ❑ **Content:** What exactly is the ad selling? An object? An experience? An idea?
   - ❑ **Argument:** How is the ad selling the product? What message is the ad sending to the audience?
   - ❑ **Medium:** What medium was the advertisement produced in? Television? Print? Radio? How did this choice suit the rhetorical purpose of the ad and accommodate the needs of a particular audience?
   - ❑ **Character and setting:** What is featured by the ad? An object? A scene? A person? How are these elements portrayed? What are the ethnicity, age, socioeconomic class, and gender of any people in the advertisement? How do these choices relate to the ad's intended audience and reflect deliberate rhetorical choices?
   - ❑ **Rhetorical appeals:** Which rhetorical appeals does the ad rely on to persuade its audience? *Pathos*? *Logos*? *Ethos*? *Kairos*? *Doxa*? How do these appeals operate both through language and through imagery?
   - ❑ **Strategies of development:** Which strategies of argumentation does the ad use? Narration? Definition? Comparison-contrast? Example or illustration? Classification? Process? Analogy? Cause and effect? How do these strategies contribute to the ad's persuasive appeal?
   - ❑ **Word & image:** What is the relationship between the word (written or spoken) and the imagery in the ad? How does this relationship affect the persuasiveness of the advertisement?

- ❑ **Layout & design:** How are the elements of the ad arranged—on a page (for a print ad) or in sequence (for a television or Internet commercial)? What is the purpose behind this arrangement? How does the ad's organization facilitate its argument? How do elements like choice or coloring of typeface, filtering or cropping of photographs, or the overall tone of the advertisement (informal, personal, authoritative, technical, comic, serious affect its persuasiveness?
- ❑ **Design:** What typeface is used? What size? What color? How do these decisions reflect attention to the ad's rhetorical situation? How do they function in relation to the ad's rhetorical appeals?
- ❑ **Tone:** What voice does the text use to reach its audience? How does it convey this tone? Through words? Images? Color? Music? Is the tone technical, informal, personal, or authoritative? Is it comic or serious?
- ❑ **Historical context:** In what country and at what historical moment was the advertisement produced? How do the demands of context shape its persuasive appeals? How does the ad reflect, comment on, challenge, or reinforce contemporary political, economic, or gender ideology? How does this commentary situate it in terms of a larger trend or argument?
- ❑ **Cultural resonance:** Does the ad use famous events or places or recognizable symbols to increase its persuasiveness? If so, how does that establish audience or a relationship to a cultural moment?

Seeing Connections
To consider how to best insert your images as evidence in your paper, see Chapter 8.

2. **Rhetorical Analysis:** Building on your brainstorm in Assignment #1, develop your thoughts into a cohesive rhetorical analysis essay, driven by a strong thesis statement and drawing on evidence from the advertisement to support your claim. As you work with your notes from Assignment #1, be selective in which details you include in your essay: your goal is not to produce a list of all your observations, but to produce a focused analysis that argues for how the advertiser used specific rhetorical appeals or strategies to produce a persuasive argument. *For added challenge,* perform your rhetorical analysis on two or three ads for the same products, comparing how the advertisers adjusted the strategies to accommodate different rhetorical situations, audience, media, or purposes.

3. **Rhetorical Analysis: Fallacies.** Working alone or with a group, select a print ad or commercial that includes a misuse of either *pathos*, *logos*, or *ethos* as a persuasive strategy. As an essay (or a PowerPoint or Prezi), define the fallacy and then analyze how it functions in the ad. In your conclusion, suggest how the ad itself could be altered to avoid this line of argument. *For added challenge*: instead of finding an existing ad, work with a group and film your own "commercial" that clearly hinges on a particular fallacy of argument. In the

beginning of your video, define the fallacy you'll be illustrating; after your commercial segment, provide a brief verbal analysis in your conclusion to underscore your point for your audience.

4. **Cultural Analysis:** Write a paper in which you compare two ad campaigns and examine the ideology behind specific constructions of our culture. Does one campaign portray gender- or race-specific ideas? How do the tools of persuasion produce each message? What message is conveyed by the reliance on such cultural ideals or notions of identity? What representations of sexuality, gender roles, or class are presented by these ads? Present your findings to the class, holding up examples of the ads to discuss in support of your analysis.

5. **Collaborative Historical Analysis:** Working in groups, look at several ads from different time periods produced by the same company, such as ads for cigarettes, cars, hygiene products, or personal computers. Each member of your group should choose a single ad and prepare a rhetorical analysis of its persuasive appeals. Share your analyses to explore how this company has modified its rhetorical approach over time. Collaborate on a paper in which you chart the evolution of the company's persuasive strategies and how that evolution was informed by *kairos*.

CHAPTER 3

Composing Arguments

Chapter Preview Questions

3.1 How do the canons of rhetoric determine the content, shape, and style of arguments?

3.2 What is the role of invention in creating persuasive arguments?

3.3 How does the canon of arrangement influence a reader's response to a text?

3.4 How can style be used to compose a powerful argument?

3.5 What techniques can I use to create strong titles, introductions, and conclusions?

3.6 How can I write a persuasive position paper?

When you skim news stories online or watch media coverage of dramatic events, you are in fact reading about an issue through a filter: the newscaster's selection of images and quotations as well as the reporter's choice of words in composing a story about that event. Such writing aims to persuade you to read further—to stay on the website, share the link with friends, or post a comment with your response—and in that way even the news functions as argument. Let's consider an example. Imagine that it is September 2005 and the United States is still reeling from the aftermath of Hurricane Katrina. As you click through several news sites, you pause to look at the images they display. One features a striking photo of a military helicopter dropping supplies to the citizens of New Orleans (see Figure 3.1). Another shows an African-American mother clutching two small children and wading through waist-deep water. Yet another displays the image of a mob of angry people, packed together and arguing as they try to evacuate the city. A final site uses the

FIGURE 3.1 A photograph of supplies being dropped to survivors of a hurricane in New Orleans.

picture of a child's dirt-smeared doll, swept into a pile of debris on the road, as its poignant commentary on natural disaster.

Based on these images, which site would you visit? How does each image make a different argument about what happened? How might the words that accompany the photo shape your interpretation of the visual texts? How does the choice of a particular visual-verbal combination present a specific *point of view* or argument about an event in the news?

Photographs and captions on news sites or in newspapers work through the tools of persuasion that we examined in earlier chapters. In this chapter, we'll continue to explore how visual and verbal rhetoric shapes our reality. We'll become acquainted with the *canons of rhetoric*—five classifications of argument established by Aristotle—and we'll work through the process of composing an argument: coming up with ideas, structuring those ideas, and developing a style for your position, or stance, on an issue. We'll also delineate specific strategies for how you can write compelling titles, introductions, and conclusions for your own essays about visual rhetoric.

UNDERSTANDING THE CANONS OF RHETORIC

3.1 How do the canons of rhetoric determine the content, shape, and style of arguments?

In ancient Greece, all communicative acts were classified into five categories, or what Aristotle called the **canons of rhetoric**:

- **Invention:** creating and constructing ideas
- **Arrangement:** ordering and laying out ideas through effective organization
- **Style:** developing the appropriate expression for those ideas
- **Memory:** retaining invented ideas, recalling additional supporting ideas, and facilitating memory in the audience
- **Delivery:** presenting or performing ideas with the aim of persuading

Each one of these canons is necessary for persuasive communication, whether that be through spoken word, written discourse, or, more recently, multimedia texts. For our discussion of composing arguments in this chapter, we'll focus on the first three canons.

Seeing Connections
See Chapter 9 for explanation of the canons of Memory and Delivery.

INVENTION IN ARGUMENT

3.2 What is the role of invention in creating persuasive arguments?

When you craft language with the purpose of persuading your audience, you are **inventing** an argument. That is, you are generating ideas about a topic. Aristotle defined *invention* as methods for "finding all available arguments." Methods you might use to "invent" arguments include:

- **Definition:** What does the text *mean*? What are other examples?
- **Division:** What *parts* are comprised within the text?
- **Comparison:** Does the text mean something new now versus years ago? How does the text *compare* to other texts?
- **Classification:** What is the *purpose* of the text? Cause and effect? Consequence?
- **Testimony:** What do *others* say about the text?

Invention is the "discovery of valid or seemingly valid arguments to render one's cause probable."

—*Cicero,*
De Inventione, I.vii

To develop ideas, you can use a range of **rhetorical strategies**, including those you learned in the previous chapter: invoking *pathos*, using *ethos* or appeals to character, or employing *logos* to reason with your readers or listeners. Your task as a writer is to forge a powerful text that argues your point—the focus of your *invention*—and to convince others to agree with you. In composing arguments, you can look for examples in texts all around you, and learn from them how *invention* generates particular perspectives that the author wishes to convey to the audience.

Consider pictures. We might think that a photograph provides a window on another person's reality. But in fact photographs, like written works, are texts of *rhetorical invention*. The "reality" that photographs display is actually a *version* of reality created by a photographer's rhetorical and artistic decisions: whether to use color or black-and-white film; what sort of lighting to use; how to position the subject of the photograph; whether to opt for a panorama or close-up shot; what backdrop to use; how to crop, or trim, the image once it is printed. In effect, when we see photographs in a newspaper or art gallery, we are looking at the product of deliberate *strategies of invention.* In photography, these strategies include key elements of composition, such as selection, placement, perspective, and framing. In written texts, the same elements—selection, placement, perspective, and framing—are critical to making an argument.

Figure 3.2, an image captured by photojournalist Margaret Bourke-White, shows a line of homeless African Americans, displaced by the 1937 Louisville flood, waiting in line to receive food and clothing from a local Red Cross center. Does the photo merely document a moment in the history of Kentucky? Or have the choice of subject, the cropping, the angle, the background, and the elements within the frame been selected by the

FIGURE 3.2 Margaret Bourke-White, "At the Time of the Louisville Flood," 1937.

photographer to make a specific argument about race and American culture during the first half of the twentieth century?

In your own writing, you could use this photograph as a springboard for inventing an argument. Perhaps you would write a historically focused argument that examines the catastrophic 1937 Louisville flood and its impact on the local community. Or you could refer to this photograph as visual evidence in a paper that examines the link between social status, race, and disaster relief. Either argument could draw on the power of the photograph, which reveals the invention strategies of the artist.

Let's look more closely at how invention factors into the way photographers and writers compose arguments. Consider two famous photographs by Dorothea Lange (see Figure 3.3 and Figure 3.4 on the next page), which offer very different representations of migrant workers during the Great Depression. In each case, we see a migrant family huddled inside a tent. The subjects seem to be poor, hungry, and struggling to make a living. Their material conditions are bleak.

FIGURE 3.3 Dorothea Lange's wide shot gives a stark sense of the experience of migrant farmers.

FIGURE 3.4 The close-up focuses on the struggles of the migrant mother.

But notice the effects of the different perspectives. In Figure 3.4, we get an intimate look inside this woman's eyes, where we can see her concern. The lines on her face, visible in this close-up, are evidence of her hard life and worries. The photograph in Figure 3.3 has a wider frame that encompasses the tent and the barren ground. This perspective makes a different kind of argument, one that addresses the condition of the soil, the landscape, the living quarters. We can hardly make out the woman huddled in the darkness of the tent. When we look for visual evidence of the living conditions of migrant workers in the American West during the 1930s, each photograph offers different angles on our argument. Which one would we use to support a thesis about the labor conditions of migrant workers? Which one would we use to argue that the human body is scarred by hardship? Depending on our purpose, we would choose one photograph over the other to serve as evidence for our claims about the Great Depression. Each photograph demonstrates a particular strategy of invention, creating and constructing ideas in visual form about the "reality" of life for migrant workers. We, in turn, can invent different arguments based on our starting point: which photo do we use as evidence for our thesis?

Similarly, in written documents, divergent perspectives on the same topic can yield different arguments. Commentary on Lange's *Migrant Mother* photographs exposes the variety of perspectives not only on the photographs' status as "documentary" evidence from the Great Depression but also on the way our historical understanding of that period itself is constructed by the invention or arguments of others. For instance, the following excerpt from historian James Curtis's article "Dorothea Lange, Migrant Mother, and the Culture of the Great Depression" demonstrates the way in which Lange's photos are often interpreted as windows into that period:

> In addition to being a timeless work of art, *Migrant Mother* is a vital reflection of the times. Examined in its original context, the series reveals powerful cultural forces of the 1930s: the impact of the increasing centralization and bureaucratization of American life; the anxiety about the status and solidarity of the family in an era of urbanization and modernization; a need to atone for the guilt induced by the destruction of cherished ideals, and a craving for reassurance that democratic traditions would stand the test of modern times.

For Curtis, the images function both as what elsewhere in the article he calls "a timeless and universal symbol of suffering in the face of adversity" as well as the key to understanding Lange's relationship to the evolving genre of documentary photography. For journalist Geoffrey Dunn, however, Lange's series prompts a different response:

> The photographs taken by Lange and her colleagues at the Resettlement Administration (later to become better known as the Farm Security Administration) have been widely heralded as the epitome of documentary photography. The eminent photographer and curator Edward Steichen called them "the most remarkable human documents ever rendered in pictures."
>
> In recent years, however, the FSA photographs have come under a growing criticism. Many view them as manipulative and condescending, to the point of assuming a "colonialistic" attitude toward their subjects. Still others have argued that they are misleading and disingenuous, and in some instances, fabricated.
>
> In a compelling essay entitled "The Historian and the Icon," University of California at Berkeley professor Lawrence Levine has argued that the FSA photographers focused their lenses on "perfect victims," and in so doing, rendered a caricatured portrait of the era.

> "Americans suffered, materially and physically, during the years of the Great Depression to an extent which we still do not fully fathom," Levine asserted. "But they also continued, as people always must, the business of living. They ate and they laughed, they loved and they fought, they worried and they hoped . . . they filled their days, as we fill ours, with the essentials of everyday living."
>
> With the notable exception of FSA photographer Russell Lee, and later, Marion Post Wolcott, whose largely overlooked bodies of work actually capture the dimensions of "everyday living," Lange and her colleagues focused almost exclusively on human suffering. That is most certainly the reason that people like Florence Owens Thompson [the mother in these photographs]—and many others who appeared in FSA images—resented their photographic portrayal.
>
> "Mother was a woman who loved to enjoy life, who loved her children," says Thompson's youngest daughter, Norma Rydlewski, who appears as a young child in Lange's classic photograph. "She loved music and she loved to dance. When I look at that photo of mother, it saddens me. That's not how I like to remember her."

Like Curtis, Dunn uses the photographs as the basis for an argument about Lange's practice of documentary photography; however, Dunn considers first-person accounts from other witnesses of that historical moment and arrives at a different argument. He concludes that the series exemplifies not reflection but misrepresentation.

All texts—whether written accounts or photographs—are actually shaped by individual perspective and point of view. Texts are "invented" for a specific audience. Your own writing is a text informed by your invention strategies, your purpose, your point of view, and the rhetorical situation of your argument. In your writing, you are like a photographer, making important compositional decisions: What will be the subject of your text: an individual, a group, an institution? How will you pose that subject to best convey your own perspective? Should you zoom in, focusing on one particular example as a way of addressing a larger concern? Or should you take a step back, situating your argument in relation to the broader context that surrounds the issue? The choices you make will determine the ultimate impact of your argument: like photographs, effective writing persuades the viewer to look at a topic through the lens of the author's interpretation.

WRITER'S PRACTICE

Examine the picture in Figure 3.5, taken by photographer Todd Heisler, of a soldier's coffin returning home on a civilian flight into Reno, Nevada, being draped with the American flag prior to being unloaded from the plane. What argument is Heisler making about Americans' response to the war and casualties? Now consider this image as the basis for inventing your own position: What types of arguments might you construct that would use this image as visual evidence? What other sorts of images or evidence would you use to develop your argument?

FIGURE 3.5 Photograph of the arrival of a soldier's coffin in Reno, Nevada.

ARRANGEMENT IN ARGUMENT

3.3 How does the canon of arrangement influence a reader's response to a text?

After invention, the second canon of rhetoric, **arrangement**, becomes your key consideration because the way in which you present material on the page will shape a reader's response to your ideas. In many cases, attention to *arrangement* takes the form of the way you order elements in your argument—whether that be the layout of images and text on a newspaper front page or the way you structure a written argument in an academic paper. It is the *arrangement* of an argument that separates a spontaneous reaction or stream-of-consciousness freewrite from a carefully developed position paper or logical essay on a specific issue or topic.

Here are common strategies of arrangement that will help you transform a set of free associations into a convincing and well organized argument:

- **Chronological structure:** Demonstrate change over time. Chronology relies on examples arranged in a temporal sequence, such as the transformation in the Apple computer marketing campaign from the Macintosh to the iPad.
- **Cause-effect:** Show how one event causes another. An essay confronting the issue of sexist imagery in rap music videos might start by exploring how women are represented in popular rap videos (*cause*) and then conclude by discussing the impact of this representation on the self-esteem of young girls (*effect*).
- **Problem-solution:** Define the problem, then offer a solution. A paper about violence and video games might devote the first half of the paper to exploring the *problem* of desensitization and then focus in the second half of the paper on proposing a possible *solution*.
- **Block structure:** Work your way systematically through a series of examples or case studies. For instance, you might sequentially analyze individual James Bond films in an essay about the relationship between real-world political climates and spy narrative.
- **Thematic structure:** Organize by themes or subtopics. An essay on reality TV might include sections on voyeurism, capitalism, and Darwinism (*the themes*), integrating examples from *Survivor*, *American Idol*, and *America's Next Top Model* as evidence in each section.
- **Deferred thesis:** Begin with a question and locate your thesis in the conclusion. Substitute a thesis question for a thesis statement at the beginning of your essay, such as "How do images featured in the news define our understanding of the impact of natural disasters upon specific communities?" Place your thesis at the end of your paper as a way of synthesizing the evidence explored in the paper itself.

Let's look to photography to see the way a successful argument relies on strategies of arrangement. Figure 3.6 through Figure 3.9 offer a selection of photographs from Ansel Adams's 1944 photo essay, *Born Free and Equal,* which captures his impressions of the Japanese-American

Seeing Connections
See Chapter 8 for more discussion of analyzing photo essays.

residents of the Manzanar internment camp during World War II. Adams explained his purpose for writing the book most clearly to his friend, Nancy Newhall: "Through the pictures the reader will be introduced to about twenty individuals . . . loyal American citizens who are anxious to get back into the stream of life and contribute to our victory." The work as a whole follows a *thematic structure*, moving the reader from "The Land" to "The Place," "The History," "The People," and finally "The Problem." On the surface, Adams seems to have arranged the sections to move from broader context, to the individuals, to the articulation of the social and political realities of the internment process. However, closer analysis shows that his strategy is much more complicated; he interweaves portraiture with his more panoramic, contextualizing photographs so as to constantly remind his audience of the fact that the people who have been imprisoned in this way are Americans—everyday people with everyday lives.

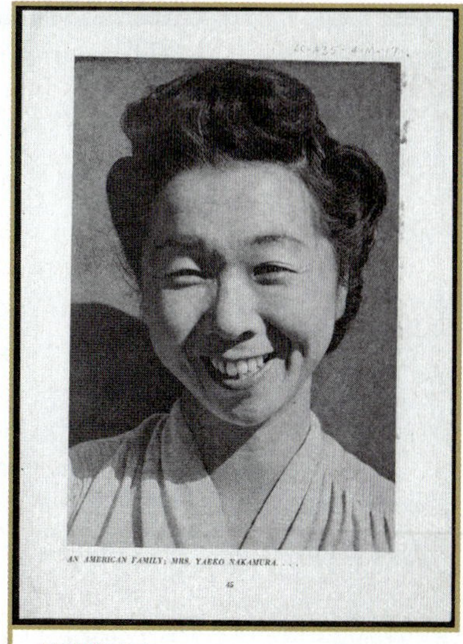

FIGURE 3.6

The selections gathered here are from the "People" chapter; note how the strategic arrangement amplifies many of the concepts that Adams stresses in his summary to Newhall. Figure 3.6 and Figure 3.7 first create an emotional connection with the reader by focusing on individual example. By showing close-ups of mother and daughter, with the caption strategically emphasizing the fact that these are "An American Family," Adams suggests the unfairness of the relocation process. Subsequently, he widens his frame to show "A Manzanar Household" (Figure 3.8), portraying a quotidian family scene, little girl at her desk doing homework, family clustered around in a typical domestic setting. From here, we can see Adams' next move in strategic arrangement in Figure 3.9: the pair of adorable young boys eating at a mess hall. Having engaged the reader once more, Adams broadens his scope yet

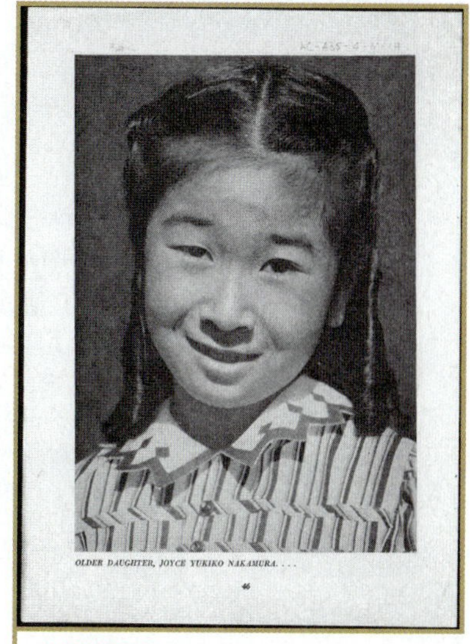

FIGURE 3.7

FIGURE 3.8

OLD AND YOUNG ALIKE EAT IN THE BLOCK MESS HALLS.

THE EVACUEES WAIT IN LINE FOR THEIR MEALS. . . .

50

FIGURE 3.9

again to give us context for this scene. We are no longer inside the faux middle class home; we see the barracks, the food lines, and the unforgiving landscape. As we saw with Dorothea Lange's *Migrant Mother* series, Adams uses shifting perspectives rhetorically, and in tandem, in order to emphasize his argument about in the injustices of the internment process.

Using Classical Strategies of Arrangement

Adams made strategic choices in arranging his photo essay to create a visually and conceptually striking argument, including image selection, cropping, layout, and complementary text. As a writer, you have many methods at your disposal to help you similarly arrange the elements of your argument. If we return to classical rhetoric, we can find other models for structuring strong arguments. Consider the strategies represented in the table to the right; notice the way these structures balance making your own argument with taking into account diverse perspectives on the issue.

Note that the models of arrangement in the Strategies of Arrangement table are not designed to be rigid parameters. Instead, they should suggest possibilities and potentially effective strategies of arrangement; in your own writing, you will have to select the most productive way to lay out your argument, depending in part on your thesis, your background or context materials, and your evidence.

Strategies of Arrangement

A Classical Speech or Oration

1. Introduction
2. Statement of facts
3. Division
4. Proof
5. Refutation
6. Conclusion

Option A

Use when you want to ground the reader in your argument before bringing up opposing perspectives.

1. Introduction, identification of rhetorical stance
2. Thesis
3. Statement of background, definition, or context
4. Evidence and development of argument
5. Opposing opinion, concession, qualification, refutation
6. Conclusion

Option B

Establish opposing opinion up front so that the entire piece functions as an extended rebuttal or refutation of that line of argument.

1. Introduction and opposing viewpoint
2. Thesis and identification of rhetorical stance
3. Evidence and development of argument
4. Conclusion

Option C

Treat diverse viewpoints as appropriate during the development of your argument and presentation of your evidence.

1. Introduction, identification of rhetorical stance
2. Thesis
3. Statement of background, definition, or context
4. Evidence, opposing opinion, concession, qualification, refutation
5. Conclusion

In considering these various modes of arrangement, you might also notice that writing persuasively sometimes involves more than just identifying your own point of view. Often, you may need to understand and acknowledge different perspectives on the issue. As you consider diverse viewpoints, ask yourself:

- Do they corroborate your argument? *Then you could include them as supporting evidence.*
- Do they offer points of view that you can disprove? *Then you might present the opinion and provide a rebuttal, or refutation of the points, demonstrating why they are not valid.*
- Do they offer points of view that you can't disprove? *Then you might concede the validity of their argument but go on to qualify their points by showing why your own argument is nonetheless persuasive.*

The key is to treat these other voices with respect; always represent their points of view fairly and without bias, even if you disagree with them. Let's look at how two more modern models of argumentation balance attention to the author's claim with engagement with alternate perspectives.

Using Toulmin to Arrange or Analyze an Argument

The Toulmin model of argumentation was developed by British philosopher Stephen Toulmin in 1969 as a way to define a system of persuasive reasoning. Toulmin suggests that a logical argument has several parts: claim, grounds, warrants, backing, rebuttal, and response. Let's look at how Toulmin's approach could help you construct an argument about images such as the one shown in Figure 3.5.

Here's the context: until 2009, the Pentagon banned the publication of photographs (and other media coverage) showing the caskets of American soldiers who had been killed in the Middle East. Coming into office, President Obama was faced with the decision about whether to lift the ban.

Here's the question: should the media be allowed to publish such images?

- The **claim** is the *thesis*, or central argument. In other words, the claim is a statement that you ask your audience to accept as true.

  Claim: The Pentagon should not ban publication of photographs of fallen American soldiers.

- The **grounds** are the reasons you think the claim should be believed and the evidence that supports those reasons (statistics, expert testimony, etc.).

  Grounds: The Constitution guarantees freedom of speech and of the press.

- The **warrants** are assumptions that explain *how* the grounds support the claim. If the warrants are not clear or are implied, they may also need supporting evidence, called **backing**.

  Warrants: Freedom of speech and the press imply a right to *listen* to and *read*—that is, to access information.

- The **rebuttal** is a listing of anticipated counterclaims and your **response**.

Rebuttal: Publishing images of fallen Americans could negatively affect public morale during wartime.

Response: People have a constitutional right to access information, and openness about American casualties is necessary to produce transparency in government as well as to provide opportunities to memorialize those who sacrificed their lives for our country.

Using the Toulmin model can provide you with a framework to help you think through the complexities of your claim and produce a more nuanced argument. You can rely on the Toulmin method to compose a claim of your own, support it with appropriate evidence, and explain clearly how and why that evidence does in fact prove, or support, your claim. You can also use the Toulmin approach when analyzing arguments made by others; that is, you would evaluate a writer's essay based on the categories we've discussed here: claim, warrants, grounds, backing, rebuttal, and response.

Considering Rogerian Arguments

An alternative mode of argumentation was developed by rhetoricians Richard Young, Kenneth Pike, and Alton Becker in 1970. Drawing from the communication practices of Carl Rogers—an influential psychologist—Young, Pike, and Becker modeled a process of persuasion based upon a deep understanding and appreciation of an opponent's perspective. Their model of argumentation was empathic rather than adversarial, putting into practice Rogers' suggestion from 1951 that such communication based on finding common ground can help resolve emotionally intense situations such as found in negotiations or diplomacy.

As a writer, you might wonder how the Rogerian approach differs from other types of argument. Consider this example from an argument about Facebook profile pictures:

> Some media watchdog groups argue that parents should be able to arbitrarily override their teenagers' Facebook account settings so that the parents can remove any photos they deem objectionable, a clear violation of the right to free speech.

On the one hand, in this statement, the author clearly articulates her opinion. On the other hand, however, she offers only a dismissive and cursory glimpse of the opposing viewpoint, closing down any possibility of dialogue or negotiation. Notice how an exchange using a Rogerian approach fosters a greater possibility for a productive conversation on this issue:

> Some media watchdog groups worry that teenagers post pictures on their Facebook profile pages without considering the future implications of the images. They believe that provocative photos (featuring teenagers in sexualized poses or engaged in reckless activities) might produce unforeseen results, such as limiting the Facebook user's college or employment prospects later in life, or even attracting sexual predators. For this reason, they argue, Facebook should put into place parental overrides to allow a parent to monitor and safeguard their children's well-being. This raises an important question: would this mechanism impinge on the teenager's right to free speech?

The revision entails more than simply removing inflammatory or biased language; it involves offering acknowledgment and fair assessment of the counterposition. For this reason, a Rogerian argument hinges greatly on establishing a sense of **common ground** between diverse opinions, and, as Douglas Brent has argued, necessitates "imagining [the counterposition] with empathy." By fostering more open and nonjudgmental dialogue, a Rogerian approach can help transform volatile exchanges into opportunities for productive consensus. To adopt this strategy in your own writing, incorporate the following steps into your writing process:

1. When you introduce the issue, be sure to restate your opponent's position in a respectful way that shows a rich knowledge and understanding of that stance.
2. In discussing the opposing opinion, elaborate on the contexts in which such a stance might be valid.
3. In stating your own position, likewise be sure to suggest the contexts in which your stance might be valid.
4. As the closing moment in your argument, move toward compromise or conciliation, suggesting how your opponent's stance might benefit from incorporating components of your own position. Ideally, you would demonstrate how the positions can complement each other, rather than showing which one "wins."

Keep in mind that while you can use a Rogerian method to shape your entire essay, you can also employ it in certain sections of your argument, such as when you are restating counterarguments to show your own nuanced understanding of your topic.

STYLE IN ARGUMENT

3.4 How can style be used to compose a powerful argument?

Inventing a thesis or main idea and *arranging* the elements of your writing are two steps in completing your task of written persuasion. You also need to spend some time considering what tone, word choice, and voice you will use in your writing. This is where **style**—the third canon of rhetoric—enters the scene. While "style" often suggests basic grammar or mechanical correctness, from the vantage point of classical rhetoric, *style*—according to the Roman rhetorician Cicero—concerns choosing the appropriate expression for the ideas of your argument; these choices relate to language, tone, syntax, rhetorical appeals, metaphors, imagery, quotations, level of emphasis, and nuance.

Indeed, we often translate *style* into *voice* to indicate how a writer's perspective is manifested in word choice, syntax, pacing, and tone. To construct a successful argument, you need to be able to employ the voice or style that best meets the needs of your rhetorical situation. As Cicero famously stated: "For I don't always adopt the same style. What similarity is there between a letter and an oration in court or at a public meeting?" Now consider two more contemporary examples of style, both focused on President Obama. The first is an excerpt of writing from a *Sports Illustrated* piece:

> Obama's erect carriage and lefthandedness led me to think of Lionel "Train" Hollins, who commanded the Portland Trail Blazers' backcourt when the kid then known as "Barry O'Bomber" was making his way through high school.

Using basketball lingo ("backcourt") and casual vocabulary ("the kid" and "making his way"), the writer Alexander Wolff describes Obama as someone who speaks the language of popular readers—what Cicero would have called "*plain style*." Moreover, the naming of famous players gives credibility or *ethos* to Wolff himself as someone who knows the players and even their nicknames. In this way, his style or writing contributes to building his authority as an author.

Seeing Connections
For more on Cicero's idea of style as Levels of Decorum, see Chapter 8.

In contrast, a writer from the academic journal *Rhetoric & Public Affairs* uses what Cicero called *high style*, or elevated diction, in making a critique of President Obama:

> While Obama's rhetoric of *consilience* approximates dialogic coherence, it nonetheless falls short of the discursive demands of racial reconciliation.

By using sophisticated concepts—such as "dialogic coherence" and "discursive demands"—familiar only to a highly educated academic audience, writer Mark McPhail uses the style of an erudite member of the intellectual class. His "backcourt buddies" can be understood as the colleagues who understand that "dialogic coherence" and "discursive demands" refer to ways of speaking and writing. While McPhail's style is radically different from Wolff's, it has a parallel function in that it builds his authority as a writer for those familiar with the journal's conventions.

Similarly, your choice of style should address a specific audience and can thus build your ethos with those readers. If you are wondering, how to move from invention and arrangement to developing your own style, then it is time to learn about constructing a *persona* and developing a *rhetorical stance* in your writing.

Constructing Your Persona

When you select a certain set of words, tone, style, or set of metaphors to shape your argument and try to persuade your audience, you are constructing a **persona** for yourself as a writer and rhetorician. Your persona is *a deliberately crafted version of yourself as writer.* A public figure will often use *persona* as a purposeful rhetorical tool. President Barack Obama might choose to give a speech about war flanked by a group of military men and women, or a speech about health care surrounded by doctors, as we see in Figure 3.10.

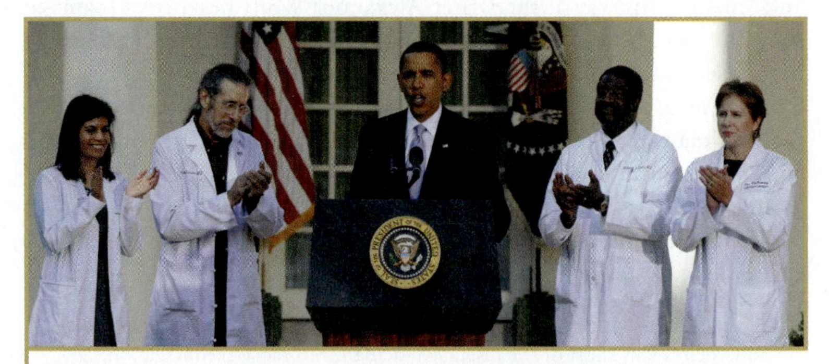

FIGURE 3.10 When President Barack Obama talks about health care surrounded by white-coated medical personnel, he creates a persona for himself as a friend and supporter of physicians.

The same principle governs the writing process. When you compose a text (verbal, visual, or multimedia), you decide how to use language to shape your particular *persona*. That is, you create a portrait of yourself as the author of your argument through tone (formal or informal, humorous or serious); word choice (academic, colloquial); sentence structure (complex or simple and direct); use of rhetorical appeals (*pathos*, *logos*, *ethos*); and strategies of persuasion (narration, example, cause and effect, analogy, process, description, classification, or definition). Creating a persona requires care. A well-designed one can facilitate a strong connection with your readers and therefore make your argument more persuasive. However, a *poorly constructed persona*—one that is, for instance, biased, inconsistent, or underdeveloped—can have the opposite effect, alienating readers and undercutting your text's overall effectiveness.

Choosing a Rhetorical Stance

To be persuasive, you must not only create a persona that responds appropriately to your specific rhetorical situation and engages both audience and text, but you must also convey a *position* that Wayne Booth, one of the most important revivalists of classical rhetoric, defined as the **rhetorical stance**. In essence, a writer's rhetorical stance refers to the position the author assumes in relation to subject, audience, and context; it is a careful and deliberate navigation of the rhetorical situation and appeals with an intent to persuade an audience. Booth argued that communication failed between people (or a text failed to persuade a reader) if the writer takes on a stance that ignored the balance of the rhetorical situation.

We see examples of inappropriate rhetorical stances constantly: the TV evangelist who moves his congregation with a polished sermon that completely distracts them from flaws in his moral character; the used-car salesman who pads his sales pitch with offers of free gifts,

AT A GLANCE

Three Poorly Constructed Personas

The famous rhetoric scholar Wayne Booth identified three ways in which communication can break down, resulting in a failure that indicates a lack of balance among author, audience, and text. Booth emphasized that a poorly constructed persona leads to this demise, so you should avoid these situations in your own writing:

- **The pedant or preacher:** the text is paramount and both the audience's needs and the speaker's character are ignored.
- **The advertiser:** the effect on the audience is valued above all, ignoring the quality of the text and the credibility of the speaker.
- **The entertainer:** the character of the speaker is elevated above the text and the audience.

rebate specials, and low percentage rates; the actor who uses her celebrity status to drive a product endorsement, rather than clearly articulating the merits of that product itself. In each case, the *rhetorical situation*—the relationship between author, audience, and text—is out of balance, and the argument itself, ultimately, is less persuasive. In your own writing, therefore, you need to pay special attention not only to the *persona* you create but also to the *rhetorical stance* you assume in relation to your specific situation.

3.5 What techniques can I use to create strong titles, introductions, and conclusions?

WRITING WITH STYLE: TITLES, INTRODUCTIONS, AND CONCLUSIONS

In writing, you indicate your *persona* and *rhetorical stance* through stylistic choices: your diction, sentence structure, tone, and imagery. These choices shape reader's understanding of your argument. Let's zoom in now on three key features of writing an argument through style.

Title. Your reader's first encounter with your topic and argument comes through your **title**; in this way, the title itself operates as a rhetorical act that provides a frame and sets up the argument. Consider, for instance, Figure 3.1. Many newspapers featured this image on their front pages on September 2, 2005—but with different headlines. Figure 3.11 and Figure 3.12 are two examples. Notice how each newspaper indicates its rhetorical stance through the visual-verbal arguments contained on its front page.

WRITER'S PRACTICE

In writing your own essays, you should spend some time brainstorming your titles. Some writers find constructing a powerful title to be a useful *invention* activity to start their composition process; others construct the title only after completing the first draft of their paper, as a way of synthesizing the argument and bringing it into sharper focus. As you work with a title, think about its role in setting up your stance on your topic, indicating to your readers not only the scope of your analysis but also your angle on it. Try the following techniques in writing your title:

- Play with language.
- Link the title to your main point.
- Describe key image you discuss.
- Name an underlying metaphor or motif.
- Raise a larger issue raised by your argument.
- Test your working title by sharing it with a partner in class.

How does the headline "Mayor Sends 'Desperate SOS'" (see Figure 3.11) suggest a different argument than "Rising rage: Descent into anarchy" coupled with the same image? The difference in tone, perspective, and rhetorical stance apparent from these contrasting examples underscores the role a headline—or title—plays in forming a reader's expectations for

Anchorage Daily News

Final Edition

■ **BEDLAM:** *Fistfights, fires erupt at Superdome where 30,000 try to evacuate by bus.*

■ **RELIEF STALLS:** *Gunfire slows rescue efforts; looters rage in New Orleans streets.*

■ **EVACUATION:** *Houston Astrodome is declared too full to accept any more refugees.*

Mayor sends 'desperate SOS'

Refugees seethe, wonder why help is so slow to arrive

Offers of help, money pour in to dispossessed

■ **GENEROSITY:** Some go to shelters, seeking families to house and feed.

Katrina inside

Hurricane overwhelmed government preparations

■ **DRILLS:** Magnitude of catastrophe outdistanced planners' imaginations.

$375,000? IS HE PULLING OUR TURKEY LEGS?

Humble food stands, in the right hands, are hot parcels of land

Change in fair policy allows vendors to sell their leases to non-family

INSIDE

Fall movies offer thrills, chills, laughs and tears WEEKEND W1

Utah's 8.9% rise in home prices ranks 31st in U.S. BUSINESS D12

Time for a new Itty Bitty Salt Lake City contest LIFE C1

DESERET

Morning News

SALT LAKE CITY, UTAH

Video links London bombings to al-Qaida

Al-Jazeera tape shows terrorists praising blasts

Rising rage

Descent into anarchy

Chaos spreads as law breaks down

Utahns rally to aid victims of hurricane

Utahns race to pumps as prices soar

INSIDE

deseretnews.com

New public-housing complex may allow convicted killers

FIGURE 3.11 Front page of the *Anchorage Daily News*, September 2, 2005.

FIGURE 3.12 Front page of the *Deseret Morning News*, September 2, 2005.

the argument that follows. In effect, a *title* is the first step in writing an interpretation or making an argument.

Introduction. Like your title, your introduction is a matter of style. It offers your readers insight into the persona and rhetorical stance that will characterize your essay as a whole. In your opening paragraphs (since an introduction may be more than one paragraph), you establish your voice (informal? formal?), your tone (measured? firm? angry? cautious?), your persona, and your stance on your topic through careful attention to word choice, sentence structure, and strategies of development. Most introductions also provide the first articulation of your argument as well, moving from a general statement of topic to a more focused statement of your *thesis*.

However, perhaps just as importantly, the introduction is the place where you capture the attention of your reader, often through a stylistic device that we call a "hook." For instance, let's return to Ansel Adams's work, *Born Free and Equal*. In the opening pages of his book, he hooks his audience through a combination of word and image. On one page, he reproduces the Fourteenth Amendment to the U.S. Constitution, which states, "No state shall make or enforce any law which shall abridge the privileges or immunities of citizens of the United States . . ."; he then juxtaposes that line with the smiling face of the "American School Girl" shown in Figure 3.13. Here *logos* and *pathos* work side by side to prompt readers to wonder about this apparent contradiction. This is the hook that gets readers interested—and compels them to keep reading.

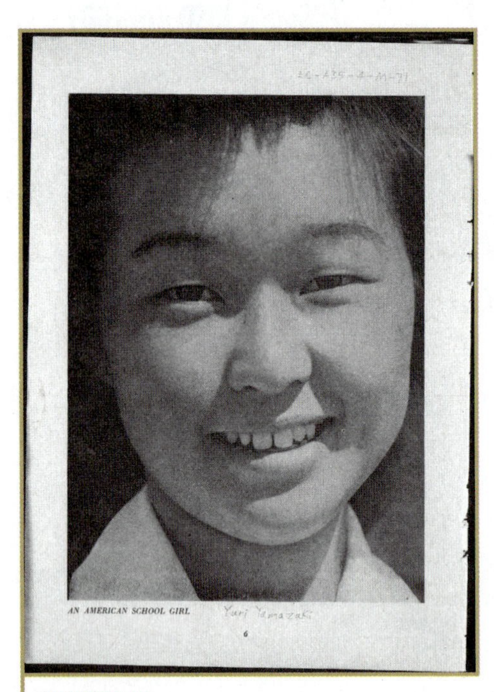

FIGURE 3.13

Let's look at how one student, Michael Zeligs, took style into consideration while composing his introduction to a rhetorical analysis essay on the photography of Robert Frank:

> "Robert Frank, Swiss, unobtrusive, nice, with that little camera that he raises and snaps with one hand he sucked a sad poem right out of America onto film, taking rank among the tragic poets of the world."
>
> In his introduction to Robert Frank's *The Americans*, Jack Kerouac captures the photographer's responsible position as a concerned observer of his time, as the first person to sweep away dominating prejudice and expose what post-World War II America really represented. In his book, Frank pushes the limits of traditional art photography—limits that required clear foregrounds and backgrounds, clear subject and exposure and level tilt—and this enables him to focus more on scenes that dominate his eye and inspire emotional arguments. The America that Frank addresses, however, is not one of fulfilled dreams and two-car garages. It is a struggling foreground for change, founded in the two beautifully conflicting scenes of "Charleston, South Carolina," and "Trolley," where unique photographic elements merge to advance a critique of racial inequality during America's post-war crisis of identity.

What hooks the reader first is the quotation that heads the introduction: an abstract, lyrical statement that refuses to sacrifice its vision by adhering to conventional punctuation. This quote announces the essay's topic at the same time that it provides a sharp contrast for the writing style of the main body of the introduction that follows. By comparison, Michael's voice or writing style seems crisp, focused, and academic, establishing a *persona* that shows he is both informed on his subject and knowledgeable about the larger context; from the introduction, we tell that he has not only analyzed Frank's photographs but has read the introduction to the book as well. Michael fashions his first sentence to serve as a bridge between his opening hook and the rest of the paragraph. Rather than using the epigraph simply as a snappy device to capture the reader's attention and then abandoning it, Michael creates an *ethos* appeal by identifying the quotation's author (Jack Kerouac, an iconic critic of American culture) and then restates the meaning of the quote in a way that pulls it in line with his own argument about Robert Frank's photography. The rest of the paragraph moves from general (a description of the project of Frank's larger book, *The Americans*, and a definition of traditional photographic methods) to specific (clarification of the two images Michael is most interested in), ending ultimately with a clear articulation of Michael's rhetorical stance and thesis statement.

WRITER'S PRACTICE

In written texts, you can use your introduction to hook your readers through one of several methods. Try the following techniques:

- Define your terms (especially if you're writing on a subject that may not be familiar to everyone).
- Include a significant quotation or a startling statistic or fact.
- Present an overview of the issue you're discussing.
- Use an anecdote or narration.
- Incorporate a vivid example.
- Draw on a relevant analogy or metaphor.
- Use the second-person pronoun (*you*) to invite readers to make personal connections.

Your choice of hook will depend to a large extent on your broader stylistic decisions about your essay and the way in which you want to develop your argument.

Conclusion. If the introduction offers the writer the opportunity to hook the audience while providing a rhetorical stance on a subject, the **conclusion** is the final opportunity to reinforce an essay's argument while making a lasting impact on readers. For this reason, although a conclusion by its nature should include some elements of summary (synthesizing the key points from the essay), it should also have a *rhetorical power of its own*. Let's look at how Michael Zeligs concluded his essay on Frank's photographs:

> Robert Frank, in his images from *The Americans*, takes compelling pictures of a socially conflicted south to expose the growing struggle of race in 1950's America. His images spark from a new ideology of the photographer—a lack of concern for absolute photographic perfection allows him to document situations that really *mean* something. He chooses conflicting lives, black and white together on the page but unequal, his film subtly showing sympathy for the downtrodden worker and the weary traveler. Careful lines and deliberate tones show two opposing worlds where skin color can change the appearance of an entire backdrop, where stark white prison bars show us the walls we have erected within ourselves. These are not simple pictures of ordinary people. They are an artist's whisper about the elusiveness of equality, how in the war against bigotry, we are not done yet.

While providing a summary of his evidence, Michael takes care to make his conclusion as stylistically sophisticated as his introduction. Notice his careful word choice ("takes compelling pictures," "expose") that works in tandem with the subject of his essay by returning to the task of redefining

American photography that he began in his introduction. Moreover, the conclusion makes implicit reference to his analysis of the images themselves in the main body of his paper ("downtrodden worker and weary traveler," references to "lines" and "tones"). Finally, Michael broadens his topic to raise larger, ongoing issues of race relations. His conclusion thus leaves readers with more than a simple summary of points. It prompts them to reflect on the ongoing state of race relations in America.

WRITER'S PRACTICE

Consider ways to make your own conclusion a powerful part of your argument. Try the following techniques:

- Use a key quote, example, or reference that either epitomizes or synthesizes your points.
- Return to an opening example or analogy, offering a slightly different, perhaps more informed perspective on it to connect introduction and conclusion as a frame for your argument.
- Use a chronological structure to move from the past to recent times, perhaps ending with a projection into the future.
- Use your conclusion to suggest broader implications that could increase the reader's sense of personal connection to the topic or its urgency.

No matter which strategy you choose, remember to maximize the persuasive potential of your conclusion as a means of reaffirming the strength of your argument with your readers.

WRITING A POSITION PAPER

3.6 How can I write a persuasive position paper?

One way to put into practice the canons of rhetoric—*invention, arrangement*, and *style*—is to write a position paper on your topic. By definition, a **position paper** offers you the opportunity to write your opinion on an issue. This can take the form of a letter to the editor of a newspaper, a form we call the **op-ed** (for opinion editorial), or it can take the form of a *white paper* in politics or a *memory aid* in law. In each case, the writer focuses in on an issue an presents opinion backed by evidence. Sometimes, a *position paper* will be very strong in tone, taking one side of a controversial issue, much as you would find in a debate, and actively argue in direct opposition to alternative positions on the issue. In such cases, you would follow either the classical or Toulmin modes of arrangement.

Within these modes of argumentation, you might make a further choice of micro-organization. Should you set up a block structure in order to separate your treatment of the opposition's claims from the section where you focus on your own position? Or do you want to use a more point-by-point model, where you present a series of counterarguments, debunking each in turn before developing your own position? See the At a Glance box for different micro-organizational structures for a position paper that resembles a debate.

Other times, a *position paper* might be less adversarial. *Position papers* can also use the Rogerian technique of understanding the issue from another's point of view in order to communicate that material to a third party, such as found in policy statement papers delivered to the United Nations, or law briefs, or statements one original research. Because of such variance, when you write a position paper, you should select your strategy of arrangement as carefully as you craft your style for the essay. Moreover, both organization and style should relate to your purpose and audience, in support of the main point of invention.

Let's take a closer look at how position papers use the canons of rhetoric and strategies of argument we've discussed in *Envision* so far by considering

AT A GLANCE

Two Models for Organizing a Paper as a Debate

Block Structure

1. Introduction
2. Summary of opposing position
3. Rebuttal, concession or qualification of the opposing position
4. Your argument, supported by evidence
5. Conclusion

Point-by-Point Structure

1. Introduction
2. Opposing Claim #1/ Rebuttal/Concession/Qualification #1
3. Opposing Claim #2/ Rebuttal/Concession/Qualification #2
4. Opposing Claim #3/ Rebuttal/Concession/Qualification #3 (etc.)
5. Reassertion of your argument, supported by evidence
6. Conclusion

an example. Lindsay Funk, an undergraduate student, composed a powerful *position paper* during her internship at the online news site PolicyMic.com. Her writing offers a strong argument in response to a Senator's remarks about US foreign aid. We can learn from analyzing her essay the way in which *invention, arrangement,* and *style* work in writing. We'll also look closely at her writing of the title, introduction, and conclusion, in order to understand the significance of her rhetorical choices. In Lindsay's case, she employs both classical structures and the Toulmin logic of claims and warrants to persuade readers of PolicyMic.com of her position.

Rand Paul Asks Does Foreign Aid
Make Us Safer? Yes, It Does

Today, Senator Rand Paul wrote in PolicyMic that the U.S. trying to "protect the entire globe" through a combination of foreign aid and military action makes the U.S. "less secure, not more." Full quote below:

"Another part of our debt woes is the trillions of dollars we spend fighting decade-long wars and sending foreign aid all over the world. America must always maintain a strong national defense, but young people can imagine a world in which the United States doesn't have to be involved in every part of it. We can't continue borrowing money from China or spending ourselves into debt to protect the entire globe. We simply cannot afford it. It is not what's best for our country. It makes us less secure, not more."

Paul is returning to one of his favorite punching bags: foreign aid, and the argument that it makes the U.S. less secure. So does foreign aid make us safer? I'm going to tackle

The **title** is both informative and catchy. It tells us about the main idea yet also sets up a provocative **claim** that the article will later support.

Lindsay uses *kairos* in writing her **introduction** by evoking a quotation the Senator made that day. Her opening **style** is objective, typical of news reports.

She then provides the full text of the Senator's words in quotation marks, standard practice for online writing.

Consider the style of the Senator's words. He uses repetition by beginning two sentences the same way—"It is not . . . It makes us"—in order to produce emphasis.

When Lindsay launches her own position, she uses strong emotional language ("his favorite punching bags") to indicate her **rhetorical stance.**

Notice how her use of "I" creates a **persona** of authority; she builds her *ethos* by suggesting that she knows a lot about different kinds of aid as well as the goals behind such aid. She then she uses *logos* to present two main categories for analysis.

Her concrete example here serves as evidence—an **illustrative strategy of argumentation**—to support her claim about US goals in giving aid.

The position paper then moves from macro to micro, using a strategy of **arrangement** that takes the reader from considering "people" in general to Senator Paul in particular (the focus of her argument).

While she argues her thesis with forceful language in semi-formal prose, she also evokes other authorities in order to back up her perspective. This **appeal to research** functions as Toulmin's **grounds** in the form of expert testimony.

this question by talking about how the kinds of foreign aid that the U.S. doles out interact with our national security interests.

There are many different kinds of foreign aid, but I'm going to divide them into two main categories for our purposes: military and structural. These categorizations reflect the U.S.'s goal in giving this aid. Military aid usually reflects some specific U.S. national security interest in that country providing a military service on our behalf. A great example of this would be U.S. military aid to Pakistan, which allows U.S. use of Pakistani airfields for their Afghanistan operations. By contrast, structural aid has the primary goal of improving the recipient country, whether it be through humanitarian aid, loans, technical assistance, etc.

When people think of foreign aid, they usually think of structural aid. Critics of this kind of aid (such as Rand Paul) usually point to deficits in America and ask whether the U.S. can afford to be funding education or healthcare in other countries when these areas also require funding at home. Military aid, which is channeled both through the Department of Defense and the State Department, often escapes this kind of criticism except in particularly egregious cases.

Both of these forms of aid support U.S. counter-terrorism efforts, although structural aid does so more indirectly. Numerous scholars and studies have argued that foreign aid can be a key tool for counter-terrorism. After all, terrorism does not simply "spring up" in a country. It usually arises from a combination of grievances that might include corruption, poor governance, poor basic services like education or health care or roads, or a generalized lack of access to resources or political power. Ameliorating these conditions can be a powerful tool for preventing terrorist groups from forming or gathering support. However, these same studies have also noted that in some cases, foreign aid can exacerbate the conditions that lead to terrorism, as in particularly repressive countries foreign aid can fuel corruption or keep ineffective leaders in power.

She moves from grounds to **warrants** and includes **backing.**

Structurally, her article then includes a **counter-argument,** and then **concession**, with the line that that "in some cases, foreign aid can exacerbate" bad situations leading to terrorism. Here, she evokes **invention** by creating the case of "particularly repressive countries" as an example of her point.

Military aid has a more self-evident relationship with U.S. national security. An example of this would be the wars against Al-Qaeda proxies in Africa: ECOWAS and the French have been fighting Al-Qaeda in the Islamic Maghreb (AQIM) in Mali, while AMISOM has been fighting Al-Shabaab in Somalia. The U.S. has helped fund and assist both of these interventions, though no American boots are technically on the ground.

With her **rebuttal**, she returns to her original **thesis and continues** to build her argument by naming specific instances where US aid has served to counter terrorism.

Now, military aid also has its drawbacks. International forces in both Somalia and Mali have been accused of also committing atrocities, albeit less than Al-Shabaab and AQIM. Foreign interventions are not always popular with the local populace, and can lead to retributive violence down the line.

The more casual term "Now" introduces complexity into her argument, offering yet another turn in the strategy of arrangement. In classical rhetoric, this is called a **qualification.**

So does foreign aid make us safer? It's hard to tell what the long-term implications of military or structural aid will be

Returning to her original question and strategically repeating the words of the title anchors the reader back to her main purpose.

In developing her **refutation**, Lindsay uses more plain or low style diction, such as "It's hard to tell" and "though" in order to engage the reader's attention and **respond** to the issue at hand.

Her strong **conclusion** makes a closing assertion through a vivid image and a clear declarative sentence: "a concept of strong national defense cannot be so easily decoupled from foreign aid."

She ends with a flourish of *pathos*, warning that "disavowing" aid "ignores" reality. In this way, she soundly clinches her argument.

on U.S. national security. At the moment, though, there's no question that it's being used in the service of defeating Al-Qaeda affiliates and preventing similarly aggressive successors from taking hold.

Despite what Rand Paul might say, a concept of strong national defense cannot be so easily decoupled from foreign aid. Now, there's probably a solid case to be made for evaluating the effectiveness of our current counter-terrorism policy and tactics, including revisiting our foreign aid. But advocating for a strong national defense while simultaneously disavowing foreign aid ignores the very real role that the latter currently plays in the former.

Writing a Position Paper that Considers Multiple Arguments

Lindsay Funk's article demonstrates interesting possibilities for developing your own persuasive writing when tackling one opponent in a position paper. But sometimes we seek to include many voices, in the way that Lindsay quoted Rand Paul. Recall our earlier discussion of photographs: each photograph suggests a different angle, a unique "version" of an event, and the perspective of a particular persona. When we bring all these different sides to light, we find that suddenly an incident or issue that might have seemed polarized—or "black and white"—is actually much more complex. While counterargument, concession, rebuttal, and qualification can begin to suggest this complexity, another writing strategy you can use is to consider multiple arguments by quoting a number of sources. This is a technique often used in news reporting, and it indicates that there are many "positions" lurking beneath the surface of an issue. While we will learn how to respond in depth to such voices through model of "a research conversation" in Part II of *Envision,* at this point it is worth looking at how even a short

WRITER'S PRACTICE

After reading Lindsay Funk's position paper on US foreign aid and its relation to national security and terrorism, take a few moments to analyze the elements of the photograph in Figure 3.14. Next, using the canon of *invention*, brainstorm your own *rhetorical stance* on the photo. What argument can you make about US foreign aid—either military aid or structural aid—that might accompany this image in an opinion article? Work through one of the structures of *arrangement* and draft an outline for your position paper. Identify your *claim*, and then cite your *grounds* the way Lindsay did before expanding on your *warrants*. Move through your points of argument by including the counter argument, concession, qualification, and rebuttal. When you are done drafting, go back and compose an engaging *introduction* and *conclusion* using the strategies you learned in this chapter. Finally, play with *style* as you cap your article with a title that both informs and entices the reader into wanting to know your view on the issue.

FIGURE 3.14 The powerful image of doves in front of a tank in the Middle East offers multiple interpretations on military and structural foreign aid.

position paper or op-ed can engage a spectrum of differing perspectives. As you turn to write your own arguments, consider how you can explore different viewpoints, including other voices as well as through experimentation with diction, syntax, style, image selection, arrangement of argument, and voice. See how Richard Woordward does so below.

ONE 9/11 PICTURE, THOUSANDS OF WORDS: RORSCHACH OF MEANINGS

Richard B. Woodward

Notice how Woodward begins by identifying the specific assumptions (i.e., about photography, objectivity and evidence) he will devote much of his essay questioning. This strategy effectively establishes the *kairos* for the argument to follow.

Faith in the camera as an infallible eyewitness was supposed to have died for good with the advent of Photoshop. Critics have opined for years that the popularity of such digital trickery would erode the truth- value of all photographs. What attorney would risk introducing an 8-by-10 print as evidence of a murder scene if jury members knew how to rotate bodies and paintbox skin tones on their home computers?

So far, nothing of the sort has happened; indeed, quite the reverse. Despite the shame visited this summer upon certain photojournalists for their "fauxtography" in Lebanon—darkening skies, adding smoke and fire to scenes of battle—evidence produced by cameras has never been so prevalent or taken for granted. The view that photographs accurately reflect the chaos of events or inner states of mind remains stubbornly unshaken, and some of the most zealous believers are photographers themselves.

Here is where the author introduces his first major claim. And Again, word choice ("glib interpretation") is critical to determining what his argument is.

The eruption in the media and on photo blogs last week over an image taken on 9/11 by the German photographer Thomas Hoepker—and the glib interpretation put upon it by Frank Rich in the *New York Times*—has proved once again that we don't need Photoshop to doctor the meaning of an image. Our minds do this job, adding or eliding information as we see fit, better than any computer program.

For those who tuned in late, Mr. Hoepker's photograph depicts five young white New Yorkers on the Brooklyn waterfront engaged in conversation while smoke from the World Trade Towers billows above and behind them. The scene includes a park bench and a bicycle, blue sky and water. The quintet seem to be concentrating on each other on a gorgeous day with the disaster purely as background

As reported by David Friend in his new book "Watching the World Change: The Stories Behind the Images of 9/11," Mr. Hoepker saw the people in his photograph as "totally relaxed like any normal afternoon. They were just chatting away. It's possible they lost people and cared, but they were not stirred by it. . . . I can only speculate [but they] didn't seem to care."

That was enough for Mr. Rich to declare in his column this Sept. 10 that "from the perspective of 9/11's fifth anniversary, Mr. Hoepker's photo is prescient as well as important—a snapshot of history soon to come. What he caught was this: Traumatic as the attack on America was, 9/11 would recede quickly for many. This is a country that likes to move on, and fast. The young people in Mr. Hoepker's photo aren't necessarily callous. They're just American."

The next day the journalist Daniel Plotz wrote a piece on Slate that disputed Mr. Rich, calling his reading of the image a "cheap shot.." In Mr. Plotz's view the five have not ignored or moved beyond 9/11 but have "turned toward each other for solace and for debate." He asked any of the people in the photograph to contact Slate and describe the event from their side of the lens.

First to respond was Walter Sipser, a Brooklyn artist. "A snapshot can make mourners attending a funeral look like they're having a party," he wrote. "Had Hoepker walked fifty feet over to introduce himself he would have discovered a bunch of New Yorkers in the middle of an animated discussion about what had just happened." Another figure in the picture who wrote in was Chris Schiavo, a professional photographer. She bitterly chastised both Mr. Rich and Mr. Hoepker for their "cynical expression of an assumed reality." As a "third-generation native New Yorker, who knows and loves every square inch of this city," whose "mother even worked for Minoru Yamasaki, the World Trade Center

He focuses here on viewer reaction to the photographs. The accumulation of quotations increases his *ethos* as a researcher and also gives weight to their criticism, even though it is a reaction Woodward does not share.

Woodward transitions here into the discussion of an example that more directly supports his own argument (i.e. that visual evidence is subjective), but uses this example only to hint at his argument rather than state it outright.

Woodward again uses emotionally charged language ("simplistic"; "inscrutable oblivion") as part of his *pathos* appeal. In this case, such language is being deployed to more directly present his central argument—namely, that we cannot pass definitive judgment on what a photograph means (claim) because the meaning of a photographic image is "inherently unstable" (grounds).

Fleshing out the context for his discussion even further, Woodward pivots to a series of examples that serve as evidence to bolster his main argument. Think about the order in which he chooses to present them. The examples move in a historical progression from events that are more distant (the Spanish Civil War) to those that are more recent (the Al-Aqsa Intifada). Why does Woodward organize his evidence in this way?

architect," she stated that "it was genetically impossible for me to be unaffected by this event."

It can't be fun to have your public moment of emotional confusion hijacked by a Magnum photographer and turned into a national symbol of moral disgrace by a *New York Times* columnist.

Mr. Hoepker and Mr. Rich interpreted the picture for their own purposes, claiming to know from the relaxed gestures of the group and the context of the event what the five were talking about and thinking.

But their simplistic reading of the image, however mistaken in the view of those in it, is more naïve than malicious. Their translation is not absurd and can be supported by elements in the image. The meanings of photographs are inherently unstable. Without captions to nail down who, what, why, where, when, they tend to drift away into the inscrutable oblivion—one reason the medium was so beloved by the surrealists. The poignancy (or hilarity) of many found photographs is that they have lost their original context, the storyline that made them necessary at the time.

These free-floating mysteries require a narrative to be understood, even if it is distorted, incomplete, or flat wrong. Historic photographs assumed to be straightforward records of events by some have been seen as anything but by others. Robert Capa's "Fallen Soldier" from the Spanish Civil War in 1936 was subject to decades of innuendo and slander against Capa for supposedly having faked the soldier's death. Conspiracy theorists of the JFK assassination have detected in the 486 frames of the Zapruder film second and third gunmen, CIA agents and mafiosi. Attorneys defending the Los Angeles police officers accused of brutalizing Rodney King slowed down George Holliday's 81-second video into still photos and convinced a jury in Simi Valley that the supine Mr. King was still a threat.

More recently, during the Al-Aqsa Intifada of 2000 an Associated Press photograph, of a man with a bloodied head and a baton-wielding Israeli policeman behind him, was broadly published and labeled as the beating of a Palestinian by an Israeli officer. In fact, the bloodied man was Tuvia Grossman, a Jewish-American student from Chicago, and the photograph actually showed his rescue by the policeman from a mob of Palestinian rioters. The captioned villain was really the savior, not the scourge. In 2002 a Paris court forced the AP and the French newspaper Libération to pay Mr. Grossman €4500 ($5,700) for falsely representing him in the picture.

Mr. Hoepker suppressed his photograph of the "blasé" New Yorkers for four years because, he said, it did not express the rage and suffering that he and millions felt that day. The image didn't fit the accepted narrative of the event. As Mr. Friend writes in his book, "it did not meet any of our standard expectations of what a September 11th photograph *should* look like."

With the passage of time, however, Mr. Hoepker has gone back and re-evaluated the image. Last year he was proud enough to choose it as the catalog cover for his retrospective in Munich. He now compares it to Breughel's "Landscape with the Fall of Icarus," the painting in which most of the 16th-century figures seem unaware or unconcerned by the body of the Greek boy plummeting from the sky into the sea.

Having reassessed the image in light of all the other less ambiguous pictures published from that day, he believes it "has grown in importance." In effect, he has Photoshopped it in his mind so that it now belongs neatly in a more contemporary storyline of this nation's culpability for world unease. The German press has reproduced the photograph widely and seems to have read it, as Mr. Rich did, to upbraid Americans for their hedonism and short memories. Funny, but I don't know many New Yorkers who have moved past 9/11, certainly none who has done so "fast." Thomas Hoepker may be the exception.

This description seems at first to undermine Woodward's main point by suggesting that "standard expectations" can—and perhaps should—dictate what photographs are allowed to be publicly displayed.

Woodward quickly challenges this suggestion, however, by describing how Hoepker "re-evaluated" his own decision. Note Woodward's decision to highlight the parallel Hoepker draws between his photograph and the famous painting of Icarus. What does this comparison suggest about the nature of photographic images? How does it support or reinforce Woodward's overall argument?

While acknowledging that many continue to indict Hoepker's photograph for the indifference and "hedonism" it supposedly displays, Woodward concludes by criticizing many of the voices he has quoted in his position paper. In this way, he gets the last word on how to "read" this controversial photo.

Look at the closing paragraph and how Woodward uses the *conclusion* to present his own argument despite quoting so many other voices in his piece. In this way, he places his main idea, the *invention* in his thesis statement, in the final paragraph for the answer. As for the *arrangement* of his essay, we see that Woodward strategically quotes multiple viewpoints on the issue, allowing readers to become acquainted with those who believe in the objective reality of visual images, before he offers a series of counter-examples that challenge this view. By organizing his essay in this way, Woodward focuses the public reaction to the Hoepker's photograph through the lens of his own argument. His style also reserves his strongest language for the very end, such that invention, arrangement, and style all privilege his own view above that of others.

As you turn now to write your own arguments, recall the many options available to you and select the ones that best meet the needs of your rhetorical situation.

THE WRITER'S PROCESS

In this chapter, you've learned to harness the canons of rhetoric—*invention*, *arrangement*, and *style*—to compose effective arguments of your own. You've developed strategies for crafting *titles, introductions*, and *conclusions*; you've explored the importance of *persona* and *rhetorical stance* in argument. You've learned the differences between three models of argumentation—classical, Toulmin, and Rogerian—and how they relate to your purpose and your audience. Now it's time to implement these skills. Practice inventing a position on an issue, arranging claims and evidence for your argument (including working with images as evidence for your points), developing a rhetorical stance, and working on persona through style by crafting your prose with care.

WRITING ASSIGNMENTS

1. **Written Analysis of a Photograph**: Select a photograph to analyze: you might select the work by a well-known photographer such as Ansel Adams, Dorothea Lange, Carrie Mae Weems, W. Eugene Smith, or Cindy Sherman; one from the Library of Congress "American Memory" archives online; or even a photograph from a newspaper, news magazine, or *Life* magazine's photographer website. Practice the textual analysis lessons you've learned in this chapter by writing out answers to the questions on the checklist below. When you are done, draft two captions or titles that represent alternate perspectives or interpretations of the image. Compare your analysis and your captions/titles with a partner.

- ❑ **Content:** What, literally, does the photograph depict? Who or what is the subject of the photo? What is the setting?
- ❑ **Argument:** What argument or stance is the photographer conveying through the image? What is its underlying message? For instance, while the photo might show a group of people standing together, its argument might be about love, family unity across generations, or a promise for the future.
- ❑ **Photographer:** Who took this photograph? What is her or his reputation? What style of photography or famous photos is she or he known for?
- ❑ **Audience:** Who was the photographer's intended audience?
- ❑ **Context:** What was the historical and cultural context of the photograph? Where was it reproduced or displayed (an art gallery, the cover of a magazine, the front page of a newspaper)? If it "documents" a particular event, person, or historical moment, how prominently does this photograph factor into our understanding of this event, person, or place? (For instance, is it the only known photograph of an event, or is it one of a series of pictures taken of the same subject?)
- ❑ **Purpose:** What is the photograph's purpose or motive for capturing this image? Is it intended to be overtly argumentative and to move its audience to action? Or is the argument more subtle, even to the point of seeming objective or representational?
- ❑ **Rhetorical stance:** How does the composition of the photo convey a sense of the rhetorical stance or point of view of the photographer? Pay attention to issues of focus (what is "in focus"? This may differ from the ostensible "focus" of the picture); cropping (what is "in" the picture, and what has been left "out"?); color (is the picture in black and white? color? sepia?); setting (what backdrop did the photographer choose?); and perspective (are we looking down? up?).
- ❑ **Representation versus reality:** Does this photograph aspire to represent reality, or is it an overtly abstract piece? Is there any indication of photo manipulation, editing, or other alteration? If so, what rhetorical purpose does this serve—what argument does this alteration make?
- ❑ **Word and image:** Does the photo have a caption? Does the image accompany an article, essay, or other lengthy text? How does the image function in dialogue with this verbal text? Does it offer visual evidence? Does it argue an independent point? Does it provide a counterargument to the print text?

2. **Draft Alternate Introductions.** Building from your work in Assignment #1, draft two alternate introductions for a rhetorical analysis essay on your photograph. First review the section on Introductions earlier in this chapter. Next identify your claim or thesis statement for your rhetorical analysis, using the techniques you practiced in Chapter 1. Then develop two possible introductions for the essay, utilizing different strategies for each one. As you craft the introductions, ask yourself:

   - ❑ Do you want to prioritize facts (*logos*), an emotional connection with the reader (*pathos*), your own authority on the subject (*ethos*)?
   - ❑ Do you want to use comparison-contrast? Definition of terms? Process? Classification? Description? Narration? Definition? Cause-effect?
   - ❑ Do you want to include a startling statistic? A relevant quotation or question? A vivid statement of the problem? An intriguing anecdote? A representative example or examples?
   - ❑ What type of persona will you construct? How will you use word choice, syntax, and tone to establish style?

   Keep in mind that you may employ several techniques or strategies in each introduction. Your goal is to imagine two alternate possibilities for how to introduce your topic and argument to your reader. When you have drafted the two introductions, share them with a partner in class and assess which offers the strongest foundation for your argument.

3. **Compose an Argument:** Write a position paper about an issue that moves you and about which you can take a strong stance. Be sure to anticipate counterclaims and to address them through rebuttal, concession, or qualification. Consider basing your argument on the analysis of a powerful image, building from your work in Assignments #1 & #2 above. If you do so, include your interpretation of the photograph as part of your paper.

4. **Consider Multiple Perspectives:** Identify different positions on an issue, then assign various members of your group each to write a position paper on one of those stances. You might, for instance, write about the conflict between your college campus and the surrounding town: one student could write a position paper that represents the staff perspective, another one on the administrator's perspective, another the City Council's perspective, and a fourth person could represent the study body's perspective. Collaboratively write an introduction and conclusion for this series of papers that provide an overview of the topic and the conversation between the multiple perspectives.

Part II

RESEARCH ARGUMENTS

CHAPTER 4

Planning and Proposing Research Arguments

Chapter Preview Questions

4.1 How do I get started on formulating a research topic?
4.2 How do I generate a productive topic and research questions?
4.3 What prewriting techniques can I use to narrow my topic?
4.4 What are the steps for developing a strong research plan?
4.5 How do I write a formal research proposal?

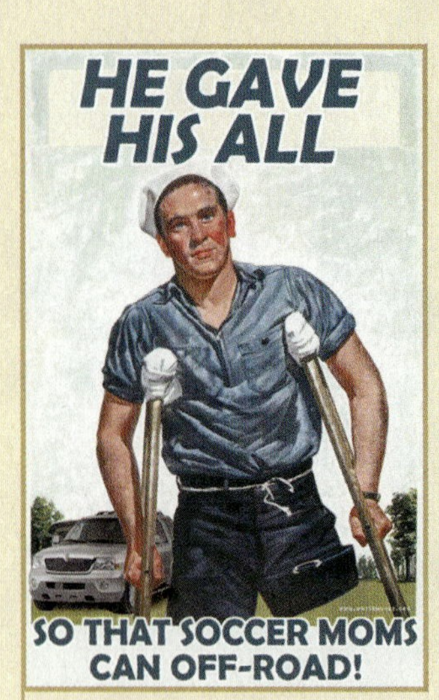

FIGURE 4.1 How does this parody propaganda poster use visual elements to challenge the government's official rationale for going to war in Iraq?

When we approach the task of research, it becomes clear that we can use many of the skills of analysis that we've practiced in previous chapters to help us interpret the meaning of texts and provide us with a starting point for our own line of inquiry. For instance, take a look at the poster shown in Figure 4.1. What you probably see first is a sailor, making direct eye contact with you, drawn in the style of a vintage World War II poster. However, closer scrutiny complicates this initial impression. How does your realization that he's an amputee, paired with the header "He Gave His All," enrich your understanding of his identity—as a hero, a veteran? Relatedly, how does the picture of the SUV, inserted discretely in the lower left, sharpen your sense of the poster's context? How does the reference to "Soccer Moms" further transform your understanding of the poster's argument or its exigency? At some point, as you begin to assess these different elements, you realize that this patriotic image is being repurposed here to offer a pointed critique of the recent war in Iraq. By ironically yoking the "giving his all" appeal with the gas-guzzling car and the "Soccer Moms" stereotypically presumed to drive them, this poster implies a connection between the war with Iraq and the oil trade. These observations will help you begin to develop an argument about the poster, but in order to back up or substantiate your claims about its meaning, you need to do some research. That is, you need to place the rhetorical elements of the poster in their historical and critical contexts, including the military recruitment campaigns from World War II and the debate over the more recent war in Iraq.

Research can be conducted in any number of ways, including interviews, fieldwork, and the exploration of sources both online and in print. However, the starting point of any research effort is to determine what questions to ask, what inquiries to pursue. In this chapter, you will learn how to become an active participant in a research community and begin to develop the skills for narrowing your research question and creating an effective research plan and a solid research proposal.

ASKING RESEARCH QUESTIONS

4.1 How do I get started on formulating a research topic?

The discussion in this chapter focuses on the subset of persuasive images—propaganda posters—because such texts make very powerful public statements and because, for many of us, to understand the motives and purpose behind a propaganda poster, we have to perform a certain amount of research. Often this research involves seeking answers to questions we have formulated about the poster. In fact, most research begins with the act of asking questions.

One way you can get started on your research is to pick a text that moves you and start brainstorming questions about it. Let's say that you came across the 1917 American enlistment poster shown in Figure 4.2 in an exhibit on campus or as part of a class discussion about World War I posters. Approaching it for the first time, you and your peers probably will start to analyze the visual rhetoric, much as we did in the earlier chapters of this book.

What are your eyes drawn to first, the words or the image? Maybe you look first at the simian figure in the middle, roaring menacingly at you, and then at the swooning, semi-naked woman in his arms. In contrast, maybe the person next to you is attracted first to the bold yellow text at the top and then to the bottom, where the words "U.S. Army" in black are superimposed on the imperative "Enlist." In synthesizing various responses to the

FIGURE 4.2 This World War I propaganda poster offers a wealth of detail for historical analysis.

text, you most likely would find yourself with more questions than answers—a good thing, for those questions can be the beginning of your research inquiry.

You might ask: Is that gorilla King Kong? Your research would allow you to confidently answer, No, since you would discover that the poster was made decades before the movie was released. That same research might lead you to discover several books that discuss the wartime practice of casting enemies as subhuman creatures, offering a possible explanation for why the enemy nation is portrayed as a threatening gorilla in this poster. Adding to that your observation that "*culture*" is spelled "Kultur" (on the club the gorilla is holding), you probably would realize that the enemy symbolized here is in fact Germany.

Then you might ask: What is the significance of that bloody club? Why is the woman unconscious and partly naked? More research might provide insight on how bestiality emerged as a wartime theme in World War I enlistment posters. If a nation's women were threatened with potential attack by such "monsters," these posters implied, then the men would surely step up to save and protect their wives, daughters, sisters, and mothers.

By asking questions about your text, you can move beyond an initial response and into the realm of intellectual discovery. In fact, your first questions about a text will lead you to ask more pointed questions about the context, political environment, key players, and social trends informing your text. For the propaganda poster in Figure 4.2, such questions might include:

- What conflict was America involved in during 1917?
- What was the meaning of the word on the gorilla's hat, "Militarism," at that time?

- How would an appeal to enlist factor into that historical situation?
- Who is the audience for this poster, and how is this poster part of a series of wartime propaganda images?

If you were to work through these questions, you might begin to develop ideas for a feasible research topic—one that could yield an interesting paper on war propaganda and the relationship between America and Germany in 1917.

As you investigate your research topic, your questions will likely become more specific:

- Do other posters of the same historical period use similar imagery and rhetorical strategies?
- How do the techniques used in early twentieth-century posters differ from those used during World War II?
- How are the rhetorical strategies used in this poster similar to or different from enlistment posters you might encounter today?
- In what ways have enlistment posters changed over time?

In all cases, what these questions lead to is a focused *research topic* and, ultimately, a written essay that draws on and contributes to the arguments that others have made about such texts. Generating a range of interesting and productive questions is the first step in any research project; the process of inquiry itself helps you to define a project and make it your own.

Constructing a Research Log

From the very beginning of your research process—as you move from asking questions about a text to identifying a productive topic, to gathering information and taking notes—keep track of your ideas in a *research log*. This log will help you organize your ideas, collect your materials, chart your progress, and assemble the different pieces of your research.

Your research log can take many forms, from a handwritten journal, to a series of word

AT A GLANCE

Constructing a Research Log

To start your research log, include a variety of entries related to the initial stages of the research process:

- Write freely on possible topic ideas.
- Insert and annotate clippings from newspaper or magazine sources that offer interesting potential topics.
- Paste in and respond to provocative images related to potential topics.
- Write a reaction to ideas brought up during class discussion.
- Insert and annotate printouts from emails, blog posts, or other collaborative work on research ideas.
- Track preliminary searches on the Internet and in your library catalog.
- Develop your research plan.
- Vent anxieties over your project.

processing documents, a personal blog, or a collection of bookmarked webpages. It can contain primarily written text, or it can include images, video, or audio files as well. The key lies not in what your research log looks like, but in the way you use it to help you develop an interesting and provocative research project that keeps careful track of the sources you encounter along the way.

4.2 How do I generate a productive topic and research questions?

GENERATING TOPICS AND RESEARCH QUESTIONS

If you think back to our discussion of *invention* in Chapter 3, you'll understand that one of the most crucial aspects of starting a research project is selecting a viable and engaging topic. The word *topic*, in fact, comes from the ancient Greek word *topos*, translated literally as "place." The earliest students of rhetoric used the physical space of the papyrus page—given to them by their teachers—to locate their topics for writing. Similarly, your teacher may suggest certain guidelines or parameters for you to follow when it comes to your topic; for instance, you may be given a specific topic (such as representations of race in Dr. Seuss cartoons) or you may be limited to a theme (the rhetoric of political advertisements on television, radio, and the Internet).

AT A GLANCE

Looking for the "Perfect" Topic

1. ***Look inward.*** What issues, events, or ideas interest you? Are there any hot-button topics you find yourself drawn to again and again? What topic is compelling enough that you would watch a news program, television special, YouTube video, film, or relevant lecture on it?
2. ***Look outward.*** What are the central issues of student life on campus? Do you walk by a technology-enhanced classroom and see the students busy writing on laptops or using plasma screens? Topic: technology and education. Do you see a fraternity's poster about a "dry" party? Topic: alcohol on campus. Do you see workers outside the food service building on strike? Topic: labor relations at the college.
3. ***Use creative visualization.*** Imagine that you are chatting casually with a friend when you overhear someone talking. Suddenly, you feel so interested—or so angry—that you go over and participate in the conversation. What would move you so strongly?
4. ***Use the materials of the moment.*** Perhaps the *topos* might be closer to the classical Greek model; although not a roll of papyrus, your class reading list or a single issue of a newspaper can house many topics. Scan the front page and opinion section of your school or community newspaper to see what issues people are talking about. What issues are gripping the community at large?

In some cases, you may not have any restrictions at all. But regardless of the degree to which your topic has been mapped out for you, you still can—and should—make it your own. You do this partly by generating your own **research questions**, a set of questions that will guide your work and lead you to your final argument. You can generate these questions by responding to the rhetorical situation provided by your assignment and by considering what interests *you* most about the topic. Even if your whole class is writing on the same topic, each person will present a different argument or approach to the issue. Some will use a different stance or persona, some will rely on different sources, some will use different rhetorical appeals, and all will argue different positions about the topic. The way you make a research project your own is by developing powerful research questions.

To understand how this works, let's look at one student's project on propaganda posters to see how he moved from a series of images to a more fully developed research topic. When asked to choose a topic for a research paper, student Tommy Tsai found he was interested in propaganda posters from World War II. Looking at a selection of images (see Figures 4.3 through 4.5), Tommy started by asking some questions, such as the ones that follow:

FIGURE 4.3 This Uncle Sam poster from 1917 was reissued for World War II.

FIGURE 4.4 Anti-Nazi propaganda relied on religiously charged rhetoric.

FIGURE 4.5 American war efforts employed extreme visual messages to galvanize support.

- Who is depicted in these posters? Are these depictions positive or negative?
- What is the purpose of each poster?
- What strategies are these posters using to persuade their audiences?
- How do these posters reveal cultural prejudices?

Through the process of asking such questions, Tommy was able to identify his preliminary topic as "the rhetoric of World War II propaganda." He wrote in one research log entry that he wanted to analyze these posters in their historical contexts: "In particular, I plan to focus on the propaganda posters that appeared in the three most active countries in that time period: the United States, Germany, and Japan. My research paper will report my findings from the comparison of the different rhetorical strategies employed by the three nations." By generating a set of preliminary research questions, he was able to focus more clearly on the dialogue between those posters and his interest in them. In this way, he was able to turn an overly broad initial topic into one that was more specific and workable.

As you consider your own possible research topics, keep this key principle in mind: successful topics need to interest you, inspire you, or even provoke you. Even with assigned topics, you should be able to find some aspect of the assignment that speaks to you. That is, there needs to be a *connection* between you and your topic to motivate you to follow through and transform it into a successful argument.

In addition, while selecting your topic, you might consider the type of research you'll need to do to pursue it; in fact, you might select your topic based mostly on the sorts of research it allows you to do. For instance, a student writing on propaganda of the prohibition era will draw extensively on paper sources, which might involve archival work with original letters, posters, or government documents from that time period. A student writing on visual advertising for ethnic-theme dorms on campus will be more likely to complement paper sources with interviews with the university housing staff, student surveys, and first-person observations. A student writing on sexualized rhetoric in student campaign materials might take a poll, gather concrete examples, and research both print and online coverage of past and present elections. Think

WRITER'S PRACTICE

Exploring a Potential Topic

Before selecting a topic for a research project, it's important to carefully evaluate it to understand its viability. Choose a tentative topic, and put it to the test by answering the following questions:

1. **What is interesting about this topic?** We write best about ideas, events, and issues that we connect with through curiosity, passion, or intellectual interest.
2. **Can I make a claim or argue a position about this topic?** At this stage, you may not have developed a position on the topic, but you should see promise for advancing a new perspective or for taking a stand.
3. **Will I be able to find enough research material on this topic?** Brainstorm some possible sources you might use to write this paper.
4. **Does this sort of research appeal to me?** Since you will be working with this topic for an extended period of time, it is best to have a genuine interest in the type of research that it will require (for instance, doing archival work, reading scholarly sources, conducting original research or engaging in fieldwork).

broadly and creatively about what kinds of research you might use and what types of research—archival work versus fieldwork involving interviews and survey taking—appeal most to you. Finally, consider whether you can actually get your hands on the source material you need to construct a persuasive argument.

NARROWING YOUR TOPIC

4.3 What prewriting techniques can I use to narrow my topic?

Once you have selected a topic and generated some research questions, the next step in the research project involves *narrowing* your topic to make your research project feasible and focused. A productive way to do this is through **prewriting**, or writing that precedes the official drafting of the paper, but, practically speaking, can take many forms. Lists, scribbled notes, informal outlines, drawings—all different types of *prewriting* can help you move from a broad topic to a much more focused one.

Brainstorming Topics Visually

The practice of **graphic brainstorming** provides writers with a great way to develop topics. This technique transforms traditional **brainstorming**—jotting down a series of related words and phrases on a topic—into a more

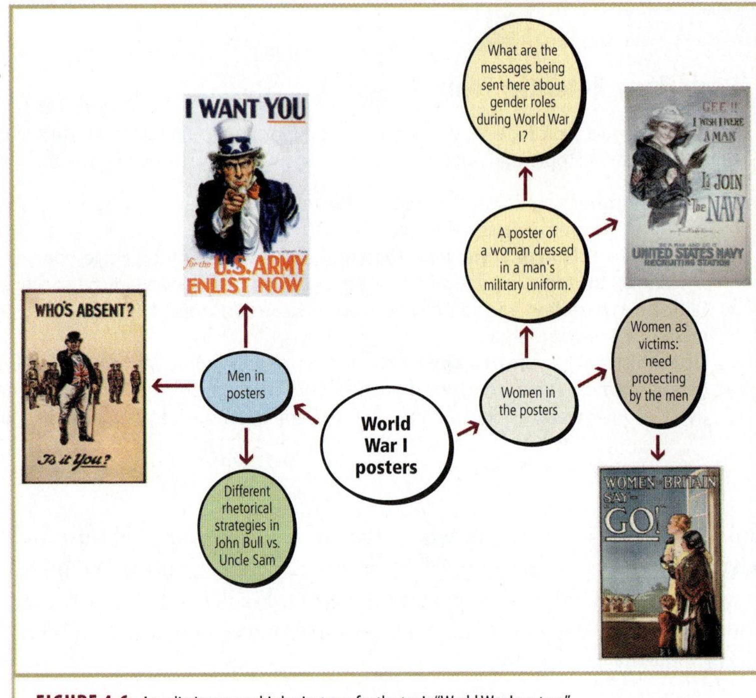

FIGURE 4.6 A preliminary graphic brainstorm for the topic "World War I posters."

visible process. Also called *webbing*, *clustering*, or *mapping*, the goal of *graphic brainstorming* is to help you develop your topic by exploring relationships among ideas. You can brainstorm by hand or on a computer; in either mode, begin by writing a topic in a circle, and then come up with ideas and questions about that topic. Next arrange them in groups around your main circle to indicate the relationships between them. As you answer each question and pose more developed ones in response, you begin to narrow your topic. You'll notice that Figure 4.6 shows how we might start to do this by writing questions that differentiate between various World War I posters and by grouping them by gender issues. In addition, in our brainstorm, we use various types of notations—including words, phrases, and questions—and insert lines and arrows to indicate the relationship between the concepts. We even use images and color to further emphasize these

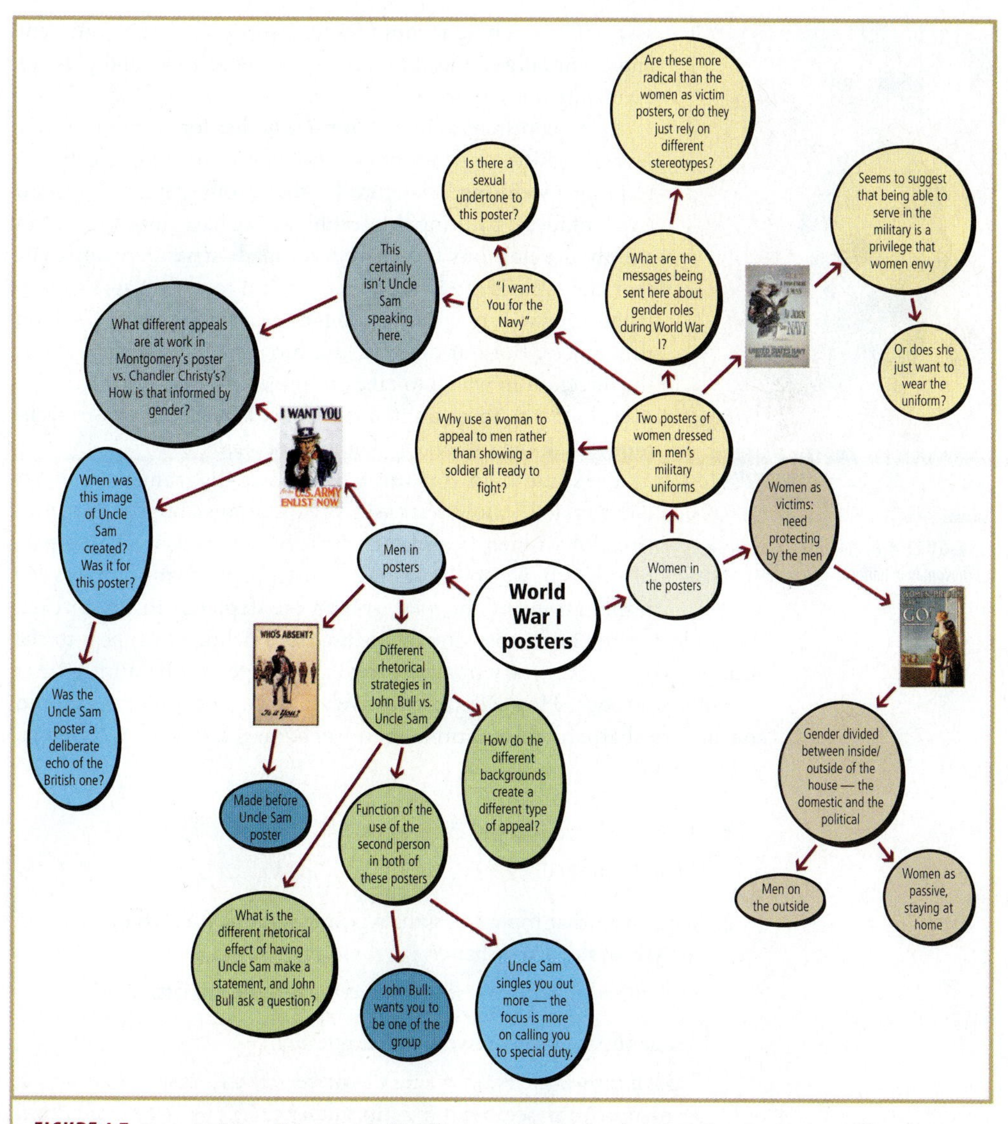

FIGURE 4.7 A more detailed graphic brainstorm for "World War I posters," showing how the author explores the many facets of this topic.

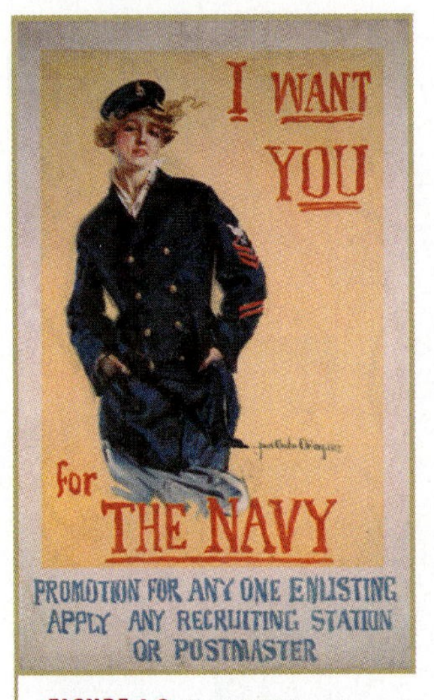

FIGURE 4.8 This 1917 U.S. poster uses a woman in uniform to present its message to enlist.

associations. These techniques help us develop the argument and eventually can lead to a more narrowed topic and perhaps even a preliminary thesis.

As we continue to brainstorm—whether for an hour or over several sessions—it becomes clear why some people call this technique **webbing**. As Figure 4.7 shows, our graphic turns into a web of ideas. By using this technique, we have done more than simply develop our topic: we have made it visually apparent that our topic is too broad for a standard research paper assignment. Our web now offers enough ideas for an entire book on the subject. But our diagram also provides us with clues about the direction in which to take our project. We can pick a *subsection* of ideas to focus on in our writing. When you try this technique, pick the subsection that interests *you* most.

Let's zoom in on one part of our diagram—the part, color-coded yellow, that asks key questions about representations of women in military posters. Working with this part of the web, we could write a focused paper that examines the implications of the way women are depicted in these texts. We could explore how cross-dressing is used as a deliberate appeal to the audience, or how military posters evoke the image of wife and mother to mobilize troops. However, to effectively narrow our topic, we should continue to sharpen our questions about such images, like the one shown in Figure 4.8.

1. Write down your topic.

   Topic formulation: gender roles in World War I.

2. Work with that topic by asking a pointed question based on close analysis of the text at hand.

   First question: Is there a sexual undertone to the posters?

3. Refine the topic by answering that question.

   Topic narrowing: Yes, in one of the posters, the woman is standing in a provocative pose, looking at the audience in a sexual manner, but in another, the women seem more identified with family (mother, daughter) than with sexuality.

4. Revise the narrowed topic to be more specific.

   Revised topic formulation: the different constructions of femininity in World War I propaganda posters.

5. Identify significant aspects of that topic to explore.

   Second question: How so? In what way? What is the significance?

6. Use the answers to these questions to focus the topic.

   Final topic focus: the use of the Madonna-whore stereotype as a persuasive strategy in World War I recruitment posters.

In working with the webbing process and then asking key questions in this way, we have just completed one of the most important steps in developing a viable research topic: narrowing a large subject to a more manageable one. By asking such questions—and we could come up with many others along different lines of inquiry (such as race, sexuality, international representations, and nationalism)—we begin to develop a *focused* topic that will offer us the opportunity for close analysis, rigorous research, and a sharp argumentative stance. That is, we can move from a topic loosely concerned with gender roles in World War I, to one that focuses specifically on a subset of recruitment posters and how they deploy a particular sexist stereotype (the virgin-whore trope) as a persuasive strategy. With this narrowed topic, we'll be able to contribute a new opinion about war posters and write an essay that adds to the ongoing dialogue that we find in our research sources.

WRITING ABOUT YOUR RESEARCH PLANS

4.4 What are the steps for developing a strong research plan?

After you have narrowed your topic, you need to develop a plan for your research process. If you find yourself concerned that you don't have the knowledge necessary to write this essay or are worried that the gaps in your own knowledge will prevent you from answering those questions in a satisfactory way, then realize that you are in good company. All researchers and scholars fear the limitations of their knowledge. The key is to develop a concrete plan to guide you as you move forward with your project.

WRITER'S PRACTICE

Working in a group or on your own, try out this practice of *narrowing a topic* with a selection of posters from the 2011 Occupy Movement. Examine the posters shown in Figures 4.9 through 4.11, and then complete a *visual brainstorm* to develop a feasible topic for your essay. Be sure that you narrow your topic from "Occupy posters" to a more focused one that you might pursue in a research paper. You might decide during your graphic brainstorm to focus your topic by identifying which images you'd like to write about or by generating key questions to ask about particular texts: How do the words and images work together in these posters? How do they work against each other? How does symbolism operate in these posters? The more specific the questions you ask, the more focused your topic will be.

FIGURE 4.9

FIGURE 4.10

FIGURE 4.11

The Research Freewrite

One way to start planning your research process is to freewrite about your ideas in your research log. In completing your freewrite, follow a **three-paragraph model**: in the *first paragraph*, announce your topic and state a preliminary thesis so that you can begin the project with a critical and focused perspective; in the *second paragraph*, identify the sources you plan to use to investigate this topic; in the *third paragraph*, speculate on obstacles or problems you might encounter in your research and how you might avoid or solve these problems. This freewrite will help you concretize your topic and assess your next steps in research.

AT A GLANCE

The Research Freewrite

- Write your ideas in full sentences.
- Use a three-paragraph model to focus your answers:
  - Paragraph 1: Announce the topic and state your preliminary thesis.
  - Paragraph 2: Identify key sources.
  - Paragraph 3: Anticipate problems.

Let's look at a freewrite from student Bries Deerrose, who shaped his research inquiry around a piece of contemporary propaganda: a leaflet dropped in Afghanistan by the U.S. military.

Research Freewrite

In the early 2000s, Over the past decade, as America's image fell increasingly under the scrutiny of our allies and enemies alike, President George W. Bush established the Office of Global Communications, the stated purpose of which was "to advise . . . on utilization of the most effective means for the United States Government to ensure consistency in messages that will promote the interests of the United States abroad, prevent misunderstanding, build support for and among coalition partners of the United States, and inform international audiences." In this paper,

This first paragraph introduces the research topic and describes what Bries thinks the main focus of his paper might be. At the end of the paragraph, he includes a tentative thesis to help him focus his interest and argument as he begins researching this topic.

I will examine how this office fulfilled its mission, especially through visual rhetoric. I will examine how the world, especially the Middle East, responded to such propaganda, and I will examine what image the office portrayed, whether this was an accurate image of America's role in Afghanistan or an example of political rhetoric. Finally, I will discuss whether such marketing was beneficial or detrimental, from both a foreign and American perspective. *Preliminary Thesis:* America has been actively projecting an image of itself using various forms of visual rhetoric; this image responds to the *kairos* of negative scrutiny abroad and uses rhetorical tactics to show how America is trying to help a war-torn Afghanistan.

In the second paragraph, Bries discusses the sources he intends to use. Notice the broad range of possibilities he considers: flyers, television commercials, radio broadcasts, and both American and international sources.

To research this topic, I hope to examine firsthand government-generated materials: flyers, commercials, radio broadcasts, publications, etc. I will also attempt to find any commentaries on this effort as well as on domestic conceptions of what America is and what its image should be. I will compare this with international opinions regarding America's image and reactions to the American marketing techniques. To do this, I will need to find foreign commentaries, including visual rhetoric responding to American visual rhetoric. I will need secondhand sources concerning international opinions.

The most difficult part of this assignment will be finding sources in English, since I am not fluent in other languages. I will also need to form my own opinion about the effectiveness, morality, and accuracy of these rhetorical tactics. Such issues are always sticky and will require much thought and a wide array of perspectives.

In the third paragraph, Bries anticipates the difficulties he might face and how he can solve them. Bries concludes with a concrete example of the visual rhetoric he will use in his research paper, a leaflet dropped in Afghanistan by the United States military.

Office of Global Communications leaflet air-dropped in Afghanistan.

Drafting the Research Hypothesis

In reading Bries's freewrite, you might have noticed that as he developed his topic, he was simultaneously experimenting with how to formulate an argument. That is, in Bries's first paragraph, he moves from the open-ended language of a proposal ("I will examine," "I will discuss") to a restatement of his subject in terms of a *tentative thesis statement* at the end of the paragraph. But how do you make a claim about a topic that you have not yet researched completely? This is often a frustrating question for many writers. Realize, however, that you've already taken the first step

Seeing Connections
See Chapter 1 to review how to develop a strong preliminary thesis statement.

just by asking pointed questions about your topic. From these questions, you can develop a **hypothesis**, or a working thesis that makes an argumentative claim that you'll attempt to prove. It is crucial for you to try to formulate a tentative *hypothesis* for your research as a way of looking at your project with an analytical eye. Of course, you will probably revise your hypothesis—and maybe your entire approach to the subject—several times over the course of your research. Indeed, this revision process is a natural part of what happens when you actually begin to read your sources, take notes in your research log, and read what your sources have to say about your topic.

One way to develop your detailed hypothesis is to rewrite one of your more narrowed questions from the research proposal as a **polished declarative statement** that you intend to prove. For example, while Tommy Tsai started by asking himself, "How were representations of race used in World War II propaganda?" after looking at his sources, he soon transformed that question into a potential thesis: "Representations of race deployed in World War II propaganda functioned as a way to justify the internment of innocent civilians." As he continued drafting, he focused his hypothesis even further, shifting from a general focus on race in World War II propaganda posters to a compelling criticism of America's use of race in its portrayal of its German and Japanese enemies. Tommy's process demonstrates that a hypothesis is only the beginning of making a strong, focused research argument.

4.5 How do I write a formal research proposal?

DRAFTING A RESEARCH PROPOSAL

In many academic contexts, you will be asked to formalize your research plan through composing a **research proposal**. This type of text—common in many disciplines and professions—is used by writers to develop agendas for research communities, secure funding for a study, publicize plans for inquiry and field research, and test the interest of potential audiences for a given project. In the writing classroom, the research proposal provides a similar formal structure for developing a project, but it also serves another purpose: it is a more structured means of organizing your thoughts to help you solidify your topic and move into the next stages of the research process. For these reasons, the *genre, organization,* and *content* of the research proposal differ in important ways from other kinds of popular and academic writing that you might do. To write your proposal, include the following elements:

- **Background:** What do I already know about my topic? What do I need to find out more about?
- **Methods:** How am I going to research this topic? What research questions are driving my inquiry?
- **Sources:** What specific texts will I analyze? What additional scholarly or popular sources can I research to help build my knowledge and my argument?
- **Timeline:** What are my goals for the different stages of research, and how can I schedule my work to most effectively meet these milestones?
- **Significance:** What do I hope to accomplish in my research? What are the broader issues or implications of my research? Why do these matter to me and to my readers?

As this list suggests, your proposal should explain your interest in your chosen subject and establish a set of questions to guide your inquiry. The proposal should delineate the timeline for your research and writing process—a crucial time management strategy.

Your proposal serves to clarify your research intentions, but it should also *persuade* an audience of the feasibility and significance of your project. In fact, perhaps the most important step in launching your research inquiry is to address the issue of your project's larger relevance or, as some writing instructors call it, the "So What?" part of the project. It is the "So What?"—an awareness of the *significance* of the topic you're addressing and the questions you're asking—that moves the proposal from being a routine academic exercise to a powerful piece of persuasive writing. When addressing the "So What?" question, consider why anyone else would care enough to read a paper on your topic. Ask yourself:

- What is at stake in your topic?
- Why does it matter?
- What contribution will your project make to a wider community?

Let's look at an example: a research proposal Molly Fehr developed on digital manipulation.

Molly's research proposal begins with a title that actually reflects her focused research question. In this way, she is sure to offer a more narrowed approach to her topic than the research freewrite.

The proposal opens with background, based on common knowledge.

In the last three sentences of the paragraph, Molly articulates her increasingly narrowed focus: from speeches to powerful rhetoric, to violent propaganda. This narrowed focus will help prevent her project from being too broad.

Chilton 1

Molly Fehr
Dr. Alyssa O'Brien
PWR 2: Rhetoric and Global Leadership
Final Research Proposal

Inspiring Nazi Germany:

How Hitler Rose to Power through the Use of Propaganda and Rousing Rhetoric

World War II involved all of the major world powers and was the deadliest conflict in human history. The men who lead these powers into battle were extraordinary historical figures ranging from Winston Churchill to Franklin D. Roosevelt to Joseph Stalin. Perhaps the most infamous historical leader of all time, Adolf Hitler, was a major component of World War II. For this research project I will examine how Hitler used powerful rhetoric to inspire his followers. The speeches that Hitler gave to the German public were effective enough to convince an entire country to go to war to fight for his beliefs. His powerful rhetoric influenced a generation of German citizens to adopt his ideology and practice his principles. In addition to persuading countless people to embrace his ideas, he used a widespread and violent propaganda campaign to effectively silence his opposition.

There are many different facets of World War II leadership and Hitler's power that one could explore. I will be focusing on Hitler specifically and how his use of violent rhetoric influenced both his supporters and his opposition. Some

Chilton 2

questions I will attempt to answer are: what part of his campaign was the most convincing? My focus will be on his overt use of violence and how that impacted his rise to power. So, what part did violence play in Hitler's rise to power? How did Hitler use fear as a rhetorical strategy? Is violent or emotional imagery the most powerful type of rhetoric? Then, more generally, how did Hitler's leadership affect Germany's role in the war? And finally, how does our understanding of his use of violence impact our view of Hitler as a leader?

As she generates specific research questions, Molly keeps her focus on "violence" as her main line of inquiry.

Hitler's extremely lengthy and provocative speeches will be the cornerstone of my research as they are excellent examples of both ethos and pathos. I will examine several of Hitler's most famous speeches, focusing on those given each year on the anniversary of his rise to power. In each of these speeches he spoke of the superiority of the German race and his future plans for the great nation. My discussion of Hitler's leadership and rhetorical style will also include with an analysis of his book, *Mein Kampf,* which outlines his core beliefs. There have been several scholarly books and articles written about *Mein Kampf* that I will use as secondary sources in my analysis. One book in particular that I will devote time to is Felicity Rash's *The Language of Violence* in which she discusses how the linguistic style of *Mein Kampf* created powerful imagery and elicited strong emotions. Other secondary sources that I will explore include John Angus's article "Evil As the Allure of

Turning to research methods, Molly names and describes the texts she plans to analyze. This makes her proposal seem quite feasible and builds her *ethos* as a scholar.

She includes book that have made important contributions to her topic.

She also includes field research, identifying a professor she might interview to learn more about the field.

Molly ends the formal writing of the proposal with a strong statement of significance. Listing the "So What?" will help her focus on the importance of her work as a writer and researcher. This section on implications is often the most crucial to readers who evaluate proposals for merit and funding.

Chilton 3

Protection," and Monika Zagar's *Knut Hamsun*. These sources and others investigate the violent imagery of Nazism and how its effects were far-reaching and dramatic. A possible field resource that I could interview might be a Stanford professor specializing in World War II. I could also interview one of the Stanford research librarians, specifically, either Nathalie Auerbach who specializes in German history or Patricia Harrington who is a general reference librarian.

This project has significant implications for the manner in which historical and contemporary leaders inspire their followers into controversial actions. Understanding how Adolf Hitler employed violent rhetoric to convince people that genocide was not only acceptable but desirable is crucial to unraveling the power of other infamous leaders. Additionally, it is interesting to explore why Hitler was so successful. If certain types of rhetoric such as emotional imagery or evocation of pride are so profoundly effective, how can they be used for good? This brings me to my final point: practical application. There are relatively few historical examples of people who succeeded in amassing so many followers to support a cause that is inherently wrong. A closer look at how Hitler managed to propagandize and affect a nation could reveal important lessons about how contemporary leaders can mobilize their supporters. Or, conversely, it could give important wisdom

Chilton 4

about how to prevent or combat such an influential leader in the future.

Timeline

1/20: Research Proposal due

1/21–1/23: In-depth research of speeches; write-up notes

1/22–1/27: Read secondary sources and write-up notes; search for more articles using online databases

1/27–2/1: Review notes and write a preliminary thesis; talk with peers and instructors for advice on thesis as well as for guidance on argument. Evaluate sources in research log and continue to read sources.

2/2–2/7: Outline due: decide on major argument. Use subheads to indicate sections of the essay.

2/8–2/10: Conduct field research interviews, using my argument and questions.

2/12–2/17: Write first draft of argument. Compose topic sentences for each section. Include evidence for my claims in drafting the argument.

2/18–2/21: Peer review feedback and instructor conference (get feedback).

2/22–3/2: Additional research and revision, as necessary.

3/5: Submit second full draft for feedback.

3/8–3/12: Final revisions, proofreading, works cited list, format paper, include images where appropriate.

3/15: Submit final revision. Done!

In her timeline, Molly lists not only deadlines assigned by her instructor, but also key steps in the research process: finding books, evaluating sources, reading and taking notes, constructing a thesis, peer review, a second round of research, drafting, and revising.

With this detailed timeline, Molly shows her careful time management and builds her *ethos* by demonstrating her understanding of the research process.

Chilton 5

Preliminary Bibliography

Auerbach, Nathalie. [Bibliographer for Germanic collections, Stanford Library]. Interview February 2013.

Campbell, John Angus. "Evil As the Allure of Protection." *Rhetoric & Public Affairs* 6.3 (2003): 523–530. Academic Search Premier. Web. 22 Jan. 2013.

Harrington, Patricia R. [Coordinator of Content Delivery, General Reference, Stanford Library]. Interview February 2013.

Hitler, Adolf, and Ralph Manheim. *Mein Kampf*. Boston: Houghton Mifflin, 1943. Print.

Hitler, Adolf. *Germany's Declaration of War Against the United States*. Reichstag Speech of December 11, 1941. Web. <http://www.ihr.org/jhr/v08/v08p389_Hitler.html>

———. *Speech Before the Reichstag*. 30 Jan. 1937. Web. <http://www.worldfuturefund.org/wffmaster/Reading/Hitler%20Speeches/Hitler%20Speech%201937.01.30.html>

———. *Speech at the Berlin Sportspalast*. 30 Jan. 1940. Web. <http://www.worldfuturefund.org/wffmaster/Reading/Hitler%20Speeches/Hitler%20Speech%201940.01.30.htm>

———. *Speech at the Berlin Sportspalast*. 30 Jan. 1942. Web. <http://www.worldfuturefund.org/wffmaster/Reading/Hitler%20Speeches/Hitler%20Speech%201942.01.30.htm>

Chilton 6

Jowett, Garth S, Victoria O'Donnell, and Garth Jowett. *Readings In Propaganda and Persuasion: New and Classic Essays*. Thousand Oaks, CA: SAGE, 2006. Print.

Maser, Werner. *Hitler's 'Mein Kampf': an Analysis*. London: Faber, 1970. Print.

Rash, Felicity J. *The Language of Violence : Adolf Hitler's Mein Kampf*. New York: Peter Lang, 2006. Print.

Žagar, Monika. *Knut Hamsun: the Dark Side of Literary Brilliance*. Seattle, WA: University of Washington Press, 2009. Print.

THE WRITER'S PROCESS

Now that you've learned about the process of generating research questions, narrowing your topic, developing a hypothesis, and then writing up your plans for research in a three-paragraph freewrite or a formal proposal, what can you argue about the first poster of this chapter (Figure 4.1)?

In answering this prompt, you might start to work through the writing activities related to the research process that we've discussed. You might develop a research focus that begins with questions and ends with a "So What?" or statement of significance. You might speculate about which sources that you could use to answer your questions and on opportunities and obstacles you might encounter when pursuing this project. You might try to develop a proposal that concludes with a clear statement of your future authority on this topic as a researcher. Try the strategies for keeping track of your ideas and work in progress in a research log, a key tool that you'll be using in the next chapter as we turn to gathering and evaluating sources for your topic. It's time to get started on the research process for writing a persuasive argument about an issue that matters to you.

WRITING ASSIGNMENTS

1. **Written Analysis of Propaganda Posters:** Select a propaganda poster (for instance, from the Library of Congress online archive) and practice the textual analysis strategies you have learned in this chapter by following the checklist below and writing out your answers.

   ❑ What is the poster's underlying message?

   ❑ What are the specifics of the rhetorical situation informing this piece of propaganda? Who produced the poster? Who was its intended audience? How was it distributed or shared?

   ❑ What is its historical context? In what country was the poster produced? What was the contemporary social and political situation? How does an understanding of its context affect our understanding of its message?

   ❑ What types of rhetorical appeals does the poster feature? Does it rely primarily on *logos, pathos, ethos, kairos*, or *doxa* to make its point? How does attention to this appeal manifest itself visually in the poster?

   ❑ Recalling the discussion of exaggerated use of appeals from Chapter 2, does the poster rely on any logical fallacies? Any exaggerated use of *pathos*? Any fallacies of authority? If so, how do these work to persuade the audience?

   ❑ What is the relationship between word and image in the poster? How do design elements such as color, font, layout, and image selection (photograph or illustration) operate as persuasive elements in this text?

   ❑ Does the poster use stereotypes or symbols to convey its message? How do these operate as rhetorical devices in this situation? How do they place the poster in the context of a larger cultural discussion?

   ❑ What research questions can you develop about this poster?

   ❑ What kinds of sources might you look at to develop a more complex understanding of this poster and its message?

2. **Research Freewrite:** Freewrite about your research ideas by first writing out answers to the questions provided in the "Prewriting Checklist" for Assignment #1 and then developing them into a three-paragraph freewrite. In the first paragraph, introduce your research paper topic and describe what you think the main focus of the paper might be. Include a preliminary thesis in this paragraph. In the second paragraph, discuss the sources that you intend to use. In the third paragraph, speculate on what obstacles you foresee in

this project and/or what you anticipate to be the most difficult part of the assignment. If appropriate, use an image to complement your written text. Show your answers to your instructor or your peers for feedback.

3. **Research Proposal:** Write a detailed research proposal that discusses your topic, planned method, and purpose in depth. Be sure to cover your topic, your hypothesis, your potential sources and problems, your method, timeline, and, most importantly, the significance of the proposed project. When you are done, present your proposal at a roundtable of research with other members of your class. Answer questions from your classmates to help you fine-tune your topic and troubleshoot your future research.

4. **Peer Review:** Collaboratively peer review your research proposals. Assume that you are on the review board granting approval and funding to the best two proposals of each group. Complete research proposal review letters for each member of your group. When you are done, discuss your letters and what changes you can recommend. Then revise your proposals to make them stronger, better written, and more persuasive. See Chapter 6 for more discussion of effective peer feedback sessions.

CHAPTER 5

Finding and Evaluating Research Sources

Chapter Preview Questions

5.1 What does the research process look like?

5.2 How do I develop effective search terms for my research?

5.3 What is the difference between a primary and a secondary source?

5.4 How do I critically evaluate both print and online sources?

5.5 How do I pursue field research for my project?

5.6 How can I understand the conversation my sources are having about my topic?

5.7 What is an annotated bibliography, and how can it help me develop my argument?

As you move from planning to conducting research, you'll need to investigate resources and evaluate them for your project. You can use your analytical skills to make important distinctions when locating, evaluating, and using research sources for your research project. Look, for instance, at the covers in Figure 5.1 and Figure 5.2. Although they focus on the same topic—climate change—the visual rhetoric suggests that the content of each journal will be quite different. The audience for *Science* magazine differs from that of *Newsweek*, and, consequently, the writing styles within the articles will be different as well. The cover of each magazine previews the distinct content inside. Studying the covers can help you look back in history to understand how climate change has been understood in the past. In this way, you are finding and evaluating research sources for your project.

FIGURE 5.1 Cover of *Science*, March 24, 2006.

Specifically, the cover of *Science* in Figure 5.1 conveys how the editors chose to represent global warming to their audience in 2006. It features a photograph of an ice-covered lake that appears to have been taken with a "fish-eye" lens, bringing several ice fragments into prominence in the foreground. Ask yourself: What is the argument conveyed by the visual rhetoric of the cover? What is the significance of the choice to use the lake as the "main character" in the image? How is color used strategically? What kind of stance toward the dangers of global warming does the cover suggest?

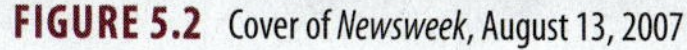
FIGURE 5.2 Cover of *Newsweek*, August 13, 2007

In contrast, the *Newsweek* cover from over a year later (see Figure 5.2) provides a very different perspective on the topic, pairing a striking close-up image of the sun with a provocative claim. Consider the way that the words and image work together and how the asterisk complicates *Newsweek's* stance on the topic. How is this cover specifically designed to appeal to its more mainstream, popular audience?

Clearly, the editors deliberately located, evaluated, and used materials for the covers that would reflect their magazine's contents. As a researcher, you can use your skills in rhetorical analysis to help you evaluate sources for your own research project, looking to the different elements of a text—from the cover design, to the table of contents, the index, and the writing itself—to better understand the text's perspective on your topic and its usefulness for your project.

Your task as a researcher is quite similar to that of the editors of *Science* and *Newsweek*. As you begin gathering and evaluating sources for your own research argument, keep in mind that you will need to shape the argument into a paper addressed to a particular audience: your writing class, a group of scientists, a lobbying organization, an advertising firm, or browsers on the Web. To take part in any of these conversations, a researcher needs to learn

- what is being talked about (the *topic*),
- how it is being discussed (the *conversation*), and
- what the different positions are (*research context*).

VISUALIZING RESEARCH

5.1 What does the research process look like?

To grasp the specifics of the topic, the conversation, and the research context, it is helpful to take a moment to visualize the research process. When you think of the act of research, what comes to mind? Surfing the Web?

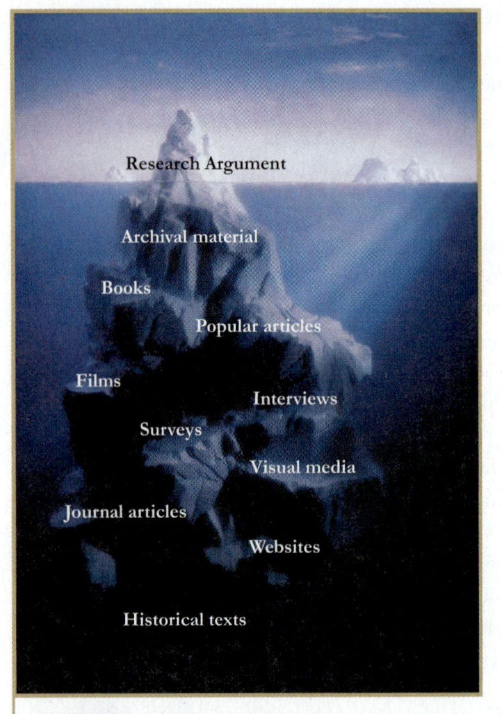

FIGURE 5.3 The iceberg of research demonstrates the many sources you will consult in building your argument.

Looking through a library? Interviewing experts in the field? All these images represent different research scenarios. The material you gather in each situation will compose the foundation for your research; it will inform your essay, but not all of it will find its way into your final paper. Nevertheless, you need to research widely and thoroughly to be fully informed about your topic and write a compelling research-based argument. One helpful way of visualizing the relationship between the *process* and the *product* of research is through the metaphor of the **iceberg of research** (see Figure 5.3). In essence, your final argument will be a synthesis of your research; beneath the surface lie the many different sources you will explore: books, journal articles, websites, field surveys, historical materials, interviews, multimedia, and more. All these constitute the research material. Your task as a researcher is to move beyond a surface knowledge of your topic; you need to gather, assess, keep, throw out, and ultimately use a variety of sources. By exploring such a wide range of material, you will encounter a rich array of scholarly and popular perspectives on your topic. In many ways, your research argument will be, in fact, a discussion with those research sources themselves. You add your voice to theirs. But your final paper may appear as only the "tip of the iceberg" or a result of your careful study of the work of others.

Sometimes, this process of building on others can be intimidating; we fear that we will have nothing new to add to the conversation. Yet if we think of research sources as texts written by people who were once, like us, struggling to figure out what they were trying to say, then we can see the process of gathering and assessing sources as a very social one, a process in which you *respect* and *acknowledge* the ideas of others and then seek to add your own voice to an ongoing conversation. One way to begin that conversation is to discover what others before you have said, thought, written, and published—and to keep track of that process in your research log, as explained in Chapter 4.

In this chapter, we'll use the metaphor of the *conversation* to accentuate the point that the research process is an act of composing a response to an ongoing dialogue about a topic. By gathering, synthesizing, and sorting the perspectives of others, you begin to shape your own stance on a research topic. By adding your voice as a writer, you are responding to others. Research is a *relationship* that you develop with the source material and the writers you encounter along the way.

DEVELOPING SEARCH TERMS

5.2 How do I develop effective search terms for my research?

The first step in the research process lies in locating relevant and interesting sources to draw into your conversation. This involves finding the best **search terms** to use in looking for sources on your topic. Your search terms will change depending on whether you are searching the Internet, an academic database, or a library catalog. You will need to identify the most productive keywords for searching in each of these situations.

Let's take as our example a project about Internet advertising. In a preliminary Web search, specific terms such as "pop-up ads," "Facebook ads," and "ethics & advertising online" probably yield more results than generic terms like "Internet advertising" and "Internet advertisements." If you search a database such as LexisNexis (a resource for news articles as well as legal, medical, and business articles), your keywords might be closer to your preliminary topic. Using the phrase "Internet advertising" in a database search would provide you with more than 90 citations in popular magazines and journals, while "pop-up ads" might yield fewer than 20 hits—the opposite of your results with a basic Internet search. Finally, you would likely find that a successful search of your library catalog requires still *different terms*—typically more academic terminology, such as "electronic commerce," "social media marketing," or "Internet marketing," because those phrases appear in scholarly book titles.

In many initial searches, the list of potential sources returned to you will be much larger than you can efficiently process. Your main task, then, will be to find ways to narrow your search. Experimenting with a range of terms—particularly more limited ones—can help you with this task by finding materials specific to your topic. For instance, you might use the narrower term "Internet advertising & law" to eliminate irrelevant sources and focus on the legal aspect of the issue, if that interests you. Through such experimentation you will find the search term that yields the most productive results; be sure to record your terms in your research log to track which ones prove most useful.

AT A GLANCE

Tips for Using Search Terms

- ***Web:*** Use popular or colloquial terminology in your Internet searches because search engines pick up actual terms from the webpages they index.
- ***Library:*** The Library of Congress has created a set of terms, called Library of Congress Subject Headings (LCSHs), used by librarians to catalog information. These headings may not always be obvious to you. (For example, the Library of Congress calls the Vietnam War the "Vietnamese Conflict, 1961–1975." A search under "Vietnam War" will produce no results.) You can find the LCSH terms in two ways: by looking at a library record online or by consulting the print index. By plugging the official subject headings into your library catalog, you can access information for your project more efficiently.
- ***Databases:*** Since databases can house a wide range of materials, from academic publications to popular articles, you will have to customize your language based on the database you have selected. Match your search terms in diction and formality to suit the type of resource you are exploring.

5.3 What is the difference between a primary and a secondary source?

UNDERSTANDING PRIMARY AND SECONDARY SOURCES

Your initial searches will yield a range of sources—from magazine articles to books, video recordings, and perhaps even manuscripts or a photograph collection. Each of these sources can play a vital role in your research. Scholars divide research into primary and secondary research, and sources, likewise, into **primary sources** (original texts you analyze in your research paper) and **secondary sources** (sources that provide commentary on your primary material or on your topic in general).

Seeing Connections
See some of Tommy Tsai's primary sources on p. 111.

Consider, for instance, Tommy Tsai's project, examined in detail in Chapter 4. Propaganda posters were Tommy's *primary sources*, and the articles, books, and transcribed interviews providing analysis of those posters were his *secondary sources.* His own paper, when completed, became *another* secondary source, one that contributes to an ongoing intellectual discussion about the meaning and power of the posters.

But as you search for your research materials, keep in mind that no sources are *inherently* primary or secondary; those terms refer to *how you use them* in your paper. For instance, if you were working with the topic of Internet advertising, you might use actual Facebook ads and Flash animations as your primary sources, as well as press releases and advertising websites. For secondary sources you might turn to articles that discuss innovations in social media marketing, a website on the history of digital advertising, and perhaps even a book by a famous economist about the impact of technology on corporate marketing strategies. However, imagine that you shift your topic slightly, making your new focus the economist's theories about the corruption of traditional advertising by multimedia technology. Now, that same book you looked at before as a *secondary* source becomes a *primary* source for this new topic.

AT A GLANCE

Primary and Secondary Sources

- ***Primary sources:*** materials that you will analyze for your paper, including speech scripts, advertisements, photographs, historical documents, film, artwork, audio files, and writing on websites. Primary sources can also include testimonies by people with firsthand knowledge or direct quotations you will analyze. Whatever is under the lens of your own analysis constitutes a *primary source.*
- ***Secondary sources:*** the additional materials that help you analyze your primary sources by providing a perspective on those materials; these include scholarly articles, popular commentaries, background materials (in print, video, or interview format), and survey data reinforcing your analysis. Whatever sources you can use as a lens to look at or understand the subject of your analysis constitutes a *secondary source.*

As you can see, your inquiry will determine which sources will be primary and which will be secondary for your argument. In most cases, you will need to use a combination of primary and secondary materials to make a persuasive argument. The primary sources allow you to perform your own analysis, whereas the secondary sources offer you critical viewpoints that you need to take into account in your analysis and integrate into your argument to build up your *ethos*. How you respond to and combine your primary and secondary sources is a matter of choice, careful design, and rhetorical strategy.

Finding Primary Sources

Searching for **primary sources**—original texts you analyze in your research paper—can be challenging, but they can be found in many places: in your library (whether in the general stacks, archives, or multimedia collections); at community centers such as library exhibits, museums, and city hall; or even in online digital archives such as the one maintained by the Library of

Congress. These materials can be some of the most exciting sources to work within your research process and might include:

- Original documents (examples: a handwritten letter by Mahatma Gandhi or Charles Lindbergh's journals)
- Rare books and manuscripts (examples: a first edition of a Charlotte Brontë novel or Roger Manvell's manuscripts on the history of the Third Reich)
- Portfolios of photographs (examples: photos of Japanese-American internment camps or of Black Panther demonstrations from the 1960s)
- Government documents (examples: U.S. censuses and surveys, reports from the Department of Agriculture or congressional papers)
- Other one-of-a-kind texts (examples: AIDS prevention posters from South Africa, a noted artist's sketchbook, or a series of leaflets produced by the U.S. Psychological Warfare Department)

In many cases, you can work directly with these materials so you can perform your own firsthand analysis of that piece of cultural history.

Consider the sources that student James Caputo used in his project on media representations of the early years of the NASA space program. James had many primary sources to choose from: John F. Kennedy's inspirational speeches about the formation of the space program; front pages of both American and Russian newspapers detailing the successful completion of the first Apollo mission; publicity shots of the astronauts; the first images—both still and moving—from the moon's surface. He chose to focus on multiple magazine covers and images from magazine articles for his primary source materials (see Figure 5.4 and Figure 5.5).

The image in Figure 5.4 originally appeared in an article published in *Collier's* magazine on October 23, 1948, concerning the military applications of space travel. James analyzed it and postulated that it was intended to warn American readers of the consequences of falling behind in the "space race" with the Russians. Similarly, he observed that the cover shot from *National Geographic's* December 1969 issue (Figure 5.5) relied on *pathos* to influence American readers' understanding of the U.S. space program; more specifically, he recognized that the image, with its strong nationalist argument that American astronauts were the "First Explorers on the Moon," cast the successful Apollo 11 mission once again in terms of the Cold War and the American-Soviet space race. Through this initial analysis of primary

FIGURE 5.4 James used this illustration, "The Rocket Blitz from the Moon," which originally accompanied a 1948 *Collier's* magazine article, as a powerful primary source for his research paper.

FIGURE 5.5 James also analyzed other primary sources, including magazine covers like this one from *National Geographic*.

sources, James was able to develop a preliminary claim for his essay. He then tested his hypothesis through further research using secondary sources, which provided him with key background information and critical perspectives on his topic.

Searching for Secondary Sources

As James's example suggests, while primary materials play an important role in your research, just as important are your **secondary sources**—texts that provide commentary on your topic and often analyze the texts you have chosen as primary sources. The writers of these texts offer the voices with which you will engage in scholarly conversation as you develop the substance of your argument.

Although your instinct may send you directly to the Internet, your first stop in your search for secondary sources should actually be your library's reference area, the home of reference librarians—people trained to help you

AT A GLANCE

Finding Secondary Sources

- ***Dictionaries, guides, and encyclopedias*** provide helpful background information for your topic.
- ***Library catalogs*** allow you to search the library holdings for relevant books or documentaries.
- ***CD-ROM indexes and bibliographies*** contain vast amounts of bibliographic information.
- ***Electronic databases and indexes*** are available on the Internet through subscription only; many provide access to full-text versions of articles from a range of sources.
- ***Electronic journals and ebooks*** offer access to the full digital versions of books and academic journals from a wide range of disciplines.
- ***Google scholar and Google books*** can be helpful resources, but should be used in conjunction with academic databases and library catalogs.

find what you need—as well as a treasure trove of encyclopedias, bibliographies, and other resource materials. These storehouses of information can be invaluable in providing you with the *foundational sources* for your project, including basic definitions, historical background, and bibliographies. Yet, while such "background" materials are necessary to help you construct a framework for your research argument, they represent only one part of your iceberg of research. For more rigorous analysis, you should turn to books and articles that provide critical analysis and arguments about your specific research subject. To locate these more specific secondary sources, you might search your library catalog for relevant books and films and other published materials.

You can also consult databases and indexes, indispensable research guides that will provide you with bibliographic citations for academic articles on your topic. Databases can come in many forms: collections of electronic journals, Internet resources, or CD-ROMs. Although some databases provide bibliographic citations that you can use to locate the source in your library catalog, many include a detailed abstract summarizing a source's argument, and others link you to full-text electronic copies of articles.

AT A GLANCE

Using One Source to Locate Additional Sources

1. Locate one relevant source through the library catalog. Take note of the LCSH listed on the citation.
2. Retrieve the source from the library stacks.
3. Spend some time looking over books in the same area to discover additional books on the same topic.
4. Conduct an additional catalog search, this time narrowing your search using the official subject headings you noted for your first source. Retrieve those books.
5. Assess briefly the applicability of each text to your project, and check out the ones most valuable to you.
6. Look at the bibliographies in the backs of your most useful books to locate sources that were helpful to the authors and may be of use to you.
7. Repeat the process often to build your iceberg of research.

Finally, although databases, catalogs, and search engines provide indispensable tools for conducting your research, remember also that your classmates can serve as secondary sources you might consult or even interview. Ask others who are working on similar topics to share resources, and help each other along the route of your research. This is particularly true for the stage in your research when you produce a **preliminary bibliography**—a working list of the sources for your iceberg of research.

AT A GLANCE

Recording Searches in Your Research Log

Use your research log to keep careful track of the dates, details, key terms of your searches and to organize your sources and your notes.

- Date each entry in your log to keep track of your progress and show the evolution of your ideas.
- Keep a running list of your sources by call number, author, and title.
- Write down complete identifying information for any source you consult, including online images or articles, print copies of journals or magazines from the library, articles from library databases, and book chapters.
- Double-check transcribed quotations for accuracy while you still have the source before you, and include page numbers (or paragraph numbers for website articles). Be sure to include quotation marks around each direct quote you transcribe, even in your research log.
- Include printouts (or digital copies, if your log is electronic) of relevant articles or database entries, and especially of online articles, images, or websites that might disappear when their site is updated.
- Annotate the entry by including an evaluation of the source and an indication of how you might use it as part of your final paper.

5.4 How do I critically evaluate both print and online sources?

Seeing Connections
See Chapter 3 for a more complete discussion of rhetorical stance

EVALUATING YOUR SOURCES

Implementing these research strategies to locate primary and secondary materials will provide you with access to many interesting sources, but how do you discriminate among them to find those that are credible, reliable, and authoritative? How do you know which ones will be the most useful for your argument? The key rests in understanding the argumentative perspective, or *rhetorical stance*, of each source. At times, the source's stance may be self-evident: you may automatically gravitate toward experts in the field, well known for their opinions and affiliations. It is just as likely, however, that you may not be familiar with the names or ideas of your sources. Therefore, it is essential to develop a method for evaluating the sources you encounter.

For many of us, when we hear the words "research paper," our first impulse is to log onto the Internet and plug our topic into a search engine such as Google or Bing. That will certainly provide a start, but the best research involves investigating a range of different sources—both print and online. Imagine, for example, you were writing a research paper on the stem cell debate. While you might be tempted to dive right into a Google search, a better approach for this topic would be to consult library and database sources. Your first stop might be to the library's reference area, where you look up foundational information in the *Encyclopedia of Bioethics.* After getting an overview from the Encyclopedia entry on "Stem Cells," including references to key debates, events, actors, and subtopics related to this issue, you're now ready to search the library catalog for books that can provide you with a more in-depth treatment of the topic. In addition, you might want to complement book sources with material from journal articles, which often represent the most current discussions on a topic. To find relevant articles, you begin searching the electronic databases that most closely suit the specific focus of your project, such as SciSearch, MEDLINE, Legal Periodical, or BIOSIS. You produce an impressive list of citations and even retrieve a few full-text articles that you save to your research log.

Your first search complete, you can now retreat to a quiet space and assess the significance and value of your findings. Imagine that your search has directed you to a recent article in the journal, *Stem Cells*, featured in Figure 5.6. You notice that the editors chose to feature an actual image of embryonic cells on its cover, signaling a focus on cellular biology and scientific applications. Opening up the issue, you search the table of contents for the article. As you do so, you evaluate the listed contents as a whole: they provide an overview of the more specific research questions and projects this journal explores, helping you better understand the scope, focus, and possible bias of the journal.

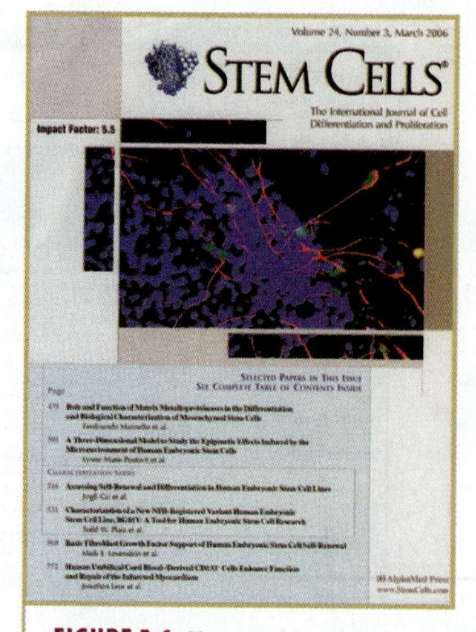

FIGURE 5.6 The cover of *Stem Cells* emphasizes its scientific approach in choices of cover image and text.

Next, turning to the article itself, you scan key elements on the page. Underneath the title and author's name, this particular article lists the author's academic affiliation, providing a way to evaluate her *ethos*. A quick look helps you categorize this text as following the conventions of a scientific article: it lists the article's key words at the top of the page (providing possible alternative search terms); it contains an abstract—a brief overview of the topic and the author's argument (allowing you to easily evaluate the article's contribution to the conversation on this topic); it is broken into clearly labeled subsections (giving you insight into the structure of the argument); it contains visual evidence in the form of information graphics (suggesting a reliance on quantitative data); and it provides an extensive references section at the end (offering you a springboard for further reading). Reading the first few paragraphs of the introduction confirms your impressions. The article utilizes the objective, academic style of scientific writing, suggesting that this source will provide an authoritative, well-researched, and empirically-driven perspective on stem cell research. Since you've narrowed your focus to recent scientific advances in this field, the article suits you well; however, keep in mind that if your focus was on media representations of the stem cell debate, this same article—despite its *ethos* and authority on the subject—might not be a good match as a primary or secondary source.

Seeing Connections
See Chapter 8 for a full discussion of academic abstracts.

Now let's examine how you might supplement your library research with a search for online sources. Imagine that your first online search for this topic produced the following hit: the Stem Cell Information website (Figure 5.7). Even as you click the link, you notice that the URL ends with ".gov," indicating that this is a government website, not a commercial (".com"), educational (".edu") or personal site; the homepage itself confirms this as it appears on your screen, with clear headers associating it with the U.S. Department of Health & Human Services and the National Institutes

FIGURE 5.7 A screenshot of the NIH Stem Cell Information page.

of Health (NIH), granting it a strong *ethos* appeal. Next, your eye is drawn to the page title, "Stem Cell Information," which suggests that this page is intended to be informational—to get the basic facts out. As you scan the homepage's layout, you see that it functions as a table of contents, linking to relevant articles and information sites; main articles, with eye-catching representative images, are given priority in the center frame, while links to Frequently Asked Questions, Tools, and news articles are listed in the left and right sidebars. One other element catches your attention: the article titles are prominent and bolded, but there are no authors listed. Clearly, this site privileges information over authority in a way quite different from the strategy we previously observed in the *Stem Cells* journal article.

Just as you moved from the contents of the journal to the specific article above, now you click on a particular link of interest: "The Promise of Stem Cells." The link title seems to indicate the website's bias: using the word "promise" implies a positive stance on this issue that complicates your initial impression of its objectivity. However, arriving at the page itself, you notice something interesting: the word "promise" no longer appears. Instead, the header "Stem Cell Basics" reasserts the objective tone, reinforced by an introductory paragraph that uses clear and unbiased language. The page's features are typical of those found in online writing: short chunked paragraphs (allowing you to move quickly through the argument); bullet lists of questions or important points (increasing the scannability of information); links that take you deeper into the site or to related pages (providing options for customizing your further reading); a notation at the bottom as to when the date was last modified (speaking to *kairos* and relevance); and a "contact us" link (suggesting the organization's willingness to be accountable for its online publication). Other features contribute to the page's *ethos*, such as a link about accessibility, a privacy statement, a glossary and site map. Lastly, you notice that it provides the citation information at the very bottom of the page: clearly this is a page designed to be used for those doing serious research on this subject.

As you can see, for both the print and online source, it is not enough simply to locate them: you need to use your skills of rhetorical analysis to assess their viability for your individual project. Whether examining a journal article or a website homepage, analyzing the rhetorical strategies at work is essential to understanding its argument and therefore its suitability as a research source.

USING FIELD RESEARCH

5.5 How do I pursue field research for my project?

In addition to the primary and secondary sources you will consult as you develop your research project, you may also have the chance to go out across campus, into the community, or into the virtual world to engage with people's opinions and use that information in your essay. That is, your project might provide you with the opportunity to enrich your argument by carrying out your own **field research**—conducting *interviews*, developing *surveys*, and engaging in *fieldwork*. Consider the possibilities: for an essay on YouTube mash-ups and copyright infringement, you could interview a faculty member who has written extensively on the Digital Millennium Copyright Act; for a project investigating cyberbullying, you could use your own survey of fifty college students to bring the voices of cyberbullying victims—and perhaps even bullies—into your paper; for an essay about

AT A GLANCE

Questions for Evaluating Sources

- Who is the author? Is he an expert on the topic? What institution or organization is he affiliated with? What else has he written on this subject? Have other sources that you've read referenced him or his work?

  Tip: Look the author up online or in a bibliography index to assess his ethos.

- Who published the source? Is it a university press or online academic journal (suggesting peer-reviewed scholarship) or a trade press or commercial website (suggesting a commercial venture)? Is it published by a foundation or organization (suggesting a political agenda) or self-published (suggesting the author's struggle to have his or her views accepted for publication)? If it's an online source, does the site include a gesture of accountability for the information it publishes, such as a "contact us" link?

  Tip: For online sources, look at the URL to see if it's a ".gov" (government-affiliated site), ".com" (commercial site), ".org" (an organization's site), ".mil" (a military website) or ".edu" (educational or university site).

- When was it published? Is it a recent contribution or an older study? If it's an electronic source, does it have a "last updated" notation? If not, do embedded links still work?

  Tip: Don't dismiss older materials too quickly; sometimes an older source can provide historical context or provide a foundational perspective on your issue. However, usually you should use the more recent sources to engage the most timely perspectives on your topic.

- What was the occasion for the source? Was it written in reaction to a specific text or event or in response to a particular research question? Was it designed to inform? To instruct? To provide a call to action?

  Tip: Sometimes the purpose or occasion might be explicit; other times it is less obvious. A quick online search (of author or the name of a key event or cited publication) can help you understand cultural or historical context if it not readily apparent; understanding the purpose behind the source can help you better assess the source's argument and motives.

- Who is its intended audience? Scholars? Experts in the field? A popular audience? A particular demographic, such as college students, parents, teens, or senior citizens? How is the argument and language shaped to address this audience? Does the author use rhetorical strategies—such as definition or community-specific terms (like jargon) to speak to his audience? Are you a member of the intended audience? If not, how that does affect the persuasiveness of the argument?

  Tip: Keep in mind that there sometimes is a difference between the audience that an author intended to address and the audience who actually reads the argument. Is the argument flexible enough to speak to both types of readers?

- What is the source's argument? Does the author have a clear argument? Are there any implicit or unstated assumptions underlying the argument? Check the opening paragraphs, preface or introduction to the text: does the author lay out his theoretical framework or a roadmap of how he will structure his argument?

  Tip: As you work with a source, always write a paraphrase of its main claim in your research log for easy reference. To see others's critical assessments of a source's argument, consider looking at book reviews or literature reviews that discuss the text; for more popular reactions to electronic texts, check the "comments" section, if available, beneath blog posts or online articles.

- What types of evidence does the author use to support his claim? Does he use primary research, such as analysis of primary texts or his own surveys or interviews? Does he use secondary sources as evidence? Does he use a combination of the two? Does he include a variety of sources or perspectives, or does he seem to cherry-pick his examples? Does he address counterarguments? Does he treat them respectfully? Does he cite his sources ethically and appropriately? Does he provide a works cited or list of references at the end? If it's an online source, does the author provide links to any Internet sources he cites?

  Tip: Use your source's citations as the starting point for further research; if you find a cited quotation or piece of evidence from your source's argument particularly striking, use the associated link or the citation in the works cited to track down that additional source and read it to see how it might contribute to your own project.

- What is the tone of the source? Does it use objective language? Is its tone comic? Serious? Scholarly? Casual? Does it seem to represent a particular political, cultural or ideological position or world view (i.e., feminist, conservative, fundamentalist, American)?

  Tip: Just because a source is associated with a particular ideological position doesn't mean that you need to disqualify it from your research; however, you'll need to take into account how any bias might influence the strength of its argument and the evidence it provides for your research.

- How might you use this source in your own research? Would it operate as a primary or a secondary source for your argument? Does the approach (popular, scientific, scholarly, informational) seem appropriate to your project's focus and goals? Does it offer a counterargument or a different disciplinary perspective?

  Tip: You don't need to use every source that you discover in your research. Sometimes you might need to set aside sources even though they have extremely strong ethos or arguments because they represent a focus or stance that is not useful for your purposes. Be sure to keep a record of such sources, however, in your research log in case you have cause to return to them later in your research.

urban murals, you could visit several local murals, take photographs, and even talk with local artists. In each case, you would be using *field research* to complement your text-based research and to strengthen your research-based claim.

Conducting Interviews

One of the most common forms of *field research*, an interview provides you with the opportunity to receive in-depth information from an expert on your topic. The information you gather from these interviews can supplement the material you've found in published sources, providing you with the opportunity to make an original research claim or unique contribution to the scholarly conversation on your topic. Keep in mind, however, that conducting interviews involves much more than simply having a chat with someone; it involves a careful process of planning and preparation before the meeting even takes place. If you decide to conduct an interview as part of your field research, you might incorporate these steps into your research process:

1. ***Identify your purpose:*** Even before setting up an interview, you need to clarify your research goals. What information would an interview provide that other types of research would not? What do you hope to get out of the interview?
2. ***Decide upon your interview subject:*** Who would provide you with the most insight into your topic? Is the best source for your field research a professor at your college who is an expert in this area? A professional from the community? Peers in your class, dorm, athletic team, or town?
3. ***Determine your preferred interview format:*** Interviews can be conducted in many ways: face to face; over the phone; through videochat or textchat; by email. You'll need to choose the method that best suits your needs and your interviewee's preferred mode of communication.
4. ***Prepare:*** Know your interviewee: read an online biography or browse an online resume or curriculum vita; familiarize yourself with what he or she has written and read any articles related to your topic; understand your interviewee's position on your research issue. This information will help you both construct useful questions and also cultivate your own *ethos* during the interview by showing you've taken the time to prepare.
5. ***Develop questions:*** Your questions will provide the framework for your discussion, so craft them with care. Design interview questions to elicit usable quotations, and avoid sentence constructions that would turn an open-ended question ("What is your opinion on the recent Faculty Senate vote?") into a Yes-No question ("Do you agree with the recent Faculty Senate vote?") that would leave less opportunity for elaboration. Use neutral terms and watch out for biased or leading questions: for instance, a question such as "Don't

you agree that there need to be more female faculty in the Math Department?" suggests the interviewer's opinion in a way that might influence the answer. In general, use specific language and ground your questions in your knowledge about your subject and your interviewee's areas of expertise. Finally, review your drafted questions with your instructor or a classmate to get feedback for revision before you finalize them for the interview.

6. ***Make contact:*** In contacting your potential interviewee, clearly explain who you are, the topic of your research, and your goal for the field research. If you are planning a face-to-face interview or a video or text-based chat, suggest two or three possible times for the session; for all types of interviews, include your timeline in your request. In addition, provide a summary of the types of questions you might ask so that your interviewee can think them through before meeting with you. Follow up unanswered requests with polite emails or phone calls. Don't hesitate to persist, but do so respectfully. Once you've set up the interview, be sure to confirm time and place the day before for a face-to-face interview or chat session.

7. ***Maintain your ethos:*** Your persona as an interviewer can be key to a successful session. Dress nicely, maintain a professional tone throughout the meeting, and have your materials organized before you start. Respect your interviewee's time: arrive on time for the interview, and keep it within the agreed upon time span. Use your interview questions as a guide, but don't follow them too rigidly; listen to your interviewee's answers and follow up on key points even if it means asking a question that's not on your list. Conversely, be careful not to digress. Keep the conversation focused on the research topic.

8. ***Record and document:*** In your notes, be sure to write down the full name of the person, his or her title, and the time, date, and location of the interview; you will need this information to properly cite the interview in your essay. While you'll want to take some notes during the interview, recording the session can help you resist the impulse to transcribe the conversation word for word. However, be sure to ask your interviewee's permission before recording the meeting. At the end of the interview, get written permission from your interview

Seeing Connections
See Chapter 7 for instructions on how to cite an interview in a research paper.

subject to use direct quotations from the conversation in your essay. It is possible that she or he might ask be quoted anonymously, in which case you'll need to respect that request when incorporating material from the interview into your paper.

9. ***Analyze the conversation:*** If you record an interview, create a transcript as soon as possible after the meeting. Take some time to process the information you received, highlighting key quotes or ideas in your notes or on the transcript, listing ideas or readings for further research, and reflecting on connections to your other sources. If you conducted a face-to-face or videochat interview, analyze the conversation or transcript shortly after it happens, while your impressions are still fresh.
10. ***Follow-up:*** Send a thank-you note to the person you interviewed and offer a copy of your completed paper.

Developing a Survey

In your research, you may come across published surveys that can provide important statistical data for your project, whether in scientific journals, newsmagazines like *Time*, or research organizations such as the Pew Research Center. Alternately, you might consider developing your own survey in order to retrieve information tailored to your particular research question or line of inquiry. The benefit of a survey is that it enables you to accumulate data from a broad range of participants; it works particularly well for gathering quantitative data, but can also yield deeper insightful perspectives on your topic through short answer questions.

As you compose your survey, remember that it is like any other writing project in that it benefits a careful drafting process, one that takes into account the rhetorical situation and purpose of your project. The following steps can help you develop an effective survey:

1. ***Identify your purpose:*** The first step in developing any survey is clarify your goals. What research question are you trying to answer? What type of results would be most useful to your research? Do you want to gather statistical data? Do you want to solicit reflective or detailed responses that can use for qualitative analysis? The answers to these questions will help determine the shape of your survey.

2. ***Determine your survey population:*** In order to receive useful answers, you need to carefully target your survey population. You might select your survey subjects by age (i.e., teenagers, college students, parents, senior citizens); by occupation (i.e., students, instructors, administrators, athletes, artists); by location (i.e., residents of your town, your college campus); or by other characteristics, such as gender, political or religious affiliation, or even nationality.
3. ***Aim for a representative sample:*** To insure the most reliable results, don't skew your sample out of convenience (for instance, only distributing your survey to your fraternity brothers when the research question requires both a male and female perspective). In addition, consider how sample size influences the viability of your results: the results from a survey of ten students is less likely to yield persuasive findings than a survey of forty students.
4. ***Develop your questions:*** In many ways, your purpose will determine the format of your survey. You have a many options available to you:
   - Close-ended questions tend to generate quantitative data and offer no little or no opportunity for elaboration. Two typical formats for these questions include multiple choice (where the subject chooses one or more of a variety of options) and ranked questions (where the subject ranks a series of items according to a clear scale).
   - Open-ended questions invite reflection and nuanced responses, whether they be as short as a single sentence or as long as a paragraph.

   In general, it is best to design surveys that balance short, multiple choice questions, which yield primarily statistical data, with short answer questions that will produce more complex responses. Keep your survey short; the longer your form, the fewer completed surveys will probably be returned to you.
5. ***Draft your Survey:*** As with any rhetorical text, you should craft your survey carefully:
   - Assess the best delivery method for your survey given your target population: Paper survey? Email? Electronic form? Your choice of medium might influence your survey design.

- Consider the canon of *arrangement*. Put your questions in a logical order; use subcategories to help organize information; consider giving your survey subjects a sense of the scope of the survey (i.e., including an introduction that states, "This survey contains 10 questions...") or markers that indicate their a progress through it (i.e., if your survey is divided into pages, include a header with a notation such as "Page 3 of 4").
- Focus on style. Use clear, concise language, and avoid creating Yes-No questions ("Was your freshman orientation session effective?") when you want to generate more nuanced responses ("Please comment on the most effective and least effective aspects of your freshman orientation session"). Avoid biased language or leading questions.
- Construct an expository frame for the survey: a very brief introduction of a sentence or two that indicates the purpose and relevance of the survey; a concluding sentence that appears after the last question, thanking the participant for completing the survey.

6. ***Test and Revise your Drafted Survey:*** As with any rhetorical text, It is important to take into account *audience* as you construct your argument. Test your draft by having a friend complete your survey and give you feedback on its clarity, organization, length, and the relevance of its questions to your purpose. Use that feedback to revise.
7. ***Distribute your Survey:*** State your deadline clearly, and make sure the respondents know where and how to return the form.
8. ***Analyze the results.*** As you read through the completed surveys, look for patterns or trends in the responses and categorize them in a table or "code" the survey responses using a highlighter or jotting key terms in the margin; start to think about how to best organize and showcase data (through percentages? charts? graphs?); highlight key comments in the open-responses to include as direct quotations in your research paper. Most of all, *listen* to your respondents, even if the data does not necessarily confirm your hypothesis: your developing research claim should be informed by your research findings.
9. ***Follow-up:*** Consider sharing your findings with survey participants, if possible, through an article in a local newspaper or college publication.

Seeing Connections
See Chapter 7 for instructions on how to cite a survey in your research paper.

WRITER'S PRACTICE

What types of technology can be used most effectively in the college classroom? Please explain your answer.

Which types of technology are the most effective in the classroom as learning tools? Select as many apply.

- Overhead projectors
- Smartboards
- Laptops
- Desktop computers
- iPads or Tablets
- Cellphones

How effective are the following types of technology in the college classroom as learning tools?

	Very Ineffective	Ineffective	Somewhat Ineffective	Neither Effective nor Ineffective	Somewhat Effective	Effective	Very Effective
Overhead projectors	○	○	○	○	○	○	○
Smartboards	○	○	○	○	○	○	○
Laptops	○	○	○	○	○	○	○
Desktop computers	○	○	○	○	○	○	○
iPads or Tablets	○	○	○	○	○	○	○
Cellphones	○	○	○	○	○	○	○

For a research project on the use of technology in the college classroom, one writer decided to construct a survey to collect student perspectives on this issue. During the drafting process, she experimented with different variations of the same question to consider how format influenced the answers she might receive. Look over each variation carefully.

What is the implied purpose behind each question? Is it the same for each one? How might the questions elicit different responses? What would the author need to do to make sure she received useful responses from this survey? What revisions might you suggest?

Other Models of Fieldwork

While interviews and surveys represent two modes of fieldwork available to you, you might take your research even more actively into the "field." Let's look at a more ambitious approach to this type of research. Student Vincent Chen used field research quite prominently in his research project about the rhetoric of climate change. Specifically, he included photographs he took while attending the Copenhagen Conference on Climate Change in December of 2009. Included in this conference was a special session on the "15th Conference of the Parties to the UNFCCC (United Nations Framework Convention on Climate Change)," commonly known as "COP15." At the COP15, Vincent conducted impressive field research, such as taking photographs of people milling through the halls, attending talks, and listening to speakers present position statements about the environment. But Vincent's most powerful field research was a single photo, showing the crowds of attendees stopping mid-motion to hear the speech of Mohamed Nasheed, then-President

FIGURE 5.8 Vincent Chen's field research includes this photo of Mohamed Nasheed, president of the Republic of Maldives, making a powerful speech to a riveted audience at the 2009 Copenhagen Climate Conference. © Vincent Chen 2009.

of the Republic of Maldives. The photo became central to making his argument that President Nasheed strongly differentiated himself from other climate leaders at the conference through his inflammatory rhetoric about the danger of rising seas as well as the *logos* argument of his country's small size and limited economic power. To argue this position, Vincent used a photo he took as visual evidence documenting the power of President Nasheed's conference-stopping speech (see Figure 5.8). He also included additional field research in the form of interviews with other students who attended at the conference and an interview with Professor Stephen Schneider of the Interdisciplinary Environmental Studies Program at his university.

This field research added depth and power to Vincent's argument by allowing him to include his own evidence as strategic argumentative support for his argument. With regard to the photo in Figure 5.8, rather than just asserting his claim to be true, Vincent could allow his readers to *see* the evidence that would support his point that President Nasheed, out of all leaders at the climate conference, made people stop and listen to an argument for action.

Of course, not all fieldwork involves trips around the world. Sometimes you can gather your own evidence for your research project by using resources available within your local community. Consider these scenarios: if you were studying the impact of a new park in your community, you might meet with a city planner or the landscape architect responsible for the project and look a blueprints or concept art for the project; if you were writing about a city water reservoir, you might visit the site, take photographs, and meet with the site manager; and, if you were writing on the marketing strategies of a local baseball team, you might even write a letter to that team's marketing coordinator to set up an interview or gather information. Fieldwork such as this allows you to take your research to the next level and make a truly original contribution of your own.

Evaluating Field Research Sources

When you conduct interviews and surveys, you are looking for materials to use in your paper as secondary sources. But keep in mind the need to evaluate your field research sources as carefully as you assess your web and print sources. If you interview a professor, a marketing executive, a witness, or a roommate, consider the rhetorical stance of that person. What kind of bias does the person have concerning the topic of your project? If you conduct a survey of your peers in your dorm, assess the value and credibility of your results as rigorously as you would evaluate the data of a published study. Don't fall into the trap of misusing statistics when making claims if you haven't taken into account the need for **statistical significance**, or to paraphrase the social psychologist Philip Zimbardo, the measure by which a number obtains meaning in scientific fields. To reach this number, you need to design the survey carefully, conduct what's called a *random sample*, interview a *large enough* number of people, and ask a *range of different people*. These are complex parameters to follow, but you will need to learn about them to conduct survey research that has reliable and credible results.

"Statistics are the backbone of research. They are used to understand observations and to determine whether findings are, in fact, correct and significant. . . But statistics can also be used poorly or deceptively, misleading those who do not understand them."

—*Philip Zimbardo* (595)

As Professor Zimbardo points out, statistics—though we often think of them as Truth—actually function rhetorically. Like words and images, numbers are a mode of persuasion that can mislead readers. You need to be especially vigilant when using a survey or statistics as a supposedly "objective" part of your iceberg of research, particularly if you plan to depend on such materials in your argument.

Take as much care with how you convey information visually as you do with how you convey it in writing. Consider David Pinner's project about grade inflation. David accumulated enough quantitative information through fieldwork and primary research to compose his own charts. He discovered a wealth of information in archived faculty senate minutes, which he sorted through during his research. From that work, he came across important statistical data that reflected the change in grade distribution at Stanford over the course of 25 years. In addition to including the numbers in his written text, he created two pie charts (see Figure 5.9), using a visual comparison of statistics to underscore his point. His argument was more powerful not just because of his impressive field research but also because of how he represented it graphically through responsible use of statistics.

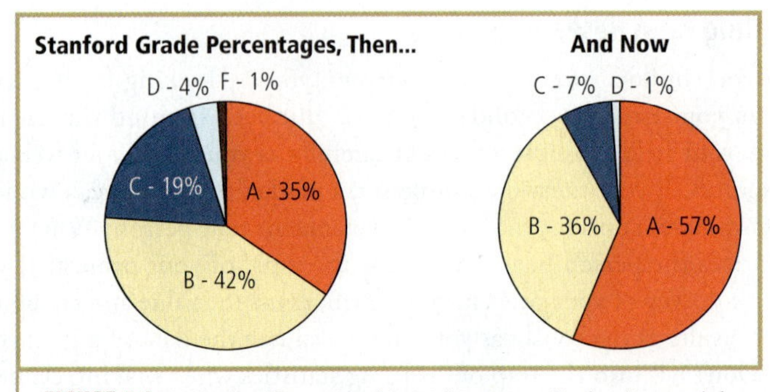

FIGURE 5.9 Student David Pinner created these information graphics from his research data to suggest the difference in grade distribution between 1968 and 1992.

5.6 How can I understand the conversation my sources are having about my topic?

CREATING A DIALOGUE WITH YOUR SOURCES

Throughout this chapter we have emphasized that research is social, a conversation with the people whose ideas and writing came before yours. As you gather, assess, and use sources, you are contributing to this conversation, building on the work of others, and adding a new perspective. Indeed, this notion of writing as communal is the reason why you need to use the author's name when citing a quotation or an idea; remember that all your sources are authored sources; each source mentioned in this chapter was composed by a person or a group of people. If you think of these texts as written *by people like you*, you will have an easier time remembering to acknowledge their ideas and integrate their quotations into your essay. In the process, you will go a long way toward avoiding unintentional plagiarism. You can begin this process through an exercise we call a **dialogue of sources**—a fictional conversation among the primary and secondary sources of your research paper designed to help you identify each one's central argument and main idea.

Seeing Connections
See Chapter 7 for a more complete discussion of plagiarism and intellectual property.

To prepare for her research paper on tobacco advertisements, Amanda Johnson (AJ) wrote this dialogue between several sources she had found: RJ Reynolds Tobacco Co. (RJRT); Larry C. White (LW), author of *Merchants of Death*; and Hugh High (HH), a professor of economics, finance, and law who published a collection of tobacco studies titled *Does Advertising Increase Smoking?* among others, which she presents in a literal dialogue with herself acting as scholarly moderator.

AT A GLANCE

Creating a Dialogue of Sources

- ***Identify the key players*** from your research log and your notes. Which ones have the most influential or important arguments?
- ***Create a cast of characters list*** with a short "bio" for each speaker, including yourself. Describe each person's credentials and rhetorical stance—his or her *ethos* and argument. (You may even want to create identifying icons or pictures to give "faces" to the participants.)
- ***Draft the script.*** Write the key questions you want to ask your sources about your topic. Use quotes from your sources to respond where possible, and include page numbers.
- ***Consider what your sources would say to each other.*** Write their fictional conversation by using quotes from your sources.
- ***Don't just play the "objective" moderator.*** Respond to the sources and, in the process, start to develop your own argument.
- ***Conclude with a synthesis statement.*** Use the closing paragraph to tie together the various views presented in your "dialogue of sources" and then indicate how you will build on that collection of knowledge. In this way, you offer both a summary and a synthesis, by bringing together and then adding to the conversation of research.

Dialogue of Sources [excerpt]

AJ: I would like to thank the panel for joining us this afternoon. We have quite a diverse group of writers, researchers, spokespeople, and a professor here to discuss the focus and objectives of current tobacco advertising. Since I know your comments on this subject vary widely, I suppose I will start off by asking you to talk about what you believe to be the focus of tobacco advertising as it exists today.

RJRT: RJ Reynolds tobacco products are among the best advertised in the industry, and we take pride in our

Amanda's complete dialogue begins with a list of speakers and their bios. Then she introduces the topic of her research project. She reproduces the argument of each source, both print and interview, through paraphrase.

By allowing debate to evolve, Amanda begins to see how she might use quotations from these sources in her paper.

commitment to maintaining honest advertising to the public. We do not intend for our advertising to manipulate nonsmokers into trying our products, nor do we choose to target these audiences. Advertising is simply a method by which we are able to maintain our share of the market and compete with other tobacco manufacturers.

LW: How can you possibly claim to avoid targeting specific audiences and replenishing your older dwindling population with new younger smokers!?! The whole point of advertising is to get more people to buy your product, and, since market shares don't change all that much for large companies like yours, the best way to get more people to buy your product is to increase the number of overall smokers. Youth are your best option because if you can get them hooked now, you will have a steady flow of income for several decades to come.

HH: Mr. White, you make a good point about general economic objectives. However, studies show that advertising does very little to change the number of new smokers. Countries that have banned advertising for tobacco-related products have seen very little decline in the number of consumers that buy their product. As RJRT stated previously, advertising is only successful at making adjustments within the market concerning the relative amounts each company is able to sell.

AJ: I recently reviewed a chart concerning the prevalence of smoking among U.S. adults and found that over the past 40 years since the surgeon general first warned about cigarettes' cancerous effects, the steady decline in smokers has slowed to rest around 25 percent of the population over the age of 18. With the number of people dying each day, it is surprising that this number does not continue to go down. How would you account for the slowed change?

Most importantly, she begins to develop her own argument in the context of this conversation. She does this by questioning the responses, adding facts from her research, and moving the argument forward as she'll need to do in her essay..

Notice how Amanda's work allowed her to write out the process of research *as a conversation.* This process will help her avoid unintentional plagiarism since she is giving credit to her sources. Moreover, she can conclude the dialogue with a summation of the arguments she has uncovered through her research and predict how she will build upon them as she develops her thesis for her own research-based argument.

WRITING AN ANNOTATED BIBLIOGRAPHY

5.7 What is an annotated bibliography, and how can it help me develop my argument?

As you move further into your research, you might want to use your notes to create what researchers call an **annotated bibliography**—a list of research sources that provides informational notes about each source and how you might use it as you turn to drafting your paper. An annotated bibliography can work in conjunction with your research log and active note-taking to encourage you to think critically, helping you to understand the larger research conversation on your topic and start to develop your own persuasive claim.

The format of an annotated bibliography follows a fairly standard pattern. For each source, you compose an entry containing

Seeing Connections
For a discussion of MLA style and guidelines, see Chapter 7.

- The **bibliographic citation**, correctly formatted to follow a particular citation form (such as MLA, APA, or Chicago Style)
- A **brief annotation** that concisely summarizes the content of the source and indicates its relevance to your project.

Some researchers distinguish between two different types of annotation: the *descriptive annotation* and the *analytic annotation*. In writing the first type of annotation, you essentially create your own brief academic abstract for the source, providing an overview of its features and argument and suggesting its relevance to the larger conversation. In doing so, you would refer many of the elements we discussed above in relation to evaluating sources: author; place of publication; date of publication; purpose; audience; argument; evidence; tone; and relevance. For instance, consider these examples of *descriptive annotations* from a research project on teenagers and online privacy.

Ivester, Matt. *lol...OMG! What Every Student Needs to Know About Online Reputation Management, Digital Citizenship, and Cyberbullying.* NV: Serra Knight Publishing, 2011. Print.

In *lol...OMG*, Matt Ivester provides an overview of the changing nature of digital citizenship; Ivester argues that in today's world we need to be conscious creators and curators of our online identities. A Duke University and Stanford Business School alumnus, Ivester was also creator of the infamous gossip website, JuicyCampus, providing him with an informed perspective on the more problematic elements of online culture. The book analyzes several powerful examples from the media of the dangers of digital citizenship, including the Duke Sexlist Powerpoint scandal, Alexandra Wallace's YouTube Rant, and the Tyler Clementi cyber-bullying tragedy. Of particular interest is Chapter 7, "Active Reputation Management," which provides seven steps readers can take to check their own online reputation. Aimed at a college audience and written in a direct and no-nonsense style, this book provides both valuable insight into the changing definitions of digital citizenship for the millennial generation and a concrete course of action that people can take to protect themselves online.

Keller, Jared. "Teens Care About Online Privacy—Just Not the Same Way You Do." *Pacific Standard* 22 May 2013. Web. 29 May 2013.

Written for a popular audience, this online article provides an overview of a new research study conducted jointly by the Pew Research Center and the Berkman Center for Internet Society that examined how much information teens are sharing about themselves online. Keller, a journalist who specializes in social media, reports that while the study indicates that teens are sharing more information through social networks (for instance, 91% of all teens report having uploaded a photo of themselves online in 2013, as opposed to 79% in 2006), they are more proactive in managing their online privacy. Keller puts the study in context of other scholarly work: Susan Barnes's theory of the "privacy paradox," as well as research by danah boyd, Nicole Ellison, Charles Steinfield, and Cliff Lampe. He concludes that the Pew study indicates that the privacy paradox is becoming less pronounced than it was when Barnes coined the phrase seven years ago, offering a useful snapshot of how teenagers manage their online identities within both a social and a technological framework.

Notice that in each case, the annotation provides specific details about the source, including a summary of the argument; however, while the final sentence suggests the source's relevance, it refrains from critiquing the argument, producing an annotation that focuses more on summary than analysis.

An *analytic annotation* follows the same model as the descriptive version, with one addition: it moves past simple summary to critique. For this reason, you'll find the *analytic annotation* an even more useful tool in your research process. Let's look at an example of this type of annotation for a research project on social activism and video games.

McGonigal, Jane. *Gaming Can Make a Better World.* TED Talks. Feb 2010. Web. 23 April 2013.

In this TED talk, video game designer Jane McGonigal passionately argues that we can use video games to solve larger cultural problems, such as the energy crisis and world hunger. Using examples from massive online games such as *World of Warcraft*, McGonigal insists that we embody the best qualities of ourselves when we play computer games: that we collaborate more readily, think more creatively, and have more self-confidence. In a provocative moment at the beginning of the talk, she suggests that we need to play video games more, not less – but that we need to play games designed to harness these qualities toward positive social good. While she offers some interesting examples of such games drawn from her work at the Institute of the Future (such as *World without Oil*), she discusses them only in the last four minutes of her twenty minute talk, so that key component of her argument (implementation) remains under-defined and under-developed. Overall, despite her compelling personality and her "exuberant" enthusiasm (11.43), her argument lacks in *logos* and evidentiary support; she provides some intriguing ideas for a future that unites gaming with social activism but does not convince her audience that it is actually possible.

This annotation has much in common with the two *descriptive annotations* that we looked at earlier: it addresses the credentials of the author, summarizes the argument, includes specific relevant detail, describes tone, and suggests its relevance. However, note the way the annotation's author integrates her own critique of McGonigal's claim throughout paragraph; she looks at this source through a critical lens, indicating that she will bring a similar approach to her treatment of this source material in her research paper. In some cases, you might even expand on the analytic model by including a final sentence that specifically indicates how you will use this source in relation to your own research. In this way, you would provide your readers with more than a critical review of the text; you would offer them an understanding of how that source contributed to the way you were developing your own claim.

As the examples above demonstrate, writing an annotated bibliography involves more than merely recording information: it is a way for you to identify arguments and add your response to what the source has to say about your research topic.

WRITER'S PRACTICE

Choose two sources from your preliminary research. Using the At A Glance box below as a model, answer the questions listed there to help you evaluate the sources. Now write a *descriptive annotation* for one source and an *analytic annotation* for the other, drawing on the information from your evaluation. Be concrete and descriptive, but also concise, writing no more than 150 words for each paragraph. Reflect on the two annotations when you have finished. How did each help you better understand your source material and how each text relates to your overall project and the development of your own thesis claim on the topic?

THE WRITER'S PROCESS

As you begin to articulate your contribution to the research conversation about your topic, use the strategies that you've learned in this chapter. These include visualizing research as a conversation that you are joining and understanding the process of researching your argument as a movement from surface to depth. As you learn to search and locate both primary and

AT A GLANCE

Composing an Annotated Bibliography

1. Put your sources into alphabetical order; you can also categorize them by primary and secondary sources.
2. Provide complete identifying information for each source, including author's name, title, publication, date, page numbers, and database information for online sources.
3. Compose a concise annotation for each source:
   - Summarize the main argument or point of the source; use concrete language. Include quotations if you wish.
   - Take into account the writer's ethos and stance. How credible or biased is this source?
   - Consider the usefulness of this source to the conversation on this topic. Does the source provide background information? Does it offer a contrasting perspective to other sources you have found? Does it provide evidence that might back up your claims?

secondary sources, you can engage in critical evaluation of these texts in your research log. You can also engage in innovative fieldwork of your own to generate original resource material to use in your argument. In writing your own annotated bibliography, remember that effective annotations and note-taking practices can help you develop the strategies of an academic writer and that these practices will move you toward finalizing your own argument about the topic.

Along the way, be sure to take careful notes. This is a crucial step in your writer's process. Many students make sense of the rich and diverse perspectives they encounter during their research through careful note taking. You can use the dialogue of sources method as a note-taking strategy while you work through your research sources. Or, you can take notes using a software program such as Endnote or Citelighter, bookmark pages and PDFs on your computer, or use the time-tested method of paper note-cards. Whatever your method, be vigilant in your practice now so you won't have to retrace your steps and relocate your sources or quotations later. By putting into practice the techniques and lessons of this chapter, you will start to see connections among various research sources and begin to articulate your own research-based argument.

AT A GLANCE

Note-Taking Strategies

As you read through your sources, take notes on materials that you could use in your paper:

- Particularly memorable quotations
- Background information
- A well-written passage providing context or a perspective useful to your argument

Be sure to double-check your notes for accuracy, use quotation marks for direct quotes, and include complete source details and page numbers.

WRITING ASSIGNMENTS

1. **Write About Magazine or Journal Covers:** Browse the online cover collection maintained by *Time* magazine or *Life* magazine, or choose a selection of covers from magazines at your local library. Look at two covers on a particular topic, such as global warming, presidential elections, a recent natural disaster, or computer technology. Practice the techniques of rhetorical analysis that we used in relation to images 5.1 and 5.2, and brainstorm an argument for how the cover of each magazine reflects its stance on the issue in question. Use the checklist below to guide your rhetorical analysis.

   ❑ What images are featured on the cover? What style is used? Are the images photographs (in black & white, color, sepia, etc.)? Are they hand-drawn? Are they sketches or polished artwork? Are they cartoons or more realistic? Are the images zoomed in (close-ups), portraits, or panoramic? What is the rhetorical effect of the style of the images?

- ❑ Does the cover feature people? Places? Symbols or abstract concepts? What do the cover images suggest about the contents of the larger text? How do they suggest a specific rhetorical stance or point of view?
- ❑ How do the words on the cover work in conjunction with the image to suggest the entire text's rhetorical stance? Do the words complement the image? Do they offer a contrast to the image?
- ❑ To what extent do you see the cover utilizing rhetorical appeals? How does it make an appeal based on facts, reason or logic? How does it appeal to the audience through emotion? How does it create an appeal based on credibility or authority?
- ❑ How does the layout function rhetorically? Does the cover use juxtaposition? symmetry or asymmetry? How does it indicate emphasis through the placement of elements on the cover? To what extent does it draw the audience's eye through a pre-determined and strategic path?
- ❑ Does the cover rely on any specific strategies of development to make its argument about its contents? Does it use narration? Comparison/contrast? Definition? Analogy? Example? Categorization? Process? How does its use of strategies make an argument about its contents?

2. **Research Log Entries:** Keep a running commentary/assessment of potential research sources for your project. Realize that careful research notes are a crucial part of the process and will help you avoid unintentional plagiarism of material. Include a combination of typed notes, highlighted photocopies, emails, sources from databases, note cards, scanned images, and other means of processing all the information you encounter.

3. **Working with Your Preliminary Bibliography:** Create a *dialogue of sources* or an *annotated bibliography* to showcase the primary and secondary sources you'll employ in the major paper. Be sure that your writing provides a range of primary and secondary sources. Include both print and electronic sources and, if appropriate, include images to demonstrate the kinds of materials you'll be analyzing in the project.

4. **Collaborative Peer Review:** Present your annotated bibliographies to one another in groups. Pull the "greatest hits" from your research log, and tell the class about how your research is going. In other words, *present a discussion of your work in progress.* Identify obstacles and successes so far. You'll get feedback from the class about your developing research project.

CHAPTER 6

Organizing and Writing Research Arguments

Chapter Preview Questions

6.1 What strategies of organization will work for my essay?

6.2 What strategies can I use to create an outline for my argument?

6.3 How can I balance my argument with my research?

6.4 How do I integrate research sources responsibly and rhetorically?

6.5 What are the best ways to get started writing a full draft?

6.6 What strategies can I use to revise my draft?

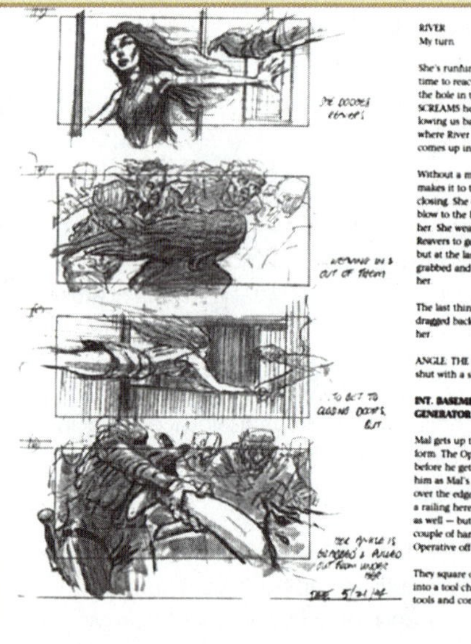

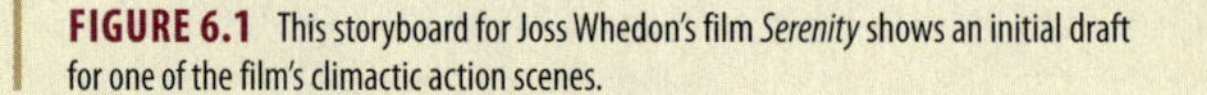
FIGURE 6.1 This storyboard for Joss Whedon's film *Serenity* shows an initial draft for one of the film's climactic action scenes.

Constructing a research argument is a complex and ongoing process. From selecting a topic to locating and evaluating sources and taking notes, it involves a series of interrelated steps. This is true of the *drafting* stage as well. In fact, organizing, drafting, and revising information is a prominent part of the process of creating any text—an academic essay, a television commercial, a radio essay, or even a film. Figure 6.1, for instance, lets us glimpse the drafting process behind a film called *Serenity* (2005). In this scene, one of the main characters, River, fights a roomful of Reavers—the cannibalistic bad guys of the film—to protect her brother and friends. What you see in Figure 6.1 are the storyboards for this scene—an artist's draft that lays out the action in chronological increments, mapping out not only the movement of the characters but also the camera angles and thus the audience's experience of the events depicted. Notice the way it captures a sense of motion by rapidly changing perspectives and how it creates a narrative tension in the last panel with the close-up of the Reavers grabbing River to drag her back during her attempted escape. Storyboards like this clearly operate as visual outlines, an organizational strategy that underlies almost all films. The polished final version seen in the theater is actually made possible by drafting steps like this one.

In many ways, the process of writing is like film production:

- Both have many small steps that support a grounding vision or main idea
- Both have a carefully planned structure
- Both involve rigorous editing

Because producing a film and producing a research argument share such rich similarities, we'll use the medium of film throughout this chapter to understand the process of writing a research paper: from constructing a visual map and formal outline to integrating sources, key quotations, and evidence. We'll talk about incorporating sources responsibly in a way that sustains the conversation you began in the previous chapter, and we'll walk through the drafting and revision process. Just as filmmakers leave many scenes on the cutting room floor, you too will write, edit, cut, and rearrange much of the first draft of your research paper before it reaches its final form. You'll find that the process of completing your research argument is as collaborative as film production. Additionally, both film and writing require you to consider issues of length, cost, and time as you work to produce the best possible text. So let's get started moving from notes to writing the complete paper.

ORGANIZING YOUR DRAFT IN VISUAL FORM

6.1 What strategies of organization will work for my essay?

It can be quite challenging to turn on the computer and try to crank out a complete draft without first arranging materials into some kind of order. Storyboards like those shown in Figure 6.1, or the bubble webs or graphic flowcharts described in this section, can be productive ways to prewrite through visual means. You can use various forms of graphically organizing your research notes and argumentative points in order to sort, arrange, and make connections between ideas.

The most basic way to get organized is physically to stack your research books and materials and then write labels for each pile. Alternatively, you might write your main ideas and notes about your sources on post it notes, then arrange and re-arrange them on a table or wall to visualize different modes of arrangement. These organizational strategies offer concrete ways to categorize the resources you have and figuring out, visually, how they relate to one another.

Another method would be using a computer to turn your handwritten visual map into a **bubble web**, in which you arrange your ideas into categories using shapes and colors. You could also try more hierarchical or linear graphic flowcharts as a means of organizing your materials. In **graphic flowcharts**, you list one idea and then draw an arrow to suggest cause and effect and to show relationships among items. Figure 6.2, for example, presents Ye Yuan's graphic flowchart of his ideas about war photography, arranged in a tree structure. This visual hierarchy helped him assess his project by asking questions and checking to see if he had enough research or points to make:

- Is each point developed thoroughly?
- Do I have a balance among the sections?
- Is there a coherent whole?

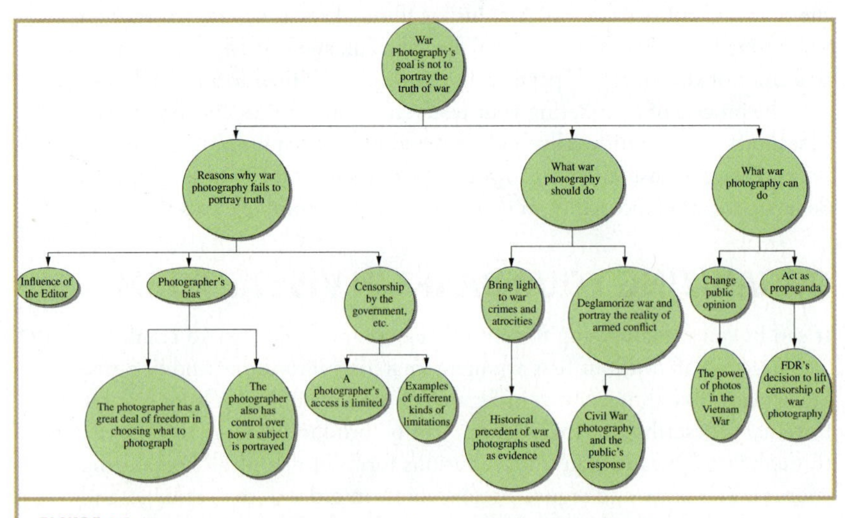

FIGURE 6.2 This graphic flowchart by Ye Yuan allowed him to visualize the sections of his written paper.

LEARNING OUTLINE STRATEGIES

6.2 What strategies can I use to create an outline for my argument?

Visual maps can help you sort out your materials and prepare you for the next step: the detailed, written **outline**. For a longer, more complex paper, such as a research-based argument, an *outline* is an extremely useful method of arranging ideas and expediting the drafting process. Outlines offer a plan for your paper and should show the relationships among the various sections in your argument. If your outline simply consists of a list of topics, you won't be able to see the argument of the whole paper, nor will you be able to check for a strong progression between your individual points. In other words, the secret to producing a successful outline—and by extension a successful paper—is to pay special attention to the flow or development of ideas.

It's often hard to know for certain the best way to put together points in an outline. We can learn a lot from films about the ways in which various texts are organized. Consider how a film's trailer provides a brief *outline* of the key scenes, the main conflict, the crucial characters, and the message of the movie. Figure 6.3 (on the next page) shows still shots from one of the several theatrical trailers for *Avatar*.

Structured loosely as a narrative, this trailer suggests an outline of the film, moving from an introduction of the human characters, to scenes showing the main avatar (Jake) and his Na'vi girlfriend, to scenes of the final physical conflict between the two civilizations. In doing so, the trailer reproduces one of the central themes of *Avatar*: the identification of both good and evil in the human civilization, and the conflict between the corporate part of that civilization and the spiritual Na'vi civilization. There are many ways in which these elements might have been arranged, each suggesting a different argument for the film—and indeed, different *Avatar* trailers made different arguments. The power of the trailer as an organizational tool or outline is that it allows filmmakers to experiment with order and, ultimately, meaning.

Keeping the idea of the trailer in mind, take your ideas from the visual map you have created and craft them into a **formal outline**, a detailed list that uses numbers and letters to indicate subsections of your argument. Rather than list three sections only—such as Introduction, Body, and Conclusion—create several points within the body to show the development of your argument.

FIGURE 6.3 These still shots from one of several trailers for the film *Avatar* transition the viewer from the human perspective into the world of Pandora, and then into the climactic conflict between the worlds.

As you organize your ideas, remember that formal outlines can help you work step by step through the process of arguing your position. That is, they can save you a lot of time as you approach writing the essay itself. Consider using full sentences to most clearly articulate your thoughts or inserting sources right into the outline; these techniques can help you troubleshoot areas where you might need to do supplemental research or expand your argument.

Another benefit of outlining is that it allows you to work with the rhetorical canon of **arrangement**, experimenting with different organizational structures. Depending on your topic, you might try several approaches. You might start your paper with a question, move through evidence, and then arrive at a declarative thesis statement toward the end of the essay. Alternatively, begin with a firm thesis statement up front, followed by an accumulation of supporting evidence that broadens out to a larger issue. Or, try moving thematically through your research offering a progressive argument. See the "At a Glance" box above for additional ways to organize your material in an outline.

AT A GLANCE

Useful Organization Strategies for Writing

- ***Chronological:*** relevant for historical discussions
- ***Thematic:*** helps with diverse case studies
- ***Cause and effect:*** focuses on consequences
- ***Problem-solution:*** useful for social issue papers
- ***Illustrative:*** emphasizes examples of a pattern
- ***Macro to micro:*** moves from the general to the specific
- ***Micro to macro:*** moves from the specific to the general
- ***Narrative:*** employs the personal experience

Seeing Connections
See Chapter 3 for more on the canon of arrangement.

Outlines with Argumentative Subheads

Outlines can also help you develop the complexity of your research argument if you incorporate subheads and transitions into your writing. **Subheads**, or labeled headings for each subsection of your outline, are a terrific way to structure your ideas into discrete units to show the progression of your argument and help your readers make sense of a

AT A GLANCE

Assessing Outlines

- ***Thesis:*** Is it complex, arguable, and interesting?
- ***Argument:*** Is there a logical and fluid progression of ideas? Does each one relate back to the thesis? Is there extraneous information that you can cut? Do more points need to be developed?
- ***Sources:*** Are primary sources identified for analysis in the paper? Are secondary sources listed to provide support and authority for the argument? Are there sufficient sources listed for each point? Are visual texts included as argumentative evidence?
- ***Format:*** Are there argumentative subheads? Do they move the argument of the essay along?

complex argument. Subheads work particularly well for longer, research-based essays. You can transform the key parts of your outline into a short list of **argumentative subheads**, or subheads that indicate the progression of your argument at each point.

If you were writing a detailed outline, you might insert into the body of your paper subheads that indicate specific parts of your argument. You can feel free to get creative by connecting your subheads thematically or by using a single metaphor to add a rich layer of vivid words to your essay. Look at how Dexian Cai met this challenge by incorporating argumentative subheads into his outline.

Dexian Cai
Dr. Alyssa O'Brien

Research Paper—Outline

I. Introduction: Ronald Targets Asia

1. Hook: A brief description of a current McDonald's video advertisement. While ostensibly American and Western, the interesting aspect is that this video is in fact an ad targeting an Asian market.
2. Thesis: McDonald's video advertising in East Asia has evolved over time, adapting to trends and changes in Asian societal values. The paper will argue that McDonald's both shapes and is shaped by these evolving trends, creating a dynamic relationship between the restaurant and consumers.
3. Implications: What are the effects of McDonald's influence on Asian values and societal evolution? Is this a healthy trend or merely a restaurant moving with

Notice how Dex includes the opening line for his paper, the hook, right in the outline, setting the tone for the paper.

His thesis comprises two sentences since this argument is complex, although he could develop the "how so" part of the thesis more.

He ends the intro with questions to engage the reader.

the times? Are accusations of cultural imperialism or degradation of morals justified?

II. Backstory to the Food Chain Empire
- A brief history of McDonald's entry into the various East Asian markets. In particular, research will center on Japan, Hong Kong, Korea, Taiwan, China, and Singapore.
- A summary of McDonald's image and *ethos* in the United States.

III. McDonald's: From Homely to Hip

Then
- Rhetorical analysis of ads from the 1970s and 1980s, when McDonald's first broke into the Asian markets.
- Argument that McDonald's was using *pathos*, attempting to portray itself as a family restaurant that made children feel special. Highlight the fact that the campaigns differed across the various countries because McDonald's tailored each campaign to the specific market's characteristics and perceived needs.
- Compare and contrast with contemporary American campaigns. Family vs. fast food.
- Source: McDonald's Corporation. (Pending the approval of a request sent via e-mail.)
- Secondary Source: Watson, James L. *Golden Arches East: McDonald's in East Asia*. Palo Alto, CA: Stanford UP, 1997.

After a brief background section, Dex moves on to the heart of his argument. The subhead "From Homely to Hip" reflects in words the point Dex will make in this section, namely, that McDonald's has changed its brand image from conservative to trendy. The play on words in the subhead helps keep Dex on track to interest the reader.

Note that he includes his sources right in his outline so he'll be sure to weave them into his paper.

Now

- Rhetorical analysis of most recent video ads.
- Argument that McDonald's marketing strategy has evolved to embrace East Asia as an "assimilated market," as the campaign and slogan are standardized the world over. There is no longer a uniquely Asian campaign; instead it is replaced by the homogeneous American set of ads.
- Image of fun and relaxation is interspersed with images of McDonald's products. Using youth to drive the campaign is a clear signal of the target audience and the aim of creating a "cool" and "hip" image for the franchise. This contrasts the familial tone of ads from the "early days." A switch from *pathos* to *ethos*.
- Sources: McDonald's Country websites

IV. Getting Behind the Arches

- Key Question: What has brought about this evolution in advertising strategies in East Asia? Why the shift in image?
- Argument: The dynamics of influence are mutual and interactive. Although McDonald's largely responds to perceived societal trends, it also seeks to influence attitudes and sell its version of "hip" or "cool," especially to Asian youth.

Since his paper focuses on the visual rhetoric of McDonald's advertising in Asia, it is appropriate for Dex to include images in his outline. These images will serve as evidence for his argument. [Images were removed for copyright purposes but appeared in Dex's original outline.]

He includes a key research question as a transition into this section. His next subhead again uses language to convey this point in the progression of his argument; with such argumentative subheads, he can be certain that his argument is building in significance.

- Analyze how the Asian case is reflective of McDonald's marketing strategy internationally. Discuss the moral/ ethical implications of such strategies.
- Consider the McDonald's "Culture of Power" argument in Kincheloe's book. Are the claims leveled against the franchise valid?
- Source: Kincheloe, Joe L. *The Sign of the Burger: McDonald's and the Culture of Power*. Philadelphia: Temple UP, 2002.

V. Amer-Asia? A Peek at the Future of Fast Food

- Synthesize the arguments of the paper.
  Raise Larger Questions
- Given the trend of increasing global integration, is homogenization under American leadership an inevitable end of modern civilization?
- Discuss ways in which this is not so ("dissenting opinion"). Asia's cultures continue to greatly influence McDonald's, causing wide variations between McDonald's image in Asia and in America.
- Answer these bigger concerns: What are the implications of changing societal trends for Asian youth? How does McDonald's advertising affect and influence these trends? Do the ads exacerbate/speed up the "Americanization" of Asian youth? or do they merely reflect what is already present?

He is still working on points of the argument, even in the outline, as shown in his question about whether to bring in Joe Kincheloe's argument as a secondary source here.

The final section is not titled "Conclusion" but instead uses an argumentative subhead to transition into the closing argument of the paper, namely that the presence of McDonald's is potentially changing distinctions between nations, blurring cultures into a combined identity Dex calls "Amer-Asia."

As you can see from Dex's writing in this outline, using an appropriate metaphor in the subheads provides consistency in language that in turn can help the flow of the essay and make it engaging to read. In addition, each subhead offers a mini-preview of the points to come, and therefore writing them can help you keep your overall argument on track.

Transitions

You can also enhance the flow of your writing with careful attention to **transitions**—phrases that provide the connections between the paragraphs or sections in your paper. When creating transitions, even during your outlining phase, think about how you can signal the next idea, build on the previous idea, or reiterate the key terms of your thesis as you advance your argument. Many students like to think of the game of dominoes when composing transitions: each domino can only touch another domino with a matching number; two connects with two, three with three. Using this notion of progressive, connecting terms, you can incorporate transitions within sections of your outline to give it overall structure and flow. Then, when you turn to writing the paper, you will avoid big jumps in logic.

6.3 How can I balance my argument with my research?

SPOTLIGHT ON YOUR ARGUMENT

As you turn now from writing an outline to fleshing out the full draft, consider the decision before you concerning what kind of voice or rhetorical stance to take in the language of your prose. Again, we can learn a lot from filmmakers as they face similar decisions.

In his 2012 documentary, *How to Survive a Plague*, filmmaker David France recounts the strife, struggle and controversy surrounding the early efforts to respond to the AIDS epidemic. While France includes many voices in his film—from doctors to protesters to politicians—he ultimately emphasizes his own argument about the decisive role grassroots activist organizations like ACT UP played in changing public attitudes and public policy regarding this disease. Of course, the film relies on research as background material, presenting interview segments and providing extensive archival footage. But as the image in Figure 6.4 suggests, France's views about the power of popular protest form the foundation for everything disclosed in the film, making his rhetorical stance a prominent part of the text.

You also should consider diverse ways to present your argument. Sometimes you want to put your sources center stage and direct from behind the scenes, and sometimes you will want to step out of the shadows and articulate your argument more explicitly to the audience. Whichever way you go, you should decide what role you, the writer, will play in your paper. The key is to choose the role that will produce the most effective argument on your topic, one that fits the needs of your rhetorical situation. Your voice is your **spotlight on your argument**; it should have rhetorical purpose and complement the content of your project.

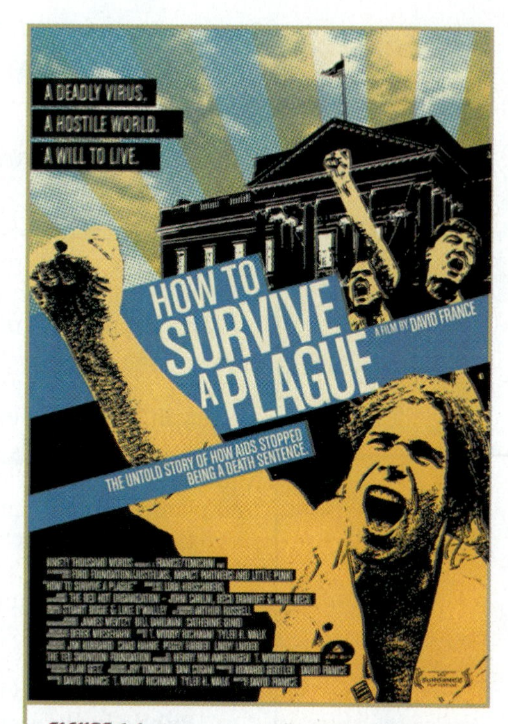

FIGURE 6.4 This promotional image for *How to Survive a Plague* reveals the way film emphasizes its argument about the role popular protest played in shaping the national response to the AIDS crisis in the 1980s.

Analyzing a Published Argument

As you outline your research paper and consider ways to bring your sources into your argument, you should study carefully the writing found in articles that you encounter throughout your research project. You can learn a lot about how to organize and spotlight your own argument from a *rhetorical analysis* of the formal properties of your secondary sources. Examine the article which follows by Bret Schulte, posted in both the print and online editions of *U.S. News & World Report*. The article provides an excellent snapshot back in time of the rhetorical situation from 2006—when *An Inconvenient Truth* first appeared in cinemas and people were beginning to learn about global warming. Schulte's piece demonstrates many of the writing techniques we've been learning in this chapter, including arranging his points into a progression of ideas and making his own voice quite strong as a spotlight on his argument. Specifically, you'll see that the piece uses interview research and reformats it into an argument that reflects the writer's own perspective on the film. The piece structures itself with subheads that are argumentative, cites interview with quotations, integrates statistics as research, and ends with a memorable conclusion.

Notice how Schulte's voice emerges immediately when he calls *An Inconvenient Truth* a "docu-horror film." The alliteration (public-perils-PowerPoint presentation) and exaggerated *pathos* further develop Schulte's rhetorical stance.

SAYING IT IN CINEMA

By Bret Schulte

Posted 5/28/06: *U.S. News & World Report*

President Bush doubts he'll see it, but millions of other people undoubtedly will. Former Vice President Al Gore's docu-horror film about the frightening future promised by global warming—an apocalyptic world of deadly hurricanes, rising oceans, disease, drought, and famine—is pushing the debate to a new level. While tracking Gore's political ascent and contentious loss of the presidency in 2000, the film zeroes in on Gore's newest campaign: to educate the public about the perils of global warming one PowerPoint presentation at a time. Although Gore insists he has no plans to run for national office, the film has thrust him back into the national limelight and sparked an industry of "Al Gore for president" speculation. His well-publicized movie has also provoked critics to run campaign-style ads challenging climate change science. Gore spoke with *U.S. News* about the film, *An Inconvenient Truth,* already playing in select cities and slated for 125 markets by July 4. Excerpts:

Rather than enclosing direct quotations from Gore's interview in quotation marks, Schulte opts for an innovative structure. He pairs a rhetorical subhead of his own (his argument) with an excerpt from interview (his source). The merger of Schulte's and Gore's voice provides a unique rhetorical effect on the reader.

Public indifference. We are dumping tens of millions of tons [of carbon dioxide] into the atmosphere every day, and it has literally changed the relationship between the Earth and the sun. It's a challenge to our moral imagination to understand we are now like a bull in the china shop. [And] there has been a very well-organized and lavishly funded effort by a few irresponsible polluters to intentionally confuse the American people by spending millions of dollars a year on pseudo-science reports—the same way the tobacco industry used that technique to stave off action to save the lives of smokers.

Saving the Earth vs. saving the economy. The companies that are doing well... are the ones that have become more efficient. Reducing pollution actually creates jobs and strengthens the economy. Pollution is waste, and the modern approach to pollution reduction dovetails with successful business making higher profits.

Gore's stiff personality. I benefit from low expectations.

Losing the presidency. I don't cry over spilled milk. It's very difficult in a national campaign for any candidate to be seen and heard without the distortions his or her opponent makes on an hourly basis. I think I've been through a lot since the 2000 campaign, and that old cliche, "What doesn't kill you makes you stronger," is sometimes true.

At this point, the sarcasm in the subhead "Gore's stiff personality" indicates that you should not take the article as a literal transcription of an interview. Instead, the writer crafts an argument about Gore through strong references to history, in this case the 2000 election.

Global warming and the media. The debate over global warming is over. The slide [in my presentation] people most ask me about is the one that contrasts the massive study of 10 years of peer-reviewed scientific articles on global warming, zero percentage of which disagreed with the consensus, and the study of 14 years of newspaper articles, 53 percent of which expressed doubt about whether the problem is real or not. That is really a striking contrast.

Here, the writer refers to research incorporated by Gore in his film, primarily *logos*.

The Competitive Enterprise Institute's TV campaign. I'm not surprised. They're funded by Exxon Mobil, and they put a lot of money into trying to confuse people. Unfortunately, they have succeeded. I'm hopeful they will soon be recognized for what they are and put in the same category as people who still believe the moon landing was staged in a movie lot.

The references to the TV campaign—and to people not believing the truth of other events—builds the argument.

Looking back on the Senate's turndown of the Kyoto Protocol. I did push as hard as I knew how to. The truth is that Congress was not willing to ratify it. It was already controlled by the Republicans, but if it had been controlled by the Democrats, I dare say at that point, the result would have been nearly the same. I think that is changing.

Lobbying the people, not the politicians. Nothing is going to change in Washington until the sense of urgency felt and expressed by the American people changes. I'm concentrating on that task.

Practicing what you preach. We have a hybrid car and all the new light bulbs. My family is completely carbon neutral. That means reducing as much carbon dioxide as we possibly can and then buying offsets to cancel out the rest.

The subtle allusions to steps Gore recommends we take to save the environment serve to build the writer's *ethos*, as they show his strong familiarity with the content. At the same time, these references mock Gore's film.

If Gore were president. One difference is that you might see George W. Bush doing a cold opener on *Saturday Night Live* from an alternate universe.

By ending with humor, the writer packs a memorable punch.

6.4 How do I integrate research sources responsibly and rhetorically?

INTEGRATING RESEARCH SOURCES

After you decide on your approach to working with sources—as a strong explicit narrator or as the synthesizer of information—you need to start turning your outline into a rough draft. In order to introduce and weave these voices into your written prose, you will need to include your sources appropriately (to avoid plagiarism) and rhetorically (to decide on how much of a presence you will have in the paper) but also strategically (to provide a range of quotations and supporting evidence for your paper). We call this process **integrating sources**, and it's a complex process that occurs in three basic ways:

- **Summary:** synthesizing a great deal of information from a source
- **Paraphrase:** putting a source quotation into your own words
- **Direct quotation:** excerpting a specific passage from a source, enclosing it in quotation marks

You'll want to alternate among these methods while incorporating your sources for stylistic variety and to accommodate the different ways you'll be using your research as evidence for your argument. This means knowing your options as a writer and selecting the best method for each rhetorical

AT A GLANCE

Integrating Sources Appropriately and Effectively

- ***Read.*** Read the source actively and carefully, underlining passages that suggest moments of deep meaning or that might contribute to your argument. If you are working with online texts, cut and paste the citation into a document and note the paragraph number (for websites) or page number. Always note the page number if you transcribe quotations as you read.

  You'll need this part in order to provide the citation in your own writing.
- ***Record.*** Keep a notebook or an annotated file of citations in which you record your reactions to a particular passage you've read. Does this passage strike you as important? Does it reveal the theme of the text, the climax of a scene, the point of the argument, the purpose of the passage?

  You'll need this part in order to provide your interpretation of the citation.
- ***Relate.*** Integrate the source material and your interpretation in an appropriate place in your own essay. Think about where in the essay, and in which particular paragraph, the information should appear. Think about the context—what comes before and after the summary, paraphrase, or quotation? How does it related to the text around it?

  You'll need this part in order to integrate your source material effectively.

situation within your research essay. Realize that you have many choices for how to integrate research sources, and your decisions should be determined by the specific need of each part of your argument as well as the value of the research to build your *ethos*, provide background, offer an alternative perspective, or convey foundational knowledge.

Selecting Summary

A **summary** is a brief version—in your own words—of the content of a text. You might want to summarize the plot of a film or a book in a review, or you might want to summarize the basic argument presented by one of your sources in order to respond to it. Summaries are not analyses; you are not exploring your own ideas when you summarize but merely laying out the ideas explored by another writer in another text. You need to make sure that you tell your readers exactly what you are summarizing and provide complete bibliographical information at the end of your paper. For example, a research paper about the Italian films produced after WWII might include a summary that begins:

Seeing Connections
For an example of summary paragraph in an annotated bibliography, see Chapter 5.

> In their influential study *Italian Neorealism and Global Cinema*, cultural critics Laura Ruberto and Kristi Wilson provide a concise history of film innovations at the turn of the twentieth century and argue that Italian documentaries allowed international conflicts to seem real to viewers...

Your summary would follow, and your list of works cited at the end of your paper would include the following reference:

> Ruberto, Laura E. and Wilson, Kristi M. *Italian Neorealism and Global Cinema*. Detroit: Wayne State UP, 2007. Print.

If you wanted to include a brief quote within the body of your summary, then you would use quotation marks and a page number, as follows:

> In their influential study *Italian Neorealism and Global Cinema*, cultural critics Laura Ruberto and Kristi Wilson provide a concise history of film innovations at the turn of the twentieth century and argue that Italian documentaries "had a way of making the global seem local" (2).

Note that in this case, you are still writing a summary, but you include a direct quotation because it is rhetorically concise and powerful (with *pathos*-laden language), but also because citing the text gives you more *ethos* or authority as a writer.

Picking Paraphrase

Unlike a summary, a **paraphrase** focuses in and restates one part of a text. While a summary is often shorter than the text it summarizes, a paraphrase may be longer or shorter than the text it paraphrases. You might want to paraphrase a text to help your readers understand it, particularly if the original text is dense or difficult. Or you might simply want to paraphrase to make sure that you understand the source yourself—to offer yourself an opportunity to think clearly about the words you are reading. For instance, you might select the following lines to paraphrase:

> "Film had a way of making the global seem local, and the effect of movement, and, later, sound created an immediacy that still photos and written narratives could not approach" (Ruberto and Wilson 2).

Your paraphrase might read as follows:

> Italian film brought world events home to viewers, especially through moving images and audio (Ruberto and Wilson 2).

Note that you replace all the words, not just some of them, for a paraphrase. You need to be careful that you are using your own words to create a new text, not simply cutting and pasting the words of your source together in a different order. For instance, the following sentence represents a failed and problematic paraphrasing:

> Film made the global seem local, and the effect of motion and audio tracks constructed a connection to the audience that photographs and books could not (Ruberto and Wilson 2).

Notice the strong echo of the original text: if you follow both the structure and the language of the source closely, substituting only an occasional synonym to avoid directly quoting, then you are actually plagiarizing—even if you do so accidentally and even if you provide an appropriate citation. You are plagiarizing because you are not informing your reader that the structure, ideas, and much of the language used in your paper were created by someone else.

Seeing Connections
See Chapter 7 for a more detailed discussion of plagiarism and intellectual property.

How to avoid this problem? As you paraphrase, try not to look at the original sentence; move beyond its specific wording to try to get at its meaning. Double-check after you've written your paraphrase to be sure that you don't too strongly replicate the original in phrasing or structure. In addition, be sure to provide your reader with the appropriate bibliographical information about your source by offering a lead-in phrase ("As Ruberto and Wilson argue in their book *Italian Neorealism and Global Cinema* ...") and then list the complete reference for this source at the end of your paper. Or you can provide a parenthetical citation after the summary or paraphrase including the author's name and, for a paraphrase, the page number where the passage you are paraphrasing appears in the original text. When in doubt, consider using a direct quotation instead of a paraphrase to bring your source's voice directly into your essay.

Using Direct Quotations

Quoting directly from a source may seem much simpler than paraphrasing or summarizing, but quotations should be included to accomplish a specific rhetorical purpose, and they must be integrated responsibly so that you give the original writer credit. Consider how you might feel if someone took your writing and recycled it without acknowledging that it was your work. More importantly, realize that naming the author and background of a great passage can build your authority and *ethos* as a writer, so it is a wise move to name your sources in your paper. However, be careful not to swing to the opposite extreme and fill your paper with quotations from others. If a quotation does not fit into any of the categories listed in the "At a Glance" box, consider paraphrasing or summarizing it. What you want to avoid is a paper dominated by unnecessary quotations; in such a case, your argument—what readers expect most in your paper—gets buried. It's similar to what happens in film when the filmmaker splices together too many different scenes; the audience becomes lost in the montage and can no longer follow the narrative.

Working with Quotations in Your Writing

But how, practically, do you go about *integrating* direct quotations appropriately and effectively? The key is to think carefully about how you are using the source material first and then choose an appropriate structure. Your

AT A GLANCE

Reasons to Use Direct Quotations

- ***Evidence:*** the quotation provides tangible evidence for part of your argument.
- ***Ethos:*** the original author is a primary source or an expert on the subject, and including a direct quotation would increase the *ethos* of your argument.
- ***Language:*** the original author used memorable phrasing or has a particular voice that would be lost in paraphrase.

temptation might be simply to "drop" a quote in between two of your sentences, as in the example below:

> More recently, *Hunger Games* protagonist Katniss has challenged the anti-feminist stereotype prominent in today's young adult fiction. "She's Jo March as coal miner's daughter in hunting boots, the opposite of Bella, the famously drippy, love-obsessed heroine of the *Twilight* books—and unlike clever and self-possessed Hermione of the *Harry Potter* series, she's the lead, not the sidekick" (Pollitt 10). Translated to the big screen in a blockbuster film, Katniss solidifies this image, providing a much-needed positive model for today's young women.

While Pollitt's sentence merits being quoted directly because of its language, the danger in this method is that you are using the quotation not as evidence, but as a substitute for your own writing. The original writer (Katha Pollitt) is given little credit for her work besides the parenthetical citation, making her more a ghostwriter than a source for your argument.

Rather than using a drop quote, integrate direct quotations strategically into your writing so as to leverage them more effectively as you develop your claim. One typical practice is to use a **signal phrase** to indicate the context of the quotation and to orient it in terms of your argument. A signal phrase can be located in many different positions relation to the quotation, but most often it appears as an introductory phrase or clause that refers to the original author or title of the source, to heighten the *ethos* of the source.

> In her 2012 article, Kate Pollitt argues, "She's Jo March as coal miner's daughter in hunting boots, the opposite of Bella, the famously drippy, love-obsessed heroine of the *Twilight* books – and unlike clever and self-possessed Hermione of the *Harry Potter* series, she's the lead, not the sidekick" (10).

An alternate method would be to limit the amount of text quoted and **integrate small sections into your own sentence**. This strategy works particularly well when you are trying to capture a unique turn of phrase or concept from the original text and tends to maintain the strength of your own voice as a writer. For example, consider how in this example, the author integrates a few words of direct quotation into her sentence so as to spotlight Pollitt's memorable characterization of Bella Swan's character:

> Pollitt argues that, unlike the "famously drippy, love-obsessed" Bella from the *Twilight* series, Katniss offers a smart, positive role model for today's young women (10).

In another variation, the author includes a slightly longer section of the original text that works in conjunction with paraphrase:

> Kate Pollitt offered a persuasive intertextual interpretation of Katniss's character when she suggested that Katniss is "Jo March as coal miner's daughter in hunting boots," directly opposing the model of femininity embodied by *Twilight*'s Bella (10).

This model can also be adapted to allow the writer to follow up the quotation with an end comment that advances the argument.

A third integration strategy involves **appending the quotation to one of your own sentences with a colon**. The syntactical function of the colon implies that what follows it (the quote) is directly related to what precedes the colon (your own observation). For this reason, this structure works well to suggest that the direct quotation operates as an elaboration of your point or as evidence.

> Pollitt argues that Katniss represents a new-and-improved model of female heroine: "She's Jo March as coal miner's daughter in hunting boots, the opposite of Bella, the famously drippy, love-obsessed heroine of the *Twilight* books—and unlike clever and self-possessed Hermione of the *Harry Potter* series, she's the lead, not the sidekick" (10).

At times, you may even decide to include a lengthier quotation in your essay, perhaps because of the strength of the author's argument or because you intend to analyze the passage. For direct quotations of four lines or longer, set the passage off from the rest of the text as a **block quote**. Here's an example using Pollitt once again.

> In discussing Katniss's role in revitalizing the female pop culture protagonist, Pollitt argues,
>
> > She's Jo March as coal miner's daughter in hunting boots, the opposite of Bella, the famously drippy, love-obsessed heroine of the *Twilight* books – and unlike clever and self-possessed Hermione of the *Harry Potter* series, she's the lead, not the sidekick. We're worlds away from the vicious-little-rich-girls of *Gossip Girl* and its knockoffs, where everything revolves around looks, clothes, consumerism, social status, and sexual competition. (10)
>
> As Pollitt suggests, some of Katniss's appeal lies in how she embodies the intelligence and fortitude of previous female protagonists, qualities that have been increasingly obscured beneath superficiality and sentimentality in more recent years.

It's worth noting some technical details here: the quotation as a whole is indented one inch from the left margin; quotation marks are omitted in block quotes because the formatting itself marks it as a direct quotation; the final period precedes the parenthetical citation for a block quote; the author's analysis ("As Pollitt notes...") resumes flush with the left margin, indicating it is part of the same paragraph and same line of argument.

While including blocks of text might be tempting, especially when dealing with a particularly rich source, be judicious in your use of lengthy quotes. Including too many of them can fragment your argument, interrupt the flow of your essay, and drown out your own voice. Always follow up a block quote with analysis to clarify to your reader how it contributes to your argument and to return the spotlight onto your own research and claim.

As you work with direct quotations in your own writing, you might find these additional strategies helpful:

- To quote a source within a source, use (qtd. in ——) to indicate where *you* found the quotation, for instance:

  > Film critic Millicent Marcus argues that "neorealism is first and foremost a moral statement" (qtd. in Ruberto and Wilson 7).

  If you don't include the author's name in the signal phrase, use an alternate model:

  > A different perspective might argue that "neorealism is first and foremost a moral statement" (Marcus qtd. in Ruberto and Wilson 7).

- To edit part of a quote, use square brackets as such [ ]. This abridgement allows you to get concisely to the heart of the issue in your chosen quotation. For instance, you might edit the Pollitt quote above:

  > Kathy Pollitt argues in her 2012 article from *The Nation*, Katniss is "the opposite of Bella [...] and unlike clever and self-possessed Hermione [...], she's the lead, not the sidekick" (10).

Experiment with these strategies in your own writing to determine which best serve your rhetorical purpose. One key to remember is to avoid overusing any one type of integration strategy; in that case, your writing style might become monotonous, like a film that relies too heavily on the same types of shots. For instance, if you want to draw attention to the *author* of a quotation to add *ethos* to your argument, you might opt to integrate using an introductory clause; however, if you want to emphasize *information* rather than authorship, an incorporated structure might be more effective. Remember that the purpose of integrating sources is to demonstrate your work as a researcher and to show that you are building your argument on the work of others. Therefore, choose what types of integration strategies work best for each source and for each part of your paper.

WRITER'S PRACTICE: CHECKING YOUR SOURCE INTEGRATION

In your efforts to integrate sources effectively, keep in mind that source material should *support* your argument, not supplant it. If you're worried that you have integrated too many sources (and lost your own voice), spend some time reviewing the draft and ask yourself:

- Am I still the moderator of this conversation?
- Is my voice clear, compelling, and original?
- Do I allow my own argument to emerge as foremost in this piece?

Documentation During Integration

When integrating sources into your draft, be sure to include citations for each quotation or paraphrase. This would also be a good time to begin drafting your preliminary bibliography or MLA Works Cited list, in order to save time later. The purpose of documentation is not only to provide a "list of credits" for your references but also to supply interested readers with the resources to continue learning about your topic. Just as you undoubtedly found certain articles inspiring while investigating your topic and used them as springboards for more focused research, so too might your paper serve as a means of leading your readers to intriguing ideas and articles. You can go back over the correct format for citations in your final edit, following the guidelines in Chapter 7 for documentation to do so.

AT A GLANCE

Check for Integrating Sources

- Did you ***introduce the quote*** in various ways?
- Did you ***link the reference*** to your argument to show the relevance?
- Did you ***comment*** on it afterward to advance your argument?
- Did you ***cite*** it properly using the appropriate documentation style for your subject area?

6.5 What are the best ways to get started writing a full draft?

DRAFTING YOUR RESEARCH ARGUMENT

As you continue to forge ahead with your research argument, turning it from an outline to a full draft or composing sections of your argument in separate time blocks, remember that there are many strategies for getting it done. Also realize that to write is to struggle with the process, as noted by Stanford University psychologist David Rasch: "Almost all writers are familiar with the experience of feeling stuck, blocked, overwhelmed, or behind schedule in their writing." What can help? Staying motivated and relying on others. The key is to start and then just keep writing. Try out one of the many methods described in the "At a Glance" box.

AT A GLANCE

Strategies for Drafting

- ***Following the linear path:*** Start at the beginning, write the introduction, and then move sequentially through each point of argument.
- ***Fleshing out the outline:*** Gradually transform the outline into a full draft, moving from a keyword outline to a prose outline by systematically expanding each of the sections; as you add more detail, the keywords fall away, leaving behind drafted paragraphs.
- ***Writing from the middle:*** Start writing from a point of greatest strength or start with a section you can complete easily; then write around it and fill out sections as you go.
- ***Freewrite and then reverse outline:*** First, freewrite a few pages; then compose a **reverse outline** in which you record the point of each paragraph to assess the argument's flow and structure; and finally, reorder and rewrite the paper until it begins to take the proper form for the argument.

Keeping Your Passion

As you move deeper into the writing process, integrating quotations and working out the flow of your argument, don't lose sight of your enthusiasm for your subject. Reread your earliest freewrites and your entries in your research log. What goals prompted you to begin the project? What aspects of your topic excited you, angered you, or inspired you? What contribution did you imagine yourself making to this discussion? Remember, your audience will be reading your paper to learn *your* particular point of view on the subject.

You should also allow yourself well-needed energy breaks. Brief periods away from the writing process can often recharge and reinvigorate your approach to the paper and help you think through difficult points in the argument. Ironically, a pause in drafting can also help you avoid writer's block by allowing you to remember what interested you about this project in the first place.

Finally, if you are having trouble getting through the draft process, allow yourself to write what Anne Lamott, author of *Bird by Bird*, famously calls the "shitty first draft." In the words of Lamott, "All good writers write them. This is how they end up with good second drafts and terrific third drafts." That is, you should realize that the first version by no means has to be perfect or even close to what the final paper will look like. It is instead simply your first attempt at getting your ideas on paper. Freeing yourself to write something—anything—can help you escape from the weight of perfectionism or the fear of failure that often paralyzes writers. You will have plenty of opportunities to rework the material, show your draft to others, and move forward with the writing process.

Analyzing a Student's Draft of a Research-Based Essay

Let's examine now the draft of Stanford student Wan Jin Park, who developed a research project comparing Gore's film *An Inconvenient Truth* (2006) to Gore's more recent PowerPoint slide show during his talk at TED, a conference organized to showcase innovative thinking. Wan Jin conducted a range of academic and field research, wrote a detailed outline, and then composed his draft. After feedback from his course instructor and his classroom peers, he revised his first partial draft and outline substantially, as demonstrated later in this chapter. But throughout, Wan Jin kept his passion for his project and his respect for Gore as a leader trying to use rhetoric to persuade people of the importance of attending to climate change. We can study his first draft and conduct a *rhetorical analysis* of his writing strategies to see how you, too, can approach writing your research argument.

You'll see that the excerpt from Wan Jin's draft integrates research sources in a variety of ways, begins to showcase Wan Jin's own voice as a writer, and effectively relies on the outline as a prewriting tool.

Wan Jin Park

Working Draft + Outline

Environmental Leadership:

How Al Gore Illuminated an Overlooked Crisis

Rising levels of carbon dioxide emissions do not contribute to global warming. It has become silly and naïve to argue thus

Wan Jin's working title is strong and raises a problem—but in the revision, he will introduce his argument more forcefully.

His organizational strategy is to open with a counterargument, acknowledging that, today, even middle-schoolers know about global warming.

even before a group of middle school students. The awareness of the dangers of our carbon addicted lifestyle, however, would not be as widespread as it is today had it not been for the one man spearheading the global movement against climate change: Al Gore. Gore's rise to environmental influence is in large part due to Davis Guggenheim's documentary *An Inconvenient Truth*, which was then followed by a revised presentation at the TED Conference in March 2008. What strikes the audience, however, is not the revision of data and graphics in the slides, but rather, it is the change in Gore's rhetoric. In *An Inconvenient Truth*, Gore focuses on drawing in the audience and persuading them to join the environmental movement through the depiction of himself as a warm, dedicated, but lonely leader in the face of a global crisis; by contrast, at the TED presentation, Gore has garnered huge support, but senses a lack of change in the United States, and thus focuses on pushing the public toward increased initiative through his urgent and passionate rhetoric.

Then he introduces the film fully as well as his second primary source: Gore's 2008 TED talk.

Even in his draft, Wan Jin has strongly developed his thesis—this work will sustain him through the rest of the paper. He can use the key terms of the thesis to structure the remaining sections of the essay.

Gripping the Flames: Gore Leading the Environmental Movement

Wan Jin's subheads show his gift for creative language—he uses *pathos* but also indicates this new part of his argument with the subhead.

At the forefront of the global environmental movement against climate change is Al Gore. In fact, The Nielsen Company, a leading global marketing and advertising research company, conducted a survey in conjunction with Oxford University which serves as a testament to Gore's environmental prominence. In a survey of 26,486 people across 47 countries,

Already bringing in research, Wan Jin starts with facts and statistics (*logos*) from survey and field research.

Gore has been voted as "the most influential spokesperson to champion the global warming debate," even "ahead of former United Nations" Secretary General Kofi Annan (Nielsen).

Gore has been active with the environmental movement since the beginning of his political career; however, his lasting, and perhaps, most influential contribution did not come until the release of Davis Guggenheim's *An Inconvenient Truth* in May 2006. Although based on lectures "that Gore has been presenting in one form or another for nearly three decades," *An Inconvenient Truth* has achieved levels of popularity and influence unrivalled by those of any other medium employed in the environmental movement (Rosteck and Frentz). Earning over $49 million, it currently ranks as the fifth-highest-grossing documentary in the history of the United States. Further indicative of the documentary's influence are the results of another survey conducted by The Nielsen Company in April 2007. Of the viewers who have seen *An Inconvenient Truth*, eighty-nine percent reported to have become "more aware of the problem"; sixty-six percent "changed their mind about global warming"; and most importantly, seventy-four percent changed their habits as a result (Nielsen).

Next, he provides background and cites an article from his research (Rosteck and Frentz).

Considering the fact that *An Inconvenient Truth* is Gore's most influential rhetorical medium, an analysis of the documentary will thus illuminate the key characteristics that define the success of Gore's environmental leadership.

At this point, Wan Jin offers a road map for the rest of his essay, referring back to his title and his thesis in a way that offers powerful coherence for the essay.

As Wan Jin gets into the body of his essay, he takes his evidence one piece at a time, first providing a strong rhetorical analysis of the visual and audio elements of the film, then quoting directly from Gore's voice-over.

With the word, "However," Wan Jin lets us know his view, introducing his argument.

The careful analysis of specific words such as "gearshift" make this rhetorical argument persuasive.

Contrasting Images: the Beautiful and the Doomed

An Inconvenient Truth begins with a beautiful depiction of nature. The camera focuses close-up on a branch full of small green tree leaves. The green hue is accentuated by the bright sunlight that is reflected off of the leaf blades. After a few seconds, the camera shifts to the right to reveal a sparkling river. The soft piano music in the background adds to the calm and peaceful mood. Al Gore then narrates in the background, purposefully emphasizing the sibilants as if to imitate the sounds of the river and the rustling leaves:

> You look at that river gently flowing by. You notice the leaves rustling with the wind. You hear the birds. You hear the tree frogs. In the distance, you hear a cow. You feel the grass. The mud gives a little bit on the riverbank. It's quiet; it's peaceful. (Inconvenient)

The first thirty seconds of the film is beautiful. However, Gore interjects and introduces human neglect of nature by stating, "all of a sudden, it's a gearshift inside you and it's like taking a deep breath and going 'Oh yeah, I forgot about this'" (Inconvenient). By using the word "gearshift," Gore metaphorically compares the audience to machines that are equipped with a gear; in essence, Gore argues that we have become the products of our industrial production, and have thus become so separate from our nature that we have completely forgot about it.

The consequences of our neglect are horrifying. After the establishment of our neglect, Gore's presentation shows images of the damages we made to nature. We see images of factories emitting thick black smog that obscures the sun. In one of the images, the hue of the sky is grayish purple; considering how the corpses of formerly sick bodies usually show this hue, this image is suggestive of the damage we have done to nature. Furthermore, as a demonstration of how global warming has aggravated natural disasters, we see footages of the aftermath of Hurricane Katrina. We see footages of crying babies without shelter and caretakers, a bloated dead body lying face down in the water, and a man stroking the forehead of his dead wife. Although Hurricane Katrina has been an American natural disaster, these footages shock even the most foreign audience.

The presentation of these images after Gore's argument that we have forgotten about our nature compels the audience to feel guilt and responsibility. In effect, Gore induces the audience to personalize the issue of climate change, thereby making us more receptive to Gore's message of change.

The Dedicated Leader

- After fear, Gore portrays himself as a dedicated leader
- autobiographical threads in the documentary
- vulnerable moments in Gore's personal history
- Source: these stories "strengthen[ed] the hero's resolve"
- Secondary source: Kathryn Olson, Director of the Rhetorical Leadership Graduate Certificate Program at University of

Just as he analyzed the words in the film, Wan Jin carefully analyzes the images, building his argument. His own voice as a writer here becomes adamant and urgent, evoking the mood of the film but also forcing us to take his argument seriously.

This section ends with a mini summary and strong statement of Wan Jin's argument. In this way, he creates an effective organization for his larger paper, and from here can go about completing it one section at a time.

The next sections of the draft show in outline form the content Wan Jin plans to cover, including his main arguments, his section of evidence, and his secondary source citations.

He provides an *ethos*-building introduction for his secondary source.

By working with more than two sources in this section—Inhofe and Olson—Wan Jin shows potential to move from merely quoting sources (as we saw in Chapter 3) to synthesizing them in conversation with one another. He can then build on their combined ideas as he advances his own argument.

By selecting and arranging quotes in his draft, Wan Jin can approach the writing with a keen sense of his argument and overall plan for persuading the reader. He has chosen his evidence and uses the draft to sort through it effectively.

Wisconsin-Milwaukee, claims the autobiographical threads "persuasively documents Gore's single-mindedness in pursuing his public cause, often at his own expense, through a lifetime of disappointments and sacrificing a comfortable retirement to carry the message globally."

- Gore in a Beijing taxi on way to Tsing Hua University.

Lonely Leader

- personal footages depict Gore as "emotional suffering"
- Senator James Inhofe attacks Gore's ideas
- Secondary Source: Gore "inviting impression that encourages auditors to join him or her in social action" (Olson).

TED Presentation

- More passionate; more religious; his sense of urgency is raised
- His tone of voice, joking, moral issue
- Quote: "The only two countries that didn't ratify—and now there's only one. Australia had an election. And there was a campaign in Australia that involved television and Internet and radio commercials to lift the **sense of urgency** for the people there. And we trained 250 people to give the slide show in every town and village and city in Australia"
    - There has been progress: Gore contributed to the change through his environment
- "The cities supporting Kyoto in the US are up to 780"
- Returning to religious rhetoric, passion, urgency

- Evidence; He does not begin his presentation about how far we have come since 2006, when the documentary film *An Inconvenient Film* was released. Instead, he begins by quoting Karen Armstrong (I believe she is someone prominent in religious studies) who said "religion really properly understood is not about belief, but about behavior."
- In arguing this, he essentially says that what we lack with our response to climate change is a change in behavior
    - "But, as important as it is to change the light bulbs, it is more important to change the laws. And when we change our behavior in our daily lives, we sometimes leave out the citizenship part and the democracy part."

Once more considering multiple sources, here Wan Jin demonstrates careful *source evaluation*, a process that will in turn help him write a stronger argument. For more on evaluating sources, see Chapter 5.

As shown by Wan Jin's paper, a working draft should have a strong and well-developed thesis. This will drive the entire argument. Then, you can begin to work through the sections of an outline, providing specific evidence and secondary source support in what in Chapter 5 we called "a conversation with your sources." As you continue, fill in parts of your draft and rely on your peers for support and feedback.

REVISING YOUR DRAFT

6.6 What strategies can I use to revise my draft?

As many professional writers can attest—and Wan Jin would agree with this based on his drafting experience—a text goes through numerous drafts on its way to becoming a polished final product. Even filmmakers produce multiple drafts of their movies before they release their film, experimenting with different sequencing, camera shots, and pacing to create what they consider to be the fulfillment of their artistic vision. We've all seen the results of this process: deleted scenes or *outtakes* from popular films or television programs. What these segments represent are moments of work (writing, producing, and shooting) that, after review and editing, were removed to streamline the film.

As you might imagine, often it's difficult or even painful to reshape your work during revision; it's hard to leave some of your writing behind on the cutting room floor. However, as your project develops, its focus may change: sources or ideas that seemed important to you during the early stages of research may become less relevant, even tangential; a promising strategy of argumentation may turn out to be less suitable to your project; a key transition may be no longer necessary once you reorganize the argument. As you turn to your draft with a critical eye, what you should find is that in order to transform your paper into the best possible written product, you'll need to move beyond proofreading or editing and into the realm of macro changes, or **revision**.

Troubleshooting

Proofreading remains a critical part of the revision process. Careless grammatical and punctuation errors and spelling mistakes can damage your *ethos* as an author, and they need to be corrected. It is very probable that you've been doing such *micro-revision* throughout the drafting process—editing for style, grammar, punctuation, and spelling. However, sometimes it's difficult to do *broader revisions* until you have a substantial part of your paper written. It is only once your argument starts coming together that you can recognize the most productive ways to modify it in order to optimize its effectiveness. This is the key to successful revision: you have to be open to *both* microediting and large-scale, multiple revisions. Think of this process as **re-vision**, or seeing it again with new eyes, seeing it in a new light.

Let's look at decisions some students made during the revision process:

- **Content Overload.** Reading over her draft about the propagandistic elements in World War II films, Jennifer realized that she had gotten so caught up in presenting background information that her paper read more like a historical report than an argument.

  Revision: Jennifer sharpened her focus, cut down on some of the background information, and brought her own argument to the forefront.

- **Lack of Reliance on Sources.** Miranda had the opposite problem; in her draft she made a compelling argument about the literary status of graphic novels but did not really quote from or mention any of her sources, so she wasn't showcasing her work as a researcher.

Revision: She more prominently integrated her source material into her argument, both by referring to specific authors and articles she had read and by using additional direct quotations. In doing so, she greatly increased her *ethos* and the persuasiveness of her argument.

- **Overly-Broad Thesis.** After drafting her paper on hip-hop and gender identity, Sharita realized that her thesis was too broad and that in trying to cover both male and female imagery, she wasn't able to be specific enough to craft a really persuasive argument.

  Revision: Realizing that her interest really lay in exploring the conflicted stereotype of powerful, sexualized women in hip-hop videos, Sharita cut large sections of her paper revolving around the male imagery. The result was a provocative argument based on concrete, persuasive examples.

- **Overreliance on Design.** Max, a dedicated Mac user, wrote his draft on the aesthetics of design in the Apple product line. The first

AT A GLANCE

Revision Strategies

1. ***Read your essay out loud or have someone read it to you.*** You can hear mistakes and inconsistencies that you unknowingly skipped over when reading silently.
2. ***Gain critical distance.*** Put your essay away for a few hours, or even a few days, and then come back to it fresh.
3. ***Answer peer review questions for your essay.***
4. ***Don't be chained to your computer.*** Print out your draft, making revisions by hand. We conceptualize information differently on paper versus on a screen.
5. ***Look at your writing in different ways.*** Take a paragraph and divide it into distinct sentences, which you line up one under another. Look for patterns (for instance, is the repetition deliberate or accidental?), style issues (is sentence structure varied?), and fluidity of transitions between sentences.
6. ***Take into account feedback even if initially it doesn't seem significant.*** You might not decide to act on the advice, but at least consider it before dismissing it.
7. ***Revise out of order.*** Choose paragraphs at random and look at them individually, or begin at the end. Sometimes our conclusions are the weakest simply because we always get to them last, when we're tired; start revision by looking at your conclusion first.
8. ***Look at revision as a whole.*** As you correct mistakes or prose problems, consider the impact that the revision makes on the rest of the essay. Sometimes it is possible just to add a missing comma or substitute a more precise verb, but often you need to revise more than just the isolated problem so that the sentence, paragraph, or essay as a whole continues to "fit" and flow together.

version of his paper was visually stunning, detailed, and eloquently written. But it was so one-sided that it read more like a marketing brochure than an academic argument.

Revision: His task in revision was to provide a more balanced perspective on the Apple computer phenomenon. After further research, he incorporated a greater diversity of perspectives in his paper and softened some of his language to be less biased in favor of Apple products.

As these examples indicate, you need to enter into the research process looking not just for mistakes to "fix" but also for larger issues that might relate to your structure, your thesis, your scope, or the development of your ideas.

Collaboration Through Peer Feedback

In addition to your own assessment of your writing, you should take into account **peer evaluations** of your drafts; you might consider your peer feedback sessions to be "advance screenings" with your audience. In the film industry, such test screenings are standard practice, and through this process the audience becomes a collaborator with the director, producer, screenwriters, film editors, and actors in determining the final form of a film. Many films have been altered after audience feedback during test screenings, from their titles (*Licence to Kill*) to their narrative structures (*Blade Runner*), length (*Titanic*), and, most typically, their endings (*Pretty Woman, Fatal Attraction, 28 Days Later, Australia*). In each case, test audience feedback shaped the final edit and made evident the rhetorical relationship between audience, writer and text. Similarly, writing needs to take into consideration the audience's expectations; we write to show our audience our thoughts, our research, and our claim, so we need to respond to audience needs when we write and revise our texts.

Peer feedback sessions provide you with an opportunity for a test screen of your argument. While a casual conversation about your draft with a peer can provide useful insights, taking a more structured approach can provide you with a stronger foundation for revision. To facilitate a productive peer review session,

- Write a cover memo that points your readers to specific questions you have about your draft. Your peer reviewers can customize their responses to address the particular issues that concern you as a writer.
- Write down peer feedback; don't rely exclusively on oral comments. You can take notes during your peer review session, or each of your

partners could bring written comments to the meeting. This will give you more tangible feedback to work with as you revise.

- Model good peer review behavior for your partners in how you work with their drafts: come prepared to the session, having read their essays and prepared written comments; praise the strengths of their work; offer constructive feedback in an even tone, pointing to specific points in the draft that need revision; balance attention to micro editing (stylistics, punctuation, grammar, usage) with discussion of higher order thinking (argument, structure, use of evidence).
- Listen to the feedback you receive. Don't become defensive about your writing. Take the suggestions in the spirit of collaboration, and ask questions to be sure that you understand your readers' comments.

Sometimes you'll find that your peer reviewers vocalize ideas that echo your own concerns about your draft; other times you may be surprised by their reactions. Keep in mind that their comments are informed *suggestions*, not mandates; your task, as the writer, is to assess the feedback you receive and implement those changes that seem to best address the needs of both your argument and your audience as you move forward with your revision process.

AT A GLANCE

Questions for Peer Review on the Draft

- ***Argument consistency:*** Do the introduction and conclusion argue the same points, or has the argument shifted by the end?
- ***Organization and progression:*** Does the paper flow logically, developing one idea seamlessly into the next? Does the author provide important theoretical foundations, definitions, or background at the beginning of the paper to guide the audience through the rest of the argument?
- ***The author's voice in relation to the sources:*** Does the essay foreground the author's argument, or does it focus primarily on the sources' arguments, locating the author's point of view primarily in the conclusion?
- ***Information:*** Are there any holes in the research? Does the author need to supplement his or her evidence with additional research, interviews, surveys, or other source materials?
- ***Opposition and concession:*** Does the author adequately address counterarguments? Does he or she integrate opposing perspectives into the argument (i.e., deal with them as they arise), or does he or she address them in a single paragraph?

ANALYZING A STUDENT'S REVISION OF A RESEARCH-BASED ESSAY

Let's return now to Wan Jin's draft paper and see how he used his own self-assessment and peer review suggestions to revise his paper and strengthen his argument.

Wan Jin's revised title actually conveys part of his argument—he has traded the general claim "Illuminates" to offer several new terms: soft, passionate, and dynamic rhetoric.

His introduction has a new sense of urgency, shown in short and long sentence variety, strong diction, and sign-posting (the two-part rhetoric).

Moreover, Wan Jin spends a great deal of time advancing a more developed thesis, naming Gore as lonely leader with soft rhetoric and then as passionate leader with dynamic rhetoric. With this thesis, the paper will offer a more forceful argument.

Most importantly, Wan Jin ends the opening with a "So What?" significance statement.

Park 1

Wan Jin Park

Research-Based Argument–Final

March 15, 2010

Balancing the Soft and the Passionate Rhetorician: Gore's Dynamic Rhetoric in His Environmental Leadership

At the forefront of the global environmental movement is one man with the power to blur national boundaries, urge political leaders to adopt reforms, and motivate hundreds of thousands. That man is Al Gore. Gore has been a pivotal leader, attracting unprecedented levels of support for the once overlooked issue, especially through Davis Guggenheim's *An Inconvenient Truth*. The success of the documentary can be attributed to Gore's two-part rhetoric. He first induces fear and guilt in us, the audience, making us more receptive to his message. He then portrays himself as a warm, dedicated, but lonely leader, thereby arousing our desire to join him in social action. Despite the success of his soft rhetoric, Gore sets it aside two years later at the TED2008 Conference and adopts a heightened sense of passion and urgency. The shift in rhetoric mirrors a change in Gore's agenda, and it is this dynamic rhetoric that Gore molds to fit specific goals that defines the success of his leadership. An understanding of Gore's rhetoric offers us invaluable insight on how to use dynamic rhetoric to bring overlooked social issues into the light.

Park 2

Before showing us a change in his rhetoric, Gore uses soft rhetoric in *An Inconvenient Truth.* Soft rhetoric, a newly coined term, refers to a rhetorical tool that draws in a guarded audience, not through impassioned words, but through the appeal to the audience's sense of guilt and the establishment of a warm and inviting *ethos*. Because the public was still guarded toward the issue of climate change before the release of the documentary, Gore shies away from passionate speech that are meant to inspire, and instead focuses on convincing his audience to join him through soft rhetoric.

He introduces his own term—one he made up. Wan Jin did not want to use "I" so he speaks in third person, but he clearly establishes his own argument in this revision.

His microedits to style and descriptive language make his writing even more vivid and memorable.

Contrasting Images: the Beautiful and the Doomed

Gore begins his soft rhetoric by inducing fear and guilt in us, the audience, through the juxtaposition of beauty and doom. He first offers us a beautiful depiction of nature. The camera focuses close-up on a branch full of green tree leaves. Bright sunlight reflects off of the leaf blades, accentuating the green hue. After a few seconds, the camera turns to the right to reveal a glistening river. The river is a mix of green and blue, both defining colors of nature. The soft piano music in the background adds to the calm and peaceful mood. Gore then narrates in the background, purposely emphasizing the sibilants as if to imitate the sounds of the river and the rustling leaves:

In the revision, Wan Jin begins with a topic sentence that conveys his argument, rather than just launching into the rhetorical analysis of the film's details.

> You look at that river gently flowing by. You notice the leaves rustling with the wind. You hear the birds. You

Since Wan Jin quotes more than four lines in this passage, he formats the citation as a **block quote**.

He has also incorporated more research, so he is not over-relying on only one source.

Here, Wan Jin cites the article analyzed earlier in this chapter. He picks a strong quotation, sets it up by building the *ethos* of the source, and then, most importantly, comments on it in the next paragraph, emphasizing "frightening" and the building on Schulte's reading to develop his point about guilt.

> hear the tree frogs. In the distance, you hear a cow. You feel the grass. The mud gives a little bit on the riverbank. It's quiet; it's peaceful. (*An Inconvenient Truth*)

The sequence of images and narration encapsulates the beauty of nature so well that Professors Thomas Rosteck and Thomas Frentz write in "Myth and Multiple Readings in Environmental Rhetoric: The Case of *An Inconvenient Truth*" that "we experience, visually and through Gore's voiceover, the awe, sublime beauty, and wonder of Earth" (5).

Gore suddenly interrupts the experience and interjects that we have forgotten about nature in spite of its beauty: "all of a sudden, it's a gearshift inside you and it's like taking a deep breath and going 'Oh yeah, I forgot about this'" (*An Inconvenient Truth*). Through the use of the word "gearshift," Gore metaphorically compares us, the audience, to machines that are equipped with a gear; in essence, he argues that we have become so addicted to the industrial age that we have transformed into its products, becoming separate from and oblivious to our nature.

* * *

The images arouse such horror that Bret Schulte, Assistant Professor of Journalism at University of Arkansas, writes that Gore shows us "the frightening future promised by global warming—an apocalyptic world of deadly hurricanes, rising oceans, disease, drought, and famine" (Schulte).

Park 4

By deliberately introducing the "frightening" images only after his "gearshift" metaphor, Gore compels us to feel not only frightened, but also responsible and guilty for the damages done to nature (Schulte; *An Inconvenient Truth*). The arousal of guilt is crucial in shaping *An Inconvenient*

Truth into an effective environmental medium, as it "sets up the rhetorical tension with which Gore will leverage his message" (Rosteck and Frentz). Kathryn Olson, the author of "Rhetorical Leadership And Transferable Lessons For Successful Social Advocacy In *An Inconvenient Truth*," agrees and elaborates on what Gore's message is: "he asks [us]...to share the guilt of insufficient action with him and to redeem [our] selves...now that [we] grasp the gravity...of climate change" (11). The arousal of guilt, the first part of Gore's soft rhetoric, thus draws in a once guarded and reluctant public into the environmental movement.

Dedication Molded by Frustration and Failure

After rendering us more receptive through the appeal to our sense of fear and guilt, Gore portrays himself as a warm, vulnerable, and dedicated leader. Rosteck and Frentz also explore the second part of Gore's soft rhetoric and argue that Gore establishes such *ethos* through "personal images of frustration and failure" that are interspersed throughout the documentary (9). In fact, Gore expresses his frustration right from the beginning of *An Inconvenient Truth*, confessing that

Notice here, he offers a strong conversation with many of his sources: Rosteck and Frentz, Olson, and looking back to Schulte.

Most powerfully, he ends with his own point, making sure the spotlight is on his argument.

The revised subheads show his advanced thinking and reflect the suggestions of his classmates from peer review.

Park 5

"I've been trying to tell this story for a long time, and I feel as if I've failed to get the message across" (*An Inconvenient Truth*). We then meet a naively optimistic Gore who fails to change the world through the first Congressional hearings on global warming; he almost loses his son to a car accident; he loses the presidential election in 2000; and his family, a group of tobacco farmers, loses Gore's sister, Nancy, to lung cancer (*An Inconvenient Truth*).

He has fleshed out the points from his working draft and outline. He strategically cites the words from his research sources (Rosteck and Frentz) to show how he views the text through the lens of those sources.

What these stories of failure and pain have in common are that they "strengthen[ed]" Gore's "resolve" and dedication to the environmental movement (Rosteck and Frentz 7). His son's near-death-accident taught him how anything taken for granted, even our beautiful environment, can easily vanish. His sister's death taught him the importance of connecting the dots, of connecting our actions to future consequences. His presidential election "brought into clear focus the mission that [he] had been pursuing all these years," convincing him to "[start] giving the slideshow again" (*An Inconvenient Truth*).

Here, Wan Jin demonstrates **writing as synthesis**, in that he puts the many sources in conversation with one another and adds his own voice to that dialogue.

Because these stories "persuasively [document] Gore's single-mindedness in pursuing his public cause, often at his own expense, through a lifetime of disappointments," Olson also agrees with Rosteck and Frentz that the stories of personal failure and frustration are essential to Gore's portrayal as a human, vulnerable, but dedicated leader (Olson 99). This portrayal places us "in a position to hear demand for action in

Park 6

a more sympathetic light," and when coupled with our sense of guilt, it renders Gore's message irresistible (Rosteck and Frentz 10). And Gore's message is clear. He "shows his evolution from interested observer to committed activist" with the goal of "invit[ing] our own journey of transformation" through the environmental movement (5).

Rosteck, Frentz, and Olson's arguments have merit. Gore's transformation into a dedicated leader as a result of his frustrations and failures does create an "inviting impression that encourages [us] to join him ... in social action" (Olson 102). However, they leave unexplored a crucial aspect of Gore's rhetoric. What is more responsible for creating the warm and inviting *ethos* is the portrayal of Gore as a lonely leader.

* * *

No Longer the Soft Leader

Despite the success of his soft rhetoric as a lonely leader in *An Inconvenient Truth,* Gore sets it aside and instead adopts a heightened level of passion and sense of urgency two years later in his follow-up presentation at the TED 2008 Conference. The change reflects a shift in Gore's primary agenda. Gore's primary goal is no longer attracting support for the environmental movement, as he already achieved that goal. Gore even acknowledges in his TED presentation the extent of his success. He claims that "68 percent of Americans now

At this point, Wan Jin will credit the research that has come before him and then build upon it.

Through effective synthesis, he acknowledges the opposing positions before him, but then adds to them, as if adding another brick on a foundation. His original contribution as a writer is to focus on the concept of *ethos*.

After a significant amount of evidence (excerpted), Wan Jin moves to the next point in his argument. His heading refers to terms in his title, using diction to offer coherence and force in the writing.

He sets up the argument about Gore's 2008 TED talk through citing Gore's own words and leading the reader through the *logos* from his rough draft.

Park 7

believe that human activity is responsible for global warming, [and] 69 percent believe that the Earth is heating up in a significant way" (Gore 9.21). Furthermore...

* * *

In this revision, Wan Jin took the suggestion of his peers: he analyzes not only the images and words, but also the embodied rhetoric or body language of Gore's persona.

Even his body language is imbued with the increased level of passion. As he delivers the line, "we need a worldwide, global mobilization for renewable energy, conservation, efficiency, and a global transition to a low carbon economy," he not only stresses each word, but also moves his hands up and down as he speaks, visually emphasizing each word (Gore, 4.39). He also twists his upper body from left to right, with his arms extended, as he says, "the political will has to be mobilized," visually enacting the word "mobilized" (Gore, 4.57).

Introducing new concepts such as "honor" and "heroism," Wan Jin increases the power of his words and the significance of his argument. He chooses then to use a direct quote as evidence.

The heightened passion in Gore's rhetoric becomes fully manifested near the end of the presentation when Gore appeals to honor and heroism, both qualities we have treasured throughout history, as he stresses the need for a hero generation:

> What we need is another hero generation. We have to... understand that history has presented us with a choice. And we have to find a way to create, in the generation of those alive today, a sense of generational mission. (Gore, 17.39)

Gore then alludes to the "hero generation that brought democracy to the planet...another that ended slavery...and that gave women the right to vote" in order to illustrate the level of passion and dedication that we need to emulate as we

Park 8

fight the climate crisis (Gore, 18.44). The climate crisis is no longer just a global issue, but is now the "opportunity to rise to a challenge that is worthy of our best efforts" (Gore, 20.12). In his last efforts to move the audience toward increased sense of urgency and initiative, Gore closes with the line:

> We are the generation about which, a thousand years from now, philharmonic orchestras and poets and singers will celebrate by saying, they were the ones that found it within themselves to solve this crisis and lay the basis for a bright and optimistic human future. (Gore, 20.47)

The appeal to *pathos,* the appeal to honor, heroism, and love for our children and the ensuing desire to promise them a better future illustrates how Gore sets aside his soft rhetoric and transforms into an impassioned leader, urging his audience to become heroes of our generation.

He carefully chooses his lines and concludes with a strong interpretation of their meaning.

Seesaw: Balancing the Soft and the Passionate Rhetorician

Gore adopts different styles of rhetoric in *An Inconvenient Truth* and in his follow-up presentation for the TED2008 Conference. Gore uses a two-part soft rhetoric in *An Inconvenient Truth* in order to draw in a guarded audience. He first compels us to feel fear and guilt through the juxtaposition of images of the beautiful and the doomed, making us more receptive to his environmental message. He then builds his *ethos* as a warm, dedicated, but still lonely leader, creating the inviting impression that draws us in and encourages us to join him in

Park 9

social action. When Gore delivers his TED presentation, his primary goal changes to motivating increased initiative and political will; he thus sets aside his soft rhetoric and adopts a heightened level of passion and sense of urgency.

Moving to his conclusion, Wan Jin explains the final term in his paper: dynamic rhetoric.

He also brings in contemporary events, appealing to *kairos* to make the reader receptive to his argument.

The impassioned tone in Wan Jin's own writing suggests that he is moving toward the end of his paper, and indeed he closes with a compelling call to action.

This dynamic rhetoric, which Gore molds to fit his specific agenda, is the key to Gore's successful environmental leadership. He can be the warm, authentic, and soft leader when he wants to disarm a guarded audience. He can be the energized leader when he needs to inspire increased initiative in those that look up to him. In light of the recent sufferings caused by earthquakes in Haiti and Chile, the understanding of Gore's rhetoric offers us invaluable insight. In order to bring the countless pertinent but overlooked issues into the light à la Gore, we need to learn how to mold our rhetoric and master the art of balancing the soft and the passionate rhetorician in us.

Park 10

Works Cited

The Works Cited, on a separate page, provides proper MLA citation for all the research Wan Jin quoted, paraphrased, or summarized in the paper.

An Inconvenient Truth. Dir. Davis Guggenheim. Perf. Al Gore. Paramount Classics, 2006. DVD.

Gore, Al. "Al Gore's New Thinking on the Climate Crisis." Lecture. *TED: Ideas Worth Spreading*. TED.com, Apr. 2008. Web. 15 Jan. 2010. http://www.ted.com/talks/lang/eng/al_gore.html.

Park 10

__________. "Al Gore on Averting Climate Crisis." Lecture. *TED: Ideas Worth Spreading*. TED.com, Feb. 2006. Web. 20 Jan. 2010. http://www.ted.com/talks/lang/eng/al_gore.html.

Nielsen Company. *Global Consumers Vote Al Gore, Oprah Winfreyand Kofi Annan Most Influential to Champion Global Warming Cause: Nielsen Survey. Nielsen: Trends & Insights*. 2 July 2007. Web. 18 Jan. 2010. http://nz.nielsen.com.

Olson, Kathryn M. "Rhetorical Leadership and Transferable Lessons for Successful Social Advocacy in Al Gore's An Inconvenient Truth." *Argumentation & Advocacy* 44.2 (2007): 90–109. *Communication & Mass Media Complete*. EBSCO. Web. 24 Feb. 2010.

Rosteck, Thomas, and Thomas S. Frentz. "Myth and Multiple Readings in Environmental Rhetoric: The Case of An Inconvenient Truth." *Quarterly Journal of Speech* 95.1 (2009): 1–19. *Communication & Mass Media Complete*. EBSCO. Web. 24 Feb. 2010.

Schulte, Bret. "Saying It In Cinema." *U.S. News*. 28 Mar. 2006. Web. 17 Jan. 2010. http://www.usnews.com/usnews/news/5warming.b.htm.

MLA suggests that writers include URLs in their Works Cited only when absolutely necessary to find the original source, but this student's professor required that they be included as part of the assignment.

Wan Jin shows a well balanced "iceberg of research"—including scholarly journals, popular articles, videos, and surveys.

He might also have included field research in the form of interviews with professors or surveys with students who had watched any of Gore's presentations.

The strong ending of Wan Jin's paper shows how careful revision can help you develop a compelling argument and use the last lines to leave your reader with your own memorable rhetoric. Consider, too, how the ending of Wan Jin's essay expanded to encompass a broader frame and then addressed the reader directly, using "you." Finally, you might notice that his revised essay analyzed rhetoric in all the ways we have learned to understand it through the chapters in this book: that is, rhetoric as texts that are spoken, written, visual, multimedia, as well as embodied. As you turn to craft your own research-based argument, keep in mind the many approaches to rhetoric explored here, and offer your own original insights by building on the work of writers and scholars who have come before you.

WRITER'S PRACTICE

To assess the writing you have done on your research-based argument, exchange your essay with a peer in class. Then, create annotations using the Comment Feature of your word-processing program and indicate what strategies are at work in each section of the essay. You might compare the draft to the final revision in those comments.

Alternatively, you could comment on your own essay, adding marginal notes about what improvements you made from the draft to the final revision. Then, you can summarize your revisions in a concluding reflective paragraph. That will inform both you and your instructor about your progress as a writer, researcher, and rhetorician.

THE WRITER'S PROCESS

In this chapter, you have learned strategies for visual mapping, organizing, outlining, drafting, and revising your research paper. You have explored ways of casting your argument and acquired concrete methods for integrating both written sources and visual texts as evidence for your argument. Chances are you have written the first full draft of your paper. But don't forget revision. Revision shows us the way that all *writing is rewriting*.

Sometimes, when writing, we may continue to revise our papers even after we have "finished." While you may be satisfied with your final research product when you turn it in, it is possible that you have set the groundwork for a longer research project that you may return to later in your college career. Or you may decide to seek publication for your essay in a school newspaper, magazine, or a national journal. In such cases, you may need to modify or expand on your argument for this new rhetorical situation; you may produce your own "director's cut"—a paper identical in topic to the original but developed in a significantly different fashion. Keep in mind that revision is indeed "re-vision."

WRITING ASSIGNMENTS

1. **Written Analysis of a Film Trailer.** Put your strategies of rhetorical analysis into practice and analyze a film trailer. Use the pre-writing checklist below to help guide your analysis.

   - ❑ Assess the genre of the film (comedy? horror? drama? documentary?) and how this affects the audience's response to its content. Does the trailer combine elements of different genres? What is the rhetorical effect of this combination?
   - ❑ What is the "plot" of the trailer? What is the organizational structure?
   - ❑ Is this plot arranged chronologically? In parallel sequences? Thematically? What is the rhetorical significance of arrangement?
   - ❑ What is the message conveyed to its audience? What argument is it making about the longer film?
   - ❑ What notable types of shots does the filmmaker use in the trailer? Jot down one or two instances where cinematic techniques (zoom-in, cuts between scenes, fade in/fade out, montage) are used for rhetorical effect.
   - ❑ Is there a narrator? Voice-over? What is the effect on the audience?
   - ❑ Is there any framing—a way of setting the beginning and end in context?
   - ❑ How is time handled? Does the trailer move in chronological order? Reverse chronological order? What is the significance of such rhetorical choices on the meaning and power of the trailer? Does it use flashbacks? If so, what effect is achieved through the use of flashbacks?
   - ❑ How are *pathos*, *ethos*, and *logos* produced by the different cinematic techniques? For instance, is *pathos* created through close-ups of characters? Is *ethos* created through allusions to famous films or filmmaking techniques? Is *logos* constructed through the insertion of a narrator's viewpoint?

- ❑ What is the audience's point of identification in the trailer? Is the audience supposed to identify with a single narrator or protagonist? Does the film negotiate or manipulate the audience's reaction in any specific ways? How?
- ❑ How is setting used to construct a specific mood that affects the impact of the message of the trailer?

2. **Visual Map or Outline:** Create a visual representation of your research argument: a bubble map, flowchart, hierarchical set of bubbles, or handmade construction paper model. Write an annotation for each part of your drawing, model, or storyboard to help you move from mass of material to coherent research-based essay.

3. **Detailed Written Outline:** Working with your research materials and notes, create a written outline of your ideas, using numbers and letters to indicate subsections of your argument. Rather than simply calling the second section "II. Body," create several points within the body to show the development of your argument. You may want to start with a topic outline, but ideally you should aim for argumentative subheadings. Include your working thesis statement at an appropriate place in your outline, and include visuals that you will analyze in the essay itself. After you draft the outline, go back and insert your primary and secondary sources in the outline. Insert actual quotations (with page numbers) from your research where possible, and don't forget to cite your sources for both paraphrase and summary. This outline might easily turn into the paper itself. Use it to check the balance of sources, the progression of ideas, and the complexity of your argument.

4. **Research-Based Argument:** Write a 12- to 15-page argumentative research paper on a topic of your choice. If you wish to analyze and research visual rhetoric, consider the images that shape a debate, tell a certain history, or persuade an audience in a certain way. In other words, address an issue through a visual rhetoric lens. You should integrate research materials that can include articles, books, interviews, field research, surveys (either published or that you conduct yourself), TV programs, Internet texts, and other primary and secondary sources, including visuals. Keep in mind that, because this is a research paper, you need to balance primary and secondary materials. Ultimately, your goal should be proving a thesis statement with apt evidence, using appropriate rhetorical and argumentative strategies.

4. **Reflection Essay:** After you have completed your essay, compose a one-page reflection letter that serves as a self-evaluation. Think back on the development of your argument through research and revision. Include comments on the strengths of the essay, the types of revisions you made throughout your writing process, and how the collaborative process of peer review improved your essay. Conclude by explaining how you might continue to write about this issue in future academic or professional situations.

CHAPTER 7

Avoiding Plagiarism and Documenting Sources

Chapter Preview Questions

7.1 What do the terms "intellectual property" and "plagiarism" mean?
7.2 What are the conventions of documentation style?
7.3 How do I produce a Works Cited list in MLA style?

"Creativity always builds on the past." For many writers, the debt to those who have written before them is carefully acknowledged—whether through direct references, parenthetical citations, or a list of sources. Even visual artists and multimedia writers *name their sources explicitly* to show that they belong to a larger community of writers and that they respect the work of others.

FIGURE 7.1 Justin Cone's film, *Building on the Past*, remixes visuals and sound to emphasize how all our ideas rely on the works of those before us.

But Justin Cone, a designer and animator based in Austin, Texas, makes this point more emphatically through the multimedia montage shown in Figure 7.1, from a short film called *Building on the Past*, which recycles and modifies public-domain film footage to make an argument about the relationship between creativity and legislation. The visuals are accompanied by a musical score and a voice-over that repeats the same sentence intermittently throughout the film: "Creativity always builds on the past." In the scene shown here, which opens the film, Cone re-edits the public-domain footage to run in reverse, showing the children running backward uphill instead of forward downhill, offering a powerful argument about how we rely on others for our own creativity. Cone expresses that idea visually, through his strategy of organization, word choice, and design.

Your research project, too, will undoubtedly draw its strength from previous work on the subject. It should be a merger of your argument and the already existing dialogue on the topic. So even as you "re-edit it" to suit the purpose of your paper—by selecting passages to quote, paraphrase, summarize, or even argue against—it is crucial that you let your readers know *where* the ideas originated by providing what we call complete and ethical **source attribution**, or the acknowledgment and identification of your sources.

In this chapter, you'll learn how the rhetorical art of *imitation*—the process by which we all learn to write, compose, speak, and produce texts—differs from the theft of others' ideas, which is called **plagiarism**. We'll discuss why it is important to respect the work of others—which in legal terms is now called *intellectual property*—and you'll acquire strategies for avoiding *unintentional plagiarism*. Finally, we'll provide a means of understanding the process of constructing in-text and end-of-paper citations, and we'll explain the logic of MLA, APA, CSE, and Chicago documentation styles. You'll discover that there is actually logic governing the arrangement of elements in documentation practices, much as there is logic shaping mathematical or chemical formulas, and that the specific order of a style addresses the values of a particular audience. Moreover, you'll find that correct *source attribution* actually builds your *ethos* as a writer and researcher by confirming your membership in that scholarly community.

7.1 What do the terms "intellectual property" and "plagiarism" mean?

UNDERSTANDING INTELLECTUAL PROPERTY AND PLAGIARISM

In ancient times, **rhetorical imitation**, or the practice of taking after others, was a celebrated form of instruction. Students would copy a celebrated speech out word by word, studying the word choice, organization, rhythm, and art of the work. That is, students would compose a rhetorical analysis (as you have done in earlier chapters) to understand the speech's strategies of argumentation, use of rhetorical appeals, and organization. Finally, students would rearrange and re-use elements of the speeches they studied, including content (words) and form (arrangement), to create their own speeches. Through this process of imitation and re-editing, the earliest students learned to become great rhetors.

This ancient process is actually very similar to your task as a modern writer. After analyzing articles and studying argumentative strategies from samples of student writing, at some point you need to move on to create your own text, inspired by what you learned and perhaps re-editing parts, since "creativity builds on the past." But importantly, today, we don't just borrow and recycle the ideas of others without acknowledgement. We need to be aware that ideas, not just actual words but also the concepts developed by others, must be considered in terms of **intellectual property**, that is, words and ideas often legally belong to someone else as a form of property. In this increasingly litigious society, you need to understand when to stop imitation and when to start acknowledging your sources so that you preserve the rights of others and protect yourself as an developing writer.

Plagiarism—using another person's idea as your own—was not a crime in classical times, according to scholars Peter Morgan and Glenn Reynolds. But with the invention of printing technology, copyright law, and a cultural emphasis on the profitability of intellectual concepts came a concern about taking someone else's ideas—and therefore their *earning potential*—whether intentionally or unintentionally. Consequently, in colleges and universities today, plagiarism can lead to suspension or even expulsion because the perpetrator is charged with literally stealing the *intellectual property* of someone else. In professional circles, charges of plagiarism can ruin a career and destroy the credibility of the writer.

But there is another reason for acknowledging sources and avoiding plagiarism: keeping in mind the principle discussed in Chapter 5—that research is always a conversation with those who came before. This reason is an ethical, not legal one. As you work with sources, realize that the claims you are able to make are in fact based on the foundation provided by others. Identifying your sources thus becomes an ethical writing strategy that you practice out of respect for those who have come before you. By acknowledging their names, ideas, and words, you contribute to a body of knowledge, graciously extending thanks to those who have paved the way. Therefore, while there are legal issues related to intellectual property, copyright law, and "fair use" that you need to know about, if you keep the *respect principle* in mind, you will rarely fall into the trap of inadvertently "stealing" someone's work.

AT A GLANCE

Avoiding Unintentional Plagiarism

Remember that you must document your sources when you:

- Quote a source word for word
- Summarize or paraphrase information or ideas from another source in your own words
- Incorporate statistics, tables, figures, charts, graphs, or other visuals into your work from another source

You do not need to document the following:

- Your own observations, ideas, and opinions
- Factual information that is widely available in a number of sources ("common knowledge")
- Proverbs, sayings, or familiar quotations

Avoiding Unintentional Plagiarism

As we have discussed, plagiarism—or using someone else's ideas without acknowledgment in their original or even altered form—is a serious offense, even if it occurs unintentionally. Indeed plagiarism can happen for many reasons: fatigue, oversaturation of information, poor memory, or sloppy note taking. Regardless of the circumstances, many colleges and universities have plagiarism policies that do not distinguish between intentional and unintentional plagiarism; the act will bring consequences ranging from a failure in the course to expulsion.

Working with Images and Multimedia as Sources

When you choose to include visuals or multimedia in your writing, keep in mind that it is not enough to include just the source and provide the citation for it. You also need to spend a few moments thinking about issues of **copyright** and **permissions**. Since oral culture gave way to print culture, copyright—or the *right* to *copy*—has been a pressing legal issue. However, with the advent of digital technologies, the problem has been exacerbated; with the prevalence of photo scanners, digital copy and paste tools, seemingly omniscient search engines, and the ever-expanding reach of the Internet, the possibilities for copying, sharing, and distributing materials are in more people's reach than ever before. As a writer yourself, it is important that you respect copyright restrictions and ethically attribute all your sources that you use in your own writing—including visual texts.

When you browse through catalogs of images, you need to record the source of each image you decide to use. If you have copied an image from the Internet, you need to note as much of the full source information as you can find: the website author, the title, the sponsoring organization, and the date. If you have found a visual (photograph, chart, ad) from a print source and scanned it into a computer, you need to list the print source in full as well as information about the original image (the name of the photographer, the image title, and the date). Listing Google as your source is not sufficient; be sure to find the original source and list it in full. Keep careful track as you locate images, give appropriate credit when you use them in your essay, and ask for permission if necessary by writing the owner of the image.

UNDERSTANDING DOCUMENTATION STYLE

7.2 What are the conventions of documentation style?

So far in this chapter, we've emphasized the importance of *source attribution* as a means of avoiding plagiarism. But it might interest you to know that the method you use to provide information about your source

DOCUMENTATION STYLE	COMMUNITY OF WRITERS	DEFINING FEATURES	PURPOSE OF FEATURES	EXAMPLE
MLA	Modern Language Association (language, literature, writing, philosophy, and humanities scholars and teachers)	Citation begins with author's name (last name first, full first name), then publication information, date, medium of publication (then, if a website, date you accessed it).	Knowledge advances based on individual author's contributions; thus, names are prioritized over dates; place of publication matters for building *ethos*.	McCloud, Scott. *Understanding Comics*. New York: Harper Perennial, 1994. Print.
APA	American Psychological Association (psychologists and social scientists)	Publication date immediately follows designation of author, multiple authors may be listed (last name and initials), titles are in sentence style (first word capitalized, rest lowercase)	Since knowledge advances based on dated contributions to the field, dates are prioritized; most writing is collaborative, so up to six authors are listed; titles, typically long and technical, are in lowercase.	Bruce V., & Green, P. (1990). *Visual perception: Physiology, psychology, and ecology* (2nd ed.). London, England: Erlbaum.
CSE	Council of Science Editors (such as biology and physics)	References include last name and date; often superscript numbers are used	Like APA style, emphasis is on knowledge advancing through studies and scientific research; a heavily cited style of writing	[1]Goble, JL. Visual disorders in the handicapped child. New York: M. Dekker; 1984. p. 265.
Chicago	University of Chicago (business writers, professional writers, and those in fine arts)	Sources are listed as footnotes or endnotes and include page numbers	Knowledge is incremental, and readers like to check facts as they go along	[2]Scott McCloud, *Understanding Comics* (New York: Harper Perennial, 1994), 33.

corresponds to the values of a particular academic community. This is where **documentation** comes in—the responsible and correct acknowledgment of your sources and influences according to a specific *style*. Today, with software programs that can format your source attributions for you, it may seem confusing or even frustrating to worry about which documentation style to use. But realize that the guidelines for each style have a rhetorical purpose corresponding to the way that knowledge is constructed for that community (see the table on the previous page). Taking a moment to understand the logic behind the styles will help you practice proper citation without having to look up every instance of how to do it. In the process, you build your *ethos* as a writer by showing that you speak the language of a particular academic community.

In-Text Citations: Documentation as Cross-Referencing

In addition to responsible source attribution, documentation also functions as a *road map* for your audience to locate the source—both in your bibliography and in the library or online. Accordingly, for sources appearing as **in-text citations** —or quoted right in the essay itself—the purpose of proper documentation is to point readers clearly to the list of sources at the end of the paper. The way this works is through **cross-referencing**, such that the reference in the text of the essay should correspond to the first word of the source listed in the bibliography.

Let's take a look at an *in-text citation* from Michael Rothenberg's paper on the Twin Towers. MLA style always places such references inside parentheses to set them off from the rest of the writing. Notice that the last name and page number in parentheses point the reader directly to the author's name in the "Works Cited" list.

Michael has alphabetized the list by authors' last names, which corresponds to MLA style documentation and the logic of the humanities as an academic community. Readers need only scan down the page to look for the last name of the source cited earlier. This makes it very easy, and once you understand that this *cross-referencing logic* governs all MLA documentation, then you can begin to understand how to document sources—even new multimedia sources.

> ...the Twin Towers were so enormous that together they encased a staggering 11 million square feet of commercial space (Czarnecki 31).
>
> * * *
>
> Works Cited
>
> Bravman, John. Personal interview. 13 May 2003.
>
> Bruno, Lisa D. "Studio Daniel Libeskind." *Baltimore Sun*. Baltimore Sun, 6 Nov. 2002. Web. 1 June 2003.
>
> Czarnecki, John E. "Architects at the Forefront as They Show Ground Zero Aspirations." *Architectural Record*. Nov. 2002: 31–50. Print.

If there is no author to put in your parentheses, begin with the first word of the source entry on the Works Cited page. Here is an example from Tanner Gardner's paper on the globalization of the NBA, where he quotes an article from the journal *The Economist.* Many of the articles in this journal are collectively written, so no authors are named. In this case, Tanner uses the first words of the title. See how the cross-referencing logic of MLA style helps readers find the source in the Works Cited list:

> The relationship between Nike and basketball is actually reciprocal, as their promotions actually promote basketball internationally by providing publicity for the sport ("The Yao").
>
> * * *
>
> Works Cited
>
> "The Yao Crowd." *The Economist* 9 Aug. 2003: 55. Print.

Using this system, you will easily direct your readers to the correct source. But there are two additional cases that can be tricky. First, if you are citing an author and a passage that you have discovered within another source, then you need to use the cross-referencing system to indicate the source that has the passage in it. If you wanted to incorporate the quotation that Michael listed above, namely the line from Howard Decker, you would not put (Decker) as your source, since the you would have no other information to add to this name. Instead, you need to attribute its location to where you found it, namely, as part of Michael's research log. Therefore, your citation would look like this:

> "The motivations for it are complicated. Commerce. Capitalism. Ego" (Decker qtd. in Rothenberg, Research Log).

Your Works Cited entry would look as follows:

> Rothenberg, Michael. Research Log. 2003. Microsoft Word file.

The second tricky case concerns a situation in which the author you are quoting has multiple sources that will be included in the bibliography. Putting only the last name in the parentheses would not suffice since the reader would not know which source to consult. You need to list *both* the author's name and the first major keyword of the correct title. Then, in the Works Cited list, you need only state the author's last name once and use three short dashes to indicate repetition. Look at how Stephanie Parker mastered this situation. Here are two examples from her essay—which appears in full later in this chapter—where Stephanie cites from different works by Daniel Shim. Notice how the keyword following the author's last name functions as the *cross-reference* to the correct source:

Example 1: Here, since Stephanie mentioned the author in the sentence, she needs only include the keywords and the page number if there was one, but since this is an online text, there is no page number to cite.

> Daniel Shim relates his own experience: "I was born in Canada in white communities & I grew up to be like them. Soompi has given me knowledge about Asian culture that I would not get from my school or family" (Online interview).

Example 2: In this next case, Stephanie has not mentioned the author by name in the sentence, so she includes the author's last name as well as the first keyword of the source title in her MLA in-text citation. Moreover, since she is citing an article title, she includes the quotation marks; for a book title, she would italicize the keyword:

> . . . his YouTube videoblog, in which he comments on events in his daily life and makes fun of Asian stereotypes, has almost 30,000 subscribers and is the 4th most popular comedy blog in all of Canada (Shim, "Shimmycocopuffsss's . . . ").

Now let's look at the Works Cited list to locate those two sources. Note the color coding to see how the *cross-reference* system operates.

Works Cited

Shim, Daniel. Online interview. 12 November 2008.

—. "Shimmycocopuffsss's Profile Page" YouTube. 27 November 2008. Web. 28 November 2008.

—. "Wasabi Boy-No Engrish." YouTube. 5 March 2008. Web. 28 November 2008.

Using Notes for Documentation

Although MLA style relies primarily on in-text citations and a final bibliography—unlike Chicago style, which uses primarily footnotes or endnotes—there are two specific cases when you will want to include a note. First, if you want to include extra explanatory information (definitions of key terms, background material, alternative perspectives, or historical data) but don't want to break the flow of your argument, you can provide that information for the reader either in an **endnote**, which appears at the end of your paper, before the bibliography, or as a **footnote**, which appears at the bottom or *foot* of the page.

7.3 How do I produce a Works Cited list in MLA style?

PRODUCING A WORKS CITED LIST IN MLA STYLE

You've seen how documentation works as a *cross-referencing system*, in which the in-text citation within parentheses points the reader directly to the source in the bibliography. In MLA style, the bibliography is called a **Works Cited** list because it refers explicitly to the works (or sources) you have cited (or quoted) in your paper. Sometimes a Works Cited list is accompanied by another section called a **Works Consulted** list, which names all the other sources you may have read and studied but did not actually quote from in your final revision. You can also combine the two by creating a **Works Cited** and **Consulted List.**

Realize that this list of sources provides a moment of *ethos* building as well: by listing both works *cited* and works *consulted*, you demonstrate your research process and new knowledge. You also invite your readers to explore the topic in depth with you.

LOGIC OF MLA STYLE

AUTHOR'S NAME	TITLE	PUBLICATION INFORMATION
List the author's name first, by last name. If there are multiple authors, include them all, following the order listed in the publication. If there is no author, use the publishing organization (if available) or just move on to the title.	The title comes next. For books and films, italicize the title. For shorter pieces (such as articles, TV shows, songs, etc.), put the title in quotation marks, with the larger publication (the collection of essays, TV series, or album) italicized.	Last comes publication information: place, publisher or company, date, and medium of publication. For shorter pieces, include the complete range of page numbers, followed by a period. For online articles, list the medium of publication (Web) followed by a period and conclude with a date of access

Satrapi, Marjane. *Persepolis: The Story of a Childhood.* New York: Pantheon, 2004. Print.

Yagoda, Ben. "You Need to Read This: How Need to Vanquished Have to, Must, and Should." *Slate.* Washington Post Newsweek Interactive, 17 July 2006. Web. 20 July 2006.

Documentation for Print and Online Text-Based Sources

Below, you'll find example citations for print and online text-based sources that apply the logic of MLA style. Use them as a reference to guide your own citation practices:

- Single-Author Book
- Multiple-Author Book
- Electronic Books (e-books)
- Anthology or Edited Collection of Essays
- Introduction, Preface, Forward or Afterward in a Book
- Two or More Books by the Same Author
- Article in a Collection of Essays
- Article from a Print Journal
- Article from a Journal Published Only Online
- Article from a Popular Magazine Published Monthly (print and online)
- Article from a Newspaper (print and online)
- Article found through a Database (including Google Books)
- News Article from a Website
- Definition
- Letter to the Editor
- Newspaper Op-Ed
- Letter or Memo
- Dissertation (Unpublished)
- Government Publication
- Interview
- Survey
- Email
- Blogpost
- Facebook Post
- Tweet
- Reddit Post
- Text Message, Chat Room Discussion, or Real-time Communication

Single-Author Book

Satrapi, Marjane. *Persepolis: The Story of a Childhood*. New York: Pantheon, 2004. Print.

Multiple-Author Book

Heath, Joseph, and Andrew Potter. *Nation of Rebels: Why Counterculture Became Consumer Culture*. New York: Harper, 2004. Print.

Booth, Wayne C, Gregory G Colomb, and Joseph M Williams. *The Craft of Research*. 3rd ed. Chicago: University of Chicago Press, 2008. Print.

For an e-book, list the type of medium at the end of the citation (i.e., Nook file, Kindle file, iBooks file, Google Books file). When in doubt, use the term "Digital file" at the end instead.

Electronic Books (e-books)

Brooks, Max. *World War Z: An Oral History of the Zombie War.* N.p.: Crown Publishing Group, 2006. iBook file.

Davis, Mike. *City of Quartz.* N.p.: Verso, 2006. Nook file.

Anthology or Edited Collection of Essays

Waggoner, Zach, ed. *Terms of Play: Essays on Words That Matter in Videogame Theory*. Jefferson, NC: McFarland & Company, Inc., Publishers, 2013. Print.

Andrews, Maggie, and Mary M. Talbot, eds. *All the World and Her Husband: Women in Twentieth-Century Consumer Culture*. London: Cassell, 2000. Print.

Introduction, Preface, Foreword, or Afterword in a Book

Gerbner, George. Foreword. *Cultural Diversity and the U.S. Media*. Eds. Yahya R. Kamalipour and Theresa Carillia. New York: State U of New York P, 1998. xv–xvi. Print.

Cohen, Mitchell, and Dennis Hale. Introduction. *The New Student Left.* Ed. Cohen and Hale. Boston: Beacon Press, 1967. xvii–xxxiii. Print.

When you have two or more texts by the same author in your works cited, use dashes in the place of the author's last name for the second book. Alphabetize by the title of the book or article.

Two or More Books by the Same Author

Palmer, William J. *Dickens and New Historicism*. New York: St. Martin's, 1997. Print.

—. *The Films of the Eighties: A Social History*. Carbondale: Southern Illinois UP, 1993. Print.

Article in Collection of Essays

Boichel, Bill. "Batman: Commodity as Myth." *The Many Lives of the Batman*. Eds. Roberta Pearson and William Uricchio. New York: BFI, 1991. 4–17. Print.

Article from a Print Journal

Roberts, Garyn G. "Understanding the Sequential Art of Comic Strips and Comic Books and Their Descendants in the Early Years of the New Millennium." *Journal of American Culture* 27.2 (2004): 210–17. Print.

Article from a Journal Published Only Online

Martin, Paul. "The Pastoral and the Sublime in Elder Scrolls IV: Oblivion." *Game Studies* 11.3 (2011): n. pag. Web. 8 Nov 2012.

Parish, Rachel. "Sappho and Socrates: The Nature of Rhetoric." *Kairos* 17.1 (2012): n. pag. Web. 12 Dec 2012.

Note that for online sources, the most the most recent MLA Handbook states, "You should include a URL as supplementary information only when the reader probably cannot locate the source without it or when your instructor requires it" (182).

Article from a Popular Magazine Published Monthly (print and online)

Maney, Kevin. "The New Face of IBM." *Wired* July 2005. Web. 18 Aug. 2005.

Sontag, Susan. "Looking at War." *New Yorker* 9 Dec. 2002: 43–48. Print.

Article from a Newspaper (print and online)

Haughney, Christine. "Women Unafraid of Condo Commitment." *New York Times* 10 Dec. 2006, Sec 11:1. Print.

Cowell, Alan. "Book Buried in Irish Bog Is Called a Major Find." *New York Times*. New York Times, 27 July 2006. Web. 31 July 2006.

Article found through Database (including Google Books)

Chun, Alex. "Comic Strip's Plight Isn't Funny." *Los Angeles Times* 27 Apr. 2006, Home ed.: E6. *LexisNexis*. Web. 4 May 2006.

Gottesman, Jane. *Game Face: What Does a Female Athlete Look Like?* NY: Random House, Inc., 2001. *Google Book Search*. Web. 15 July 2004.

Rosette, Ashleigh Shelby and Robert W. Livingston. "Failure is Not an Option for Black Women: Effects of Organizational Performance on Leaders with Single versus Dual-Subordinate Identities." *Journal of Experimental Psychology* 48.5 (2012): 1162–1167. *Academic Search Premier*. Web. 5 Jan. 2013.

If you use a database (such as ProQuest, LexisNexis, or EBSCO) to locate an article, you include that information in your citation. The MLA Handbook includes Google Books under this category.

Articles (and books) with no author are listed alphabetically by title

News Article from a Website

"Hillary's American Dream." *The Economist* 29 July 2006: 32. Print.

Quade, Alex. "Elite Team Rescues Troops Behind Enemy Lines." CNN.com. Cable News Network, 19 Mar. 2007. Web. 19 Mar. 2007.

Yagoda, Ben. "You Need to Read This: How Need to Vanquished Have to, Must, and Should." *Slate*. Washington Post Newsweek Interactive, 17 July 2006. Web. 20 July 2006.

Definition

"Diversity." *American Heritage Dictionary of the English Language*. 4th ed. Houghton, 2000. Print.

"Greek Mythology." *Wikipedia*. Wikimedia Foundation, 16 Apr. 2010. Web. May 5, 2010.

Letter to the Editor

Tucker, Rich Thompson. "High Cost of Cheap Coal." Letter. *National Geographic* July 2006: 6–7. Print.

Newspaper Op-Ed

Woodlief, Wayne. "Op-Ed; Time Heals Biden's Self-Inflicted Wound." *Boston Herald* 26 Jan. 2007: 19. Print.

Letter or Memo

Greer, Michael. Letter to the authors. 30 July 2006. Print.

Dissertation (Unpublished)

Li, Zhan. "The Potential of America's Army: The Video Game as Civilian-Military Public Sphere." Diss. Massachusetts Institute of Technology, 2004. Print.

Government Publication

United States. Census Bureau. Housing and Household Economics Statistics Division. *Poverty Thresholds 2005*. US Census Bureau, 1 Feb. 2006. Web. 20 May 2006.

Interview

Tullman, Geoffrey. Personal interview. 21 May 2006.

Cho, Ana. Telephone interview. 4 June 2005.

When writing a citation for an interview, include the mode of interview (i.e. telephone interview, Skype interview).

Survey

Meyer-Teurel, Fiona. "Hacking and Modding in Video Games." Survey. 23 May 2013.

For a survey you conduct yourself, list yourself as the author, then the name of the survey (or the word survey), and the date you conducted it.

Email

Tisbury, Martha. "Re: Information Overload." Message to Max Anderson. 27 Mar. 2008. Email.

Blog Post

Gardner, Traci (Tengrrl). "Oh Internet, You Pandora's Box!" *Pedablogical.* Pedablogical, 13 Apr. 2009. Web. 14 June 2013.

When citing an online posting (from a blog, Twitter, Reddit, etc.), use the author's real name if you know it, followed by the username in parenthesis. If the real name is unknown, simply list the username.

Facebook Post

Pond, Amelia. "Time travel is possible ..." Facebook.com. 24 April 2010. Web. 25 April 2010.

The White House. "Spurring Innovation, Creating Jobs." Facebook. com. 5 Aug. 2009. Web. 13 February 2010.

Tweet

Booker, Cory (CoryBooker). "I'd rather have my ship sunk at sea than rot in the harbor. To exceed our limits we must test them; to fly we must risk falling." 11 June 2013, 6:51 a.m. Tweet.

When writing a citation for a Tweet, include the entire tweet as the title.

Reddit Post

Examples of Good. "My Mom Made Me Lunch." Reddit.com. Fri. 23 Apr. 2013.

Text Message, Chat Room Discussion, or Real-time Communication

Zhang, Zhihao. "Revision Suggestions." *Cross-Cultural Rhetoric Chat Room*. Stanford U. 25 May 2006. Web. 5 June 2008.

Documentation for Visual, Audio, and Multimedia Sources

MLA documentation style was devised principally with text-based images in mind. However, since many of the materials for your research project might be visual or multimodal texts, you need to consider ways to adapt the principles of MLA citation style to these different forms.

This may seem daunting at first, but if you remember the *logic of MLA style*, you'll find you can apply the basic principles of this format to any medium. In a humorous but informative YouTube video, "How to Cite a Cereal Box in MLA 2009," Martine Courant Rife makes exactly this point by taking her viewer through the steps for citing a cereal box (because, as she says, "if you can cite a cereal box, you can cite anything"). The key is to examine and evaluate your source closely—for a cereal box, looking at each side of the box, even inside—and then consider how the information provided there helps you fill out the categories of *author*, *title*, and various *publication* information that we discussed above.

Consider how we might cite this Special K box. As Figure 7.2 shows, while there is no clear author, we can identify the title as "Kellogg's Special K: Original." Publication data can be found on the side: as seen in Figure 7.3, we can

FIGURE 7.2 Examining the front of the cereal box provides us with the title for our citation.

FIGURE 7.3 Close analysis of the side shows us the place of publication, publisher, and the date of production.

find place of publication (Battle Creek, MI), publisher or corporate sponsor (Kellogg Sales Co.), and date of production or publication (2013) in the fine print. The medium itself is clear: it's a cereal box. Our citation, then, following the model of a citation for a print text, might look something like this:

"Kellogg's Special K: Original." Battle Creek, MI: Kellogg Sales Co., 2013. Print Cereal Box.

While there may be no official way to confirm the accuracy of this particular citation, the principles we used to create it follow the rationale of MLA form. Below, you'll find example citations for many types of media texts you might use in your research paper. However, if the type of source you are using does not appear in the list below, simply follow the logical steps for citing print and online sources (as we did with Special K).

- Cartoon or Comic
- Photograph
- Painting
- Screenshot
- Advertisement
- Cover (Magazine, Book, CD, etc.)
- Map
- TV Program
- Film
- Online Video
- Internet Site
- Homepage
- Computer Game
- Radio Essay
- Lecture
- Speech or Sound Recording
- Performance

Editorial Cartoon or Comic Strip

Grondal, Cal. "Reasonable Search." Cartoon. *Cagle.com* 11 June 2013. Web. 12 June 2013.

Pastis, Stephen. "Pearls before Swine." Comic strip. *Comics.com* 18 Apr. 2006. Web. 16 May 2006.

Wilkinson, Signe. Cartoon. *San Francisco Chronicle*. 1 June 2010: A13. Print.

When writing a citation for a photograph you took yourself, list yourself as the photographer, then the title or location of the photo, the year you took it, then the file type.

Photograph

Alfano, Christine. "Golden Gate Bridge, San Francisco." 2004. JPEG file.

Goldin, Nan. *Jimmy Paulette & Misty in a Taxi, NYC*. 1991. Photograph. San Francisco Museum of Modern Art, San Francisco.

Liss, Steve. "Trailer-Park Picnic in Utah, 1997." *Great Images of the 20th Century*. Ed. Kelly Knauer. NY: Time Books, 1999. 41-42. Print.

Sherman, Cindy. *Untitled Film Still*. 1978. Museum of Modern Art. *The Complete Untitled Film Stills of Cindy Sherman*. Web. 7 July 2006.

Painting

Warhol, Andy. *Self Portrait*. 1986. Andy Warhol Museum, Pittsburgh. *The Warhol: Collections*. Web. 3 Aug. 2006.

Screenshot

Fielding, Geri. "Happy Doggie." *Instagram,* 24 Feb. 2010. Web. 26 Feb. 2010.

"Star Wars Galaxies." Sony Online Entertainment, n.d. Web. 5 Feb. 2005.

Advertisement

Diet Coke. Advertisement. *Wired Magazine*. Oct. 2012: 78. Print.

Doritos. Advertisement. ESPN. 7 June 2013. Television.

Nike. "We Are All Witnesses." Advertisement. *Nikebasketball*. 3 Jan. 2006. Web. 15 June 2006.

Palmolive Soap. "Would Your Husband Marry You Again?" *Harper's Bazaar*. 1921. *Ad*Access*. Web. 25 Feb. 2013.

Cover (Magazine, Book, CD, etc.)

Adams, Neil. "Deadman." *Comics VF.com*. Comics VF, 1978. Web. 23 Oct. 2005.

Cover. *Gameinformer*. May 2013. Print.

Map

Hong Kong Disneyland Guide. Map. Disney, 2006. Print.

"Providence, Rhode Island." Map. *Google Maps*. Google, 11 Mar. 2012. Web. 1 Mar. 2012.

TV Program

"The Diet Wars." *Frontline*. PBS, 2004. Web. 16 Aug. 2006.

"Farmer Guy." Prod. Seth McFarlane, et al. *Family Guy*. Fox Broadcasting Company, 12 May 2013. *hulu*. Web. 15 May 2013.

Film

Beyond Killing Us Softly: The Impact of Media Images on Women and Girls. Dir. Margaret Lazarus and Renner Wunderlich. Prod. Cambridge Documentary Films, 2000. Film.

"A Brief History of America." *Bowling for Columbine*. Dir. Michael Moore. United Artists, 2002. *Bowling for Columbine*, n.d. Web. 13 June 2006.

Online Video

Ingham, Ben. "An African Race." Vimeo. 7 June 2013. Web. 13 June 2013.

Wesch, Michael. "A Vision of Students Today." YouTube. 12 Oct 2007. Web. 31 March 2010.

Internet Site

Cartoonists Index. MSNBC, n.d. Web. 4 Nov. 2005.

Homepage

Corrigan, Edna. Home page. *Ednarules*. N.p., n.d. Web. 24 Oct. 2005.

Computer Game

Infinity Ward. *Modern Warfare 2.* Activision. 2009. Playstation 3.

Rovio Entertainment. *Angry Birds Space*. Apple App Store. 2012. iPhone.

Second Life. Your World. Linden Labs, n.d. Web. 7 May 2006.

Radio Essay

Ydstie, John. "Book Marketing Goes to the Movies." *Morning Edition*. Natl. Public Radio. 18 July 2006. Radio.

Lecture

Connors, Fiona. "Visual Literacy in Perspective." English 210B. Boston U. 24 Oct. 2004. Lecture.

Delagrange, Susan and Ben McCorkle. "What is a Public Service Announcement (PSA)?" Writing II: Rhetorical Composing. Coursera. May 2013. Lecture.

Speech or Sound Recording

Bu, Lisa. "How Books Can Open Your Mind." TED Conference Feb. 2013. Lecture. *TED: Ideas Worth Spreading*. TED, May 2013. Web. 23 May 2013.

Jobs, Steve. Commencement Address. Stanford U., Palo Alto, 12 June 2005. *iTunes U*. Apple. Web. 27 July 2006.

Reagan, Ronald. "The Space Shuttle *Challenger* Tragedy Address." 28 Jan. 1986. *American Rhetoric.* Web. 5 Mar. 2006.

Rheingold, Howard. "Technologies of Cooperation." Annenberg Center for Communication. U of Southern California, Los Angeles. 3 Apr. 2006. Speech.

Performance

Phedre. By Jean Racine. Dir. Ileana Drinovan. Pigott Theater, Memorial Hall, Stanford, 10–13 May, 2006. Performance.

Student Paper in MLA Style

To see how texts you might encounter in your research process today will range across varied formats and media, let's consult a student paper by Stephanie Parker, who focused on how digital communities, such as Soompi (a Korean pop culture website), have transformed ideas of racial identity. Stephanie incorporated an impressive array of both print and electronic sources in her project, including books, book chapters, and journal articles; e-books, online newspaper articles, telephone and online interviews; YouTube videos, websites, screenshots, blog posts, and more.

Parker 1

Stephanie Parker
Dr. Christine Alfano
PWR 2 Cultural Interfaces
7 December 2008

Soompi and the "Honorary Asian": Shifting Identities in the Digital Age

Every morning at 7:00 AM, Norwegian James Algaard turns on his computer and joins Soompi IRC: a chatroom for members of a Korean Pop Culture discussion forum. James' daily entrance into the chatroom is enthusiastically greeted by online acquaintances who know him as <SeungHo>, a connoisseur of Korean Hip Hop and a collector of limited edition sneakers. Seungho Lee was born in South Korea, but was adopted by a Norwegian family; websites like Soompi are his only connection to Korean culture. Thousands of miles away in Los Angeles, it is 10:00 PM when I, an American with a strong interest in Asia, join the same chatroom to spend time with Seungho and thirty other "Soompiers," people from around the world who have come together to form a strong and tight-knit online community. The chatroom itself [...] is visually mundane—a window that gradually fills with text as different users type, but Soompi IRC is an organic and multicultural part of cyberspace where people communicate in English, Korean, Mandarin, Cantonese, Spanish, Norwegian, Swedish, Vietnamese, Japanese, Tagalog, and French about every topic imaginable, 24 hours a day.

We Soompiers are representatives of "Generation I"—we have grown up with the Internet and are using it to define ourselves in a more globalized society (Gates 98). A decade ago, cultural identity for people like Seungho and me was limited by factors like geography, language, and ethnicity; with the emergence of new technology and online communities, we have access to an ever-growing variety of choices for personal expression. Soompi and other cyber communities are at the forefront of a larger movement towards redefining how we culturally relate to one another. This movement will extend past the reach of the

Stephanie heads her paper in proper MLA form, with her name, her instructor's name, the class title, and the date, all flush to the left margin.

Stephanie lists both the author and page number in her citation. Notice that she is citing this source even though she is only paraphrasing his ideas.

Stephanie closes her introduction with a two-sentence thesis that outlines the claim that she will support through her textual and cultural analysis in the rest of the paper.

Stephanie's page numbers skip to 9 here since we've abridged her paper.

Parker 9

Internet and act as a catalyst for cross-cultural interaction and understanding on a level never seen before.

* * *

In this section, midway through her paper, Stephanie synthesizes a variety of different types of sources to make her point.

"This Site is My Life": Soompi Addicts and the Asian Fix

For the past decade, most academic research on cyber culture has focused on the type of social interaction that takes place within the digital medium. Scholars Howard Rheingold, Elisabeth Reid, Amy Jo Kim, and Lisa Nakamura have all helped to build the foundations for the study of online group behavior. But there is also another important part of Internet life that is only beginning to develop with the current generation of web users—how membership in an online group affects a person's self-perception in relation to others in real life. Nessim Watson is a Professor of Communication at Westfield State College, and has devoted years to the study of American mass media and cultural representations. After spending two years participating in and studying an online fan club, he concluded that, "those youth formed a community which created not only individual benefits for participants but also a group strength" (102). It is those "individual benefits" that should provide the next source of material for research. The strong allegiance to a web-based group is not something that an Internet user logs in and out of—they take this allegiance with them and it influences their decisions and behavior in the real world: their mode of personal expression, their opinions about other groups, and especially their cultural identity.

Stephanie cites the page number for the print source from which she took this direct quote. Notice that because she used the author's name earlier in the sentence, she does not need to include it again in her parenthetical citation.

Soompi is one of the best venues to observe the brand new phenomenon of people gaining a real sense of culture from an online source. According to Quantcast, a free internet ratings site, Soompi.com has 26 million page views per month, with a full 66% accomplished by "Addicts," or users who log on more than once every day ("Traffic Stats ..."). For them, Soompi is the most convenient place to get their fix of Asian culture. This makes sense, and is in line with a report published in 2001 by the Pew Internet & American Life Project, "Asian-Americans

She cites the source for the statistics she uses. Since her source had no author, she refers to it here with an abbreviation of its title, which she places in quotation marks since it is the title of the article. In the Works Cited, she lists this source by its title as well, so it is easy for the reader to cross-reference.

Parker 10

and the Internet: The Young and Connected." According to the study, English-speaking Asian-Americans "are the Net's most active users ... and have made the Internet an integral part of their daily lives" (Spooner 2). For hundreds of thousands of people in this demographic, Soompi has definitely become an important force in their personal lives and decisions, and in some cases, is the only website visited besides social utilities like Facebook ("What Would You ..."). They can use Soompi to build their knowledge of Asian culture, and to form new connections with other people they can relate to around the world. In September of 2008, a discussion topic was posted on the Forums: "What Would You Do Without Soompi?" Certain self-proclaimed "addicts" left replies such as, "I probably wouldn't be so into Asian stuff," and "I would be a lot less knowledgeable about the world" ("What Would You ..."). For thousands of Soompiers, the Forums are where they learn Asian-specific modes of fashion, style, speech patterns, and other cultural behaviors of expression.

This part of personal development is extremely important in the case of Asian-Americans living in predominantly non-Asian areas, without an "Asian group" of friends to participate in cultural activities with. Prominent scholars in Asian-American studies constantly emphasize the unique relationship between the Asian-American community and New Media, and its power to change traditional ideas about identity, culture, and the potential fluidity of both (Nakamura, *Digitizing Race* 184). Lisa Nakamura recognizes in *Digitizing Race: Visual Cultures of the Internet* that "[i]nteractive media like the Web can question identity while building discursive community in ways that other static media cannot" (184). It allows anyone who wishes to contribute to the evolution of Asian-American culture to effectively "log in" and express their approval, resistance, or creativity in the largest Forum on the planet, all while strengthening the bonds of a real community. Daniel Shim relates his own experience: "I was born in Canada in white communities & I grew up to be like them. Soompi has given me knowledge about Asian culture that I would not get

Even though Stephanie reads this as an electronic file, Spooner's study was in PDF form and therefore has page numbers that she could refer to in her citations.

This source is a discussion thread from the website that Stephanie is discussing, but for the purposes of citation, she refers to it by its title, just as she would for an article that had no author listed.

Since Stephanie is working with two different texts written by Nakamura, here she specifies which she is referring to by including the title as well as the author and page number in the citation.

The second time that Stephanie references Nakamura's book, she does not need to include the author or title in the citation since they are exactly the same as in the previous citation.

Since this is from an interview, there is no page number to cite. However, since Stephanie lists more than one source from Shim in her Works Cited, here she includes a citation that makes it clear that this quote was taken from her online interview with him.

Stephanie includes a parenthetical reference to Figure 6 to draw her visual evidence into dialogue with her main written argument.

Stephanie once again takes a direct quote from an interview she conducted and so does not cite a page number or author here. The curious reader would look up "Kang" on the Works Cited and discover that the quote came from a personal interview.

Parker 19

from my school or family" (Online interview). To follow that point further, in her book, Nakamura argues that the Internet provides a Forum for "questioning a rigid and essentialized notion of Asian American 'authenticity'" (185). This is extremely important—the idea of culture being inextricably linked to ethnicity, language, and geographic location becomes irrelevant in the face of rising online communities, the organic and global nature of which forces the issue of what makes a person "Asian," or "American."

Since Daniel joined Soompi and began to use the Internet as a tool for personal expression, his popularity online has grown enormously: his YouTube videoblog, in which he comments on events in his daily life and makes fun of Asian stereotypes, has almost 30,000 subscribers and is the 4th most popular comedy blog in all of Canada (Shim, "Shimmycocopuffsss's . . ."). Without having grown up around many Asian young people, Daniel has been extremely successful in navigating the cultural landscape with the help of his online community, even producing his own ideas about Asian-American identity as a New Media celebrity (see Figure 6). For young people like Daniel in Toronto and Seungho in Norway, Susan Kang says that "online is pretty much the only place they feel like they can connect to other Asians." Soompi makes it not only possible, but easy for Asians who live in a non-Asian place to immerse themselves in Asian culture and comment on it—an unprecedented step in the separation of culture and a static location.

Figure 6. Daniel Shim's parody video, "Wasabi Boy-NoEngrish" confronts Asian stereotypes with comedy and has been viewed almost 200,000 times. Author screenshot.

Works Cited

Bell, David. *An Introduction to Cybercultures*. London: Routledge, 2001. Print.

Chen, Louie Haoru. Online interview. 16 November 2008.

"Crazy Sale for Korean Fashion." Advertisement. *Yesstyle*. 10 November 2008. Web. 10 November 2008.

Dator, Jim, and Yongseok Seo. "Korea as the Wave of a Future: The Emerging Dream Society of Icons and Aesthetic Experience." *Journal of Futures Studies* 9:1 (2004): 31–44. Print.

Gates, Bill. "Enter 'Generation I.'" *Instructor* March 2000: 98. Print.

Gulia, Milena, and Barry Wellman. "Virtual Communities as Communities: Net Surfers Don't Ride Alone." Eds. Smith, Mark A. and Kollock, Peter. *Communities in Cyberspace.* New York: Routledge, 1999. 167–194. Print.

Herring, Susan C. "Questioning the Generational Divide: Technological Exoticism and Adult Constructions of Online Youth Identity." *Youth, Identity, and Digital Media*. Ed. David Buckingham. Massachusetts: MIT Press, 2000. 72–95. Print.

Jones, Steven G. *Virtual Culture: Identity & Communication in Cybersociety*. London: Sage Publications Ltd, 1997. Print.

Kang, Susan. Online interview. 25 October 2008.

Kim, Amy Jo. *Community Building on the Web*. Peachpit Press, 6 April 2000. Web. 24 October 2008.

Ko, Shu-ling. "GIO Looking to Take Foreign Soap Operas off Prime Time TV." *Taipei Times* 11 January 2006. *AsiaMedia*. 11 January 2006. Web. 20 November 2008.

"Korea Wave Hits Middle East." *Dae Jang Geum* 13 December 2005. Web. 1 November 2008.

This Works Cited represents an abridged version of the much longer Works Cited that Stephanie included with her full paper.

All the sources in the Works Cited listed in alphabetical order by author's last name, or, in the cases where there is no identified author, by title.

Stephanie lists a variety of sources here, from academic journal articles, to books, newspaper articles, advertisements, and even online sources such as webpages, YouTube videos, and discussion list postings.

Notice the formatting of the entries: the first line of each entry is flush left, with a hanging indent in the wrapped lines so readers can skim the Works Cited easily.

When there is no author, the title is listed first.

When an author's name appears more than once, three hyphens (—) stand in for the name in the second and subsequent entries, and the entries by the same author are alphabetized by title.

Notice here how in the Watson entry, Stephanie cross-references with the Jones citation above so as not to be redundant.

.Parker 20

Lee, HyukMin. Telephone interview. 15 October 2008.

Nakamura, Lisa. *Cybertypes*. New York: Routledge, 2002. Print.

—. *Digitizing Race: Visual Cultures of the Internet*. Minneapolis, MN: University of Minnesota Press, 2008. Print.

Reid, Elisabeth. "Electropolis: Communications and Community on Internet Relay Chat." Honors Thesis. University of Melbourne, 1991. Print.

Rheingold, Howard. *The Virtual Community: Homesteading on the Electronic Frontier*. Addison-Wesley Publishing Company, 1993. Print.

Shim, Daniel. Online interview. 12 November 2008.

—. "Shimmycocopuffsss's Profile Page" YouTube. 27 November 2008. Web. 28 November 2008.

—. "Wasabi Boy-No Engrish." YouTube. 5 March 2008. Web. 28 November 2008.

Spooner, Tom. "Asian-Americans and the Internet: The Young and Connected." *Pew Internet and American Life Project*. 12 December 2001. PDF file.

"Traffic Stats for soompi.com." Quantcast.com. 1 November 2008. Web. 1 November 2008.

"Wannabe Asians/Wasians" 1721 Posts. *Soompi*. Started 28 July 2006. Web. 1 October 2008.

Watson, Nessim. "Why We Argue About Virtual Community: A Case Study of the Phish.net Fan Community." Jones 102–110. Print.

"What Would You Do Without Soompi? How would your life be different?" 95 posts. *Soompi*. Started 1 September 2008. Web. 1 October 2008.

Yang, Jeff. "On Top of YouTube: Happy Slip, Choi, KevJumba." *The San Francisco Chronicle* 6 June 2008. Web. 20 October 2008.

THE WRITER'S PROCESS

In this chapter you've learned about the importance of source attribution, the concept of intellectual property, the dangers of plagiarism—whether accidental or not—the rhetorical purpose for documentation styles, the cross-referencing system of in-text citations, and the logic behind constructing entries for your MLA Works Cited and Consulted list. Now it's time for you to implement these practices in your own writing.

Take a look at your own research sources as they appear in your written draft. Have you acknowledged all your sources in full? Are the names of authors "hidden" in parentheses or in notes listing a range of sources? Should you instead name the authors in the prose of your essay and include just the page numbers in parentheses? In that way, you make your conversation with these authors move overt, and your source attribution of their work is more respectful.

Now take a look at all your online, visual, and multimedia sources. Did you include proper and concise parenthetical attributions for each one in the paper? Does your Works Cited list provide an alphabetized account of all your research, even the materials that may be so new that we haven't invented ways to cite them yet? Realize that you, as an emerging writer, can use the lessons from this chapter in order to think through the logic of documentation, include the newest sources in your essay, and develop your contribution to an ongoing research conversation.

WRITING ASSIGNMENTS

1. **Documentation Log:** Develop your own system of note taking and ethical citation of sources to avoid unintentional plagiarism. Create citations for your works cited using MLA form. Follow the order in the checklist below in formatting your citation; keep in mind, depending your source, not all of these categories may apply.

- ❑ Author or authors
- ❑ Title of book or article
- ❑ If an article, title of journal or book within which it was published
- ❑ Place of publication

- ❑ Publisher
- ❑ Date of publication
- ❑ If a printed or PDF article, page span
- ❑ If online article from a database, the database or search engine
- ❑ Medium of publication
- ❑ If an online source, date you accessed it
- ❑ The URL for a website, if your instructor requires it, or if the site would be difficult to find without it

2. **Citations Peer Review:** Share your draft paper with your peers and have them check to see which sources need citation. Does your paper contain knowledge you must have obtained from a source? If so, you need to acknowledge the source of that knowledge. Do certain passages seem to be common knowledge? If so, you don't need to cite them. What paragraphs could go into notes? What aspects of your paper need more explanation and could use a note?

3. **Writing with Technology:** You might find it helpful to turn to one of the scholarly tools for producing a Work Cited list. These include *Easybib, Ref Works, End Note, Citelighter,* and *Zotero*. Many researchers and scholars depend on these tools, keeping notes right in the program, inserting all identifying information for a source, and then selecting the documentation format needed for their papers. The technology then produces a list in the chosen documentation style. However, you will definitely need to double-check the list for accuracy, using what you learned in this chapter.

Part III

DESIGN AND DELIVERY

CHAPTER 8
Designing Arguments

CHAPTER 9
Delivering Presentations

CHAPTER 8

Designing Arguments

Chapter Preview Questions

8.1 What is decorum, and how does this rhetorical principle govern document design?

8.2 What are the conventions for academic writing?

8.3 What techniques can I learn to integrate images effectively into my writing?

8.4 How can I compose an abstract about my essay and a "bio" about myself as a writer?

8.5 How do audience and purpose affect my document design?

8.6 How can I create multimodal arguments, such as op-ads, photo essays, and websites?

FIGURE 8.1 The cover of Michael Chaitkin's research essay offers a carefully designed visual argument.

This third part of *Envision* invites you to consider how you can communicate your ideas, research, and writing in various formats—including the conventional academic paper, but also expanding out to include creative cover pages, multimedia representations in word and image, and even texts that combine voice, moving images, and animation. We'll provide specific *document design* guidelines for academic essays, including line-spacing, margin size, page numbering and other considerations. You'll learn how to write an academic abstract to provide an overview of your argument and a short biography (or "bio") to build your credibility as the author, as well as how to insert images correctly into your written essay. Then, in the second half of the chapter, we'll examine ways you can compose effective arguments in more popular, less academic formats through op-ads, photo essays, newsletters, brochures, websites, online videos, and other multimodal projects. But whether your project is conventional or creative, you need to learn the principles of **document design**—the guidelines that determine the best medium and method of communicating your idea in a specific format.

Michael Chaitkin, for example, moved from the conventional to the creative when he turned the cover page of his research paper into a **visual argument**—a graphic representation of a written argument—that served as a compact visual depiction of his thesis (see Figure 8.1). In the essay itself, Michael explored the significance of Michelle Bachelet becoming Chile's first elected female president; he contended that although she was the daughter of a convicted traitor who was tortured to death by Chilean dictator Augusto Pinochet, she offered the promise of "healing history's wounds" by bridging the political and cultural gap between fighting communities in Chile. Michael then attempted to convey this argument visually through the following design strategies: by placing the photograph of Bachelet in the center of his collage; by using a picture of Pinochet as a somewhat oppressive top border for the page; by placing images of the Chilean communities on both sides of Bachelet to indicate that she serves as the bridge between them; and by locating his central research question, in blue, between those texts. In this way, he deliberately employed the strategies of *invention*, *arrangement*, and *style* to produce a collage that served both as a cover for his written research paper and as an argument in its own right. You'll learn how to produce similar texts that showcase your argument in the pages that follow.

UNDERSTANDING DOCUMENT DESIGN AND DECORUM

8.1 What is decorum, and how does this rhetorical principle govern document design?

But first, in order to grasp the concept of document design more fully, let's return to Alex, our hypothetical student from Chapter 1. For one of her classes, she has completed a research paper on humanitarian aid efforts in third world countries. She now needs to format her paper to submit it to her teacher, and she also is considering submitting it for publication in her college's undergraduate research journal. Moreover, her teacher wants her to convert her paper into a visual argument to appear in a class exhibit. She therefore has an important task in front of her: to learn appropriate design strategies for both academic essays and visual arguments. In each case, she has four key decisions to make: Alex must identify her *argument* (her main point), her *audience* (whom she intends to reach), her *medium* (printed article, abstract, advertisement, photo essay, or multimedia montage), and the specific *form* (the layout and design aspects) for her composition. What governs her choices is a matter of document design strategy, or the choices writers make in formatting their work.

To use terms from classical rhetoric, the decisions you face for document design have to do with **decorum**—a word defined as "appropriateness." In everyday language, someone who exhibits decorum in speaking knows the right kinds of words and content to use given the circumstances and audience. For example, you might swear or shout with joy at a baseball game, but not at a job interview when talking about how your team won the game. But decorum as a rhetorical principle extends beyond choosing the right words and phrases for the occasion.

Seeing Connections
Chapter 3 offers additional discussion of considering style in relation to argumentative writing.

In the Roman rhetorical tradition, Cicero separated decorum into three levels of style that he assigned to different argumentative purposes. Cicero defined the *grand style* as the most formal mode of discourse, employing sophisticated language, imagery, and rhetorical devices; its goal is often to move the audience. He considered *middle style* less formal than grand style but not completely colloquial; although it uses some verbal ornamentation, it develops its argument more slowly in an attempt to persuade the audience by pleasing them. The final level, *plain style,* mimics conversation in its speech and rhythms, aiming to instruct or inform the audience in a clear and straightforward way. By adding decorum to our rhetorical toolkit, we can make decisions about how to design documents. As demonstrated in the "Levels of Decorum" table, we can attend to argument, audience, medium, and form by understanding the *level of style* for a particular occasion. Like our classical counterparts, we must understand our rhetorical situation and use a style that best suits the circumstance.

LEVELS OF DECORUM

LEVEL	CHARACTERISTICS	EXAMPLE: WRITTEN ARGUMENT	EXAMPLE: VISUAL ARGUMENT
Grand or high style	Ornate language; formal structures; many rhetorical devices	Academic paper to be published in a scholarly journal	An information graphic in a scholarly journal
Middle style	Some ornamentation; less formal language; argument is developed at a leisurely pace	Feature article or editorial column	A photo essay for a school exhibit
Plain or low style	The least formal style; closest to spoken language; emphasis on clarity, simplicity, and directness	A blog post or contribution to an online forum	A series of Tumblr posts, showcasing personal perspective or experience

For the rest of this chapter, we'll look at various models for document design, examining the way in which we need to adjust our choice of style according to the formal and rhetorical demands of each situation.

UNDERSTANDING ACADEMIC WRITING CONVENTIONS

8.2 What are the conventions for academic writing?

From the perspective of *decorum*, the conventional academic essay falls under either grand or middle style, depending on the preferences of your audience. Characteristics of academic writing include:

- Using language more sophisticated than ordinary speech
- Using formal structures to organize your paper, including the following elements:
  - An informative and catchy title that comes under your identifying information
  - A complete introduction containing your *thesis statement*
  - Clear subsections for each part of your argument, often using argumentative subheads
  - A substantial conclusion in its own paragraph
- Accurately and ethically acknowledging your sources and providing a Works Cited list

Seeing Connections
See Chapter 6 for guidance on writing Argumentative Subheads at the outline stage.

AT A GLANCE

Key Elements of Academic Document Design

- Double-space all pages.
- Provide 1-inch margins on all sides.
- Use a professional but easily readable font, such as Times New Roman or Arial
- Number pages at the top right; include your last name before the page number.
- Use subheads to separate sections.
- Use in-text citations to acknowledge research sources.
- Use endnotes or footnotes for additional information.
- Include a list of references at the end, preferably a Works Cited and Consulted list.
- Staple, clip, or bind the paper together.

Adhering to these characteristics in the document design of your writing signals your membership in a scholarly community, since you demonstrate knowledge of the format conventions for academic papers. It's similar to using table manners in a particular community or waiting in line to pay at a store; the conventions reflect consensus concerning shared expectations or practices that in turn to promote unity, consistency, and familiarity.

These guidelines are very pragmatic in nature, driven by a deeper purpose than simply following rules. Most have to do with the rhetorical relationship between yourself, your text, and your readers. By double-spacing your document and providing 1-inch margins on all sides, you leave ample room for reviewers to comment on lines or paragraphs. You include page numbers and your name on the corner of your essay to enable readers to keep track of whose paper they are reading and to easily refer to your writing by page number when commenting on a specific point. By using subheads, you help structure what might be a complicated argument to make it more accessible to your audience. Finally, when you include citations, footnotes, and references, you demonstrate your *ethos* as a writer and researcher by giving credit to your sources.

Seeing Connections
See Chapter 3 for a discussion of crafting a rhetorically effective title.

It might seem like an overstatement to argue that a detail as basic as the spacing and alignment of words on a title page can contribute to your ethos. However, consider the different rhetorical force of the three cover pages reproduced in Figures 8.2, 8.3, and 8.4. The first contains all the relevant information: the title, the author's name, the date, and the class for which the essay was written, yet it makes a less powerful impression than the other examples. Why is that? In 8.3, Alex took into account very simple design principles when formatting the page. She changed to a more accessible font, to increase *readability*. She used *contrast* to differentiate the title, with its large, bold font, from the rest of the words on the page. She experimented with *proximity*, grouping related items together to help her reader conceptualize levels of importance. In 8.4, she took the process one step further. She used the principle of *alignment,* moving elements into visual connection with one another on the page so as to give a sense of rhetorical purposefulness behind the layout;

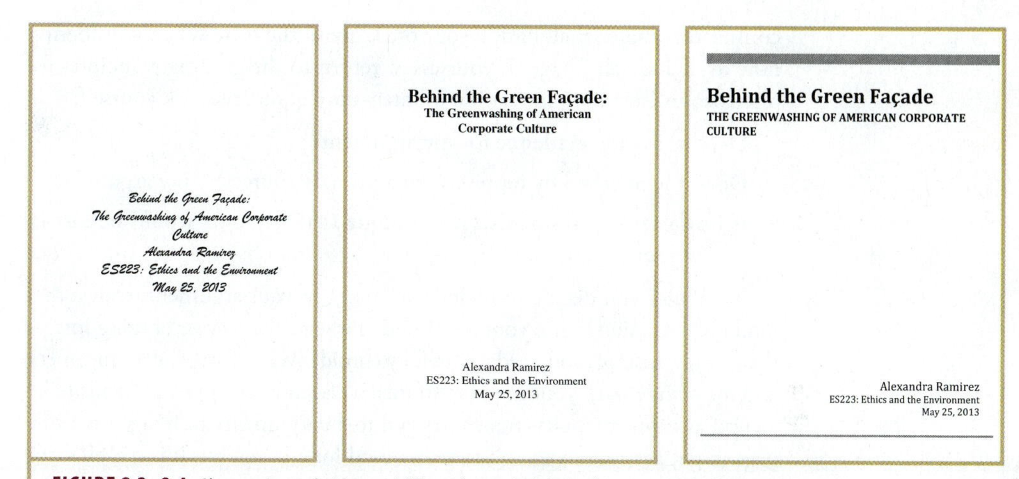

FIGURE 8.2–8.4 Alex experimented with several different formats in designing her cover page for her research project.

finally, she decided to re-format her subtitle in small capitals, a technique she would use for her subheads in the rest of the essay, to give the entire document a sense of coherence through strategic *repetition.* She could even have integrated a relevant cover image or quotation to set the mood for her essay.

As these examples indicate, format is not something simply imposed upon you and your writing. It involves a set of *rhetorical acts* that influence the way that your readers encounter, experience, and are persuaded by your argument.

INTEGRATING IMAGES IN ACADEMIC WRITING

8.3 What techniques can I learn to integrate images effectively into my writing?

Just as there are proper academic conventions for designing the writing and layout of your essay, there exist specific guidelines for how best to integrate images into your writing. But first, consider the rhetorical purpose of your images. If they are just for decoration, then they are not essential to your argument. By contrast, if your essay focuses on a visual topic, such as the analysis of ads or films, then you probably want to include images or screen shots as *primary sources* to analyze in the essay itself. Moreover, if your argument relies on images—such as political campaigns from billboards or websites—as supporting *evidence* for your thesis, then you also want to allow your readers to consult that material alongside your prose about the text. When considering how to include an image in your essay, return to the guiding principles we discussed in Chapter 6 in relation to integrating quotations; ask yourself:

Does it provide **evidence** for my argument?

Does it lend **ethos** by representing a primary source for my argument?

Is its design or **composition** so unique that elements would be lost in written description?

Even once you decide to include an image in your argument, realize that randomly inserting it into your paper does not serve the *purpose* of using images rhetorically. Instead, you need to carefully consider your strategy of arrangement and the *placement* of your images. An image placed in an appendix tends to be viewed as supplementary, not as integral to an argument; an image on a title page might act as an epigraph to set a mood for a paper, but it is less effective as a specific visual example. If you want to use your images as *argumentative evidence*, you need to show them to your readers as you analyze them; therefore, placing them beside the words of your argument will be most successful. Each decision is both a stylistic and rhetorical choice.

Once you have determined the placement that best serves your rhetorical purpose, you need to insert the image in a way that maximizes its impact on your argument. Like a quotation, an image cannot be dropped into a text without comment; it needs to be **signposted**, or connected to your argument through deliberate textual markers. You can accomplish this by making explicit **textual references** to the image—for example, "shown in the image at the right" or "(see Figure 3)"—and by taking the time to explain the rhetoric of the image for readers. Just like words quoted from a book or an interview that you might use as evidence, visual material needs *your interpretation* for readers to view it the way you do. Your analysis of its meaning will advance your argument by persuading readers to see the image as you do, and in the process, readers will pause to consider the evidence rather than skip over it.

It is also crucial to draft a **caption** for the image that reiterates the relationship between the point you are making in the paper and the

AT A GLANCE

Including Visuals in a Paper

- Decide whether it's appropriate to include an image based on assessing its function in terms of evidence, *ethos*, and composition.
- Position it strategically and describe its relevance in your main text so that your readers don't skim over it.
- Include a figure number and caption, or brief description that explains how the image contributes to your argument.
- Refer to the figure number or image title when writing the prose of your essay (for example, "See Figure 1")
- List the complete image source information in your bibliography

visual evidence you include. This dialogue between image and ideas will help remind you to use your images rhetorically and analytically, as evidence, rather than just as decoration. Remember, however, that what is most important is the analysis of the image you include in the body of your paper; don't hide the meaning of the image in the caption. Captions should be concise; they should not do the work of the written argument.

Design of Academic Papers

A page from student Zachary Templeton's essay on using video games to combat depression provides an example of both effective academic writing conventions and the strategic placement and captioning of visuals (see Figure 8.5). Since Zachary was writing on a series of software programs that his readers probably had never encountered, he decided to include screenshots as evidence. Rather than relegate these pictures to an appendix, Zachary positioned them in the paper with the text wrapped around them, making the visuals an integral part of his argument that resonated with the surrounding text. He then emphasized the importance of each image by giving it a meaningful, rhetorical caption that paraphrased his central point.

Zachary's careful attention to academic conventions—from his page number at the top, to the readable typeface, clear structure, and purposeful integration of an image as evidence for his central claim—adds *ethos* to an already articulate and well-researched argument.

TOOLS OF DESIGN FOR ACADEMIC AUDIENCES

8.4 How can I compose an abstract about my essay and a "bio" about myself as a writer?

In addition to attending to the format of the research paper itself and integrating visuals as evidence correctly, you may also need to write supplemental materials that provide readers with a preview of your argument and information about yourself as the author. These materials are commonly known as the *academic abstract* and author *bio*. Both texts are standard components of conventional academic writing; by learning their formal design properties, you can confidently add them to your toolkit of writing strategies.

Writing an Abstract

The **research abstract** is a professional academic genre designed to present the research topic and to lay out the argument. Abstracts differ depending treatment options. Since SuperBetter does not feature overt references to cognitive behavior therapy (CBT) like SPARX does, it may be more appropriately used for patients whose depression is under control or in remission. In this case SuperBetter would help patients lead a healthy and balanced lifestyle that would reduce their chances of relapse. McGonigal advocates this point of view in *Reality Is Broken*: "SuperBetter, of course, isn't meant to replace conventional medical advice or treatment. It's meant to augment good advice, and to help patients take a more active role in their own recovery" (141). As an example of this type of use, therapists could begin with traditional face-to-face CBT and then once their patients' symptoms are manageable, forego frequent appointments to be replaced by SuperBetter and infrequent check ups. In spite of this proposed model, SuperBetter may become more of a stand-alone alternative like SPARX. Researchers in the Penn study are using a power pack that includes predesigned power-ups, quests, allies, and bad guys, which are directly developed from CBT principles (Goligoski); the iPhone App version of SuperBetter integrates a "Being Awesome" module, designed to be integrated with main quests accomplish similar goals (Figure 3). Even users themselves are creating their own power packs based on CBT to be distributed to the greater SuperBetter community (Magladry). Clearly, SuperBetter has a lot of unexamined potential in treating depression and other mental illnesses.

Figure 3. While this iPhone screenshot does not showcase the power pack from the Penn study, it features the "Being Awesome" power pack, which focuses on self-acceptance. (Author screenshot)

Promoting Engagement and Flow

While SPARX and SuperBetter differ in their format and applicability to traditional treatment, they and other successful therapy games share several underlying themes. Many games provide such a high level of engagement for players that they often achieve flow, a state of mind in which a person becomes completely immersed in an activity because of "an

FIGURE 8.5 This excerpt from Zachary's essay, "Video Games: A Viable and Accessible Treatment Option for Depression," provides an example of polished academic design.

on the disciplinary audience and the purpose of the writing: When applying to academic conferences in the humanities, for example, scholars often must write abstracts that predict the paper's argument, research contribution, and significance, while writers in the sciences or social sciences typically write abstracts *after* the paper has been completed to serve as a short summary of the article. You will encounter abstracts when you begin searching for research articles; they often precede a published paper or accompany bibliographic citations in online databases. Abstracts can range from a few sentences to a page in length, but they are usually no longer than two paragraphs. The key in writing an abstract is to explain your argument in one brief, coherent unit. While some characterize an abstract as simply a summary, others suggest it can have a more complex structure. In their seminal work, *The Craft of Research,* Wayne Booth, Gregory Colomb, and Joseph Williams propose the following model for abstracts: Context + Problem + Main Point or Launching Point. According to their interpretation, an abstract clarifies not only the topic, but a tension in that topic and the way that the written piece addresses that tension. As you read the abstract below, which originally accompanied an article on video games that Zachary could easily have referenced in his essay, consider the ways in which the author adheres to this structure.

Seeing Connections
Chapter 5 discusses how you might evaluate published abstracts during your research.

Serious games have received much positive attention; correspondingly, many researchers have taken up the challenge of establishing how to best design them. However, the current literature often focuses on best practice design strategies and frameworks. Fine-grained details, contextual descriptions, and organisational factors that are invaluable in helping us to learn from and reflect on project experiences are often overlooked. In this paper, we present five distinct and sometimes competing perspectives that are critical in understanding factors that influence serious game projects: *project organisation, technology, domain knowledge, user research*, and *game design*. We explain these perspectives by

In the first sentence, the authors establish the context for their research.

The second and third sentences convey the tension or problem that their particular project addresses.

In the final sentences of the abstract, the authors suggest both their main point and some of their methodology, providing the reader with a clear overview of what to expect when reading the whole paper and their contribution to the conversation on this topic.

providing insights from the design and development process of an EU-funded serious game about conflict resolution developed by an interdisciplinary consortium of researchers and industry-based developers. We also point out a set of underlying forces that become evident from viewing the process from different perspectives, to underscore that problems exist in serious game projects and that we should open the conversation about them.

In composing your abstract, you will need to make several rhetorical decisions, outlined in the questions in the "At a Glance" box.

Constructing Your Bio

While the abstract offers a concise statement of the argument, the **bio**, short for *biography*, is a brief paragraph that conveys aspects of the author's experiences or credentials to the intended audience. In this way, the bio functions as a short written account of your *persona*. Its purpose is to

AT A GLANCE

Design for composing an Abstract

- What level of decorum do you wish to use?
- How will the style predict the tone of your essay and establish your persona as a researcher?
- If you use "I" in the prose, can it be *ethos*-based in terms of your research or experience?
- How much specificity should you include from the essay?
    - Do you want to identify key examples you analyze in your writing?
    - Do you want to give an overview of your argument?
    - Should you name any important sources you use in making your argument?
    - What is your major research contribution?
    - What is the larger significance of your essay?

persuade readers of your depth of knowledge about or research into your topic. Moreover, a successful bio usually connects aspects of the research topic to the writer's experiences, interests, and motivations for engaging in research work. Molly Cunningham's bio for her paper on Hollywood depictions of Africa follows this model, resembling the polished "About the Author" paragraph that you might find at the back of a book or in the headnote of an academic article:

> Molly Cunningham is a sophomore planning to double major in Cultural Anthropology and English. After spending time in East Africa, she became interested in exploring cultural constructions of the orphan within the community in light of the AIDS pandemic. Involved in fundraising for a Kenyan orphanage, she also has developed research plans for examining the attitudes that determine the amount of foreign aid going into Africa. She has used this research essay on Hollywood depictions of Africa to expand her thinking on this topic while learning to convey her findings to wider audiences.

Molly names specific qualifications and experiences she has had that make her an authority in this area.

She ends the bio with her future plans in this area of research that suggest her pursuit of a "research line" or academic path of scholarly inquiry.

When formatting your own bio, you might decide to include a photograph of yourself. Select your picture carefully, with attention to its rhetorical impact in conveying your *persona*. Many students who choose to write a traditional bio like Molly's opt for a formal school portrait; other students might choose a more humorous picture to complement the tone of their bios. One student, when writing about online gaming communities, even used Photoshop to create a portrait of herself standing next to her onscreen avatar identity to represent the two perspectives she was bringing to her research. As you can tell, the picture works with the bio not only to construct a *persona* for the writer but also to suggest that writer's rhetorical stance.

8.5 How do audience and purpose affect my document design?

FORMATTING WRITING FOR AUDIENCE AND PURPOSE

The format of a page matters to an audience: from the paragraph indents to the margins and double-spaced lines, to the rhetorical placement of images—all these design decisions are ways of conveying your level of decorum and your purpose to your specific audience. When we say "first impressions," we often mean how well a writer meets the conventions anticipated by the audience.

When your argumentative purpose and your audience allow you to move an exclusive focus on written text, you have the opportunity to produce a **multimodal composition**—literally a composition that operates in more than one mode, such as visual, aural, or written. A feature article for a magazine; a newsletter aimed at a community audience; or an online article for diverse readers: each of these texts has the potential to operate through multimodality. An important factor to keep in mind in designing such texts is that research conducted by Adbusters, an organization devoted to cultural criticism and analysis, has shown that readers notice the *visual part* of any page significantly more than any text on the same page (see Figure 8.6). Adbusters uses this finding to provide advice for creating ads, but we can apply the insight to all rhetorical compositions—whether academic or popular—that combine multiple elements.

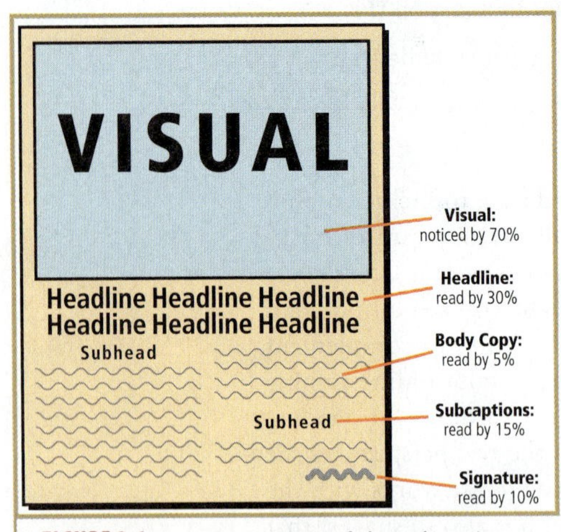

FIGURE 8.6 A graphic representation of what readers notice most on a page: visuals grab attention most.

Let's look at how this attention to design informs a style of writing that is increasingly common in today's society: the online article. In the following reading, originally published online, the author employs many conventional elements of document design, including a title, subheads, references, and a list of sources at the end. But notice how it adapts some of these elements to meet the viewing needs of online readers. The author also includes hyperlinks, ALL CAPS for some titles, and sections of varying lengths. Finally, is not just the format that sets this article apart from traditional academic discourse: the writing style itself has been changed to meet the expectations of the online writing audience.

WHAT'S WRONG WITH THE BODY SHOP?

—a criticism of 'green' consumerism—

REFERENCED VERSION—all the facts and opinions in THE London Greenpeace A5 'Body Shop' leaflet validated. Note: most references are given just by way of example.

The Body Shop have successfully manufactured an image of being a caring company that is helping to protect the environment [1] and indigenous peoples [2], and preventing the suffering of animals [3]—whilst selling 'natural' products [4]. But behind the green and cuddly image lies the reality—the Body Shop's operations, like those of all multinationals, have a detrimental effect on the environment [5] and the world's poor [6]. They do not help the plight of animals [7] or indigenous peoples [8] (and may be having a harmful effect), and their products are far from what they're cracked up to be [9]. They have put themselves on a pedestal in order to exploit people's idealism [10]—so this leaflet has been written as a necessary response.

Companies like the Body Shop continually hype their products through advertising and marketing, often creating a demand for something where a real need for it does not exist [11]. The message pushed is that the route to happiness is through buying more and more of their products. The increasing domination of multinationals and their standardised products is leading to global cultural conformity [12]. The world's problems will only be tackled by curbing such consumerism—one of the fundamental causes of world poverty, environmental destruction and social alienation [13].

FUELLING CONSUMPTION AT THE EARTH'S EXPENSE

The Body Shop have over 1,500 stores in 47 countries [14], and aggressive expansion plans [15]. Their main purpose (like all multinationals) is making lots of money for their rich shareholders [16]. In other words, they are driven by power and greed. But the Body Shop try to conceal this reality by continually pushing the message

The title is in plain style and all capital letters, with the subtitle in lowercase. This font decision makes it appealing to online readers.

The numbers correspond to notes and sources at the end. These notes are *hyperlinked*, so readers can jump there easily while reading on the web.

Here, the writing itself verges on *low style* with the contraction and the slang work "cracked" – this serves to entice online audiences to keep reading.

The article employs British spelling for many words, such as standardised, colours, criticised, and organise, since the authors are located in Britain. Moreover, as this line indicates, the article against the Body Shop is one in a series of pieces that critique multinational corporate practices.

The article uses argumentative subheads, as might an academic paper. They convey points of argument being made in the article. Moreover, they keep readers interested.

that by shopping at their stores, rather than elsewhere, people will help solve some of the world's problems [17]. The truth is that nobody can make the world a better place by shopping.

20% of the world's population consume 80% of its resources [18]. A high standard of living for some people means gross social inequalities and poverty around the world [19]. Also, the mass production, packaging and transportation of huge quantities of goods is using up the world's resources faster than they can be renewed and filling the land, sea and air with dangerous pollution and waste [20]. Those who advocate an ever-increasing level of consumption, and equate such consumption with personal well-being, economic progress and social fulfillment, are creating a recipe for ecological disaster [21].

Rejecting consumerism does not mean also rejecting our basic needs, our stylishness, our real choices or our quality of life. It is about creating a just, stable and sustainable world, where resources are under the control of local communities and are distributed equally and sparingly—it's about improving everyone's quality of life. Consuming ever more things is an unsatisfying and harmful way to try to be happy and fulfilled. Human happiness is not related to what people buy, but to who we are and how we relate to each other. LET'S CONSUME LESS AND LIVE MORE!

Notice how the article uses all CAPS to draw the online reader's attention and even begins a new section with a two-word question.

MISLEADING THE PUBLIC

Natural products? The Body Shop give the impression that their products are made from mostly natural ingredients [22]. In fact like all big cosmetic companies they make wide use of non-renewable petrochemicals, synthetic colours, fragrances and preservatives [23], and in many of their products they use only tiny amounts of botanical-based ingredients [24]. Some experts have warned about the potential adverse effects on the skin of some of the synthetic ingredients [25]. The Body Shop also regularly irradiate certain products to try to kill microbes—radiation is generated from dangerous non-renewable uranium which cannot be disposed of safely [26].

* * *

CENSORSHIP

As the Body Shop rely so heavily on their 'green', 'caring' image, they have threatened or brought legal action against some of those who have criticised them, trying to stifle legitimate public discussion [46]. It's vital to stand up to intimidation and to defend free speech.

Some sections are very short, a common feature in online writing, where information is "chunked" into accessible segments.

WHAT YOU CAN DO

Together we can fight back against the institutions and the people in power who dominate our lives and our planet. Workers can and do organise together to fight for their rights and dignity. People are increasingly aware of the need to think seriously about the products we use, and to consume less. People in poor countries are organising themselves to stand up to multinationals and banks which dominate the world's economy. Environmental and animal rights protests and campaigns are growing everywhere. Why not join in the struggle for a better world? London Greenpeace calls on people to create an anarchist society—a society without oppression, exploitation and hierarchy, based on strong and free communities, the sharing of precious resources and respect for all life. Talk to friends and family, neighbours and workmates about these issues. Please copy and circulate this leaflet as widely as you can.

The article uses direct address, the pronoun you, to engage readers. This design strategy again indicates the use of the plain style.

The conclusion's turn to ask a rhetorical question and then end with a strong call to action also reflect a writing style more common to online writing than to conventional essays, which are often more subdued in tone.

REFERENCES

1. See "Fuelling Consumption" paragraphs in the leaflet and associated references.
2. See "Exploiting Indigenous Peoples" paragraphs in the leaflet and associated references.
3. See "Helping Animals?" paragraph in the leaflet and associated references.
4. See "Natural products?" paragraph in the leaflet and associated references.

[...]

Since these notes are positioned far down on the page, they can go into more detail because they assume that only very interested readers will be accessing this part of the composition.

10. [Numerous publications, statements, advertisements, etc. by the Body Shop.] For example, the company's Mission Statement (1998) says that they are dedicating their business "to the pursuit of social and environmental change" and are trying to ensure that their business "is ecologically sustainable, meeting the needs of the present without compromising the future."" For us, animal protection, human rights, fair trade and environmentalism, are not just fads or marketing gimmicks but fundamental components in our holistic approach to life of which work and business are a part" [Gordon Roddick (Chairman) quoted in 1996 *Body Shop* publication "Our Agenda".] "I'd rather promote human rights, environmental concerns, indigenous rights, whatever, than promote a bubble bath" said Anita Roddick (the *Body Shop* founder and Chief Executive) [speech at 'Academy of Management', Vancouver (Aug 95).]

Back to 'Beyond McDonald's—Retail' Section
London Greenpeace Press Release
WWW Body Shop FAQ
London Greenpeace reply to Body Shop statement
A5 Version of 'What's Wrong with the Body Shop'

From a design perspective, the final series of links for future reading signifies one of the great benefits of writing in a digital environment.

As you can tell from this article, the same strategies of design that shape academic research papers also apply to other modes: what is most important in each is a consideration of *purpose, audience,* and *argument.* Think about how readers will interact with your writing—whether as a print copy handed in for comments (in which case you double-space and follow academic guidelines); as a newsletter (in which case you might open with a powerful image, lay out the writing in columns or boxes, and use an interesting page size); or as a piece to be read on the web (in which case you include hyperlinks, single-space, create shorter chunks, and use font strategically).

In your own writing, you likewise will have the opportunity to present your arguments in multiple modes. In the pages that follow, we'll walk through some of the most common forms you might encounter and consider how to apply the design strategies we have discussed so far to a diverse range of texts.

DESIGNING ARGUMENTS IN POPULAR FORMATS

8.6 How can I create multimodal arguments, such as op-ads, photo essays, and websites?

While it is important to understand the conventions of academic writing, increasingly teachers are inviting students to experiment with alternative forms of making arguments, often modeled on popular or non-academic texts. Many of these—such as op-ads, photo essays, websites, or short films—are visual or multimodal in nature, yet still rely on the same foundations of rhetoric that govern persuasion as a whole. When you construct an argument in a more popular format, you should still apply strategies for inventing, arranging, and producing the design, just as you would for a conventional essay. The goal is the same: to design a powerful text to persuade your audience to agree with your message.

Keep in mind, however, that each medium structures information in a distinct way. A photo essay is set up differently than a webpage, just as a webpage is set up differently than an online video. Therefore, part of creating a powerful multimodal argument lies in identifying your chosen medium's conventions of structure and style and adjusting the form of your argument—its layout, design, style, and organization of information—to be the most appropriate choice for your project.

Crafting an Op-Ad

The **op-ad,** or **opinion advertisement**, is one of the most concise forms of visual argument. Most op-ads promote an opinion rather than try to sell a consumer product. Many nonprofit organizations, special interest groups, and political parties find the op-ad to be a particularly effective way to reach their target audiences. Like all ads, the op-ad is a compact persuasive text, one that uses rhetorical appeals to convey its message. In addition, like other types of ads, an op-ad may rely partially on written text, but it tends to work through the visual components of its argument.

In Figure 8.7, for instance, the op-ad makes its point through a strategic combination of visual and verbal elements. The Body Shop has crafted an innovative image that communicates a powerful message: the realistically proportioned doll, set in a confident, casual pose reclined on the sofa, produces a strong counterstatement against standards of body image in the mass media that promote exceptional thinness for feminine beauty.

Seeing Connections
See Chapter 2 for strategies for analyzing op-ads rhetorically.

FIGURE 8.7 This Body Shop opinion advertisement relies on a powerful visual argument to shock readers into questioning concepts of beauty.

In many ways, the figure of the heavyset Body Shop doll evokes Barbie; op-ads often rely on this rhetorical strategy—**parody**, or the use of one text's formal properties to subvert the meaning of the original and make an independent argument. The words, "There are 3 billion women who don't look like supermodels and only 8 who do," are arranged to reinforce the visual argument of the doll's curvy body. The image creates an argument based on *pathos*, while the statistics draw on *logos*. In this way, the op-ad uses the way readers attend to information on a page: image first, headline second. The design of the op-ad thus works through visual and verbal strategies to make people think twice about body image.

To understand how to compose your own op-ad, let's look at the process by which one student, Carrie Tsosie, constructed her visual argument. After writing an effective research paper that presented the dangers of allowing uranium mining on or near Navajo reservations, Carrie decided to reformulate her argument as an op-ad to reach a larger audience. Her initial considerations were her visual format and her headline—two elements of her ad that underwent some revision. She explained:

> My first idea was to have an image of a deformed lamb because then the audience would see what radiation poisoning can do. I wanted to use the phrase "Stop mining before it starts," but it seemed like that phrase was overdone, and I don't think that my audience could really relate to the deformed lamb because they do not know how important it is to some Navajo people and their lives. (Tsosie, reflection letter)

As shown in her completed op-ad (see Figure 8.8), Carrie decided against the *pathos*-based image of a sick animal.

She opted instead to feature different human environments through her strategic choices of images. In addition, rather than base her ad on a strong imperative such as "Stop Mining," she chose to soften her voice and reach her audience by asking them to question their assumptions about alternative energy. In her final op-ad, she composed a heading with the provocative question "Alternative Energy for Whom?" and then followed the words with a striking visual argument. It is here, in the image, that we find the main work of argumentation. Carrie combined an image from the urban landscape with a stereotypical image from the reservation to produce a striking effect, using what we call *visual juxtaposition*, or the combination of multiple images, as a rhetorical device to call attention to the discrepancy between these ways of life and inform readers about her critique.

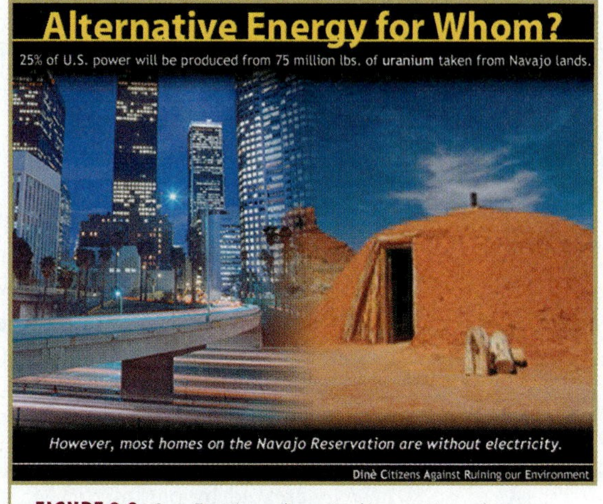

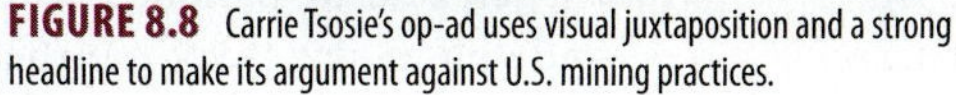
FIGURE 8.8 Carrie Tsosie's op-ad uses visual juxtaposition and a strong headline to make its argument against U.S. mining practices.

Producing a Photo Essay

Although an op-ad offers a concise, forceful argument, you may wish to develop your points more thoroughly than one page allows or use visual space to show the range of material with which you've been working. If so, consider the **photo essay**—a text in which photographs, rather than print text, convey the central argument. In a word-based essay, the verbal text takes priority, and images often appear as isolated points of evidence. In a photo essay, by contrast, the visual either collaborates with the verbal or becomes the *primary mode* of argumentation and persuasion.

AT A GLANCE

Designing an Op-Ad

- Decide on your purpose (to inform, to persuade, to move to action).
- Identify your audience.
- Know your argument.
- Determine which appeals to use (*pathos, logos, ethos*).
- Select key images for your ad.
- Write your print text; decide how it will function in relation to your image(s).
- Draft a gripping headline to complement your image.
- Experiment with layout—arrangement, image size, organization of text—to arrive at the most effective design.

As a genre, the photo essay first emerged in 1936 with the launching of *Life* magazine, whose mission statement was "to see life; to see the world." Over the 63 years it remained in print, *Life* hosted many of America's most famous photo essays, covering a range of topics from the space race to the Vietnam War, the civil rights movement, and rock and roll. But the photo essay can assume many different forms and use diverse media: it could be a series of documentary photographs and articles about southern sharecroppers published together in book form, such as Walker Evans's and James Agee's *Let Us Now Praise Famous Men* (1941); it could be a book-length photo essay that juxtaposes images with first-person narratives, such as Lauren Greenfield's *Girl Culture* (2002); it could be a striking 27-page color spread in a magazine, such as William Albert Allard's "Solace at Surprise Creek" in the June 2006 issue of *National Geographic*; or it could even be an online arrangement of captioned photos, such as *A Rescue Worker's Chronicle*, created by paramedic Matthew Levy. In each case, the photographs and written text work together, or the images themselves carry the primary weight of the argument.

Seeing Connections
Ansel Adams's photo essay about Japanese-American internment camps is discussed in Chapter 3.

Today electronic photo essays are essential conveyers of important events, a result of Internet news sources like CNN.com, Time.com, and MSNBC.com, which routinely publish photo essays as "picture stories" on their websites. Such texts are composed of a series of images and words that work together to convey an argument about a person, event, or story. Each electronic photo essay typically contains (1) a photo, (2) an accompanying caption, (3) an audio option, and (4) a table of contents toolbar that allows readers to navigate through the images. The result is an electronic text that maintains many structural similarities to print text: it offers readers a clear sense of progression from beginning to end while investing its argument with the rhetorical force of multiple media (word, image, sound).

FIGURE 8.9 Through this photo essay, the author makes a visual argument about art on campus.

Let's now consider how Conor Henriksen created a photo essay to fulfill an assignment about outdoor art on campus. Figures 8.9 and 8.10 represent two different pages from the longer piece, in which the author complemented photographs he took himself of sculpture and fountains around campus with brief captions, descriptions, and relevant quotations from secondary sources. The photographs themselves clearly appeal to the reader most directly through their vibrant color, strategic arrangement, and visual composition. Despite the surface similarities in layout, we can see that there are different strategies at work: in Figure 8.9, Conor paired a wide shot of the sculpture with a close-up of one figure to give a dual perspective on the installation; in Figure 8.10, he provides a variety of vantages on the fountain, each designed to focus on a different way of understanding it in context. The text he includes works in conjunction with the images it accompanies, but does not dominate. While it provides a conceptual frame, the photographs themselves provide the most forceful argument about the beauty and significance of outdoor art on campus.

FIGURE 8.10 A second page from Conor's photo essay.

The photo essay works best if you have a topic that can be effectively argued through an accumulation of visual evidence presented as a sequence of images. Keep in mind that designing a photo essay is like drafting a research paper: you may take pages of notes, but the task of crafting the argument involves sifting through information, deciding between relevant and irrelevant materials, and arranging the most powerful evidence in your finished product. In addition, while images have priority in a photo essay, keep in mind the importance of strategically selected and deployed text to

AT A GLANCE

Designing a Photo Essay

1. Decide on the argument for your project.
2. Arrange your images so they support this argument.
3. Draft written text to accompany or preview each image or set of images.
4. Determine your layout by experimenting with ways of formatting the words and images.

accompany your visual argument. Overall, remember to shape your photo essay around your argument through carefully made rhetorical choices about purpose, audience, and medium.

Composing in Newsletter or Magazine Format

Another familiar multimodal format is the newsletter or magazine article. Even with the explosion of online texts, publishers have gone to great lengths to devise ways for articles to retain this popular format even when they appear on the screens of Nooks, Kindles, and iPads. The advice from Adbusters is particularly resonant when we consider the design principles of this form of writing. As Figure 8.6 suggests, a much higher percentage of readers notice visuals than any other component, with the headline being second in significance. We can see the truth in this assertion every time we open an issue of *Time, Wired,* or *Vogue.* An engaging image captures our eye; a provocative headline draws us in; only then do we settle in to dive into the main body of the article.

Taking this into account, consider the importance of visuals as you approach designing your own articles of this sort. Choose images with rhetorical impact to hook your reader and position supporting images strategically in the main body to complement your main points. As for your headline, follow a suggestion from Adbusters: "The most important thing to remember here is that your headline must be short, snappy and must touch the people that read it. Your headline must affect the readers emotionally, either by making them laugh, making them angry, making them curious or making them think." Clearly, headlines work through rhetorical appeals: you need to think carefully about which appeal—*pathos, ethos,* or *logos*—would provide the most effective way to engage your audience.

Let's look at the design decisions Miranda Smith made in formatting her writing project on the topic of famine relief in Africa. The assignment invited her to experiment with a

AT A GLANCE

Designing a Newsletter or Magazine Article

1. Decide on the thesis for your project.
2. Categorize your images, arranging them within thematic groups.
3. Organize them into different configurations: by chronology, concept, and subject.
4. Draft written text in the form of headings, captions, and paragraphs.
5. Determine your layout by experimenting with formatting the words and images.

AFRICA | CHARITIES

Charities Taking Action Against Hunger

ACF International, a charity focused on ending malnutrition in countries, takes stand against the famine in Africa.

BY MIRANDA SMITH

Recently, word has spread about a charity called Action Against Hunger | ACF International, an organization that focuses on providing aid to countries in need. ACF has 30 years of expertise and operates in 40 countries. While providing many communities with viable solutions to hunger and access to clean and safe water, ACF saves lives of children all over the world.

With 55 million children throughout the world suffering from acute malnutrition, ACF administers and help prevent these forms of malnutrition through direct invention.

In order to address this crisis, ACF provides community-based, outpatient programs and inpatient care designed to help people recover from the effects of malnutrition. The ACF also provides Ready-to-Use-Foods to discharged patients as well as children in communities that cope with seasonal

IMAGE COURTESY OXFAM EAST AFRICA

13

500,000 people have received lifesaving support from ACF across the Horn of Africa in 2011.

215 TONS of food assistance was delivered to 12,608 Somalis in August 2011.

10,000 malnourished children were treated by ACF in Kenya as of July 2011.

There are many diseases linked to malnutrition, including diarrhea, dysentery, and cholera. Unfortunately, many of the diseases are obtained through unhygienic living conditions and unclean water.

ACF helps communities at risk by teaching the people healthy practices and constructing water filters using basic materials. In addition, in order to make living conditions more hygienic, ACF groups build hand washing stations and latrines, along with distributing hygiene kits.

ACF also recognizes the need to deal with unclean water in communities. To address this problem, they drill and decontaminate wells where the water is either unsafe or lacking. As far as protecting existing clean water, they try hard to protect all natural springs. During droughts and water shortages, ACF installs emergency storage tanks and reservoirs full of water into the affected areas.

ACF focuses much of its efforts on Africa. Some of the African countries they are helping include Burkina Faso, the DRC, Ethiopia, Kenya, Niger, and Somalia.

"We strive to deliver effective humanitarian assistance wherever it's most needed."

Burkina Faso is currently experiencing a shortage of natural resources (from crops, to water), which is a significant problem due to the fact that they are dependent on an agricultural economy. The ACF is currently sending supplies their way.

In the Democratic Republic of Congo, they are enduring many outbreaks of very bad malnutrition. In response, Action Against Hunger is focusing on improving the health care system. In 2010, they supplied 476 treatment centers and trained 4,000 public health workers. From this action, 42,000 malnourished people received care that saved their lives.

In Ethiopia, it is expected that Action Against Hunger will aid over 285,000 people by the end of 2011. Already 150,000 have been aided. The Ethiopians need assistance because approximately 5 million people are at risk to drought-related health problems.

In addition, the ACF is intensifying the emergency nutrition programs in Kenya as the crisis of food shortages and drought build up in the Horn of Africa. These programs are expected to help 50,000 to 65,000 children who are suffering from severe acute malnutrition.

14

ACF is also active in Niger. In 2010, ACF's cash-for-work programs along with the dispersion of tools and seeds saved 5,600 families in that country.

In Somalia, there are a very few organizations besides Action Against Hunger providing aid throughout the current drought and famine. In Mogadishu, teams from Action Against Hunger are supplying help to the people, and in July of this year, they provided 130,000 with assistance. They delivered over 215 tons of food this August to needy Somalians.

Although ACF deals with many politically troubled countries, it focuses on help, not politics.

As it states on its website, "As a humanitarian agency we are apolitical. But when it comes to human suffering, we are not neutral: We strive to deliver effective humanitarian assistance wherever it's most needed."

Get involved: visit the Action Against Hunger website at wwww.actionagainsthunger.org

15

FIGURE 8.11 Miranda Smith's research project on famine relief in Africa, presented in the form of a feature article.

popular publication format, so Miranda decided to create her own feature article from a news magazine, taking *Time Magazine* as her model. In designing her text, she not only took into account her argument but also, as Figure 8.11 makes clear, deliberately designed the layout, placement of images, font size, color, and overall look of the piece with painstaking care. Her rhetorical choices establish a hierarchy of information: she strategically uses a header and subheader; she pulls out a key quote on her second page to accentuate an important point; she uses the *logos* of statistics to frame and define the information in the second half of the article; lastly, she selects several images to complement her written argument. Her article ends powerfully with a *pathos*-based appeal, namely, a small child looking directly at the reader as if inviting her to "get involved," a visual echo of the call to action positioned above his head. We can see here how the visual and verbal operate in tandem as powerful persuasive tools for this multimodal composition.

Composing a Website

If you decide to move your project online and produce a website, your readers will then encounter your visual argument as a series of interlinked pages (or *hypertext*). Web authors construct a framework for an argument

FIGURE 8.12 The homepage for Causes.org is organized to provide structure while encouraging exploration.

through the **homepage** (the site's introduction), the **navigation scheme** (the site's organizational structure), and the contents of individual pages, offering both internal and external links designed to guide readers through the various levels of argument and evidence. In effect, a *hypertext argument* is produced by the interactive collaboration between the author's direction and the readers' participation, so that the audience plays an active role in the construction of meaning.

This dynamic determines the argumentative structure for Causes.org's homepage (see Figure 8.12). The site's target audience is one that is probably already predisposed to participate in social activism or community service, therefore much of the page is designed to provide readers with examples of opportunities and prompt them to action. The site's primary level of decorum is plain style: through simple language, clean, uncluttered design, and engaging visuals, the website seeks to persuade viewers that they too can make a difference in the world.

Seeing Connections
See Chapter 3 for instructions and advice on writing a hook for the introduction of your essay.

Part of the power of this multimodal argument lies in its engaging opening hook—similar to the hook you would find in the introductory paragraph of an academic essay—which centers the audience's attention on an example of a person who took action for social good. The *homepage* cycles through a series of such examples, such as Paul who protected the rainforests, Kellie who is protecting pets, Jo who speaks out against animal cruelty, and Eric who fought cancer (see Figure 8.12). Looking closely at Eric in Figure 8.12, we can see the effective design decisions at work: the header is punchy and succinct, putting us on a first-name basis with the character and clearly identifying his accomplishment; the realistic cartoon, with Eric dressed in business casual attire, making eye contact with the audience, relies on *pathos*; the more detailed explanation below the header creates *ethos* by mentioning Eric's full name and also draws the readers even deeper into the site with the lure, "read the whole story." Taken together, these elements effectively personalize the Causes.org experience to appeal to its audience.

Even more significant than the example itself is the way it operates in tandem with the website frame. Text above and below the central example deliberately encourages audience participation. The top menu offers the principal navigational menu for the site, organized thematically around particular issues. The intent is not linearity, but that exploration of the site will be guided by the visitor's interests; the prominence of the search field in the upper left attests to this as well. Similarly, in the upper right, the audience is prompted to "Start a Campaign," a call to action that is articulated even more forcefully beneath the image. In the footer beneath Eric, in large font, the visitor is asked to put himself in Eric's (or Jo's, or Kellie's, or Paul's) shoes: "How will you use Causes to make a difference?" The shift to second person, coupled with the green "Get Started" imperative that follows, makes clear the argument of this site: its entire design is geared toward providing visitors with possibilities and inspiration that will prompt them to start their own activist campaign.

Clearly, while the Causes.org website on the surface seems simplistic and minimalist, its design was informed by strategic rhetorical decisions that took into account audience and purpose. Based on this example, the process of authoring your own website may seem daunting at first. However, in many ways drafting text for the web resembles drafting the complex argument of a long research paper: in both cases, you need to identify the necessary elements of your composition, and then you need to follow a process of careful planning and organization.

In designing your website, you will need to account for three levels of information: a *homepage* at the **primary level** (which will serve as the introduction to your site and draws your audience further into your site); a *series of topic pages* at the **secondary level** (which will contain both content and, sometimes, links to further, more specialized subtopic pages); and the *subtopic pages* at the **deep level** (which will contain content and perhaps even more links). There is no limit on the number of topic and content pages you can include; you should determine the scope of your project and number of pages based on your assessment of how to make your argument most effectively.

WRITER'S PRACTICE

In terms of design, composing a website resembles the process of outlining a research paper. Yet there are important differences between digital writing and writing for print readers. For a website:

- *Chunk* your information—or divide it into manageable parts.
- *Strive for consistency* of theme, font, and/or color throughout your site; avoid visual clutter and ineffectual use of images.
- *Consider creating* a *template,* or visual precedent, that establishes the key elements for the rest of the site, much as an introduction in a written paper often sets the style and conventions for the rest of the argument to follow.
- *Use subheads* to structure your argument and help readers navigate your text.

Let's look now at a student's web project on the visual rhetoric surrounding the 1963 March on Washington. In designing the site, Hailey Larkin intended to encourage readers to engage with the primary texts within the framework of a researched argument.

The homepage for this site (see Figure 8.13) models the composition of the entire project. The most striking element is the photograph, used here to underscore the author's argument. Notice the way the homepage

- pairs image with text
- uses a quote (in blue) as an epigraph
- explicitly states its argument in bold
- meticulously cites its sources (with parenthetical, hyperlinked references to the Sources page)
- shows careful attention to copyright issues by using a public domain image

FIGURE 8.13 This project on the 1963 March on Washington uses a carefully designed website as its medium.

On the subpages, Hailey supports her researched argument through reference to secondary sources and analysis of the primary texts. For instance, on the "Celebrities" page, she analyzes photographs of Joan Baez, Bob Dylan, Harry Belafonte, Sammy Davis Jr., and Charlton Heston. The homepage also demonstrates the site's attention to organization. The tabbed menu at the top is duplicated by the visual menu below, where each subpage is assigned a representative image. Color is used strategically in both instances (white font; yellow border) to help the viewers locate themselves in relation to the larger structure of the argument.

As you compose your own website as a visual argument, be sure to consider **usability**—how user friendly your hypertext is and how accessible to users with disabilities. Even a site with professional design and a state-of-the-art graphic interface is ultimately ineffective if the audience cannot navigate it. Learning to write with attention to diverse readers will make you a more rhetorically savvy and effective communicator.

AT A GLANCE

Designing a Website

- Decide on your audience and purpose.
- Draft a header; include an image in it.
- Map a logical organization for your site to help readers find information easily and understand your purpose and argument.
- Be consistent in imagery and font; avoid jarring color combinations or visual clutter.
- Be strategic in your use and placement of images; be clear in your word choice.
- Link to subpages and external sites.
- Provide a feedback link for comments, and include a "last updated" notice.
- Test your site for usability—both in terms of its general user friendliness and its accessibility to users with disabilities.

Creating an Online Video

If given the opportunity to choose a popular format for your argument, you might consider one that you encounter everyday on the channels of Vimeo, YouTube, and the like: the online video. Whether you watch weekly videoblogs, technology product reviews, make-up or fashion tips, celebrity gossip reports, or even gaming walk-throughs, chances are you are quite familiar with one of the genres of homegrown video currently available on the Internet. And with camera hardware and editing software coming hardwired on more and more smartphones, laptops, and tablets these days, more and more people find themselves with the opportunity to be their own cameraman, director, producer, and film star.

FIGURE 8.14 The vlogger of popular video blog *danisnotonfire* carefully designs each of his videos, despite their seemingly casual tone.

Consider the Internet sensation *danisnotonfire*. British-born Dan Howell rose quickly to fame in 2010–2011 for his vlog and, as of May 2013, his YouTube channel boasted 1.6 million subscribers. His video blogs often center on personal narrative; in typical YouTube style, he directly addresses the audience, looking into the camera as if to make eye contact (see Figure 8.14); his pieces incorporate occasional cuts between takes to enhance continuity, create a story structure, and emphasize certain ideas. He also at times superimposes text onto the screen to accentuate a point. While clearly gravitating toward a plain or low style, he creates an engaging text defined by his own persona and through a perspective that keeps his viewers coming back for more.

If creating a video, take into account how best to persuade your audience. While you might narrate or appear in the video, you might also use footage of events, interviews, locales, or even animation to drive your argument.

- For a collaborative project on the impact of the Nintendo 64, one group of students constructed its video around a series of interviews they conducted, creating an argumentative structure in which they presented the interview question in type on the screen, following each with "answers" in the form of footage from the interviews. The *ethos* of the interviewees and the careful selection of sound bytes drove home their argument.
- Another student designed a short video argument about current war protests, showing an escalating sequence of images—news photographs of the war-torn landscape, of protest demonstrations, and politicians speaking about the military campaign—set against the soundtrack of the song "Wake Me Up" by Evanescence. The rapid succession of images paired with stirring music provoked an emotional reaction in the audience, without the need for verbal commentary.

AT A GLANCE

Designing an Online Video

1. Decide on how you might approach video as a medium to best engage your audience.
2. Use storyboarding to brainstorm or *invent* your ideas.
3. Create a script and build on your storyboard to develop a visual outline.
4. Practice your drafted scenes; if you film the drafts, do a self-assessment or peer review to help you revise.
5. Film your revised scenes, labeling each "draft" as a take for future analysis.
6. Use the strategies you learned in Chapter 6 for revision as you edit your film.
7. When you feel the text is complete, pre-screen it with a test audience and receive feedback.
8. Finally, submit it to your audience and then write up a reflection on your work.

- Yet another group, designing a video argument on *locavorism* (the movement to eat foods grown locally rather than those shipped from around the world), filmed footage inside two markets: the local Albertsons (a big chain supermarket) and their nearby Whole Foods (a natural food market). Using a news reporting style, they examined fruits and vegetable in the produce section in both locales, comparing price, availability and quality so as to make their argument about the feasibility of adhering to a locavore diet.

In your own film project, use *invention*—perhaps drafting your ideas on a storyboard, as discussed in Chapter 6. Consider levels of style—plain, middle, or grand—and how to best convey these through tone, choice of images, types of camera shots, and persona or voice. Work with the canon of arrangement, as discussed in Chapter 3, to consider how edits, order of scenes, and transitions can contribute to the persuasiveness of your argument.

THE WRITER'S PROCESS

In this chapter, you've learned how to design and produce your texts in ways that meet your purpose and match the expectations of your audience. Often this means knowing, understanding, and adhering to conventions set forth by a community of scholars, readers, or writers. This is the case for the document design of your research essay, cover page, abstract, and bio. At other times, this means exploring innovative approaches to design in multimedia contexts. It is also the case for the document design of visual and multimodal arguments. All modes of design depend on your rhetorical expertise in choosing a level of decorum, in knowing what strategies best work for your situation, in deciding on your medium and your format, and then in having these choices support your purpose in designing your work. By examining academic essays, op-ads, photo essays, websites, and short videos, you have seen that the rhetorical principles of audience, argument, form, and purpose carry across diverse media. With the ever-changing features of modern media, you have an increasing number of choices for designing arguments with purpose, power, and creativity. It's time now for you to make your contribution. Write out your brainstorming ideas, and begin to design your own argument.

WRITING ASSIGNMENTS

1. **Write an Analysis of a Visual/Verbal Argument.** Select an argument (a YouTube video blog, a work of graffiti art from a community center, a parody poster from a campus organization, for instance) and using the strategies developed in this chapter, analyze how it uses style and design elements to construct its argument. Use the checklist below to help you with this process.

   - ❑ **Argument:** What is the text's topic? What is its argument? What evidence is used to support the argument? What is the rhetorical stance and point of view on the topic? What role does verbal, visual, or multimedia play in persuasion in this text? Are words and images complementary or does the argument work primarily through one means?
   - ❑ **Audience:** Whom is the argument intended to reach? What response seems to be anticipated from the audience? Sympathetic? Hostile? Concerned?
   - ❑ **Medium:** Is the medium used appropriate for the argument and its target audience? What type of interaction does the medium create with its audience?
   - ❑ **Form:** What are the specific characteristics of the medium? Consider layout, images, style, and font. How are these elements organized?
   - ❑ **Purpose:** What is the purpose in presenting the argument to the audience in this design? To move them to action? Inform them? Teach them? What type of decorum or style (grand, middle, or plain) is used to realize this purpose?

2. **Design Elements to Accompany Your Final Essay Revision:** Write an abstract and bio for your research paper. Adhere academic document design. Post all your documents online as a showcase of your work as a writer and researcher.

3. **Visual Argument:** Create a photo essay based on the argument from your research paper or as part of an independent project. The images you use in your photo essay may be from your paper, or you can use a completely new set, particularly if you did not use images in your original essay. Your argument may mirror that found in your research paper, or you may focus on a smaller portion of your overall argument. The style, arrangement, medium, and rhetorical strategies of your photo essay should match your audience and your purpose. Include written text in your photo essay strategically. Once you have finished, write a one-page reflection on the strategies you used in this project.

4. **Multimodal Argument:** Transform your written essay into one of the creative formats you've learned in this chapter: try creating an op-ed, a website, an online film, a visual collage, or text combining multiple modes, such one that uses words or audio strategically as part of the text's persuasive power. If using audio, match your images to a recorded argument. Alternatively, combine visual images with a soundtrack, and post your work on a website that you design; pick your music carefully, and time each image to match a particular mood or moment in the music. If you are transforming your essay into an short online film, modify your organization, arrangement, text selection, and even order of images to accommodate this shift in medium. Once you have finished, write a one-page reflection on your work.

CHAPTER 9

Delivering Presentations

Chapter Preview Questions

9.1 How do the branches of oratory help me understand my presentation rhetorically?

9.2 Can I identify audience, purpose, and persona to shape my presentation options?

9.3 What strategies can I learn to transform a written argument into a presentation?

9.4 How do I know when to give a speech, a poster session, a PowerPoint, or a live performance?

9.5 How will the canons of memory and delivery help me draft and perform my presentation?

FIGURE 9.1 Barack Obama delivers his argument at the 2004 Democratic National Convention.

Perhaps, by this point, you've finished your written argument and submitted it to your instructor according to proper academic conventions. Maybe you even translated it into a visual argument, such as an op-ed, photo essay, or website. But what if you are asked to do more: to present your argument to an audience in the form of a "live" presentation? Today, students increasingly need to learn strategies for presenting research-based writing and original ideas to both academic and public audiences. You may even be asked to present your research proposal orally, or with multimedia, *before* you get started on drafting your research essay. In such cases, you might turn to the lessons of this chapter, to learn how to approach "writing" and "giving" a presentation.

In the following pages, we'll learn from famous speakers and performers, such as Martin Luther King, Jr., Barack Obama, Steve Jobs—and even rock stars Bono and Lady Gaga. We'll attend to an author's choice of *embodied rhetoric* and *gestures*, such as the one shown in Figure 9.1, which captures then-candidate Barack Obama giving his speech at the 2004 Democratic National Convention. Notice how Obama's hand emphasizes the words he speaks at that moment, he holds his body still, and he makes strong and eye contact with part of the audience. On the podium sits the *script*, or written version of the speech, which was carefully drafted, reviewed by his campaign, and then revised for Obama to give to a live audience. With strategically chosen language, the speech laid out the basic themes of his campaign—"There's not a black America and white America and Latino America and Asian America; there's the United States of America"; "Do we participate in a politics of cynicism or a politics of hope?"—and in this way he used the rhetorical techniques of repetition and asking questions to persuade the audience to accept his argument for a multi-racial, unified America. The convergence of well-crafted language, passionate delivery, and deliberate gesture produced a memorable moment in American history.

As you approach drafting your own presentation, you might look to Obama and other orators as powerful models and explore the many possibilities available to you for this act of effective communication. You can also benefit from understanding the *branches of oratory* as rhetorical concepts that determine the way you might speak at particular occasions. In addition, we'll discuss how attending to *audience, purpose,* and *persona* will enable you to focus your writing and drafting process in order to produce the most successful presentation for the situation. You'll also learn effective strategies for translating your written argument into various multimedia presentations, methods for drafting a script and designing visuals, and techniques for a memorable and effective delivery of your argument.

BRANCHES OF ORATORY

9.1 How do the branches of oratory help me understand my presentation rhetorically?

While today we turn to rhetoric to shape any verbal or visual argument, rhetoric originally evolved as a technique in classical Greece for teaching people how to speak both eloquently and persuasively in public. Classical rhetoricians such as Aristotle divided such public speaking into three **branches of oratory** based on time, purpose, and content.

- **Judicial or forensic discourse** involves defending or accusing and deals with the *past.* It deals with right and wrong.

  Relevant Situations: You might employ judicial oratory to argue about a past action in debate team, or moot court or law school, using verbal arguments as well as charts, graphs, photos, and other visual evidence arranged and designed to persuade your audience.

- **Deliberative or legislative discourse** concerns policy and typically argues for or against specific actions that might take place in the *future.* It concerns what is beneficial or harmful for a population.

  Relevant Situations: You might employ deliberative oratory to exhort or dissuade an audience in promoting the passage of a bill in Congress, or a plan for a fund-raising campaign. Your presentation might include memos, a financial plan, and specifications concerning the worthiness of the enterprise; you might employ PowerPoint slides, charts, images, prototypes, models, and animation to support your argument.

- **Epideictic or ceremonial discourse** generally deals with the *present.* It concerns praising or blaming.

  Relevant Situations: You might employ ceremonial oratory at a wedding or graduation, a senior thesis presentation, a company party, an advertising campaign celebration, a political party rally designed to praise (or blame) a candidate, or even a funeral.

Since strategies differ from one rhetorical branch to another, you'll find it helpful to assess which branch best addresses the demands of your particular situation, and to that end, we can turn to rhetorical concepts we already know well.

BRANCHES OF ORATORY: CONTEMPORARY EXAMPLES

JUDICIAL OR FORENSIC DISCOURSE: involves accusing or defending

Johnny Cochran's 1995 defense of O. J. Simpson represents a notable instance of forensic discourse when Cochran used powerful visual and verbal rhetoric to clear O. J. Simpson of murder charges.

Notice the way Cochran makes his point visually by slipping on gloves that had been used in the crime to underscore his defense: "If it doesn't fit, you must acquit."

DELIBERATIVE OR LEGISLATIVE DISCOURSE: argues for or against specific actions

In her 2010 TED talk, "Why We Have Too Few Women Leaders," Facebook COO Sheryl Sandberg employs deliberative discourse to argue for greater gender equality in the upper levels of business leadership.

By insisting that women learn to "take a seat at the table," Sandberg persuades more women to become leaders.

EPIDEICTIC OR CEREMONIAL DISCOURSE: entails praise or blame

Eulogies, such as Obama's speech delivered at Senator Edward Kennedy's funeral in 2009, are a typical form of epideictic discourse in that they center on praising and celebrating people's lives.

Although colleagues told funny stories about Ted Kennedy, their remarks were celebratory of his accomplishments, and their demeanors solemn and respectful.

9.2 Can I identify audience, purpose, and persona to shape my presentation options?

AUDIENCE, PURPOSE, AND PERSONA

When crafting successful presentations, consideration of the rhetorical situation helps focus the task. That is because the concepts of *audience, purpose,* and *persona*—which we've discussed in relation to written and visual texts—are key elements for oral rhetoric as well. For instance, consider how attention to purpose, audience, and persona determines the presentations shown in Figures 9.2 and 9.3. Notice rock star Bono's trademark sunglasses as he presented his views to world leaders at the Davos economic forum in Figure 9.2. Compare this to Steve Jobs and his very rehearsed 2008 presentation at MacWorld, where he stood in his predictable black turtleneck and jeans, gesturing emphatically to underscore his point (see Figure 9.3). In each case, the speaker chose *presentation strategies*—including words, visuals, props, and

FIGURE 9.2 U2 leader Bono addresses world financial leaders at the annual symposium in Davos, Switzerland.

FIGURE 9.3 Steve Jobs, co-founder and former Apple CEO, presenting a new product at MacWorld 2008.

gestures—to fit the *audience* and *purpose* of his rhetorical situation. The way each presenter appeared—in terms of dress, accessories, tone of voice, and even attitude—defined his *persona* as a speaker. Keep this in mind when you design a presentation, select words and visual material, and practice a form of delivery that is specific to your rhetorical situation. You, too, can carefully construct your presentation to be a powerful visual and verbal argument.

You may find yourself presenting to your class using a podium and a project for slides, to a larger academic audience as part of a conference panel where various speakers take turns with mostly oral arguments, to college administrators or a university forum where you'll want to have handouts or documentation of your points, or even to a public audience, such as at a TEDx organized by your school. In each case, you'll have many choices to make. You can start determining the possibilities for your situation by using the focusing questions in the "At a Glance" box, designed to help you identify your audience, purpose, and persona.

AT A GLANCE

Identifying Your Audience, Purpose, and Persona

1. **What format will my presentation take** (oral speech, multimedia slideshow, interaction drama, etc.)?
2. **Who is my audience?** What do they know or not know about this topic already? How receptive will they be to my material? Are they experts in the area or will they need a lot of background explanation?
3. **What is my purpose?** What do I hope to accomplish? What is my ultimate goal with this presentation?
4. **What branch of oratory does my presentation represent?** Is it designed to defend or accuse? To argue for a position or policy? To celebrate or condemn a person or an event?
5. **What persona do I want to convey** (knowledgeable, friendly, impassioned, concerned, expert, peer, etc.)? How do I visualize myself as a presenter? How might I dress, stand, gesture, and use facial expressions?
6. **What kind of tone do I want to use** (fun, serious, informative, concerned, alarmed, practical, etc.)?
7. **What supporting materials do I plan to use** (quotes from research, photographs in a PowerPoint slide or on a handout, film or commercial clips, graphs, charts, posters, etc.)?

9.3 What strategies can I learn to transform a written argument into a presentation?

TRANSFORMING RESEARCH WRITING INTO A PRESENTATION

Whether you are a student preparing for a class presentation or a polished public speaker, creating an effective oral argument involves a process of *planning, drafting, revision, rehearsal,* and finally, *performance*. Figure 9.4 provides us a glimpse into this composition process; shown here are President Obama's handwritten edits of his September 9, 2009, speech to Congress about health care reform. Through consultation with his speechwriter Jon Favreau, the President carefully crafted and revised his word choice, structured sentences, and organized examples in order to produce a compelling argument on the need for a new health care plan.

Like the President in this example—who drew on a vast corpus of research, including medical statistics, historical references, and national values in producing this speech—when composing your presentation, you will need to consider how best to transform your research into a writing meant for oral delivery. To achieve this goal, you need to think about *transforming* your research argument from one kind of writing to another—from *writing for readers* to *writing for listeners*. This process involves taking into account scope, content, and style. If you have 15 written pages of argument, it would probably take 40 minutes or more to read your words out loud. Thus, you'll need to cut down the sheer amount of material you can convey. Moreover, you would certainly not choose to simply read your written paper; writing meant to be read silently differs from writing meant to be read out loud. Only in certain academic circles is there a preference for complex, written prose as a formal speaking style. By contrast, in most cases, audiences desire clear, well organized speech that is easy to follow. Finally, think about ways to present it in an interesting, memorable way, using a more conversational tone than in formal writing. You can accomplish all these goals through a process of *selection, organization*, and *translation*.

FIGURE 9.4 President Barack Obama's speeches are products of a careful process of drafting and revision, as is apparent in this picture of the President's annotated speech for a September 9, 2009, address to a joint session of Congress.

Selection

Always plan for a shorter presentation time than what you actually have allotted. Most of us speak for longer than we realize; so if you are planning material for a 10-minute presentation, aim for 8; a 15-minute presentation, aim for 12; a 5-minute presentation, aim for 3. One way to keep your time frame manageable is to **select** only a subset of material to present. That is, if your written argument comprises three main areas, plan to cover only one in

AT A GLANCE

Key Steps in Transforming Your Research Argument into a Presentation

- ***Scope:*** How do I convert 10, 15, or even 20 pages of written argument into a 5-, 10- or 15-minute oral presentation?

  Answer: Selection

- ***Content:*** How do I reframe the content so that it makes sense to my audience?

  Answer: Organization

- ***Style:*** How do I change the written word to a spoken, visual, and digital medium?

  Answer: Translation

AT A GLANCE

Focusing Your Argument

1. What matters most about this project?
2. What two or three points can I make to convey my answer to the above question?
3. What do I want my audience to walk away thinking about when I am done?

your presentation. Also, if you plan on speaking extemporaneously (or improvising), be sure that you build this into your schedule for your presentation. Finally, remember to be as selective with your visual evidence as you are with your overall information. You might opt to use only the most powerful images, or you might decide to center your presentation on a single case study and therefore feature only those materials relevant to that narrower focus.

You should find the "At a Glance" focusing questions helpful for moving through the process of selection. Question 1 will help you identify the crux of your presentation. This may be your thesis, but you may have found that what really matters most is the need to raise awareness about an issue, the need to publicize potential solutions to a problem, or the need to advocate for a particular research agenda. Question 2 will help you narrow your project to a few points designed to convey your project's significance to the audience. Question 3 will help you confirm your purpose and ensure that your presentation is engaging and memorable.

Organization

As you transform your research into an oral presentation, you have an opportunity to **reorder** your written argument to meet the expectations of a listening audience. You might, for instance, begin with your conclusion and then convey the narrative of your research. Or you might want to show your visual evidence first, ask questions, and then provide your thesis at the end. In other words, your presentation doesn't need to be miniature version of your written argument. Be innovative in your organization; think about what structure would be the most effective for your audience.

To draft with attention to organization, create a flowchart, outline, or block graphic of each element of your presentation. Don't forget your opening "hook" and closing message as you work on structuring your presentation. Try matching each component to a minute-by-minute schedule to make sure that you are within time limits. And finally, consider creating a

visual outline by drawing or pasting in images next to your verbal cues to show how and when you will use images as a part of your presentation.

To grasp what this *visual outline* might look like, let's look at an excerpt of the presentation aid composed by Nicholas Spears for his research proposal presentation on the rhetoric of Lady Gaga as a political activist. Examining Figure 9.5, we can see that Nicholas carefully paired his choice of slides (on the left) to the words he intended to speak (on the right). In this way, he could clearly map the relationship between the multimedia and spoken elements of his presentation, creating a strong organizational structure.

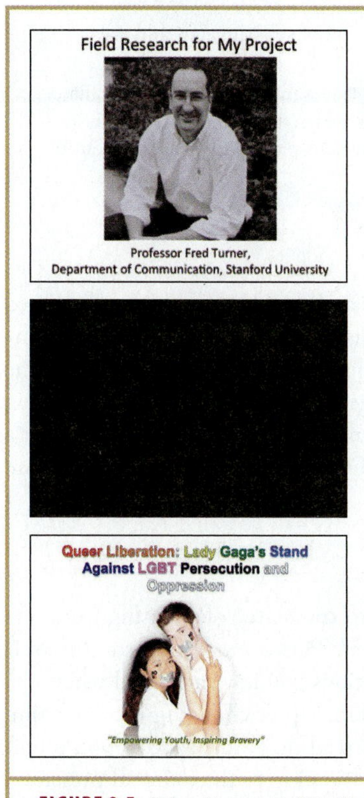

Finally, I will do some field research by interviewing my Communications Professor Fred Turner **[cue slide showing professor]** who specializes in media and popular culture studies.

I will also interview some friends who are involved in LGBT activism and hopefully glean some information as to how Gaga is perceived by these individuals, preferably both on subjective and objective levels

[cue blank slide]
I hope to find a greater significance behind Lady Gaga's hand in activism, delving into her creation of the Born This Way Foundation, the organization she co-founded with her mother, Cynthia, to combat bullying of LGBT youth and to inspire them to be themselves.

Ultimately, I hope that my research will help me explain why Gaga is so focused on the LGBT youth population and why these youth respond so well to both Gaga's public persona and her activism.

[Click to Final Slide for second close]:
I would like to thank you for listening to my proposal. I am excited to dig deeper into this topic and provide you all with my findings in a few weeks. This project really matters to me, because as you can see from this NOH8 photo of me, I am deeply committed to activism myself.

But if all else fails, I will dress up like Gaga and sing her songs. Facebook photos will not be allowed . . . unless I look really fierce.

Paws up little monsters!

FIGURE 9.5 Nicholas Spears created this slide-based presentation script in order to help him keep track of which slides to click on as he worked through the words of his presentation on Lady Gaga's activism.

AT A GLANCE

Key Questions to Shape Organization

- **How can I "hook" my audience?** What would be an effective way to open my presentation? Should I appeal to emotion? to reason? Should I establish my authority as a researcher? What parts of my research would help me do so?
- **What strategies can I use to organize my content?** Narration? Example? Cause and effect? Problem-solution? Process? Definition? Which strategies would be most useful for conveying my argument clearly and effectively to my audience?
- **What main points do I want to use as central evidence?** Do I want to focus on a single case study or on multiple examples?
- **When do I want to present my thesis?** Do I want to start with a question or line of inquiry and then end with my argument in my conclusion? Or do I want to start strong with my thesis within the first moments of my talk and then prove it with evidence?
- **How do I want to close my presentation?** Do I want to conclude by summing up my points or by pointing to the future or further implications? Do I want to end with a call to action or with a provocative question? What strategy would create the greatest impact on my audience?

He even used a **blank slide** to focus the audience back on him as he stated the significance of his project, and finished strongly after the question-answer session. As you can learn from this excerpt of Nicholas's script, the key is to see a presentation as its own genre of writing and to draft a text that meets the needs of both your audience and your purpose. Use the at a glance box on Key Questions to Shape Organization to shape the structure of your own presentation.

Translation

The final step of the transformation is to **translate** your writing from text *meant to be read to text meant to be heard.* This is more important than it may first appear. Think about presentations you have attended where the speaker read from a script without looking up or changing the inflection of his or her voice. If you sat down and read that same speech, you might have found it interesting; however, just listening to the material presented in that way, you probably found yourself bored, confused, or both. The point here is that there are important differences between these types of writing, and you need to carefully *translate* your research into a more conversational script that is accessible to your listening audience.

- **Examine your language:** assess the length of your sentences, the complexity of your diction. Most listeners find shorter sentences, repetition, conversational language, and clear or concrete word choice important for understanding oral discourse.
- **Avoid jargon:** define any terms with which your audience might not be familiar.
- **Add clear signposting**: include verbal "signs" that indicate the steps (or signs along the way) of an argument. More often than not, listeners need more explicit *signposting* than do readers of essays.

AT A GLANCE

Signposting as Structural Devices

Help listeners by including these terms to indicate the logical order of your ideas:

- First
- Second
- Third
- On one hand
- On the other hand
- For example
- Consider
- But
- Yet
- In conclusion

Listeners also respond to humor, direct address, familiar examples, and even questions. These strategies are designed to engage your audience's attention. Finally, as you write your script, *annotate* your written copy with places where you pause, emphasize words, look up, or laugh. Finally, include reminders of when to point to visuals or advance your slides.

WRITING AND DESIGNING A PRESENTATION

9.4 How do I know when to give a speech, a poster session, a PowerPoint, or a live performance?

Let's look in more depth at the work that Nicholas Spears did for his research proposal presentation on the activism of Lady Gaga, and learn from how he transformed his entire written research proposal into a script for his oral and multimedia research presentation. As you read through it, consider the creative rhetorical strategies Nicholas used to captivate and engage his audience, and then try some of them yourself.

Nick opens with a powerful question that immediately gains the attention of the audience.

He continues this strategy, after putting images and words on the screen.

Now his tone shifts, as he mimics Lady Gaga's own expressions, states his name, and identifies his research purpose.

For background, Nick creates a visual montage to match his oral discussion of Lady Gaga's rise to fame.

Lady Gaga Research Proposal "Script"

How many LGBT youth do you think took their own lives because of anti-gay bullying this past year?

[cue slide: photos and numbers on screen]

Another question: How many servicemen and women during the last decade lost their jobs in the military because their fellow service members felt "uncomfortable" fighting alongside them simply because of their sexuality?

Well those numbers are to come later on, but I can tell you that these figures are shockingly and unacceptably high.

Hello all you lovely, beautiful people, my name is Nicholas Spears and my research proposal is on Lady Gaga's involvement in LGBT activism.

[cue slide: animation—montage of photos of Lady Gaga when younger and her rise to fame]

Stephanie Germanotta started out as a student at the NYU Tisch school of music. She had a big dream to one day break into the industry and become a big star. Stephanie would become one of the biggest pop stars in history, selling out arenas and making platinum level albums, oh... and maybe a few Grammys here and there as well. Her transformation into Lady Gaga brought about a shocking, yet avant-garde and captivating public persona. Her unique look is easily recognized by anyone who has some sense of popular culture. To this end, Gaga's influence on society has been noteworthy.

[cue slide: Lady Gaga at Rally]

Due to her stature and popularity, Gaga decided to tackle a big issue that she feels very strongly about, LGBT rights. You can hear her talk about these issues in the following clip **[cue audio-video of Gaga at Rally]**

[cue slide: hypothesis]

Based upon my preliminary research, my hypothesis is as follows:

Lady Gaga combines her star power with personal anecdotes about being bullied growing up, and the power and support of her large gay fan base to become an activist of the people, specifically, the LGBT community.

And that brings me to my research questions.

[cue slide: Research Questions—click AFTER set up]

Through my research, I hope to answer some important questions: "why Gaga? What makes Gaga an authority on LGBT rights? "What is it about Gaga's shocking public persona that resonates with so many people, specifically the LGBT community?" "How has Gaga's music, full of political and social rhetoric, circulated around the world so effectively?" "How has she been able to create so much social change and awareness as she has?"

[cue slide: animation of research sources]

To answer these questions, I will turn to some very useful primary and secondary sources.

In terms of primary sources, **[click to advance]** I will look at Gaga's various speeches on LGBT rights. Namely, her speech in Maine asking that the government repeal the Don't Ask

Now Nick gets to the heart of the matter: Lady Gaga's activism. He uses an audio-video clip as evidence for his point.

Next, he writes his hypothesis on a slide. But in his delivery, he reads the words off his script, not his slide, so that he never turns his back on the audience.

With fluid transitions, and careful control of slides (including clicking AFTER the set up), Nick moves on to state specific research questions.

Using animation features, Nick next presents all his sources in a visually engaging manner.

In order to support his claim about Lady Gaga's "beauty of music and art," Nick plays a short selection of her work.

He then uses the rhetorical terms from Chapter 2 to focus on his future argument.

The script allows Nick to plan how visual and verbal materials will work together.

The script includes delivery directions, such as "look up" and "smile," reminding him to connect with his audience.

Don't Tell policy, and her speech at the National Equality March addressing President Obama to make all US citizens equal.

[click to advance]

I also thought I would analyze Gaga's various socially and politically charged songs. The beauty of music and art in general is that it is open for interpretation. While some of her songs are explicitly pro-LGBT rights in both meaning and feeling, others are not. Here is a taste of the songs I will analyze.

[cue audio clips]

These songs will be a perfect way to address how Gaga makes use of certain rhetorical tools such as *pathos, ethos,* and logos to captivate her audience.

[cue slide: Secondary Sources – showing screenshots and covers of books]:

In terms of secondary sources, I will analyze various interviews such as her *60 Minutes* interview

[cue animation showing second Gaga interview] and her interview with Barbara Walters.

[cue animation showing second Gaga interview] These interviews show a more vulnerable side of Gaga and help render Gaga as more relatable. **[look up and smile]**

[cue animation showing screenshots of articles]

I will also analyze scholarly articles about Gaga's involvement in LGBT activism found in various publications such as the *Advocate* and on Academic Search Premier.

As shown in Figure 9.5, the script from here forward then covers his choice of field research, his hopes for his future presentation, a blank side for significance, and then a "second close"—a last statement that allows Nicholas to leave the audience with a powerful final message and a strong impression. He chooses to conclude with a photograph of himself as an activist again Prop 8, as well as with words of humor. He even quotes Lady Gaga herself. His script is the writing that reminds him to click to the final slide and end in such a memorable manner. Notice, too, that the script includes directions such as "Look up" and "smile," ensuring that he will connect effectively with his audience.

Strategies of Presentation Design

As you can tell from Nicholas's presentation script, careful script writing is key step in communicating your argument powerfully and persuasively not only because it helps you see how your rhetorical choices of selection, translation, and organization will play out in your live performance, but also because you can anticipate—or even draft out—ideas you have for the **design** of your presentation. In Nick's case, his combination of a powerful opening hook using photos and numbers, his slide with his focused research questions, and his turn from seriousness to playfulness as indicated by the script all combined to create a compelling presentation. What other models of presentation design might you consult as you devise your own strategies? Consider these examples:

- Jessica Luo centered her talk about the media coverage of the Tiananmen Square uprising in 1989 on photographs from both Chinese and European presses. She created pairs to demonstrate the arguments made through photos by each media organization. Jessica wanted to move a mainly American student audience into caring about an incident that happened in China more than 20 years ago. Thus, she decided to transform her "objective" writer's voice into a personal narrative and used rhythmic, repetitive terms that explained the rhetorical significance of each image.
- For a project on land mines, Stewart Dorsey showed two PowerPoint presentations side by side on large projection screens. He stood between the two screens to suggest that his argument offered a feasible compromise between polarized camps.
- Max Echtemendy used a mixture of media and interactivity in his research presentation on fantasy violence. First, he set up a table showing horror

novels, DVD boxes, articles in magazines, music videos, and many other examples of "fantasy violence all around us." Then he asked students to complete a brief questionnaire, and he worked with their answers as he discussed the key elements of his argument. He ended by showing a clip from *The Lord of the Rings* and asking for audience response.

- Tom Hurlbutt, exploring the implications of Internet surveillance, created a dynamic PowerPoint presentation that linked to websites, asked students to log on to Amazon, and revealed code that showed their search history from previous class sessions. In this way, he integrated graphic effects in a rhetorically purposeful way.
- Eric Jung, for a presentation on art and technology, transformed the classroom into a twenty-second-century museum, complete with "exhibits" of technologically produced art. He assumed the role of museum guide and gave the class a "tour" of the exhibits, concluding with a "retrospective" lecture about the early twenty-first-century debate over how digital media changed popular conceptions of art.

These innovative projects suggest the many effective ways to use strategies of *selection*, *organization*, and *translation* to write and design the most intriguing, powerful, and appropriate presentation for your purposes.

As you can tell from our list of possibilities above, presentations vary greatly in their design strategies, depending on the rhetorical situation. At times, you may be asked to give an exclusively *oral presentation*, in which

WRITER'S PRACTICE

Take 10 minutes to brainstorm the design possibilities for your presentation. Complete the following questions:

1. What format will my presentation take?
2. What materials do I plan to use in my presentation?
3. What might be a potential outline for my presentation?

Now peer-review your responses with a partner. Have each person suggest changes, new ideas, and alternative ways of designing the presentation. You might also use this time to begin practicing the presentation. Finally, to get a sense of how your presentation will change according to your audience, consider how your answers would change depending on whether you presented to a class audience or a group of friends in the dorm, a review panel at a company, or a potential employer. Experiment to find the most effective ways to design your presentation.

you make your argument without the use of any visuals. We are most familiar with this form of public speaking: great civil rights leaders, peace activists, and political leaders rarely cue up a PowerPoint slide to make their points. Yet, even the shortest talks can be augmented by strategically chosen visual texts that enhance the persuasiveness of an argument. For your own assignments, you will probably be given the option of incorporating visuals in your presentations, so it is important that you develop strategies for doing so effectively—that is, with rhetorical purpose.

Writing for Poster Sessions

Posters communicate arguments both verbally and visually. The presentation style is used most frequently in the sciences, where **poster sessions** are common at conferences and large conventions. Visitors walk through exhibit halls where hundreds of posters are on display, stopping to read those that interest them and often requesting copies of the complete research paper. If you plan on pursuing a science major, you might want to ask your instructor if a poster presentation is acceptable to report research findings.

To create posters, researchers select salient points from their work and organize the content into short summaries with complementary visuals. The goal of a poster presentation is to produce a visual-verbal display that conveys the research accurately, engagingly, and concisely. Figure 9.6 show an award-winning poster from a student research symposium. The poster demonstrates certain key features:

- Bold headings offer clear titles that are easy to read from a distance
- Clear, vertical hierarchies provide key information
- Concise written content is paired with compelling images

AT A GLANCE

Guidelines for a Poster Presentation

- Make sure your poster is readable from a distance; size your fonts accordingly.
- Put the poster's title, authors, and academic affiliation at the top.
- Avoid visual clutter; consider using white space to offset various elements, including tables, figures, and written texts.
- Arrange materials in columns, not rows.
- Avoid long passages of texts; rely primarily on visual persuasion.
- Always check with the conference organizers for their specific guidelines.

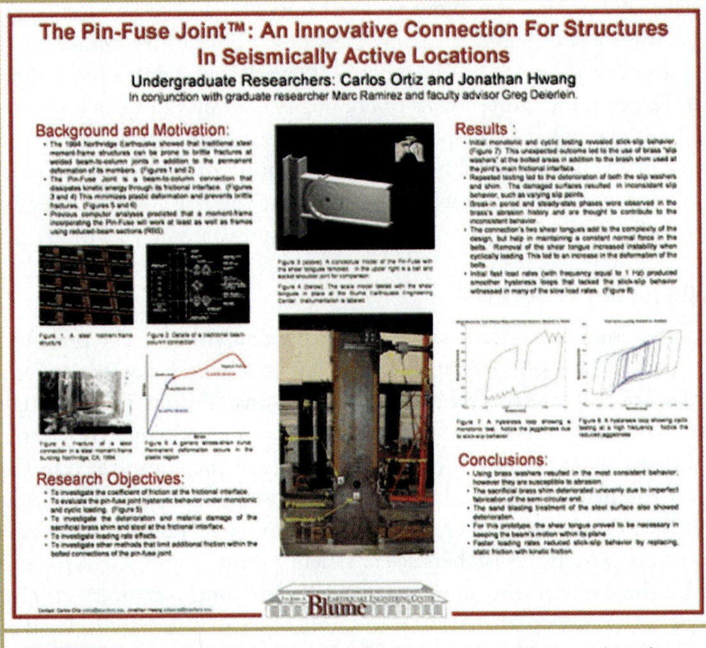

FIGURE 9.6 Co-researchers Carlos Ortiz and Jonathan Hwang transformed their research into this award-winning poster for the 2005 Stanford Symposium of Undergraduate Research in Progress.

Writing for Multimedia Presentations

In today's increasingly high-tech environment, multimedia presentations have become very popular in both academic and professional contexts. There are a range of options available to today's presenter: PowerPoint, Keynote, Prezi, or Google slides; film or audio clips; screencasts; projection of digital images; even live Web browsing or video-conferencing with guest speakers. Many factors will influence your choice of multimedia, including your access to technology, the capabilities of the room in which you are presenting, the requirements of your presentation assignment, and your own technological expertise. However, any time you consider incorporating multimedia into a presentation, be sure to keep in mind the following: these multimedia components are *secondary* to your argument. Start by planning what to say, and then choose the rhetorical tools to help you make the most powerful presentation.

Working with Slideshows

For many presenters, the default tool for presentations is PowerPoint. We commonly overhear students saying, "I have to give a PowerPoint" rather than "I have to give a presentation." The first step in constructing a successful presentation—whether using PowerPoint, Keynote, Prezi, or other presentation software—is to remember that you need to prioritize your *argument*, not the fonts, templates, graphics, and animation.

This is a rule clearly observed by dynamic presenters, from Steve Jobs to Lawrence Lessig, who over time successfully integrated slides into their presentations. Specifically, they moved away from text-heavy slides filled with bullet lists of information, to a more visually dynamic, minimalist style that balanced text with image and that served as visual evidence (some might even say visual punctuation) to their oral arguments.

Seeing Connections
Use the concepts of *readability, contrast, proximity, repetition* and *alignment* discussed in chapter 8 to help you design powerful slides.

If you are composing a slide-based presentation, think strategically about how to use those slides to your best advantage. Will you use them to analyze primary sources (images, film clips, information graphics)? To structure your argument, outlining claims and subclaims? To reinforce key terms or concepts? To showcase definitions or key quotations? To feature an in-depth case study or example? To move your audience emotionally through *pathos* or appeal to their intellect through compelling *logos* of data? Keep in mind, too, that it's not just what slides you create that matters; it's how you use them.

Morgan Springer, for instance, felt that using a map in his slideshow would strengthen his argument on self-determination in Kosovo and East Timor. Having selected a map graphic, he then customized it to his argument by coloring in red those countries experiencing political wars and military dictatorships. As a final touch, after presenting that slide to the audience, he used slide *animation* to circle the two countries that he was going to focus on in his own particular project (see Figure 9.7).

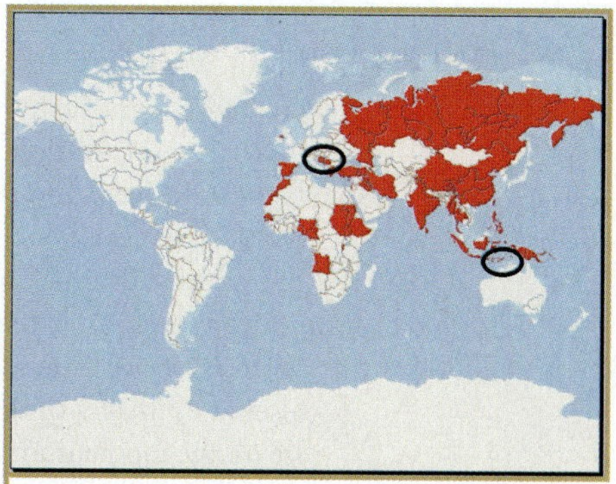

FIGURE 9.7 One of Morgan Springer's map slides from his PowerPoint presentation on national self-determination.

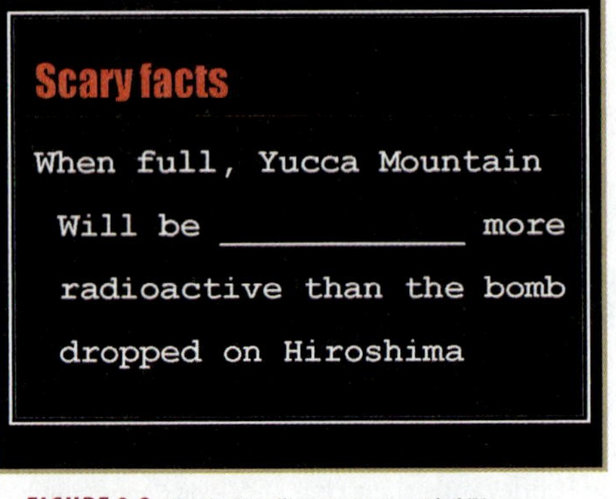

FIGURE 9.8 Natalie Farrell's presentation titled "Yucca Mountain and Nuclear Waste: Gambling with the Future of the Human Race," slide 5.

FIGURE 9.9 Slide 6, in which Natalie dramatically fills in the blank.

Similarly, Natalie Farrell wanted the class to guess at the power of a projected nuclear disaster on Yucca Mountain before shocking them with the actual numbers, so she created slides with blanks left in the list of statistics (Figure 9.8). After a moment of audience participation during which she asked questions and invited the audience to fill in the blanks verbally, she then clicked to a slide that revealed the true statistics (see Figure 9.9), and the audience gasped at the dramatic information revealed on the screen.

For his project, Frank Li decided to embed a screenshot in his slideshow. While previewing it, however, he realized that although the image created a significant visual impact, the screenshot was overall too text-heavy for the audience to read. To solve this problem, he highlighted a key quote from the text and put it in a larger font so that his audience would have the benefit of being able to read the quotation while seeing the screenshot image.

Conversely, Alex Bleyleben's use of slides is notable for his understanding of when *not* to use them. In his presentation about global activism, Alex projected a series of images of the slaughter of the endangered black rhino. To capitalize on the momentum of this *pathos* appeal, Alex turned the screen blank after quickly showing a series of gruesome pictures so as to shift the audience's attention back to his own presence at the podium as he delivered the key points of his argument.

AT A GLANCE

Writing an Effective Multimedia Presentation

- Use purposeful visuals, not clip art.
- Plan to spend time discussing the images you use as visual evidence.
- When using a film or audio clip, be selective in how much to show so it doesn't overwhelm your presentation.
- Don't put too much text on each slide or rely too heavily on bullet lists.
- Use slide animation to stagger the amount of information you present.
- Keep fonts consistent in style, size, and color to avoid distracting the audience.
- Break complicated ideas into multiple slides.
- Use clear, interesting headers to help visually structure your argument.
- Tie your slides together with a visual theme or template that, if possible, reflects the content of your topic.
- Include sound effects and animation rhetorically rather than for flair or flash.
- Give a handout with full quotations or info-graphics as necessary.

These examples suggest many purposeful, rhetorical ways of writing for slide-based presentations. The most important thing to remember is that a slideshow is not a *script* for you to use, but rather a *rhetorical act of persuasion* that should engage your audience.

Beyond the Slideshow

In some cases, you may wish to close down your slideware and experiment with more innovative ways to optimize the power of multimedia for your argument.

In "Redefining the Essay," Caroline Chen embedded audio clips from her interview with rhetoric scholar Andrea Lunsford into her presentation, reinforcing the key points from their discussion by transcribing select phrases on a handout for the audience to read as they listened to the audio.

When composing her presentation on social media shopping, Michelle Pan decided to emphasize the nonlinear functionality of the presentation software program, Prezi. The zooming technique allowed her to "frame" her points and focus in on the details of her argument, so she could literally move from the big picture of her argument (that successful social media advertising relies on audience, voice, and content), to focus in on specific examples,

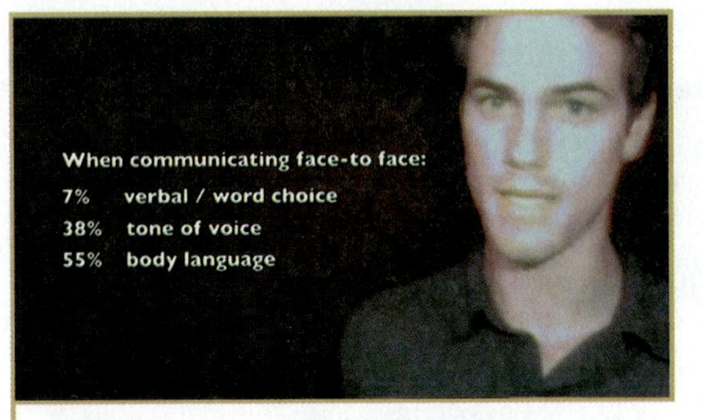

FIGURE 9.10 Max Oswald created a YouTube-type video as the core of his presentation about the distancing effects of modern technology.

and then broaden her frame once again to consider the big picture. The unique Prezi animation format allowed her to show the different relationships between her points that would not have been possible had she used a conventional, linear slide program.

Max Oswald, for his presentation on the effects of technology on modern life, composed the first eight minutes of his talk as a YouTube-style video, complete with spliced scenes and dramatic camera angles, to make his point about the distancing effect of technology (Figure 9.10). Then for the final three minutes of his presentation, he turned off the video and delivered his conclusion in person, dramatically underscoring his argument about the difference between technologically mediated and live encounters.

Rather than browsing the Internet live during her presentation, Rose Emerson used screen capture software to record a segment of gameplay from *Modern Warfare 2*. She then played the footage in the background as she delivered her argument about hyper-masculinization and hyper-militizarization in video games, pausing the recording at pre-designated moments so she could approach the screen and point out key elements to support her argument. She timed her presentation carefully so that she gave her final lines as the gameplay culminated in her character's death.

AT A GLANCE

Presenting Multimedia Effectively

- Practice your timing; experiment with the way you introduce and analyze the media that you present.
- Make eye contact; look at your audience, not the screen.
- If you are using slides, don't read off them, but instead read off a separate script; that will enable you to keep facing the audience and making eye contact.
- Always rehearse a multimedia presentation at least once before giving it live, especially if you are using slides with animations, video footage, or audio clips.

CHOOSING METHODS OF MEMORY AND DELIVERY

9.5 How will the canons of memory and delivery help me draft and perform my presentation?

As the above examples of student presentations reveal, the *way you present* your visual materials is just as crucial as the content you draft for that presentation. In other words, after *selection, arrangement,* and *design* of materials, you need to think about strategies of *presenting* you work, and for that, we can turn to the last two canons of rhetoric: **memory** and **delivery**. According to classical rhetoricians, these two canons made possible the stunning live performances that entranced audiences and won legal cases in course. We can understand them as follows:

- **Memory** entails both literally memorizing one's argument to communicate it to the audience as well as evoking commonly known or familiar phrases held in *cultural memory*.
- **Delivery** concerns all bodily strategies of presenting your argument to an audience, as well as how your voice and body work with any multimedia you might include.

Harnessing Memory for Live Performances

You might ask, won't the content convey the persuasiveness of the argument? While that might be true in written texts, when you are presenting your work orally to a live audience, you also need to attend to *how* you communicate your argument, and it helps to think of such presentations as a form of **performance**. Indeed, ancient rhetoricians categorized and taught the canons of rhetoric to students who then gave elaborate live performances to wealthy patrons. The Greek poet Simonides of Ceos, for example, apparently discovered the importance of memory when he was the only survivor of the banquet hall crashing down and killing all revelers after his speech; Simonides was able to name the bodies by recalling the location of where each man sat.

Artistotle, Cicero, and Quintilian wrote extensively on the "Art of Memory" as a means of engaging and persuading audiences. Aristotle argued that speakers should place striking visual images in certain places and align a point of speech to each one to aid retention. The Roman rhetorician Cicero subsequently refined this technique into a form of visual organization called an **architectural mnemonic technique** in which you associate a phrase to a room or a part of a house you know well. Then, as you work through your presentation or long speech, you walk through your "memory house" in your imagination and at each step, the visual clues trigger your memory of what to say. This technique is still used by memory masters today, who win contests for recalling strings of words or numbers.

In its second sense, *memory* entails learning and storing quotations, phrases, and stories to present at live performances and pass down from generation to generation. Rhetoricians would pull from their "memory treasuries" the appropriate phrase or story to share with that specific audience. This still happens when speakers tell a tale that evokes the shared values of a specific community or use memorized statistics to make a timely point. Consider how graduation speakers share anecdotes from the past year, or presidential inauguration speeches refer to the vision of the Founding Fathers.

Seeing Connections
In this way, the Canon of Memory relies heavily on *kairos* and *doxa*; see Chapter 2 for discussion of these concepts.

WRITER'S PRACTICE

Try out these techniques by writing a humorous speech to share with your class on the last day of the term. First, compose a "memory treasury" by writing down material you might use in that speech. If you were to give such a reflection or "graduation" speech to your class, you would want to quote familiar sayings, share anecdotes of funny moments, tell stories about specific members of class, and even list out the numbers of pages you had to read or write, or the number of revisions you made on your assignments.

Then, take your "memory hoard" and devise an organizational plan for the order of your points. Draw a basic diagram of the classroom, school, or your own home. Assign one point to each location within that drawing in order to use the *architectural mnemonic technique.* Make your associations as vivid as possible to help trigger your memory, such as placing your point about working long hours on a window, since that location might remind you that you rarely saw the light of day while completing your assignment. Run through the diagram with its assigned points of memory several times and then share your speech with your class.

Mastering Delivery for Live Performances

After *memory* comes *delivery*, the last canon or rhetoric, and it entails the way you bring all the previous canons together. Indeed, *delivery* is so important that when asked which three of the five canons of rhetoric he considered most valuable to successful public speaking, the Greek orator

Demosthenes replied, "delivery, delivery, delivery." In other words, so crucial is this fifth canon that it can supersede the rest. Without an effective performance, your ideas and words will have little impact on the audience. Thus, one core aspect of the canon of *delivery* is the *sound* of the presentation: how speakers use tone of voice, pacing, strategic pauses, or changes in volume or inflection to make their arguments memorable and effective. Demosthenes himself practiced reciting his speeches with rocks in his mouth, or while running, or standing before the ocean, in order to improve the articulation, stamina, and projection of his voice.

AT A GLANCE

Fundamental Elements of Delivery

- ***Voice:*** use of pitch, tone, loudness, softness, and enunciation
- ***Stance or posture:*** use of the body to convey confidence and authority
- ***Embodied rhetoric:*** dress or outfit, appearance, mannerisms
- ***Gesture:*** use of hands to communicate information
- ***Pacing:*** speed of words, visuals, and overall argument
- ***Visuals:*** incorporation of complementary slides, posters, graphics, handouts
- ***Style:*** inclusion of elements such as repetition, allusion, metaphor, stories, personal narrative, jokes, and pauses

If you think of some of the most prominent speakers of recent history—Barack Obama, Ronald Reagan, Hillary Rodham Clinton—you probably can hear in your head the rhetorically powerful ways they used **voice**, or the sound of language itself. You can likewise prepare yourself for effective oral delivery through *voice* by *annotating* your script to indicate places where you will pause, emphasize a key word, or use the strength of your voice to underscore a point. Written cues like this can help you to deliver a memorable, moving, and convincing oral argument.

However, it is not just the *sound* of delivery that affects the persuasiveness of a presentation but the *look* of that presentation as well. How many times have you seen a talk in which the speaker dressed up to make a point or used the rhetoric of his or her body to persuade the audience? This form of presentation is called **embodied rhetoric**, and it refers to the way in which the body becomes a visual means of communicating the message. In most presentations, you employ *embodied rhetoric* through the clothes you wear, how you stand, and even how you hold the materials you use to convey your argument. When Liz Kreiner delivered her presentation on sexual assault on campus, for instance, she made very strategic decisions about her embodied rhetoric: to emphasize the seriousness of her subject, she dressed conservatively and stood absolutely still at the podium as she recounted the disturbing stories of date rape that she had uncovered during

FIGURE 9.11 During her presentation on sexual assault on campus, Liz Kreiner opted against using multimedia, relying instead on her voice and embodied rhetoric to convey the seriousness of her subject.

her research. Her somber demeanor, reinforced by her serious tone of voice, produced an extremely powerful rhetorical moment (see Figure 9.11).

In most cases, we see *embodied rhetoric* at work through **gesture**. Often, when we think about the term *gesture* in relation to public speaking, we think of very overt or intentional hand motions that public speakers make for emphasis, like that made by Jake Palinsky in Figure 9.12, in which he directs the audience's attention by pointing to the diagram he is describing. Our eyes follow his finger to focus on the part he is explaining at that moment.

The *gesture* is a careful rhetorical move: it has purpose and works effectively as a strategy of communication. Sometimes gestures in public speaking seem less carefully composed, such as the one in Figure 9.13. Here we see the speaker in midsentence, her hands opened as if in an involuntary accompaniment to her words. But notice how the open palm, extended toward members of the audience, invites them to listen; it is tilted down to allow words to travel and open the space between the speaker and the audience. This subtle instance of delivery techniques invites the listeners into the argument and demonstrates a moment of connection.

Although we all use gestures without realizing that we do, we can in fact train ourselves to use the rhetoric of the body more carefully, and even

FIGURE 9.12 In his presentation on recent developments in stem cell research, Jake Palinsky used gesture deliberately to help his audience understand a scientific diagram.

FIGURE 9.13 In a moment of explanation, Alina Lanesberg uses a subtle gesture to emphasize her point and draw her audience into her argument.

WRITER'SPRACTICE

Analyze the gestures used by one of the most famous public speakers, Martin Luther King, Jr. (see Figure 9.14 and Figure 9.15). Write a brief account of the suggested meaning and purpose of each gesture, describing each of the images as you make your argument. Then select the words you might match to the gesture. This exercise will help you explore strategies to use in your own presentations.

FIGURE 9.14 Martin Luther King, Jr. gesturing at a press conference.

FIGURE 9.15 Martin Luther King, Jr. emphasizes his point at a mass rally in Philadelphia, August 4, 1965.

strategically, as an integral part of our overall presentation design. Your purpose in using gestures as part of a presentation should be to harness the power of the body effectively to communicate ideas. Therefore, as you draft and deliver your presentation, remember that your *entire* body—from voice to body language to clothes, posture, expression, and gestures—participates in communicating your ideas and information. All work together to ensure the successful delivery of your live performance.

PRACTICING YOUR PRESENTATION

Speakers like Martin Luther King, Jr. dedicate much of their time to practicing delivery. Similarly, two ideologically opposed political figures, Adolf Hitler and Winston Churchill, relied extensively on practice to develop their delivery techniques.

- Hitler recorded himself speaking and using hand gestures, then would watch the films over and over again, selecting the motions that he felt were most powerful. Next, he would practice that form of delivery—the tone of voice, the pacing, the bodily stance, and the hand gestures—until he felt it was perfect. Finally, he would destroy the recordings so that no one would know how carefully he practiced. The practice made his delivery seem natural.
- Churchill used voice alone to persuade the British public to withstand the waves of Nazi attacks night after night in the bombing of Britain. Over the radio wires, his practiced and powerful words—delivered with the perfect amount of confidence and encouragement—helped the British persevere during those dark days.

These examples reveal the power of practice in strengthening delivery and its capacity to persuade audiences. Likewise, you should incorporate repeated practice into the process of drafting and revising your presentations. As with any assignment, your argument will benefit from peer review, so consider performing a "dress rehearsal" for a friend or roommate to get feedback on the clarity of your ideas, your use of multimedia or visual aids, and the effectiveness of your delivery. Better yet, become your own peer reviewer by filming your "dress rehearsal" and then critiquing your performance "draft." By becoming a member of the audience yourself, you can better see how to revise your presentation into a truly powerful argument.

Anticipating Problems and the Question-and-Answer Session

As you practice your presentation, don't forget to consider problems that might arise, such as faulty technology, a bored or confused audience, or even hecklers. To troubleshoot technology, visit the room you'll be presenting in and test the equipment in advance. Make sure you have backup for the technology: save your work on a flash drive, or email it to yourself. Bring handouts in case your multimedia doesn't work, and be prepared to talk without technology if necessary. Also, be ready to cut down or extend the length of your talk by indicating on your script places you might cut or points you might discuss in more detail. Realize that the more comfortable you are with your material, the more you can adapt on the spot to the needs of your audience.

Successful adaptation includes handling the **question-and-answer session** well; this part of a presentation, usually located at the end, serves as the final opportunity to clarify your argument and convince your audience. A successful presenter anticipates and, in some cases, even sets up the framework for the question-and-answer session. For instance, during his presentation on Marilyn Manson, Ben Rosenbrough realized he didn't have time to develop the link he saw between Elvis Presley and Manson in his formal presentation, and so he made only a passing reference to the connection, hoping that the audience would be intrigued and ask about it after his talk. When they did, he advanced his PowerPoint beyond his conclusion slide to **a secret slide** documenting these connections in a powerful way. Similarly, you can anticipate what questions your audience might have by delivering your presentation to a classmate, seeing what questions your presentation generates, and even practicing trial responses. Consider having some new evidence, a stunning visual, or even a handout prepared to answer a question that you hope might be asked after your presentation.

DOCUMENTING YOUR PRESENTATION

Design. Delivery. Practice. What is left? After all your hard work on your presentation, you probably want to leave some kind of trace, a written artifact, or a form of textual memory of the presentation. **Documentation**—*some form of written or visual evidence of your presentation's argument*—is the answer. Documentation serves an important rhetorical function: to inform and persuade. This might take the form of a **handout** that provides additional information in the form of an annotated bibliography, a summary of your key points and thesis, visual rhetoric from your presentation, references for further reading, or a printout of your PowerPoint presentation. You should put your contact information on it so the audience can ask you further questions.

Documentation might also consist of a **text** or **script** for your presentation. This can either be the annotated printout of your PowerPoint presentation, a full speech, or a typed set of notes in outline form with placeholders for your slides or media aids such as shown in Nicholas Spears's visual outline (see Figure 9.5). More innovatively, you might document your presentation with a **creative take-away** that reflects a key aspect of your presentation. Consider Wendy Hagenmaier's handout for her project on media coverage of the bombing of Hiroshima and Nagasaki (see Figure 9.16). The cover of the *New York Times* from August 1945 is attached to a small candle; Wendy's caption reads, "Light this candle in remembrance of how the August 1945 atomic

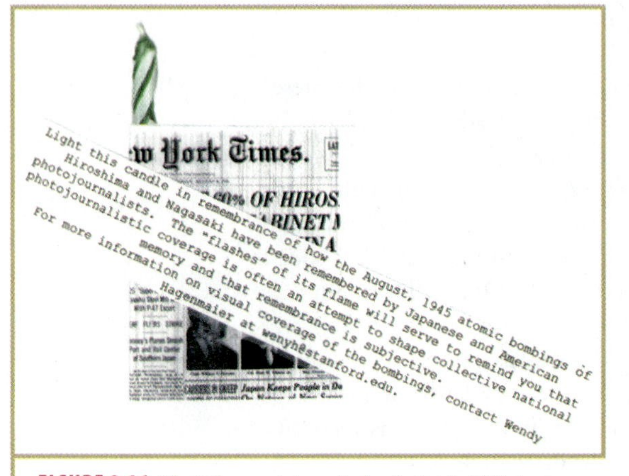

FIGURE 9.16 Wendy Hagenmaier's creative handout on the 1945 atomic bombings of Hiroshima and Nagasaki.

bombings of Hiroshima and Nagasaki have been remembered by Japanese and American photojournalists. The 'flashes' of its flame will serve to remind you that photojournalistic coverage is often an attempt to shape collective national memory and that remembrance is subjective." Another student, Falco Pichler, presenting his research finding on Nike marketing strategies, created a "backstage pass" to what he called the "Nike Show" and invited students to read his paper online. Aaron Johnson, presenting his research on media representation of athletes who take performance-enhancing drugs, made a mock subscription card with the title "Sports Exaggerated" as creative documentation for his presentation (see Figure 9.17). Using Photoshop, he embedded a cover of *Sports Illustrated* into the subscription card and listed the main points of his argument as "advertising points" for his presentation. Notice his complete contact information at the bottom of the card.

DO YOU WANT TO BECOME AWARE OF HOW SPORTS ILLUSTRATED HAS EXAGGERATED THE ISSUE OF DRUGS IN SPORTS?

A PRICE SO LOW IT'S LIKE GETTING

8 FREE ISSUES!

SUBSCRIBE NOW! Get 12 issues of Sports Exaggerated for just $12.

You'll SAVE 74% off the cover price - *that's like getting the first 8 issues free.*

$1 an issue

With each issue you get:

- An IN-DEPTH look at SI's overportrayal of the issue
- A better idea of how serious the drug issue really is
- An awareness of how this exaggeration is harming the athletes and fans alike

or contact Aaron Johnson with questions: ajohn999@stanford.edu.

FIGURE 9.17 Aaron Johnson's creative presentation take-away for his research project on *Sports Illustrated*.

These examples begin to show the range of creative documentation strategies you might pursue as the final part of your presentation. Taking the lead from Aaron, you might even craft an interactive visual take-away such as a graphic montage, a minibook, or other forms of visual argument. The importance of such texts—whether conventional prose handouts or compelling visual creations—lies in their power to make your presentation memorable, convincing, and engaging. So consider your strategies for documentation as carefully as you design your entire presentation.

THE WRITER'S PROCESS

In this chapter, you have explored possibilities for presentations; learned how to convert a written argument into a spoken, visual, multimedia presentation or performance; and worked through the different ways of writing for presentations. Recall the strategies of *design*, *memory*, and *delivery* you have studied, and keep in mind the importance of both *voice* and *embodied rhetoric* as ways of communicating your message and your purpose to your particular audience. Finally, as you craft your own presentation, remember the old adage, "Practice makes perfect." Peer review and revision are as important to your presentation as collaboration on drafts and revision are to your written work. They enable you to anticipate problems and harness your creativity as you shape your ideas into a memorable, moving, and persuasive form of rhetorical communication.

WRITING ASSIGNMENTS

1. **Write Your Analysis of a Presentation:** As part of the necessary preparation for writing your own presentation, conduct field research in the form of observing three public speeches, presentations, or oral/multimedia arguments. If possible, take a camera with you and document your observations of each kind of presentation. Type up a brief rhetorical analysis on the delivery, rhetorical strategies, and effectiveness of each one. Use the Prewriting Checklist below. Then indicate what strategies you plan to use in your own presentation. These presentations can include lectures in any of your classes, speakers visiting campus or your dorms, or the practice presentation of a member of your class.

   - ❑ What is the presenter's purpose given the different branches of oratory? Did the presentation successfully accomplish that purpose?
   - ❑ What is the presenter's relationship to the topic? Is she or he an expert? A novice? Fairly well-informed? What do you make of the speaker's *persona*?
   - ❑ How was the presentation structured? Was an outline or summary provided for the audience to follow, either orally, on a whiteboard, in a handout, or on a slide? Did the argument follow the designated structure? Did the presenter clearly and persuasively develop his or her claim?
   - ❑ Did the presenter modify the presentation to accommodate the audience's reaction? For instance, did he or she notice some confusion in the audience and pause to explain a difficult point?

- ❑ How did the presentation begin? Did the presenter use any effective oral or visual devices to "hook" the audience?
- ❑ Were the main points clearly developed? How was the scope of the presentation? Was there too much information? Too little?
- ❑ Was there a clear conclusion? How did the presenter both summarize his or her main points and argue for the larger relevance of the topic?
- ❑ How appropriate were the sentence structures and the word choice to the occasion, audience, and subject matter? Did the presenter use any formal devices—figurative language, deliberate repetition, literary allusions?
- ❑ How effective was his or her vocal delivery? Consider elements such as voice projection, vocal pacing (speaking slowly or quickly), enunciation (speaking clearly), and the use of emphasis (stressing certain words or using deliberate pauses).
- ❑ Consider the presenter's embodied rhetoric. Did he or she stand or sit? Remain stationary, or move around? Did the presenter use gestures, facial expression, or even costume to add to the rhetorical effect of the argument? How careful was the presenter to make sure his or her body did not block the audience's line of sight to any slides or whiteboard, unless for rhetorical effect?
- ❑ Did the presenter make eye contact (indicating a direct relationship with the audience) or simply read from a prepared text (indicating a focus on the material rather than the audience)?
- ❑ How did the presenter use visuals? Did he or she show slides, bring in posters, write on a blackboard, distribute handouts, pass around books, or bring in material evidence for the presentation? Were the visual components rhetorically purposeful or did they seem an afterthought?
- ❑ If the presenter used posters, were they clear and accessible to the audience? Were the words large enough to read from a distance? Did the poster avoid visual clutter? Did it contain a clear title and use information graphics effectively?
- ❑ If the presenter used a slide program such as PowerPoint, was the visual design of the slides effective? Did the slides have a unity of theme, color, and layout? How much text was on each slide? Were there innovations in the slideshow, such as using dual screens, animation, or embedded clips or Internet links? Were these effective or distracting?
- ❑ If the presenter used technology, were there any technical difficulties? Did the presenter overcome them smoothly (for instance, having a backup plan)?
- ❑ Did the presenter finish within the allotted time? How did he or she handle the question-and-answer session?

2. **Design and Deliver a Formal Presentation:** Create a timed presentation of your research argument for your class (ask your instructor for the precise time limit). You should include the appropriate media (visual rhetoric, PowerPoint slides, websites, movie clips, performative or interactive aspects). In addition, the oral delivery of your presentation might include a handout that you distribute to the class to provide information—for example, an annotated bibliography, a summary of your key points and thesis, visual rhetoric from your presentation, references for further reading, or a printout of your PowerPoint presentation—formatted in the proper manner (or in a creative way if that works for your presentation) with your complete contact information on it. Also compose a script for your presentation. This can either be the annotated printout of your PowerPoint presentation, a full speech, or notes in outline form (with placeholders for your slides or multimedia). Include references in the text or script of your presentation to any materials you use (handouts and printouts of multimedia).

3. **Create a Collaborative Presentation:** Work in groups of two to four to design and deliver a presentation to the class. You might want to divide the tasks of selecting material, brainstorming strategies of presentation, and designing your visual materials. Will you take turns speaking throughout the presentation, or will each person be responsible for a distinct segment of the presentation? Will one person write the script, another person deliver it—perhaps from memory—while a third creates the slides? Choose the strategy that best suits your audience and your purpose. Don't forget to practice together, and when your group is presenting, look at the others who are speaking to keep the class's attention focused on your group presentation.

4. **Prepare a Community Writing Presentation:** Either in groups or individually, rewrite a presentation that you designed for your writing class to meet the audience expectations of a specific community audience; think about how to adapt your message to persuade this broader audience. How would you need to shape your presentation differently if you were delivering it, for instance, to a group of local politicians, to school administrators, or to a national student group? After you revise your presentation in this way, consider contacting that broader group to set up a meeting to deliver your presentation.

Part IV

READINGS

CHAPTER 10
You Are What You Eat

CHAPTER 11
Life Online

CHAPTER 12
Imagining the Ideal Body

CHAPTER 13
Playing Against Stereotypes

CHAPTER 14
Crisis and Resilience

CHAPTER 15
Claiming Citizenship

CHAPTER 10

You Are What You Eat

We take as the title for this chapter the phrase "You Are What You Eat" because never before has this simple idiom held such complex meanings. The dinner table has long been a site of negotiation between children and parents, but the conflicts have moved from whether to eat your vegetables and finish what's on your plate to a much larger arena. Food studies as a field have become a battleground between epicureans and nutritionists, ranchers and activists, and local growers and big business. Thinking about food and its impact on the individual, the environment, and the future has become a new obsession.

Let's consider the ways that our discussions about food have moved out of the kitchen. Walk into any bookstore and you'll not only find glossy-covered gourmet magazines and fully illustrated cookbooks, but you'll probably also encounter a display adorned with copies of Maria Rodale's *Organic Manifesto*, Bryant Terry's *Vegan Soul Kitchen*, Peter Singer's *The Ethics of What We Eat*, and numerous copies of Michael Pollan's best-selling books: *Cooked, In Defense of Food*, and *Food Rules.* Feel like watching a film? You can select from a variety of movies that celebrate food, relationships, and community: from *Julie and Julia* to *Chocolat, Tampopo, Eat Drink Man Woman, Babette's Feast, Jiro Dreams of Sushi,* and even *Willy Wonka & the Chocolate Factory*. Perhaps you simply decide to browse online. You're likely to come across a recipe site aggregating family recipes; a food blogger photo-documenting his every meal; or a food activist providing commentary on the latest incursion against processed foods, GMOs, and fast food chains. Turning on the television will have similar results; shows like *Cake Boss, Top Chef, Hell's Kitchen*, and *Kitchen Nightmares* grow every week in popularity, and the Food Network has carved out its own niche on cable TV. Even a stroll down the street will bring food culture in sharp focus, from the rampant spread of Jamba Juices, Starbucks, and McDonald's into the empty nooks and crannies of our consumer spaces to the rise of specialty markets like Trader Joe's and Whole Foods. Food provides more than just sustenance; it increasingly has come to shape and mediate our understanding of ourselves and our culture.

Perhaps because of the omnipresence of food culture, we are also witnessing a growing critique of it. To see this, we need look no further than our local movie theater and the release of several documentary films over the past ten years that have challenged us to reevaluate the role of food in our lives. While *Fast Food Nation* and *Super Size Me* began the trend in the mid-2000s by targeting the fast food industry and its deleterious effects on American health, these two ground-breaking films were followed by a series of similarly food-focused documentaries. One standout example is the 2009 film *Food, Inc.*, which shifted attention from individual eating habits to corporate farming and industrialized agriculture. The theatrical release poster, shown in Figure 10.1, succinctly epitomizes this critique. What we notice first in the poster is the stereotypical scene of bucolic America, a cow standing in a green field under a vivid blue sky, with an iconic red barn in the background. However, one detail disrupts this idealistic vision: the large barcode branded broadly across the cow's side. This film's goal, the poster argues, is to challenge our romantic notions of food culture, to expose the inner workings of this big business industry, and to problematize our understanding of our relationship to our food.

FIGURE 10.1 This poster for *Food, Inc.* challenges the romantic ideal of the food industry.

In the readings that follow, you'll be introduced to the range of commentaries on food culture today, from the food bloggers who memorialize each meal with a highly pixelated photo and pithy commentary to activists who draw a link between American food obsession, a sedentary lifestyle, and the rise of obesity among American children. We'll look carefully at the government nutritional information graphic, and also consider ways that people define themselves according to their eating choices: as locavore, globavore, vegetarian, and vegan. Finally, we'll delve into the controversy surrounding genetically engineered crops, looking at their viability as a solution to world hunger. As you read through these selections, we invite you to contemplate your own eating habits and ask yourself: How are food and culture linked? How does what we eat, how we eat, where we eat, and who we eat with shape our ideas of ourselves and our community?

REFLECT & WRITE

- ❑ Notice the subtitle to *Food, Inc.* at the top of Figure 10.1. How does it complement and complicate the argument of the poster's central image and main title?
- ❑ Considering that this film exposes some of the more controversial practices in the food industry, why do you think the poster designers chose this image rather than one that would have more shock value?
- ❑ **Write.** Compose a rhetorical analysis of this image that uses a strong thesis statement and specific references to the visual composition of the poster. Argue about the significance of this image in relation to the film's title and main idea.

In this article, The New York Times *journalist* **Kate Murphy** *describes the culture of "food blogging," the practice of keeping an online food diary, complete with photos. This article originally appeared in* The New York Times *on April 7, 2010.*

First Camera, Then Fork

Kate Murphy

JAVIER GARCIA, a 28-year-old neuroscientist at the University of California, Irvine, was in the campus pub recently having a grilled cheese sandwich. But before he took a bite, he snapped a digital picture of it, cheese artistically oozing between toasted white bread, just as he has photographed everything he has eaten in the last five years.

Every other week he posts the photos on his Web site, ejavi.com/javiDiet, providing a strangely intimate and unedited view of his life and attracting fans from as far away as Ecuador. The nearly 9,000 photos leave nothing out, not even snacks as small as a single square of shredded wheat.

When he lost his iPhone while visiting New York last month, he pleaded with exasperated friends to take pictures of his food and to e-mail them to him, lest his record be incomplete. "It was a nightmare," Mr. Garcia said, particularly because the unfocused pictures "were not the quality I'm used to."

In 1825, the French philosopher and gourmand Jean Anthelme Brillat-Savarin wrote, "Tell me what you eat, and I will tell you what you are." Today, people are showing the world what they eat by photographing every meal, revealing themselves perhaps more vividly than they might by merely reciting the names of appetizers and entrees.

5 Keeping a photographic food diary is a growing phenomenon with everything from truffle-stuffed suckling pig to humble bowls of Cheerios being captured and offered for public consumption. Indeed, the number of pictures tagged "food" on the photo-sharing Web site Flickr has increased tenfold to more than six million in the last two years, according to Tara Kirchner, the company's marketing director. One of the largest and most active Flickr groups, called "I Ate This," includes more than 300,000 photos that have been contributed by more than 19,000 members. There would be more, but members are limited to 50 photos a month. The same phenomena can be found on other sites like Twitter, Facebook, MySpace, Foodspotting, Shutterfly, Chowhound and FoodCandy.

Nora Sherman, 28, the deputy director of the City University of New York's Building Performance Lab, which promotes sustainable construction, finds that the pictures she takes of her food are her most popular posts on Facebook, Twitter and on her blog, Thought for Food, (noraleah.com). The immediate and enthusiastic commentary on, say, an arugula and feta salad or a plate of fried okra have given her a sense of connection and community since moving to Manhattan from New Orleans in 2006.

"People I have never met follow my blog and know me through the food I eat," Ms. Sherman said. She was even introduced to her boyfriend through someone she came to know through his comments on the food pictures on her blog, and who thought the two might be a match.

She said she takes pictures of at least half the meals she eats, omitting, for example, multicourse meals when it might "interrupt the flow." But she has noticed lately that it's becoming harder to suppress the urge to shoot. "I get this 'must take picture' feeling before I eat, and what's worse is that I hate bad pictures so I have to capture it in just the right light and at just the right angle," Ms. Sherman said.

She uses a Canon PowerShot S90 and uploads pictures to her Web site daily, sometimes several times a day, which takes at most 30 minutes a day. The camera, she said, is small but works well in low light. She doesn't style her photos, saying, "I like to take shots that no pro would ever take—holding an oyster in my hand about to slurp it down, or a bagel with a bite out of it."

10 Her impulse to photograph her food and do so artistically has made her a more adventurous eater. "It's driven me to seek out interesting, photogenic foods," she said. She is now more likely to eat foods she would have once avoided, like beef tendon, heart and tripe at an Asian shopping mall in Flushing, Queens. And, she said, photographing the food has kept her honest when she has started diets: "When I decided to have salad for dinner during a juice fast, I snapped and posted that."

Photos are also a means of self-motivation for Mr. Garcia, who began photographing his food after he lost 80 pounds. "It's definitely part of my neuroticism about trying to keep thin," he said. "It keeps you accountable because you don't want to have to see that you ate an entire jar of peanut butter."

And, ever the scientist, he hopes to one day use the photographs to calculate how much money he spends to consume a calorie versus how much he spends in gym memberships and sports gear to burn a calorie. "People I have dated haven't been that into it," he said of his food photojournaling. "But it's never been a deal breaker."

Pamela Hollinger, 36, an independent radio programmer and announcer in Stephenville, Tex., said her husband of eight years is resigned to her taking pictures of her food. "When we were dating, it was like, 'What are you doing?'" she said. "Now it's a quirk he's come to accept."

Her habit began in 1997 as a way to show her mother what she ate on vacations, but she now photographs almost everything she eats, leaving out only insignificant snacks and anything unappealing looking, like a bowl of oatmeal. "I think getting an iPhone had a lot to do with it," Ms. Hollinger said. "It's so easy to just take a quick picture of what I'm eating and no one really notices." Or maybe they think she is just texting at the table.

15 She e-mails the pictures directly from her phone to a few friends and posts some of them on her Facebook page as well as on Chowhound. "I like to show off what I'm eating or something I've made that I'm proud of, like a pork rib-eye roast that became pulled pork sandwiches and then pork tacos and then pork salad," she said. "I get more comments on my food pictures than anything else. Within seconds, I get, 'Oh, I'm jealous,' or 'Hey, can I come over?'"

That some people are keeping photographic food diaries and posting them online does not surprise psychotherapists. "In the unconscious mind, food equals love because food is our deepest and earliest connection with our caretaker," said Kathryn Zerbe, a psychiatrist who specializes in eating disorders and food fixations at Oregon Health and Science University in Portland. "So it makes sense that people would want to capture, collect, catalog, brag about and show off their food."

Photographing meals becomes pathological, however, if it interferes with careers or relationships or there's anxiety associated with not doing it. "I'd have to ask if they would feel O.K. if they didn't do it," said Tracy Foose, a psychiatrist at the University of California, San Francisco, who treats patients with obsessive-compulsive disorders. "Could they resist the urge to do it?"

Joe Catterson, the general manager of Alinea restaurant in Chicago, said that, increasingly, people can't. "One guy arrived with the wrong lens or something on his camera and left his wife sitting at the table for an hour while he went home to get it," he said.

Such compulsion is apparent even at restaurants where the plating is less elaborate. "They've got to take a picture of their pancakes and send it to their friend," said John Vasilopoulos, the manager at the Cup & Saucer, a diner on the Lower East Side. "I don't get it because their food gets cold, but I take it as a compliment."

20 Evidently aware of the trend, manufacturers like Nikon, Olympus, Sony and Fuji have within the last two years released cameras with special "food" or "cuisine" modes, costing around $200 to $600. "These functions enable close-up shots with enhanced sharpness and saturation so the food colors and textures really pop," said Terry Sullivan, associate editor of digital imaging technologies at Consumer Reports.

This bemuses Tucker Shaw, the food critic for The Denver Post, who made do with a basic point-and-shoot digital camera to take pictures of everything he ate in 2004; he published the photos in his book, "Everything I Ate: A Year in the Life of My Mouth."

"It used to turn heads if you took a picture of your food, and I even got in trouble at a few restaurants," he said.

"Now it's ubiquitous and just shows that we are in a spastic food era—we couldn't get more obsessive."

Nonetheless, Mr. Shaw said the year he spent photographing his food (and a year was enough for him) resulted in an achingly honest account of his life that revealed far more than the fact that he ate too few leafy green vegetables: "The pictures, I realize now, are incredibly personal, and by looking at them you can probably deduce the type of person I am." Moreover, the pictures set off memories and emotions in a way a written journal could not. "I remember every single day, who I was with, what I was feeling," he said.

Unlike a picture of a flower or friend, a picture of a meal recalls something smelled, touched, tasted and ultimately ingested. Carl Rosenberg, 52, a Web site developer who divides his time among San Francisco; Austin, Tex.; and Addis Ababa, Ethiopia, photographs his food along the way with a Nikon D3.

25 "You have more of a direct connection with your food, so it forms a more essential memory of an occasion," he said. He often places a small stuffed animal, a sheep, which he calls the Crazy Sheep, next to his food before taking a picture; reminiscent of the globe-trotting garden gnome in the French film "Amélie."

"I think photographing food is a more accurate way to document life," said Mr. Rosenberg, who shares photos with family and friends but does not post them. "Food isn't going to put on a special face when you take a picture of it."

REFLECT & WRITE

- ❑ What strategy does Murphy use to hook her readers into the article?
- ❑ Find the original article online and look at the use of visual evidence. What do the images contribute to Murphy's argument? How does the visual rhetoric change your experience as a reader?
- ❑ According to the article, what effect does food photography have on the photographer? In terms of community? In terms of eating habits?
- ❑ Why do you think Murphy includes the opinion of psychiatrists? How does their opinion change your understanding of the practice of food blogging? How might the article have been different if she had omitted that section?
- ❑ **Write.** Murphy quotes one of her sources, Carl Rosenberg, as saying, "I think photographing food is a more accurate way to document life . . . Food isn't going to put on a special face when you take a picture of it." Do you agree that photographs of food document life more accurately than other types of photographs? Why would that be the case? Write a personal essay that draws a connection between your food practices (how you snack; your food addictions or favorite foods; childhood memories associated with food; your grocery shopping habits; when or where you eat) and a larger commentary about who you are and your overall approach to life.

Circulated through social networks like Flickr and Facebook, photographs such as these not only document food, but also are composed in deliberate ways to make a specific argument about that food.

Food Photographs

FIGURE 10.2 Laura Thal first shared her image of "happy-go-latte" on Facebook.

FIGURE 10.3 Stella HaYoung Shin originally shared this photo with her Facebook friends, captioning it with the name of the restaurant that made the meal.

FIGURE 10.4 Originally saved on Facebook by Caroline Grant, co-editor of *The Cassoulet Saved Our Marriage*, this photograph of homemade mint stracciatella ice cream was tagged #happysummer.

REFLECT & WRITE

- ❑ Consider the title of Laura Thal's photograph in Figure 10.2: "happy-go-latte." How does the composition of the photo work together with the title? What argument about culture is the photograph making?
- ❑ Look at the perspective of Stella's photograph (see Figure 10.3). What impression do the layout, the framing, and the angle make on the audience? What is the photo's argument?
- ❑ What argument is Caroline making about her ice cream in Figure 10.4? What distinguishes this photo from other food blog photographs that you have seen? What is it about the photograph that makes that argument persuasive?
- ❑ **Write.** Visit the "I Ate This" pool on Flickr.com. Select three images that work in dialogue to make a specific argument about food or food consumption: draft a thesis statement that presents your interpretation. Now, working with the canon of arrangement, order the images strategically in a

slideshow to make that claim. Present the slideshow to your classmates and ask them to identify your argument. At the end of your discussion, share your thesis statement with them and discuss to what extent the audience's experiences of the argument were the same as your authorial purpose.

WRITING COLLABORATIVELY

How is eaters' relationship to food influenced by the way in which that food is offered to them? This is the question you'll answer for the collaborative writing project in which you and a group will visit three types of restaurants: a fast food restaurant, a family style chain restaurant, and an upscale gourmet restaurant. For each one, perform a rhetorical analysis of the menu. How, when, and where is the menu presented to the eater? How is it designed in terms of color, layout, and even the materials used? What is contained on the menu? Price? Ingredients? Calories? Which information is presented as the most important to the eater? How can you tell? If you have permission from the establishment, take photographs of the menu to use as visual evidence. Having performed your analysis, write a summary of your findings as a team and develop a claim about how the rhetoric of menus mediates or influences the customer's encounter with the restaurant's food. Present your analysis (with the photographic examples, if you have them) to the class.

According to the official White House press release, the "Let's Move!" campaign is designed to "combat the epidemic of childhood obesity through a comprehensive approach that builds on effective strategies, and mobilizes public and private sector resources." Spearheaded by First Lady Michelle Obama, *the mission of "Let's Move!" is to marshal government, educational, and medical resources to support parents in creating healthier eating and lifestyle habits among children, with the goal of solving the problem of childhood obesity within a generation. What follows are the remarks prepared for the First Lady to deliver at the launch in Washington, DC, on February 9, 2010.*

Remarks of First Lady Michelle Obama As Prepared for Delivery Let's Move Launch

Washington, DC
February 9, 2010

Hello everyone, thank you so much. It is such a pleasure to be here with all of you today.

Tammy, thank you for that wonderful introduction and for your outstanding work in the White House garden.

I want to recognize the extraordinary Cabinet members with us today—Secretaries Vilsack, Sebelius, Duncan, Salazar, Donovan and Solis—as well as Surgeon General Benjamin. Thanks to all of you for your excellent work.

Thanks also to Senators Harkin and Gillibrand, and Representatives DeLauro, Christensen and Fudge for their leadership and for being here today.

5 And I want to thank Tiki Barber, Dr. Judith Palfrey, Will Allen, and Mayors Johnson and Curtatone for braving the weather to join us, and for their outstanding work every day to help our kids lead active, healthy lives.

And I hear that congratulations are in order for the Watkins Hornets, who just won the Pee Wee National Football Championship. Let's give them a hand to show them how proud we are.

We're here today because we care deeply about the health and well-being of these kids and kids like them all across the country. And we're determined to finally take on one of the most serious threats to their future: the epidemic of childhood obesity in America today—an issue that's of great concern to me not just as a First Lady, but as a mom.

Often, when we talk about this issue, we begin by citing sobering statistics like the ones you've heard today—that over the past three decades, childhood obesity rates in America have tripled; that nearly one third of children in America are now overweight or obese—one in three.

But these numbers don't paint the full picture. These words—"overweight" and "obese"—they don't tell the full story. This isn't just about inches and pounds or how our kids look. It's about how our kids feel, and how they feel about themselves. It's about the impact we're seeing on every aspect of their lives.

10 Pediatricians like Dr. Palfrey are seeing kids with high blood pressure and high cholesterol—even Type II diabetes, which they used to see only in adults. Teachers see the teasing and bullying; school counselors see the depression and low-self-esteem; and coaches see kids struggling to keep up, or stuck on the sidelines.

Military leaders report that obesity is now one of the most common disqualifiers for military service. Economic experts tell us that we're spending outrageous amounts of money treating obesity-related conditions like diabetes, heart disease and cancer. And public health experts tell us that the current generation could actually be on track to have a shorter lifespan than their parents.

None of us wants this kind of future for our kids—or for our country. So instead of just talking about this problem, instead of just worrying and wringing our hands about it, let's do something about it. Let's act . . . let's move.

Let's move to help families and communities make healthier decisions for their kids. Let's move to bring together governors and mayors, doctors and nurses, businesses, community groups, educators, athletes, Moms and Dads to tackle this challenge once and for all. And that's why we're here today—to launch "Let's Move"—a campaign that will rally our nation to achieve a single, ambitious goal: solving the problem of childhood obesity in a generation, so that children born today will reach adulthood at a healthy weight.

But to get where we want to go, we need to first understand how we got here. So let me ask the adults here today to close your eyes and think back for a moment . . . think back to a time when we were growing up.

15 Like many of you, when I was young, we walked to school every day, rain or shine—and in Chicago, we did it in wind, sleet, hail and snow too. Remember how, at school, we had recess twice a day and gym class twice a week, and we spent hours running around outside when school got out. You didn't go inside until dinner was ready—and when it was, we would gather around the table for dinner as a family. And there was one simple rule: you ate what Mom fixed—good, bad, or ugly. Kids had absolutely no say in what they felt like eating. If you didn't like it, you were welcome to go to bed hungry. Back then, fast food was a treat, and dessert was mainly a Sunday affair.

In my home, we weren't rich. The foods we ate weren't fancy. But there was always a vegetable on the plate. And we managed to lead a pretty healthy life.

Many kids today aren't so fortunate. Urban sprawl and fears about safety often mean the only walking they do is out their front door to a bus or a car. Cuts in recess and gym mean a lot less running around during the school day, and lunchtime may mean a school lunch heavy on calories and fat. For many kids, those afternoons spent riding bikes and playing ball until dusk have been replaced by afternoons inside with TV, the Internet, and video games.

And these days, with parents working longer hours, working two jobs, they don't have time for those family dinners. Or with the price of fresh fruits and vegetables rising 50 percent higher than overall food costs these past two decades, they don't have the money. Or they don't have a supermarket in their community, so their best option for dinner is something from the shelf of the local convenience store or gas station.

So many parents desperately want to do the right thing, but they feel like the deck is stacked against them. They know their kids' health is their responsibility—but they feel like it's out of their control. They're being bombarded by contradictory information at every turn, and they don't know who or what to believe. The result is a lot of guilt and anxiety—and a sense that no matter what they do, it won't be right, and it won't be enough.

20 I know what that feels like. I've been there. While today I'm blessed with more help and support than I ever dreamed of, I didn't always live in the White House.

It wasn't that long ago that I was a working Mom, struggling to balance meetings and deadlines with soccer and ballet. And there were some nights when everyone was tired and hungry, and we just went to the drive-thru because it was quick and cheap, or went with one of the less healthy microwave options, because it was easy. And one day, my pediatrician pulled me aside and told me, "You might want to think about doing things a little bit differently."

That was a moment of truth for me. It was a wakeup call that I was the one in charge, even if it didn't always feel that way.

And today, it's time for a moment of truth for our country; it's time we all had a wakeup call. It's time for us to be honest with ourselves about how we got here. Our kids didn't do this to themselves. Our kids don't decide what's served to them at school or whether there's time for gym class or recess. Our kids don't choose to make food products with tons of sugar and sodium in super-sized portions, and then to have those products marketed to them everywhere they turn. And no matter how much they beg for pizza, fries and candy, ultimately, they are not, and should not, be the ones calling the shots at dinnertime. We're in charge. We make these decisions.

But that's actually the good news here. If we're the ones who make the decisions, then we can decide to solve this problem. And when I say "we," I'm not just talking about folks here in Washington. This isn't about politics. There's nothing Democratic or Republican, liberal or conservative, about doing what's best for our kids. And I've spoken with many experts about this issue, and not a single one has said that the solution is to have government tell people what to do. Instead, I'm talking about what we can do. I'm talking about commonsense steps we can take in our families and communities to help our kids lead active, healthy lives.

25 This isn't about trying to turn the clock back to when we were kids, or preparing five course meals from scratch every night. No one has time for that. And it's not about being 100 percent perfect 100 percent of the time. Lord knows I'm not. There's a place for cookies and ice cream, burgers and fries—that's part of the fun of childhood.

Often, it's just about balance. It's about small changes that add up—like walking to school, replacing soda with water or skim milk, trimming those portion sizes a little—things like this can mean the difference between being healthy and fit or not.

There's no one-size-fits-all solution here. Instead, it's about families making manageable changes that fit with their schedules, their budgets, and their needs and tastes.

And it's about communities working to support these efforts. Mayors like Mayors Johnson and Curtatone, who are building sidewalks, parks and community gardens. Athletes and role models like Tiki Barber, who are building playgrounds to help kids stay active. Community leaders like Will Allen who are bringing farmers markets to underserved areas. Companies like the food industry leaders who came together last fall and acknowledged their responsibility to be part of the solution. But there's so much more to do.

And that's the mission of Let's Move—to create a wave of efforts across this country that get us to our goal of solving childhood obesity in a generation.

30 We kicked off this initiative this morning when my husband signed a presidential memorandum establishing the first ever government-wide Task Force on Childhood Obesity. The task force is composed of representatives from key agencies—including many who are here today. Over the next 90 days, these folks will review every program and policy relating to child nutrition and physical activity. And they'll develop an action plan marshalling these resources to meet our goal. And to ensure we're continuously on track to do so, the Task Force will set concrete benchmarks to measure our progress.

But we can't wait 90 days to get going here. So let's move right now, starting today, on a series of initiatives to help achieve our goal.

First, let's move to offer parents the tools and information they need—and that they've been asking for—to make healthy choices for their kids. We've been working with the FDA and several manufacturers and retailers to make our food labels more customer-friendly, so people don't have to spend hours squinting at words they can't pronounce to figure out whether the food they're buying is healthy or not. In fact, just today, the nation's largest beverage companies announced that they'll be taking steps to provide clearly visible information about calories on the front of their products—as well as on vending machines and soda fountains. This is exactly the kind of vital information parents need to make good choices for their kids.

We're also working with the American Academy of Pediatrics, supporting their groundbreaking efforts to ensure that doctors not only regularly measure children's BMI, but actually write out a prescription detailing steps parents can take to keep their kids healthy and fit.

In addition, we're working with the Walt Disney Company, NBC Universal, and Viacom to launch a nationwide public awareness campaign educating parents and children about how to fight childhood obesity.

35 And we're creating a one-stop shopping website—LetsMove.gov—so with the click of a mouse, parents can find helpful tips and step-by-step strategies, including healthy recipes, exercise plans, and charts they can use to track their family's progress.

But let's remember: 31 million American children participate in federal school meal programs—and many of these kids consume as many as half their daily calories at school. And what we don't want is a situation where parents are taking all the right steps at home—and then their kids undo all that work with salty, fatty food in the school cafeteria.

So let's move to get healthier food into our nation's schools. That's the second part of this initiative. We'll start by updating and strengthening the Child Nutrition Act—the law that sets nutrition standards for what our kids eat at school. And we've proposed an historic investment of an additional $10 billion over ten years to fund that legislation.

With this new investment, we'll knock down barriers that keep families from participating in school meal programs and serve an additional one million students in the first five years alone. And we'll dramatically improve the quality of the food we offer in schools—including in school vending machines. We'll take away some of the empty calories, and add more fresh fruits and vegetables and other nutritious options.

We also plan to double the number of schools in the HealthierUS School Challenge—an innovative program that recognizes schools doing the very best work to keep kids healthy—from providing healthy school meals to requiring physical education classes each week. To help us meet that goal, I'm thrilled to announce that for the very first time, several major school food suppliers have come together and committed to decrease sugar, fat and salt; increase whole grains; and double the fresh produce in the school meals they serve. And also for the first time, food service workers—along with principals, superintendents and school board members across America—are coming together to support these efforts. With these commitments, we'll reach just about every school child in this country with better information and more nutritious meals to put them on track to a healthier life.

40 These are major steps forward. But let's not forget about the rest of the calories kids consume—the ones they eat outside of school, often at home, in their neighborhoods. And when 23.5 million Americans, including 6.5 million American children, live in "food deserts"—communities without a supermarket—those calories are too often empty ones. You can see these areas in dark purple in the new USDA Food Environment Atlas we're unveiling today. This Atlas maps out everything from diabetes and obesity rates across the country to the food deserts you see on this screen.

So let's move to ensure that all our families have access to healthy, affordable food in their communities. That's the third part of this initiative. Today, for the very first time, we're making a commitment to eliminate food deserts in America—and we plan to do so within seven years. Now, we know this is ambitious. And it will take a serious commitment from both government and the private sector. That's why we plan to invest $400 million a year in a Healthy Food Financing initiative that will bring grocery stores to underserved areas and help places like convenience stores carry healthier food options. And this initiative won't just help families eat better, it will help create jobs and revitalize neighborhoods across America.

But we know that eating right is only part of the battle. Experts recommend that children get 60 minutes of active play each day. If this sounds like a lot, consider this: kids today spend an average of seven and a half hours a day watching TV, and playing with cell phones, computers, and video games. And only a third of high school students get the recommended levels of physical activity.

So let's move. And I mean that literally. Let's find new ways for kids to be physically active, both in and out of school. That's the fourth, and final, part of this initiative.

We'll increase participation in the President's Physical Fitness Challenge. And we'll modernize the challenge, so it's not just about how athletic kids are—how many sit-ups or push-ups they can do—but how active they are. We'll double the number of kids who earn a Presidential Active Lifestyle Award in the next school year, recognizing those who engage in physical activity five days a week, for six weeks. We've also recruited professional athletes from a dozen different leagues—including the NFL, Major League Baseball, and the WNBA—to promote these efforts through sports clinics, public service announcements and more.

45 So that's some of what we're doing to achieve our goal. And we know we won't get there this year, or this Administration. We know it'll take a nationwide movement that continues long after we're gone. That's why today, I'm pleased to announce that a new, independent foundation has been created to rally and coordinate businesses, non-profits, and state and local governments to keep working until we reach our goal—and to measure our progress along the way. It's called the Partnership for a Healthier America, and it's bringing together some of the leading experts on childhood obesity, like The Robert Wood Johnson Foundation, The California Endowment, The Kellogg Foundation, the Brookings Institution, and the Alliance for a Healthier Generation, which is a partnership between the American Heart Association and the Clinton Foundation. And we expect others to join in the coming months.

So this is a pretty serious effort. And I know that in these challenging times for our country, there are those who will wonder whether this should really be a priority. They might view things like healthy school lunches and physical fitness challenges as "extras"—as things we spring for once we've taken care of the necessities. They might ask, "How can we spend money on fruits and vegetables in our school cafeterias when many of our schools don't have enough textbooks or teachers?" Or they might ask, "How can we afford to build parks and sidewalks when we can't even afford our health care costs?"

But when you step back and think about it, you realize—these are false choices. If kids aren't getting adequate nutrition, even the best textbooks and teachers in the world won't help them learn. If they don't have safe places to run and play, and they wind up with obesity-related conditions, then those health care costs will just keep rising.

So yes, we have to do it all . . . we'll need to make some modest, but critical, investments in the short-run . . . but we know that they'll pay for themselves—likely many times over—in the long-run. Because we won't just be keeping our kids healthy when they're young. We'll be teaching them habits to keep them healthy their entire lives.

We saw this firsthand here at the White House when we planted our garden with students like Tammy last Spring. One of Tammy's classmates wrote in an essay that her time in the garden, and I quote, ". . . has made me think about the choices I have with what I put in my mouth . . ."

50 Other wrote with great excitement that he'd learned that tomatoes are both a fruit and a vegetable and contain vitamins that fight diseases. Armed with that knowledge, he declared, "So the tomato is a fruit and is now my best friend."

Think about the ripple effect when children use this knowledge to make healthy decisions for the rest of their lives. Think about the effect it will have on every aspect of their lives. Whether they can keep up with their classmates on the playground and stay focused in the classroom. Whether they have the self-confidence to pursue careers of their dreams, and the stamina to succeed in those careers. Whether they'll have the energy and strength to teach their own kids how to throw a ball or ride a bike, and whether they'll live long enough to see their grandkids grow up—maybe even their great grandkids too.

In the end, we know that solving our obesity challenge won't be easy—and it certainly won't be quick. But make no mistake about it, this problem can be solved.

This isn't like a disease where we're still waiting for the cure to be discovered—we know the cure for this. This isn't like putting a man on the moon or inventing the Internet—it doesn't take some stroke of genius or feat of technology. We have everything we need, right now, to help our kids lead healthy lives. Rarely in the history of this country have we encountered a problem of such magnitude and consequence that is so eminently solvable. So let's move to solve it.

I don't want our kids to live diminished lives because we failed to step up today. I don't want them looking back decades from now and asking us, why didn't you help us when you had a chance? Why didn't you put us first when it mattered most?

55 So much of what we all want for our kids isn't within our control. We want them to succeed in everything they do. We want to protect them from every hardship and spare them from every mistake. But we know we can't do all of that. What we can do . . . what is fully within our control . . . is to

give them the very best start in their journeys. What we can do is give them advantages early in life that will stay with them long after we're gone. As President Franklin Roosevelt once put it: "We cannot always build the future for our youth, but we can build our youth for the future."

That is our obligation, not just as parents who love our kids, but as citizens who love this country. So let's move. Let's get this done. Let's give our kids what they need to have the future they deserve.

Thank you so much.

REFLECT & WRITE

- ❑ Look at the first six paragraphs of the speech. To what extent do they serve a rhetorical purpose in relation to the rest of the speech or in terms of the First Lady's assessment of the audience and rhetorical situation?
- ❑ How does the First Lady establish *ethos* in her speech? What types of authority does she invoke? Find specific phrases or passages where she establishes her credibility. Why does she establish *ethos* in this way? How does it contribute to the persuasiveness of her speech?
- ❑ Where does the call to action begin in the speech? How does she build up to it? Is it an appropriate place in the speech to shift to a call to action? Would you have done it earlier? Later? Why?
- ❑ Analyze the movement in this speech from the focus on the individual, to the community, to the government. How effective is this structure for her argument?
- ❑ Consider the rhetorical repetition of the phrase "let's move." What multiple meanings does it hold?
- ❑ Look carefully at the language and word choice Michelle Obama uses in the conclusion of her speech. What deliberate rhetorical choices did she make to bring her speech to a powerful close?
- ❑ **Write.** Clearly this argument was written to be delivered orally. Condense this speech into a 1½–2 page memo between a local representative of "Let's Move!" and a community's Parent Teacher Organization. What changes in content, development, style, and format do you need to institute to accommodate the shift in rhetorical situation and genre?

Since World War II, the United States Department of Agriculture (USDA) *has used information graphics to represent the recommended daily intake of different food categories. The following images represent diagrams released over a span of 70 years.*

USDA Nutritional Information Graphics

FIGURE 10.5 The USDA first published "The Basic Seven" diagram in 1943 as a way of helping to maintain attention to nutrition despite World War II food rationing.

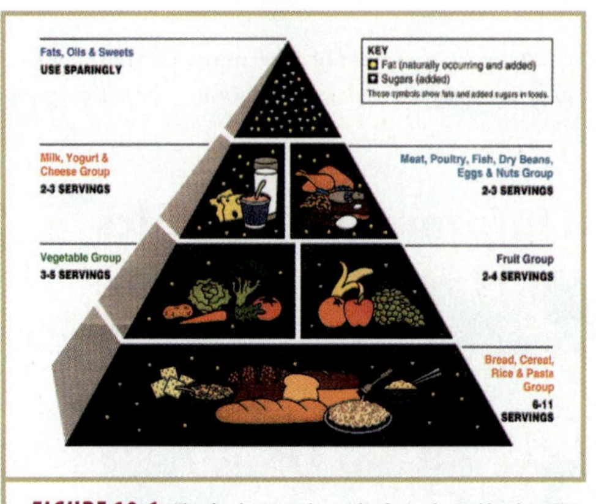

FIGURE 10.6 This food pyramid was the first released by the USDA in 1992 and was based on a similar model published in Denmark in 1978. Many food packages still feature this original pyramid.

FIGURE 10.7 Released in 2005, the MyPyramid graphic revised the pyramid design to reflect shifts in the American approach to "a healthier you."

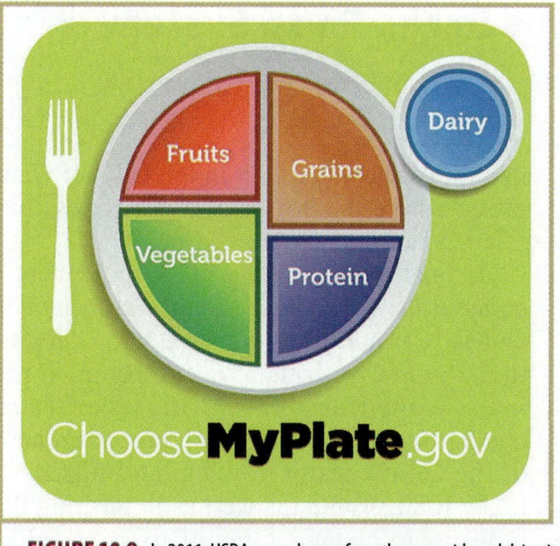

FIGURE 10.8 In 2011, USDA moved away from the pyramid model, instituting instead a plate-based framework to structure its nutritional recommendations.

REFLECT & WRITE

- ❑ How does the shape of the information graphics influence the way that each makes its argument about nutrition? What different impressions does the idea of a pie chart (Figure 10.5), a pyramid (Figure 10.6 and Figure 10.7), and a plate (Figure 10.8) make on the audience?
- ❑ Consider the differences between the graphics, from their titles, to layout, style, and content. How do these revisions alter the USDA's argument? How does the shift in *kairos* reflect a similar shift in cultural approaches and attitudes (*doxa)* with regard to eating and health?
- ❑ **Write.** Take the information from the MyPlate chart, and rework it into two different types of information graphics (for instance, a bar graph and a pie chart). How does the change in the delivery of the argument transform the argument itself?

In recent years, ***Michael Pollan*** *has become one of America's leading writers on food culture. Some of his most notable works include* Cooked *(2013);* Food Rules: An Eater's Manual *(2009), a guide to sensible eating;* In Defense of Food: An Eater's Manifesto *(2008), which won the James Beard Award; and* The Omnivore's Dilemma *(2006), which has won numerous awards and was named one of the ten best books of 2006 by both the* Washington Post *and* The New York Times. *In the following piece, originally published in the October 3, 2011, issue of the* Nation, *Pollan exposes the rift between the food movement's power to change public sentiment and its ability to affect federal legislation.*

How Change Is Going to Come in the Food System

Michael Pollan

In the forty years since the publication of Frances Moore Lappé's *Diet for a Small Planet*, a movement dedicated to the reform of the food system has taken root in America. Lappé's groundbreaking book connected the dots between something as ordinary and all-American as a hamburger and the environmental crisis, as well as world hunger. Along with Wendell Berry and Barry Commoner, Lappé taught us how to think ecologically about the implications of our everyday food choices. You can now find that way of thinking, so radical at the time, just about everywhere—from the pages of *Time* magazine to the menu at any number of local restaurants.

To date, however, the food movement can claim more success in changing popular consciousness than in shifting, in any fundamental way, the political and economic forces shaping the food system or, for that matter, in changing the "standard American diet"—which has only gotten worse since the 1970s. Recently there have been some political accomplishments: food movement activists played a role in shaping the FDA Food Safety Modernization Act and the Child Nutrition Reauthorization Act, both passed in the last Congress, and the last couple of farm bills have thrown some significant crumbs in the direction of sustainable agriculture and healthy food. But the food movement cannot yet point to legislative achievements on the order of the Clean Air Act or the Clean Water Act or the establishment of the Environmental Protection Administration. Its greatest victories have come in the media, which could scarcely be friendlier to it, and in the food marketplace, rather than in the halls of Congress, where the power of agribusiness has scarcely been disturbed.

The marked split between the movement's gains in the soft power of cultural influence and its comparative weakness in conventional political terms is faithfully mirrored in the White House. While Michelle Obama has had notable success raising awareness of the child obesity problem and linking it to the food system (as well as in pushing the industry to change some of its most egregious practices), her husband, after raising expectations on the campaign trail, has done comparatively little to push a reform agenda. Promising anti-trust initiatives to counter food industry concentration, which puts farmers and ranchers at the mercy of a small handful of processors, appear to be languishing. Efforts to reform crop subsidies during the last farm bill debate were halfhearted and got nowhere. And a USDA plan to place new restrictions on genetically modified crops (in order to protect organic farms from contamination) was reportedly overruled by the White House.

There are two ways to interpret the very different approaches of the president and the first lady to the food issue. A cynical interpretation would be that the administration has decided to deploy the first lady to pay lip service to reform while continuing business as usual. But a more charitable interpretation would be that President Obama has determined there is not yet enough political support to take on the hard work of food system reform, and the best thing to do in the meantime is for the first lady to build a broad constituency for change by speaking out about the importance of food.

5 If this is the president's reading of the situation, it may well be right. So far, at least, the food movement has only a small handful of allies in Congress: Tom Harkin, Jon Tester and Kirsten Gillibrand in the Senate; Earl Blumenauer and Jim McGovern in the House. The Congressional committees in charge of agricultural policies remain dominated by farm-state legislators openly hostile to reform, and until big-state and urban legislators decide it is worth their while to serve on those committees, little of value is likely to emerge from them. Whatever its cost to public health and the environment, cheap food has become a pillar of the modern economy that few in government dare to question. And many of the reforms we need—such as improving conditions in the meat industry and cleaning up feedlot agriculture—stand to make meat more expensive. That might be a good thing for public health, but it will never be popular.

So what is to be done? The food movement has discovered that persuading the media, and even the president, that you are right on the merits does not necessarily translate into change, not when the forces arrayed against change are so strong. If change comes, it will come from other places: from the grassroots and, paradoxically, from powerful interests that stand to gain from it.

The most promising food activism is taking place at the grassroots: local policy initiatives are popping up in municipalities across the country, alongside urban agriculture ventures in underserved areas and farm-to-school programs. Changing the way America feeds itself has become the galvanizing issue for a generation now coming of age. (A new FoodCorps, launched in August as part of AmeriCorps, received nearly 1,300 applications for fifty slots.) Out of these local efforts will come local leaders who will recognize the power of food politics. Some of these leaders will run for office on these issues, and some of them will win.

It's worth remembering that it took decades before the campaign against the tobacco industry could point to any concrete accomplishments. By the 1930s, the scientific case against smoking had been made, yet it wasn't until 1964 that the surgeon general was willing to declare smoking a threat to health, and another two decades after that before the industry's seemingly unshakable hold on Congress finally crumbled. By this standard, the food movement is making swift progress.

But there is a second lesson the food movement can take away from the antismoking campaign. When change depends on overcoming the influence of an entrenched power, it helps to have another powerful interest in your corner—an interest that stands to gain from reform. In the case of the tobacco industry, that turned out to be the states, which found themselves on the hook (largely because of Medicaid) for the soaring costs of smoking-related illnesses. So, under economic duress, states and territories joined to file suit against the tobacco companies to recover some of those costs, and eventually they prevailed.

10 The food movement will find such allies, especially now that Obama's Patient Protection and Affordable Care Act has put the government on the hook for the soaring costs of treating chronic illnesses—most of which are preventable and linked to diet. No longer allowed to cherry-pick the patients they're willing to cover, or to toss overboard people with chronic diseases, the insurance industry will soon find itself on the hook for the cost of the American diet too. It's no accident

that support for measures such as taxing soda is strongest in places like Massachusetts, where the solvency of the state and its insurance industry depends on figuring out how to reduce the rates of Type 2 diabetes and obesity.

The food movement is about to gain a powerful new partner, an industry that is beginning to recognize that it, too, has a compelling interest in issues like taxing soda, school lunch reform and even the farm bill. Indeed, as soon as the healthcare industry begins to focus on the fact that the government is subsidizing precisely the sort of meal for which the industry (and the government) will have to pick up the long-term tab, eloquent advocates of food system reform will suddenly appear in the unlikeliest places—like the agriculture committees of Congress.

None of this should surprise us. For the past forty years, food reform activists like Frances Moore Lappé have been saying that the American way of growing and eating food is "unsustainable." That objection is not rooted in mere preference or aesthetics, but rather in the inescapable realities of biology. Continuing to eat in a way that undermines health, soil, energy resources and social justice cannot be sustained without eventually leading to a breakdown. Back in the 1970s it was impossible to say exactly where that breakdown would first be felt. Would it be the environment or the healthcare system that would buckle first? Now we know. We simply can't afford the healthcare costs incurred by the current system of cheap food—which is why, sooner or later, we will find the political will to change it.

REFLECT & WRITE

- ❑ How does Pollan use Lappé to frame his argument? How does the Lappé reference operate in his introduction? Why do you think he chose to return to him again in his conclusion?
- ❑ Look carefully at that first time that Pollan refers to President Obama. What is the impact of his referring to him in this way? How does he follow up on this initial strategy in the way he refers to the president later in his article?
- ❑ How does Pollan use the analogy to the tobacco industry and the antismoking campaign to shore up his argument? Is this an effective rhetorical technique?
- ❑ **Write.** Right now, Pollan's piece follows the form of an op-ed (or opinion editorial) in that it offers an informed and persuasive opinion on a current issue. Revise it into more of a call to action, either one that is intended to be print-based or that follows more of the op-ad model discussed in Chapter 8. Use at least two to three facts or points from Pollan's piece to inform your call-to-action.

Originally published in August 2011 on the Mother Nature Network website, this information graphic provides an overview to define the difference between a "locavore" and "globavore" approach to food consumption.

Information Graphic: Locavorism vs. Globavorism

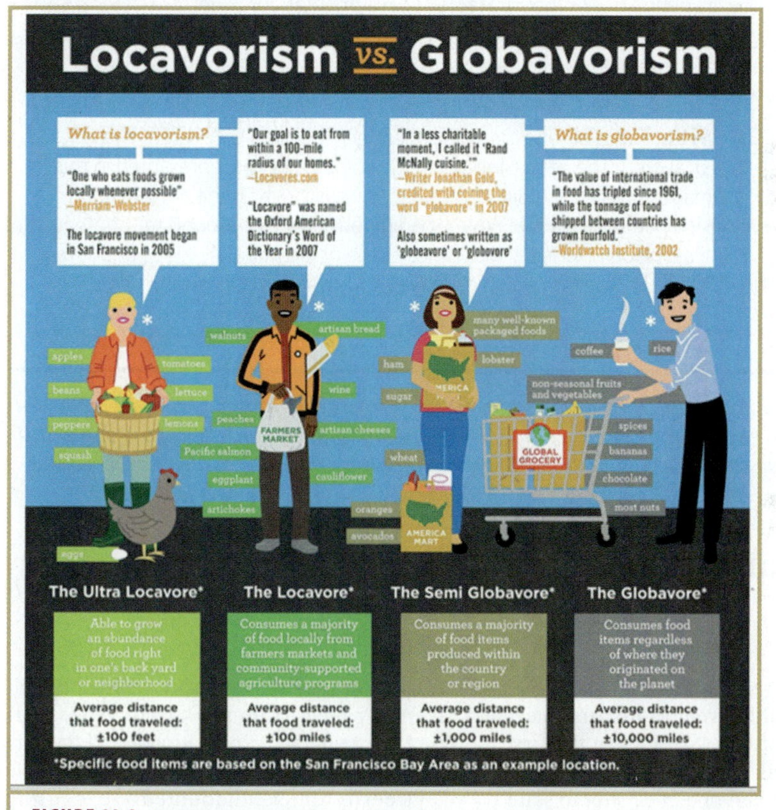

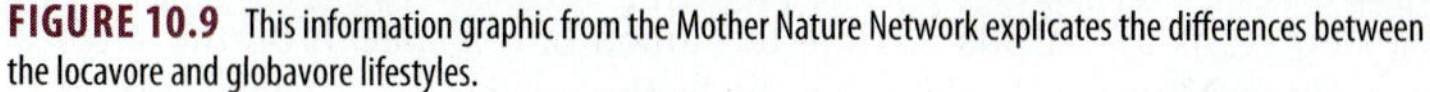

FIGURE 10.9 This information graphic from the Mother Nature Network explicates the differences between the locavore and globavore lifestyles.

REFLECT & WRITE

- ❑ The MNN editors called this image a "beginner's guide to what being a 'locavore' or 'globavore' really means." How is this infographic composed to appeal to "beginners"? Consider content, style, and design in your analysis.

Seeing Connections Refer to Chapter 2 for more on rhetorical appeals and strategies of argumentation.

- ❑ How does the infographic utilize *ethos*, *pathos*, and *logos* in developing its definitions? What strategies of argumentation do you see at work?
- ❑ This infographic suggests that it is simply informative, providing definitions, but it implicitly makes an argument. What is the claim it makes about locavorism vs. globavorism? How does it suggest this position on the issue?
- ❑ **Write.** Focus on one individual identity ("The Ultra Locavore"; "The Locavore"; "The Semi Globavore"; The Globavore") as represented in this image, looking carefully at the various ways in which the artist defined each particular stance. Write a paragraph organized around the strategy of *definition* in which you synthesize the different points made about that character type into a single, unified, and cohesive paragraph.

In this article, originally published in Slate *in May 2008,* **Taylor Clark** *takes a closer look at the way vegetarianism has been defined in our culture. Based in Portland, Oregon, Clark has contributed pieces to magazines such as* GQ *and* Psychology Today *and is the author of two books:* Starbucked *(2008) and* Nerve *(2011).*

Meatless Like Me

Taylor Clark

Every vegetarian remembers his first time. Not the unremarkable event of his first meal without meat, mind you. No, I mean the first time he casually lets slip that he's turned herbivore, prompting everyone in earshot to stare at him as if he just revealed plans to sail his carrot-powered plasma yacht to Neptune. For me, this first time came at an Elks scholarship luncheon in rural Oregon when I was 18. All day, I'd succeeded at seeming a promising and responsible young man, until that fateful moment when someone asked why I hadn't taken any meat from the buffet. After I offered my reluctant explanation—and the guy announced it *to the entire room*—30 people went eerily quiet, undoubtedly expecting me to launch into a speech on the virtues of hemp. In the corner, an elderly, suited man glared at me as he slowly raised a slice of bologna and executed the most menacing bite of cold cut in recorded history. I didn't get the scholarship.

I tell this story not to win your pity but to illustrate a point: I've been vegetarian for a decade, and when it comes up, I still get a look of confused horror that says, "But you seemed so ... *normal.*" The U.S. boasts more than 10 million herbivores today, yet most Americans assume that every last one is a loopy, self-satisfied health fanatic, hellbent on draining all the joy out of life. Those of us who want to avoid the social nightmare have to hide our vegetarianism like an Oxycontin addiction, because admit it, omnivores: You know nothing about us. Do we eat fish? Will we panic if confronted with a hamburger? Are we dying of malnutrition? You have no clue. So read on, my flesh-eating friends—I believe it's high time we cleared a few things up.

To demonstrate what a vegetarian really is, let's begin with a simple thought experiment. Imagine a completely normal person with completely normal food cravings, someone who has a broad range of friends, enjoys a good time, is carbon-based, and so on. Now remove from this person's diet anything that once had eyes, and, *wham*!, you have yourself a vegetarian. Normal person, no previously ocular food, end of story. Some people call themselves vegetarians and still eat chicken or fish, but unless we're talking about the kind of salmon that comes freshly plucked from the vine, this makes you an omnivore. A select few herbivores go one step further and avoid *all* animal products—milk, eggs, honey, leather—and they call themselves vegan, which rhymes with "tree men." These people are intense.

Vegetarians give up meat for a variety of ethical, environmental, and health reasons that are secondary to this essay's goal of increasing brotherly understanding, so I'll mostly set them aside. Suffice it to say that one day, I suddenly realized that I could never look a cow in the eyes, press a knocking gun to her temple, and pull the trigger without feeling I'd done something cruel and unnecessary. (Sure, if it's kill the cow or starve, then say your prayers, my bovine friend—but for now, it's not quite a mortal struggle to subsist on the other five food groups.) I am well-aware that even telling you this makes me seem like the kind of person who wants to break into your house and liberate your pet hamster—that is, like a PETA activist. Most vegetarians, though, would tell you that they appreciate the intentions of groups like PETA but not the obnoxious tactics. It's like this: We're all rooting for the same team, but they're the ones in face paint, bellowing obscenities at the umpire and flipping over every car with a Yankees bumper sticker. I have no designs on your Camry or your hamster.

Now, when I say that vegetarians are normal people with normal food cravings, many omnivores will hoist a lamb shank in triumph and point out that you can hardly call yourself normal if the aroma of, say, sizzling bacon doesn't fill you with deepest yearning. To which I reply: We're not *insane*. We *know* meat tastes good; it's why there's a freezer case at your supermarket full of woefully inadequate meat substitutes. Believe me, if obtaining bacon didn't require slaughtering a pig, I'd have a BLT in each hand right now with a bacon layer cake waiting in the fridge for dessert. But, that said, I can also tell you that with some time away from the butcher's section, many meat products start to seem gross. Ground beef in particular now strikes me as absolutely revolting; I have a vague memory that hamburgers taste good, but the idea of taking a cow's leg, mulching it into a fatty pulp, and forming it into a pancake makes me gag. And hot dogs ... I mean, *hot dogs*? You *do* know what that is, right?

5 As a consolation prize we get tofu, a treasure most omnivores are more than happy to do without. Well, this may stun you, but I'm not any more excited about a steaming heap

of unseasoned tofu blobs than you are. Tofu is like *fugu* blowfish sushi: Prepared correctly, it's delicious; prepared incorrectly, it's lethal. Very early in my vegetarian career, I found myself famished and stuck in a mall, so I wandered over to the food court's Asian counter. When I asked the teenage chief culinary artisan what was in the tofu stir-fry, he snorted and replied, "Shit." Desperation made me order it anyway, and I can tell you that promises have rarely been more loyally kept than this guy's pledge that the tofu would taste like shit. So here's a tip: Unless you know you're in expert hands (Thai restaurants are a good bet), don't even try tofu. Otherwise, it's your funeral.

As long as we're discussing restaurants, allow me a quick word with the hardworking chefs at America's dining establishments. We really appreciate that you included a vegetarian option on your menu (and if you didn't, is our money not green?), but it may interest you to know that most of us are not salad freaks on a grim slog for nourishment. We actually enjoy food, especially the kind that tastes good. So enough with the bland vegetable dishes, and, for God's sake, *please* make the Gardenburgers stop; it's stunning how many restaurants lavish unending care on their meat dishes yet are content to throw a flavorless hockey puck from Costco into the microwave and call it cuisine. Every vegetarian is used to slim pickings when dining out, so we're not asking for much—just for something *you'd* like to eat. I'll even offer a handy trick. Pretend you're trapped in a kitchen stocked with every ingredient imaginable, from asiago to zucchini, but with zero meat. With no flesh available, picture what you'd make for yourself; this is what we want, too.

For those kind-hearted omnivores who willingly invite feral vegetarians into their homes for dinner parties and barbecues (really! we do that, too!), the same rule applies—but also know that unless you're dealing with an herbivore who is a prick for unrelated reasons, we don't expect you to bend over backward for us. In fact, if we get the sense that you cooked for three extra hours to accommodate our dietary preferences, we will marvel at your considerate nature, but we will also feel insanely guilty. Similarly, it's very thoughtful of you to ask whether it'll bother me if I see you eat meat, but don't worry: I'm not going to compose an epic poem about your club sandwich.

Which leads me to a vital point for friendly omnivore-herbivore relations. As you're enjoying that pork loin next to me, *I am not silently judging you*. I realize that anyone who has encountered the breed of smug vegetarian who says things like, "I can hear your lunch screaming," will find this tough to believe, but I'm honestly not out to convert you. My girlfriend and my closest pals all eat meat, and they'll affirm that I've never even raised an eyebrow about it. Now, do I think it strange that the same people who dress their dogs in berets and send them to day spas are often unfazed that an equally smart pig suffered and died to become their McMuffin? Yes, I do. (Or, to use a more pressing example, how many Americans will bemoan Eight Belles' fatal Kentucky Derby injury tonight at the dinner table between bites of beef?) Would I prefer it if we at least raised these animals humanely? Yes, I would.

Let's be honest, though: I'm not exactly St. Francis of Assisi over here, tenderly ministering to every chipmunk that crosses my path. I try to represent *for* the animal kingdom, but take a look at my shoes—they're made of leather, which, I am told by those with expert knowledge of the tanning process, comes from dead cows. This is the sort of revelation that prompts meat boosters to pick up the triumphant lamb shank once again and accuse us of hypocrisy.

Well, *sort of*. (Hey, *you* try to find a pair of non-leather dress shoes.) My dedication to the cause might be incomplete, but I'd still say that doing something beats doing nothing. It's kind of like driving a hybrid: not a solution to the global-warming dilemma but a decent start. Let's just say that at the dinner table, I roll in a Prius.

10 Finally, grant me one more cordial request: Please don't try to convince us that being vegetarian is somehow wrong. If you're concerned for my health, that's very nice, though you can rest assured that I'm in shipshape. If you want to have an amiable tête-à-tête about vegetarianism, that's great. But if you insist on being the aggressive blowhard who takes meatlessness as a personal insult and rails about what fools we all are, you're only going to persuade me that you're a dickhead. When someone says he's Catholic, you probably don't start the stump speech about how God is a lie created to enslave the ignorant masses, and it's equally offensive to berate an herbivore. I know you think we're crazy. That's neat. But seeing as I've endured the hassle of being a vegetarian for several years now, perhaps I've given this a *little* thought. So let's just agree to disagree and get on with making fun of Hillary Clinton's inability to operate a coffee machine.

Because, really, peace and understanding are what it's all about: your porterhouse and my portobello coexisting in perfect harmony—though preferably not touching. We're actually not so different, after all, my omnivorous chums. In fact, I like to think that when an omnivore looks in the mirror, he just sees a vegetarian who happens to eat meat. Or, no, wait, maybe the *mirror* sees the omnivore through the *prism* of flesh and realizes we all have a crystalline animal soul, you know?

This is excellent weed, by the way, if you want a hit. Hey, while you're here: Have I ever told you about hemp?

REFLECT & WRITE

- ❑ What level of decorum (high style, middle style, plain style) does Clark use to make his argument? What elements of his writing style contribute to the level of decorum he chose?
- ❑ Throughout the essay, Clark integrates second person (you) to draw in the reader. Did this explicit reference to you—the reader—engage you more or less in his argument? Why?
- ❑ Clark is clearly taking aim at some of the cultural stereotypes of vegetarians. What alternative profile of a "vegetarian" does he present here? How does this portrait challenge or rewrite these cultural stereotypes?
- ❑ "[O]ne day," Clark writes, "I suddenly realized that I could never look a cow in the eyes, press a knocking gun to her temple, and pull the trigger without feeling I'd done something cruel and unnecessary." How persuasive a defense of vegetarianism do you find it to be? What rhetorical appeals is Clark using here? How else might he have presented his point if he wanted to use a different appeal? Which do you think would be most persuasive?

- Consider Clark's conclusion. Why do you think he chose to end his essay in this way? To what extent does it reinforce—or perhaps even undermine—his argument?
- **Write:** Clark invites us to reflect on the environmental or ecological effect our eating choices have. Write an essay in which you evaluate the validity of this perspective. Do you think it is important to consider the global implications of our eating choices? What are the benefits of adopting this perspective? What are the disadvantages? Try to adopt a similar voice and style to the one found in this essay in making your argument.

In 2005, photojournalist **Peter Menzel** *and his wife, writer* **Faith d'Aluisio**, *published* Hungry Planet, *an extensive look at eating habits around the world through photographs and essays. This work received numerous awards, including the 2006 James Beard Foundation award for Book of the Year and the 2006 Harry Chapin World Book of the Year award from the World Hunger Media Foundation. A selection of the images from* Hungry Planet *were published by* Time *magazine as a photo essay called "What the World Eats," with the subtitle "What's on family dinner tables around the globe?" The images and captions that follow are taken from that photo essay.*

Photographs from *Hungry Planet*

FIGURE 10.10 United States: The Revis family of North Carolina
Food expenditure for one week: $341.98
Favorite foods: spaghetti, potatoes, sesame chicken

FIGURE 10.11 **China:** The Dong family of Beijing
Food expenditure for one week: 1,233.76 Yuan or $155.06
Favorite foods: fried shredded pork with sweet and sour sauce

FIGURE 10.12 **Mexico:** The Casales family of Cuernavaca
Food expenditure for one week: 1,862.78 Mexican Pesos or $189.09
Favorite foods: pizza, crab, pasta, chicken

FIGURE 10.13 **Chad:** The Aboubakar family of Breidjing Camp
Food expenditure for one week: 685 CFA Francs or $1.23
Favorite foods: soup with fresh sheep meat

REFLECT & WRITE

- ❑ Look carefully at the captions, reproduced as they originally appeared in the *Time* photo essay. What information is included? Judging by this information, what types of comparisons does the photo essay encourage the readers to make between the different families?
- ❑ Consider the staging of the food and the use of space. How do these elements contribute to each photograph's argument?
- ❑ Which photograph surprised you the most? Why? Did any of them seem to reinforce common stereotypes? Did any of them resist those stereotypes?
- ❑ **Write.** First, choose one of the pictures and write a rhetorical analysis of its argument, referring to specific elements in the photo and caption as evidence. Then, find a copy of *Hungry Planet* in your local library or bookstore. Look through the book to find the photo you selected and

examine it within this different context, reading through the text that accompanies it in *Hungry Planet* as well. Now, as an addendum to your initial analysis, write a reflection on how your understanding of the argument of the photograph changes with the different rhetorical situations. Be sure to take into account the issue of audience, purpose, and medium (book versus online photo essay) in your writing.

Few developments have more dramatically impacted our eating habits than the rise of genetically modified food. Taking stock of the debates surrounding this trend, James McWilliams offers readers food for thought on what has come to be known as "Frankenfood." McWilliams is an associate professor of history at Texas State University, and the author of Just Food: Where Locavores Get It Wrong and How We Can Truly Eat Responsibly *(2010). He has published a number of op-eds in* USA Today, *the* Christian Science Monitor, *and* The New York Times, *and is a regular contributor to the online journal, Slate, where this article appeared in January 2009.*

The Green Monster

James McWilliams

I'm sitting at my desk examining a $10.95 jar of South River Miso. The stuff is delicious, marked by a light, lemony tang. The packaging, by contrast, is a heavy-handed assurance of purity. The company is eager to tell me that the product I've purchased is certified organic, aged for three weeks in wood (sustainably harvested?), unpasteurized, made with "deep well water," handcrafted, and—the designation that most piques my interest— *GMO free*.

GMO refers to "genetically modified organisms." A genetically modified crop results from the laboratory insertion of a gene from one organism into the DNA sequence of another in order to confer an advantageous trait such as insect resistance, drought tolerance, or herbicide resistance. Today almost 90 percent of soy crops and 80 percent of corn crops in the United States sprout from genetically engineered seeds. Forty-five million acres of land worldwide contain genetically engineered crops. From the perspective of commercial agriculture, the technology has been seamlessly assimilated into traditional farming routines.

From the perspective of my miso jar, however, it's evident that not all consumers share the enthusiasm. It's as likely as not that you know GMOs by their stock term of derision: *Frankenfoods*. The moniker reflects a broad spectrum of concerns: Some antibiotech activists argue that these organisms will contaminate their wild cousins with GM pollen and drive native plants extinct. Others suggest that they will foster the growth of "superweeds"—plants that develop a resistance to the herbicides many GMOs are engineered to tolerate. And yet others fear that genetic alterations will trigger allergic reactions in unsuspecting consumers. Whether or not these concerns collectively warrant a ban on GMOs—as many (most?) environmentalists would like to see—is a hotly debated topic. The upshot to these potential pitfalls, however, is beyond dispute: A lot of people find this technology to be creepy.

Whatever the specific cause of discontent over GM crops, popular resistance came to a head in 2000, when the National Organic Program solicited public input on the issue of whether they should be included. In response, sustainable-food activists deluged officials with a rainforest's worth of letters—275,000, to be exact—beating the measure into oblivion. Today, in the same spirit, environmentalists instinctively deem GMOs the antithesis of environmental responsibility.

5 Many scientists, and even a few organic farmers, now believe the 2000 rejection was a fatal rush to judgment. Most recently, Pamela Ronald, a plant pathologist and chair of the Plant Genomics Program at the University of California-Davis, has declared herself one such critic. In *Tomorrow's Table: Organic Farming, Genetics, and the Future of Food*, she argues that we should, in fact, be actively merging genetic engineering and organic farming to achieve a sustainable future for food production. Her research—which she conducts alongside her husband, an organic farmer—explores genetically engineered crops that, instead of serving the rapacity of agribusiness, foster the fundamentals of sustainability. Their endeavor, counterintuitive as it seems, points to an emerging green biotech frontier—a hidden realm of opportunity to feed the world's impending 9 billion a diet produced in an environmentally responsible way.

To appreciate how "responsible genetic modification" isn't an oxymoron, consider grass-fed beef. Cows that eat grass are commonly touted as the sustainable alternative to feedlot beef, a resource-intensive form of production that stuffs cows with a steady diet of grain fortified with antibiotics, growth hormones, steroids, and appetite enhancers that eventually pass through the animals into the soil and water. One overlooked drawback to grass-fed beef, however, is the fact that grass-fed cows emit four times more methane—a greenhouse gas that's more than 20 times as powerful as carbon dioxide—as regular, feedlot cows. That's because grass contains lignin, a substance that triggers a cow's digestive system to secrete a methane-producing enzyme. An Australian biotech company called Gramina has recently produced a genetically modified grass with lower amounts of lignin. Lower amounts of lignin mean less methane, less methane means curbed global warming emissions, and curbed emissions means environmentalists can eat their beef without hanging up their green stripes.

Another area where sustainable agriculture and genetic modification could productively overlap involves nitrogen fertilizer. A plant's failure to absorb all the nutrients from the fertilizer leads to the harmful accumulation of nitrogen in the soil. From there it leaches into rivers and oceans to precipitate dead zones so choked with algae that other marine life collapses. In light of this problem, Syngenta and other biotech companies are in the process of genetically engineering crops such as potatoes, rice, and wheat to improve their nitrogen uptake efficiency in an effort to diminish the negative consequences of nitrogen fertilization. Early results suggest that rice farmers in Southeast Asia and potato farmers in Africa might one day have the option of planting crops that mitigate the harmful effects of this long-vilified source of agricultural pollution.

Animals, of course, are just as modifiable as plants. Livestock farmers have been genetically tinkering with their beasts for centuries through the hit-or-miss process of selective breeding. They've done so to enhance their animals' health, increase their weight, and refine their fat content. Breeding animals to reduce environmental impact, however, hasn't been a viable option with the clunky techniques of conventional breeding. But such is not the case with genetic engineering.

Case in point: Canadian scientists have recently pioneered the "enviropig," a genetically modified porker altered to diminish the notoriously high phosphorous level of pig manure by 60 percent. Like nitrogen, phosphorous runoff is a serious pollutant with widespread downstream consequences. But with the relatively basic insertion of a gene (from E. coli bacteria) that produces a digestive enzyme called phytase, scientists have provided farmers with yet another tool for lessening their heavy impact on the environment.

10 When commercial farmers hear about GM grass, increased nitrogen uptake, and cleaner pigs, they're excited. And when they hear about other products in the works—genetically modified sugar beets that require less water and have higher yields than cane sugar; a dust made from genetically modified ferns to remove heavy metals from the soil; genetically modified and edible cotton seeds that require minimal pesticide use—they're also excited. And they're excited not only because these products have the potential to streamline production, but also because GM technology allows them to play a meaningful role in reducing their carbon footprint.

However, with the exception of the modified sugar beets, the GMOs mentioned in this article are not currently on the market. The cutting-room floors of research laboratories all over the world, in fact, are littered with successful examples of genetically engineered products that have enormous potential to further the goals of sustainable agriculture. Demand for these products remains high among farmers—it almost always does—but food producers fear the bad publicity that might come from anti-GMO invective.

Given the potential of these products to reduce the environmental impact of farming, it's ironic that traditional advocates for sustainable agriculture have led a successful campaign to blacklist GMOs irrespective of their applications. At the very least, they might treat them as legitimate ethical and scientific matters deserving of a fair public hearing. Such a hearing, I would venture, would not only please farmers who were truly concerned about sustainability, but it would provide the rest of us—those of us who do not grow food for the world but only think about it—a more accurate source of scientific information than the back of a miso jar.

REFLECT & WRITE

- ❑ Consider the title and the term, "Frankenfood," that McWilliams introduces in the third paragraph? What images or associations do these terms evoke? How do these associations relate to the type of argument that McWilliams is making in this article?
- ❑ McWilliams begins this essay by presenting a stark counterpoint to a genetically modified food: a jar of "certified organic," "unpasteurized," and "GMO free" miso soup. Why do you think McWilliams chooses to open his essay this way? In what way does it prepare readers for the argument to come?
- ❑ Find the passages where McWilliams characterize the conventional critique of genetically modified food. How does he balance a fair treatment of this perspective with his own opinion on the issue?
- ❑ McWilliams uses many different rhetorical techniques in his argument, for instance: deliberate repetition; *logos*; *ethos*; definition; example. Pinpoint places in the essay where he uses these techniques and consider how they contribute to the development of his argument.
- ❑ In McWilliams' view, efforts like the GMO movement are "legitimate ethical and scientific matters deserving of a fair public hearing." How does he support his point? What examples does he provide? Do you find them persuasive? Can you think of any "ethical" concerns the GMO movement raises that McWilliams could have addressed?
- ❑ **Write**: Pushing back against the conventional critique of genetically modified food, McWilliams writes about the "hidden realm of opportunity to feed the world's impending 9 billion on a diet produced in an environmentally responsible way." Write a one-page essay in which you analyze and assess McWilliams' claim here. What does McWilliams mean by "environmentally responsible"? What examples does he use to illustrate this definition? Do you find it be an effective defense or justification for genetically modified food? Write two versions of this essay: one that uses primarily *pathos* appeals to make its point, and one that uses either *ethos* or *logos* to persuade. Share your essays with a partner and discuss how the way that prioritizing different strategies influences the effectiveness of your argument.

In the October 26, 2009, edition of the The New York Times, *the editors posed the following questions to foster debate: "What will drive the next Green Revolution? Is genetically modified food an answer to world hunger? Are there other factors that will make a difference in food production?" Below are excerpts from the responses received from a select group of nutritionists, economists, activists, and scholars.*

Can Biotech Food Cure World Hunger?

By The Editors

With food prices remaining high in developing countries, the United Nations estimates that the number of hungry people around the world could increase by 100 million in 2009 and pass the one billion mark. A summit of world leaders in Rome scheduled for November will set an agenda for ways to reduce hunger and increase investment in agriculture development in poor countries.

What will drive the next Green Revolution? Is genetically modified food an answer to world hunger? Are there other factors that will make a difference in food production?

- Paul Collier, economist, Oxford University
- Vandana Shiva, activist and author
- Per Pinstrup-Andersen, professor of nutrition and public policy, Cornell
- Raj Patel, Institute for Food and Development Policy
- Jonathan Foley, University of Minnesota
- Michael J. Roberts, economist, North Carolina State University

Put Aside Prejudices

Paul Collier *is a professor of economics at Oxford University and the director of the Center for the Study of African Economies. He is the author of "The Bottom Billion: Why the Poorest Countries Are Failing and What Can Be Done About It."*

5 The debate over genetically modified crops and food has been contaminated by political and aesthetic prejudices: hostility to U.S. corporations, fear of big science and romanticism about local, organic production.

> Refusing genetic modification makes a difficult problem more daunting.

Food supply is too important to be the plaything of these prejudices. If there is not enough food we know who will go hungry.

Genetic modification is analogous to nuclear power: nobody loves it, but climate change has made its adoption imperative. As Africa's climate deteriorates, it will need to accelerate crop adaptation. As population grows it will need to raise yields. Genetic modification offers both faster crop adaptation and a biological, rather than chemical, approach to yield increases.

Opponents talk darkly of risks but provide no scientific basis for their amorphous expressions of concern. Meanwhile the true risks are mounting. Over the past decade global food demand has risen more rapidly than expected. Supply may not keep pace with demand, inducing rising prices and periodic spikes. If this happens there is a risk that the children of the urban poor will suffer prolonged bouts of malnutrition.

African governments are now recognizing that by imitating the European ban on genetic modification they have not reduced the risks facing their societies but increased them. Thirteen years, during which there could have been research on African crops, have been wasted. Africa has been in thrall to Europe, and Europe has been in thrall to populism.

10 Genetic modification alone will not solve the food problem: like climate change, there is no single solution. But continuing refusal to use it is making a difficult problem yet more daunting.

The Failure of Gene-Altered Crops?

Vandana Shiva *is the founder of Navdanya, the movement of 500,000 seed keepers and organic farmers in India. She is author of numerous books, including "The Violence of the Green Revolution" and "Soil, Not Oil."*

Food security over the next two decades will have to be built on ecological security and climate resilience. We need the real green revolution, not a second "Green Revolution" based on genetic engineering.

> We need biodiversity intensification that works with nature's nutrient and water cycles, not against them.

Genetic engineering has not increased yields. Recent research by Doug Gurian-Sherman of the Union of Concerned Scientists published as a study "Failure to Yield" has shown that in a nearly 20 year record, genetically engineered crops have not increased yields. The study did not find significantly increased yields from crops engineered for herbicide tolerance or crops engineered to be insect-resistant.

The International Assessment of Agricultural Science and Technology for Development carried out by 400 scientists over four years has also concluded that genetic engineering does not hold much promise. Instead, small farms based on principles of agri-ecology and sustainability produce more food.

15 That is why I am so disappointed that the Gates Foundation in its global development program is supporting the use of genetically modified crops in Africa.

Green revolution technologies and strategies, reliant on monoculture and chemical fertilizers and pesticides, have destroyed biodiversity, which has in many places led to a decline in nutrition output per acre.

As I have shown in my book "Soil, Not Oil," industrial systems of food production are also a major contributor to greenhouse gas emissions and climate change. Industrial monocultures are more vulnerable to climate change since they reduce soil organic matter which is vital for moisture conservation and resilience to drought.

The claim by the genetic engineering industry that without genetically modified food we cannot respond to climate change is simply false. Climate resilient traits in crops have been evolved by farmers over centuries. In the community seed banks that I have helped create through the Navdanya movement, we have seeds for drought resistance, flood resistance and salt tolerance. This is the biological capital for the real green revolution.

The gene giants are now pirating and patenting the collective and cumulative innovation of Third World farmers. Patent monopolies on seed cannot create food security. They can only push small farmers in debt.

[20] The green revolution that we are building through Navdanya is based on conserving biodiversity and conserving water while increasing food production per acre. What we need is biodiversity intensification, not chemical intensification. What we need is to work with nature's nutrient cycles and hydrological cycle, not against them. It is time to put small farmers, especially women, at the heart of this process.

When Cheap Water and Oil Disappear

Raj Patel *is a fellow at the Institute for Food and Development Policy, and author of "Stuffed and Starved."*

The U.S. leads the world in genetically modified agricultural technology, yet one in eight Americans is hungry. Last year, with bumper harvests, more than a billion people ate less than 1,900 calories per day. The cause of hunger today isn't a shortage of food—it's poverty.

> Agriculture will need to be much more regionally controlled and locally adapted.

Addressing that will require not new agricultural technology, but a political commitment to making food a human right.

We do, however, need to transform the way we farm. Today's industrial agriculture depends on fossil fuels and abundant water. The growing and processing of food for the average American every year takes the equivalent of more than 500 gallons of oil. The future will see both cheap water and oil disappear.

[25] So how should we farm tomorrow? To answer this, we'll need the very best independent and peer-reviewed science. In 2005, the World Bank's chief scientist, Robert Watson, brought together leading natural and social scientists, representatives from government (including the U.S.), private sector and non-governmental organizations to ask how we'd feed the world in 2050, when there will be nine billion of us.

Over three years, more than 400 experts worked on a sobering report which has recently been published as "Agriculture at a Crossroads."

The scientists concluded that genetically modified crops had failed to show much promise in feeding the world. Instead, the study suggested that to feed the world, we need both political and technological change. Tomorrow's agriculture will need to be much more regionally controlled and locally adapted, and will need a diversity of approaches to meet the challenges of climate change and resource scarcity.

Among the farming techniques endorsed by the report is agroecology, which builds soil, insect and plant ecology. The result is a farming system that uses water frugally, sequesters vast amounts of carbon and doesn't require external inputs.

This is cutting edge science, but it isn't terribly profitable for large U.S.-based agricultural corporations. Perhaps that explains why, despite strong support for this report among governments overseas, the U.S. government last year refused to endorse it.

The Third Way

Jonathan Foley *is the director of the new Institute on the Environment at the University of Minnesota. His research is focused on global land use, agriculture and climate.*

The future of agriculture must address several goals simultaneously. First, it now appears that we will have to double world food production in the next 40 years given continued population growth, increasing meat consumption and pressure from biofuels.

You're either with Michael Pollan or you're with Monsanto, but neither paradigm can fully meet our needs.

We will also have to dramatically reduce the environmental impacts of our farming practices, which have caused widespread damage to soils, ecosystems, watersheds and even the atmosphere. In fact, agriculture's impacts rival climate change as a top environmental concern.

We will also have to improve food security for the world's poor. While the Green Revolution of the 1960s made it possible to feed hundreds of millions more people than in earlier eras, the number of undernourished in the world has started to rise again.

30 Finally, we will have to increase the resilience of agriculture. Today, our high-efficiency, globalized world has many benefits, but it is vulnerable to disruption, whether from drought, disease or price spikes. We must start building more resilience into food systems to better insulate us from future shocks.

Currently, there are two paradigms of agriculture being widely promoted: local and organic systems versus globalized and industrialized agriculture. Each has fervent followers and critics. Genuine discourse has broken down: You're either with Michael Pollan or you're with Monsanto. But neither of these paradigms, standing alone, can fully meet our needs.

Organic agriculture teaches us important lessons about soils, nutrients and pest management. And local agriculture connects people back to their food system. Unfortunately, certified organic food provides less than 1 percent of the world's calories, mostly to the wealthy. It is hard to imagine organic farming scaling up to feed 9 billion.

Globalized and industrialized agriculture have benefits of economic scalability, high output and low labor demands. Overall, the Green Revolution has been a huge success. Without it, billions of people would have starved. However, these successes have come with tremendous environmental and social costs, which cannot be sustained.

Rather than voting for just one solution, we need a third way to solve the crisis. Let's take ideas from both sides, creating new, hybrid solutions that boost production, conserve resources and build a more sustainable and scalable agriculture.

35 There are many promising avenues to pursue: precision agriculture, mixed with high-output composting and organic soil remedies; drip irrigation, plus buffer strips to reduce erosion and pollution; and new crop varieties that reduce water and fertilizer demand. In this context, the careful use of genetically modified crops may be appropriate, after careful public review.

A new "third way" for agriculture is not only possible, it is necessary. Let's start by ditching the rhetoric, and start bridging the old divides. Our problems are huge, and they will require everyone at the table, working together toward solutions.

REFLECT & WRITE

- ❑ In their commentaries, Collier and Shiva present opposing viewpoints. Which is more persuasive? Why? Does it have to do with facts? Evidence? Reasoning? Structure of argument? Voice? *Pathos* appeal? *Ethos*? Other factors?
- ❑ How does Shiva rely on *ethos* to bolster her argument? To what end? Find at least two points in her piece where she does so.
- ❑ How does Patel establish a different focus in his opening paragraphs from Collier's and Shiva's? How is this difference in focus maintained throughout his commentary? Is this more likely or less likely to appeal to his audience? Why?
- ❑ What does Foley mean by "the third way"? What debate is he tapping into? What are his solutions?
- ❑ **Write.** Choose the selection from this debate with which you least agree. Write a response to that stance in which you articulate your own position and complicate the writer's original argument. Be sure to use direct quotes from the text in your response.

ANALYZING PERSPECTIVES ON THE ISSUE

1. Search for food blogs online and look at examples of posts and photos, developing a sense of the format of this particular genre of writing. Now, keep your own food blog for a week, incorporating both written texts and your own photos. After a week, share your blog posts with the class and write a brief reflection about the process of food blogging and what you learned about yourself and your relationship to food by this experience.
2. Watch the video of Michelle Obama delivering her announcement of the "Let's Move!" project, available on the Let's Move website and on YouTube. As you watch, take notes, comparing it to the content and composition of the "Let's Move!" launch speech you read in this chapter. How is the rhetorical situation of the two pieces different? How did Obama modify her script for the online version? What did she emphasize more or less in her revision? Think also about her delivery and the staging of the video. What images were chosen, how were they arranged, and how do they complement oral delivery? Use these notes to produce a comparative analysis essay of the two texts.

Seeing Connections
For further discussion about translating between written and oral texts, see Chapter 9

3. Refer back to the Monsanto editorial cartoon analyzed in the sample student essay in Chapter 1. How does that cartoon's argument compare to the positions that the scholars share in "Can Biotech Food Cure World Hunger?" Whose position does it most closely mirror? Brainstorm an alternate editorial cartoon that could represent the perspective of one of the other contributors to that conversation.

FROM READING TO RESEARCH ASSIGNMENTS

1. Many doctors and scholars have looked at how American children suffer from a culture of poor eating practices. Raj Patel, one of the contributors to the "Can Biotech Food Cure World Hunger?" discussion, tackled this issue on his blog. Find and read his April 9, 2010 post, "Down on the Clown," on his website. Then write a response to his post that links your assessment of his call to action with the material contained in the Obama reading from this chapter as well as statistics and data gathered from your own independent research on this topic: be sure to use reputable sources in gathering your information. See Chapter 5 for strategies for effectively evaluating online sources.
2. Working in small groups, create your own contribution to the "What the World Eats" series by taking a "What the American College Student Eats" photograph. Consider the following: Who should be in the photo? What location or setting should you use? What foods should you represent? How should you arrange and stage them? After taking your photograph, write a caption similar to the ones found in Figures 10.10 to 10.13. Print out your photo and mount it and the caption on foam board for a class exhibit. Tour the exhibit with your class and then compare your different interpretations of the typical college diet. Discuss the results of your field research with the class.
3. Do your own primary research about American food culture by considering the visual rhetoric of food advertisements. Using the checklist found in Writing Assignment #1 in chapter 2, collect a set of ads and analyze the way in which they produce an argument about food consumption. Your ads should have a clear relationship to one another, for instance: ads for a single brand or type of food spanning several decades; contemporary food ads aimed at children (fast food, cereal, even vitamins); ads from a single food industry, such as dairy farmers or the meat industry; or even ads for a nutritional supplement or weight-loss program. Write an analysis in which you make a strong claim about how these ads use specific rhetorical

strategies to make an argument to the consumers about the food they eat. To find ads, use online advertising archives, search the Library of Congress website, or look through books and collections at your university library.

4. Since the *The New York Times* prompted the scholarly dialogue collected in "Can Biotech Food Cure World Hunger?" in 2009, the issue of Genetically Modified Organisms (GMOs) and genetically modified foods has often been in the spotlight. Research a key player or event in this debate: the agricultural biotechnology company, Monsanto; the Greenpeace anti-GMO protests; the California Prop 37 initiative (2012); Barack Obama's so-called Monsanto Protection Act (2013). Use primary and secondary sources to create an argument about the GMO controversy; include quotations from the opinions shared by Collier, Shiva, Patel, and Foley as appropriate. Be sure to use MLA form for citations.

Seeing Connections

For guidance on how to integrate direct quotes correctly, see Chapter 6. See Chapter 7 for more on MLA documentation form.

CHAPTER 11

Life Online

Everywhere you turn these days, you can see how technological interfaces have come to dominate our encounters with the world around us. We read our novels on Kindles, Nooks, and iPads, and we get our news from flash-driven websites and personalized online RSS subscriptions. We manage our lives with our iPhones, Androids, and BlackBerrys, and we measure a carrier's worth by the dimensions of its Wi-Fi coverage and its data package. Talking TomToms and Garmin devices tell us how to get from point A to point B; Siri reminds us what to buy at the grocery store or how to find the local Starbucks; and advanced GPS technology in our cell phones and even cameras helps us geolocate ourselves, our friends, and all of our photographed experiences. We spend our leisure time in immersive environments and alternate worlds, or gaming with systems that enable multiplayer campaigns or that track our physical movements and translate them to the screen. We watch our media on our iPads, smartphones, HD tablets, 50-inch plasma TVs, and in the theater in 3-D with digital surround sound. We catch our television shows on Hulu and Netflix, and we follow both friends and celebrities on Tumblr, Twitter, YouTube, Facebook and Pinterest, maybe even becoming minor Internet celebrities ourselves. We create and re-create multiple online identities and profiles, and we connect with our friends through pithy 140-character updates, textspeak-laden instant messages, opinionated blogposts, and videochat. We constantly share images with our friends: selfies and group shots on Facebook, filtered and edited photos on Instagram, pinned favorites on Pinterest, and sometimes overly candid pictures on Snapchat. In many ways, our lives have become so integrated with and mediated by online culture that we can't even imagine life without it.

We can find one prime example of this movement toward integrating lived and virtual experience in Figure 11.1, a photograph of a group of people involved in Google's new Glass project. Announced in 2012, this project focused on developing a wearable computer with a head-mounted display. In practical terms, the Google Glass allows you to interface with the Internet and its resources anytime, anywhere; it offers the everyday consumer the

FIGURE 11.1 This promotional photo from Google's Glass project shows how the device can augment face-to-face interactions.

opportunity to experience augmented reality—for a price. It can capture moments of our life, hands-free with a voice command; it can help us share our life events with our friends, however remote; it can superimpose maps and directions onto the landscape in front of us; it can even allow us to mine Google's vast knowledge network to help us better understand the world around us. However, not everyone shares Google's utopian vision for a tech-enhanced future. What happens to privacy when people around you might be filming at any time? What happens to equal access when those with visual impairments find themselves unable to take advantage of the technology? What happens to our ability to focus when we wear our distraction on our head? What happens when we are always connected, never alone?

Clearly the shift to living life online is hardly unproblematic. Scholars from many disciplines are just starting to make sense of how such online interactions are changing our lived experience. In this section, we'll explore different views on the effects of our technological dependence and will challenge you to take a careful look at the way you interface with your own experience. In doing so, we'll ask you to complicate your own relationship with technology to better comprehend how it is encoding your understanding of who you are, of how you experience the world, and of what *life* and *culture* even mean in this hyperconnected world.

REFLECT & WRITE

- ❑ How does this photograph serve its purpose of promoting the Google Glass Project? What argument is it making?
- ❑ Consider the choice of models, perspective, and setting. How might Google have made a stronger message about the everyday uses of Google Glass by changing some of these elements in the photograph?
- ❑ **Write.** Visit the Google Glass website. Watch its promotional videos and analyze the way in which the entire site functions as an advertisement for this product and defines how it can augment our lives. Write a paragraph-long rhetorical analysis; make sure you refer to particular elements of the site, use of appeals, and strategies of development to support your claim.

In this cartoon from the March 15, 2010, issue of the New Yorker, *editorial artist* **Mick Stevens** *makes a pointed statement about the ubiquity of social media in modern life.*

EDITORIAL CARTOON

FIGURE 11.2 In this cartoon, Mick Stevens provides a visual argument conveying the idea: "I text; therefore, I am."

REFLECT & WRITE

- ❑ A common scene in hospitals today would be the new parent texting about a baby's birth. What is the significance of having the texter be the infant himself? What does this add to the cultural critique at work here?
- ❑ Why do you think Stevens only shows the baby's hands? How would showing the baby's head, face, or body have changed the emphasis of the image?
- ❑ Why include the nurse in the frame? What does she contribute to the cartoon?
- ❑ **Write.** This cartoon makes an argument about one generation's interaction with technology and social media. Sketch either a single-panel or multiple-panel cartoon that provides an argument about an older generation's relationship to technology.

In this article, **Christine Erickson** *explores the newest form of self-portraiture, "the selfie"—the photographs that people take of themselves and upload to numerous social network sites, including Tumblr, Facebook, and Instagram. Her goal is to use this trend to explore deeper questions of how social media has affected our self-image. Erickson is a features writer for the Internet news blog,* Mashable, *where this article was originally published on February 15, 2013.*

The Social Psychology of the Selfie

Christine Erickson

The "selfie." I kind of cringe every time I hear that word, imagining Myspace-style angles, duck faces, peace signs and dirty mirrors. I'm not alone either. Many are hesitant to take and share photos of themselves, for fear of looking vain, vulnerable or being scrutinized.

FIGURE 11.3

But still, photo sharing sites like Facebook, Instagram and Tumblr are filled with self-portraits. Some upload entire albums to Facebook of their Mac Photo Booth sessions. Others take filtered pictures of what they wore that day, or caption a closeup with mild to severe self-deprecation.

Among the many self-portraits are ones of celebrities, like Justin Bieber or Kim Kardashian. When I asked comedian Chelsea Peretti why, another frequent self-sharer, she jokingly responded "loneliness and desperation for attention are crucial ingredients."

Self-image is important, and not always in a narcissistic way. It's how we deine ourselves, and present for others to see. We rely on others' perceptions, judgments and appraisals to develop our social self.

5 How we see ourselves in the mirror versus a regular photo is different. The mirror shows a reverse view, but also shows you alive and with movement—as Dr. Pamela Rutledge, director of the Media Psychology Research Center, points out.

"For some, this presents a more attractive (and therefore satisfactory) image as the movement and life tend to overcome flaws that might be more noticeable to an individual were the person to see him or herself in a photo," says Dr. Rutledge.

Technology is adapting, providing us with better tools to present our self-image. How often is the front-facing camera in a phone used as a compact mirror, compared to FaceTime or Skype? How many photos of yourself have you taken with your phone, and how many would you actually share online?

In an age of hyper sharing and high engagement, how has social media affected our self image?

Looking Behind the Selfie

The opinion of others has been a part of identity development for more than a century. The "looking-glass self" is a psychological concept that suggests we develop our sense of self based on the perceptions of those we interact with, said Andrea Letamendi, a doctor of psychology at UCLA.

10 "Now that we can interact with hundreds—no, thousands—of people simultaneously, we've strengthened the impact that others have on our self-value," says Dr. Letamendi.

The profile picture or avatar is a way for people to present a certain side of themselves. It also puts the person in control of their own image.

"I'd certainly rather post a photo I took as opposed to one someone else took most of the time," wrote a member of the BodyAcceptance subreddit.

Has that single chosen image become the most important representation of our online identity? It is the first place the eye is drawn to on a Facebook profile. Studies have shown that the comments on your Facebook profile picture strongly affect your level of perceived physical, social and professional attractiveness.

Dr. Rutledge says that many have argued there is no difference to how we adapt to present ourselves in real life.

15 "Is this different than how we adjust if we are going to a party versus a job interview or a family picnic?" asks Dr. Rutledge.

One of the differences between our self-image in real life and online is more ability to change our look, and also mask our identity. Even when a person posts a photo of you on social media, you can untag, delete or modify the photo to keep social presence more consistent with the self-image you want others to see.

Technology has also allowed us to shape who we are and highlight specific features in ways we couldn't do as easily offline.

"This may mean routine photoshopping to create a more 'likeable' self, or simply choosing photos that seem more like the visual self we want to present," says Dr. Letamendi.

Instagram is another example. Filters make any photo look more appealing than what the image actually looks like, let alone what the naked eye would've seen. There has been limited psychological study on the app, but one in particular showed active users were concerned with both personal production and social reception. A combined search of various hashtags, such as #selfie, #self and #selfportrait, will produce millions of results.

How Online Anonymity Hurts Self-Esteem

20 Anonymity now has a large influence on the feedback people receive about their image on social media.

We know how people respond to an image influences self perception. Today, the chance of being scrutinized is greater because more people interact through a protected, anonymous filter, potentially making any self-esteem issues more sensitive.

There are forums—like the subreddit amiugly, which has more than 22,000 subscribers—that allow anonymous users to give constructive criticism on self-submitted portraits. Most of which is positive, but this further suggests the desire to maintain an image that's accepted by society before the self.

Social Comparison

A recent study showed more online photo sharing from people whose self-esteem is based on "public contingencies," defined in this instance as others' approval, physical appearance and outdoing competition.

Humans are naturally competitive. Visual social platforms, like Facebook, Instagram and Tumblr allow quick and frequent access to others' profiles. We can see what old high school friends that you haven't talked to in years have lost weight. We know what coworkers and extended family are doing more-so than we could offline. This encourages social comparison.

25 Dr. Rutledge says this is a normal feature of human behavior, and that comparison doesn't stop when people shut the laptop or phone and go to school or work.

"It is only problematic when someone fixates or over-compares to their detriment, but that is not a function of the photos as much as the individual struggling with self-esteem," says Dr. Rutledge.

How to Overcome Your Social Self-Image

If you find yourself obsessing over the image you have or have not presented accurately online, Dr. Letamendi suggests limiting access to sites, especially those that are more likely to present negative feedback.

"People who tend to have low self-esteem and depression are more likely to engage in recurrent distorted cognition about the self (such as negative self-statements). Finding ways to interrupt those thoughts can prevent them from reinforcing a negative focus on the self may be helpful in improving self-esteem and lifting mood," says Dr. Letamendi.

There are also easy ways to improve self-portraits, specifically ones that don't require Photoshop. Photographer Leanne Surfleet says the lighting is always important.

30 "The main thing with a self-portrait is you are trying to show the viewer something about yourself," says Surfleet. "You, on your own, can be a powerful statement."

Knox Bronson, founder of P1xels, an online iPhone art gallery, suggests looking into the lens and be natural.

"Also, smile," says Bronson. "It's okay to show some teeth. Unless you are going for the moody poet look."

REFLECT & WRITE

- ❑ Many would consider "selfies" to be a frivolous or shallow topic for an essay. How does Erickson give it merit and traction as a persuasive argument? How does she establish her own authority, and what other authorities does she evoke to make her points convincing?
- ❑ How does Erickson draw in the reader? Find at least two particular strategies that she uses in the article that are designed specifically to engage her audience.
- ❑ In one paragraph, Erickson argues that a study has shown "more online photo sharing from people whose self-esteem is based on 'public contingencies.'" Find that passage. Do you agree with this assertion? Why or why not? How do your own social media patterns reflect on your reliance on "public contingencies"?
- ❑ **Write.** In the original blog version of this article, Erickson concluded the article in this way: "How has social media changed your self-image? Are we utilizing it to present us for the better or worse? Share your thoughts and tips in the comments below." Write a response to this prompt, including "tips" as she suggests for effective self-representation. If you want, find her original article online and leave your response as part of the comment thread, taking into account the other public responses that are already posted in developing your own.

■ *The profiles that follow are taken from the book* Alter Ego: Avatars and Their Creators, *which complicates stereotypes of gaming and virtual identity by exploring the different identities that people create for themselves online. The book is a product of a three-year study by* **Robbie Cooper**, *a photojournalist and video artist, and his co-author, virtual ethnographer* **Tracy Spaight**. *It launched simultaneously in bookstores and in the virtual world Second Life in 2007.*

Profiles from *Alter Ego: Avatars and Their Creators*

FIGURE 11.4
Name: Jason Rowe
Born: 1975
Occupation: None
Location: Crosby, Texas, USA
Average hours per week in-game: 80
Avatar name: Rurouni Kenshin
Avatar created: 2003
Game played: *Star Wars Galaxies*
Server name: Radiant
Character type: Human marksman/rifleman
Character level: 55
Special abilities: Ranged weapon specialization

The difference between me and my online character is pretty obvious. I have a lot of physical disabilities in real life, but in *Star Wars Galaxies* I can ride an Imperial speeder bike, fight monsters, or just hang out with friends at a bar. I have some use of my hands—not much, but a little. In the game I use an onscreen keyboard called 'soft-type' to talk with other players. I can't press the keys on a regular keyboard so I use a virtual one. I play online games because I get to interact with people. The computer screen is my window to the world. Online it doesn't matter what you look like. Virtual worlds bring people together—everyone is on common ground. In the real world, people can be uncomfortable around me before they get to know me and realize that, apart from my outer appearance, I'm just like them. Online you get to know the person behind the keyboard before you know the physical person. The internet eliminates how you look in real life, so you get to know a person by their mind and personality. In 2002 at the *Ultimate Online* Fan Faire in Austin, I noticed that people were intrigued by me, but they acted just like I was one of them. They treated me as an equal, like I wasn't even the way that I am—not disabled, not in a wheelchair, you know. We were all just gamers.

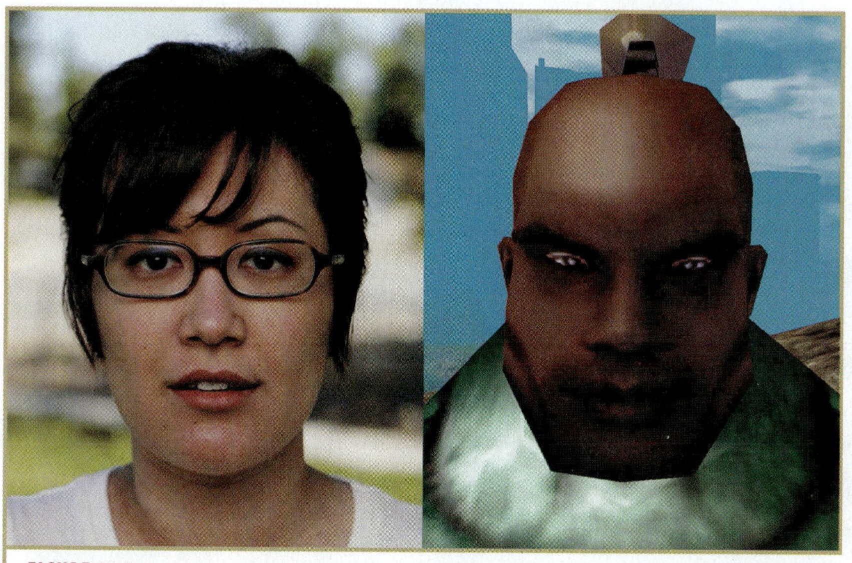

FIGURE 11.5
Name: Rebecca Glasure
Born: 1980
Occupation: Housewife
Location: Los Angeles, California, USA
Avatar name: Stygian Physic
Avatar created: 2005
Game played: City of Heroes
Character type: Elf

My avatar in *City of Heroes* is my complete opposite. Stygian Physic is big, black, and male. I created him that way because I didn't want to get hit on all the time. I wanted to be noticed for my skills, not my pixel-boobs. By playing as a guy, I found that people treated me differently. Being a guy enabled me to form relationships that I would never otherwise be able to experience. The guys just assume I'm a guy. If I'm the leader, I can make a call and they'll all just follow. And they'll open up about problems with their girlfriends and so on. When I play as a female character, I get challenged a lot more and have to argue about everything. No thanks. I've made some good friends playing as a guy. To this day they don't know I'm really a chick. I don't lie about it. They just assume that I'm a guy and never ask.

I have a six-year-old daughter who's needed more of my attention lately, and because of that I've cut back on my playing hours a lot. I would say that I used to be a 'hardcore' player, because I would spend literally all day sitting at my computer. But now my daughter's getting older, I just don't have that luxury any more. It's my hope that she grows up to like games, so we can all play together. That would blow my mind. My husband and I used to play together for the first year. When we're old and grey our reminiscences will probably consist of things like, "Remember that time we slaughtered the Hydra and got level 40 at the same time?"

FIGURE 11.6
Name: Cassien Guier
Born: 1985
Occupation: Student
Location: Lyon, France
Average hours per week in-game: 8
Avatar name: La blonde
Avatar created: 2005
Game played: *City of Heroes*
Server name: Vigilance
Character type: Human female
Character level: 30

Seeing Connections: To consider how to best use the canon of Arrangement in your *Alter Ego* revision, see chapter 3.

First of all you have to know I'm not a good player. In the game I spend more time and money making my character look good and changing her hairstyle than I do playing. By the way, thanks to all the players for giving me money to make it possible for me to change my hair every day!

5 I decided to make a superhero reflecting my inner self so I created La blonde, the supra super heroine! She's wonderful, in pink and yellow clothes and splendid shoes. She has the biggest breasts you have ever seen. Just like a real blonde, her wardrobe changes every week. She likes to smile, and people must think she looks pretty stupid because they never take her seriously. Her attitude amazes all the other superheroes! The world can collapse but La blonde will remain optimistic. She often dies. I'm not sure why but the monsters kick her out first. As if a blonde could be dangerous!

I don't really know why people like to have her in their group when fighting the bad monsters. Probably because of her pretty smiley face. Actually she must be the most useless character in the world of MMORPGs.

REFLECT & WRITE

- ❑ How do the people from *Alter Ego* defy or reinscribe common stereotypes about gamers? Mention concrete visual details in answering this question.
- ❑ Perform a rhetorical analysis of these selections. Where are *pathos*, *logos*, and *ethos* located in the different components of the profiles?
- ❑ Consider the gender-crossing found in both Cassien's and Rebecca's choices of avatars. In each case, what do their choices say about their understanding of gender dynamics in virtual environments? How do their choices reflect certain stereotypes?
- ❑ Look carefully at the layout of the profiles. How are the elements of the profiles (photos, demographics, descriptive paragraphs, avatar portraits) arranged to make a specific argument about the relationship between avatars and their creators? What is this argument in each case?
- ❑ **Write.** As the question above suggests, the layout of *Alter Ego* contributes powerfully to its argument. Make a copy of one of the *Alter Ego* profiles and, using scissors and a fresh sheet of paper, cut and paste the words and images into a new layout that is designed specifically to produce a different argument about the relationship between avatars and their creators. You can also use word processing to turn the information on the right side into a formal paragraph if you'd like, or you can use the scaling feature on your copying machine to change the size of the images. Once you are done with your new design, write a short reflection on how your design reflects your argument about avatar identity.

The **Pew Internet & American Life Project** *conducts studies examining the impact of the Internet on twenty-first-century culture, including families, education, and civic life. The project, which sent out its first survey in 2000, is one of seven projects that comprise the Pew Research Center, an organization focused on investigating the social forces and trends that shape contemporary American life. What follows is a section from its report "Teens, Kindness and Cruelty on Social Network Sites," which was published in November 2011. The lead author of the report is Amanda Lenhart, the director of the project's research on teens and their families; its findings were based primarily on a survey of 799 teens (aged 12–17) between April and July 2011.*

Excerpt from "Teens, Kindness and Cruelty on Social Network Sites"

Amanda Lenhart, Mary Madden, Aaron Smith, Kristen Purcell, Kathryn Zickuhr, and Lee Rainie

Part 2: Social Media and Digital Citizenship: What teens experience and how they behave on social network sites

Section 1: The majority of teens have positive online experiences, but some are caught in an online feedback loop of meanness and negative experiences.

The majority of social media-using teens say their experience is that their peers are mostly kind to one another on social network sites, but their views are less positive when compared with similar assessments from online adults.

We asked teens the following question about what they see in social network spaces: "Overall, in your experience, are people your age mostly *kind* or mostly *unkind* to one another on social network sites?" Most of the 77% of all teens who use social media say their experience is that people their age are mostly kind to one another on social network sites. Overall, 69% of social media-using teens say their experience is that peers are mostly kind to each other in social network spaces. Another 20% say their peers are mostly unkind, while 11% volunteered that "it depends." However, in a similar question asked of adults 18 and older, 85% of social media-using adults reported that their experience was that people are mostly kind to one another on social network sites, while just 5% reported that they see people behaving in mostly unkind ways.

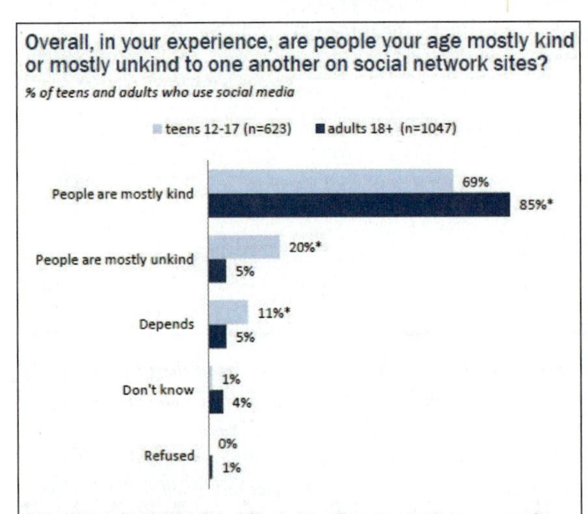

Note: The question wording for adults was "Overall, in your experience, are people mostly kind or mostly unkind to one another on social networking sites?" * indicates a statistically significant difference between bars.

Source: The Pew Research Center's Internet & American Life Teen-Parent survey, April 19-July 14, 2011. N=799 for teens and parents, including oversample of minority families. Interviews were conducted in English and Spanish. Data for adults is from Pew Internet's August Tracking survey, July 25-August 26, 2011. Nationally representative, n=2260 adults 18+, includes cell phone & Spanish language interviews.

Girls ages 12–13 have the most negative assessment of social network spaces.

While teens across all demographic groups generally have positive experiences watching how their peers treat each other on social network sites, younger teenage girls (ages 12–13) stand out as considerably more likely to say their experience is that people are mostly unkind. One in three (33%) younger teen girls who uses social media says that people her age are mostly unkind to one another on social network sites, compared with 9% of social media-using boys 12–13 and 18% of boys 14–17. One in five older girls (20%) who uses social media says that in her experience people her age are mostly unkind to one another on these sites.

How peers treat one another on social media

% of teens who use social media

	Mostly Kind	Mostly Unkind	Depends	Don't Know
Race/ethnicity				
White	72%*	20%*	9%	0%
Black	56%	31%*	9%	4%
Hispanic	78%*	9%	13%	0%
Location				
Urban	68%	23%*	8%	0%
Suburban	73%	14%+	13%	0%
Rural	57%	28%	12%	3%
Household income				
Less than $30K	61%	22%	16%	2%
$30-49K	67%	25%	9%	0%
$50-75K	78%	15%	7%	0%
$75,000 or more	72%	18%	10%	0%
Age				
Teens ages 12-13	70%	22%	8%	0%
Teens ages 14-17	68%	19%	12%	1%
Sex				
Girls	66%	23%	10%	0%
Boys	71%	16%	12%	1%
Age + sex				
Girls 12-13	65%	33%*	3%	0%
Boys 12-13	77%	9%+	14%	0%
Girls 14-17	67%	20%	13%	0%
Boys 14-17	69%	18%+	12%	1%

Note: * indicates statistically significant difference between rows within each column and section. In sections with +, the data point with the * is only statistically significantly different than the data points with + symbol.

Source: The Pew Research Center's Internet & American Life Teen-Parent survey, April 19-July 14, 2011. N=799 for teens and parents, including oversample of minority families. Interviews were conducted in English and Spanish.

Black teens are less likely to say their experience is that people their age are kind to one another on social network sites.

Black social media users are less likely than white and Latino users to report that people their age are mostly kind online. While 72% of whites and 78% of Latino youth say that their experience is that people are usually kind on social network sites, just over half (56%) of blacks say the same.

Teens tend towards negative words when describing how people act online.

5 As a part of this project, we conducted seven focus groups with teens ages 12 to 19 to ask teens more in-depth questions about their experiences interacting with others on social network sites. In the groups, we asked the teen participants questions about how people usually acted online. In some cases, we asked students to tell us about their observations of online behavior and then tell us how they thought people *should* act in online spaces. In one exercise, we asked the participants to write down words or phrases that they felt captured these concepts. As the word clouds [1]20 created from the words they shared suggest, teens overwhelmingly chose negative adjectives to describe how people act online. Words that appeared frequently included "rude," "mean," "fake," "crude," "over-dramatic," and "disrespectful." Some teens did use positive words

[1]Word clouds were created with wordle.net. The size of the word increases the more frequently it is found in the set of words included in the cloud. So, the most frequently occurring words are the largest

like the frequently mentioned "funny" and the less common "honest," "clever," "friendly," "entertaining," and "sweet," but overall the frequency of positive words was substantially lower. Other terms shared by participants could be interpreted differently depending on the context of use—these include the popular term "different" and others like "emotional,"

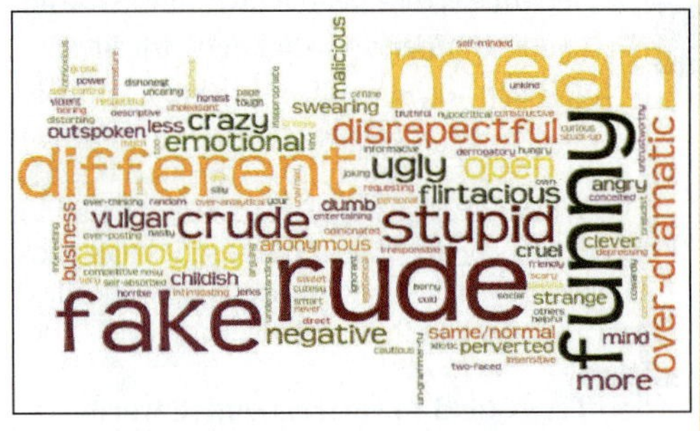

"cautious," "outspoken," "strange," and "open."

Of the teens who were asked about how they thought people *should* act online, the responses were substantially more positive and included words like "respectful," "nice," "friendly," "mature," "peaceful," and phrases

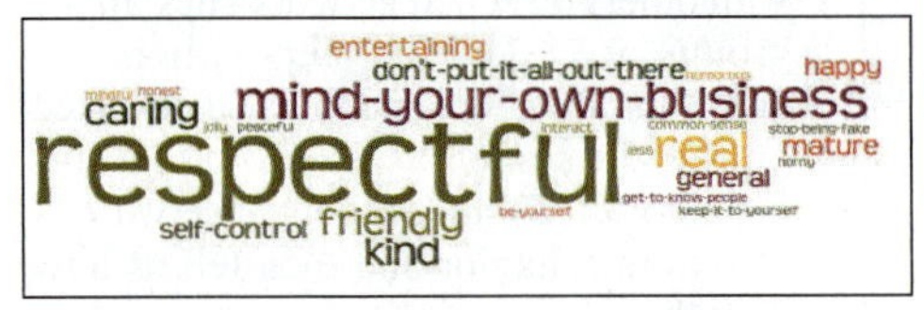

like "mind your own business" and "don't put it all out there."

After the exercise, we asked the focus group participants follow-up questions to plumb the discrepancies between the way they had witnessed people acting on social media and how they thought people *should* act on the sites.

Many teens told us that they just felt like different people on these sites and thought that people they see online often act very differently on social media from how they act in person and at school.

- *MIDDLE SCHOOL GIRL: That's what a lot of people do. Like, they won't say it to your face, but they will write it online…*
- *MIDDLE SCHOOL BOY: I know people who, in person, like refuse to swear. And online, it's every other word.*
- *MIDDLE SCHOOL GIRL: I think people get—like when they get on Facebook, they get ruthless, stuff like that.… They act different in school and stuff like that, but when they get online, they like a totally different person. You get a lot of confidence.*
- *HIGH SCHOOL BOY: [There's] this real quiet girl who go to my school, right, but when she's on Facebook she talks like some wild—like, be rapping and talking about who she knew and some more stuff and you would, like, never think that's her. You would think that's somebody else…*

Teens also identified specific online social spaces—open comment spaces and question and answer sites—that feel particularly unwelcoming:

- *HIGH SCHOOL BOY: YouTube comments are pretty bad. They're, like, oh my God.*
- *HIGH SCHOOL BOY: I have a friend who came out and he had a Formspring[2] and, like, a bunch of people from this school, like, attacked his Formspring and, like, wrote really, really homophobic things on it.*

---

[2]Formspring is an anonymous question and answer website.

10 Often teens felt bolder, ruder, or more empowered because they did not fear physical violence in the online space. One middle school girl told us that she thought people were ruder online "because you can't hurt anybody online. You can't punch nobody through the screen."

- *MIDDLE SCHOOL GIRL 1. I think I act ruder to online people.*
- *MODERATOR. You act ruder? How come?*
- *MIDDLE SCHOOL GIRL 2. Because she doesn't have to see them, so they can't beat her up.*

For some teens we spoke with—particularly middle school girls—fights and drama on social media flowed back and forth between school, the street, and Facebook, often resulting in physical fights during the in-person portions of the conflict.

- *MIDDLE SCHOOL GIRL: I read what they were talking about online, then I go offline and confront the person who was saying something to her.*
- *MIDDLE SCHOOL GIRL: . . . Like that's how most people start fighting because that's how most of the fights in my school happen—because of some Facebook stuff, because of something you post, or like because somebody didn't like your pictures.*

One middle school girl detailed the circular flow of conflict between her social network site and her in-person life, and the ways that she, at her mother's behest, tries to break the cycle.

"...the other day, Monday, I was not cool with somebody and so they tried to put on their status something about me. But I didn't reply to that because my mother told me not to say nothing back because she didn't want anything more to happen."

She further explains a physical fight she was supposed to have and the ways in which others taunted her offline and online about her allegedly skipping out on the conflict. She describes her attempts to ignore online comments made about her "ducking" the fight, until the taunting escalated to insulting her friend. "...I was supposed to be fighting somebody Monday, but the security guard picked me up and brung me back inside the school. Yeah, they were like, 'oh my man, [MIDDLE SCHOOL GIRL] ducked it.' I was like, that's crazy, but I didn't reply back and then she said something about my best friend..."

15 For other teens, the fact that they can act differently on social media translates into more real, positive experiences. Instead of seeing social media as a place that fomented conflict or bad behavior, some teens felt as though it increased a sense of closeness and allowed people to be authentic or more real than they could be offline:

- *HIGH SCHOOL GIRL: I think people act different on Facebook because that's like their—I mean, I think the self that they show you on Facebook could be their true self, like who they actually want to be.*
- *MIDDLE SCHOOL GIRL: Yeah, I act the same how I act in school. Like online I'm still goofy and stuff like that.*

Several teens told us that they find friends and romantic interests easier to talk to and more open in these online social spaces.

- *HIGH SCHOOL GIRL: But I feel like, since it's on Facebook, I guess it's easier to talk to people, or like, admit things and, like, you just have, like, open conversations because they're not, like face-to-face, so it's not as, like—they're not, like, embarrassed or nervous or something.*

- *HIGH SCHOOL BOY: [O]n Facebook definitely people... can be more open in some ways than in real life. Like, they'll say more than they will because it's not, like, face-to-face, so. Like, some things that might be awkward in real life won't be that awkward in a conversation on Facebook.*

At least one teen with whom we spoke attributed the ease of conversation in social media with a sense of privacy in social chat spaces:

- *MIDDLE SCHOOL BOY: I don't know, it just feels like in person, it can be awkward and weird if you're trying to tell something, like, personal and secret because you're looking at them... But like on a Facebook chat, it is very—it's like there's no one unless it's like a hacker or something. But that's rare. You can talk where you can actually tell them lots of things, or send them a private message, not, like, public.*

And others do not find friends changed when they talk to them online:

- *HIGH SCHOOL GIRL: I don't really have a like, kind of, issue, I guess. I mean, when I talk to someone online—like... my best friend since sixth grade—she doesn't change when she's online or when I see her in person. I don't really get to see her that often because she goes to a different school, but no, she doesn't ever change.*

Other teens spoke of the challenges of managing disparate friend groups in the same public space visible to all of them:

- *HIGH SCHOOL GIRL: Well, I think—I still—I think people still make personas in real life too. It's just, like, like if I'm with a different group of friends I'll be more one way than I am with another group of friends just because that's how—it's more comfortable for them and it makes it fun for the group.*

REFLECT & WRITE

- ❑ Which is the most surprising statistic contained in this section of the report. Why?
- ❑ How do the report's assertions about the relationship between race, gender, age, and online behavior resonate with your own observations?
- ❑ Which was the most persuasive part of this section? Why?
- ❑ This section contains both traditional information graphics as well as word art. What different purposes do these serve as visual rhetoric? Is one more effective than the other? Why or why not?
- ❑ **Write.** In one section of the article, the researchers discuss how they "asked the participants to write down words or phrases" that they felt summarized their observations about online behavior, which they used to generate a word cloud. Conduct a similar experiment with at least 20 of your friends; use the online program Wordle or the software of your choice to generate a similar word cloud about online behavior and then write a one-page reflection on the results you observed from your survey.

The authors of the following piece are two of the most prominent researchers of teens and social media in the U.S. today. **danah boyd** *is a fellow at Harvard University's Berkman Center for Internet and Society and a social media researcher at Microsoft Research New England. Her most recent book is titled,* It's Complicated: The Social Lives of Networked Teens. **Alice Marwick** *is an assistant professor of communication and media studies at Fordham University and also works with boyd as a researcher at the Berkman Center. Like boyd, Marwick focuses her research principally on youth and social media, a topic about which they both have presented and written frequently. The following is an excerpt from their essay "Social Privacy in Networked Publics: Teens' Attitudes, Practices, and Strategies," which they originally prepared as a presentation for a 2011 Symposium on the Dynamics of the Internet and Society.*

Excerpt from "Social Privacy in Networked Publics: Teens' Attitudes, Practices, and Strategies"

danah boyd and Alice Marwick

Waffles, 17, NC:[1] *Every teenager wants privacy. Every single last one of them, whether they tell you or not, wants privacy. Just because an adult thinks they know the person doesn't mean they know the person. And just because teenagers use internet sites to connect to other people doesn't mean they don't care about their privacy. We don't tell everybody every single thing about our lives. We tell them general information—names, places, what we like to do—but that's general knowledge. That's not something you like to keep private—"Oh, I play games. I better not tell anybody about that." I mean—that's not something that we do. So to go ahead and say that teenagers don't like privacy is pretty ignorant and inconsiderate honestly, I believe, on the adult's part.*

There's a widespread myth that American teenagers don't care about privacy. The logic is simple: Why else would teenagers share so much on Facebook and Twitter and YouTube?[2] There is little doubt that many—but not all—American teens have embraced many popular social media services.[3] And there is little doubt that those who have are posting

[1]The names used in this article are pseudonyms. Some were chosen by the participants themselves; others were chosen by the authors to reflect similar gender and ethnic roots as are embedded in the participants' given names. All identifying information in teens' quotes has been altered to maintain confidentiality.

[2]A 2008 Harris Interactive/CTIA survey about teens' relationship to their mobile was publicized as indicating that kids don't care about privacy because only 41% indicated that they were concerned about privacy and security issues when using their mobile: http://files.ctia.org/pdf/HI_TeenMobileStudy_ResearchReport.pdf In 2010, Chris Jay Hoofnagle, Jennifer King, Su Li, and Joseph Turow found that young people's attitudes about privacy parallel adults' attitudes, but their skills in managing privacy online are often lacking.

[3]As of September 2009, the Pew Internet and American Life Project found that 73% of American teens ages 12–17 use a social network site; only 8% of teens in their sample used Twitter. See Lenhart et. al. 2010.

photos, sharing links, updating status messages, and commenting on each other's posts.[4] Yet, as Waffles explains above, participation in such networked publics does not imply that today's teens have rejected privacy as a value. All teens have a sense of privacy, although their definitions of privacy vary widely. Their practices in networked publics are shaped by their interpretation of the social situation, their attitudes towards privacy and publicity, and their ability to navigate the technological and social environment. As such, they develop intricate strategies to achieve privacy goals. Their practices demonstrate privacy as a social norm that is achieved through a wide array of social practices configured by structural conditions. How teens approach privacy challenges the ways in which privacy is currently conceptualized, discussed, and regulated.

What is Privacy?

Privacy is a fraught concept, with no clear agreed-upon definition. Philosophers and legal scholars have worked diligently to conceptually locate privacy and offer a framework for considering how and when it has been violated.[5] Yet, fundamentally, privacy is a social construct that reflects the values and norms of everyday people. How people conceptualize privacy and locate it in their life varies wildly, highlighting that a universal notion of privacy remains enigmatic.[6] When we asked teens to define privacy for us, their cacophonous responses reveal the diverse approaches that can be taken to understand privacy.[7] While these discussions do not help to determine a precise definition of privacy, how teens attempt to explain privacy demonstrates its importance to them.

When trying to locate privacy, young people circle around the tropes that adults use to

[4]Of teens who are on social network sites, Pew found that 86% comment on friends' posts. They also found that 38% of teens ages 12–17 shared content online; 14% keep a blog. See Lenhart et. al. 2010.

[5]The definitions of privacy are numerous. Helen Nissenbaum (2010) relates multiple definitions of privacy and groups them based on whether they are normative or descriptive; emphasize access vs. control; or emphasize promoting other values vs. protecting a private realm. These include definitions from Ruth Gavison ("a measure of the access others have to you through information, attention, and physical proximity") (68); Jeffrey Reiman ("the condition under which other people are deprived of access to either some information about you or some experience of you") (1976, 30); Westin's "the claim of individuals, groups, or institutions to determine for themselves when, how, and to what extent information about them is communicated to others (Westin 1967, 7), and Anita Allen (who defines three types of privacy: physical privacy, informational privacy, and proprietary privacy, 71). See Nissenbaum 2010 for a full discussion.

[6]Anthropologists have found wild variations in how different communities understand and prioritize privacy. John L. Locke's *Eavesdropping: An Intimate History* (2010) weaves together many of these different accounts.

[7]Teens are not alone in having diverse views about what constitutes privacy. Diverse adult perspectives are well documented in Christena Nippert-Eng's *Islands of Privacy* (2010).

discuss privacy. They speak of secrets and trust, and highlight particular spaces as more or less private. Throughout these conversations, teens consistently come back to the importance of control and personal agency. They believe that privacy has to do with their ability to control a social situation, how information flows, and when and where they can be observed by others. Unfortunately, teens often struggle to assert control over situations, particularly when technology usurps their control or when their agency is undermined. More often than not, teens acknowledge this lack of control when people who hold power over them—e.g. their parents—insist on violating boundaries that teens create or social norms that they declare. Therein lies the key hypocrisy surrounding teens and privacy. Alongside adults' complaints that teens don't care about privacy when it comes to online activities is an ongoing belief that teens do not have the right to privacy when it comes to their physical spaces—or, in many cases, their online activities.[8] Parents often use the accessibility of teens' online vocalizations as justification for violating teens' privacy.

5 In 2006, 17-year-old Bly Lauritano-Werner from Maine created a Youth Radio episode to highlight this hypocrisy. In it, she argued "*My mom always uses the excuse about the internet being 'public' when she defends herself. It's not like I do anything to be ashamed of, but a girl needs her privacy. I do online journals so I can communicate with my friends. Not so my mother could catch up on the latest gossip of my life.*"[9] In doing so, Bly is arguing an age-old refrain; she wants the right to be let alone[10] even—and perhaps especially—when she's socializing with friends.

Teens like Bly lack the agency to be able to assert social norms and adults regularly violate teens' understandings of social decorum. Consider what happened in Old Saybrook, Connecticut when local law enforcement and teachers put together an assembly for students on privacy.[11] To make a point about privacy, the educators put together a slide show of images grabbed from students' Facebook profiles and displayed these images to the student body. Students were furious. One student told a reporter that this stunt is "a violation of privacy." Most adults find this incredulous given that the content was broadly accessible—and that the students in the school had already most likely seen many of these images because they certainly had

[8]Marwick, A., Murgia-Diaz, D., & Palfrey, J. (2010). *Youth, privacy and reputation (literature review)* (Berkman Center Research Publication No. 2010-5). Boston: Berkman Center for Internet and Society at Harvard University. Retrieved from http://papers.ssrn.com/sol3/papers.cfm?abstract_id=1588163

[9]Youth Radio broadcast "Reading My LiveJournal" by Bly Lauritano-Werner: http://www.youthradio.org/oldsite/society/npr060628_onlinejournal.shtml

[10]Warren, S.D. & Brandeis, L.D., (1890). Right to Privacy. Harvard Law Review, 4, 193.

[11]Misur, S. (2011, April 11). Old Saybrook High School makes privacy point; Some perturbed when real students shown in social-media slide show. *Shoreline Times*. New Haven, CT. Retrieved from http://www.shorelinetimes.com/articles/2011/04/11/news/doc4da2f3cb5caae518276953.txt

access to them. Yet, by taking the images out of context, the educators had violated students' social norms and, thus, their sense of dignity, fairness, and respect. As one student explained to a reporter, "I kind of thought, it's like if you put it online, anyone can see it, but then at the same time, it's like kind of not fair for the police officers to put that on display without their permission and without them knowing." This incident does not reveal that teens don't understand privacy, but rather, that they lack the agency to assert social norms and expect that others will respect them. Those who have power over them—their parents and the police—can use their power to violate teens' norms, using accessibility as their justification. In this way, adults further marginalize young people, reinforcing the notion that they do not have the social status necessary to deserve rights associated with privacy.

In an era of social media where information is often easily accessible, it's all too easy to conflate accessibility with publicity. Yet, just because teens are socializing in a public setting doesn't mean that they want to be public figures nor does it mean that they want to be the object of just anyone's gaze. What's at stake concerns not just the right to be invisible, but who has the right to look, for what purposes, and to what ends. Finding a way to manage boundaries is just one of the challenges that teens face in navigating networked publics because privacy isn't simply about control over the social situation; it also requires enough agency to affect these situations.

As they enter into networked publics, teens are grappling with the tensions that surround privacy and publicity. They are trying to find ways to have agency and assert control in settings where both the architecture and their social position make it very difficult for them to control the flow of information. Yet, in exploring strategies for maintaining social privacy in networked publics, they reveal how social norms are enacted. Privacy is both a social norm and a process; it is not something that is had so much as something that is negotiated. And the practices which teens engage in while attempting to negotiate privacy show that this social construct is not disappearing simply because technology introduces new hurdles.

Variations in Privacy Norms and Practices

Even though all the teens we interviewed expressed an appreciation for privacy at some level, they did not share a uniform set of values about privacy and publicity. Just as some teenagers are extroverted and some introverted, some teens are more exhibitionist and some are more secretive. Variations among individuals are shaped by local social norms; sharing is viewed differently in different friend groups, schools, and communities. There's also a gendered component to it, with teens having different ideas of what is appropriate to share that map to stereotypical understandings of male and female emotional behavior. When 17-year-old Manu emphasizes that he's "not that kind of person," he's also enacting fairly widespread norms of masculinity:

danah: When you broke up with your girlfriend, did you write anything about it on Facebook?

Manu, 17, NC: No. I'm like—I'm not that kind of person—I find it really weird to have my emotions or anything on Facebook or Twitter, and it's just—I don't do stuff—I know other people do, but I feel like I'll get judged or just—I'm not that kind of person to let stuff out like that. I don't do statuses, actually, either.

10 Privacy must be contextualized. Teen understandings of privacy and how they carry these out varies by individual, by community, by situation, by role, and by interaction. In other words, privacy—and the norms surrounding privacy—cannot be divorced from context.[12]

When teens share information about themselves, thereby increasing their exposure, they do so because they gain something from being visible. There is always a trade-off, as teens account for what they might gain and what they might lose and how such cost-benefit analyses fit into their own mental models of risk and reward. Thus, when teens are negotiating privacy, they aren't simply thinking about a "loss"; they're considering what they might gain from revealing themselves.

Consider the words of Meixing, a bubbly 17-year-old from Tennessee who shares extensively on Facebook:

Meixing, 17, TN: Most of the time I'm a pretty extroverted person so I share a lot of things with people anyways…

danah: That means you don't care about privacy?

Meixing: I mean I do care about privacy, but if I found someone that I could trust then my first instinct would be to share stuff with that person. For example, I think, like my last boyfriend and I we were really close and then we had each other's passwords to Facebook and to emails and stuff. And so if I would get something that I didn't know about then he would notify me and look over my stuff… It made me feel safer just because someone was there to help me out and stuff. It made me feel more connected and less lonely. Because I feel like Facebook sometimes is kind of like a lonely sport, I feel, because you're kind of sitting there and you're looking at people by yourself. But if someone else knows your password and stuff it just feels better.

Meixing is highlighting the trade-offs that she faces when she's thinking about privacy. On one hand, she cares about privacy, but she's willing to expose herself in intimate situations because it makes her feel more connected. Her barriers to sharing are rooted in her sense of trust. She's not willing to expose herself to just anyone; she shares both because and as a signal that she trusts someone.

Trust is a very significant issue for teenagers and it regularly emerges in discussions about privacy. Many teens aren't confident that they can trust those around them, even their closest friends. All too often, teens use the information that they gather about others to "start drama," performing gossip and social conflict for a wide audience on social media.[13] This makes some teens very nervous about sharing, even with their closest friends. Taylor, a 15-year-old in Massachusetts, questions

---

[12]Nissenbaum 2010.

[13]Marwick, Alice and boyd, danah. (2011). "The Drama! Teens, Gossip and Celebrity." *Popular Culture Association/American Culture Association Annual Meeting*, San Antonio, TX, April 20–24.

the motivations behind her friends' decisions to invade her privacy.

Taylor, 15, MA: So I usually give people the light version because I don't want them in my business and I really don't think that they have any right to be in my business.

danah: Why do they think they have a right?

Taylor: Because they're my friends, so they put themselves in my business sometimes, so they think that they should be there to help me and protect me with things but I can deal with it myself.

15 Taylor doesn't want her friends "in her business" because she's worried that she'll lose control, so she purposely avoids sharing anything that is personal or intimate. But this doesn't stop her from sharing altogether. A photographer, she regularly uploads her work to Facebook precisely because she wants feedback and public validation.

Taylor, 15, MA: [A comment] gives me input and it makes me feel good. . . . Even if it's negative I'd probably like it as a comment. It's just like a message is more personal, which I appreciate, but when people can see that they like my work, I like it when people can see that other people like it because I don't know, I just like getting lots of comments on one picture and seeing people read them.

In choosing to share her photographs but not her personal thoughts, Taylor is trying to assert control, thereby enacting privacy by selecting what should and should not be shared. She is not alone in this approach. Many teens who seemingly share a lot online are actually consciously limiting what is available. Consider Abigail's perspective:

Abigail, 17, NC: I actually know everybody I'm friends with [on Facebook] . . . But I'm not good friends with everybody on Facebook. The people that I go to school with I know I know what they're doing. That's why I'm friends with them on Facebook but they don't need to know what I'm exactly doing today. I'm eating breakfast, then I'm going to swim practice, then I'm doing my history homework, then I'm going to do this. They don't need to know all that. I can just put an overview like "Practice, homework, then Allie's," or something. I don't need to say exactly everything I'm doing at times and stuff.

The affordances of networked publics that make widespread sharing possible also motivate teens to use more private channels of communication—like text messaging or Facebook chat—to discuss things that are embarrassing or upsetting, intimate or self-exposing. Although most teens are quite conscious about what they choose to share, they don't always have complete control over what others share about them. Facebook, Flickr and other social media sites let users tag pictures of other users, while Twitter creates affiliations between users through @replies. In North Carolina, 17-year-old Jacquelyn finds it "weird" and embarrassing that her mother regularly posts pictures of her on Facebook. While she's uncomfortable with her mother sharing photos of her, she also understands the impulse. *"I guess as a parent, it's different than being a teenager because we're her kids so she wants to show all her college friends and high school friends what we're up to because obviously, we're not going to friend her high school friends because we don't know them. It makes sense, I guess. I don't know."*

20 In trying to navigate privacy, teens must not only contend with what they choose to share, but what others choose to share about them. While networked privacy is not unique to networked publics, the affordances of networked publics magnify this issue, reifying the public-by-default nature of such environments. Those who are more inclined to share often expect those who don't want information shared to speak up. Abigail, for example, posts all photos from her camera to Facebook because it's easier for her than filtering. She goes through her photo albums and tags the photos with her friends' names, deleting any photos that are blurry. Most of the pictures she puts up have multiple people in them, so she's not inclined to delete them, but understands if her friends untag themselves. If a friend is "really bothered" by a photo and complain to her directly, she'll delete it. The assumption in Abigail's friend group is that content is public-by-default. Such a setting forces teens to make a conscious choice about what to obscure, rather than what to publicize.

The public-by-default nature of networked publics is especially acute on Facebook and Twitter because of the role that social streams play in those environments. Facebook's news feed broadcasts both implicit actions (e.g., a broken heart when two people stop being "in a relationship") and shared content (e.g., newly uploaded photographs). The news feed and Twitter's stream are central to those sites and the first thing that most participants see when they login. While Facebook's news feed was controversial when it first launched,[14] it's now a fundamental part of Facebook's architecture. Teens share updates to be seen by their friends, but they also recognize that not everything shared through this mechanism is actually seen by their friends. While some teens expect their friends to read every update and picture that they post, others see the public-by-default dynamic as an opportunity to reduce expectations. Consider why Vicki, a 15-year-old from Georgia, posts status updates in lieu of sending private messages:

Vicki, 15, GA: Because a status update, everybody can read. Like, everybody who wants to read it can read it, but they're not obligated to read it. Like, when you send a message, it's, "Oh my gosh, this person sent me a message. Now I have to read this." But, when it's an update, it's, like, if I don't want to read your status, I'm not going to read yours. But I'm going to read the next person's, like, if I want to read theirs. You don't have to look at it if you don't want to.

Content that is publicly accessible is not necessarily universally consumed. Likewise, information that is publicly accessible is not necessarily intended to be consumed by just anyone. While teens may be negotiating privacy in a public-by-default environment, social norms also serve a critical role in how teens do boundary work.

[14]boyd, danah. 2008. "Facebook's Privacy Trainwreck: Exposure, invasion, and social convergence." *Convergence: The International Journal of Research into New Media Technologies* 14 (1): 13–20.

References

Allen, A. L. (1999). Coercing Privacy. William and Mary Law Review 40 (3): 723–724.

boyd, danah. (2008a). "Facebook's Privacy Trainwreck: Exposure, invasion, and social convergence." Convergence: The International Journal of Research into New Media Technologies 14 (1): 13–20.

Gavison, Ruth. (1980). Privacy and the limits of the law. Yale Law Journal 89: 421–471.

Hoofnagle, Chris Jay, Jennifer King, Su Li, and Joseph Turow. (2010, April 14). "How Different are Young Adults from Older Adults When it Comes to Information Privacy Attitudes and Policies?" Working paper available at: http://papers.ssrn.com/sol3/papers.cfm?abstract_id=1589864

Lenhart, Amanda, K. Purcell, A. Smith, and K. Zickuhr. (2010). Social media and young adults. Washington, DC: Pew Internet & American Life Project, February 3. http://pewinternet.org/Reports/2010/Social-Media-and-Young-Adults.aspx.

Locke, John L. (2010). Eavesdropping: An Intimate History. New York: Oxford University Press, USA.

Marwick, Alice, Murgia-Diaz, D., & Palfrey, John. (2010). Youth, privacy and reputation (literature review) (Berkman Center Research Publication No. 2010-5). Boston: Berkman Center for Internet and Society at Harvard University. Retrieved from http://papers.ssrn.com/sol3/papers.cfm?abstract_id=1588163

Marwick, Alice and danah boyd. (2011b). "The Drama! Teens, Gossip and Celebrity." Popular Culture Association/American Culture Association Annual Meeting, San Antonio, TX, April 20–24.

Misur, S. (2011, April 11). Old Saybrook High School makes privacy point; Some perturbed when real students shown in social-media slide show. Shoreline Times. New Haven, CT. Retrieved from http://www.shorelinetimes.com/articles/2011/04/11/news/doc4da2f3cb5caae51 8276953.txt

Nippert-Eng, Christena E. (2010). Islands of Privacy. Chicago: University of Chicago Press.

Nissenbaum, Helen. (2010). Privacy in Context: Technology, Policy, and the Integrity of Social Life. Palo Alto, CA: Stanford University Press.

Reiman, J. (1976). Privacy, intimacy and personhood. Philosophy and Public Affairs 6(1): 26–44.

Warren, S.D. & Brandeis, L.D., (1890). Right to Privacy. Harvard Law Review, 4, 193.

Westin, A. (1967). Privacy and Freedom. New York: Atheneum.

REFLECT & WRITE

- ❑ Perform a quick rhetorical analysis of this selection from boyd and Marwick's essay. Where do they rely on *logos*? *Ethos*? *Pathos*? How is each of the appeals used strategically in the essay?
- ❑ How do the authors use quotations, paraphrase, and summary in this piece? Which are from primary sources? Which are from secondary sources? How do their choices about working with her sources affect the persuasiveness of their argument?
- ❑ How might boyd and Marwick have used visual evidence to support their points? How might inserting photographs of teenagers produce a different impact than integrating screenshots from Facebook? Which types of visual rhetoric do you think would most strongly underscore their argument?
- ❑ **Write**. Draft a response to boyd and Marwick in the form of a blog comment in which you confirm, refute, or qualify their assessment of how teens understand the concept of privacy in their online interactions. Refer to specific passages from their article in your response as well as evidence drawn from your own experience.

Seeing Connections: Refer to Chapter 6 for a more detailed discussion of choosing between summary, paraphrase, and direct quotation in your own writing.

A writer for The New York Times Magazine, **Clive Thompson** *specializes in writing about technology and society. He is also a columnist for* Wired *magazine and contributes articles to* Fast Company. *Thompson also posts his insights on collisiondetection.net, his blog about technology and culture. In this article, which was published originally in the September 7, 2008, issue of* The New York Times, *Thompson writes about the implications of the integration of the News Feed feature into Facebook.*

I'm So Totally, Digitally Close to You

Clive Thompson

On Sept. 5, 2006, Mark Zuckerberg changed the way that Facebook worked, and in the process he inspired a revolt.

Zuckerberg, a doe-eyed 24-year-old C.E.O., founded Facebook in his dorm room at Harvard two years earlier, and the site quickly amassed nine million users. By 2006, students were posting heaps of personal details onto their Facebook pages, including lists of their favorite TV shows, whether they were dating (and whom), what music they had in rotation and the various ad hoc "groups" they had joined (like "Sex and the City" Lovers). All day long, they'd post "status" notes explaining their moods—"hating Monday," "skipping class b/c i'm hung over." After each party, they'd stagger home to the dorm and upload pictures of the soused revelry, and spend the morning after commenting on how wasted everybody looked. Facebook became the de facto public commons—the way students found out what everyone around them was like and what he or she was doing.

But Zuckerberg knew Facebook had one major problem: It required a lot of active surfing on the part of its users. Sure, every day your Facebook friends would update their profiles with some new tidbits; it might even be something particularly juicy, like changing their relationship status to "single" when they got dumped. But unless you visited each friend's page every day, it might be days or weeks before you noticed the news, or you might miss it entirely. Browsing Facebook was like constantly poking your head into someone's room to see how she was doing. It took work and forethought. In a sense, this gave Facebook an inherent, built-in level of privacy, simply because if you had 200 friends on the site—a fairly typical number—there weren't enough hours in the day to keep tabs on every friend all the time.

"It was very primitive," Zuckerberg told me when I asked him about it last month. And so he decided to modernize. He developed something he called News Feed, a built-in service that would actively broadcast changes in a user's page to every one of his or her friends. Students would no longer need to spend their time zipping around to examine each friend's page, checking to see if there was any new information. Instead, they would just log into Facebook, and News Feed would appear: a single page that—like a social gazette from the 18th century—delivered a long list of up-to-the-minute gossip about their friends, around the clock, all in one place. "A stream of everything that's going on in their lives," as Zuckerberg put it.

5 When students woke up that September morning and saw News Feed, the first reaction, generally, was one of panic. Just about every little thing you changed on your page was now instantly blasted out to hundreds of friends, including potentially mortifying bits of news—*Tim and Lisa broke up; Persaud is no longer friends with Matthew*—and drunken photos someone snapped, then uploaded and tagged with names. Facebook had lost its vestigial bit of privacy. For students, it was now like being at a giant, open party filled with everyone you know, able to eavesdrop on

what everyone else was saying, all the time.

"Everyone was freaking out," Ben Parr, then a junior at Northwestern University, told me recently. What particularly enraged Parr was that there wasn't any way to opt out of News Feed, to "go private" and have all your information kept quiet. He created a Facebook group demanding Zuckerberg either scrap News Feed or provide privacy options. "Facebook users really think Facebook is becoming the Big Brother of the Internet, recording every single move," a California student told The Star-Ledger of Newark. Another chimed in, "Frankly, I don't need to know or care that Billy broke up with Sally, and Ted has become friends with Steve." By lunchtime of the first day, 10,000 people had joined Parr's group, and by the next day it had 284,000.

Zuckerberg, surprised by the outcry, quickly made two decisions. The first was to add a privacy feature to News Feed, letting users decide what kind of information went out. But the second decision was to leave News Feed otherwise intact. He suspected that once people tried it and got over their shock, they'd like it.

He was right. Within days, the tide reversed. Students began e-mailing Zuckerberg to say that via News Feed they'd learned things they would never have otherwise discovered through random surfing around Facebook. The bits of trivia that News Feed delivered gave them more things to talk about—*Why do you hate Kiefer Sutherland?*—when they met friends face to face in class or at a party. Trends spread more quickly. When one student joined a group—proclaiming her love of Coldplay or a desire to volunteer for Greenpeace—all her friends instantly knew, and many would sign up themselves. Users' worries about their privacy seemed to vanish within days, boiled away by their excitement at being so much more connected to their friends. (Very few people stopped using Facebook, and most people kept on publishing most of their information through News Feed.) Pundits predicted that News Feed would kill Facebook, but the opposite happened. It catalyzed a massive boom in the site's growth. A few weeks after the News Feed imbroglio, Zuckerberg opened the site to the general public (previously, only students could join), and it grew quickly; today, it has 100 million users.

When I spoke to him, Zuckerberg argued that News Feed is central to Facebook's success. "Facebook has always tried to push the envelope," he said. "And at times that means stretching people and getting them to be comfortable with things they aren't yet comfortable with. A lot of this is just social norms catching up with what technology is capable of."

10 In essence, Facebook users didn't think they wanted constant, up-to-the-minute updates on what other people are doing. Yet when they experienced this sort of omnipresent knowledge, they found it intriguing and addictive. Why?

Social scientists have a name for this sort of incessant online contact. They call it "ambient awareness." It is, they say, very much like being physically near someone and picking up on his mood through the little things he does—body language, sighs, stray comments—out of the corner of your eye. Facebook is no longer alone in offering this sort of interaction online. In the last year, there has been a boom in tools for "microblogging": posting frequent tiny updates on what you're doing. The phenomenon is quite different from what we normally think of as blogging, because a blog post is usually a written piece, sometimes quite long: a statement of opinion, a story, an analysis. But these new updates are something different. They're far shorter, far more frequent and less carefully considered. One of the most popular new tools is Twitter, a website and messaging service that allows its two-million-plus users to broadcast to their friends haiku-length updates—limited to 140 characters, as brief as a mobile-phone text message—on what they're doing. There are other services for reporting where you're traveling (Dopplr) or for quickly tossing online a stream of the pictures, videos or websites you're looking at (Tumblr). And there are even tools that give your location. When the new iPhone, with built-in tracking, was introduced in July, one million people began using Loopt, a piece of software that automatically tells all your friends exactly where you are.

For many people—particularly anyone over the age of 30—the idea of describing your blow-by-blow activities in such detail is absurd. Why would you subject your friends to your daily minutiae? And conversely, how much of their trivia can you absorb? The growth of ambient intimacy can seem like modern narcissism taken to a new, supermetabolic extreme—the ultimate expression of a generation of celebrity-addled youths who believe their every utterance is fascinating and ought to be shared with the world. Twitter, in particular, has been the subject of nearly relentless scorn since it went online. "Who really cares what I am doing, every hour of the day?" wondered Alex Beam, a Boston Globe columnist, in an essay about Twitter last month. "Even I don't care."

Indeed, many of the people I interviewed, who are among the most avid users of these "awareness" tools, admit that at first they couldn't figure out why anybody would want to do this. Ben Haley, a 39-year-old documentation specialist for a software firm who lives in Seattle, told me that when he first heard about Twitter last year from an early-adopter friend who used it, his first reaction was that it seemed silly. But a few of his friends decided to give it a try, and they urged him to sign up, too.

Each day, Haley logged on to his account, and his friends' updates would appear as a long page of one- or two-line notes. He would check and recheck the account several times a day, or even several times an hour. The updates were indeed pretty banal. One friend would post about starting to feel sick; one posted random thoughts like "I really hate it when people clip their nails on the bus"; another Twittered whenever she made a sandwich—and she made a sandwich every day. Each so-called tweet was so brief as to be virtually meaningless.

15 But as the days went by, something changed. Haley discovered that he was beginning to sense the rhythms of his friends' lives in a way he never had before. When one friend got sick with a virulent fever, he could tell by her Twitter updates when she was getting worse and the instant she finally turned the corner. He could see when friends were heading into hellish days at work or when they'd scored a big success. Even the daily catalog of sandwiches became oddly mesmerizing, a sort of metronomic click that he grew accustomed to seeing pop up in the middle of each day.

This is the paradox of ambient awareness. Each little update—each individual bit of social information—is insignificant on its own, even supremely mundane. But taken together, over time, the little snippets coalesce into a surprisingly sophisticated portrait of your friends' and family members' lives, like thousands of dots making a pointillist painting. This was never before possible, because in the real world, no friend would bother to call you up and detail the sandwiches she was eating. The ambient information becomes like "a type of E.S.P.," as Haley described it to me, an invisible dimension floating over everyday life.

"It's like I can distantly read everyone's mind," Haley went on to say. "I love that. I feel like I'm getting to something raw about my friends. It's like I've got this heads-up display for them." It can also lead to more real-life contact, because when one member of Haley's group decides to go out to a bar or see a band and Twitters about his plans, the others see it, and some decide to drop by—ad hoc, self-organizing socializing. And when they do socialize face to face, it feels oddly as if they've never actually been apart. They don't need to ask, "So, what have you been up to?" because they already know. Instead, they'll begin discussing something that one of the friends Twittered that afternoon, as if picking up a conversation in the middle.

Facebook and Twitter may have pushed things into overdrive, but the idea of using communication tools as a form of "co-presence" has been around for a while. The Japanese sociologist Mizuko Ito first noticed it with mobile phones: lovers who were working in different cities would send text messages back and forth all night—tiny updates like "enjoying a glass of wine now" or "watching TV while lying on the couch." They were doing it partly because talking for hours on mobile phones isn't very comfortable (or affordable). But they also discovered that the little Ping-Ponging messages felt even more intimate than a phone call.

"It's an aggregate phenomenon," Marc Davis, a chief scientist at Yahoo and former professor of information science at the University of California at Berkeley, told me. "No message is the single-most-important message. It's sort of like when you're sitting with someone and you look over and they smile at you. You're sitting here reading the paper, and you're doing your side-by-side thing, and you just sort of let people know you're aware of them." Yet it is also why it can be extremely hard to understand the phenomenon until you've experienced it. Merely looking at a stranger's Twitter or Facebook feed isn't interesting, because it seems like blather. Follow it for a day, though, and it begins to feel like a short story; follow it for a month, and it's a novel.

20 You could also regard the growing popularity of online awareness as a reaction to social isolation, the modern American disconnectedness that Robert Putnam explored in his book "Bowling Alone." The mobile workforce requires people to travel more frequently for work, leaving friends and family behind, and members of the growing army of the self-employed often spend their days in solitude. Ambient intimacy becomes a way to "feel less alone," as more than one Facebook and Twitter user told me.

When I decided to try out Twitter last year, at first I didn't have anyone to follow. None of my friends were yet using the service. But while doing some Googling one day I stumbled upon the blog of Shannon Seery, a 32-year-old recruiting consultant in Florida, and I noticed that she Twittered. Her Twitter updates were pretty charming—she would often post links to camera-phone pictures of her two children or videos of herself cooking Mexican food, or broadcast her agonized cries when a flight was delayed on a business trip. So on a whim I started "following" her—as easy on Twitter as a click of the mouse—and never took her off my account. (A Twitter account can be "private," so that only invited friends can read one's tweets, or it can be public, so anyone can; Seery's was public.) When I checked in last month, I noticed that she had built up a huge number of online connections: She was now following 677 people on Twitter and another 442 on Facebook. How in God's name, I wondered, could she follow so many people? Who precisely are they? I called Seery to find out.

"I have a rule," she told me. "I either have to know who you are, or I have to know of you." That means she monitors the lives of friends, family, anyone she works with, and she'll also follow interesting people she discovers via her friends' online lives. Like many people who live online, she has wound up following a few strangers—though after a few months they no longer feel like strangers, despite the fact that she has never physically met them.

I asked Seery how she finds the time to follow so many people online. The math seemed daunting. After all, if her 1,000 online contacts each post just a couple of notes each a day, that's several thousand little social pings to sift through daily. What would it be like to get thousands of e-mail messages a day? But Seery made a point I heard from many others: awareness tools aren't as cognitively demanding as an e-mail message. E-mail is something you have to stop to open and assess. It's personal; someone is asking for 100 percent of your attention. In contrast, ambient updates are all visible on one single page in a big row, and they're not really directed at you. This makes them skimmable, like newspaper headlines; maybe you'll read them all, maybe you'll skip some. Seery estimated that she needs to spend only a small part of each hour actively reading her Twitter stream.

Yet she has, she said, become far more gregarious online. "What's really funny is that before this 'social media' stuff, I always said that I'm not the type of person who had a ton of friends," she told me. "It's so hard to make plans and have an active social life, having the type of job I have where I travel all the time and have two small kids. But it's easy to tweet all the time, to post pictures of what I'm doing, to keep social relations up." She paused for a second, before continuing: "Things like Twitter have actually given me a much bigger social circle. I know more about more people than ever before."

25 I realized that this is becoming true of me, too. After following Seery's Twitter stream for a year, I'm more knowledgeable about the details of her life than the lives of my two sisters in Canada, whom I talk to only once every month or so. When I called Seery, I knew that she had been struggling with a three-day migraine headache; I began the conversation by asking her how she was feeling.

Online awareness inevitably leads to a curious question: What sort of relationships are these? What does it mean to have hundreds of "friends" on Facebook? What kind of friends are they, anyway?

In 1998, the anthropologist Robin Dunbar argued that each human has a hardwired upper limit on the number of people he or she can personally know at one time. Dunbar noticed that humans and apes both develop social bonds by engaging in some sort of grooming; apes do it by picking at and smoothing one another's fur, and humans do it with conversation. He theorized that ape and human brains could manage only a finite number of grooming relationships: unless we spend enough time doing social grooming—chitchatting, trading gossip or, for apes, picking lice—we won't really feel that we "know" someone well enough to call him a friend. Dunbar noticed that ape groups tended to top out at 55 members. Since human brains were proportionally bigger, Dunbar figured that our maximum number of social connections would be similarly larger: about 150 on average. Sure enough, psychological studies have confirmed that human groupings naturally tail off at around 150 people: the "Dunbar number," as it is known. Are people who use Facebook and Twitter increasing their Dunbar number, because they can so easily keep track of so many more people?

As I interviewed some of the most aggressively social people online—people who follow hundreds or even thousands of others—it became clear that the picture was a little more complex than this question would suggest. Many maintained that their circle of true intimates, their very close friends and family, had not become bigger. Constant online contact had made those ties immeasurably richer, but it hadn't actually increased the number of them; deep relationships are still predicated on face time, and there are only so many hours in the day for that.

But where their sociality had truly exploded was in their "weak ties"—loose acquaintances, people they knew less well. It might be someone they met at a conference, or someone from high school who recently "friended" them on Facebook, or somebody from last year's holiday party. In their pre-Internet lives, these sorts of acquaintances would have quickly faded from their attention. But when one of these far-flung people suddenly posts a personal note to your feed, it is essentially a reminder that they exist. I have noticed this effect myself. In the last few months, dozens of old work colleagues I knew from 10 years ago in Toronto have friended me on Facebook, such that I'm now suddenly reading their stray comments and updates and falling into oblique, funny conversations with them. My overall Dunbar number is thus 301: Facebook (254) + Twitter (47), double what it would be without technology. Yet only 20 are family or people I'd consider close friends. The rest are weak ties—maintained via technology.

30 This rapid growth of weak ties can be a very good thing. Sociologists have long found that "weak ties" greatly expand your ability to solve problems. For example, if you're looking for a job and ask your friends, they won't be much help; they're too similar to you, and thus probably won't have any leads that you don't already have yourself. Remote acquaintances will be much more useful, because they're farther afield, yet still socially intimate enough to want to help you out. Many avid Twitter users—the ones who fire off witty posts hourly and wind up with thousands of intrigued followers—explicitly milk this dynamic for all it's worth, using their large online followings as a way to quickly answer almost any question. Laura Fitton, a social-media consultant who has become a minor

celebrity on Twitter—she has more than 5,300 followers—recently discovered to her horror that her accountant had made an error in filing last year's taxes. She went to Twitter, wrote a tiny note explaining her problem, and within 10 minutes her online audience had provided leads to lawyers and better accountants. Fitton joked to me that she no longer buys anything worth more than $50 without quickly checking it with her Twitter network.

"I outsource my entire life," she said. "I can solve any problem on Twitter in six minutes." (She also keeps a secondary Twitter account that is private and only for a much smaller circle of close friends and family—"My little secret," she said. It is a strategy many people told me they used: one account for their weak ties, one for their deeper relationships.)

It is also possible, though, that this profusion of weak ties can become a problem. If you're reading daily updates from hundreds of people about whom they're dating and whether they're happy, it might, some critics worry, spread your emotional energy too thin, leaving less for true intimate relationships. Psychologists have long known that people can engage in "parasocial" relationships with fictional characters, like those on TV shows or in books, or with remote celebrities we read about in magazines. Parasocial relationships can use up some of the emotional space in our Dunbar number, crowding out real-life people. Danah Boyd, a fellow at Harvard's Berkman Center for Internet and Society who has studied social media for 10 years, published a paper this spring arguing that awareness tools like News Feed might be creating a whole new class of relationships that are nearly parasocial—peripheral people in our network whose intimate details we follow closely online, even while they, like Angelina Jolie, are basically unaware we exist.

"The information we subscribe to on a feed is not the same as in a deep social relationship," Boyd told me. She has seen this herself; she has many virtual admirers that have, in essence, a parasocial relationship with her. "I've been very, very sick, lately and I write about it on Twitter and my blog, and I get all these people who are writing to me telling me ways to work around the health-care system, or they're writing saying, 'Hey, I broke my neck!' And I'm like, 'You're being very nice and trying to help me, but though you feel like you know me, you don't.' " Boyd sighed. "They can observe you, but it's not the same as knowing you."

When I spoke to Caterina Fake, a founder of Flickr (a popular photo-sharing site), she suggested an even more subtle danger: that the sheer ease of following her friends' updates online has made her occasionally lazy about actually taking the time to visit them in person. "At one point I realized I had a friend whose child I had seen, via photos on Flickr, grow from birth to 1 year old," she said. "I thought, I really should go meet her in person. But it was weird; I also felt that Flickr had satisfied that getting-to-know you satisfaction, so I didn't feel the urgency. But then I was like, Oh, that's not sufficient! I should go in person!" She has about 400 people she follows online but suspects many of those relationships are tissue-fragile. "These technologies allow you to be much more broadly friendly, but you just spread yourself much more thinly over many more people."

35 What is it like to never lose touch with anyone? One morning this summer at my local cafe, I overheard a

young woman complaining to her friend about a recent Facebook drama. Her name is Andrea Ahan, a 27-year-old restaurant entrepreneur, and she told me that she had discovered that high-school friends were uploading old photos of her to Facebook and tagging them with her name, so they automatically appeared in searches for her.

She was aghast. "I'm like, my God, these pictures are completely hideous!" Ahan complained, while her friend looked on sympathetically and sipped her coffee. "I'm wearing all these totally awful '90s clothes. I look like crap. And I'm like, Why are you people in my life, anyway? I haven't seen you in 10 years. I don't know you anymore!" She began furiously detagging the pictures—removing her name, so they wouldn't show up in a search anymore.

Worse, Ahan was also confronting a common plague of Facebook: the recent ex. She had broken up with her boyfriend not long ago, but she hadn't "unfriended" him, because that felt too extreme. But soon he paired up with another young woman, and the new couple began having public conversations on Ahan's ex-boyfriend's page. One day, she noticed with alarm that the new girlfriend was quoting material Ahan had e-mailed privately to her boyfriend; she suspected he had been sharing the e-mail with his new girlfriend. It is the sort of weirdly subtle mind game that becomes possible via Facebook, and it drove Ahan nuts.

"Sometimes I think this stuff is just crazy, and everybody has got to get a life and stop obsessing over everyone's trivia and gossiping," she said.

Yet Ahan knows that she cannot simply walk away from her online life, because the people she knows online won't stop talking about her, or posting unflattering photos. She needs to stay on Facebook just to monitor what's being said about her. This is a common complaint I heard, particularly from people in their 20s who were in college when Facebook appeared and have never lived as adults without online awareness. For them, participation isn't optional. If you don't dive in, other people will define who you are. So you constantly stream your pictures, your thoughts, your relationship status and what you're doing—right now!—if only to ensure the virtual version of you is accurate, or at least the one you want to present to the world.

40 This is the ultimate effect of the new awareness: It brings back the dynamics of small-town life, where everybody knows your business. Young people at college are the ones to experience this most viscerally, because, with more than 90 percent of their peers using Facebook, it is especially difficult for them to opt out. Zeynep Tufekci, a sociologist at the University of Maryland, Baltimore County, who has closely studied how college-age users are reacting to the world of awareness, told me that athletes used to sneak off to parties illicitly, breaking the no-drinking rule for team members. But then camera phones and Facebook came along, with students posting photos of the drunken carousing during the party; savvy coaches could see which athletes were breaking the rules. First the athletes tried to fight back by waking up early the morning after the party in a hungover daze to detag photos of themselves so they wouldn't be searchable. But that didn't work, because the coaches sometimes viewed the pictures live, as they went online at 2 A.M. So parties simply began banning all camera phones in a last-ditch attempt to preserve privacy.

"It's just like living in a village, where it's actually hard to lie because everybody knows the truth already," Tufekci said. "The current generation is never unconnected. They're never losing touch with their friends. So we're going back to a more normal place, historically. If you look at human history, the idea that you would drift through life, going from new relation to new relation, that's very new. It's just the 20th century."

Psychologists and sociologists spent years wondering how humanity would adjust to the anonymity of life in the city, the wrenching upheavals of mobile immigrant labor—a world of lonely people ripped from their social ties. We now have precisely the opposite problem. Indeed, our modern awareness tools reverse the original conceit of the Internet. When cyberspace came along in the early '90s, it was celebrated as a place where you could reinvent your identity—become someone new.

"If anything, it's identity-constraining now," Tufekci told me. "You can't play with your identity if your audience is always checking up on you. I had a student who posted that she was downloading some Pearl Jam, and someone wrote on her wall, 'Oh, right, ha-ha—I know you, and you're not into that.' " She laughed. "You know that old cartoon? 'On the Internet, nobody knows you're a dog'? On the Internet today, everybody knows you're a dog! If you don't want people to know you're a dog, you'd better stay away from a keyboard."

Or, as Leisa Reichelt, a consultant in London who writes regularly about ambient tools, put it to me: "Can you imagine a Facebook for children in kindergarten, and they never lose touch with those kids for the rest of their lives? What's that going to do to them?" Young people today are already developing an attitude toward their privacy that is simultaneously vigilant and laissez-faire. They curate their online personas as carefully as possible, knowing that everyone is watching—but they have also learned to shrug and accept the limits of what they can control.

45 It is easy to become unsettled by privacy-eroding aspects of awareness tools. But there is another—quite different—result of all this incessant updating: a culture of people who know much more about themselves. Many of the avid Twitterers, Flickrers and Facebook users I interviewed described an unexpected side-effect of constant self-disclosure. The act of stopping several times a day to observe what you're feeling or thinking can become, after weeks and weeks, a sort of philosophical act. It's like the Greek dictum to "know thyself," or the therapeutic concept of mindfulness. (Indeed, the question that floats eternally at the top of Twitter's website—"What are you doing?"—can come to seem existentially freighted. What are you doing?) Having an audience can make the self-reflection even more acute, since, as my interviewees noted, they're trying to describe their activities in a way that is not only accurate but also interesting to others: the status update as a literary form.

Laura Fitton, the social-media consultant, argues that her constant status updating has made her "a happier person, a calmer person" because the process of, say, describing a horrid morning at work forces her to look at it objectively. "It drags you out of your own head," she added. In an age of awareness, perhaps the person you see most clearly is yourself.

REFLECT & WRITE

- ❑ What strategy does Thompson use to start his article? To what extent is it successful in drawing the reader in and setting up background for the rest of the essay?
- ❑ What, according to Thompson, is the "paradox of ambient awareness"?
- ❑ How does Thompson use historical context and social sciences to bolster his commentary? How do these choices influence the persuasiveness of his claims?
- ❑ Look for places where Thompson includes personal narrative and experience in the article. How might that be strategic? What do those moments accomplish?
- ❑ **Write.** In the conclusion of the piece, Thompson suggests, "In an age of awareness, perhaps the person you see most clearly is yourself." Over the course of five days, use microblogging as a mode of self-expression. Either Tweet or update your status feed on Facebook or Google+ at least three times a day (you can do more if you like): if you don't have a Facebook, Google, or Twitter account, create one, or keep a log of your simulated micro-blogs in a Word document. Use the updates to capture a moment in your day; link to a reading you liked; provide commentary; work through your thoughts; or contemplate an issue, event, etc. Do not exceed 140 characters in your posts. At the end of the five days, cut and paste all your micro-blogs into a Word document. Read through them, and beneath, write a short reflection about what they say about you. Is Thompson right? Do you see yourself more clearly? Did writing in this way help you process your experiences? Feel free in your reaction to respond directly to the claims found in his article.

WRITING COLLABORATIVELY

Pull up a random profile page on Facebook (note: if you are going to work with the profile page of one of your Facebook friends, ask his/her permission before sharing it with the group). Analyze the visual rhetoric of the page, paying special attention to the layout, use of color, content, design, and organization. How do these elements combine to create an impression about the persona of the page's author? What "argument" is the author making about him or herself on the profile page? Now, perform the same analysis, but this time on a random Tumblr page or, if you have access, a LinkedIn page. As a group, compare your findings, and develop a claim about the different ways in which Tumblr, Facebook, and LinkedIn help their users construct an online identity.

Created by software programmer **Randall Munroe**, *xkcd is a "webcomic of romance, sarcasm, math, and language" that has garnered a large cult following and has been reproduced in mainstream publications such as* The New York Times *and the* Guardian.

"Online Communities 2"

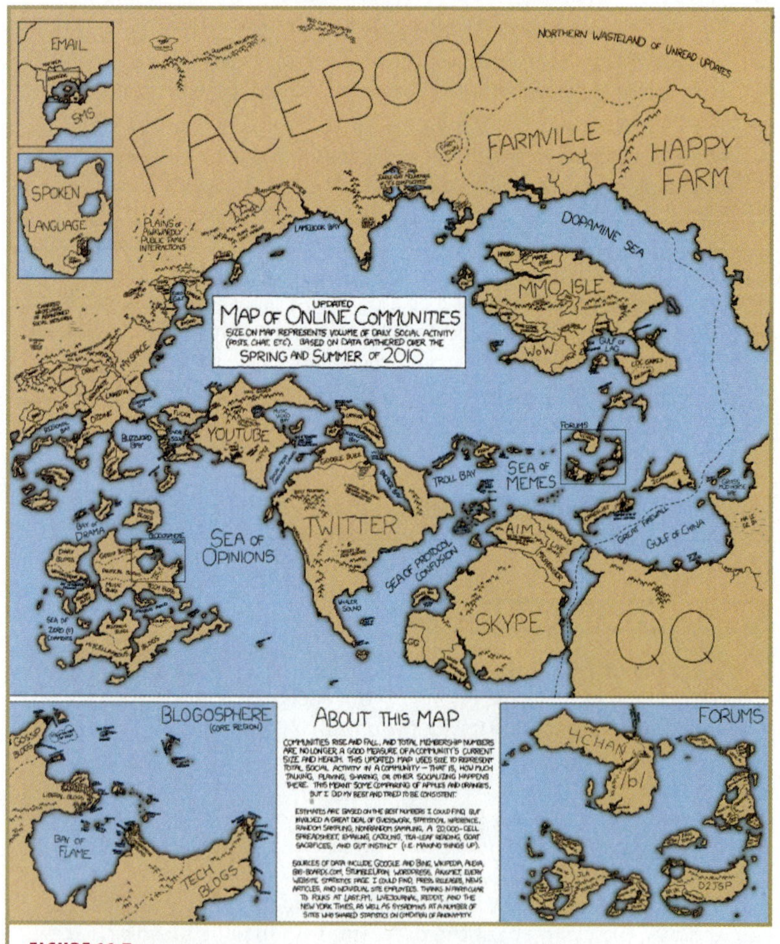

FIGURE 11.7 This xkcd comic literally "maps" the influence of various online communities in 2010.

REFLECT & WRITE

- ❑ What overall argument is the cartoon making? Try to write out the claim or thesis as a single sentence.
- ❑ Do you find the genre of cartography an appropriate one for making an argument about online communities? Why or why not? What alternate genres or modes of design might work well to make a similar graphic argument?
- ❑ How are position, spacing, and size used to connote importance and connections? Choose one subset of the map (such as the northern most part or the bottom left or right, for instance) and clarify what claim the section is making about those particular communities based on their position and representation on the map.
- ❑ **Write.** This cartoon is called "Online Communities 2" because it is a revision of a previous cartoon, published in 2007, called "Online Communities." Look up that original cartoon online and write a brief comparison-contrast essay in which you explore the way xkcd argues that the composition, distribution, and impact of online communities changed between 2007 and 2010.

Seeing Connections: Refer to Chapter 1 for guidance on analyzing cartoons and composing effective thesis statements.

A professor of communications at Webster University, **Art Silverblatt** *is best known for his writings on media and communication. His publications include* Media Literacy: Keys to Interpreting Media Messages *(1995);* International Communications *(2004); and* Genre Studies in Mass Media: A Handbook *(2007). In this article, he links Twitter feeds to "Newspeak," the linguistically and conceptually truncated form of writing prophesied by George Orwell in his dystopian novel,* 1984. *This article was originally published in the September/October 2009 issue of the* St. Louis Journalism Review.

Twitter As Newspeak

Art Silverblatt

It can be argued that Twitter has emerged as a legitimate form of communication that could influence how children will spell—and think—in the future. Both Fox News and CNN have adopted the form and syntax of Twitter for their closed-captions, so that Twitter is no longer merely a computer shorthand but has become an integral facet of our mainstream media.

To illustrate: On September 11, 2001, Fox News carried a story about President Bush's immediate response to the terrorists' attacks that adopted Twitter as the style for their closed-caption account (he "did rht thin").

This year, a new keyboard was introduced called "Tweetboard." The traditional keyboard has been reconfigured, so that Twitter symbols assume prominent positions on the top row: @ (reply), # (hashtags), RT (retweet), and via @. Another key is for shortening URLs.

One way to understand the impact of Twitter is to consider another language that is predicated on the elimination and abbreviation of words—the language of Newspeak, found in George Orwell's futuristic novel, 1984. In the Appendix of 1984, Orwell observes that "Newspeak differed from most all other languages, in that its vocabulary grew smaller instead of larger every year."

5 Reduction of vocabulary was regarded as an end in itself, and no word that could be dispensed with was allowed to survive. Newspeak was designed not to extend but to diminish the range of thought, and this purpose was indirectly assisted by cutting the choice of words down to a minimum . . . The Newspeak vocabulary was tiny, and new ways of reducing it were constantly being devised.

Like Newspeak, the syntax of Twitter is based on economy. Only 140 characters are allowed in a single tweet. Thus, in an online article, entitled "7 Tips to Improve Your Twitter Tweets," the first tip involves ways to cut the copy:

> Abbreviate. If you can say it with less letters, do so! . . . There are only 140 characters allowed in a single tweet, so shortening a word or using a bit of slang is completely acceptable. Instead of "are," say "r." the same goes for "you" and "u."

Orwell's comments about the impact of Newspeak on thought may also be applicable to Twitter, in the following respects:

Ideas Are Reduced to Literal Meaning

In these reductive languages, the meaning of words is reduced to a literal level; there is no space to examine the implications of meaning. Orwell explains:

10 "The A vocabulary consisted of the words needed for the business of everyday life—for such things as eating, drinking, working, putting on one's clothes . . . Their meanings were far more rigidly defined. All ambiguities and shades of meaning had been purged out of them."

To illustrate: Danny Ayalon, the Assistant Foreign Minister of Israel, issues daily Tweets to the public. The problem, of course, is reducing the complexity of a 2500-year religious, cultural, and political conflict to 140 characters. On September 9, Ayalon tweeted, "Dilemma is placed on international community by Iran. Need to turn the tables and place dilemma back on Iran. Only with strong sanctions." This missive provides only surface information, leaving numerous questions unaddressed.

What is the "dilemma"? Why has this dilemma been placed on the international community by Iran? What is meant by "strong sanctions"? How do strong sanctions "place the dilemma" back on Iran? What other options (in addition to sanctions) exist, and what are their relative strengths and weaknesses?

No Context to Information Is Provided

Both Twitter and Newspeak operate in an eternal present; there is no room to discuss ideas within a historical or cultural context. Orwell declares, "When Oldspeak had been once and for all superseded, the last link with the past would have been severed." Thus, Ayalon's tweet leaves unanswered essential background information, such as:

When was this "dilemma" placed on the international community by Iran? Have sanctions been tried before? When, and with what results? What was the role of other countries in this activity—Israel, United States and Western Allies, other Arab nations.

Language Assumes a Neutral Tenor

15 The use of abbreviations eliminates the emotional connotation of content. Orwell explains:

"Even in the early decades of the twentieth century ... the tendency to use abbreviations was most marked in totalitarian countries and totalitarian organizations. Examples were such words as Nazi, Gestapo, Comintern, Inprecorr, Agitprop. In the beginning the practice had been adopted as it were instinctively, but in Newspeak it was used with a conscious purpose. It was perceived that in thus abbreviating a name one narrowed and subtly altered its meaning, by cutting out most of the associations that would otherwise cling to it."

One major difference between Newspeak and Twitter, of course, involves function. Newspeak's purpose was ideological; the government of Big Brother instituted this language as a way of controlling the masses. In contrast, the form and format of Twitter is technologically driven; Twitter has been designed to reach targeted groups of people throughout the virtual world instantaneously. But regardless of intention, Twitter is anti-democratic. It helps create a young generation that not only cannot spell but is also incapable of examining the implications of ideas, challenging information, and thinking independently.

REFLECT & WRITE

- ❑ How does Silverblatt see Twitter-style communication permeating popular media? What does he consider to be the larger implications of this stylistic shift?
- ❑ By choosing an Orwellian analogy for Twitter, what type of approach does Silverblatt signal he is taking toward the trend? Why?
- ❑ Who is the audience for Silverblatt's article? How can you tell?
- ❑ Look carefully at Silverblatt's examples. How persuasive are they?
- ❑ **Write.** Do you agree with Silverblatt's assertion that Twitter is helping to create "a young generation that not only cannot spell but is also incapable of examining the implications of ideas, challenging information, and thinking independently"? Write a one-page response to Silverblatt confirming, refuting, or qualifying his statement. Be sure to locate your argument in relation to Twitter—its usage and its style.

Evgeny Morozov *is best known for his work as a contributing editor to* Foreign Policy *and for running* "Net Effect," *the magazine's blog about global politics and the Internet age. Currently a Yahoo! Fellow at Georgetown University's Institute for the Study of Diplomacy, Morozov has published broadly in many venues, including in the* Economist, *the* Wall Street Journal, Newsweek, *the* Times Literary Supplement, *and the* San Francisco Chronicle. *The following article was first posted on September 5, 2009, to the* "Net Effect" *blog.*

From Slacktivism to Activism

Evgeny Morozov

Below is the text of a talk about "slacktivism"—a subject that has received considerable attention on this blog and elsewhere—that I delivered at Festival Ars Electronica this morning (the session was dedicated to "cloud intelligence").

As someone who studies how the Internet affects global politics, I've grown increasingly skeptical of numerous digital activism campaigns that attempt to change the world through Facebook and Twitter. To explain why, let me first tell you a story about a campaign that has gone wrong.

If you have been to Copenhagen, you probably have seen the Stork Fountain, the city's famous landmark. A few months ago, a Danish psychologist Anders Colding-Jørgensen, who studies how ideas spread online, used Facebook to conduct a little experiment using the Stork Fountain as his main subject. He started a Facebook group, which implied—but never stated so explicitly—that the city authorities were planning to dismantle the fountain, which of course was NEVER the case. He seeded the group to 125 friends who joined in a matter of hours; then it started spreading virally. In the first few days, it immediately went to a 1000 members and then it started growing more aggressively. After 3 days, it began to grow with over 2 new members each minute in the day time. When the group reached 27,500 members, Jørgensen decided to end the experiment. So there you have it: almost 28,000 people joined a cause that didn't really exist! As far as "clouds" go, that one was probably an empty one.

This broaches an interesting question: why do people join Facebook groups in the first place? In an interview with the Washington Post, Jørgensen said that "just like we need stuff to furnish our homes to show who we are, on Facebook we need cultural objects that put together a version of me that I would like to present to the public." Other researchers agree: studies by Sherri Grasmuck, a sociologist at Temple University, reveals that Facebook users shape their online identity implicitly rather than explicitly: that is, the kind of campaigns and groups they join reveals more about who they are than their dull "about me" page.

This shopping binge in an online identity supermarket has led to the proliferation of what I call "slacktivism", where our digital effort make us feel very useful and important but have zero social impact. When the marginal cost of joining yet another Facebook group are low, we click "yes" without even blinking, but the truth is that it may distract us from helping the same cause in more productive ways. Paradoxically, it often means that the very act of joining a Facebook group is often the end—rather than the beginning—of our engagement with a cause, which undermines much of digital activism.

Take a popular Facebook group "saving the children of Africa." It looks very impressive—over 1.2 million members—until you discover that these compassionate souls have raised about $6,000 (or half a penny per person). In a perfect world, this shouldn't even be considered a problem: better donate a penny than not to donate at all. The problem, however, is that the granularity of contemporary digital activism provides too many easy way-outs: too many people decide to donate a penny where they may otherwise want to donate a dollar.

So, what exactly plagues most "slacktivist" campaigns? Above all, it's their unrealistic assumption that, given enough awareness, all problems are solvable; or, in the language of computer geeks, given enough eyeballs all bugs are shallow. This is precisely what propels many of these campaigns into gathering signatures, adding new members to their Facebook pages, and asking everyone involved to link to the campaign on blogs and Twitter. This works for some issues—especially local ones. But global bugs—like climate change—are bugs of a different nature. Thus, for most global problems, whether it's genocide in Darfur or climate change, there are diminishing returns to awareness-raising. At some point one simply needs to learn how to convert awareness into action—and this is where tools like Twitter and Facebook prove much less useful.

This is not to deny that many of the latest digital activism initiatives, following the success of the Obama electoral juggernaut, have managed to convert their gigantic membership lists into successful money-raising operations. The advent of micro-donations—whereby one can donate any sum from a few cents to a few dollars—has enabled to raise funds that could then be used—at least, in theory—to further advance the goals of the campaign. The problem is that most of these campaigns do not have clear goals or agenda items beyond awareness-raising.

Besides, not every problem can be solved with an injection of funds, which, in a way, creates the same problem as awareness-raising: whether it's financial capital or media capital, spending it in a way that would enable social change could be very tough. Asking for money could also undermine one's efforts to engage groups members in more meaningful real-life activities: the fact that they have already donated some money, no matter how little, makes them feel as if they have already done their bit and should be left alone.

10 Some grassroots campaigns are beginning to realize it: for example, the web-site of "Free Monem", a 2007 pan-Arab initiative to free an Egyptian blogger from jail carried a sign that said "DON'T DONATE; Take action" and had logos of Visa and MasterCard in a crossed red circle in the background. According to Sami Ben Gharbia, a Tunisian Internet activist and one of the organizers of the campaign, this was a way to show that their campaign needed more than money as well as to shame numerous local and international NGOs that like to raise money to "release bloggers from jail", without having any meaningful impact on the situation on the ground.

That said, the meager fund-raising results of the Save the Children of Africa campaign still look quite puzzling. Surely, even a dozen people working together would be able to raise more money. Could it be that the Facebook environment is putting too many restraints on how they might otherwise have decided to cooperate?

Psychologists offer an interesting explanation as to why a million people working together may be less effective than one person working alone. They call this phenomenon "social loafing". It was discovered by the French scientist Max Ringelmann in 1913, when he asked a group of men to pull on a rope. It turned out they each pulled less hard than when they had to pull alone; this was basically the opposite of synergy. Experiments prove that we usually put much less effort into a task when other people are also doing it with us (think about the last time you had to sing a Happy Birthday song). The key lesson here is that when everyone in the group performs the same mundane tasks, it's impossible to evaluate individual contributions; thus, people inevitably begin slacking off. Increasing the number of other persons diminishes the relative social pressure on each person. That's, in short, what Ringelmann called "social loafing".

Reading about Ringelmann's experiments, I realized that the same problem plagues much of today's "Facebook" activism: once we join a group, we move at the group's own pace, even though we could have been much more effective on our own. As you might have heard from Ethan Zuckerman, Facebook and Twitter were not set up for activists by activists; they were set up for the purposes of entertainment and often attracted activists not because they offered unique services but because they were hard to block. Thus, we shouldn't take it for granted that Facebook activism is the ultimate limit of what's possible in the digital space; it is just the first layer of what's possible if you work on a budget and do not have much time to plan your campaign.

So far, the most successful "slacktivist" initiatives have been those that have set realistic expectations and have taken advantage of "slacktivist" inclinations of Internet users rather then deny their existence. For example, FreeRice, a web-site affiliated with the UN Food Program, which contains numerous education games, the most popular of which are those helping you to learn English. While you are doing so, it exposes you to online ads, the proceeds of which go towards purchasing and distributing rice in the poor countries (by FreeRice's estimates, enough rice is being distributed to feed 7,000 people daily).

15 This is a brilliant approach: millions of people rely on the Internet to study English anyway and most of them wouldn't mind being exposed to online advertising in exchange fo a useful service. Both sides benefit, with no high words exchanged. Those who participate in the effort are not driven by helping the world and have a very selfish motivation; yet, they probably generate more good than thousands of people who are "fighting" hunger via Facebook. While this model may not be applicable to every situation, it's by finding practical hybrid models like FreeRice's that we could convert immense and undeniable collective energy of Internet users into tangible social change.

So, given all this, how do we avoid "slacktivism" when designing an online campaign? First, make it hard for your supporters to become a slacktivist: don't give people their identity trophies until they have proved their worth. The merit badge should come as a result of their successful and effective contributions to your campaign rather than precede it.

Second, create diverse, distinctive, and non-trivial tasks; your supporters can do more than just click "send to all" button" all day. Since most digital activism campaigns are bound to suffer from the problem of diffusion of responsibility, make it impossible for your supporters to fade into the crowd and "free ride" on the work of other people. Don't give up easily: the giant identity supermarket that Facebook has created could actually be a boon for those organizing a campaign; they just need to figure out a way in which to capitalize on identity aspiration of "slacktivists" by giving them interesting and meaningful tasks that could then be evaluated.

Third, do not overdose yourself on the Wikipedia model. It works for some tasks but for most–it doesn't. While inserting a comma into yet another trivia article on Wikipedia does help, being yet another invisible "slacktivist" doesn't. Finding the lowest common denominator between a million users may ultimately yield lower results than raising the barrier and forcing the activists to put up more rather than less effort into what they are doing. Anyone who tells you otherwise is insane. Or, worse, a slacker! Thank you.

REFLECT & WRITE

- ❑ Think carefully about Morozov's choice for an opening example. How would starting the essay with a positive example of online activism have changed his reader's understanding of the topic?
- ❑ What is "social loafing," and why is it an important concept for Morozov's definition of online activism?
- ❑ Toward the end of the article, Morozov moves from an article focused on example and analysis to one that operates as a call to action. Why did he make that transition? How would the article have been different if he hadn't?
- ❑ **Write.** Early in his article, Morozov suggests that "Facebook users shape their online identity implicitly rather than explicitly: that is, the kind of campaigns and groups they join reveal more about who they are than on their dull 'about me' page." However, some readers have contended that a factor missing from Morozov's analysis is the role of peer pressure, namely that many times users join a group, "like" a cause, or share an activist-oriented image because of the influence of their friends, not because they are deliberately trying to craft an online persona. Using examples from your own Facebook experience or that of friends, write a one-page position paper that assesses Morozov's claim in terms of this idea of social pressure.

Daniel Terdiman *specializes in writing about technology and Internet culture, and has contributed articles to* The New York Times, *Salon.com,* Time *magazine, and* Wired. *He has been a game development advisor for the BBC and NPR's Talk of the Nation. In 2006, he was part of a CNET news team that won an online journalism award from the Society of Professional Journalists for its series* Taking Back the Web. *The article that follows first appeared in the April 22, 2004, edition of* Wired.

Playing Games with a Conscience

Daniel Terdiman

At first, the game looks like so many other first-person shooters: cross hairs aiming missiles at a raft of enemy targets.

But *September 12th* isn't like other games. Because when a missile shot at Arab terrorists kills an innocent bystander in the game's fictional Afghani village—and it's nearly impossible not to—other villagers run over, cry at their loss and then, in a rage, morph into terrorists themselves.

"The mechanics of the game are about this horrible decision, whether to do things, to take actions that will inevitably kill civilians," says Noah Wardrip-Fruin, co-editor of *First Person,* a collection of essays about the relationship between stories and games.

Indeed, *September 12th* has a point to make: that our actions have consequences, and that we should try to understand why other people take to arms. As Wardrip-Fruin puts it, the goal of the game is to develop in the player "empathy for the people who will become terrorists out of that experience, of having seen innocent people killed."

5 Earlier this week, the Simon Wiesenthal Center issued its annual report looking at websites and online games that promote hate, racism and anti-Semitism.

The report seeks to raise awareness about how hate groups are exploiting technology to spread their message, says Mark Weitzman, director of the center's Task Force Against Hate.

Such use of technology "teaches us that there always have been people in our society that will use whatever means is available to send out a message of hate," Weitzman says. "Our concern is how to deal with it."

He points to games like *Concentration Camp Manager, Ethnic Cleansing, Ghettoopoly* and others as examples of games put out by extremist groups.

"There's suicide-bombing games, (and) the full range taken from today's headlines," says Weitzman. But "you won't find them advertised, especially because some of them are rip-offs of legitimate games. I don't think the people at Monopoly would be very happy about *Ghettoopoly.*"

10 But rather than focus on games that disseminate messages of hate, Wardrip-Fruin, *September 12th* designer Gonzalo Frasca and Persuasive Games founder Ian Bogost would prefer that people instead consider games that foster understanding and tolerance of other cultures.

"I think that what is essential is allowing players to freely experiment within a virtual environment and encourage them to discuss what they play with their peers," says Frasca. "*September 12th* carries its own humanistic message, but I think that eventually, it would be even better if players would be able to use games as small laboratories for exploring—and contesting—their own beliefs."

Bogost says there are a growing number of games that promote positive messages and mutual understanding. For example, he thinks that *Real Lives 2004* does a good job of helping players see what it would be like to experience life as a member of another culture.

"You're taking on the role of another person who is not you," says Bogost. "Maybe (it's) a person from rural India. You're implicating yourself in all the trials or tribulations or difficulties that you might not think of."

Another game Bogost likes is *Civilization III*, because of the way it makes players work together, regardless of race or religion.

15 To Wardrip-Fruin, it's just as important to look at how a game is built as it is to look at a game's message.

"It's important to think about the structure of the game," he says, "not just from these hate sites, but from mainstream publishers, if we're going to understand these issues."

He thinks that hate groups are doing no more than exploiting a style of game—for example, first-person shooters—for their own purposes.

"If you think about what these people are doing on these hate sites, they're taking a set of well-understood game mechanics that are about hating someone—about hating the Germans during World War II—and finding them and killing them," Wardrip-Fruin explains. "So it's very easy to just slap (on) the image of the group you hate. I would argue the message is the same: Find the group you hate and go and kill them."

Frasca agrees.

20 "Keep in mind that a lot of commercial games—following the Hollywood tradition—use token enemies like Arabs (and) Vietnamese," he says, "which are shot in these games without the players thinking twice about the ideological message that these games carry. Lots of people start thinking about this when, say, Hezbollah launches an anti-Israel game, but there are plenty of anti-Arab games that are available at Wal-Mart at $39.95."

Still, that's not to say that all violence discourages mutual understanding.

"I do not think that killing virtual people is wrong, though—it is a lot of fun, indeed," Frasca says. "But virtual killing is totally different from real killing. As long as we can make that difference within a critical attitude, the situation does not need to be problematic."

But Frasca also says there are countless games that promote neither hate nor violence.

Wardrip-Fruin concurs, and says open-ended simulation games like *The Sims* do a very good job of encouraging constructive thought in game players.

25 "It's very hard to imagine one that is about hating some ethnic or religious other," he says. "I'd say that the fundamental thing about a computer game is the structure of what you do as a participant, and the structure

of something like *SimCity* or *The Sims* is about understanding a system, and trying to make it grow in the way you want it to grow."

Frasca goes so far as to say that some massively multiplayer games, even ones involving violence, help players understand each other better.

"Online games such as *EverQuest* foster cooperation between players from all over the world," he explains. "Even if there can be language barriers that can interfere with the communication, *EverQuest* allows players to work together based on their skills, without focusing on their gender, age, nationality (or) religion."

According to Bogost, there is a bright future for games that promote mutual tolerance and understanding.

But right now, says Frasca, games with such agendas are few and far between.

"Games for tolerance are (in) their infancy," he says. "But I think they have a great potential because games always allow you to be in somebody else's shoes and viewing the world through their eyes. And that is the essential requirement for tolerance: Understanding that other people have different realities that may not be the same (as) ours."

REFLECT & WRITE

- ❑ What is the argument made by this article? How does Terdiman's selection of which games to mention and which descriptions to develop factor into the construction of this argument?
- ❑ At one point in the article, Terdiman mentions that Gonzalo Frasca suggests that even violent multiplayer games have their positive side. Do you agree with this assertion? Why or why not?
- ❑ **Write.** Draft a response to the Terdiman piece that argues for the benefits of venting "hate" online through gaming. You might choose to develop the position offered by Chris Kaye in the October 2004 issue of *Esquire*. In his article, "Joystick Jihad," he wrote, "Casting our enemy as the villain [in video games] can be as lucrative as a Halliburton contract in an oil-rich war zone (and a hell of a lot more fun)" (p. 114).

The following screenshots are taken from games linked through the website for **Games for Change,** *an organization devoted to using persuasive games to produce "real world impact." These are "serious games," or games with an agenda, which, by definition, means that they are designed to argue a specific position about issues as varied as the environment, human rights, and world hunger.*

Screenshots: Games for Change

FIGURE 11.8 This screenshot from *Ayiti: The Cost of Life* shows how the game invites the player to help the Guinard family to make choices about schooling, work, community, and leisure to help them thrive in their homeland, Haiti.

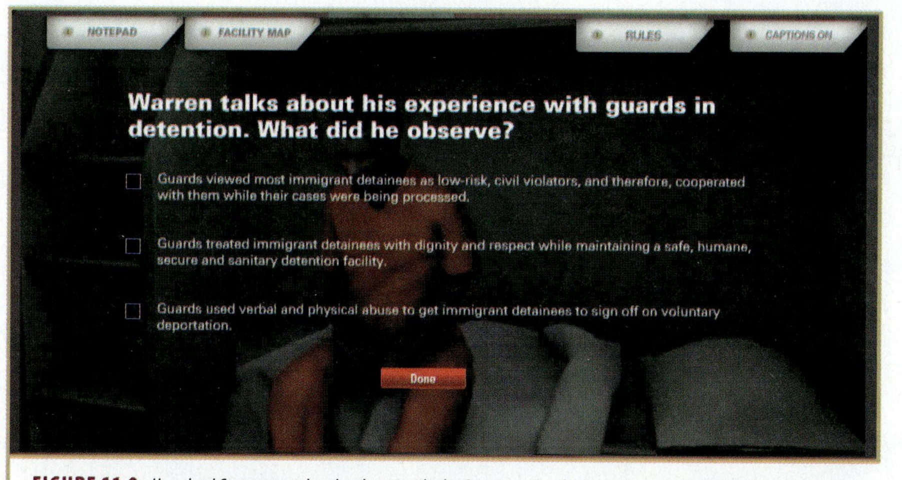

FIGURE 11.9 *Homeland Guatanamo* takes the player inside the Guantamo Bay facility in the role of a reporter investigating a "questionable"death of an inmate being held there.

REFLECT & WRITE

- ❑ Examine the interface provided by each game. Is the player invited in through a "God view" (looking down from above)? Does the player seem to be given a more direct, first-person perspective? How might that angle affect game play?
- ❑ How does the color palette of the game set the mood for the game play?
- ❑ Are the graphics realistic? Cartoonish? How might that affect the message of the game? How would changing the graphics to be more realistic or more cartoonish alter that message? Why do you think the designers made that choice?
- ❑ **Write.** Visit the Games for Change website, and play one of the games linked there. Write an analysis of the game that answers the following questions: Who is the intended audience? How can you tell? What type of game is it (i.e., shooter game, role-playing game, strategy game, simulation game)? How does this design choice determine the argument the game makes? What is that argument? To what extent is the game driven by *pathos*? By *ethos*? By *logos*? Can a game like this actually effect social change? Why or why not?

ANALYZING PERSPECTIVES ON THE ISSUE

Seeing Connections: For further discussion of crafting a powerful conclusion, see Chapter 3.

1. In its current edited form for this edition of *Envision*, Erickson's article on "selfies" ends rather abruptly. Review criteria for effective conclusions in chapter 3 and draft an alternative closing paragraph for this article that pulls together key points from the essay, yet which also moves beyond simple summary to function as an interesting and provocative closing paragraph on its own merits. Consider using example, quotation, key terms, voice or tone, visual evidence, stylistic resonance with the introduction, or other strategies of development to give your concluding paragraph additional power.
2. The images from Cooper and Spaight's book, *Alter Ego,* contained in this section create their own argument about what that book is "about" and what that book says about gaming avatars. Find a copy of the book at your library or local bookstore and select four to five alternate examples. Photocopy them, and then arrange them in a short booklet to make your own argument about gamer identity. Exchange these new booklets with a partner and discuss how each of you used evidence and arrangements differently to support your own individual argument about gamer identity and stereotype.
3. As boyd and Marwick's article indicates, privacy remains a hot topic in relation to any discussion of social media. How do you feel about the privacy controls currently in place on Facebook or the other social networks that you participate in? What are the dangers of lax privacy restrictions? What are the benefits of more public access to information? Draft a short satiric piece in which you convey your stance on the Facebook privacy controversy; you can create a written satire (like Jonathan Swift's *Modest Proposal* or an article from *The Onion*), a comic-based satire (like an editorial cartoon or webcomic), or even a film-based satire (like a segment from *The Daily Show*, a YouTube short, or even a clip modeled on *South Park*-styled animation).
4. Many scholars, including Morozov, are skeptical about the effectiveness of Twitter as an agent of social action. Drawing from information in the Morozov article and using the style of *xkcd*, create an editorial cartoon in which you argue for—or against—the effectiveness of Twitter as a political medium.

FROM READING TO RESEARCH ASSIGNMENTS

1. Read the full report on "Teens, kindness and cruelty" on the Pew Internet and American Life website. Using statistics and information from these two sources, storyboard a short five-minute film on this topic intended to be shown to high school and college students. Change up the title, include visual examples, strategically organize your information, select some direct quotes, and most importantly, identify and develop a claim that you want to make about social media usage. For added challenge, produce your film and share it with your class.

2. Randomly select at least five of your Facebook or Twitter friends and research their status updates or tweets for the last month. For each friend, cut and paste their updates or feeds into a Word document in chronological order, then read through them sequentially, looking for trends in the way they use the microblogging function. Do they use it to narrate their lives? For self-promotion? To advertise causes? To share links? To experiment in poetry? To quote their favorite lyrics or lines from movies? Based on your research, define at least three different categories or "types" of updates and write an analysis that describes each one and then makes a claim for how each one represents a different way of managing online identity and relationships through social media.
3. In "From Slacktivism to Activism," Morozov argues that social activism on social network sites like Facebook has little real impact for social change. Research a recent social media activist campaign, such as KONY 2012, the Human Rights Campaign's initiative in favor of marriage equality in March 2013, or another example of your choice. Drawing on both primary and secondary sources, make an argument for the efficacy of social media to produce opportunities for real activitism.
4. Working in groups, research an important issue and develop a stance. Your topic might be campus-based (workers' rights, alcohol on campus, student fees), local (tax increases, community recycling, school redistricting), or national (human rights violations, global poverty, global conflict). Conduct field research about this issue by interviewing members of the community. Draft a storyboard for an online game designed to persuade viewers to your point of view. Prepare a pitch for a fictional governing board in which you argue for the effectiveness of your game in effecting positive social change. Be sure in your pitch to include the following: whom the game will reach; how players will access the game; what the rhetorical features of the game are in terms of design and content; and why this form of interactive media would be an effective persuasive tool.

CHAPTER 12

Imagining the Ideal Body

FIGURE 12.1 A woman asserts her identity by marking her body with piercings and body art.

When you look at the photo of the woman in Figure 12.1, what do you see? What catches your eye? Is it the model's sideways glance? Her ornate tattooing or her nose piercing? Her elaborate make-up? Her eclectic outfit? How does she choose to mark herself—and how does her body consequently operate as a rhetorical text? Finally, how did you begin to draw conclusions about her identity based on your reaction to or interpretation of the markings on her body?

When we look at bodies as visual texts in society, we often participate in a social process of reading people according to certain social categories: as male or female; young or old; rural or urban; and from a certain race, class, or culture. We try to mark our bodies with signs of our identities, to announce who we are, our affiliation with a particular group or religion, our sexual orientation, and sometimes even our political stance. Hairstyles, piercings, clothing choices, tattoos, toned abs, or even painted toenails: these choices all constitute ways we "mark" ourselves in relation to our culture—or try to change the way we are perceived by remaking the signs of our identities. We may be judged by the social standards of "ideal" beauty, operating in our communities and our society at large.

Now consider the image in Figure 12.2. How does the woman's face and body evoke ideas about beauty that come from magazines such as *Vogue*, *Glamour*, *Cosmo*, or *Marie Claire*? Many aspects of the ad reproduce common elements found in fashion and cosmetics advertising: the model's direct gaze into the camera, her partially parted lips, her nearly bare neck and shoulders, her almost impossibly smooth complexion. What sort of visual argument is Figure 12.2 making about the ideal face and body, especially given that the billboard is actually an ad for a skin-lightening cream in Seoul, South Korea? Clearly, the normalizing of these distorted images of ideal beauty becomes even more problematic if we consider it in the context of racial, ethnic, and national difference.

FIGURE 12.2 Korean billboard ad for skin-lightening cream.

However, keep in mind that it's not just the female form that has been subjected to such steroetypes. Magazines like *GQ, Maxim,* and *Men's Health* are packed with advertisements for cologne, shaving products, running shoes, casualwear, and even watches that reinforce idealized notions of what it means to be an attractive man in contemporary society. Television shows—from night-time dramas to reality shows like the *The Bachelorette*—and Hollywood films similarly feature the Perfect Man in lead roles, providing somewhat unrealistic role models for boys and young men. Even video games, arguably, propose a specific type of athletic, hypermasculinity, which young teen boys are invited to play through and measure themselves against as they level up in the games. All around us, media continues to shape and craft a gendered ideal. Your rhetorical analysis of these images can help you begin to formulate your argument about how visual representations construct social notions that we come to accept as "natural."

It is important to consider what happens to our sense of self when the body we are meant to strive for is represented by an ideal that is overly thin, obviously Caucasian, unrealistically sculpted, or hyperfeminized or overly masculinized. As the articles in this chapter suggest, these representations seem to affect people's attitudes toward eating disorders, drug abuse, self-esteem, and societal norms. In the pages that follow, we will explore the complex relationship between bodies and identity by looking more closely at some of the body ideals that circulate within our culture. Who determines today's standards of "attractiveness"? How does the visual rhetoric of advertisements, films, television shows, and fashion magazines shape our notions of the "ideal body"? And how are our own bodies marked by the constructions of body image we see everywhere across cultures?

REFLECT & WRITE

- ❑ Consider the visual elements in Figure 12.1. What aspects evoke a conventional fashion ad? Which aspects subvert that convention?
- ❑ Consider Figure 12.2 carefully. What are the implications of using a Caucasian model to advertise skin-lightening cream in South Korea? How would the persuasiveness of the ad change if it featured a Korean model?
- ❑ Examine both Figures 12.1 and 12.2. What elements in each ad are gender specific? Race specific? Culturally specific? Class specific? How do the elements relate to each other?
- ❑ **Write.** Take a walk and look for billboards posters, or displays that present images of ideal beauty on your campus or in your community. Write a letter to your local newspaper, analyzing the persuasive power of these images. Include photos of the images as evidence for your claim.

■ *The following piece is an excerpt from* **Pamela Abbott** and **Francesca Sapsford's** *"Young Women and Their Wardrobes," which first appeared in the collection,* Through the Wardrobe: Women's Relationships with Their Clothes. *In their research for the article, Abbott and Sapsford interviewed a group of 16-year-old women from a town in northern England who were all enrolled in year 11 of secondary school. Their interview questions focused on the girls' choices of what to wear, and they observed them at home, at school, and while shopping. One of Abbott and Sapsford's goals was to "give a voice to ordinary young women." In this section, they set up a theoretical framework through which to consider their primary evidence—the interviews with the girls.*

Clothing the Young Female Body

Pamela Abbott and Francesca Sapsford

Fashion plays a large part in a teenage girl's life. The media bombard her with advertisements for clothes and emphasize a particular image—the 'waif' look. Teenage magazines play an important part in shaping femininity. They are concerned with personal relationships (especially those with men), with physical appearance and with defining a particular form of beauty and style. Feature articles, advertisements and advice columns are all concerned with appearance and 'getting a man'. In these magazines, appearance and relationships to men define femininity. The teenage magazines such as *Sugar* and *Bliss* not only 'sell' the image but also promise that wearing certain clothes will attract young men. The promise is used as a tool to sell clothes to young women. However, Winship (1987) indicates that girls also get pleasure from fashion and she suggests that they interpret what the magazines say. Furthermore, girls don't have to be seen as dupes. They can think for themselves: Zoe (age 13) says 'I think it is a load of rubbish. You have the models that are skinny, but that's models. I don't think they say you should be this, you just get the ideas about clothes and what to look like.' (Quoted in article entitled 'Pure Bliss' in *Young People Now*, 30.07.96, p. 20).

Chua (1992) suggests that clothes have five functions:

1. They are chosen for a particular audience.
2. They are chosen for a particular event.
3. They are prefigured in preparation for the actual display.
4. The identity information forms a whole.
5. Once public, only limited modification is possible.

He makes a distinction between being in fashion and being in the vanguard of fashion. He argues that women wish to be in fashion; that is, they wish to be wearing what is seen as the norm. McCracken (1988) argues that clothing is the material of the visual representation of one's social worth. That is, from clothing one can infer things such as class, age and so on. In other words, clothing is a cultural category.

The consumption of clothes by young people is more than a need for clothes. Clothing is a statement. Clothes are acquired for their style, for their designer label, for the statements that they make about the wearer. Fashions are used and adapted by young women to make these statements. Young women also resist attempts to transform them and to make them conform. Here we can think about resistance to school uniforms and the attempt to transform school uniforms. Young women wear make-up to school when it is forbidden, wear jewelry which they then hide—for example earrings which they place their hair over—unacceptable shoes and short skirts in an attempt to resist conformity to the rules of the school. Often in doing so they become more alike in appearance.

5 Putting on clothes, make-up, or jewelry, and/or changing piercings are termed backstage activity (Goffman, 1971). The front stage, the display, is what we become when the body is adorned. For young women, part of growing up is learning how to present the female body—how to achieve femininity by fashioning the body. From magazines, themselves, female relatives and peers, young women learn how to invest in their looks, discipline their body, decorate and clothe it. This is achieved by cooperation and competition—and it is hard work. However, most young women cannot achieve the 'ideal'—the ideal is white, youthful, able-bodied and slim. As Hill-Collins (1990) has indicated 'Judging white women by their physical appearance and attractiveness to men objectifies, but their white skin and straight hair privileges them in a system in which part of the basic definition of whiteness is superior to black.' (p. 791).

Wolf (1991) argues that the 'beauty myth' undermines girls and women individually and collectively. She argues that young women must always be concerned about the presentation of self—about their appearance. The pressures that arise from the 'beauty myth' she suggests reduces young women's confidence and saps their energy and exposes them to dieting and cosmetic surgery. Young women, she argues, are looked at and objectified and controlled in the public sphere, and this control is exercised by boys/men, who are the final arbiters of what is desirable. Wilson, for example, suggests 'Even the bizarre can be fashionable and attempts to outrage or (as often happens) to be overtly sexual, or sexual in some different way, may nonetheless remain within stylistic boundaries of clothes that still express submissiveness to a boyfriend, even if they spell rebellion at home.' (1987, p. 24).

Clothes, then, are part of the way of adorning the body, and there are the 'right' clothes; girls have to learn clothing behaviour—to wear the right clothes. Clothes, adornment and conduct form a dress code, a code to which young women feel constrained to conform. However this does not mean that clothes are a disguise that hides the 'true nature' of the body/

person, nor that young women are totally constrained by conforming to external pressure.

Goffman (1972) pointed to the social rules that provide appropriate body behaviour in public places and spaces and has also pointed to the performance or presentation of self. Mauss (1973, 1985) and Bourdieu (1986) have argued that clothing the body is an active process—a means of constructing and presenting the bodily self. Bourdieu (1984) has also indicated that the body is more than the clothes that adorn it. It is also ascribed ideologies of class, gender and race. As Craik (1994) indicates

> Women wear their bodies through their clothes. In other words, clothing does a good deal more than simply clothe the body for warmth, modesty or comfort. Codes of dress are technical devices which articulate the relationship between a particular body and its lived milieu—the space occupied by bodies, accented by bodily actions, in other words, clothes construct a personal habitat. (1994, p. 4)

We can conclude, then, that the body as a physical form is disciplined, and that appropriate behaviour includes conforming to a dress code. Fashion is pre-packaged and is sold to a mass market, resulting in common identities. However, we are not totally controlled: we are actively involved in creating an identity to present, but within limits—what is acceptable as we play the fashion game.

10 Bourdieu (1984) refers to the concept of distinction—the ways that we use consumer goods to distinguish ourselves from others. Dress is a way of adding attraction, of constructing a self on a biological body, of presenting self to others in the way we wish to be seen. Young women get pleasure from fashion, from choosing clothes and from adorning the body.

The ways in which bodies are fashioned through clothes, make-up and demeanour constitute identity, sexuality and social position. In other words, clothed bodies are tools of self-management (Craik, 1994, p. 46).

Young women have to learn to become consumers—to become able to construct a self-identity through clothes, body-decorating and piercing. However, the clothes that are available are limited and women continue to be judged by their appearance. This means that young women tend to invest time and effort into managing and constructing their bodies. Part of becoming a woman for girls is to learn how to adorn their bodies, to love clothes and to be concerned about fashion and style. Furthermore, for young women, style gives meaning, validation and coherence to their group identity—it defines who is part of the group and who is external to the group. It is a visible expression of the individual belonging to a group. Clothing is part of tribalism and of social status and, in that sense, can be seen as opposed to individuality. The group recognizes itself and is recognized by others, so it is both a statement and relational and is part of display. It can also be related to hostility and to conflict, defining those who are members and those who are not and constructing one's identity within conflicting groups. An example would be the clothing of the mods and rockers, which not only identified separate groups, but groups in conflict.

Bibliography

Bourdieu, P. (1984), *Distinction: A Social Critique of the Judgement of Taste*, London: Routledge & Kegan Paul.

Chua, B. H. (1992), "Shopping for women's fashion in Singapore", in R. Shields (ed), *Lifestyle Shopping: The Subject of Consumption*, London: Routledge.

Craik, J. (1994), *The Face of Fashion: Cultural Studies in Fashion*, London: Routledge.

Goffman, E. (1971), *Presentation of Self in Everyday Life*, Harmondsworth: Penguin.

—— (1972), *Relations in Public: Microstudies of the Public Order*, Harmondsworth: Penguin.

Hill-Collins, P. (1990), *Black Feminist Thought: Knowledge, Consciousness and the Politics of Empowerment*, London: Unwin Hyman.

Mauss, M. (1973), 'Techniques of the body', *Economy and Society*, 2, 1, pp. 70–87.

—— (1985), 'A category of the human mind: the notion of the person, the notion of self', in M. Corrithers, S. Collins and S. Lukas (eds), *The Category of Person*, Cambridge: Cambridge University Press.

McCracken, G. (1988), *Culture and Consumption: New approaches to the Symbolic Character of Consumer Goods and Activities*, Bloomington and Indianapolis: Indiana University Press.

Wilson, E. (1985/1987), *Adorned in Dreams: Fashion and Modernity*, London: Virago.

Winship, J. (1987), *Inside Women's Magazines*, London: Pandora.

Wolf, N. (1991), *The Beauty Myth: How Images of Beauty are Used Against Women*, London: Chatto & Windus.

REFLECT & WRITE

- ❑ Why is it important for Abbott and Sapsford to establish a scholarly framework before moving to the interviews with the girls? What does this section contribute to the larger argument? What would a section of first person accounts provide? How would the two work in conjunction with one another?
- ❑ Go back and look at the opening selection again with a highlighter in hand. Mark the sections in which the authors make their own claims as opposed to quoting from or referring to other scholarship. To what extent do they spotlight their own argument in relation to their sources?
- ❑ As the headnote indicates, the primary research for this article was done in England. Do you think the conclusions drawn by the authors are specific to British girls? How do clothing mores translate to young women across cultures?
- ❑ At the end of this section, the authors refer to clothing as a form of "tribalism" that helps construct group identity. Their example is "mods and rockers." What alternate examples from your own experience might you give to prove this point? Discuss how you might develop a subsequent paragraph that extends and explores your example.
- ❑ **Write.** The authors provide short summations of many theoretical positions, such as Chua's five functions of clothes, Wolf's beauty myth, and Craik's idea of clothed bodies as "tools of self-management." Choose one of these positions and write a personal essay in which you use a narrative of your own personal experience to either support or refute that position. Be sure to take time not only to tell your story but also to get at the cultural meanings behind your clothing choices or experience.

Seeing Connections
Look at the "Spotlight Your Argument" section in Chapter 3 for a discussion of how to develop your authorial stance in persuasive writing based on research.

■ *In 2010, Swedish photographer* **Rebecka Silvekroon** *took a photograph of a realistically proportioned mannequin that she had seen in the Swedish Department store, Åhléns, and posted it on her website. Almost three years later, the photo went viral after the Facebook group, Women's Rights News, posted it on their wall on the social media site. Within weeks, it had received over 1 million "likes" on Facebook and had spread on other social media sites as well.*

Photograph: Swedish Mannequins

FIGURE 12.3 Realistically-proportioned mannequins from a Swedish department store.

REFLECT & WRITE

- ❑ The mannequins that most stores use are proportioned to U.S. women's size 00. These Swedish mannequins reflect U.S. women's sizes 6 and 10. How does this sizing information influence your understanding of the messages that mannequins (these particular mannequins, but also more traditional ones) send about female body size?
- ❑ The photograph in Figure 12.3 depicts mannequins in a lingerie section of the department store. Would the image make as strong an impact if it

depicted mannequins from a dress department? An outwear department? Why or why not? What role does placement play in making an argument?

- **Write.** Create a photo essay on "Mannequins and Body Image" by visiting your own local mall or shopping center and taking photographs of the mannequins you find there. Arrange your images strategically, and write captions and accompanying text for your photographs to produce a solid and cohesive argument. Share your photo essay with your class.

Seeing Connections
Review Chapter 8's advice on creating a photo essay to help you construct your own powerful argument.

Psychotherapist and writer **Susie Orbach** *first became a leading participant in the discussion of women's body image issues with the publication of her 1978 book* Fat Is a Feminist Issue. *Since that time, she has both written and taught extensively on the issue of women's physical and emotional health and has appeared on numerous television and radio programs. This article recounts Orbach's involvement in the genesis of Dove's "Campaign for Real Beauty" and was originally published in the June 17, 2005, issue of* Campaign, *an online advertising, marketing, and public relations magazine.*

Fat Is an Advertising Issue

Susie Orbach

When O&M called Susie Orbach to ask her advice on Dove's campaign for real beauty, she jumped at the chance to turn advertising's often destructive relationship with women's body image on its head.

More than one million hits on the "campaign for real beauty" website; pictures of women on billboards all over the UK that make you smile inside; a programme to deconstruct beauty ads going into secondary schools; a fund to raise girls' and women's self-esteem; mother-and-daughter workshops on self-image; a mission to change negative feelings women can have towards their bodies . . . and all this from a soap-cum-beauty company?

In January two years ago, Mel White of Ogilvy & Mather rang me. "I'd like to book an hour of your time. Some of us working on the Dove brand have been worrying that beauty advertising has been damaging to women. We want to make sure we understand how, and what we might do to change it."

White was the global brand and category partner at O&M. She was part of a team spearheading an attempt to make a positive contribution to women's lives. "We all—at Dove and the agency—are women of a certain seniority," she said. "We think we can make a difference, a positive impact on women's lives. Dove has never sold products on the basis of stoking up insecurity. But maybe we can go further. Can you help?"

5 Could I help? To hear that creative teams were now interested in investing their energy in strengthening women was extraordinary. Years of banging on the doors of clothing manufacturers, government, the

food industry and advertising, to persuade them that by making fashion funkier and food more interesting they would increase sales, made this a dream meeting. I never thought the beauty industry would come asking. I was delighted. I was intrigued.

Could White be serious? Was this a bit of ethical window-dressing or a sincere endeavour? Could they change the grammar of beauty in an industry that had been so instrumental in promoting exclusivity? Was Dove really up for a genuinely radical transformation of the representation of women?

Would the creatives actually hear the dissatisfaction emanating from girls and women about the absolutely torturous standards of beauty they had either wittingly or unwittingly foisted on them? Could the art directors come up with some way to meet that dissatisfaction and make difference sexy, something the fashionistas could resonate with?

The first step was to persuade Unilever. Such a retool was going to take a lot of money and steady commitment. If the executives there could understand the difficulties their wives, mothers, lovers, sisters and daughters had with their own physical appearance, then maybe we had a chance. The change that the Dove team were advocating would require consciousness-raising throughout the agency and the business. The 400 or so people working on Dove would have to be behind it. This was not just a whoopee new campaign like any other.

On the advertising side, O&M assembled creative teams that knew the Dove brand and had done some of their best work on it. They also brought on board teams who did not know Dove, but who had previously done outstanding work on other accounts across the world.

10 The film O&M made for one of their first internal pitches featured the daughters of executives talking about their own bodies and the cute noses, freckles, hair and tummies they wanted to do away with or change. The poignancy of these little (and big) girls showing their dissatisfactions and their wish to be free of some of the most quintessentially adorable aspects of themselves was completely compelling. It's not possible to watch that three-minute DVD without reaching for a tissue. It was a testimony to the hurt and damage we were unintentionally doing to our daughters.

The film hinted at the longing these lovely girls had to be acceptable, to be pretty, to feel good about themselves.

That DVD and others made for internal Unilever and O&M purposes provided the opening through which I, as a psychotherapist, academic and political activist in the area of women's psychology, body image and eating problems, could now deliver the relevant clinical evidence. My writing, public speaking and research experience with thousands of women could provide the backbone to the Dove initiative, an initiative that had the potential to turn around the grief and distress that lurked inside so many girls' and women's physical experience of themselves.

I told Dove that the Harvard psychiatrist and anthropologist Anne Becker had found that three years after the introduction of TV into Fiji in 1995, 11.9% of adolescent girls were puking into the toilet bowl trying to change their Fijian build into one that resembled the Western images they were imbibing via their TV sets.

I told Unilever that just half-an-hour looking at a magazine could lower youngsters' self-esteem significantly. I told them that one in four college females has a serious eating problem and that most women wake up and feel their tummies to check how good or bad they've been the day before. Before they've even brushed their teeth, their critical selves are planning how punishing to be today.

15 I told them that without intending to, mums were passing on negative attitudes about their own bodies towards their infant girls, and that their daughters were now absorbing a shaky body sense that made them vulnerable to the blandishments of the market that purported to meet this distress while actually reinforcing it.

The women working on Dove knew how women's magazines had discreet cosmetic surgery ads in the back long before TV shows such as The Swan and Extreme Makeover came along. However expectant you felt before reading Vogue, Glamour, Cosmo or Marie Claire, you felt coshed by a mood depressant after it. And all the Dove women knew they weren't just victims of the image industries. In a sense, all of us women are complicit in these unrealistic representations of femaleness. In order not to feel entirely powerless inside a visually dominating landscape that represents beauty so narrowly, we play out our own beauty scripts inside it: not questioning it, but trying to meet it.

The psychoanalyst in me could try to explain how women's relationship to the beauty industry perfectly encapsulates the psychological essence of the abused. The victim, shunning that awful feeling of being exploited and to gain some self-respect, rejects the idea she is being used. Instead, she makes the job of appearing beautiful her own personal project. She is not being compelled to bind her feet, she does it willingly. It's the only way to be. She will involve herself in trying to look younger, skinnier, taller, bigger-breasted, smaller-breasted and making sure every surface is coiffed, painted, plucked, waxed, perfumed, moisturised, conditioned or dyed. Taking the job on for herself is her response to being targeted.

It is her refusal to, as it were, be done to.

That this can't bring women satisfaction works in the interest of the beauty industry. Having set up this relationship of insecurity, there is always another area to work on—and even if all enemies were banished, ageing would be waiting just around the corner.

20 Dove's mission was to reformulate this warped and damaging engagement with beauty and offer in its place something based not on impossibility, but on possibility. Daring and innovative, so far. But could they take the campaign through their company and into the public domain?

In May 1999, work coming out of the Women's Unit at the Cabinet Office showed eating problems and concern about the body was the number one issue for girls and women aged between 11 and 80. The UK Government held a Body Image Summit, under the leadership of Tessa Jowell and Margaret Jay. Research showed that the promotion of images of ever-skinnier, wan-looking but apparently need-free women who shoved attitude into the camera lens was creating serious (health and mental health) problems in the lives of girls and women.

The Body Image Summit included influential magazine editors, fashion designers and buyers who could have changed our narrow visual culture.

But the Summit programme collapsed at the first whiff of contempt in the media. The Government showed itself to be entirely pusillanimous, back-pedalling and equivocating at its own subsequent press conferences.

After my experience as a consultant to and keynote speaker at the Summit, I was now interested to see what the commercial sector could do. I didn't expect the same kind of inertia and collapse from business when the first criticism came along. But I also hadn't quite understood how considerable are the resources the business community can call on when it is serious.

25 I'd known that a significant part of a product's cost was spent on marketing and advertising, but I hadn't appreciated how much time, labour and money could go into the development of a brand. As my work with Dove developed, I began to feel increasingly hopeful about how we might begin to challenge the negative aspects of what I'd come to call the visual musak—the ersatz femininity—around us and to include diverse, vibrant, pleasing and sexy images of women of all sizes, ages and physical types.

One of my key objectives was to get across the idea that recent times have seen a widening, a democratising, of the idea that everyone could be beautiful. Triggered by Twiggy and then fully realised by the Kate Moss generation (as much because of their class backgrounds as their skinniness), beauty had moved from being the interest of the few to the aspiration of all girls and women. This was pretty positive stuff in itself. But the terms and the expansion of beauty faltered on a paradox. The industry was simultaneously promoting an anti-democratic ideal of beauty that was narrow (literally) and excluding. Everyone had to be thin, thinner, thinnest.

If Dove was going to turn around the limited, destructive aspects of the beauty and dieting industries, then it was going to have to produce bold, startling, appealing images of women in all their sumptuous variety that would swagger in and dent the visual field. Dove would have to find a way to meet women where they had trained their eyes to be—on those images of skinny, untouchable and yet needy sexy women—and touch them deeply and humorously enough [to] bring them to where I knew from my clinical practice they wanted to be: appreciated for their magnificent differences, their uniqueness, not their sameness.

Women have had enough of not finding themselves in the ads they look at. If Dove could get it right, other companies would be playing catch-up. And, of course, they did. Within months of the launch of the "campaign for real beauty," Revlon hired Susan Sarandon as one of its faces. It was a vindication that not only had Dove and Ogilvy caught the zeitgeist, but others would follow and the aims of the campaign would be met not just by women flocking to their brand, but also by their competitors.

What impressed the most and continues to impress me is the commitment of the leadership team at Dove—Silvia Lagnado, Alessandro Manfredi, Erin Iles and Daryl Fielding and, of course, White. They're making the campaign work. Everyone doing Dove business now asks the questions I was brought in to help them confront in order to make the campaign effective. How does this marketing help women's and girls' self esteem? In what ways could it harm them? How does this product affect me? How do I want it to affect my daughter, my niece, my sister, my wife? How can I make a positive impact and turn the scourge of body hatred around? How can I be a global player in the beauty industry spreading good feelings about women's bodies rather than promoting insecurity?

30 How can I give girls and women a chance to enter into a new, contented relationship with their bodies?

These are deep, painful and complex issues. That's why they called in the shrink. But, as their performance so far shows, it is a really good start.

REFLECT & WRITE

- ❑ In this article, Orbach chronicles the process she used to persuade Unilever, the makers of Dove beauty products, to embrace the "Campaign for Real Beauty." How did Orbach and the O&M team deploy strategies of *pathos*, *ethos*, and *logos* to accomplish their goals? Consider the order in which they used these appeals. Why did they structure their patterns of persuasion in this way?
- ❑ How might Orbach be trying to offer the same argument she makes to Unilever to the reader? In which paragraphs can you see places where she makes her case to both audiences?
- ❑ At one point, Orbach claims that in order to be successful at this campaign, Dove was going to have to "produce bold, startling, appealing images of women in all their sumptuous variety that would swagger in and dent the visual field." Look at the images from the Dove campaign that they share on their official website, on television, and in fashion magazines. Has Dove accomplished this goal? What differences do you see between Dove's campaign and advertisements produced by other beauty product companies?
- ❑ **Write.** Some might argue that the "Campaign for Real Beauty" is simply an *ethos* appeal to the consumer. Write an essay in which you argue this point, considering whether or not the campaign has the potential to enhance or detract from the popularity of Dove's products—or whether it will have no distinguishable effect overall either on the company or on the self-esteem of women and girls.

John Riviello *is a graphic designer specializing in Flash animations. The screenshots in Figures 12.4–12.15 are from a movie hosted on Riviello's website about body image issues and their relationship to the diet industry, fashion magazines, and consumers' self-perceptions.*

What If Barbie Was an Actual Person? A Flash Movie

John Riviello

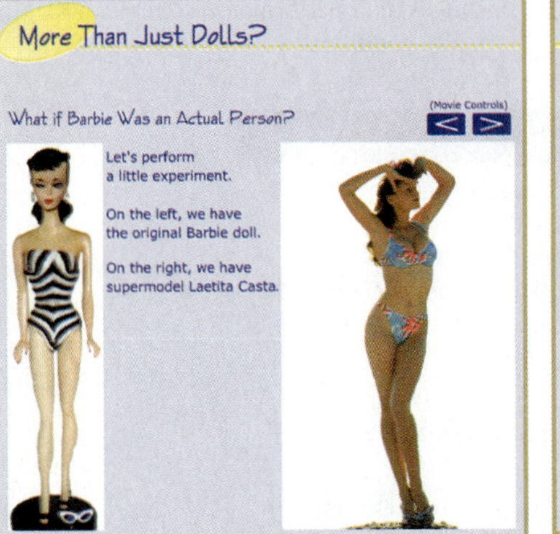

FIGURE 12.4 These screenshots from John Riviello's site juxtapose Barbie against a real model to demonstrate the differences between idealized versions of female beauty.

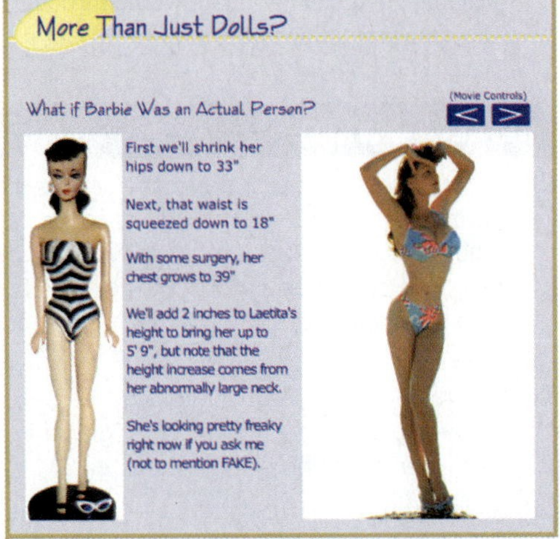

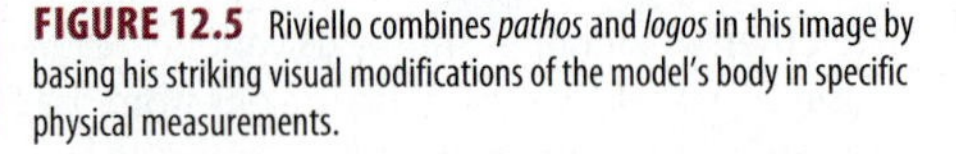

FIGURE 12.5 Riviello combines *pathos* and *logos* in this image by basing his striking visual modifications of the model's body in specific physical measurements.

REFLECT & WRITE

Seeing Connections
For an alternative critique of the Barbie paradigm, see the Body Shop Op-Ad in Chapter 8.

- ❑ In his visual argument, Riviello pairs an image of a vintage Barbie with a photo of model Laetitia Casta. To argue his point, he explains how he would transform Laetitia and then actually modifies her picture through flash animation to reflect these alterations. What are the benefits of constructing his argument in this way? Why show both Laetitia and the Barbie? Is this an effective structure for the argument? Why?
- ❑ In the last frame of the animation (not shown here), after Laetitia's eyes bulge cartoonishly in horror at her undersized feet, she disintegrates into a heap of dust, leaving us looking only at the vintage Barbie. To what extent does this strategy serve as an effective conclusion? What rhetorical appeals does it draw on?
- ❑ Visit the Flash animation itself by looking at John Riviello's "body image" website. How does watching the animation produce a different effect from simply looking at the static images alone? What does the new media component add to the argument?

- ❑ **Write.** Riviello could have written his argument as an academic essay, but he chose instead to use media animation to argue his point. Write an essay in which you move through the same process of argumentation that he does, but use a more academic style. What adjustments do you have to make to convert his argument? Is one more effective than the other? Why or why not?

This poster is part of the National Eating Disorders Association's broader campaign to promote new programs and academic curricula designed to educate the populace about the dangers of eating disorders. This campaign produces a variety of visual arguments, some of which address the problems associated with anorexia and bulimia, and others which promote girls' positive self-image and a healthy relationship with food.

Anorexia Awareness Poster

National Eating Disorders Association (NEDA)

FIGURE 12.6 2012 poster from the National Eating Disorder Association.

REFLECT & WRITE

- ❑ Analyze the visual elements of the ad. How do the multiple mirrors and the pink lipstick combine to make an argument about how images of "ideal beauty" in society can harm young girls? What might be the ad's point about the relationship between constructions of female beauty and eating disorders?
- ❑ Look at the arrangement of the ad, with the central image in white circumscribed by a black ring. How does this visual organization direct the reader's eye to the girl at the center? Why might she be shown not making eye contact back but instead holding her head in her hands?
- ❑ The copy of this ad reads: "An image problem can kill a politician, and as it turns out, a little girl." What does this claim mean? How might you translate it into your own words, as if you were giving advice to a younger relative?
- ❑ Notice the fine print at the bottom of the ad, which reads: "For millions of females with eating disorders, the stakes couldn't be higher. Because anorexia has the highest mortality rate of any mental illness." How do these aspects of the ad rely on logos? What is the effect of including statistics and categorizing eating disorders as mental illness? Also notice the logo's words: "NEDA: Feeding hope." What might be the impact of this ironic, counter-intuitive phrase?

Seeing Connections
See advice for creating your own op-ad in Chapter 8.

❑ **Write.** Search online for the Adbuster "Obsession" parody ads, Examine how they use different rhetorical strategies to make similar arguments. Sketch out a design for your own parody poster to raise awareness among young girls about the dangers of eating disorders. Include both visual and written elements. Peer review your work with a partner before presenting it to the class.

WRITING COLLABORATIVELY

The posters created by the National Eating Disorders Association (NEDA) primarily focus on body image issues and eating disorders experienced by young girls. Working as a group, identify body image problems facing boys in your community. Working in a team, create a poster (using both images and written text) aimed at addressing body image in young boys. Be sure to decide on your argument before drafting your poster: for instance, your poster could be designed either to promote positive body image or to call attention to male body image problems. Share your work with your class.

Award-winning journalist **Susan McClelland** *has written on a variety of topics, from teenage pregnancy, to sex trafficking and the children victimized during Sierra Leone's civil war. In this article, originally published in* Maclean's *on August 14, 2000, she tackles the cross-cultural implications of western body image issues.*

Distorted Images: Western Cultures Are Exporting Their Dangerous Obsession with Thinness

Susan McClelland

When Zahra Dhanani was just seven years old, her four-foot frame already packed 100 lb.—so her mother, Shahbanu, put her on her first diet. "My mother, a fat woman, daughter of another fat woman, thought if I was skinny, different from her, I would be happy," says Dhanani. The diet, and many after, did not have the desired effect. By 13, Dhanani was sporadically swallowing appetite suppressants; at 17, she vomited and used laxatives to try to keep her weight under control. There were times when she wanted to die. "I had so much self-hate," recalls the 26-year-old Toronto immigration lawyer, "I couldn't look in the mirror without feeling revulsion."

The hate reflected more than just weight. "It was race," says Dhanani, who had moved with her family to Canada from East Africa when she was 4. "I was straightening my hair—doing anything to look white." Her recovery only began when, at age 19, she started to identify with women in other cultures. "I came to realize that there were people who revered large women of colour," says Dhanani, who now says she loves all of her 200 lb. She blames part of her earlier eating disorders on the images in western media: "When you have no role models to counteract the messages that fat is repulsive, it's hard to realize that you are a lovable human being."

Body image may be one of the western world's ugliest exports. Thanks to television, magazines, movies and the Internet, rail-thin girls and steroid-built beef-boys are being shoved in the faces of people all over the world. As a result, experts say, cultures that used to regard bulk as a sign of wealth and success are now succumbing to a narrow western standard of beauty. And that, in turn, is leading to incidences of eating disorders in regions where anorexia and bulimia had never been seen before. But body-image anxiety in ethnic cultures runs much deeper than weight. In South Africa, almost six years after the end of apartheid, black women still use harmful skin-bleaching creams in the belief that whiter is prettier. "We're seeing a homogenization and globalization of beauty ideals," says Niva Piran, a clinical psychologist at the University of Toronto. "It's white. It's thin. And the result is that people come to identify less with their own cultures and more with an image in the media."

In most cultures, bigger was considered better until the 19th century. "The larger a man's wife, the more he was seen as a good provider," says Joan Jacobs Brumberg, a professor of American women's history at Cornell University and author of *Fasting Girls: The History of Anorexia Nervosa*. That began to change during the Industrial Revolution, she says, as women in the United States and Great Britain began to see thinness as a way to differentiate themselves from the lower classes. By the 1920s, fat was seen as unhealthy. And in the burgeoning magazine, movie and fashion industries, the women depicted as being successful in love, career and finances were slim and almost always white.

5 Still, eating disorders are not a modern affliction. Records of women starving themselves (anorexia) date back to the medieval period (1200 to 1500). As Brumberg notes in *Fasting Girls*, during this time, a woman who did not eat was admired for having found some other form of sustenance than food, like prayer. Yet, until the last century, the number of women who fasted was low. But, particularly over the past 30 years, the number of anorexics and women who self-induce vomiting (bulimia) or use laxatives has increased dramatically. "It's generally this obsession with the body, constant weight-watching, that introduces a person to these behaviours," says Merryl Bear of the Toronto-based National Eating Disorder Information Centre. It was commonly believed, however, that sufferers came predominantly from white, middle- and upper-class backgrounds. Experts thought ethnic minorities were immune because of their strong ties to communities that emphasize family and kinship over looks alone.

Studies done in the United States with Hispanic, black and Asian college students, however, show that women who are alienated from their minority cultures and integrated into mainstream society are prone to the same pressures of dieting as their white counterparts. In a recent study of South-Asian girls in Peel, Ont., 31 per cent responded that they were not comfortable with their body shape and size. Fifty-eight per cent compared their appearance with others, including fashion models—and 40 percent wanted to look like them.

Some of the most compelling research comes from Harvard Medical School psychiatrist Anne Becker, who was in Fiji in 1995 when the government announced that TV, including western programs, would be introduced. "Fijians revere a body that is sturdy, tall and large—features that show that the body is strong, hardworking and healthy," says Becker. "Thinness and sudden weight loss was seen as some kind of social loss or neglect."

In 1998, Becker returned to Fiji and found that this had all changed. Her studies showed that 29 percent of the girls now had symptoms of eating disorders. Many said they vomited to lose weight. But what was most alarming were the girls' responses about the role of television in their lives. "More than 80 percent said that watching TV affected the way they felt about their bodies," Becker says. "They said things such as, 'I watched the women on TV, they have jobs. I want to be like them, so I am working on my weight now.' These teenagers are getting the sense that as Fiji moves into the global economy, they had better find some way to make wages and they are desperate to find role models. The West to them means success and they are altering their bodies to compete."

Cheryl McConney has felt the pressures to alter her body, too. The black 32-year-old native of Richmond Hill, Ont., co-hosts a daytime talk show on cable TV. And although it has not been difficult for her to get where she is in her career, she is concerned about how to navigate her next step. "Looking at Canadian television, I don't see many people who look like me on air," she says. At five-foot-five, and weighing about 145 lb., McConney has never been told she should lose weight. Still, in 1998, she went on a six-month, high-protein, low-carbohydrate diet, hoping to look better in front of the camera. She shed 20 lb. "I felt good. People in the studio thought I looked great, but it wasn't easy to maintain." Within a year, she had gained it all back.

10 For McConney, race has been more of an issue. An industry insider jokingly told her that she would do better if she dyed her hair blond. And just a few months ago, she was discouraged from applying for another on-air host position because of what the casting agents said they were looking for. "They wanted the 'girl next door' and 'peaches- and-cream' pretty, not chocolate and cream," says McConney, adding: "It was pretty clear some women were not invited to participate because of their skin colour." As to the girl next door part: "I said it just depends where you live."

While McConney says she is determined to make it on-air despite the barriers, Linda, who requested *Maclean's* not use her real name, may not be around to see her success. The 19-year-old—part South African and part East Indian—has anorexia. She says trying to fit into a Canadian suburban community played a big role in her illness. "I was never proud of my different religion, different skin colour," she says. "I would put white baby powder on my cheeks just to make me look white." What alarms her now, Linda says, is that with her skin pale from malnutrition and her weight fluctuating between 75 and 85 lb., other young women often come up to her and say, "You look so good, I wish I looked like you." But she adds: "What they don't know is that my body is decaying. People glamorize eating disorders. But what it is is a lifetime of hospitalization and therapy." As long as the western media promote thinness and whiteness as the pinnacle of beauty, stories like Linda's will remain all too familiar.

REFLECT & WRITE

- ❑ In this article, Susan McClelland addresses not only the way body image relates to thinness but also its relationship to different racial features and skin color. Do you agree that the media tends to model its ideal of beauty around a Caucasian standard? What evidence can you cite from your own observations to support your opinion?
- ❑ What rhetorical appeals does McClelland utilize in this article? *Pathos*? *Logos*? *Ethos*? Which does she use most prominently and which is most powerful in solidifying her argument?
- ❑ How does McClelland's integration of direct quotations provide evidence for her claims? Make a list of all the sources she mentions in her piece. Then, evaluate them according to the criteria in Chapter 5. How rigorous is her argument, based on this selection of research sources? What credibility and power do these sources add to her piece?
- ❑ **Write.** Look at international or culturally targeted beauty magazines at your local bookstore, on the newsstand, or online. Select a few images or ads, and draft your own argument concerning how that magazine defines beauty for specific audiences. Consider bringing in *doxa*, or the appeal to shared values in a particular community. Or, argue that the image of ideal beauty reflects white, Western standards. Finally, you might ask: are the magazine ads progressive, offering new or alternative visions of bodily beauty?

Seeing Connections
See Chapter 6 for guidelines on including direct quotations in your writing.

As the NEDA ad and McClelland's article both demonstrate, debates over body ideals and body image carry very serious consequences. Taking this fact as her starting point, **Elinor Frankel** *asks whether Americans should follow the example of their Israeli counterparts in treating the promotion of female "thinness" ideals as a threat to public health. This article appeared in the website divinecaroline.com in 2012.*

Should America Follow Israel's Example and Ban Too-Thin Models?

Elinor Frankel

Each year 280 people die in the United States, suffering from an eating disorder, and about 24 millions are living with one.

Many people blame the media and the fashion industry for showing the wrong image of women's bodies and thus become a contributing factor to the increasing number of eating disorders among young girls and boys. Most victims of eating disorders cite the pressures from society and the media on being thin as a main reason for them developing their sickness.

Eating disorders are a major public health problem. 81% of all ten year olds in the United States are afraid of being fat. And half of all girls between 11 and 15 years old want to lose weight because of magazine pictures, which is a strong influence of their idea of a perfect body shape. But the body type portrayed in advertising as the ideal is possessed naturally by only 5% of American females.

So, many times, these young girls wish to obtain an image that in most cases is not real. They get fed with pictures of women that are so retouched that no human being regardless of how hard they try, are going to achieve that look.

Lisa is a girl who lived with eating disorders for many years. After severe treatment she has finally recovered, but the images and pressures of being thin, still affect her. She thinks that the way models look does affect people and especially young girls. She says that models are considered as "perfect" or at least very good looking, so of course people are influenced.

An average model weighs 23% less than the average woman. Maintaining a weight that is 15% below your expected body weight fits the criteria for anorexia, so many models, according to medical standards, fit into the category of anorexic.

Still, nobody takes responsibility, and as long as skinny sells, nothing is probably going to change. Even though advertising and media won't change by themselves, it is possible to come up with a different solution to try to protect young girls, boys, women and men. And, as the first country to do so in the word, Israel, in March 2012, decided to ban models that are too thin from the media and the catwalk, in order to prevent eating disorders and unhealthy body images. The Israeli lawmakers decided to ban models that have a Body Mass Index [a measure expressing a ratio of weight to height] of less than 18.5, as well as to require publications to disclose when they are using images where models appear thinner than they actually are.

The main person pushing this Israeli law to finally get through is the fashion photographer Adi Barkan, who began his campaign against underweight models and the prevalence of anorexia and bulimia in the Israeli modeling industry after his friend, former model Hila Elmalich, died from bulimia. It took him nearly 10 years to secure the passage of the law in Israel, but Barkan already feels that Israel can't fight alone. More countries and people have to take action against this expanding problem. That is exactly what Barkan is going to do. He wants to involve the world and create a debate.

Barkan works with the Ford modeling in New York and his next plan is to meet with Vogue's editor Anna Wintour as well as the Victoria Secret Company, where he wants to try to influence decision-makers about the importance of banning underweight models from the fashion industry.

But is it likely that a law like this really could stop people from developing eating disorders? Daniel Le Grange, professor of psychiatry and director of the eating disorder program at the University of Chicago, describes that showing unrealistic images of models in fashion magazines and on TV is not necessarily the main reason for people developing eating disorders, but it can be a contributing factor. "Developing an eating disorder is a complex process in terms of specific constellation of personality traits that one's born with. Genetic, environmental, societal things have to come together in a vulnerable individual, so it's not just one piece that makes it possible." A legislation like this can in other words achieve protection against environmental influences, but as eating disorders are so complex it is impossible to say if that is going to stop a person from developing a sickness or not.

Another complication with creating a law like this is to decide whether it undermines the freedom of the press. Donald Downs, a professor at the University of Wisconsin and an expert on the First Amendment, says that it would be very hard to create something like Israel's law in the U.S.A.:

> *In the U.S., it would be hard to justify this type of law on either legal or normative policy grounds. The complexity of eating disorders can make it difficult to justify complete legislation. In addition to the legal aspect of the case, such a law would be in tension with American cultural support for free speech in cases in which the harm is not direct or clear. We are much more wary of giving the state the power to prohibit expression in such contexts because the harm is not usually direct.*

Israel is a small country and it is hard to compare it to the USA. In Israel there is less than eight million people and in the USA there is over 310 million. Making changes in a small country is not going to be as complicated as it would be in the USA. But whether it is creating a law or not, the U.S. government should try to do something about the rising eating disorder numbers. If there is a way to save some people, by at least determining that models have a Body Mass Index of 18.5, it should be considered. It would help the models, the agencies and everybody watching.

Of course creating a law about the models weight is not going to help everybody, but every girl (and boy) that can be saved from developing a sickness, is a step in the right direction.

Hopefully, Adi Barkan and this new law can be an influence for the fashion industry and his coworkers. The more people who are willing to stand up for something like this, the better and he hopes that what he has done so far in Israel is going to reach out to the world. He points out that "No commercial success for my agency can be compared to saving lives. I'm not talking about a drastic change, only a small difference between thin and too thin, between life and death."

Hopefully, in the future, the USA will create something similar to what the Israeli lawmakers have done. Over time that could change some of the unhealthy ideals this world brings to us and progressively it could prevent young people from developing eating disorders to the same extent as they do today. With hope, that could improve and save many lives.

Works Cited

ANAD. *The National Association of Anorexia Nervosa and Associated Disorders*. Web. 15 Apr. 2012.

BBC News. "Israel Passes Law Banning Use of Underweight Models." Web. 20 Mar. 2012.

"Lisa." Personal interview. 12 May 2012.

Lubell, Maayan. "Israel Bans Use of Ultra-Skinny Models." Reuters. Web. 20 Apr. 2012.

Mazzocchi, Sherry. *EBSCOHost*, *"What You Say."* 8/11/2008, Vol. 79 Issue 31, p 4-4, 1/5p.Web. 20 Apr. 2012.

Minsberg, Talya. "What the U.S. Can—and Can't—Learn From Israel's Ban on Ultra-Thin Models." *The Atlantic*. Web. 26 May 2012.

REFLECT & WRITE

- ❑ Where do you see evidence of Frankel's appeals to authority (*ethos*)? Where can you find appeals to emotion (*pathos*)? Which appeal do you find more effective?
- ❑ Analyze the strategies Frankel uses to put this argument together. How does the essay present different perspectives on this issue? What kind of evidence does it offer to support its main claims?
- ❑ Which of the methods Frankel describes do you think will be most effective in bringing about changes in the standards over body size and beauty? World debate? Legislation on Body Mass Index? Different pictures in magazines? Exposure of photoshopped models?
- ❑ **Write.** Compose a letter to the Israeli government in which you present your view on the law banning "too thin" models. What kind of thesis do you want to advance? What tone will you adopt? What forms of rhetorical appeals will make your presentation most persuasive?

During the early twentieth century, **Charles Atlas**, *inspired by a statue of Hercules, started body building and within a few years became known as "The World's Most Perfectly Developed Man." He and partner Charles P. Roman founded Charles Atlas, Ltd., a company dedicated to selling the secrets of masculine health and fitness. His advertisements, including "Hey Skinny," "97 lb. Weakling," and "The Insult That Made a Man out of 'Mac' " (right), appeared in the back of numerous comic books and newspapers and continue to circulate as examples of vintage American advertising.*

FIGURE 12.7 Blending cartoon and advertisement, this vintage Charles Atlas ad marketed a 32-page illustrated book designed to "make a man" out of the reader.

REFLECT & WRITE

- ❑ How are *pathos*, and *logos* used in the design and layout of this advertisement to increase its persuasiveness?
- ❑ Go online to an ad archive and examine other Atlas ads from the 1940s. How do these ads use similar strategies to the one shown here? Are there any that make more effective arguments? What elements make those arguments more persuasive?
- ❑ Consider the issue of male body image. Although the Atlas ads are dated, can you find examples of similar pressures in contemporary culture? Where would you be most likely to find stereotypes of male body image? How do pressures about male body image compare to pressures about female body image? How do various cultures shape notions of the ideal male body differently than in the US?
- ❑ **Write.** Considering the pressures that face men and boys today in terms of body image, storyboard your own advertisement for a fictitious contemporary product or service that will make a "man" out of a modern-day "Mac."

This landmark article, which investigates the relationship between boys' body image and action toys, first appeared in the International Journal of Eating Disorders *in 1999. The research later was featured in a key section of* The Adonis Complex *(2000), a book-length study of male body image.* **Harrison Pope** *and* **Amanda Gruber** *are professors of psychiatry at Harvard Medical School, and* **Robert Olivardia** *is a clinical instructor at the same institution.*

Evolving Ideals of Male Body Image as Seen Through Action Toys

Harrison G. Pope, Jr., Robert Olivardia, Amanda Gruber, and John Borowiecki

Abstract: Objective: *We hypothesized that the physiques of male action toys—small plastic figures used by children in play—would provide some index of evolving American cultural ideals of male body image.* ***Method:*** *We obtained examples of the most popular American action toys manufactured over the last 30 years. We then measured the waist, chest, and bicep circumference of each figure and scaled these measurements using classical allometry to the height of an actual man (1.78 m).* ***Results:*** *We found that the figures have grown much more muscular over time, with many contemporary figures far exceeding the muscularity of even the largest human* *bodybuilders.* ***Discussion:*** *Our observations appear to represent a "male analog" of earlier studies examining female dolls, such as Barbie. Together, these studies of children's toys suggest that cultural expectations may contribute to body image disorders in both sexes.* Int J Eat Disord 26: 65–72, 1999.

Key words: *male body image; male action toys; body image disorders*

Introduction

A growing body of literature has described disorders of body image among men. For example, such disturbances are frequently documented in men with eating disorders. In one study, college men with eating disorders reported a degree of body dissatisfaction closely approaching that of women with eating disorders, and strikingly greater than comparison men (Olivardia, Pope, Mangweth, & Hudson, 1995). Other studies of men with eating disorders have produced similar findings (Andersen, 1990; Schneider & Agras, 1987). Even in studies of male students without eating disorders, the prevalence of body dissatisfaction is often striking (Mintz & Betz, 1986; Drewnowski & Yee, 1987; Dwyer, Feldman, Seltzer, & Mayer, 1969). Body image disturbances may be particularly prominent in American culture. In a recent crosscultural comparison, groups of American college men reported significantly greater dissatisfaction with their bodies than comparable groups in Austria (Mangweth et al., 1997).

Another form of body image disturbance, also frequently affecting men, is body dysmorphic disorder (Phillips, 1991, 1997; Hollander, Cohen, & Simeon, 1993). Individuals with this disorder may develop obsessional preoccupations that their facial features are ugly, that their hairlines are receding, or that their penis size is too small—to name several of the more common presentations. Recently, we have described another form of body dysmorphic disorder found in both sexes, but probably more prevalent in men, which we have called "muscle dysmorphia" (Pope, Gruber, Choi, Olivardia, & Phillips, 1997). Individuals with muscle dysmorphia report an obsessional preoccupation with their muscularity, to the point where their social and occupational functioning may be severely impaired. For example, they may abandon important social and family relationships, or even relinquish professional careers, in order to spend more time at the gym (Pope et al., 1997). Many report that they refuse to be seen in public without their shirts on because they fear that they will look too small (Pope, Katz, & Hudson, 1993). Often they use anabolic steroids or other performance-enhancing drugs, continuing to take these agents even in the face of serious side effects because of persistent anxiety about their muscularity (Pope et al., 1993; Pope & Katz, 1994).

In many ways, muscle dysmorphia appears to be part of the "obsessive-compulsive spectrum" of disorders (Hollander, 1993; Phillips, McElroy, Hudson, & Pope, 1995). It is characterized by obsessional preoccupations and impulsive behaviors similar to those of classical obsessive-compulsive disorder. If this hypothesis is correct, it is natural to ask why modern American men with muscle dysmorphia would have developed this particular outlet for their obsessions, as opposed to a more traditional symptom pattern such as hand-washing or checking rituals.

One possible explanation for this phenomenon is that in our culture, the ideal male body is growing steadily more muscular. With the advent of anabolic steroids in the last 30 to 40 years, it has become possible for men to become much more muscular than is possible by natural means. Bodybuilders who won the Mr. America title in the presteroid era could not hope to compete against steroid-using bodybuilders today (Kouri, Pope, Katz, & Oliva, 1995). The public is exposed daily, in magazines, motion pictures, and other media, to increasingly—and often unnaturally—muscular male images. Some individuals, responding to these cultural messages, may become predisposed to develop muscle dysmorphia.

5 In an attempt to provide some quantitative data bearing on this hypothesis, we examined the physiques of American action toys over the last 30 years.

Methods

Action toys are small plastic figures, typically ranging from 3 3/4 in. to 12 in. in height, used by children in play, and frequently collected by adult hobbyists. Among the best known examples are the GI Joe figures, Star Wars and Star Trek characters, Superman, Spiderman, and Batman. Contemporary versions of these figures are readily available at toy stores and vintage figures may be purchased through a vast and well-organized collectors' market. Extensive reference works, such as the 480-page *Encyclopedia of GI Joe* (Santelmo, 1997), document the evolution of these figures over the years. We chose to study these toys because, unlike cartoon characters or movie stars, they can be readily physically measured, allowing accurate comparisons between figures of different eras.

We consulted with various action toy experts to ascertain toys which had been produced in various iterations by the same manufacturer over a period of 20 years or more. To obtain an objective index of the popularity of specific toys, we consulted the 1st through 15th annual sales surveys by *Playthings* magazine, published in the December issue of each year from 1983 to 1997 (*Playthings* magazine), to confirm that the toy had been among the 10 best-selling toy product lines in several years spanning the last two decades. We also required that the toy represent an actual male human being (such as a soldier or Luke Skywalker), rather than a nonhuman creature (such as Mr. Potato Head or the Teen-Age Mutant Ninja Turtles). Two toy product lines met all of these criteria: the GI Joe series manufactured by the Hasbro Toy Company since 1964 and the Star Wars figures manufactured by the Kenner Toy Company (a subsidiary of Hasbro) since 1978. We then purchased representative examples of these figures from different time periods. We also visited a branch of a large toy store chain and purchased additional examples of toys identified by store officials and by the most recent *Playthings* surveys as the most popular contemporary male action figures. Some of these latter figures, such as Batman and the Mighty Morphin Power Rangers, might not be considered completely "human," in that they possess powers beyond those of a real human being. Others, such as the X-Men, are mutants of human beings. However, they all possess essentially human bodies.

We then measured the waist, chest, and bicep circumference of all the figures and scaled these measurements using classical allometry (Norton, Olds, Olive, & Dank, 1996) to a common height of 1.78 m (70 in.).

Results

GI Joe

The action toy with the longest continuous history is GI Joe. The Hasbro Toy Company first introduced GI Joe as an 11 1/2-in. posable figure in 1964 (Santelmo, 1997). This figure continued without a change in body style as the GI Joe Adventurer in 1970 to 1973. It developed a new body style from 1973 to 1976 as the GI Joe Adventurer with kung-fu grip and lifelike body. In the late 1970s, production of the 11 1/2-in. figures was discontinued, being replaced by a series of 3 3/4-in. figures that was introduced in 1982. These smaller figures continued through 11 series over the next 10 years, eventually attaining a height of 4 1/2 in. and culminating in the GI Joe Extreme. This was a 5-in. figure (5.8 in. with knees and waist straightened) that was introduced in 1995 and is still available on the shelves of toy stores today. Meanwhile, the 11 1/2-in. figures were reintroduced in 1991 and continue to be manufactured to the present.

We purchased three representative 11 1/2-in. figures: a 1973 Adventurer with the original body in use since 1964, a 1975

Table 1. Measurements of representative action toys extrapolated to a height of 70 in.

	Actual Measurements (in.)[a]				Extrapolated to Height of 70 in.[a]		
Toy. Date	Height	Waist	Chest	Biceps	Waist[b]	Chest[b]	Biceps[b]
GI Joe Land Adventurer, 1973 (with original body in use since 1964)	11.5	5.2	7.3	2.1	31.7	44.4	12.2
GI Joe Land Adventurer, 1975 (with new body introduced in 1974)	11.5	5.2	7.3	2.5	31.7	44.4	15.2
GI Joe Hall of Fame Soldier, 1994 (with body introduced in 1991)	11.5	4.8	7.1	2.7	29.2	43.2	16.4
GI Joe Extreme, 1998	5.8	3.0[c]	4.5[c]	2.2	36.5[c]	54.8[c]	26.8
The Gold Ranger, 1998	5.5	2.7	3.6	1.4[c]	34.4[c]	45.8[c]	17.8[c]
Ahmed Johnson, 1998	6.0	3.0	4.1	2.0	35.0	47.8	23.3
Iron Man, 1998	6.5	2.6	4.7	2.1	28.0	50.6	22.6
Batman, 1998	6.0	2.6	4.9	2.3	30.3	57.2	26.8
Wolverine, 1998	7.0	3.3	6.2	3.2	33.0	62.0	32.0

[a]Measurements estimated to the nearest 0.1 in.
[b]For comparison, the mean waist, chest, and biceps circumferences of 50 Australian soccer players, scaled to a slightly shorter height of 170.2 cm (67 in). were found to be 29.6 in., 36.3 in., and 11.8 in., respectively (19).
[c]These numbers are reduced by about 5% from actual measurments to compensate for the thickness of the figure's clothes and equipment.

FIGURE 1 GI Joe Sergeant Savage, 1982 (left); GI Joe Cobra Soldier, 1982 (middle); and GI Joe Extreme Sergeant Savage. 1998 (right) (Hasbro).

Adventurer with the newer lifelike body, and a 1994 Hall of Fame figure. A photograph of these three figures appears in Figure 1 and their dimensions are shown in Table 1. Not only have the figures grown more muscular, but they have developed increasingly sharp muscular definition through the years. For example, the earliest figure has no visible abdominal muscles; his 1975 counterpart shows some abdominal definition; and the 1994 figure displays the sharply rippled abdominals of an advanced bodybuilder. The modern figure also displays distinct serratus muscles along his ribs—a feature readily seen in bodybuilders but less often visible in ordinary men.

We also purchased several of the smaller figures for comparison—a 1982 Grunt, a 1982 Cobra soldier (GI Joe's archenemy), and a current GI Joe Extreme. As shown in Figure 1, the contemporary GI Joe Extreme dwarfs his earlier counterparts with dramatically greater musculature and has an expression of rage which contrasts sharply with the bland faces of his predecessors. Although the body dimensions of the earlier small action figures cannot be accurately estimated because of their layer of clothing, the GI Joe Extreme is more easily measured (see Table 1). If extrapolated to 70 in. in height, the GI Joe Extreme would sport larger biceps than any bodybuilder in history.

Luke Skywalker and Han Solo

A similar impression emerges upon examining the original (1978) versus the contemporary 3 3/4-in. figures of Star Wars characters Luke Skywalker and Han Solo (manufactured by the Kenner Toy Company). As shown in Figure 2, Luke and Han have both acquired the physiques of bodybuilders over the last 20 years, with particularly impressive gains in the shoulder and chest areas. Again, the clothing on these small plastic figures precludes accurate body measurements, so that they are not included in Table 1.

Modern Figures

Figure 4 [not shown here] depicts five more examples from the most popular contemporary lines of male action figures. As mentioned earlier, it might be argued that most of these characters are not entirely human, in that they possess powers beyond those of real people. Nevertheless, they are given fundamentally human bodies, but with musculature that ranges from merely massive to well beyond that of the biggest bodybuilders (Table 1).

FIGURE 2 Luke Skywalker and Han Solo, 1978 (left); Luke Skywalker and Han Solo, 1998 (right) (Kenner).

Discussion

We hypothesized that action toys would illustrate evolving ideals of male body image in the United States. Accordingly, we purchased and measured the most popular male human action figures which have been manufactured over the last 30 years. On both visual inspection and anthropomorphic measurement, it appears that action figures today are consistently much more muscular than their predecessors. Many modern figures display the physiques of advanced bodybuilders and some display levels of muscularity far exceeding the outer limits of actual human attainment.

These findings, however, must be interpreted cautiously for several reasons. First, we found only two lines of male human action toys which fully met our criterion of long-term documented popularity. Thus, it might be argued that these particular toy lines happened to favor our hypothesis by chance alone. However, on the basis of our discussions with action figure experts, we believe that the examples analyzed here are representative of the overall trend of body image in male action toys over the last several decades. The other leading contemporary toys, shown in Figure 4 [not shown here], support the impression that this trend toward a bodybuilder physique is consistent. The only notable exception to this trend is the Mattel Company's Ken, the boyfriend of Barbie. However, although the Barbie toy line overall has frequently ranked among the top 10 toy lines, Ken is but a small part of this market. Among boys in particular, Ken almost certainly ranks well below the popularity of the other male action figure discussed above (*Playthings* magazine).

Second, it is uncertain whether action toys accurately mirror trends in other media. It is our impression that comic strip characters, male models in magazines, and male motion picture actors have all shown a parallel trend toward increasing leanness and muscularity over the last several decades. However, more systematic studies will be required to confirm these observations.

Third, it is not clear to what extent these trends in toys, or parallel trends in other media, may be a cause or effect of an evolving cultural emphasis on male muscularity. Certainly, it would be premature to conclude that American men are prompted to develop disorders of body image purely as a result of boyhood exposure to muscular ideals of male physique. On the other hand, the impact of toys should not be underestimated. Male action toys as a whole accounted for $949 million in manufacturers' shipments in 1994 alone, with action figures accounting for $687 million of this total (*Playthings* magazine, 1995).

It should also be noted that similar theories have been advanced for many years regarding cultural ideals of thinness in women (Pope & Hudson, 1984; Cash & Pruzinsky, 1990). For example, one study found that both *Playboy* centerfold models and Miss America pageant contestants grew steadily thinner over the period of l959 to 1978 (Garner, Garfinkel, Schwartz, & Thompson, 1980). A recent update suggests that this trend has continued at least through 1988 (Wiseman, Gray, Mosimann, & Ahrens, 1992). Similarly, in the area of toys, the literature has documented the inappropriate thinness of modern female dolls (Norton et al., 1996, Pederson & Markee, 1991; Rintala & Mustajoki, 1992; Brownell & Napolitano, 1995). Indeed, one report has found that Mattel Company's Barbie, if extrapolated to a height of 67 in., would have a waist circumference of 16 in. (Norton et al., 1996)—a figure approaching the impossibility of our male superheroes' biceps.

In any event, these striking findings suggest that further attempts should be made to assess the relationship between cultural messages and body image disorders in both men and women.

The authors thank Erik Flint of Cotswold Collectibles, Whitbey Island, WA; Vincent Santelmo of the Official Action Figure Warehouse, New York, NY; and Jeff Freeman of the Falcon's Hangar, Auburn, IN, for their assistance in the selection and purchase of action toys and in the preparation of this manuscript.

References

Action figures duke it out. (1995). Playthings magazine, 93, 26–28.

Andersen, A.E. (Ed). (1990). Males with eating disorders. New York: Brunner Mazel.

Brownell, K.D., & Napolitano, M.A. (1995). Distorting reality for children: Body size proportions of Barbie and Ken dolls. International Journal of Eating Disorders, 18, 295–298.

Cash, T.F., & Pruzinsky, T. (Eds), (1990). Body images: Developments, deviance, and change, New York: Guilford.

Drewnowski, A., & Yee, D.K. (1987). Men and body image: Are males satisfied with their body weight? Psychosomatic Medicine, 49, 626–634.

Dwyer, J.T., Feldman, J.J., Seltzer, C.C., & Mayer, J. (1969). Body image in adolescents: Attitudes toward weight and perception of appearance. American Journal of Clinical Nutrition, 20, 1045–1056.

Garner, D.M., Garfinkel, P.E., Schwartz, D., & Thompson, M. (1980). Cultural expectations of thinness in women. Psychological Reports, 47, 483–491.

Hollander, E. (1993). Introduction. In E. Hollander, (Ed.), Obsessive-compulsive related disorders. Washington, DC: American Psychiatric Press.

Hollander, E., Cohen, I. J., & Simeon, D. (1993). Body dysmorphic disorder. Psychiatric Annals, 23, 359–364.

Kouri, E., Pope. H.G., Katz. D.L., & Oliva, P. (1995). Fat-free mass index in users and non-users of anabolic-androgenic steroids. Clinical Journal of Sport Medicine, 5, 223–228.

Mangweth, B., Pope. H.G., Jr., Hudson. J.I., Olivardia, R., Kinzi. J., & Biebl, W. (1997). Eating disorders in Austrian men: An intra-cultural and cross-cultural comparison study. Psychotherapy and Psychosomatics, 66, 214–221.

Mintz, L.B., & Betz., N.E., (1986). Sex differences in the nature, realism, and correlates of body image. Sex Roles, 15, 185–195.

Norton, K.E., Olds, T.S., Olive. S., & Dank, S. (1996). Ken and Barbie at life size Sex Roles, 84, 287–294.

Olivardia, R., Pope, H.G., Jr., Mangweth., B., & Hudson, J.I. (1995). Eating disorders in college men. American Journal of Psychiatry, 152, 1279–1285.

Petersen, E.L., & Markee, N.L. (1991). Fashion dolls; Representations of ideals of beauty. Perceptual and Motor Skills, 73, 93–94.

Phillips, K.A. (1991). Body dysmorphic disorder. The distress of imagined, ugliness. American Journal of Psychiatry, 148, 1138–1149.

Phillips, K.A. (1997). The broken mirror. New York: Oxford University Press.

Phillips, K.A., McElroy, S.L., Hudson, J.I., & Pope, H.G., Jr. (1995). Body dysmorphic disorder: An obsessive-compulsive spectrum disorder, a form of affective spectrum disorder, or both? Journal of Clinical Psychiatry, 56 (Suppl. 4), 41–51.

Playthings. (1983–1997). New York: Geyer-McAlister Publications, Inc.

Pope, H.G., Jr., Gruber. A.J., Choi, P.Y., Olivadia. R., & Phillips. K.S, (1997). Muscle dysmorphia: An under-recognized form of body dysmorphic disorder. Psychosomatics, 38, 348–557.

Pope, H.G., Jr., & Hudson, J.I. (1984). New hope for binge eaters. Advances in the understanding and treatment of bulimia. New York: Harper and Row.

Pope, H.G., Jr., & Katz, D.L. (1994). Psychiatric and medical effects of anabolic-androgenic steroids. A controlled study of 160 athletes. Archives of General Psychiatry, 51, 375–382.

Pope, H.G., Jr., Katz. D.L., & Hudson. J.I. (1993). Anorexia nervosa and "reverse anorexia" among 108 male bodybuilders. Comprehensive Psychiatry, 34, 406–409.

Rintala, M., & Mustajoki, P. (1992). Could mannequins menstruate? British Medical Journal, 305, 1575–1576.

Santelmo, V. (1997). The complete encyclopedia to GI Joe (2nd ed.). Jola, WI: Krause Publications.

Schneider, J.A., & Agras, W.S. (1987). Bulimia in males: A matched comparison with females. International Journal of Eating Disorders, 6, 235–242.

Wiseman, C.V., Gray, J.J., Mosimann, J.E., & Abrens A.H. (1992). Cultural expectations of thinness: An update, International Journal of Eating Disorders, 11, 85–90.

REFLECT & WRITE

- ❑ Summarize the thesis in your own words. How does the historical examination of action toys provide powerful evidence about social norms for male body image? At the end of your summary, write a one-line response to the argument.

- ❑ How do the images work in conjunction with the written text to create a persuasive argument? What would be lost in terms of the argument's effectiveness without them? What is gained from viewing the visual rhetoric?
- ❑ How do the pressures facing boys differ from those facing girls? What can you add from your own experience in terms of how the media shapes body image standards along gender lines?
- ❑ What do the examples used in this article tell us about the ways body ideals intersect with race, class, culture, and ethnicity stereotypes? Do different toys demonstrate this intersection differently?
- ❑ **Write.** This collaborative article was written for an academic audience. Draft a version of this article that could be published as a short opinion piece in a popular magazine or online blog. Include quotes from this article as if citing an interview.

Seeing Connections
Review the discussion of style in Chapter 3 and the discussion of the levels of decorum in Chapter 8 to help you adapt the article for a popular audience.

WRITING COLLABORATIVELY

Together with two classmates, go to a toy store or visit one online and do your own survey of recent toys for boys. Look at Transformers, Rescue Heroes, Bionicles, and comic book heroes like the Avengers, Superman, Spiderman, Batman, and the X-Men. Also look at the *Star Wars Clone Wars* line and G.I. Joe toys. Write an essay in which you use your own observations on recent toys to support, qualify, or refute the article's assertions about body image as projected through toy culture for boys. You might take digital photos of toys you find at the store and use them as visual evidence in your essay. Then, convert your writing to a multimedia presentation and share your work with the rest of the class, making sure each team member takes a turn in presenting part of the argument.

Kim Franke-Folstad, *currently a features editor at the* Tampa Tribune, *published this article in the* Rocky Mountain News *on May 24, 1999, in reaction to Harrison Pope's 1999 study on action toys and male body images.*

G.I. Joe's Big Biceps Are Not a Big Deal

Kim Franke-Folstad

Say it isn't so, Joe.

For years, I've been defending Barbie against accusations that she promotes an unrealistic body image for little girls.

And now it turns out good old G.I. Joe has been subjected to the same silly poking and probing, the same plastic-to-flesh measurement comparisons and similarly ugly allegations that he's encouraging young boys to seek an artificially enhanced physique.

Will this foolishness never stop?

5 The latest bit of bicep bashing comes from Harvard psychiatrist Harrison Pope, who's apparently spent years studying hard-bodied action figures and how they affect the way males feel their real-life bodies should look.

Big, bulging and buff.

According to Pope's research, the plastic playthings are getting ever more muscle-bound, and young men are, too—often by abusing anabolic steroids.

The doctor says he can't be sure which came first: bulked-up toys or bulked-up boys. But, either way, when a G.I. Joe's bicep measurement translates to an impossible 26 inches for a real he-man, it could mean a dangerous trend.

Here we go again.

10 Barbie's bust is too big, her waist is too small, her arches (both foot and eyebrow) are unreasonably high. G.I. Joe's arms are too thick, his chest is too chiseled and the muscles in his massive thighs are ridiculously rippled.

So what?

They are toys. We all know that. That's why we stop playing with them before we get out of grade school.

Well, most of us, anyway.

Besides, if anything, I'm more comfortable with the freakish physiques of today's action figures than I was with the more realistic and appropriately proportioned appearance of my brother's G.I. Joe back in the 1960s.

15 Now, instead of sending a dog-tagged doll that looks like your next door neighbor's older brother into battle, it's more like you've dispatched a cartoon superhero. Of course bullets bounce off his chest and he's never afraid—he's not a man, he's a mutant with a crew cut and really great accessories.

Let's face it: Boys have wanted to bulk up—and do it quickly—since Charles Atlas promised he could transform any 90-pound weakling into a muscle man proud to stroll the beach in his Speedo. These days, young men (and not so young men) may be influenced by Mark McGwire's 19-inch biceps and the knowledge that he takes an over-the-counter testosterone booster. They may have noted the equally hunky Bill Romanowski's propensity for modeling EAS apparel. Or they could be checking out the bulging necks—and wallets—of popular professional wrestlers Goldberg and "Stone Cold" Steve Austin.

But a plastic doll?

Please. To suggest that even little boys measure manliness by taking a ruler to their G.I. Joes is comical.

And from here it looks as though the "real American hero's" musculature isn't the only thing being blown out of proportion.

REFLECT & WRITE

- ❑ What is Franke-Folstad's argument in this article? Is it an effective rebuttal to Pope's claims? Do you find her argument convincing; do you find her easy dismissal of Pope's research to be compelling?
- ❑ Consider the author's tone. How do exaggeration and sarcasm characterize her voice? Does that make her writing more or less persuasive to you as a reader? Evaluate the writing in terms of levels of decorum as strategies of style. Include word choice, length of sentences, and level of language as you analyze the prose.
- ❑ Identify the logical fallacies at work in this short piece. Which ones are humorous? Which ones actually make you reconsider the implications of studying dolls and toys as rhetorical objects?
- ❑ **Write.** Franke-Folstad does not include images in her article. Imagine that you wanted to write an essay in response to the article using the photo in Figure 12.8. What is the visual argument of the three children holding very

FIGURE 12.8 Today's dolls reflect a variety of body types and identities, showcasing the diversity in our society.

specific dolls? What messages do the children's expressions send about the meaning of doll bodies? Include this image in your essay and write an appropriate caption so that it functions in support of your argument. Also consider where in the article you would place your visual rhetoric to maximize its persuasiveness. Alternatively, write a letter in response to the author and use photos of your own toys or dolls as visual rhetoric for your central claim.

As this excerpt from the November 23, 2012, issue of Wired magazine reminds us, the question of "body image" includes every aspect of the body—facial hair included. Casting an ironic glance over the mania for beards supposedly sweeping Silicon Valley, this piece (written by **Lore Sjöberg** *and illustrated by* **Kelsey Drake***) provides readers a guide to what it calls "facial topiary" of America's technology epicenter.*

Beards of Silicon Valley: A Field Guide to Tech Facial Hair

Lore Sjöberg and Kelsey Drake

There's no underestimating the importance of facial hair in the world of technology.

Look no further than the research of a man named Tamir Kahson, who in 2004 discovered the inseparable link between beards and programming languages. As Kahson so artfully demonstrated, a programming language is only as successful as the beard on the face of the man who designed it — or something like that.

OK, Grace Hopper didn't have a beard, and she was the brains behind Cobol. But she's not a man. Clearly, women are exempt the laws of tech facial hair.

In Silicon Valley, the beard is everything — unless you're a woman or you're Mark Zuckerberg and you can't grow one. For everyone else, a beard is essential to Silicon Valley success. But not just any beard. You must carefully grow your facial hair to suit your particular role in the tech ecosystem.

Confused? Don't worry. Here, we give you our Field Guide to Facial Topiary in the Tech Workplace. If you're a woman, ignore it. If you're man, start not shaving. *–Editor*

FIGURE 12.9 This information graphic provides a humorous taxonomy of male facial hair in the tech industry.

REFLECT & WRITE

- ❑ Examine the visual attributes of each beard drawing. What is the ostensible link between the facial hair and the identity of the beard owner? How does each match create an "ideal body" based on profession?
- ❑ While presented ironically, this guide may also have a more serious purpose. What larger message about body image and identity do you think these visuals are intended to get across?

- ❑ Do you see any parallels between the sorts of "profiles" presented here and the issue of racial profiling? Do these images encourage viewers to engage in a form of "profiling" that is similar?
- ❑ **Write.** Create a "field guide" for a community of which you are a member. What distinguishing feature would you choose as this group's signature characteristic? What different examples of this visual type would you create? And what would you claim this distinguishing feature ultimately tells people about your community?

ANALYZING PERSPECTIVES ON THE ISSUE

1. The National Eating Disorder Association (NEDA) poster featured in Figure 12.6 relies primarily on a *pathos* appeal to make its point. Conduct some research to locate further facts and statistics about anorexia in girls. Now, drawing on the lessons about visual arguments from Chapter 8, create an op-ad that relies on a *logos*-driven argument to make its point. Be sure to incorporate rhetorically purposeful images to substantiate and reinforce your argument.
2. Harrison Pope transformed his article, "Evolving Ideals of Male Body Image as Seen Through Action Toys" into a section of his book *The Adonis Complex* (NY: The Free Press, 2000). Locate this book in the library. Read pages 40–46 in *The Adonis Complex* and then write an essay in which you discuss the ways in which Pope developed the prose and content of his short piece into a longer research argument.

FROM READING TO RESEARCH ASSIGNMENTS

1. Use a reference book such as Charles Goodrum and Helen Dalrymple's *Advertising in America* (NY: Harry N. Abrams Inc., 1990) or your own archival work with old magazines to get a sense of how magazines constructed ideals of beauty at a particular historical moment. Using specific examples from the advertisements and/or vintage magazine articles, write a persuasive essay that defines one of the foundations of beauty for that context.
2. In 2013, the CEO of Abercrombie & Fitch, Mike Jeffries, came under fire in the media for refusing to sell clothes larger than size 10. Research this controversy, and then write a letter to Jeffries, using the Swedish mannequins as an example, asking him to reconsider his stance on this issue. Support your position with both primary and secondary research. Consider conducting a survey of female consumers or engaging in your own field work and photo-document your own research on displays, advertisements, and other messages about beauty found in Abercrombie & Fitch or similar stores.

3. What kinds of visual rhetoric might you design to address body image issues for women of different races and cultures? Research a body image related topic for a specific population (for instance, skin bleaching among African-American women or eyelid surgery among Asian women), then mock up a public service media campaign (consisting of radio spots, print ads, and posters) designed to address this issue. Pitch your campaign to the class, making sure to be clear about your underlying claim about body image anxieties within that particular demographic.

4. Research the connection between media images of "ideal bodies" and eating disorders for women and men. Are there significant differences in how these images affect men versus women? What additional factors might be involved, such as steroid use, athletic pressure, the drive for perfectionism, and even mental illness? As you research these issues, consider what prevention strategies might be possible in your community. Based on your prewriting and research, design a new campaign against eating disorders using both images and words.

CHAPTER 13

Playing Against Stereotypes

Sports figures play many different roles in contemporary culture. These roles range from models of physical perfection to embodiments of national pride; they span from representations of local identity to symbols of global community. For many viewers and readers, these figures become much larger than life.

How is the media complicit in this process? Scholar Paul Mark Pederson has suggested, "Sport and mass media are inextricably linked together in a symbiotic relationship. These two institutions rely on each other—the mass media sell sport and sport sells the mass media." In this chapter, we'll explore the way that the media constantly projects images of athletes to the consumer public, whether from the glossy covers of magazines, in flashy TV ad campaigns, or even on giant posters plastered on the sides of buses, billboards, or in the corridors of malls. Too often, images of sports celebrity remain flat and two-dimensional, even if scaled to poster size or projected in surround sound on a high-definition TV. That is, we tend to see not complex, fully developed individuals, but instead figures that feed into and perpetuate certain cultural stereotypes. So a key question emerges: how do sports—and in particular the media coverage of sports—both reinforce and dismantle such stereotypes?

We can see the complicated relationship between stereotype and media at work in Nike's famous 2004 "Tennis Instructor" commercial. In that ad, the tennis pro arrives to meet his class: a group of young teenage girls. As he starts the lesson, he flips his hair and walks among them, the girls looking adoringly after him. However, on the court, the situation changes radically. He gently tosses a ball to a young blond girl who catches it, tosses it in the air to serve it, and then changes suddenly into Serena Williams who drills the ball over the net. The pro blinks, then walks on, but the transformation repeats: all around him, the giggly young girls literally turn into Williams on the court, astounding him with their strong backhands and power returns. At the climax, he ducks to avoid a ball that narrowly misses hitting

FIGURE 13.1 Nike's "Tennis Instructor" commercial uses clever cinematography to transform a class of young tennis players into a group of Serena Williamses.

FIGURE 13.2 The tennis pro from the commercial does a double take.

FIGURE 13.3 In the final frame of the commercial, the class transforms back into a group of young girls.

him in the head. As he stands up, we see the girls through his eyes: a group of Serena Williamses, all looking at him with concern (Figure 13.1). He blinks, confused (Figure 13.2), and in the final frame they have transformed back to their teenage selves (Figure 13.3), though mirroring the poses and attitude of the multiple Williamses a moment before. It is not just the tennis pro that is schooled in this commercial; it is the viewer. Do not make assumptions about athleticism based on stereotype, Nike cautions: great athletes come in all shapes and forms.

In the readings that follow, we'll look carefully at the complex media messages about sports and uncover how sports figures become subject to gender and race stereotyping by reading articles that examine sports coverage, advertising, and photojournalism in depth. You'll learn to turn a critical eye on all future media coverage of the sports you may love—and those that may be quite new to you. In the process, you'll have a chance to contribute your own responses to this ongoing debate about sports and media.

REFLECT & WRITE

- ❑ Look at the screenshots in Figures 13.1 and 13.3. What is the effect of having the girls mirror Serena in their final poses?
- ❑ Consider Figure 13.2. How does the casting and characterization of the tennis pro feed into stereotype?
- ❑ Most of the commercial is shown through the perspective of the tennis pro. How would it have been different if he had not been part of the story? What does having his perspective add to argument?

- ❑ Some feminists have argued that this commercial is problematic because the young girls are only motivated to excel out of a desire to impress their male tennis instructor. Based on your understanding of the commercial, is this a justified critique? To what extent does this interpretation complicate the commercial's message about powerful women athletes?
- ❑ **Write.** Watch the full commercial, "Serena Williams Nike Tennis Instructor," on YouTube. Pay particular attention to the musical score and use of sound, the pacing, and how the images of Serena are integrated. Write a rhetorical analysis of this commercial that takes into account how these elements contribute to the persuasiveness of the ad. Refer to Chapter 2 for guiding questions for rhetorical analysis.

These photographs capture images of athletes who defy stereotypes about "ableness," pushing beyond physical limitations to embody examples of athletic excellence. As photojournalist Carlos Serrao, who has photographed both athletes, has stated, "In the future, disabled athletes will be 'limited' only by how fast, high and far their man-made limbs can take them. For some … the future is already here."

Defying Stereotypes of Ability

FIGURE 13.4 High-jumper Jeff Skiba, pictured here cresting the bar in his event, won a gold medal during the 2008 Summer Paralympics and was the first amputee in history to clear the 7 foot mark in the high jump—a distinction he earned at the 2008 Asuza Pacific Invitational in Los Angeles.

FIGURE 13.5 Triathlete Sarah Reinertsen is famous for more than her athleticism; she has appeared on *The Amazing Race*, starred in Lincoln car commercials, and worked as a motivational speaker.

REFLECT & WRITE

- ❑ How do these images play to stereotypes of athletes? How do they defy them? Consider the composition of the photos in your analysis, including perspective, layout, focus, and framing.
- ❑ Two what extent do these images become images of ability instead of disability? How do their messages differ from that which might be found in a photo focusing, for instance, on Jeff Skiba stretching to prepare for his event or Sarah Reinertsen in running clothes, posing for the camera?
- ❑ What differences do you see in the way the photographers chose to portray these athletes? Which photograph do you find more inspiring? Why?
- ❑ **Write.** Carlos Serrao includes photographs of both Jeff Skiba and Sarah Reinertsen in his 2008 ESPN Magazine photo essay "Anything You Can Do." Look at that photo essay online. Suggest an alternate arrangement for the nine photos featured in that piece, and write a short preface to your revised photo essay about athletes, stereotypes, and differing abilities.

Seeing Connections
Review the section on Arrangement in Argument in Chapter 3

In the following excerpt, authors **Carla Filomena Silva** *and* **P. David Howe** *interrogate the way in which the stereotype of the superstar disabled athlete depends on reinforcing and reinscribing existing paradigms of "ableness." The full article was originally published in a 2012 issue of* Journal of Sport and Social Issues.

The (In)validity of *Supercrip* Representation of Paralympian Athletes

Carla Filomena Silva and P. David Howe

Abstract

This article provides a critical overview of the viability of the "supercrip" iconography as an appropriate representation of Paralympic athletes. It focuses on its validity as a vehicle for the empowerment of individuals with impairments both within the context of elite sport and broader society. This type of representation may be seen by the able moral majority as enlightened. However, supercrip narratives may have a negative impact on the physical and social development of disabled individuals by reinforcing what could be termed "achievement syndrome"—the impaired are successful *in spite* of their disability. The authors will focus on the implications of the use of language and images embodied in supercrip iconography, relying on examples of two European Paralympic awareness campaigns disseminated through mainstream media.

> The Olympics is where heroes are made. The Paralympics is where heroes come.
>
> *Steadward & Peterson, 1997, p. 8*

***

Supercrip as a Stereotype

Supercrip can be defined as a stereotype narrative displaying the plot of someone who has "to fight against his/her impairment" in order to overcome it and achieve unlikely "success." When uncritically interpreted, this type of narrative can be regarded as positive, contesting dominant views regarding disability as "negative" and "inferior." However, it is the negative "ethos" of disability that feeds the low expectations placed on the individual labeled as *disabled* in a way that any achievement is easily glorified, no matter how insignificant. The difference in expectations between the "abled" and the "disabled" world is well articulated through the quote that introduces this article.

This is not to say that great achievements should not be praised and valued but that the distorted tendency to either "undervalue" or "overvalue" achievements whenever disability is present should be denounced. The irreducible individuality of disability experience means there is no standard reference for the "extraordinary" when disability is present, unless the social expectations are extremely low. Reinforcing low expectations is what makes supercrip iconography so problematic. Moreover, successes are generally judged in terms of the ability to conform to able-bodied norms: "if a person with a disability is 'successful', or seems to have a good life, he is seen as brave and courageous or special and brilliant. Given the intrinsic abnormality or awfulness of disability, anyone living a 'normal' life must be extraordinary"

(Charlton, 2000, p. 52). The able-bodied majority expects those who are "different" to develop and adapt, sometimes at very high personal expense, in order to be respected as citizens of equal value (Rogers & Swadener, 2001). Overcoming disability is a very lonely task that rarely requires adaptation by the able majority but can constitute significant change for a person with impairment. It rarely invokes the learning and developing of new possibilities and alternative modes of living full lives, free of stigma, prejudice, or any sense of inferiority. The verb to "overcome" is almost exclusively conjugated in the first person (Shapiro, 1994), ignoring the complexity inscribed in disability experiences and accentuating disability as an individual matter that is personal responsibility.

***

Can the Paralympics Change the (Dis) ability World?

The idea that what reality "is" is significantly influenced by the way it is represented, in an unpredictable network of connections and influences, justifies the importance of a cultural analysis of Paralympians' representations. Although the Paralympic Games have been widely understood and promoted as potentially empowering for athletes and for people with disabilities in general, the empowerment of these populations still needs to be assessed (Schantz & Gilbert, 2001; Howe, 2008). Nevertheless, the sporting global stage offered by the Paralympic Games is a golden opportunity to challenge hegemonic ideals of masculinity, physicality, and sexuality (DePauw, 1997). As Hargreaves (2000, p. 199) states, "They [Paralympic Games] also symbolize a challenge to 'ableist' ideology, a reinvention of the (dis)abled body and a redefinition of the possible." In opposition to the "dis-abled" body, the Paralympic body presents itself as productive, functional, and efficient. A body focused on possibilities instead of limits.

5 Consistent, regular, and high quality exposure of images of efficient impaired bodies can strongly influence social perceptions of (dis)-ability: "These images of athletes with a disability can, and will, alter our traditional view of the normal body (bodies) and of sport and performance" (DePauw, 2000, p. 366). They can also challenge our perception of the body, its functionality, and its role in a person's identities. Thus, the idea that the body is not only socially normalized (Elias, 1978; Foucault, 1977) but also challenges, reconfigures, and shapes the embodied world in which we live (Merleau-Ponty, 1962) legitimizes an analysis of Paralympic's representations.

Despite the obvious transgressive potential of a global event such as the Paralympic Games, inculcated perceptions of disability often jeopardize the possibility of social change. The increasing media influence and economic importance of Paralympics means, as social scientists, we should pay careful attention to the modes of representation disseminated and their possible implications. Due to the specific emotional ethos of high-performance sport, the tendency for disability supercripization may be amplified to serve interests that might not be aligned with ideals of empowerment.

"Superatletas," "Incredible Athletes," or "Freaks of Nature"

It can be argued that discourses around elite sport have always been inflated with laudatory tones that create sporting heroes, as a strategy to keep the emotional ethos of competition high and feed the sport business industry (Cashmore, 2010). This strategy explains, in part, the recurrence of supercrip narrative in Paralympic's coverage. Whereas in mainstream sport, the heroes are a few "rare" talented athletes, in disability sport the *super* label is often used indiscriminately (Howe, 2008; Peers, 2009). The expression "the Olympics is where heroes are made, Paralympics is where heroes come" (Steadward & Peterson, 1997, p. 8) is a clear example of this understanding.

***

Freaks of Nature

Freaks of Nature is the label given to the London 2012 Paralympic marketing campaign launched by the host broadcaster, Channel 4. This campaign started with a weekend devoted to Paralympic sport, during which the documentary [*Inside*] *Incredible Athletes* (presented on August 29, 2011) was the highlight. A press release dated August 9, 2010, from Julian Bellamy, Channel 4's acting chief creative officer, set the tone:

> Channel 4 sees the London 2012 Paralympic Games as an opportunity to bring about a fundamental shift in perceptions of disability in the UK, and *Inside Incredible Athletes* perfectly encapsulates this. This beautiful and insightful documentary examines the athletes' phenomenal ability and films them performing in ways that have never been seen before. The *Freaks of Nature* marketing trail is part of a bold campaign that portrays Paralympians as Channel 4 feels they should be seen—supremely talented athletes who, like their able bodied sporting counterparts, are set apart from the rest of us by their staggering ability, not their disability. And this reflects our ambitions for our coverage of the London 2012 Paralympic Games themselves—encouraging viewers to focus on the awe-inspiring ability on display throughout. (Channel 4, Press release, August 9, 2010)

In the documentary's trailer the public is invited to "meet some of the Britain's most extraordinary Paralympians." The laudatory discourse is illustrated with numeric criteria, "nine medals, one hundred and nine goals in one hundred and eleven games," so, in this sense, some evidence is presented that these athletes are actually "special" among their peers. At the end of the trailer, two of the athletes say, "We are freaks of nature." The broadcasters claimed that the expression "freaks of nature" is used in a positive sense, making the point these athletes are "set apart from the rest of us by their staggering ability, not their disability." However, this expression, uttered by athletes themselves, still created a controversy. According to good access guide website, some disability activists accused Channel 4 of breaking the United Nations (UN) 2006 *Convention on the Rights of Persons With Disabilities* when they utilize the term "freaks." The Channel 4 website quoted their "disability executive" stating that their "prime purpose was to try and draw people" and "generate a buzz about it" and that because of the "very competitive market" you sometimes "have to take a bit of a risk." (Another argument was that the expression "freak of nature"—pronounced in the trailer by the nine times Paralympic gold medalist Lee Pearson—was a "deliberate attempt to cast our athletes in the same light as Olympic athletes.")

10 This episode, surrounding the launch of the London 2012 marketing campaign, illustrates some important issues: First, the immense sensitivity around media representations of disability, second, the need for constant comparison to the Olympics Games is sign of how far the Paralympics Movement still needs to go before establishing a distinctive and legitimate identity as a high-performance sport. Finally, the controversy over the use of the word "freaks" highlights the lack of consensual representational models surrounding disability and, by extension, Paralympic sport. In essence, disability remains a social taboo.

Inside Incredible Athletes

Some features of this documentary counteract the supercrip representation made via first-person statements from participating athletes and are depicted in everyday regular activities in sporting and other contexts (home, work)—the deliberate intention to label and "market" these athletes as "super" is self-evident. Bearing this in mind, we turn our attention to the examination of some of the mechanisms of supercripization at play. Perhaps the most obvious of these mechanisms is the use of language: the superlative terminology—"incredible," "extraordinary abilities," and "amazing athletes." The video is also replete with terminology that essentialize, individualize, and reduce the success of these athletes to features hidden in their bodies: "discover the secrets inside their bodies."

The close examination, analysis, and dissection of Paralympian bodies through "state-of-the-art" technology turn their specialness into objects of scientific enquiry. This is the second mechanism at play to build in the presentation of Paralympians as "Freaks of Nature." The technological tools used to analyze sporting performance are such that allow for a deep incursion into the body, to access the secrets hidden within individual bodily boundaries, with a strong focus on the brain. It is important to analyze some of these secrets. The right hemisphere of Liz Johnson's is overdeveloped to compensate for the left hemisphere neurological damage, a result of cerebral palsy, which is used to explain her mastery of the symmetrical movement of breaststroke ("her secret lies deep inside her brain"). In similar terms, explanations for the skilful abilities of the "blind football player," David Clark, are mapped through an in-depth examination of his brain: "Could the secret lye [lie] in his brain and in his hearing ability?" David is submitted to a testing protocol where the hearing function is activated and his brain activity is recorded. Apparently David's brain reacts as it "should" in the first part of the test, but at some point, the brain areas responsible for the vision are also activated. Rhodri Cusak, neuroscientist in Cambridge University, interprets this fact as an example of brain plasticity, the capacity of human brains to adapt and redesign themselves.

In the case of the wheelchair rugby players portrayed, Mandip Sehmi and Steve Brown, are shown to have "exceptional values when compared to normative values of untrained wheelchair individuals" (as stated by Dr. Vicky Tolfrey, Loughborough University). This statement is made after they are submitted to a cardiorespiratory maximum capacity evaluation (VO_2 Max)[1] and their results shown to be better than the predicted scientific values for average wheelchair users with the same degree of function. Again, instead of something extraordinary in their bodies, it is the process of intensive training that induces adaptations, a conclusion that is explicitly conveyed when it is also said in narration that they adapt "by developing the function they still have."

Developments in cognitive and neurosciences (Clark, 2008; Sheets-Johnstone, 2011) prove what phenomenologists like Merleau-Ponty (1962) have been claiming for long time: the inextricable connection between mind, body, and world. In other words, it is more plausible to interpret Liz's brain's "specialness" as an adaptation to her "20 weekly hours of swimming and a cycle of relentless competition." Similarly, David's brain developed the ability to create pictures of "reality" due to the ways he has been using his body throughout his life. The ability to "see" the public, the coaches, the ball, the opposition, and the goal is not the result of an extraordinary hidden secret, but a fruit of years of training and competition. Body (extended),[2] mind, and world shape each other, possessing a plasticity, a certain scope for change and adaptation: "human minds and bodies are essentially open to episodes of deep and transformative restructuring in which new equipment (both physical and 'mental') can become quite literally incorporated into the thinking and acting systems that we identity as our minds and our bodies" (Clark, 2008, p. 31). Moreover, Clark goes further to affirm that the recruitment process of problem-solving resources do not exhibit any preference between "neural, bodily, and environmental resources except insofar as these somehow affect the total effort involved" (2008, p. 13). This means that adaptations happen in different forms and different locations: in the neuronal system (Liz Johnson, David Clarke), in the musculoskeletal system (Stefanie Reid, Johnny Peacock), in the cardiovascular and musculoskeletal systems (Mandip Sehmi, Steve Brown), in technical skills and abilities (Lee Pearson).

In sum, the search for the hidden secrets "Inside Paralympic Athletes" stems from a particular view that sporting success is impossible for athletes with impairment unless some "special" traits exist. However, the adaptations induced by training and hard work are largely responsible for Paralympic athlete's performances. Success is much more grounded in the flexibility and plasticity of our human gearing (body, mind, and world) than in any specific secret inside "Freaks of Nature."

The last mechanism of supercripization that we wish to illuminate is the omnipresent norm of the able-bodied. A continuous comparison seems to be needed to portray different bodies in terms that "normal people" can understand. But if the able-bodied referential stands as "right" and "beautiful," the empowerment potential of disability sport is weakened; for example, only when compared to an Olympic swimmer does Liz's impairment becomes obvious. But why is the comparison needed in the first place? Why is it interpreted as so exceptional that wheelchair athletes improve their functional abilities by training hard? Why is it so surprising that David Clarke, the captain of the British Paralympics blind football team, plays the game as well as his office colleagues? In sum, as the documentary unfolds and the secrets inside the athlete's bodies are disclosed, the "supercrip" model is deconstructed as well as, partially, reconstructed at the same time. The ultimate reasons for these athletes' sporting success presented in the documentary are not extraordinary: extensive hours of training and a certain amount of talent, as is required from any other athlete. Incredibleness is only envisioned against the background understanding of disability as exclusively negative, a perception still present in expressions such as "cope with his impairment" and "conquered her impairment." In the end, the secrets that were supposed to be hidden in these incredible bodies are translated in three words: "training," "effort," and "determination."

In the context of elite sport, it is true that athletes' images are manipulated through a media lens so that they appear superhuman, responding to the contemporary obsession for records and sporting heroes. In the highly mediatized representations of elite sport, natural ability tends to be overvalued whereas training and effort are undermined. As the press release quoted earlier highlights, although the use of expression, "The Freaks of Nature," is intended to equalize media treatment of Paralympians and Olympians, the use of this phrase still carries the weight of social stigma faced by people with disabilities. To this end it is felt that, "Freaks of Nature," "Incredible athletes," "amazing athletes," "Superatleta," and so on are still obvious markers of "Othering" processes, as opposed to the Paralympics' empowerment potential.

The social impact of media images imposes responsibilities that must be remembered by a critical and demanding audience. By re-opening the discussion over the implications of "supercrip" models in talking, writing, and showing disability, we hope to have made a contribution to an increasingly "empowering" Paralympics Games that is, at least in part, a result of a more enlightened media coverage.

Notes

[1] $V0_2$ max. expresses the maximum volume of oxygen that is possible to consume.

[2] Two main ideas ground the concept of an "extended mind": First, the mind is not only inside the head; that is, it is not related to brain functions alone as it also demands the action of the whole body; second, the mind extends beyond one's own body to include the active interaction with environment (Clark & Chalmers, 1998).

References

Cashmore, E. (2010). *Making sense of sports.* London: Routledge.

Charlton, J. L. (2000). *Nothing about us without us, disability oppression and empowerment.* Berkeley: University of California Press.

Clark, A., & Chalmers, D. (1998). The extended mind. *Analysis. 58*(1), 7–19.

Clark, A. (2008). *Supersizing the mind: Embodiment, action, and cognitive extension.* Oxford, UK.: Oxford University Press.

DePauw, K. P. (1997). The (in)visibility of disability: Cultural contexts and "sporting bodies." *Quest 49*(4), 416–430.

Elias, N. (1978). *The civilizing process.* New York, NY: Urizen Books.

Foucault, M. (1977). *Discipline and punish: The birth of the prison.* New York, NY: Pantheon.

Hargreaves, J. (2000). *Heroines of sport: The politics of difference and identity.* London: Routledge.

Howe, P. D. (2008). *The cultural politics of the Paralympic movement.* London: Routledge.

Merleau-Ponty, M. (1962). *Phenomenology of perception.* London: Routledge.

Peers, D. (2009). (Dis)empowering Paralympic histories: Absent athletes and disabling discourses. *Disability & Society, 24*(5), 653–665. doi: 10.1080/09687590903011113

Rogers, L. J., & Swadener, B. B. (Eds.). (2001). *Semiotics and dis/ability: Interrogating categories of difference.* Albany: State University of New York Press.

Schantz, O. J., & Gilbert, K. (2001). An ideal misconstrued: Newspaper coverage of the Atlanta Paralympic Games in France and Germany. *Sociology of Sport Journal, 18*(1), 69–94.

Shapiro, J. P. (1994). *No pity: People with disabilities forging a new civil rights movement.* New York, NY: Times Books.

Sheets-Johnstone, M. (2011). *The primacy of movement.* Amsterdam, Netherlands: John Benjamins.

Steadward, R. D., & Peterson, C. J. (1997). *Paralympics*. Edmonton, Alberta, Canada: One Shot Holdings Pub.

REFLECT & WRITE

- ❑ What is Silva and Howe's overarching claim? Write it out in a single sentence. To what extent do they support it through evidence? How persuasive is their argument?
- ❑ Find a spot in the article where Silva and Howe take counterargument into account. Why is this an important rhetorical move for them?
- ❑ At one point, Silva and Howe discuss the negative reaction to the term *freaks* that was used in promoting the 2012 London Paralympics. Do you find that term controversial? What is your assessment of Silva and Howe's use of the term *crip* (i.e., "supercrip") as a centerpiece of their article? To what extent does it have a negative resonance? If you were their editor, would you suggest their finding an alternative term? Why or why not?
- ❑ **Write.** Draft a one-page response to Silva and Howe's essay in which you confirm, refute, or qualify their claims about the "supercrip" stereotype. You can focus on the Paralympics or more broadly on issues of ability and disability.

Thad Mumford *has been involved in the television industry for over 30 years; as a writer and producer, his credits include work on the sitcoms* M.A.S.H., A Different World, *and* Coach. *In this article, first published in May 2004 in* The New York Times, *he invokes the concept of minstrelsy, a form of American entertainment from the nineteenth and early twentieth century characterized by actors painting their faces black with charcoal in order to perform comic skits in "blackface." A form of burlesque, minstrelsy, or black vaudeville often relied on stereotypical racist portrayals of African Americans to depict them as lazy, naïve, superstitious, or clownish.*

The New Minstrel Show: Black Vaudeville with Statistics

Thad Mumford

There has never been a better time to be a black athlete. Moneywise, it is now a sum-of-zeros game. (If only my parents had seen the long-term value of studying Rod Carew's books on hitting instead of math and chemistry.) African-Americans have turned white football and basketball players into tokens. And while our representation in baseball continues its decline, the percentage of blacks who dominate the game continues to surge. The reign of Tiger Woods and the Williams sisters could lead to a time when country club athletic equipment will be on back order in Harlem's sporting goods stores.

Advertisers now line up to have black sports figures push their products, especially to the audience they covet, with near-liturgical zeal, 18- to 25-year-old white suburban males, many of whom are mesmerized by the idiomatic hip-hop jargon, the cock-of-the-walk swagger, the smooth-as-the-law-allows attire of their black heroes.

But there is a downside to all this. The unsayable but unassailable truth is that the clowning, dancing, preening smack-talker is becoming the Rorschach image of the African-American male athlete. It casts a huge shadow over all other images. This persona has the power to sell what no one should buy: the notion that black folks are still cuttin' up for the white man.

Any ethnic group that ever found itself on the periphery of equality and acceptance has had to create coping mechanisms. Some who were victimized by bigotry secretly mimicked the prejudicial perceptions of their oppressor with exaggerated, self-deprecating depictions of their behavior, their very private burlesque that gave them brief respites from their marginalization.

5 For African-Americans, burlesque as healing balm became the essential comedic ingredient of black vaudeville. Comics would strut and cakewalk through now classic routines that savagely lampooned minstrel shows, popular staples of mainstream vaudeville in which white performers in blackface and coily-haired wigs further dehumanized their own creation, the darkie prototype.

Black vaudeville would become a casualty of expanding educational opportunities that created an evolving black middle class with deep concerns that minstrel-like characterizations were degrading and would only perpetuate the accepted attitude that the Negro was the slap-happy court jester for whites.

But a variety of factors, in particular the canonizing of youth culture, the de-emphasizing of wisdom and the glorification of the boorishness inherent in America's look-at-me culture, has played a major role in putting black vaudeville back on the boards. The featured attraction? A number of black athletes.

When we see a wide receiver strut and cakewalk to the end zone, then join teammates in the catalog of celebratory rituals, which now feature props, or hear a cackling, bug-eyed commentator speaking Slanglish ("Give up the props, dog, they be flossin' now!"), we are seeing our private burlesque, out of context, without its knowing wink and satiric spine. Minus these elements, what remains is minstrel template made ubiquitous by Stepin Fetchit and the handful of black actors who worked in the early motion pictures.

But unlike the Stepin Fetchits, left with no alternative but to mortgage their dignity for a paycheck, who often suffered tremendously under the weight of tremendous guilt and shame, some of today's black athletes have unwittingly packaged and sold this nouveau minstrel to Madison Avenue's highest bidders, selling it as our "culturally authentic" behavior, "keepin' it real," as they say.

10 Nothing could be less real or more inauthentic. Or condescending. How can 38 million people possibly have a single view of reality or authenticity? But the athletes who have exhumed the minstrel's grave keep alive these shopworn condescensions.

"The danger of the domination of these one-dimensional images is that they deny the humanity and the intellectuality of an entire people, eliminating the possibility of them being taken seriously," said Dr. Harry Edwards, a professor of sociology at San Jose State who is a consultant to the National Football League.

White adults, whose knowledge of black life is generally limited to what they see in pop culture, take burlesque at face value. This reinforces what was considered culturally authentic, that black people are funny as all get-out.

But the athletes aren't the main culprits. That, of course, would be television, which has brought its two major contributions to American culture, sex and excess, to every sport. TV has erased the line that separated sports from entertainment and created a product that encourages the marketing of black burlesque. Call it athle-tainment.

"We now allow people to take the pride and dignity from our athletes by celebrating them when they play for the camera," said Al Downing, a veteran of 15 major league seasons, now doing public relations for the Los Angeles Dodgers.

15 It can be a dizzying ride. Today's African-American athletes have been handled like porcelain eggs from the moment it became clear that preparing for the next game was of greater significance than preparing for the SAT. Then once they become seven-and eight-figure Hessians, they are walled off from the real world, and all accountability, by management, agents and corporate sponsors, who are all blessed with fertile amounts of unctuousness ("You rule, bro!"). The word no has become a museum piece. As the football Hall of Famer Deacon Jones once said, "There's no school that teaches you how to be a millionaire."

But does this mean that athletes who feel the need to pay homage to every tackle with a dance step, who triumphantly crow in the face of opponents after monster dunks, should be excused for not knowing the line between exuberance and bad sportsmanship?

"I'm more impressed by someone like a Barry Sanders, athletes who do their jobs without having to show up the opposition," said Bill White, whose major league career spanned 13 years.

Issues of cultural identity are complicated, contradictory and complex. One person's ethnic burlesque is another's sense of cultural autonomy. Questions beget more questions. If we keep our burlesque private, are we capitulating to people who feel we should be ashamed of this behavior? Aren't there more appropriate times and places to have fun with our own stereotypes? But does regulating this behavior inadvertently marginalize those African-Americans trapped in burlesquelike worlds? Is there a possible connection between the actions of the white fan who cheers rabidly after sack dances on Sunday, then may be reluctant to grant bank loans for black businesses on Monday?

Those most vulnerable to this confusion are the children, far too many growing up with mangled notions of race, manhood and sports. Black athletes who take our burlesque public could tell them, in the lingua-slanga they share, that there is a difference between having style and actin' the fool. Or that reading and speaking proper English isn't a punk white-boy thing. Or that their chances of playing professional sports are extremely remote. So, if these children do have athletic ability, they should think of using it for one purpose, to get a free education.

20 They'd get their props. Because that's keepin' it real.

REFLECT & WRITE

- ❑ What does Mumford mean when he writes that "the clowning, dancing, preening smack-talker is becoming the Rorschach image of the African-American male athlete"? Do you agree? Why or why not?
- ❑ Who, in Mumford's opinion, should bear partial responsibility for perpetuating the stereotypical image of the African-American athlete? How convincing is his argument? Explain your answer.
- ❑ Toward the end of the article, Mumford questions, "If we keep our burlesque private, are we capitulating to people who feel we should be ashamed of this behavior?" What is your response to this question?
- ❑ **Write.** Thad Mumford begins his article with an appeal to *kairos*: "There has never been a better time to be a black athlete." Considering his article appeared in 2004, do you think that this claim still holds true? What stereotypes of the African-American athlete circulate now in the second decade of the twenty-first century? Do we still see examples of "ethnic burlesque" in sports? Write a response to Mumford's article in which you update his argument, taking into account specific athletes from a variety of sports in the news today and the way in which the media represents them.

In 2012, ESPN surveyed 82 pro athletes, including members of the NBA, WNBA, NFL, NHL, MLB, and MMA, about their perceptions of race issues in sports. The following selections are from the anonymous survey responses. The results were originally published in the December 28, 2012, issue of ESPN The Magazine.

From "Black Athlete Confidential"

Who are the three most important African-American athletes ever?

Totals (Please note that because this question asked for three responses, the totals add up to more than 100 percent):

1. **Jackie Robinson:** 74 percent
2. **Muhammad Ali:** 60.5 percent
3. **Michael Jordan:** 48.1 percent
4. **Magic Johnson:** 16 percent
5. **Jesse Owens:** 14.8 percent
6. **Arthur Ashe:** 13.6 percent
7. **Wilma Rudolph, Tiger Woods:** 7.4 percent
8. **Jim Brown:** 6.2 percent
9. **Tommie Smith:**
   4.9 percent

Female Olympian: "Jackie Robinson, because in a sport that, at the time, was not played by African-Americans at the major league level, he broke through. At a time when there was segregation and black people were looking for a presence to be known as people, he was a way through athletics. He became a voice for this. He was a voice for America, which was just starting to unite. He was a gateway for African-Americans to get into sports and becoming public figures."

NBA player: "Muhammad Ali stood up for everything he believed in. He was a confident African-American athlete at a time when it was hard to be confident. Imagine if we had a draft today, and a guy like LeBron refused to go to war. Ali persevered through that. Incredible."

NBA player: "I'd say Jackie Robinson, Muhammad Ali and Michael Jordan. I'm sure MJ will be picked a lot, but I always think about how he was such an innovator. He took the barriers that Jackie Robinson, Ali, Arthur Ashe, etc. broke through and added to it. Before, the idea of a black athlete being a superstar on the court and an endorsement superstar seemed impossible."

WNBA player: "Arthur Ashe. I remember my mom always talking about Arthur Ashe and the impact he had on breaking the color barriers in the world of tennis."

WNBA player: "Without Jackie Robinson, there would be no Cam Newton or Magic Johnson."

MLB player: "Magic Johnson. I define important by how many people you've helped. Magic Johnson has helped a lot of people."

Olympic athlete: "Michael Jordan. He's probably the first athlete that people didn't even think about what color his skin was."

MMA fighter: "If I had to pick one, it would be Ali, hands down. He was the most influential athlete in sports history. No one stood for more."

Female Olympian: "Michael Jordan. During the London Olympic games, there was a documentary on the Dream Team. Originally in the interviews, he said he wasn't interested in being on the Dream Team. He thought it was a fake political statement and too much drama. Then he started talking to other players and saw this was more than just being an NBA star playing on the Olympic team. It was representing your nation and being a voice for the American people and competing on the world stage. Then you look at how he created another gateway door opening for African-Americans in sports through sponsorship deals. He really, really allowed sports to evolve in this area."

What is the image of the black athlete?

Totals:

Very positive: 8.8 percent

Somewhat positive: 42.5 percent

Neither positive nor negative: 25 percent

Somewhat negative: 17.5 percent

Extremely negative: 6.2 percent

Female Olympian: "C. I have to go in the middle. Somewhat positive, because the African-American youth look up to African-American athletes. A lot of African-American athletes in the limelight right now come from nothing to something. They're really trying to be proactive in the community and show through their story that you can make something of yourself if you're determined enough. But I also think there is a negative connotation that all we have is sports because we're not educated, and all we have is natural talent, and all we want is to make the money and not do anything to get there. So I think there is a little bit of back and forth between positive and negative."

NFL player: "Extremely negative. Everybody thinks that we spend all our money on cars, rims, etc., and that we are outspoken and not really hard workers. None of that is true."

WNBA player: "It's sad. I hate talking about it, really. The image is terrible, and to be honest, I think people and the media in general just look at the negative too much. There are a lot of strong, hard-working black athletes who do great things. But that's lost in the news."

Boxer: "Somewhat negative. Look at Floyd Mayweather. He's one of the best boxers ever. But when he was Pretty Boy, he was not a big name. Now that he's Money Mayweather, with a flashy persona, that's what people get behind. With blacks like him, probably most of white America wants to see him lose."

MMA fighter: "It's D, somewhat negative. But over the last decade, it has gotten better. Our image still suffers with some of the preconceived ideas of selfishness, overextravagance, unfaithfulness."

How does the image of the black athlete compare with reality?

Totals:

Image is the same as reality: 28.8 percent
Image is better than reality: 25 percent
Image is worse than reality: 46.2 percent

Female Olympian: "C, worse than the reality. I think if a black athlete does something that is particularly negative or shocking, the media grabs onto it right away. If it were an athlete from another race, that may not be the case."

NBA player: "C, worse than reality. White people think we're not smart. Not true. I know a lot of smart black athletes like Andre Iguodala, who's one of the smartest guys I know. People expect us just to be athletes. All throughout college and high school, I was a good athlete, and people looked at me as being a dumb athlete, a dumb jock."

NBA player: "B, image is better than reality. For black athletes, a lot of things are publicized and look really glamorous, and they are. It's amazing the things that we're able to accomplish and be blessed with. But there are also things that aren't so glamorous. Our bodies are put on the line—look at football guys who get concussions and it affects them down the line. So it's not as good as what everybody thinks it is."

Boxer: "C. Guys like Floyd Mayweather put on a bad-guy, tough-guy act. He's got bravado, all this money, people look at that and decide they can do without the antics. It's imitation Ali, it's out of control, and that gives us a black eye, it stops us from being loved. The average person can't get down with that."

On a scale of 1 to 10 (1 being absolutely not; 10 being absolutely yes), are black athletes expected to be role models for the black community?

Average answer: 8.7

Female Olympian: "10, absolutely yes. It's an unwritten rule and part of your duty. If you make it out of misfortune and hardships, then it's almost an obligation to be a role model to others who have similar situations."

Male Olympian: "Nine. Coming from a black community, there aren't a lot of people who come out of them and are able to go back and show this is what I learned, that I've been where you've been, and this is what it takes to be successful. It is a responsibility to go and show these African-American kids that their dreams can come true through a lot of work and having a team around you who believes in the same thing you want to believe in, and stay away from a lot of the negativity. Because it's out there."

NFL player: "Seven. You have people that look up to you. Now, do I agree with it? No. Don't think that just because I'm on TV, I'm a role model. I've made so many mistakes in my life, a lot of which you don't even know about. Trust me: I'm no role model. Don't look up to me."

WNBA player: "10. It's a responsibility that comes with being a professional athlete. Kids love athletes, and it's our job to give them someone to look up to outside the home."

Boxer: "Eight. It's important. But at the same time, those athletes who are role models have an obligation to use that to make sure kids know their real role models should be moms, dads, teachers, etc."

MMA fighter: "10. The kids in those communities look up to the wrong type of people—the people who make money now and deal with the consequences later. That was my existence in the inner city. I would be working out, running on the streets, and they had cars, girls, etc. It was hard to do right when you see that other guy living the extravagant lifestyle. For those fortunate enough to have had people help them see through that and get out, it's on us now to be part of the community, to be role models."

Woman Olympian: "10. We do have that obligation. But it's funny, because I bet if you asked star athletes who they most admired and who were their role models growing up, you would get some mentions of Muhammad Ali, Willie Mays, Tommie Smith, Wilma Rudolph. But you'd get more votes for moms and dads and teachers and youth coaches. I want to be a role model for my community, but I also think you got problems if young people are only looking up to athletes. That's not how most of us have achieved what we've achieved."

True or false: TV announcers use terms like "smart" and "cerebral" to describe white athletes more than black athletes.

Totals:

True: 54.4 percent

False: 45.6 percent

NFL player: "True. When you hear them talking about black athletes, you hear 'Oh, the guy is fast, he's athletic. He's got all the natural ability.' Most of the linebackers and white quarterbacks, it's 'He's smart.' But they're just as athletic as the black players, and the black players are just as smart. We all made it to the NFL, but it's just the way they describe them that is different."

NFL player: "True. I'm always hearing 'smart' and 'cerebral,' and here's another one: 'high-motor.' I'm always hearing how white players are high-motor. What does that even mean? What, they play hard? Don't black players play hard? Oh, I forgot, we rely on our talent only. Right?"

WNBA player: "True. White athletes are smart and gutsy. Black athletes are just athletic."

Male Olympian: "True. I've seen it and heard it. Or take Andrew Luck and RG III. They say Luck is smart, consistent, knows the playbook. But RG III is a great athlete, fast, strong and can throw far. People that are African-American are assumed to be naturally gifted as opposed to white players who have to work."

NBA player: "True. Put on an NBA game sometime when there is a good white player on the court and just listen to all the code words that get used. If you hear, 'scrappy,' 'tough' or 'hard-nosed,' look up and the white player probably made a steal. I don't even know what hard-nosed means. I mean, my nose seems pretty hard."

When thinking of the image of black athletes from the past, what three words come to mind?

Totals (most named words, by number of mentions):

Strong: 26

Perseverance: 21

Tough: 15

Pioneers, inspirational:
10 each
Courageous, disciplined, talented: eight each
Resilient: six

Female Olympian: "Resilient. We've come so far, and it's because those athletes were resilient enough to fight for their dreams and keep going despite how many times they were hammered down and told they can't. They said, 'No, I can,' and they pushed through."

NBA player: "Disciplined, because, I mean, if you and me walked through the hallway and people are throwing drinks and stuff at us and cussing us out and punching us and doing whatever they can to hurt us, I think me and you would have a problem with that and would react to it. But those guys went through that every game night in and night out."

MLB player: "I'd say strong. Those athletes went through more in one year than we'll ever have to deal with in our whole athletic careers. It's actually hard to get your mind around, some of the hurdles they overcame."

WNBA player: "Perseverance. You hear and read stuff about black athletes these days, and that's just crap you get on Twitter or on the Internet. Our predecessors had to persevere through that stuff in every game, in every stadium."

REFLECT & WRITE

- ❑ Reflect on the responses to the survey questions. What do they say about the stereotype of black athletes today?
- ❑ In sharing the results of their survey, the authors had to carefully sift through the responses to decide which quotations were worth including in the article. Which quotations seem particularly powerful to you? Why? Which quotations seem less impactful?
- ❑ Consider the canon of arrangement. Why do you think the authors chose to list the comments and questions in this particular order? Select a particular example of a quotation or question and analyze how its placement was rhetorically strategic.
- ❑ Why do you think the survey writers included a question about the relationship of the athlete to the larger community? Why is a question like this important when considering stereotype?
- ❑ Consider a revision of the final question of the series: When thinking of the image of black athletes, what three words come to mind? Answer that question, using tangible examples as evidence to support your claim.

- [ ] **Write.** Conduct your own similar survey, sampling at least 20 sports fans (rather than athletes) and asking the same questions listed in the preceding paragraphs. Compare their responses to the ones given by the professional athletes. Write up a short report in which you evaluate the similarities and differences between their responses, taking into account the difference in demographics (athlete vs. fan) between the original survey respondents and your own.

Called "the best sportswriter in the United States" by veteran sports journalist Robert Lipsyte, **Dave Zirin** *writes about the politics of sports for the* Nation *magazine and the* Los Angeles Times *and is host of Sirius XM Radio's* Edge of Sports Radio. *He was named one of* UTNE Reader's *"50 Visionaries Who Are Changing Your World" and was Press Action's Sportswriter of the Year in both 2005 and 2006. In this article, Zirin addresses the responsibilities that Major League Baseball has toward its Latin American–born players. This piece originally appeared in the November 14, 2005, edition of the* Nation.

Say It Ain't So, Big Leagues

Dave Zirin

In early October 30-year-old Mario Encarnación was found dead in his Taipei, Taiwan, apartment from causes unknown. His lonely death, with the lights on and refrigerator door open, ended a tragic journey that began in the dirt-poor town of Bani in the Dominican Republic and concluded on the other side of the world. In between, Encarnación, or "Super Mario," as he was known on the baseball diamond, was the most highly touted prospect in the Oakland A's organization, considered better than future American League Most Valuable Player Miguel Tejada. Tejada, also from Bani, paid the freight to bring his friend home from Taiwan. It's hard to imagine who else from their barrio could have managed to foot the bill.

Encarnación's death was not even a sidebar in the sports pages of the United States. A 30-year-old playing out his last days in East Asia might as well be invisible.

But he shouldn't be. As Major League Baseball celebrates its annual fall classic, the World Series, it is increasingly dependent on talent born and bred in Latin America. Twenty-six percent of all players in the major leagues now hail from Latin America, including some of the game's most popular stars, like David Ortiz, Pedro Martinez and Sammy Sosa. Leading the way is the tiny nation of the Dominican Republic. Just five years ago there were sixty-six Dominican-born players on baseball's Opening Day rosters. This year, there were more than 100. This means roughly one out of every seven major league players was born in the DR, by far the highest number from any country outside the United States. In addition, 30 percent of players in the US minor leagues hail from this tiny Latin American nation, which shares an island with Haiti and has a population roughly the size of New York City's.

All thirty teams now scout what baseball owners commonly call "the Republic of Baseball," and a number of teams have elaborate multimillion-dollar "baseball academies." The teams trumpet these academies. (One executive said, "We have made Fields of Dreams out of the jungle.") But unmentioned is that for every Tejada there are 100 Encarnacións. And for every Encarnación toiling on the margins of the pro baseball circuit, there are thousands of Dominican players cast aside by a Major League Baseball system that is strip-mining the Dominican Republic for talent. Unmentioned is the overarching relationship Major League Baseball has with the Dominican Republic, harvesting talent on the cheap with no responsibility for who gets left behind. Unmentioned is what Major League Baseball is doing—or is not doing—for a country with 60 percent of its population living below the poverty line. As American sports agent Joe Kehoskie says in *Stealing Home,* a PBS documentary, "Traditionally in the Latin market, I would say players sign for about 5 to 10 cents on the dollar compared to their US counterparts." He also points out that "a lot of times kids just quit school at 10, 11, 12, and play baseball full-time. It's great, it's great for the kids that make it because they become superstars and get millions of dollars in the big leagues. But for ninety-eight kids out of 100, it results in a kid that is 18, 19, with no education."

5 Considering both the poverty rate and the endless trumpeting of rags-to-riches stories of those like Sosa and Tejada, it's no wonder the academies are so attractive to young Dominicans. Most young athletes in the DR play without shoes, using cut-out milk cartons for gloves, rolled-up cloth for balls, and sticks and branches for bats. The academies offer good equipment, nice uniforms and the dream of a better life.

Sacramento Bee sportswriter Marcos Breton's book *Home Is Everything: The Latino Baseball Story* highlights the appeal of the academies: "Teams house their players in dormitories and feed their prospects balanced meals. Often it's the first time these boys will sleep under clean sheets or eat nutritious meals. The firsts don't stop there: Some of these boys encounter a toilet for the first time. Or an indoor shower. They are taught discipline, the importance of being on time, of following instructions."

The competition to get into the "baseball factories," as they are often referred to, is fierce. Sports anthropologist Alan Klein describes, in *Stealing Home*, the scene in front of one of the academies:

Every morning you would drive to the Academy, you would see fifteen, twenty kids out there, not one of them had a uniform, they all had pieces of one uniform or another, poor equipment, they would be right at the gate waiting for the security people to open up the gates and they would go in for their tryout. If they got signed, they were happy. If they didn't get signed, it didn't even deter them for a minute; they would be on the road hitchhiking to the next location. And they would eventually find one of those 20-some clubs that would eventually pick them up. And if not, then they might return to amateur baseball.

Yet even the ones who make it through the academy doors often find themselves little more than supporting players in a system designed to help pro teams ferret out the few potential stars. As Roberto González Echevarría, a Cuban baseball historian who also appears in the documentary, says, "I take a dim view of what the major leagues are doing in the Dominican Republic with these so-called baseball academies, where children are being signed at a very early age and not being cared for. Most of them are providing the context for the stars to emerge; if you take 100 baseball players in those academies, or 100 baseball players anywhere, only one of them will play even an inning in the major leagues. The others are there as a supporting cast."

10 And little is done for those very select few who make it into a major league farm system to protect them from the likely fall to the hard concrete floor of failure.

Brendan Sullivan III, a pitcher who played five seasons for the San Diego Padres, told author Colman McCarthy, "Sure, they were thrilled to have gone from dirt lots to playing in a US stadium before fans and getting paychecks every two weeks. But once a team decides a Dominican won't make it to the big leagues, he is discarded as an unprofitable resource. That's true for US players, but at least they have a high school diploma, and often college, and thus have fallback skills. Most Dominicans don't. They go home to the poverty they came from or try to eke out an existence at menial labor in the States, with nothing left over except tales of their playing days chasing the dream."

Major League Baseball seems unconcerned and uninterested in the situation it has a central role in shaping. Boston Red Sox owner John Henry speaks of the "special relationship Major League Baseball has with the people of the Dominican Republic," but it's unclear whether he believes the Bosox and Major League Baseball have any responsibilities regarding the players they employ and the families left behind.

Al Avila, assistant general manager of the Detroit Tigers, whose father, Ralph, operated the Los Angeles Dodgers' Dominican academy for decades, told ESPN.com, "Baseball is the best way out of poverty for most of these kids and their families. They see on television and read in the newspapers how many of their countrymen have made it. For parents that have kids, they have them playing from early on. The numbers show that the dream is within reach. And even if they don't make it, these Dominican academies house, feed and educate these kids in English. They become acclimated to a new culture, which is always positive. At the very least, even if they don't make it as a player, they could get different doors opened, like becoming a coach."

The question we need to ask is, Does baseball have a broader responsibility to the Dominican Republic and these 10- and 11-year-old kids who think they have a better chance of emerging from desperately poor conditions with a stick and a milk-carton glove than by staying in school? Does the highly profitable Major League Baseball have any responsibility to cushion the crash landing that awaits 99.9 percent of DR kids with big-league dreams, or the 95 percent of players who are good enough to be chosen for the academy but are summarily discarded with nothing but a kick out the door? We can probably surmise where the family and friends of Mario Encarnación fall on this question.

15 The death of "Super Mario" went unnoticed in the US press with one exception, a heart-wrenching column on October 6 in the*Sacramento Bee* by his friend Marcos Breton, who wrote, "Mario wasn't a warped athlete like we've come to expect in most ballplayers. He was big-hearted, fun-loving, a good friend.... The pressure of succeeding and lifting his family out of poverty was a weight that soon stooped Encarnación's massive shoulders."

Should it have been his responsibility alone to shoulder such a burden?

REFLECT & WRITE

- ❑ How does Zirin engage his audience in his topic from the beginning of the essay? Look at both the language he uses and the strategy of development. How might he have started the essay differently? How would that have changed the way that he constructed his argument?
- ❑ How does Zirin use *logos* in his essay? How does he use direct quotation? Where does he bring in these elements and to what effect?
- ❑ If there is a "villain" in this piece, who is it? Find specific passages in the article where Zirin creates this characterization.
- ❑ Look at the structure of Zirin's argument. How does he create a frame? How do his introduction and conclusion work together? What is the effect of that cooperation?
- ❑ **Write.** Take Zirin's argument and transform it into a 2–3 minute oral presentation designed to open up this question of responsibility to a very specific audience: Bud Selig, Commissioner of Baseball. How would you persuade him of the importance of this issue? Consider issues of arrangement, style, example, embodied rhetoric, and multimedia support in planning your presentation. Script your presentation in middle- to high-style.

Seeing Connections
Review strategies for composing effective presentations in Chapter 9.

American sports journalist **Robert Lipsyte** *has written extensively about sports culture, more specifically about the negative impact on children what he calls "Sportsworld"—an approach to sports that prioritizes winning over all else. In this piece, originally published in the August 15, 2011, issue of the* Nation, *Lipsyte dissects the predominantly male jock stereotype and how it influences broader American politics and culture.*

Jocks Vs. Pukes

Robert Lipsyte

In the spring of that hard year, 1968, the Columbia University crew coach, Bill Stowe, explained to me that there were only two kinds of men on campus, perhaps in the world—Jocks and Pukes. He explained that Jocks, such as his rowers, were brave, manly, ambitious, focused, patriotic and goal-driven, while Pukes were woolly, distractible, girlish and handicapped by their lack of certainty that nothing mattered as much as winning. Pukes could be found among "the cruddy weirdo slobs" such as hippies, pot smokers, protesters and, yes, former English majors like me.

I dutifully wrote all this down, although doing so seemed kind of Puke-ish. But Stowe was such an affable *ur*-Jock, 28 years old, funny and articulate, that I found his condescension merely good copy. He'd won an Olympic gold medal, but how could I take him seriously, this former Navy officer who had spent his Vietnam deployment rowing the Saigon River and running an officers' club? Not surprisingly, he didn't last long at Columbia after helping lead police officers through the underground tunnels to roust the Pukes who had occupied buildings during the antiwar and antiracism demonstrations.

As a 30-year-old *New York Times* sports columnist then, I was not handicapped by as much lack of certainty about all things as I am now. It was clear to me then that Bill Stowe was a "dumb jock," which does not mean stupid; it means ignorant, narrow, misguided by the values of Jock Culture, an important and often overlooked strand of American life.

These days, I'm not so sure he wasn't right; the world may well be divided into Jocks and Pukes. Understanding the differences and the commonalities between the two might be one of the keys to understanding, first, the myths of masculinity and power that pervade sports, and then why those myths are inescapable in everyday life. Boys—and more and more girls—who accept Jock Culture values often go on to flourish in a competitive sports environment that requires submission to authority, winning by any means necessary and group cohesion. They tend to grow up to become our political, military and financial leaders. The Pukes—those "others" typically shouldered aside by Jocks in high school hallways and, I imagine, a large percentage of those who are warily reading this special issue of *The Nation*—were often turned off or away from competitive sports (or settled for cross-country). They were also more likely to go on to question authority and seek ways of individual expression.

5 This mental conditioning of the Jocks was possible because of the intrinsic joy of sports. Sports is good. It is the best way to pleasure your body in public. Sports is entertaining, healthful, filled with honest, sustaining sentiment for warm times and the beloved people you shared them with. At its simplest, think of playing catch at the lake with friends.

Jock Culture is a distortion of sports. It can be physically and mentally unhealthy, driving people apart instead of together. It is fueled by greed and desperate competition. At its most grotesque, think killer dodgeball for prize money, the Super Bowl. (The clash between sports and the Jock Culture version is almost ideological, at least metaphorical. Obviously, I am for de-emphasizing early competition and redistributing athletic resources so that everyone, throughout their lives, has access to sports. But then, I am also for world peace.)

Kids are initiated into Jock Culture when youth sports are channeled into the pressurized arenas of elite athletes on travel teams driven by ambitious parents and coaches. A once safe place to learn about bravery, cooperation and respect becomes a cockpit of bullying, violence and the commitment to a win-at-all-costs attitude that can kill a soul. Or a brain. It is in Pee Wee football, for example, that kids learn to "put a hat on him"—to make tackles head first rather than the older, gentler way of wrapping your arms around a ball carrier's legs and dragging him down. Helmet-to-helmet hits start the trauma cycle early. No wonder the current concussion discussion was launched by the discovery of dementia and morbidity among former pro players.

There is no escape from Jock Culture. You may be willing to describe yourself as a Puke, "cut" from the team early to find your true nature as a billionaire geek, Grammy-winning band fag, wonkish pundit, but you've always had to deal with Jock Culture attitudes and codes, and you have probably competed by them. In big business, medicine, the law, people will be labeled winners and losers, and treated like stars or slugs by coachlike authority figures who use shame and intimidation to achieve short-term results. Don't think symphony orchestras, university philosophy departments and liberal magazines don't often use such tactics.

Jock Culture applies the rules of competitive sports to everything. Boys, in particular, are taught to be tough, stoical and aggressive, to play hurt, to hit hard, to take risks to win in every aspect of their lives. To dominate. After 9/11, I wondered why what seemed like a disproportionate number of athletic women and men were killed. From reading their brief *New York Times* memorials, it seemed as though most were former high school and college players, avid weekend recreationists or at least passionate sports fans. When I called executives from companies that had offices in the World Trade Center, I discovered it was no coincidence; stock-trading companies in particular recruited athletes because they came to work even if they were sick, worked well in groups, rebounded quickly from a setback, pushed the envelope to reach the goal and never quit until the job was done. They didn't have to be star jocks, but they did have to have been trained in the codes of Jock Culture—most important, the willingness to subordinate themselves to authority.

10 The drive to feel that sense of belonging that comes with being part of a winning team—as athlete, coach, parent, cheerleader, booster, fan—is a reflection of Jock Culture's grip on the male psyche and on more and more women. Men have traditionally been taught to pursue their jock dreams no matter the physical, emotional or financial cost. Those who realized those dreams have been made rich and famous; at the least, they were waved right through many of the tollbooths of ordinary life. Being treated like a celebrity at 12, freed from normal boundaries, excused from taking out the garbage and from treating siblings, friends, girls responsibly, is no preparation for a fully realized life. No wonder there are so many abusive athletes, emotionally stunted ex-athletes and resentful onlookers.

At a critical time when masculinity is being redefined, or at least re-examined seriously, this sports system has become more economically, culturally and emotionally important than ever. More at service to the empire. More dangerous to the common good.

Games have become our main form of mass entertainment (including made-for-TV contests using sports models). Winners of those games become our examples of permissible behavior, even when that includes cheating, sexual crimes or dog torturing. And how does that lead us to the cheating, the lying, the amorality in our lives outside the white lines? It's not hard to connect the moral dots from the field house to the White House.

The recent emergence of girls as competitors of boys has also raised the ante. Boys have traditionally been manipulated by coaches, drill sergeants and sales managers by the fear of being labeled a girl ("sissy" and "faggot" have less to do with homophobia than misogyny). Despite the many ways males can identify themselves as "real men" in our culture—size, sexuality, power, money, fame—nothing seems as indelible as the mark made in childhood when the good bodies are separated from the bad bodies, the team from the spectators. The designated athletes are rewarded with love, attention and perks. The leftovers struggle with their resentments and their search for identity.

Of course, the final score is not always a sure thing. There are sensitive linebackers and CEOs, domineering shrinks and violinists. Who won in the contest between the Facebook Puke Mark Zuckerberg and his fiercest competitors, the Olympic rowing Jocks Tyler and Cameron Winklevoss?

15 "I don't follow that stuff these days," says Bill Stowe, now living in Lake Placid, New York, after retiring as crew coach and fundraiser for the Coast Guard Academy, a far more comfortable fit than Columbia. "And I have to tell you, I don't remember separating the world into Jocks and Pukes, although it sounds good. I liked good brains in my boats, as long as they were willing to concentrate and pay the price."

Stowe, at 71, is still a conservative Republican. But he doesn't like to talk politics. "It's time to give up the torch," he says. "People are still living in ignorance, but I'm not running it up the flagpole anymore. Life's too short to fight." He surprises me when we talk sports. "The big-league thing, that's a circus. I don't understand how anyone could look up to those guys. But the real issue is with the kids. Did you read where they're building a $60 million football stadium for a high school in Texas? Just for the Jocks. Have you got any idea how much good you could do, even just in athletics, for all the other kids with that much money?"

I dutifully write all this down, which doesn't at all seem Puke-ish now. We're on the same page, the coach and I. There's hope.

REFLECT & WRITE

- ☐ Lipsyte uses the terms *jocks* and *pukes* to define the opposing stereotypes of the athlete and non-athlete. Do you see similar stereotypes in your own experience? Considering those terms derived from 1960s culture, what more current stereotypes characterize the way we understand contemporary athletes?
- ☐ Several times in his essay, Lipsyte connects jock culture with male identity. How does gender factor into stereotypes of athleticism in your experience?
- ☐ What purpose do the stories of Coach Howe serve at the beginning and the end of the piece? Why include Howe? Why didn't Lipsyte simply define his terms from the beginning on his own?
- ☐ According to Lipsyte, why does understanding the tension between "jocks" vs. "pukes" matter? What is the "So What?" of his piece?
- ☐ **Write**. Write a paragraph in which you define a current stereotype in sports culture. Be sure to pay close attention to style, sentence flow, word choice, and tone. Give concrete examples to help your reader understand this stereotype. If possible, try to complicate the stereotype that you describe; avoid creating a two dimensional portrait, instead giving your readers a more nuanced understanding of this cultural construct. Include one or more images to support your definition; be sure to cite your image sources.

During the 2009 World Championships, South African Caster Semenya won a gold medal in the women's 800 meter race with a record time of 1.55.45. Shortly afterward, the International Association of Athletics Federations (IAAF) insisted that Semenya go through a process of gender verification to prove that she was, in fact, genetically female, a request that was widely criticized. In 2010, the IAAF cleared her return to international competition. She has since won silver metals in the 2011 World Championships and the 2012 Summer Olympics. Award-winning cartoonist **Jonathan Shapiro** *("Zapiro"), also from South Africa, published the following cartoon in August 2009, at the height of the controversy.*

Jealousy of Caster Semenya

FIGURE 13.6 Zapiro's cartoon about South African runner Caster Semenya appeared in August 2009, during the height of the controversy over her gender.

REFLECT & WRITE

- ❑ What claim is the cartoon making in relation to the controversy over Caster Semenya?
- ❑ How does the cartoon play with the audience's assumptions? Looking quickly at the image, what did you think it was about? How did that change when you looked at it more carefully? Why would Zapiro play with your assumptions in this way?
- ❑ Examine how the eyes are drawn on the different characters in the cartoon. What do you notice? Why might Zapiro have drawn them this way?
- ❑ How does Zapiro portray Semenya herself? Compare her portrayal to news photographs of her that you find online. How might Zapiro have altered his depiction to create a different argument?
- ❑ **Write.** Create a revision of this cartoon (free-hand or using Photoshop) that takes a different stance about Caster Semenya. Focus less on the artistic polish of your cartoon than on the way you will change the different elements of the argument to represent this alternate position.

As a public record of American sporting history, Sports Illustrated *has charted the rise of female athletes on its covers, featuring sports figures from Mary Lou Retton to Candace Parker. Its treatment of these "cover girls" reflects the conflicted attitude toward women in sports, as demonstrated in the following three examples.*

Sports Illustrated Covers

FIGURE 13.7 The Olympic Preview issue of the *Sports Illustrated* from February 8, 2010, featured World Cup alpine ski racer Lindsey Vonn.

FIGURE 13.8 *Sports Illustrated* spotlighted the fans' love-hate relationship with tennis star Serena Williams on the cover of the magazine's July 12, 2010, issue.

REFLECT & WRITE

- ❑ Compare the way the different female athletes are portrayed in each of their cover shots; observe their facial expressions, the staging, the background, and their postures. To what extent does the accompanying text resonate with these choices?

- ❑ If these covers are about female agency—showing strong, dominant women—how do the images show this dominance in different ways?
- ❑ To what extent does an idea of gender or the female athlete influence the design of the cover? How does each one define what it means to be a woman in sports?
- ❑ **Write.** Compose a letter to the editor of *Sports Illustrated* and present your perspective on the covers, suggesting a layout, design, and caption for a cover featuring your favorite female athlete.

Title IX of the 1972 Education Amendments Act states, "No person in the United States shall, on the basis of sex, be excluded from participation in, be denied the benefits of, or be subjected to discrimination under any education program or activity receiving Federal Assistance." When this amendment was passed, the influence of Title IX was felt immediately in athletics programs, where it translated into an impetus to provide girls equal opportunities to participate in school sports. In this article, originally published in the June 22, 2012 issue of Mother Jones, **Maya Dusenbery** *and* **Jaeah Lee** *reflect on the impact of this legislation four decades after its original passage. Dusenbery is a contributor at Feministing.com; Lee is a blogger for* Mother Jones.

The State of Women's Athletics, 40 Years After Title IX

How the landmark gender-equity law has—and hasn't—evened the playing field.

Maya Dusenbery and Jaeah Lee

When Title IX, the landmark legislation that bans sex discrimination in any educational program receiving federal funding, was signed into law by President Richard Nixon 40 years ago this weekend, gender equality in sports wasn't the point. Supporters of the law had no idea this single sentence—slipped without much fanfare into an education bill—would be a game-changer for women's athletics:

"No person in the United States shall, on the basis of sex, be excluded from participation in, be denied the benefits of, or be subjected to discrimination under any educational program or activity receiving Federal financial assistance."

Bernice Sandler, who helped draft the legislation back in 1972, recently told ESPN, "The only thought I gave to sports when the bill was passed was, 'Oh, maybe now when a school

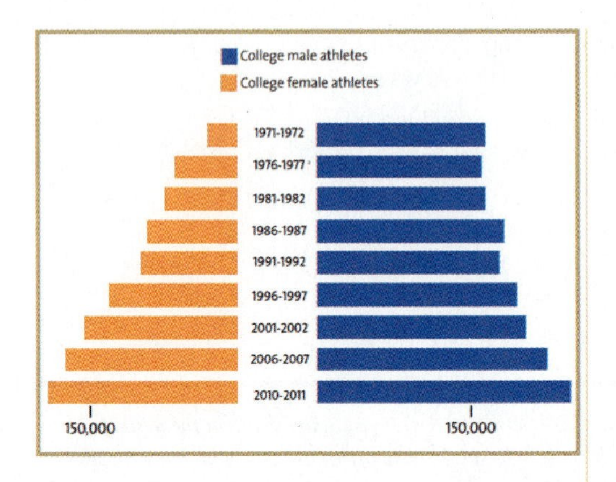

holds its field day, there will be more activities for the girls.' " During the Senate hearings on the bill—aside from one Senator's crack about coed football which drew hearty guffaws—sports weren't mentioned at all.

My, how things change. Forty years later, despite the important impact it's had in other areas, from math and science education to the rights of pregnant students, Title IX is best known for transforming women's athletics. In 1972, just 1 in 27 girls participated in high school sports; today, about two in five do, according to the Women's Sports Foundation. The number of women playing at the college level has skyrocketed by more than 600 percent. (Incidentally, these days coed football teams aren't a joke either.)

5 Yet progress towards gender equity in sports has been uneven and incomplete. Here are five charts showing what's changed—and what hasn't—since Title IX's passage in 1972.

Between 1972 and 2011, the number of girls competing in high school sports jumped from under 295,000 to nearly 3.2 million, according to data from the National Federation of State High School Associations. But girls' opportunities still haven't reached the level that boys were at back when Title IX was passed, and high schools today provide 1.3 million fewer chances for girls to play sports.

There are more women playing collegiate sports—about 200,000—than ever before. The number of female athletes at NCAA schools has increased from less than 30,000 to over 193,000 since 1972, but women still have over 60,000 fewer participation opportunities than their male counterparts.

Women now make up more than half of all college undergraduates, but they still don't get an equal portion of athletic opportunities—and schools spend proportionally less money on them. For example, in 2010 at NCAA Division I schools, women composed almost 53 percent of the aggregate student body but were under 46 percent of the schools' student athletes. Women's teams received just 41.4 percent of the money spent on head coach salaries, just 36.4 percent of the recruiting dollars, and just 39.6 percent of overall athletic expenses—a figure that's remained virtually unchanged for several years. (Most of the spending gaps can be

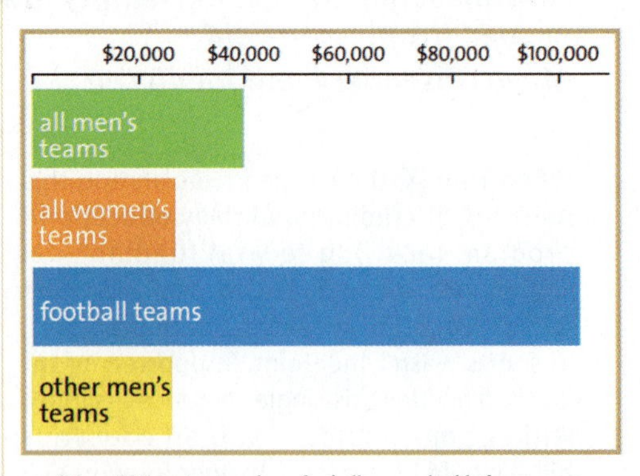

(Note: FBS institutions have football teams eligible for post-season bowl games.)

explained by the schools' money-hogging and revenue-generating men's football programs.)

Median Spending Per Athlete, NCAA Division I FBS Schools

Speaking of coaching, the spike in female athletes hasn't led to a corresponding rise in women coaches—quite the opposite, actually. While women coached more than 90 percent of women's teams in 1972, today that number has dropped to about 43 percent, according to the most recent survey of NCAA schools by Brooklyn College researchers. The percentage of men's teams coached by women has continued to hover around a negligible 3 percent.

10 And despite the fact that millions of women and girls are competing, they're unlikely to see athletic role models of their own gender in the media. A 20-year study of sports coverage by University of California and Purdue researchers shows the short shrift women's sports receives compared to men's on network news and ESPN Sportscenter: In 2009, women's sports got only 1.6 percent of the airtime, down from 6.3 percent in 2004.

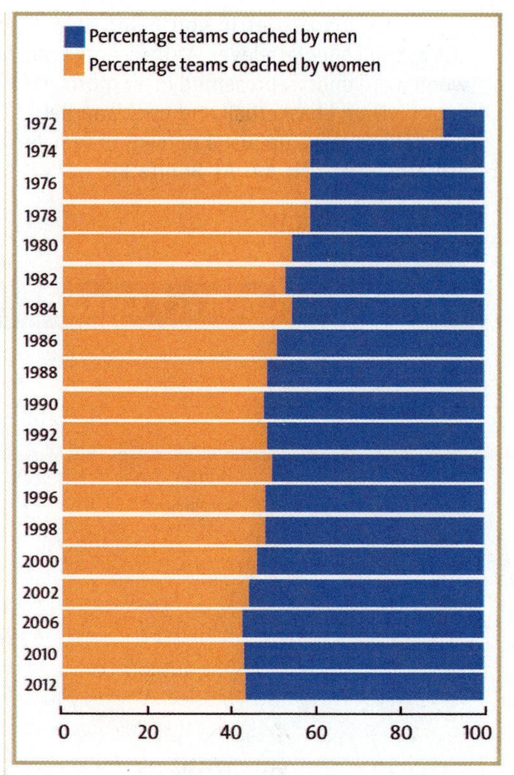

Network Air Time Breakdown for Men's and Women's Sports Teams

Most importantly, Title IX hasn't managed to extend the enormous social and health benefits of sports to all girls equally. In 2008, a national survey of third- through 12th-graders by the Women's Sports Foundation found that 75 percent of white girls play sports, compared to less than two-thirds of African-American and Hispanic girls, and about half of Asian girls. And while boys from immigrant families are well-represented in youth sports, less than half of girls from those families are playing. The gender gap is also worse in urban schools and among kids from low-income families.

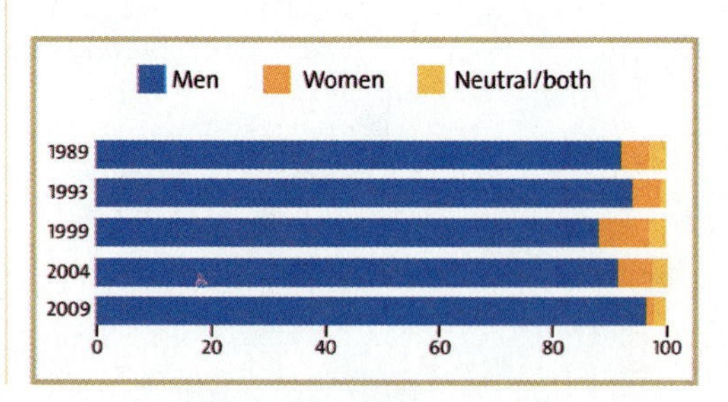

These disparities in youth sports persist at the collegiate level. African-American women are underrepresented in all sports except Division I basketball and track and field, and Latinas make up just 4 percent of female athletes in the NCAA. As Benita Fitzgerald Mosley, an Olympic gold medalist in track and field, recently explained to the *New York Times*, "[I]n the grand scheme of things, Caucasian girls have benefited disproportionately well, especially suburban girls and wealthy Caucasian girls."

REFLECT & WRITE

- ❑ What strategy do the authors use in their introduction to set up their argument? How might they have hooked their reader differently?
- ❑ What level of decorum do the authors use? High style? Middle style? Plain style? Circle or highlight key passages, words or sections that help define the article's style. To what extent does the choice of style suit the argument?
- ❑ At the end of the article, Dusenbery and Lee complicate their argument by factoring in issues of race. What is the effect of leaving it to the end in this way? How would the argument have differed had they started the piece with the discussion of race?
- ❑ The authors conclude their piece with a quote from gold medalist, Benita Mosley. Why do you think they chose to end in this way? How effective was this closing quotation in providing a conclusion for their argument?
- ❑ **Write.** Dusenbery and Lee's article appeared in a section of *Mother Jones* called "Charts," and it derives much of its power from the information graphics that are distributed throughout its argument. Using this article as the starting point for your own argument, create a multimedia presentation that using *pathos* or *ethos* rather than *logos* as the primary appeal to make a similar point about the way Title IX has (or hasn't) leveled the playing field for female athletes in the last 40 years.

Produced by the **Media Education Foundation**, *a nonprofit organization specializing in providing educational resources designed to encourage media literacy,* Playing Unfair *(2003) is a short film designed to provide analysis of the role of gender in sports 30 years after Title IX legislation mandated equal privileges for female athletes. The film integrates short clips from media footage with commentary by three prominent media scholars: Mary Jo Kane from the University of Minnesota, Pat Griffin from the University of Massachusetts, and Michael Messner from the University of Southern California.*

Transcript: Playing Unfair

The Media Education Foundation

Introduction—The Best of Times and The Worst of Times

[News voice-over] *Is the American public ready to embrace professional women's teams and the image of a tough, physical, female athlete?*

5 MARY JO KANE: As we enter a new century, we are in what I call the Best of Times and the Worst of Times with respect to media representations of female athletes. There has been both widespread acceptance and movement of women in sport that was unheard of thirty years ago, and at the same time there's been an increasing backlash about their success and their presence.

MICHAEL MESSNER: I think not too long ago, it was very easy to equate athleticism, strength, physical power, with men, and by contrast to think about women as weak, as supportive for men, purely as sexual objects. Now that landscape has changed somewhat with the tremendous growth of girls, and women's sports.

[Sports commentator] *There's Rebecca Lobo with a jumper!*

MICHAEL MESSNER: Everybody has the opportunity to see strong, powerful, physically competent, competitive women and I think that really challenges that simple gender dichotomy that we used to take so much for granted.

PAT GRIFFIN: Sport is not just a trivial activity for fun. It has real, deep cultural meaning in this society. And I think that to challenge that meaning in terms of what it means to be a man in this culture, by inviting women in and acknowledging that women are also athletic and muscular and strong, is a real challenge to that cultural norm that we live in.

MARY JO KANE: There is a cultural assumption that I think persists even to this day, that because of the definition of masculinity and sport, part of the birthright of being male in this culture is owning sport. You own sport. As women move into this once exclusive domain of male power and privilege and identity, there's been a tremendous backlash, and a desire to push back, and either to push women out of sport altogether or certainly to contain their power within in and keep them on the margins.

Out of Uniform—The Media Backlash Against Female Athletes

MICHAEL MESSNER: If you just watch the sports news, and you just watched ESPN, and if you just picked up *Sports Illustrated Magazine* for your main print source of information about what's going on in the sports world, it would be easy to continue to conclude that there is no women's sports happening.

MARY JO KANE: Women are significantly underrepresented with respect to amount of coverage, even though women represent 40% of participants nationwide in terms of sport and physical activity. What all the studies indicate is they represent about 3–5% of all the coverage. So we give viewers a very false impression if you just rely on the media, that women simply aren't participating in sports in the numbers that they are.

MICHAEL MESSNER: Over the course of a decade that we were doing research on the coverage of women's and men's sports, our dominant finding was how much the coverage of women's sports had not changed. About 5% of the airtime was given to women's sports. In our most recent study, ten years later that had gone up to about 8%, which is still miniscule. I mean it's really a tiny increase in over a ten year period in coverage of women.

[NBC News] *They are very excited. The NBA playoffs have arrived and while the Knicks are dominating…*

MICHAEL MESSNER: You set the tone and make a statement about what's most important and what the key happenings of the day were with your lead story.

[NBC News] *a big night coming up in sports as the Islanders...*

10 MICHAEL MESSNER: What we found is almost always the lead stories were about men's sports. They put a lot more production value into the men's coverage. There's tape, there's graphics, there's interviews and so forth.

[ESPN promo] *June heats up on ESPN.*

MICHAEL MESSNER: When women do kind of peak into the frame, though, it's usually in ways that are mostly dismissive or disrespectful.

[ABC News Channel 7] *Finally, a hearty erin go braugh to my countrymen and women out there, and in your honor we have a little Erin Go Bra-less.*

MICHAEL MESSNER: In our study, one of the longest stories that was done on the sports news for instance was on a female nude bungee jumper on St. Patrick's Day who had painted her body green and jumped off of a bridge and they did a very long story on this—on the sports—meanwhile ignoring all the sports women had been playing that day: a major golf tournament and so forth.

[ABC News Channel 7]
— That's wonderful; do we have to slow that down?
— That was amazing, I'll remember it forever.
— ... And so will we.

MICHAEL MESSNER: Well we all know that news isn't totally objective, but it's supposed to be a picture of what happened today in the world.

MARY JO KANE: What we know in terms of the data is that women athletes are significantly more likely than male athletes to be portrayed off the court, out of uniform, and in these hyper feminized roles. The thing that we infrequently see is images of women athletes as athletes. I think we need to talk about why that is and who benefits from *not* seeing women athletes as athletes.

15 PAT GRIFFIN: Who's controlling the images that we see in the media, and I think particularly if you look at sports media, by and large, the decisions about what images are portrayed, what images are used, who gets coverage, are still made by men. They're part of a culture that sees women in a particular

way. And so I think they prefer to see women athletes portrayed in a more feminine way, it's more comfortable.

MICHAEL MESSNER: When television does cover women's sports, they're most likely going to cover women's tennis, and during certain seasons and certainly during the Olympics, women's figure skating. There's a traditional equation of femininity with tennis and figure skating that makes some sports commentators more comfortable with covering them—they fit more in their own ideological frame about what women are supposed to look like and how they're supposed to act. There's still a tendency, we found, in the play-by-play coverage of tennis to call women athletes more often by their first names, as though there's some sort of familiarity that the commentator has with them.

[Tennis commentator] ... *to counter Jennifer's return.*
[Tennis commentator] ... *you just never know which Amelie's going to show up.*
[Tennis commentator] ... *Monica, trying to hang on, but Serena's serve...*

MICHAEL MESSNER: And to call men athletes by their last name or by their last and first name.

[Tennis commentator] ... *and Ruzesky takes the game...*
[Tennis commentator] ... *Agassi, through to the semis, and coming off his French Open win.*

MICHAEL MESSNER: People who work in an office, the boss will call the secretary by her—or his, if it's a male secretary—first name, and the referent the other way is always "Mr." or "Mrs." or some title.

PAT GRIFFIN: I think what's going on is we still have a lot of cultural anxiety about strong women and what that means about them as women. And until we can sort of move much further, as a culture in opening up the boundaries for what we consider to be OK for girls and women in sport, we're always going to have that ambivalence there.

20 MARY JO KANE: As we went into the women's World Cup soccer, nobody knew who Brandi Chastain was. We knew who Mia Hamm was, but we didn't know who Brandi Chastain was. We know who she is now.
[Newscaster] World Cup hero Brandi Chastain, throws the first pitch—tank top, no sports bra.
[ABC News Channel 7] And uh, Brandi did keep her shirt on, but did take a sweater off, during warm-ups.

[ABC News Channel 7] It was announced Nike will exploit Brandi Chastain's strip tease by attaching her to a line of sports bras.

MARY JO KANE: It immediately got turned into "Brandi Chastain took her shirt off," rather than "what fabulous athletes these women are!"

MICHAEL MESSNER: How many times did we see images of Jenny Thompson actually swimming in *Sports Illustrated*? But when she posed for *Sports Illustrated* in that way, we saw her and now we know who she is.

MARY JO KANE: What got taken up in the press and the public discourse wasn't who Jenny Thompson was and what she'd accomplished as a great swimmer, an Olympic swimmer, but what did it mean to have Jenny Thompson take her shirt off?

[Montage of images of female athletes and non-athlete models]

MARY JO KANE: And the images that you see of women being physically powerful and strong and contrast that to the images of women athletes as little sex kittens, it's an enormous difference. And it is such a powerful contrast that I would argue that is exactly why those images are suppressed. Because sport is all about physical, emotional, and mental empowerment. And so what do you do with all these women who are becoming great athletes and learning the lessons of empowerment and self respect and pride that you get from participating in sport? How are you going to keep that force at bay? And one way that you do that is to do a very time honored and tested mechanism of keeping women's power at bay and that is to sexualize them, trivialize them, and marginalize them.

There are more and more images of women athletes that bear alarming resemblances to soft pornography. What you see is an emphasis, not on their athleticism and their athletic achievements, or their mental courage and toughness, but on their sexuality, their femininity, and their heterosexuality. So what better way to reinforce all of the social stereotypes about femininity and masculinity than to pick up *Sports Illustrated* or *Rolling Stone* or *Maxim* or *Gear* and see an image of a female athlete, not as strong and powerful but as somebody that you can sexualize and feel power over. I don't think that there's a more overt example of that these days than in the world of professional tennis in the image of Anna Kournikova. She has the most corporate sponsorship of any professional female athlete and it is not because of her athletic competence because she is as of this date, still has never won any singles tournament, let alone a Major.

25 PAT GRIFFIN: What it says to me is that an athlete's sexual appeal quotient is much more important than her athletic ability quotient and her athletic accomplishment quotient. And it's very difficult to imagine the same kind of thing happening in men's tennis—a player who has never won a major tournament getting the kind of attention—media attention and endorsement in terms of money that Anna Kournikova gets. And I think that as long as that's possible, it really gives us a pretty good gauge of what are the important things in women's sports.

MICHAEL MESSNER: One of the new things over the last several years is there definitely is more media sexualization of men and men athletes in particular. Men are being viewed as sexy, mostly because of what they do. Of course they have to look good, but they're viewed as sexy primarily for what they're doing on the court or on the field, how good an athlete they are, how powerful they are, how they move when they play. Women are being viewed as sexy not for what they're doing on the court or for what they're doing on the field, but for how they look and what they wear off the field and how they pose off the field, and that's the key difference.

[ESPN: World's Sexiest Athlete] *The world's sexiest athlete? Anna Kournikova, hands down. Have you seen the billboard of it? That explains enough.*

Kournikova: *All athletes are entertainers. As long as people like what they're seeing, they're going to keep coming back, so I think that's good.*

Playing Along—Empowerment or Exploitation?

MARY JO KANE: It's not just how the media portray women athletes. It's how they are promoted and how they portray themselves. They simply feed into and keep the engine going of the way in which the media portray women athletes.

[Entertainment Tonight!: Brandi Chastain interview] *It was something that I'm glad I did and if it got attention for soccer, then good.*

MICHAEL MESSNER: Those are paradoxical images that both suggest empowerment for women and suggest that this media is still trying to frame women in conventionally sexualized ways. And I think that plays into very easily the idea that I, as an individual, need to feel empowered or do feel empowered by taking off my clothes and posing and getting myself into a major national magazine and maybe getting some endorsements.

PAT GRIFFIN: There are other women that I've talked to—young women—who see this in a real different way. They don't really see that as compromising or an expression of concern about how people see them. They just see that as—"that's just my individual way of expressing myself." And I think that certainly could be true for a certain number of them. But what I always want to say to them is it's important to look at the larger picture of pressures, that it's not just about individual choice. That if you look at how women athletes portray themselves, and how they're portrayed in the media, it's a part of a much larger cultural expectation. Is this the kind of image that we want young girls who are interested in sport to aspire to? Do we want them to think that in order to be respected as an athlete, they have to strip?

30 MARY JO KANE: And a very common retort is "what's wrong with being portrayed as feminine?" and "we want to be portrayed as well-rounded" and "there's nothing wrong with showing off our bodies. We're *proud* of our bodies." And on the surface, I think that all of those are very legitimate arguments. The problem that I have is that for women to show that they have strong and powerful bodies, it does not require them to take their clothes off. The way that those images get taken off is basically in terms of locker room titillation. It has absolutely nothing to do with men sitting around, saying, "Boy, I really respect them as fabulous athletes." It's about consuming their bodies for men's sexual pleasure. So that in no way empowers them or is done as an empowering image.

MICHAEL MESSNER: I don't think you'd have near the amount of controversy or debate if a woman occasionally decides to pose half-clothed in front of a camera for *Sports Illustrated* or something. But it's the dearth of coverage of women and the dearth of respectful coverage of women's athletics in those major media that makes those images stand out so much and be so controversial.

The Glass Closet—Homophobia in Sport and Sports Media

MARY JO KANE: Homophobia is in the bone marrow of women's athletics, you simply cannot get around it.

[ABC News] *Billie Jean King, the undisputed Queen of Tennis. Last Friday, facing what is certainly the most serious crisis of her career, thirty-seven year* *old Billie Jean admitted she had had a homosexual affair with her former secretary Marilyn Barnett.*

***[NBC News]** Billie Jean King's contract to make television ads for ER Squibb Company is not being renewed. The* New York Daily News *quotes a company official as saying she was too strong a personality, that she was overpowering the product. He denied that the company's decision had anything to do with Mrs. King's disclosure of a lesbian relationship. The* News *says Avon Products is reviewing its connection with Mrs. King cautiously.*

35 MARY JO KANE: I think it's pretty clear that if you're a female athlete and you want corporate sponsorship, you'd better project a wholesome image. And part of that wholesomeness is the assumption that you are not lesbian, that you are heterosexual. So you'll have a disproportionate number of images of women athletes with children, with boyfriends, with husbands, to clearly mark themselves as heterosexual.

PAT GRIFFIN: Sometimes I refer to that as sort of the protective camouflage of feminine drag that women athletes and coaches feel sort of compelled to monitor in themselves and in others. Certainly it's this need to reassure people—I'm an athlete, I may be a great athlete, but don't worry, I'm still a normal woman.

MARY JO KANE: The acronym for the professional golf tour is the LPGA, as in the Ladies Professional Golf Association and I think it has been widely known or feared for many years that the "L" stands for "lesbian." The LPGA and the women who've played in the Tour have taken great pains to distance themselves from that lesbian image and to again, very overtly and explicitly identify themselves as heterosexual.

***[TV ad]** Hey Laura Baugh, UltraBrite toothpaste would like to proposition you.*

***Laura:** Right here? On national television?*

MARY JO KANE: Jan Stephenson who was a well-known professional golfer was part of an LPGA calendar—"we're professional golfers by day but we're really sexy gals by night." A disproportionate amount of the coverage given to Nancy Lopez who's one of the greatest golfers ever on the Tour was about her marriage to Ray Knight who's a professional baseball player with the Mets, and her role as a mother. There were lots of pictures of Laura Baugh when she was pregnant and playing on the Tour. The LPGA rarely gets any media coverage and yet there was a lot of media coverage around "is she going to be able to get through the round and the tournament and not go into labor?" The media or the corporate sponsors or the women athletes themselves specifically identify themselves with the role of wife and mother, which clearly marks them as heterosexual.

[ABC News] *For Chris Evert this will be her nineteenth and last US Open.*

MARY JO KANE: In the late 1980s, one of the greatest professional tennis players this country has ever produced, Chris Evert, announced her retirement. *Sports Illustrated* chose to put her on the cover: "Now I'm going to be a full time wife." They chose to portray her as somebody who was giving up her career to become a full-time wife. On the inside, with the profile, they had a pictorial chronology of Evert's "career" in sport. This isn't in "Bride Magazine" or in "Heterosexual Magazine"—it's in *Sports Illustrated,* talking about her retirement as being a professional tennis player, and yet the focus, certainly in terms of the visual images you were given, was of Chris Evert as a heterosexual wife and mother.

PAT GRIFFIN: The more we focus on women athletes as heterosexual and sexy and feminine, the more lesbians in sport become invisible. It's difficult enough in many cases to be a lesbian in sport, but to be held up against that standard that is not about me—that sense of being made to feel as if I must be invisible for the sake of women's sports, for the sake of not creating controversy—it's a huge pressure, and it keeps us from really dealing with some of the key issues in women's sports which have to do with heterosexism and homophobia.

[ABC News] *It has added to the torment she has long suffered, from the public acknowledgement of her homosexuality.*

Martina: *It's much easier being heterosexual, believe me. It's much easier pretending.*

PAT GRIFFIN: There are heterosexual women in sport who are very much threatened by the idea that someone might think that they're a lesbian, or would call them a lesbian. And lesbians in sport are very much concerned—and rightly so—about being discriminated against, if they're identified in sport. And you put that together and it really drives a wedge between women in sport. And that wedge serves a larger social function of keeping women from forming alliances to really further women's sport as a whole.

[Tennis commentator] … *I mean she came out and openly declared her sexuality and in team sports of course that would be suicidal—I don't mean that literally, but I mean it would be a very, very hard thing.*

40 PAT GRIFFIN: I think it's amazing to me that in the WNBA, there is not one publicly out basketball player. And yet we know that there are many lesbians in basketball as there are in any sport. But none of them have felt personally safe enough, or I think another factor is feeling like the league itself, the women's basketball professional league, is safe enough to withstand the potential media scrutiny of acknowledging that there are lesbian players. You know, the weird thing is everyone knows there are lesbian players. So we have this strange sort of paradox of lesbians feeling that they need to hide, yet everyone knows that they're there—I often call it the "glass closet."

MARY JO KANE: The WNBA is very much aware that a large part of their fan base is lesbian. They're a new league, they are struggling to survive. So they certainly don't want to alienate any section of their fan base, especially one that's so prominent and loyal. On the other hand, they take great pains to market themselves as a family-friendly entertainment venue. And so because of homophobia and cultural stereotypes, we see that there's this contradiction on the one hand wanting to market yourself as family values entertainment, and on the other hand, what do you do with the fact that you have these lesbians in the stands?

MICHAEL MESSNER: There are stars that were put forward to promote the league, were positioned as the "girl next door," like Rebecca Lobo, a mother—Cheryl Swoops, or a fashion model—Lisa Leslie. And in doing that what they did was they pushed certain women forward as representing the league, who could exemplify what they saw as pretty conventional, heterosexual roles for women.

MARY JO KANE: I think the struggle is, how do you show athletic competence, athletic strength, athletic power—beating up and beating down your opponent—in ways that don't trigger cultural stereotypes about women athletes being too butch, being too manly, being too aggressive?

[Basketball Coach Pat Summit] *Get tough! Get tough!*

MARY JO KANE: In order for women athletes to be taken seriously as athletes, they have to be portrayed as competent, which in sports like basketball, by definition means being big, strong, tough, fast, powerful. You can't have one without the other, and yet to equate them means to challenge every stereotype and construction of femininity and masculinity we have in the culture.

Fair Play—Women Athletes in Action

45 PAT GRIFFIN: Masculinity and femininity are not natural things. You know, boys don't pop out of the womb with a football in their arm, and girls don't pop out with a doll. We have to be *taught* very carefully how we're supposed to act to conform to those artificial expectations of masculinity and femininity. And to the extent that sport is very gendered in this culture—it's one of the ways that masculinity and femininity are taught.

MICHAEL MESSNER: One of the things that people haven't really talked about that much though is that having more images of powerful women, respectful coverage of women's sports, is also potentially very good for boys. Boys are growing up in a world where they're going to have women co-workers, women bosses—the foundations for their views of women are being laid during their childhood. If what they're seeing is a sea of imagery that still suggests to them that athleticism is to be equated entirely with men and masculinity and that women are there simply as support objects or as objects of ridicule or as sexual objects, that is helping to shape the images that boys have of women. I don't believe that there's a conspiracy in the media to say "let's not cover women's sports" or "lets make fun of women athletes," but I think that especially sports desks and sports news people have not caught on to the fact yet that the culture has changed.

PAT GRIFFIN: Well, I don't think any social change happens in a nice, smooth sort of step-by-step path, onward and upward. If you look at any social change movement, whether we're talking about the black civil rights movement, the women's movement in general, the gay, lesbian, bisexual, transgender movement—when there are changes, there's always a pushback. And so change sort of happens in that way, and I think that's what we're seeing here.

MARY JO KANE: All I'm asking is, turn the camera on, and let us see what it looks like when women participate in sports. And what we'll see is that they are terrific athletes who are enormously gifted and enormously committed to something that many people in this country love, and that's sport.

REFLECT & WRITE

- ❑ What issues concerning sexuality and the female body are raised by this film transcript?
- ❑ How do the speakers raise concrete points of evidence concerning the media's unfair depiction of women in sports? Discuss the use of names, the framing, the tapes, the particular sports shown, and the focus on clothes and on sexual preference. Which of these media infractions do you think has the greatest consequences? Why?
- ❑ Do you agree with the contention that the media representation of several female athletes verges on "soft porn"? Argue for both sides of this debate.
- ❑ **Write.** Draft a letter to the *Sports Illustrated* from the perspective of Chris Evert, Rebecca Lobo, and Anna Kournikova. How would each woman respond to the arguments made by this film? Quote from passages in the transcript in your letter.

WRITING COLLABORATIVELY

Get into groups of three for this activity. Using at least three different examples of a single type of sports coverage (for instance, three news reports, three newspaper articles, or three articles in a sports-oriented magazine), explore how the amount and tone of coverage of women athletes reveal the relationship between gender stereotype and sports media. Pick two recent and concrete examples to prove your assertions. Present your findings to the class as either a slide-based presentation or a poster presentation.

In this article, Chicago Tribune *reporter* **Shannon Ryan** *discusses the WNBA's 2008 orientation for its new rookies: a makeover. This article first appeared in the May 4, 2008, issue of the* Chicago Tribune.

Banking on Beauty: Trying to Expand Fan Base by Marketing Its Players, the WNBA for the First Time Offers Rookies Lessons in Fashion and Makeup

Shannon Ryan

As a skilled instructor guided them, the WNBA's new class of rookies spent part of their orientation weekend learning how to perfect their arcs.

The trainer demonstrated how to smooth out a stroke, provided an answer to stopping runs and showed them how getting good open looks can seem effortless.

It was not Lisa Leslie or another veteran teaching basketball fundamentals but a cosmetics artist brought in by the league last month to teach the rookies how to arc their eyebrows, apply strokes of blush across their cheekbones and put on no-smudge eyeliner to receive the right attention off the court.

As part of the rookies' orientation into life as professional athletes, the WNBA for the first time offered them hour-long courses on makeup and fashion tips. The courses, at an O'Hare airport hotel, made up about a third of the two-day orientation, which also featured seminars on financial advice, media training and fitness and nutrition.

5 "I think it's very important," said Candace Parker, the Naperville product who was the league's No. 1 draft pick out of Tennessee. "I'm the type who likes to put on basketball shorts and a white T, but I love to dress up and wear makeup. But as time goes on, I think [looks] will be less and less important."

In its 12th season, the WNBA is still working to become a more profitable league with an expanded fan base. The average attendance was 7,742 per game last season. The Sky averaged 3,709 over 17 home games in 2007, compared with the 21,987 fans the Bulls averaged for 41 home games this season.

Marketing players is perhaps more important than ever, and the WNBA realizes that it's still a tough sell.

"It's all contributing to how to be a professional," league President Donna Orender said of the orientation classes. "I do believe there's more focus on a woman's physical appearance. Men are straight out accepted for their athletic ability. That's reality. I think it's true in every aspect of the work force. This is all about a broader-based education."

Physical Education

Female athletes being promoted for or encouraged to enhance their physical attributes is nothing new.

10 Tennis player Anna Kournikova, who never won a professional singles tournament, was the poster woman for marketing her sexuality in lieu of

her athletic credentials. But far more accomplished female athletes are also marketed on the basis of their appearance.

Tennis player Maria Sharapova was the second youngest woman to win Wimbledon in 2004, which prompted Sports Illustrated to put her on its cover wearing a white tennis outfit under the words "Star Power." She appeared in Sports Illustrated again in 2006, this time wearing a variety of string bikinis on a beach for the magazine's swimsuit edition.

Last month, race car driver Danica Patrick became the first woman to win an IndyCar event. She made a name for herself posing in FHM in a red bustier atop a yellow Mustang and by starring in provocative TV commercials for GoDaddy.com. One such GoDaddy commercial was rejected for airing during this year's Super Bowl.

Softball pitcher Jennie Finch, who plays for the Chicago Bandits, set an NCAA record with 60 consecutive victories in college at Arizona and won an Olympic gold medal in 2004. She wore gold again in '05, posing in a metallic bikini for Sports Illustrated.

Even this newspaper, during a five-day series of stories chronicling the origin of the Sky franchise, posed players in gowns with basketballs.

15 Susan Ziegler, a Cleveland State professor of sports psychology, said disparity in wages and media coverage between male and female athletes, along with a battle against perceived negative stereotypes, are factors in marketing female sports figures for their physicality rather than their athletic assets.

The WNBA, she said, seems to be becoming more image-conscious.

"No. 1 is, of course, the need for the image of WNBA players to be seen as real women," Ziegler said. "That comes from the lesbian homophobia that surrounds women in sports in general."

Ziegler has done extensive research on female athletes being sexualized through the media. Even with something as common as applying lipstick, promoting physical appeal can take away from the athletes' legitimacy, she says.

"Once you begin to worry about how the person looks as opposed to how she plays, you've crossed the line into dangerous play," Ziegler said. "We're not really focused on marketing them as athletes but as feminine objects."

The WNBA's New Face

20 Parker, whose appearance is considered as marketable as her basketball skills, could be just the boost the league needs to help its bottom line.

Before the draft, Los Angeles coach Michael Cooper was excited about the prospect of male fans being enticed to watch Sparks games.

"She's already changed the interest in the WNBA," Cooper said. "Hopefully we can get some of those single guys who only watch the NBA to come watch the WNBA."

Whether they are men is hard to say, but more people already are paying attention.

The Sparks sold seven times the number of season tickets in the first week after the draft as they did last season, and individual game ticket sales are up 272 percent.

25 Parker's rookie salary (around $44,000) will be a fraction of what she will make from endorsing Adidas and Gatorade.

Adidas did not release terms of Parker's multiyear contract, but she is the primary female athlete promoting the sports apparel company's products.

"She's unlike any other athlete," said Travis Gonzalez, Adidas' head of global public relations for basketball. "You look at Candace and she's the first female to dunk in a college game, probably the best female player ever. On the other side, she's an attractive girl. She's a beautiful young lady and she has a savvy sense of fashion."

For marketers, that's the complete package.

Fighting for Airtime

A league like the WNBA receives a fraction of the air time and media coverage devoted to a typical men's league, so WNBA athletes have to take advantage of any exposure they're offered.

30 "All of our public impressions are so important because women are covered so much less than men," Sky President Margaret Stender said. "They may not get a second chance. They have to be ready for the opportunity."

The WNBA has extended its contract with ESPN, the first for a women's professional league, through 2016. The new ad campaign aims to reintroduce sports fans to the league while emphasizing the vast improvement in pace and play over the years.

The Sky said Friday that its advertising campaign for the coming season will feature top draft pick Sylvia Fowles dunking while a voice says, "Yeah, we raised our game."

Marj Snyder, chief of programming and planning for the Women's Sports Foundation, says the paucity of media coverage given women athletes results in misplaced priorities.

"The problem is if only 8 percent of the coverage is on women, and the vast majority of the time we're talking about who they're married to, what clothing they're wearing, what kind of parents they are, there's not much room left to say, 'What a great athlete,' " Snyder said.

35 The WNBA works to promote its players as well-rounded role models, Stender said.

Renee Brown, the WNBA's vice president of player personnel, said the league aims to show its players as "mothers, daughters, sisters, nieces and entrepreneurs" and their "womanhood" is important to promote the league.

"You're a woman first," Brown said. "You just happen to play sports. They enjoy dressing up and trying on outfits, where back in the day, everyone just wore sweats.

"Call it what you want. We're just celebrating their womanhood."

'Game Face'

Back at the rookies' orientation, a makeup artist from the Bobbi Brown cosmetic line lectured about "a pop of blush," "brown shimmer shadow" and "twilight no-smudge" eyeliner at the rookie orientation. Parker and her colleagues paid close attention, as if a coach were a drawing up a play.

40 "You don't want to be caught without your game face on," makeup artist Faith Edwards said as she applied foundation to Charde Houston of the Minnesota Lynx.

Other players took part in a fashion show, strutting in Gucci stilettos and fuchsia evening gowns for their fellow players while taking tips from a style editor for OK! magazine.

Alexis Hornbuckle, a rookie guard with the Detroit Shock, said she rarely wears makeup but will start thinking about it more now.

"Appearance is important, whether you're an athlete or not," Hornbuckle said. "Hey, you've got to play the game. That's life."

NBA rookies go through a similar orientation, although their off-court conduct is stressed far more than their wardrobe or physical appearance. League VP Brown attended the fashion and makeup sessions, trying on some beauty products herself, and said the classes were purely "educational."

45 "I find it interesting that a lot of players do not even know how to apply mascara," Brown said. "I think as they get into it, they love it. I don't think we can run from the fact that they're women. They're so much more than basketball players."Ziegler has some advice on how the WNBA should market Parker.

"As a pure athlete," she said. "As the top athlete in the country. Leave it at that."

REFLECT & WRITE

- ❑ How does the essay use deliberate word choice in its opening lines to play with its reader's expectations? What is the effect of misdirecting the reader in this way?
- ❑ Is Ryan critical of the WNBA's marketing strategy? How can you tell? Look at specific examples from the essay for evidence.
- ❑ What is the significance of the multiple examples that Ryan uses in her "Physical Education" section? What do they contribute to her overall argument?
- ❑ How might visual rhetoric be used to complement the written argument? Consider how different types of images would affect the way the readers understood Ryan's points.
- ❑ **Write.** What Renee Brown is quoted as calling "celebrating their womanhood," some feminists might call "objectification." Take on the persona of a feminist sports critic and write a brief response to this article that discusses the WNBA's 2008 marketing strategy in terms of gender politics.

■ *During 2008, the WNBA released its "Expect Great" marketing campaign, designed to promote women's basketball. The spot transcribed here features Seattle Storm point guard Sue Bird offering her perspective on the WNBA experience.*

"Expect Great" Commercial

Sue Bird

[Opens with Sue Bird running down the court]

[Cut to Bird speaking]

BIRD: Do I like to win? Yeah.

[Cut to Bird on the court, making a basket]

BIRD: I'll hit that shot with your hand right in my face.

ANNOUNCER: ...it's Sue Bird!...

[Cut to Bird speaking]

BIRD: Lose your man?

[Cut to Bird on the court]

BIRD: . . . And I'll make the pass for an easy basket.

ANNOUNCER: ***[unintelligible excitement]***

[Cut to Bird speaking]

BIRD: Foul me going up? Score the bucket . . .

ANNOUNCER: . . . That's aggressive Sue Bird!

BIRD: . . . and one.

[Cut to Bird on the court]

BIRD: And, yes, that was me flying past you on the break.

[Cut to Bird speaking]

BIRD: Do I like to win? [shaking head with a small smile]

[Cut to Bird on the court after a successful play]

[Cut to Bird speaking]

BIRD: Expect great.

FIGURE 13.9 A close-up of Sue Bird from the WNBA "Expect Great" commercial series.

FIGURE 13.10 This frame from the "Expect Great" commercial shows Sue Bird in action on the court.

REFLECT & WRITE

- ❑ How does the commercial use a combination of imagery, sound, and spoken word to build on Sue Bird's *ethos* as a WNBA player?
- ❑ Consider the composition of this commercial in relation to the canon of *arrangement*. How would a different arrangement of these elements have affected the power of this ad?

- ❑ What other ways might you design a commercial to advertise an organization such as the WNBA? What rhetorical appeals would you feature in that commercial? How would you feature them? Why do you think that the marketing team decided on the particular approach it took with the Sue Bird commercial?
- ❑ **Write.** Several "Expect Great" ads featured a very different rhetorical approach: they featured WNBA superstars (such as Candace Parker), ventriloquizing typical comments made by critics of women's basketball ("I'm sorry, but you couldn't pay me to watch women's basketball"; "What kind of future does that league have?" "None that I can see."). Many viewers did not catch the sarcasm involved and considered the campaign to be a failure. List your own critiques of women's basketball, and use them as the basis for a new script for a Sue Bird ad. How would you integrate that text with the "Expect Great" footage to produce an ad promoting the WNBA?

ANALYZING PERSPECTIVES ON THE ISSUE

1. Consider the portrayal of athletes of different races—for instance, Kevin Garnett, Kobe Bryant, LeBron James, Serena Williams, Jeremy Lin, Tiger Woods, David Ortiz, Albert Puljols, or Robert Griffin III. How does each portrayal support or dismantle racial stereotypes? Gender stereotypes?
2. Read through the different points of view represented in "Black Athlete Confidential." Write an essay in which you make a claim about the culture of the black athletes, synthesizing the diverse points of view represented in the survey. Be sure to include direct quotes from the survey, using strategies from Chapter 6 to help you with integrating source material.
3. Compare the portrayal of Lindsey Vonn and Serena Williams on the *Sports Illustrated* covers with the way women athletes are featured in the *Playing Unfair* transcript. Write an essay in which you use these diverse representations as evidence for discussing the stereotypes and challenges facing women and girls in sports coverage today.

FROM READING TO RESEARCH ASSIGNMENTS

1. Visit *Sports Illustrated's* cover archive online, and look at the covers from a few years. Consider different ways that one particular type of athlete has been represented. Write an essay in which you analyze the stereotypes of femininity, masculinity, heterosexuality, ethnic identity, and/or race at work in these covers. Center your argument on how far the media has—or hasn't—come in its representations of athletes.

2. Choose an advertisement or series of advertisements for an athletic product, team, or event. Drawing on the readings in this chapter on the role of media in sports stereotype, develop a claim about how these ads construct or rely upon a specific stereotype about sports identity. Perform a rhetorical analysis of the advertisement(s), taking into consideration the readings on how race, gender, and sexual orientation factor into sports stereotype. Use quotations from the articles in this chapter as secondary sources, as relevant, to support your claim. You may also bring in additional primary and secondary source materials by consulting your library. See Chapter 5 for various kinds of research you might consult and Chapter 6 for strategies on incorporating sources in your writing.

3. Both "Black Athlete Confidential" and *Playing Unfair* make claims about how the news media portray athletes in terms of their race. Conduct your own study on media responses. Either identify a particular sports show (such as ESPN's *Sports Center*) and watch three to four episodes or a particular type of sporting event (a set of Sunday afternoon NFL games) and consider whether race plays a factor in the media coverage. Consider word choice in the commentary, the arguments being made, the amount of minutes of coverage, types of players and the types of plays featured, etc. Based on this evidence, write an essay in which you make a claim about race, sports, and media coverage; integrate quotations and evidence from the articles in this chapter as appropriate.

4. Explore the importance of Title IX in the history of women's participation in sports and the consequent representations of gendered athletes. Conduct research on the topic and formulate your perspective into a research argument. You might want to interview coaches as well as athletic women from diverse generations to get a range of viewpoints on this issue. Construct a list of questions based on the issues raised by the film *Playing Unfair*. For added challenge, transform your research report into a script for a film, with your interviewees as the key players in your movie.

CHAPTER 14

Crisis and Resilience

With the ubiquity of news coverage and global media today, we get our understanding of both local and world events from powerful images. From the devastation and radiation fallout after the 2011 tsunami in Japan to the disastrous effects of Hurricane Sandy in 2012, we get a glimpse into the suffering of others through vivid photos, news films, blog posts, and videos from those on the ground.

Consider the photograph in Figure 14.1, taken in the wake of the devastating floods in Boulder County and along Colorado's Front Range. The image captures a spot where the road has completely washed away from the floods.

FIGURE 14.1 In September 2013, raging floodwaters in Colorado washed away roads, cutting off entire towns and communities.

In another context, this might seem to be an environmentalist's photo of how abandoned roads can crumble and the land can return to nature. But what effect do the other photographic elements have in constructing the meaning of the text as one of crisis?

Notice how the double yellow lines just stop, leaving an eerie gap before the creek waters spill out into a cluster of rocks, tree branches, and floating debris. The shred of pink clothing on the left side of the photo is a compositional element that evokes emotion in the viewer and reminds us of the suffering of people who experienced this natural disaster. In these ways, the photo makes a power visual argument about severity of the destruction wreaked by five days of solid rainfall and extensive flooding which destroyed thousands of homes, damaged dams and sewer plans, and forced the evacuation of towns across three counties.

Analyze the written caption accompanying the photograph. How does the phrase "cutting off entire towns and communities" shape our interpretation of the visual text? How do words and image combine to place our emotional sympathy with the people experiencing this crisis? At the same time, consider the possible *motive* of the photographer. How does the rhetorical strategy of depicting the exact spot where the road ends focus our attention on the severity of the damage?

Now compare the photo in Figure 14.1 with the photo in Figure 14.2, which shows two houses crashed into one another and even collapsed into the creek. How does the inclusion of fomer homes serve to humanize this environmental disaster? Observe the details: a family's possessions still visible through a mud-splattered widow, the satellite dish that brought in entertainment now perched precariously on the roof, the overlapping layers of asphalt, sidewalk, creek barrier, and rocks making passage impossible. What is the *pathos* effect of such signs of crisis in this image? How does a photo make an argument that competes with statistics for its power?

And yet, the photo could also be interpreted as an image of resilience. Despite the ravages of nature, two houses did survive somewhat intact. The truck parked in the distance suggests the massive rebuilding that began almost immediately. Even the wet side of the house, which shows that the waters have receded, offers a glimpse of hope. The visual rhetoric of the photograph thus bridges experiences of ruin and recovery, crisis and resilience.

FIGURE 14.2 Two houses, swept from their foundations, collide in the creek in Boulder, CO.

As we see from these examples, photography offers a powerful interpretive lens on our world. By seizing a moment and turning it into a static text, the photographer (or *author*) makes an argument about the lives, experiences, emotions, and reactions of people (his *subjects*) to all kinds of events. How we read and analyze such images as *rhetorical texts* will be the focus of this chapter. In looking at images, captions, and arguments that such texts make, we'll come to a deeper understanding of how invention and selection work with regard to images we see in the media, and how the arrangement of these texts influences our understanding of events both at home and abroad, both occuring right now and recorded in history as merely one version of what happened.

In this way, we'll discover how images literally shape what is possible for us to know about a crisis on a personal, national, or even global scale. But can images also help us develop resiliency and work through difficult events? In this chapter, we'll consider all kinds of events—including flooding and fires, bomb attacks and war. Approaching visual images about these events as *rhetorical texts,* we'll question how the selection of certain photos persuades us to view the event through a particular perspective—not only to understand the destruction that occurred, but also for insight as to how people involved might go about the work of *recovery* from such incidents.

We'll also ask challenging questions about the ethics of representing the suffering of others. What does it mean to freeze identity in time and place, as many images do? On the one hand, photographs of conflict and war can serve as *testimony,* as a form of "witness," to use the words of the famous photographer James Nachtwey. But according to others, such as writer and editor Daniel Okrent, images of people in faraway places struggling through crisis can often result in sensationalism and even exploitation of that suffering in order to sell news. This chapter will engage you in this debate: between considering visual rhetoric as witness or as sensationalism, as representing a series of events and people's road to recovery or as locking history in one single—perhaps inaccurate—instant through publication in print and online.

In addition, we'll consider how the very mechanics of creating visual texts has changed with technological advances and political perspectives on who can "author" a text or create an "authoritative" version of an event through media. Indeed, since the American Civil War, photojournalism has evolved with changing technologies to include color images and film footage, political stances on how much the public can see, and ethical concerns over the consequences of war. We'll trace this process by examining the significance of photos taken by Charles Porter, an onlooker at the Oklahoma City bombing. We'll learn how people snapping cell phone shots in the London Underground can be regarded through Mark Glaser's term as "citizen paparazzi." We'll see how two photos capturing New York City's experience of Hurricane Sandy provide almost opposite perspectives on the event.

Today, just as the line between amateur and professional "author" has shifted with modern technology, the line between "objective reporter" and "expert-by-experience" has slipped too. Analyzing celebrated photos taken in the context of what the military and the media call "embedded journalism"—the practice of assigning photographers to a troop unit during war—we'll ask, with Jim Lehrer and David Leeson, how the position of the photographer shapes the argument. Finally, we'll end the chapter by asking how images can mobilize social change, as demonstrated both by the new trend in photographing abandoned buildings in America and by the example of celebrities such as Lady Gaga who use media campaigns to raise funds for survivors of crises across the world.

REFLECT & WRITE

- ❑ Analyze and compare the rhetorical properties of the photos in Figure 14.1 and 14.2. Consider the cropping, angle, color, and compositional elements for each one. How does each aspect contribute to the argument as a whole?
- ❑ What is the effect of there being no people in the photos? Recall photos from other disasters—or locate some of the Colorado floods online—that do show people caught in the crisis or engaged in rebuilding. How does the human figure change a photo's emotional appeal? Its logical argument? Its impact on your memory as a viewer?
- ❑ **Write.** Conduct historical research by looking at old newspapers from your town or community. How do photographs of past disasters—or even moments of celebration such as paving the main street, opening a church, or holding a fair—shape the story of your town's identity? What can you learn about the struggles and resilience of people from those photographs? Pick the most compelling photos from your town's historical archives and write a short rhetorical analysis essay about them.

Published on September 17, 2013 in Salon.com, *this piece by* **Drea Knufken** *explores America's growing indifference to situations of crisis. As a freelance writer, ghostwriter, and editor, Knufken maintains a blog and has co-authored the book,* The Backroads and Byways of Colorado. *She has written for BOCA Communications, Google, Blogger, and the Website Discover Los Angeles. She lives in Colorado and, since the publication of this piece, has added a list of disaster resources to her blog.*

Help, We're Drowning!: Please Pay Attention to Our Disaster

Drea Knufken

Here in the horrible Colorado flood, people are dead and homes destroyed. But the scary part is everyone's reaction.

As I write this, Colorado's Front Range is in the middle of its worst natural disaster in about 100 years. For people like me, who live here, it is a flood of tragic proportions. To the world, it is just another disaster. When many of my out-of-town friends, family and colleagues reacted to the flood with a torrent of indifference, I realized something. As a society, we've acquired an immunity to crisis. We scan through headlines without understanding how stories impact people, even those we love. Junk news melds with actual emergencies, to the point that we can't gauge danger anymore.

Even in Boulder, at the beginning of the flood, everyone welcomed the deluge. College kids rode their bikes through the knee-deep water that had settled over the bike path. Families trundled into newly formed lakes with their inner tubes. Children splashed with delight in the muddy, opaque water, the same water that would soon become a burial ground.

Night fell, and so did rain, in sheets. Families put their kids to bed; everyone attempted life as usual. Wesley Quinlan and Wiyanna Nelson, a 19-year-old couple, were driving home from a party with two friends. When their car got stuck in the torrent of water that had submerged Linden Street in North Boulder, Quinlan, Nelson and their friend Nathan Jennings climbed out of the car to swim to safety. Jennings and the other friend survived. Quinlan and Nelson drowned, their bodies concealed for hours by the muddy waters of the flood.

5 In nearby Lefthand Canyon, a firefighter was examining the damage when he saw a wall of water approaching. He climbed a nearby tree just before the water hit. Trapped above the rapids, he remained in the branches all night, the first of many captives of the flood.

It was hard to understand the full extent of the flooding that first night, though the evacuation sirens along Boulder Creek offered hints. The next morning, when images showed the mountain towns of Jamestown and Lyons transformed into islands without drinking water or electricity, when it became clear that newly formed rogue rivers were collapsing bridges and uprooting homes by their foundations, we Coloradans finally began to realize that life wasn't going to be the same for a while.

Nobody ever anticipated a FEMA-level disaster. And when it became clear to us that things were bad, the rest of the world still lacked comprehension. Perhaps disasters have become clichéd. In the same breath that we view images of destruction on the news, we text friends and read about Kardashians. We don't see our own vulnerability until we're standing knee-deep in mud in our basements.

In a matter of hours, the dry, sunny town that I call home was transformed into a delta of rubble and debris, a generic Disaster Zone.

I wanted to help, but the rain wouldn't stop. All I could do, all any of us could do was watch and wait, watch and wait.

So far, we've watched and waited for five days. Emergency management officials are saying that nearly 18,000 homes were damaged and about 1,500 destroyed. Eleven thousand, seven hundred people have been evacuated. Six are dead. No, seven. I just read it in the news.

10 Boulder is my backyard, my home. To me, the floods are urgent; they are an emergency. To others, our floods are another face in the crowd of headlines. Today alone, I read in the news that 260,000 people had to evacuate Kyoto due to a typhoon. In Washington's Navy Yard, someone murdered 13 people with a gun. There's the new episode of "Breaking Bad" and the threat of war in Syria. Every headline screams to be first in line. Everything is a crisis. And let's face it, in media language, Colorado is a small mountain state that likes to ski and smoke pot. Decimation here doesn't echo as loudly as it does in New York, Washington, D.C., or Los Angeles.

I wasn't that surprised when only one of my out-of-town friends called to check on me that first morning of the flood. People are busy. They're stoned on headlines and tweets, emails and texts. But on the second and third days of the flood, I still only had two friends contact me. When I sent my immediate family an email stating our Colorado situation in no uncertain terms, they responded with surprise. They knew about the floods, they said. But they didn't realize that I was affected.

I'd like to think that in our networked world, it's easy to comprehend how the things we read about in the news or on social media might be impacting friends and loved ones. It seems, however, that we're so drowned in data that we've become comfortably numb. Even our reactions have become passive, disconnected. Hitting "like" on Facebook or leaving a sympathetic tweet doesn't come close to the human power of a phone call, especially for someone facing the loss of their home, their health, their life. We're too disengaged to connect the dots between disaster and its human impact. And that scares me.

REFLECT & WRITE

- Compare the *pathos* appeal of the title to the calm first line of the piece. What is the effect of this sudden switch? Now trace the emotional response produced by each subsequent paragraph. How does the writer's *style* work as a persuasive tool to make you as a reader identify with her plight, then experience humor, then feel alarm or even outrage?

What is your overall sentiment at the end of reading the piece? What do you learn about using emotion in writing?

- Notice the mention of specific people in the article. How does that writing technique build the writer's *ethos* or credibility? What other elements in the piece also establish her authority as a witness and commentator on the crisis?
- The author makes a strong argument at the end of her first paragraph: "Junk news melds with actual emergencies, to the point that we can't gauge danger anymore." Scholars have termed this state "compassion fatigue." How common is "compassion fatigue" in your life? Bring to mind instances where friends or family have not taken a crisis seriously. What do you think is the writer's larger message about this situation? Locate the sentences as evidence for your answer.
- **Write.** Throughout the article, Knufken points to social media as well as news media as part of the problem. What is her argument about communication in today's networked world? Create a digital position paper in response to her argument. You can write a blog post, draft a series of tweets, or set up a photo album with captions on Facebook. Whatever medium you choose, be sure to quote some of Knufken's lines and then compose your own position as a reply.

Daniel Okrent's *article was published in the* New York Times *in the wake of the media blitz covering the tragic 2004 tsunami in Southeast Asia that claimed over 230,000 lives across fourteen countries. Okrent was the first public editor of the* New York Times, *and he has published several books, including* Last Call: The Rise and Fall of Prohibition. *He's also a baseball fan and the inventor of Rotisserie League Baseball, the best-known form of fantasy baseball.*

The Public Editor: No Picture Tells the Truth—The Best Do Better Than That

Daniel Okrent

Two Mondays ago, the scale of the Indian Ocean catastrophe was just emerging from the incomplete earlier reports (from a *Times* article the day before: a tidal wave had "killed more than 150 people in Sri Lanka"). By the 4:30 Page 1 meeting, picture editors had examined more than 900 images of devastation to find the one that would stretch across five columns and nearly half the depth of Tuesday's front page. Into a

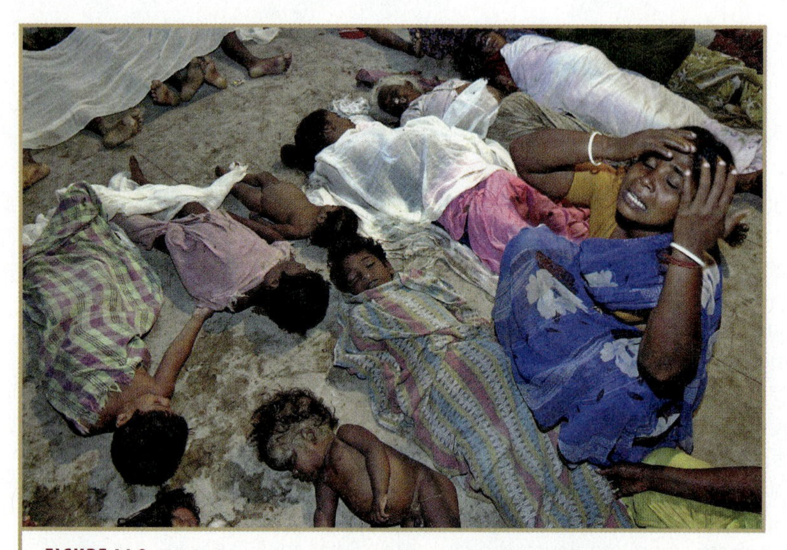

FIGURE 14.3 This shocking photo appeared on the front page of the *Times* on December 28 in the wake of the tsunami and was one of many featured in Okrent's article.

million homes came a grieving mother crouched beside the lifeless bodies of tiny children, and perhaps more horrifying, three pairs of feet extending from beneath a white sheet in an upper corner, suggesting the presence beyond the frame of row upon awful row of the tsunami's pitiless toll.

Many readers and at least a few members of *The Times*'s newsroom staff considered the picture exploitative, unduly graphic, and by its size and placement, inappropriately forced upon the paper's readers. Some felt it disrespectful of both the living and the dead. A few said *The Times* would not have published it had the children been white Americans. Boaz Rabin of Weehawken, N.J., wrote, "Lead with letters the size of eggs, use any words you see fit, but don't put a nightmare on the front page."

I asked managing editor Jill Abramson why she chose this picture. She said in an e-mail message that after careful and difficult consideration, she decided that the photo "seemed to perfectly convey the news: the sheer enormity of the disaster, as we learned one-third of the casualties are children in a part of the world where more than 50 percent of the population is children. It is an indescribably painful photograph, but one that was in all ways commensurate to the event." When I spoke with director of photography Michele McNally, who believes the paper has the obligation "to bear witness" at moments like this, she had a question for me: "Wouldn't you want us to show pictures from Auschwitz if the gates were opened in our time?"

The surpassing power of pictures enables them to become the permanent markers of enormous events. The marines planting the flag at Iwo Jima, the South Vietnamese general shooting his captive at point-blank range, the young John F. Kennedy Jr. saluting his father's passing coffin: each is the universal symbol for a historical moment. You don't need to see them to see them.

5 But in every case, someone needs to choose them. Photo editors (*The Times* employs 40) and their colleagues make hundreds of choices a week. Stories may whisper with nuance and headlines declaim in summary, but pictures seize the microphone, and if they're good, they don't let go. In most cases, a story gets a single picture; major stories may get more, but usually only one on the front page itself—and that becomes the picture that stands for the event.

This won't make every reader happy. From last year's mail:

- "The picture hardly reflects the regular Turkish population."
- "I have never been a particular [fan] of Richard Grasso, but *The Times* should not prejudge his lawsuit by publishing photos that portray him as a monster."
- "I find it appalling and disgusting that you would print an Iraqi holding up the boots of one of our dead soldiers."
- "Why are we shown the pictures of tragically mutilated U.S. civilian contractors but not slain Iraqi children?"

One reader felt that a picture of a smiling Jesse Jackson next to George W. Bush made it appear that Jackson had endorsed the president. Another believed that a photo of a dead Palestinian child in the arms of a policeman looked staged, as if to resemble the Pietà.

Richard Avedon once said: "There is no such thing as inaccuracy in a photograph. All photographs are accurate. None of them is the truth." In this Age of Fungible Pixels, when not every publication, political campaign, or advocacy organization follows the *Times* policy prohibiting manipulation of news photographs, I'm not even sure about the accuracy part. But the untruth—or, at least, imperfect truth—of any single photograph is inescapable. Some readers object to the way a picture is cropped, arguing that evidence changing its meaning has been sliced out of the frame. But meaning is determined long before that. A photographer points the camera here, then turns three inches to the left and snaps again: different picture, maybe a different reality. A photo editor selects from the images the photographer submits (should the subject be smiling? Frowning? Animated? Distracted?). The designer wants it large (major impact) or small (lesser impact). The editor picks it for Page 1 (important) or not (not). By the time a reader sees a picture, it has been repeatedly massaged by judgment. But it's necessarily presented as fact.

Last May, for an article considering whether Brazilian President Luiz Inácio Lula da Silva had a drinking problem, editors selected a seven-month-old file photo showing the president hoisting a beer at an Oktoberfest celebration. It may have been a sensible choice; drinking was the subject, and a picture of the president standing at a lectern would have been dull and disconnected. But any ambiguity in the article was steamrolled by visual evidence that may have been factual (da Silva once had a beer), but perhaps not truthful.

10 Even in the coverage of an event as photographically unpromising as a guy in a suit giving a speech, pictures convey judgment. When George J. Tenet resigned as C.I.A. director in June, a front

page shot showed him looking down, biting his lip, possibly near tears; according to Bruce Mansbridge of Austin, Tex., at other moments during the broadcast of Tenet's speech, "he appeared quite upbeat." When Donald H. Rumsfeld visited Abu Ghraib in May, *The Times* showed him flanked by soldiers, striding through the grounds of the prison, as if (wrote Karen Smullen of Long Island) "Karl Rove must have said, 'What we really need now is a photo of [Rumsfeld] leading soldiers and looking earnest and determined and strong.'" Did Rumsfeld pause at any point and laugh at a joke told by a colleague, or bark at a reporter who asked him a difficult question?

Did any of these pictures tell the whole story, or just a sliver of it?

Mix a subjective process with something as idiosyncratic as taste and you're left with a volatile compound. Add human tragedy and it becomes emotionally explosive. The day *The Times* ran the picture of the dead children, many other papers led with a photograph of a grief-racked man clutching the hand of his dead son. It, too, was a powerful picture, and it's easy to see why so many used it. But it was—this is difficult to say—a portrait of generic tragedy. The devastated man could have been in the deserts of Darfur, or in a house in Mosul, or on a sidewalk in Peoria; he could have been photographed 10 years ago, or 10 years from now. His pain was universal.

But the picture on the front page of *The Times* could only have been photographed now, and only on the devastated shores of the Indian Ocean. My colleague David House of *The Fort Worth Star-Telegram* says, "In this instance, covering life means covering death." The babies in their silent rows were as real, and as specific, as the insane act of nature that murdered them. This picture was the story of the Indian Ocean tsunami of December 2004—not the truth, but a stand-in for the truth that will not leave the thoughts of those who saw it. *The Times* was right to publish it.

REFLECT & WRITE

- ❑ What do you make of the writer's decision to use "I" in this article? How might it be a persuasive and effective tool here? How does relying on his *ethos* help Okrent make his point effectively? What other cited sources also lend authority to his argument?
- ❑ Search online for the images for the many examples Okrent mentions in his argument as standing in for the event.
- ❑ How do the images and Okrent's selection of mail comments on them work together to offer coherence and depth for his thesis? Why might he have arranged them in the order he did?
- ❑ After examining over 900 photos, the editors picked the one shown in Figure 14.3. Some readers felt "it disrespectful of both the living and the dead." Yet Okrent concludes that "covering life means covering death." What is your

position on the ethics of publishing such graphic and emotional photos? What more recent events can you recall that faced similar controversy in the media's choice of specific visual rhetoric?

- ❑ **Write.** Draft your own captions for contemporary examples of ethically troubling photographs that you find for a recent conflict in the world today. Then, compose a letter as if you were the editor of a journal defending their publication on the front page.

■ **Charles Porter** *is a bank clerk and an amateur photographer; he captured the defining images of the Oklahoma City bombing in April 1995, for which he won a Pulitzer Prize. The selection here is a transcription of his account of taking the photographs as told to BBC News, which published the article and images on its website on May 9, 2005.*

Tragedy in Oklahoma

Charles Porter

I am talking about two photographs that I took on 19 April 1995 from the Oklahoma City bombing.

One being of a policeman handing an infant to a fireman and the other of a fireman gently cradling this lifeless infant.

I have these images in front of me here, looking at them now, and there are things that strike me.

One is that the fireman has taken the time to remove his gloves before receiving this infant from the policeman.

5 Anyone who knows anything about firefighters know that their gloves are very rough and abrasive and to remove these is like saying I want to make sure that I am as gentle and as compassionate as I can be with this infant that I don't know is dead or alive.

And the second image is of this fireman just cradling this infant with the utmost compassion and caring.

He is looking down at her with this longing, almost to say with his eyes: "It's going to be OK, if there's anything I can do I want to try to help you."

He doesn't know that she has already passed away.

Spring Morning

And these images are in such contrast with the day.

It was such a beautiful, crisp, bright spring morning. And at 0902 it was just amazing.

Our building shook and I looked out the window and saw this huge brown cloud of dust and debris and papers just flying in the air, and as I ran across towards the debris cloud, I turned this corner at the building and the street was covered with glass.

There were people on the street that were injured and bleeding, and there was a gentleman that was walking towards me who had taken his dress shirt off from the office building that he was in and had it to his head, and blood was dripping from that.

I just took my camera out and instinctively started taking pictures.

I ran to the front of the building and took some images of that, and as I ran back down the side, I noticed this ambulance where these firefighters were working on these people that were wounded and mortally wounded, and I noticed something out of the corner of my eye that was running across my field of vision.

I didn't know what it was, but I trained my camera on it and it was this police officer.

And as this policeman handed this infant to the fireman, I took one frame and then as the fireman is cradling this infant I took the second frame and that is exactly how these images came to be on 19 April 1995.

After I left I got my film developed and called a friend who was the head of photography at a local university.

I called him, and he said: "If you have images that have just happened, you need to go to somebody that wants to see them, like the Associated Press or somebody like that."

I looked the address up in the phone book, I got in my car. I drove over there. I knocked on the door and I went in and said: "Hi, I've got some images of what you're seeing on TV and wanted to know if you would like to look at them?"

Speechless

20 "Chills go over me just to think about the magnitude and the enormity of where that picture went."

Wendel Hudson, who was the AP photo editor at Oklahoma City at the time, picked them out immediately and said: "We'd like to use these." And I thought: "Wow!"

It went out on the AP wire, and not knowing exactly what the AP wire is, I go home and I honestly went home and told my wife: "You know what, I just took some images and they might be in the *Daily Oklahoma* tomorrow."

I go home about 1300. About 1320 I get this phone call from this lady and she says: "Hi, I am so-and-so from the *London Times* and I want to know if you are Charles Porter."

I said: "Yes I am, but how do *you* know who I am?"

25 She said: "Well I just received your image over the AP wire . . ."

And she proceeded to explain to me what the Associated Press wire was.

I said that I didn't know how to respond and she said, "Well sir, can I ask you one question?" And this is where it hit home: "Could I get your reaction and response to what your feelings are going to be, knowing that your image is going to be over every newspaper and every magazine in the entire world tomorrow?"

I was silent and speechless, and chills go over me just to think about the magnitude and the enormity of where that picture went and the impact that picture had at that time. It was beyond my scope of comprehension and understanding, way beyond.

Joe Strupp *is Investigative Reporter and Senior Editor at* Media Matters for America. *Previously, he was Associate Editor at* Editor & Publisher, *where this article appeared one month after the Oklahoma City bombing. Strupp has been an invited media commentator on* The O'Reilly Factor, The Fox Report, *Air America Radio, National Public Radio, Wisconsin Public Radio, Voice of America, and WPIX TV News in New York City. He has won two Jesse H. Neal Business Journalism Awards, the "Pulitzer Prize" of business journalism, and also contributes to* Salon.com.

The Photo Felt Around the World

Joe Strupp

Abstract: Bank clerk Charles H. Porter took a picture of a firefighter cradling a burned infant in his arms right after the Oklahoma City bombing, in OK, in April 1995. The photograph was sold to an AP state photo editor who sent it over the wires. Different newspapers discussed how they should use such an emotionally-charged picture, and, after its publication, many readers called to ask what happened to the baby. Other readers called to protest the picture's publication. However, most newspaper officials believed that it captured the tragedy of the situation in a wordless moment. The baby died the day after the picture was taken.

Seeing Connections
Compare this professional abstract to the student samples in Chapter 8 as you learn to write your own abstract.

It sparked heated debate in several newsrooms, caused one veteran newspaper editor to cry, and, for most photo editors, became the focal front-page shot of the tragic April 19 bombing in Oklahoma City.

"It was the photo that was felt around the world," said Tommy Almon, the baby's grandfather.

President Bill Clinton even mentioned it in a televised address.

Ironically, however, the dramatic photo of firefighter Chris Fields cradling the badly burned body of infant Baylee Almon in his arms—which landed on numerous front pages the next day—was shot by a local amateur, developed at a one-hour photo shop, and nearly missed being distributed by the Associated Press.

5 Charles H. Porter IV, a 25-year-old Oklahoma City bank clerk, shot the picture of Fields holding the child, just moments after the bomb blast occurred.

He then sold the photo to AP state photo editor David Longstreath, who sent it over the wires.

"It was everything that was indicative of the bombing," said Longstreath. "It was one of those rare shots that gives the entire story, but in a way that words cannot."

Once Porter took the picture, and developed it with other bomb-blast photos, he still had nowhere to publish it. He initially took the shot to Dan Smith, a photographer at the University of Central Oklahoma, who knew Longstreath.

Longstreath said Smith called him and sent the photo over to AP to be considered. But, in the chaos that followed the explosion, Longstreath almost ignored the shot.

10 "My initial reaction when he sent it was that I was too busy," said Longstreath. "I looked at the roll he shot and took that frame. He took the rest of the roll and left that afternoon."

The infant, who had turned one-year-old the day before the explosion, was pronounced dead at the scene. The baby also was the subject of another widely distributed photo, which showed the infant being handed from police Sgt. John

Avera to firefighter Fields, just moments before the Porter picture was taken.

Once it reached the AP nationwide photo wire, the shot of Fields holding the young baby became the subject of debate for several major newspapers, and the main front-page photo for many others.

The *Philadelphia Inquirer*, which played the picture on Page One the following day, made it the solo front-page art, except for a small, inside tease photo along the left column.

"That photo showed what happened better than anything I've seen," said Ashley Halsey, the *Inquirer's* national editor. "There wasn't a photo that better captured what happened there, so we decided to use it."

15 Halsey, a 27-year newspaper veteran, said he briefly discussed the decision to play up the shot with fellow editors, but believed the tragic elements were important to the story.

"When you have an event that is this absolutely horrible, you will have this kind of photo," Halsey said. "It was deeply disturbing, but it best captured the tragedy."

Halsey said the photo sparked about a dozen phone calls from concerned readers the next day, including several who opposed its publication. But, he said, most agreed it was proper.

"It touched me very deeply because I have a child that same age," Halsey said. "After we put the paper to bed, I walked out to the parking lot and cried. I have never done that before."

Other editors, such as Morton Saltzman of the Sacramento Bee, chose not to print the photo, deciding it was inappropriate.

20 "We had a rather lengthy discussion about which photo to use on the front page, and we decided not to use it because we believed the baby was dead," said Saltzman, the *Bee*'s assistant managing editor for news. "We viewed it as a picture of a corpse, even though there was no information about the baby's condition. It was the most dramatic photo and very compelling, but we chose to go with a photo of a live child rather than a dead one."

For other newspapers, the decision to use the Porter photo or various others involving bloody victims also included lengthy discussions and compromises.

The *San Francisco Chronicle,* for example, published the firefighter photo, but did not use it as its main art. The *Chronicle* also took the unusual step of printing a short message to readers, warning them of the brutal pictures.

"There was a lot of discussion over that baby and firefighter photo, and everyone agreed that it had to be used because there were so many children who died," said Lance Iverson, the *Chronicle*'s picture editor. "But, at the same time, we didn't want to shock or offend anyone. We just wanted to tell the story and give a visual impression; that is why we ran it."

The response from readers about the baby's condition was so great, the *Chronicle* published a short story the next day explaining how the child had died.

25 "We got close to 100 phone calls asking what happened to the baby, and we had to report it was deceased," said Iverson. "We rarely get phone calls on photos; I can't recall the last time."

At the *New York Daily News,* where the shot of Avera handing the baby to firefighter Fields made Page One, executive editor Debby Krenek said the emotion of the shot made the decision easy.

"We thought it showed the gripping feeling of the situation," said Krenek. "We didn't think it was too harsh; there were a lot of other ones that we used inside that had blood running down shirts and on faces, but this was Page One."

Still, can a newspaper go too far in portraying such a tragic, bloody event as the Oklahoma City bombing? And did the dramatic firefighter/baby photo cross that line?

For Professor Tom Goldstein, dean of graduate journalism studies at the University of California at Berkeley, the answer is no.

30 "Newspapers are supposed to reflect the world, and that's what they did," Goldstein said. "There seems to be absolutely no doubt in my mind that those riveting photos should have been used, no doubt. It's not something that you necessarily want to look at during breakfast, but they are riveting."

REFLECT & WRITE

- ❑ Both Porter's and Strupp's articles cover the same event and raise the ethical question of whether or not to publish a disturbing photo of a baby who later died as a result of the Oklahoma City bombing. What is the argument of each one? How does the first-person testimony by Porter convey a different perspective than Strupp's more journalistic coverage? What rhetorical strategies are at work in each one?
- ❑ Porter's account ends with the offer of publication and Strupp's article takes up the debate among editors and officials about whether to publish. How does each one address a different audience? What is the *kairos* shaping each stance and the argument of each?
- ❑ Compare the styles of the two articles, noting rhetorical appeals, language, and even formality. How do these choices influence you as a reader?
- ❑ **Write.** Strupp's article mentions hundreds of calls and protests. Imagine that you are against the publication of this photo for ethical reasons. Consult a recent Prezi presentation created by three students who take this stance; see http://prezi.com/ddkhyxcmu35p/the-photo-felt-around-the-world/ and then compose a storyboard for your own Prezi presentation in which you include more photos and quotations from callers and writers in protest of the photo. Design your presentation to make your argument clear and sound.

Mark Glaser *is Executive Editor of PBS MediaShift and Idea Lab and an expert on online media. Formerly a freelance journalist, he wrote a weekly column for* Online Journalism Review, *where this article appeared on July 13, 2005, five days after the London bombings. Glaser has also written essays for Harvard's* Nieman Reports *and the* Yale Center for the Study of Globalization, *as well as for the* Los Angeles Times, CNET, HotWired, The New York Times, Conde Nast Traveler, Entertainment Weekly, *and the* San Jose Mercury News. *He was the lead writer for the Industry Standard's award-winning Media Grok daily email newsletter, named a finalist for 2004 Online Journalism Awards, and he won the 2010 Innovation Journalism Award. He received a Bachelor of Journalism from the University of Missouri at Columbia and lives in San Francisco.*

Did London Bombings Turn Citizen Journalists into Citizen Paparazzi?

Mark Glaser

July 7, 2005, was one of the darkest days for London, as terrorists blew up three underground trains and a double-decker bus, killing scores and injuring hundreds. But out of that darkness came an unusual light, the flickering light from survivors such as Adam Stacey and Ellis Leeper as they shot the scene underground using cameraphones and videophones.

Like the tsunami disaster in Southeast Asia, the first reports came from people at the scene who had videocameras. In this case, the cameras were smaller and built into phones. But despite the day being a major breakthrough for citizen media—from Wikipedia's collective entry to group blogs such as Londonist's hour-by-hour rundown—it also brought out the worst in some bystanders.

A London blogger who identifies himself only as Justin and blogs at Pfff.co.uk, told his story of surviving the bombing on the train that exploded near Edgware Road. His harrowing account includes this scene as he finally comes out of the underground tunnel and into the fresh air: "The victims were being triaged at the station entrance by Tube staff and as I could see little more I could do so I got out of the way and left," he wrote. "As I stepped out people with cameraphones vied to try and take pictures of the worst victims. In crisis some people are cruel."

The next day, Justin reflected a bit more on the people outside who were trying to photograph the victims.

5 "These people were passers-by trying to look into the station," Justin wrote. "They had no access, but could have done well to clear the area rather than clog it. The people on the train weren't all trying to take pictures, we were shocked, dirty and helping each other. People were stunned, but okay. The majority of the train was okay as I walked from my carriage (the last intact one) down through the train I saw no injuries or damage to the remaining four or so carriages. Just people dirty

and in shock. The other direction wasn't so pretty, but you don't need an account of this and what I saw, watching TV is enough."

While citizen media efforts became another big story, quickly picked up by the *Los Angeles Times* and *Wall Street Journal,* among many others, Justin was not so quick to exploit his story. In fact, his first impulse was not to watch any news accounts and not to give interviews to media outlets that wanted to glorify his situation.

I left a comment for him on his blog, asking him if he realized that all the people with cameraphones that day were helping to tell the story to the world. Was there a way they could tell that story in a more sensitive way?

"The news does hold a role and it's important for people to understand, comprehend and learn," Justin replied to me in another blog comment. "To ensure they're safe, systems and procedures change, that the world ultimately gets better. I don't even hold contempt really for the cameraphone people, but you must appreciate something else—were those people taking photos helping or were those people shocking the world? I've alluded to seeing [gruesome] things in the tunnel and carriage, but I've not documented them in any detail. I feel it is inappropriate and does not contribute to fact and information."

So far, gruesome images from the attacks haven't been widely distributed online or given a prominent place in Western media. That contrasts sharply with the response in the Spanish media after the Madrid train bombings on March 11, 2004, when bloody photos were on TV and in newspapers, according to a Reuters story.

The Best and Worst in All of Us

10 In fact, online news sources were at the top of their game on July 7 and beyond. The BBC Website experienced its most trafficked day ever on July 7 and was inundated with eyewitness accounts from readers—20,000 emails, 1,000 photos and 20 videos in 24 hours, according to editor and acting head of BBC News Interactive Pete Clifton.

"It certainly did feel like a step-change [on July 7]," Clifton told me via email. "We often get pictures from our readers, but never as many as this, and the quality was very high. And because people were on the scenes, they were obviously better than anything news agencies could offer. A picture of the bus, for example, was the main picture on our front page for much of the day."

The BBC and *Guardian* both had reporters' blogs that were updated as events unfolded, and group blogs such as *BoingBoing* and *Londonist* became instant aggregators of online information.

More surprising was the importance of alternative news sources such as Wikipedia and its useful entry created by volunteer hordes and the inundation of images on Flickr. Even across the pond, MSNBC.com experienced double its usual weekday traffic on July 7, with 10.2 million unique users, and set a record with 4.4 million users of streaming video that day.

Interestingly, both the BBC and MSNBC.com gave particular citizen journalists who survived a bit more room to tell their story on instant diaries set up for the occasion. The diarist on the BBC, a woman who would only identify herself as Rachel (previously just "R"), was not totally thrilled about becoming a media sensation herself.

15 "More journos phoned yesterday," Rachel wrote in one post. "I must have given my mobile to the stringer who was asking questions when I was wandering outside the hospital getting fresh air after being stitched still in shock. The *Mail* on Sunday and Metro wanted to send a photographer round! I said no way. I said I felt it was important to get witness statements out at the time as I was there and felt relatively untraumatized so I'd rather they spoke to me than shoved their mikes and cameras in the faces of those who were shell-shocked or more injured. Having done that I really do not want any more fuss. . . . I was incredibly lucky but I have no desire to become a 'Blast Survivor Girlie' one week on."

That naked impulse to tell a disaster story, glaring kleig lights and all, was once the province of mainstream and tabloid news organizations. But no longer. Now, for better and worse, our fellow citizens stand by, cameraphones in pockets, ready to photograph us in our direst times. Xeni Jardin, a freelance technology journalist and co-editor of *BoingBoing,* was aghast at the behavior of the citizen paparazzi at the scene described by Justin.

"It's like the behavior when you see with a car wreck on the highway," Jardin told me. "People stop and gawk. There's a sense that this is some sort of animal behavior that's not entirely compassionate or responsible. The difference here is that people are gawking with this intermediary device. I'm not sure if the people who did this were saying 'I've got to blog this and get it to the BBC!' But when everyone is carrying around these devices and we get used to this intuitive response of just snapping what we see that's of interest—as surreal and grotesque as that scenario sounds, I imagine we will see a lot more of that."

Jardin compared the behavior to the paparazzi that chased Princess Diana before her fatal car crash and noted that the ethical issues raised then are now applicable beyond just professional photographers.

"These are ethical issues that we once thought only applied to a certain class of people who had adopted the role of news as a profession," Jardin said. "Now that more of us have the ability to capture and disseminate evidence or documentation of history as a matter of course, as a matter of our daily lives—as a casual gesture that takes very little time, no money, not a lot of skill—those ethical issues become considerations for all of us."

Society Under Surveillance

20 Citizen paparazzi is not really a new concept, and the proliferation of cameras has continued unabated since the first point-and-shoot 35mm cameras took off right through cheap digital cameras. But while a few amateur photos might have made it into print magazines in the past, now the Internet is awash in photos and video taken by amateurs. As the term *citizen journalist* becomes part of mainstream thought—spurred on by Big Media outlets and startups—what role do these outlets play in spurring or reining in paparazzi behavior?

Dan Gillmor, founder of citizen media site Bayosphere, wrote in his landmark book *We the Media* about the proliferation of cameras in public spaces. "We are a society of voyeurs and exhibitionists," he wrote. "We can argue whether this is repugnant, but when secrets become far more difficult to keep, something fundamental will have changed. Imagine Rodney King and Abu Ghraib times a million. . . . Everyone who works, or moves around, in a public place should consider whether they like the idea of all their movements being recorded by nosy neighbors."

When I talked to Gillmor about the citizen paparazzi at the London bombing sites, he said he hoped that societies will eventually develop a zone of privacy for people in public places—but realistically didn't think it would happen.

"The line between an obviously important public event like what happened last week and public voyeurism is unclear," Gillmor said. "It's probable that there are pictures from last week floating around that are far too gruesome for any news organization to ever go near it. . . . In the end, we're going to have to develop new cultural norms, and I hope at some level that the more we wipe out the notion of privacy in a public space, the more I hope we end up with a kind of unwritten Golden Rule about privacy in public spaces and give people some space. I doubt it, but I hope people start to think about it."

Counterbalancing that was Gillmor's journalistic instinct, which said that news is news and is fair game for citizen journalists. "In a catastrophe, that's news, and I'm not going to tell people not to take photos of historic events," he said.

25 Jeff Jarvis, outspoken blogger at *Buzzmachine* and former president of Advance.net, trusts that normal folks using cameras will be more polite than paparazzi.

"The more I think about it, the more I do believe that most people will be more polite than paparazzi because they aren't motivated to get the picture no one else has to make a buck," Jarvis said via e-mail. "More reporters is merely more of what we have now. And believing in the value of news and reporting openness I think we need to see this as good. Are citizen journalists rude? Are professional journalists? Same question. Same answer."

Citizen journalism efforts are slowly coming out of beta, though there's room for more maturation in the relationship between contributors and media outlets. Andrew Locke, director of product strategy at MSNBC.com, said that his site made every effort to contact citizen journalists and pulled down contributions that didn't sit right with the editorial team.

"Jeanne Rothermich, who leads our small CJ team, has put a great deal of emphasis on fostering dialogue and partnership with individual citizen reporters," Locke told me. "We not only get more accurate information, but richer, more detailed accounts that we can share with the larger audience."

The advantage of the media sites over unmediated sources such as Flickr is that they can use the wisdom of photo and editorial staff to vet contributions and filter out insensitive or invalid material. But Locke says the next step for citizen media is more than just mentoring contributors.

30 "Over time, we want to turn those passing relationships into lasting bonds [with citizen journalists]," Locke said. "Once you have a real, ongoing relationship, then you can start sharing information and wisdom back and forth. You can develop a code of conduct that means something and can stick. It's not simply about us mentoring citizen journalists like cub reporters, it's about the community itself developing norms and standards of propriety. Yes, we'll always act as a gatekeeper, but

once you're in the gate as a citizen journalist, you should be an empowered member of the storytelling community. We still have a long way to go, but for citizen journalism to grow to its full potential we have to get there."

REFLECT & WRITE

- ❑ What might be Mark Glaser's purpose as a writer in linking this story to the 2004 tsunami in Southeast Asia? How does this strategy broaden the scope of his argument's significance?
- ❑ How do the integrated quotations work to increase the force of this argument? Consider the quotes by London blogger Justin and the email response from BBC News Interactive's Pete Clifton. Why might the writer want to include such different sources? What can you learn about the power of field research as evidence in your writing from these examples?
- ❑ What larger questions of privacy and decency are coming to light with the advent of new technologies? How is our visual world transforming? Answer by building on key passages from Glaser's article. How would you respond to Glaser?
- ❑ **Write.** Glaser raises a key issue about the ethics of everyday people—not just of photojournalists. Do you think there should be an ethical code of conduct for cell phone camera users and citizen journalists so that they don't become citizen paparazzi? Draft what such a code might look like. Use examples of infamous photo-taking during crises such as in December 2012 when a man named Ki-Suck Han was pushed into the New York Subway and photographing observers did not step in to help.

■ *During the height of Hurricane Sandy, which ravaged seven countries in the Carribean and the entire length of the eastern United States in October of 2012, two photos capture distinctly different representations of the crisis and people's response to it.*

Pictures of Hurricane Sandy

FIGURE 14.4 In this moment of crisis, water from Manhattan's East River floods East 20th Street near the FDR Drive just a few hours before the next high tide.

FIGURE 14.5 Deliverymen in NYC still working during the hurricane demonstrate resilience in spite of the havoc wreaked upon New York by Hurricane Sandy.

REFLECT & WRITE

- ❑ How do the compositional elements of Figure 14.4 suggest the surreal nature of the crisis, during which the storm surge flooded streets, subways, and tunnels across Manhattan? What emotional response does the author of the photo seek to produce in the audience?
- ❑ Now compare 14.4 to 14.5, with its caption suggesting the resilience of New Yorkers in the face of "Superstorm Sandy." How does *pathos* operate in this image through the careful selection and arrangement of visual elements?
- ❑ **Write.** Returning to what you learned in Chapter 1 on composing a comparative thesis, generate an argument about images of crisis and resilience that reveals your interpretation of the purpose and power of these photos in combination. If you like, include in your argument a position on climate change and how the photos can serve as evidence for your stance on this issue.

Seeing Connections
Follow the guidelines on crafting a thesis statement in Chapter 1.

WRITING COLLABORATIVELY

Call to mind—or search online and share with the class—other photos that have been taken by "Citizen Journalists" in times of crisis, including the Boston Marathon bombings, the New York subway death of Ki-Suck Han, the crash landing of Asiana Airlines Flight 214 in San Francisco, or events in your own community. What ethical issues are involved in the taking of such photos at the scene of the conflict and in the publication of these images on the Internet? What about images of sexual activity and assaults at parties, such as those circulated via social media from Steubenville, Ohio, or those from Saratoga, California, concerning Audrie Pott, or those from Nova Scotia, Canada, with regard to Rehtaeh Parsons? Together, develop a research-based argument about the ethical implications of such photo-documentation and digital dissemination. What print and visual campaigns might your group create to persuade viewer of your position? What might you write in an op-ed to your local or school paper about these issues?

Photographer **David Leeson** *is well known for his impressive fieldwork and powerful photography. A staff photographer for the* Dallas Morning News *since 1984, Leeson has covered stories in 60 countries across the globe: from homelessness in Texas, to death row inmates across the U.S., the apartheid in South Africa, Colombia's drug wars, and the civil war in Sudan. While on assignment in 2003, he was embedded with the Third Infantry Division in Iraq, a unit that saw a record 23 days of sustained army conflict. Leeson, along with his colleague Cheryl Diaz Meyers, was awarded a Pulitzer Prize for his work in Iraq. He has also won two Robert F. Kennedy Journalism Awards for outstanding coverage of the problems of the disadvantaged, as well as a national Edward R. Murrow award, National Headliners award, and a regional Emmy for his videos and documentaries. The text on these pages represents Leeson's own descriptive captions for the four photos he took in Iraq.*

Photographs and Stories

David Leeson

FIGURE 14.6 David Leeson's photo of a dead man's shoes from Iraq carries the haunting title "Body and Sole."

Body and Sole, Iraq

The shoes on the body of an Iraqi soldier killed as Army troops advanced north to Baghdad tell a story about a poorly equipped army. Almost all of the Iraqi dead—more than eight in this location—were wearing worn-out civilian-style shoes. Young soldiers came to view the bodies. A sergeant reminded them that 'this could 'be one of us' and that, for these war dead, 'their families will never know . . . they will just never come back home.'

FIGURE 14.7 In this photograph by Leeson, a soldier's blank stare shows the ravages of war, yet his steady body shows him carrying on with his duty in the tank.

Blank Stare

There was a tremendous firefight. Three soldiers died. I saw the blank stare of this wounded soldier as he passed by. I have no idea who he is. I never noticed his bandage until he filled the frame with my 200mm lens. It was his eyes I saw that day and remember.

FIGURE 14.8 Leeson's photo of an American military unit arresting an Iraqi civilian appeared on the front page of 43 newspapers. Leeson titled the photo "Search Party."

Search Party

3rd Infantry Division soldiers from Fort Benning, Georgia, disembark from a Bradley Fighting Vehicle to surround a man who was stopped for suspicious activity somewhere in Iraq. An AK-47 automatic rifle and ammunition were found in the man's vehicle in which he traveled with another person.

This was my first "action" photo from Iraq. My video camera was still operational and I had to make a quick decision on which camera to grab first—my still camera or the video camera. I had made a commitment to place still photos above video in every reasonable circumstance so I made the photos as quickly as possible. As soon as I was satisfied that the still image was secured I switched to video and made very similar frames. The video from this scene became part of my documentary about the invasion.

The next day I learned that this image appeared on the front page of 43 newspapers nationwide and a video I had made the day before was aired on World News Tonight. My video camera succumbed to the dust not long after I made these final frames.

FIGURE 14.9 In "Taking the Plunge," Leeson captures a moment when soldiers relax through a swim in an irrigation pond in Iraq.

Taking the Plunge

(L to R) Spc. George Gillette and Spc. Robert Boucher with Task Force 2–69 Armor, 3rd Brigade Combat Team, 3rd Infantry Division from Fort Benning, Georgia, jump into an irrigation pond somewhere in Iraq. I had a goal to shoot at least one good photo each day—if possible. This image, part of the Pulitzer portfolio, was made near sunset on the drive to Baghdad. I had not made a single image all day. I was about to give up the idea that I would see anything worth shooting when I heard that soldiers were headed to some "pond" in the desert. The truth is I was very tired and was almost disappointed that I was going to have to grab my camera and follow. But, duty called and I went. Both of these soldiers stood on the side of the irrigation pond and discussed if they would get in trouble if they jumped.

I kept my mouth shut and watched. I knew if they jumped it would make a great photo but also knew that journalistic integrity meant that I could not enter into their decision-making process on whether to jump or not. Of course, they finally decided it was worth the risk and made the plunge. After making the photo—I jumped too. The water was very cold but after weeks without a bath it was a wonderful respite from the reality of war.

REFLECT & WRITE

- ❑ How does each photographic text—as a visual reading—offer a specific perspective on the battle in Iraq and on war more generally? What rhetorical aspects shape the composition of the text? How does Leeson's position as an embedded journalist make his photos different from those we have studied so far?
- ❑ Look closely at Figure 14.6, "Body and Sole." How might you analyze the various visual elements, including what kind of shoe you see? How do visual signs such as shoes provide readers with *context* about persona, nationality, economic status, and history? What kind of argument would a different set of shoes make on this Iraqi—expensive combat boots, religious slippers, or bare feet? How do the words of the photo's title shape your interpretation of the argument made by the photo?
- ❑ In the text for Figure 14.7, "Blank Stare," Leeson asserts that he "never noticed his bandage until [the soldier] filled the frame with my 200mm lens." How might the camera enable the photographer to see more details in times of war? How is the camera as a tool of photojournalism a vehicle for helping us see? For helping viewers develop compassion?
- ❑ Consider how Leeson's stories operate in conjunction with his images to produce a particular perspective on the war. How do his comments reshape your interpretation of the images? How do the images suggest different meanings without his stories about the images? How does the last image suggest Leeson's construction of a solder's journey from crisis to resilience, or what he calls "a wonderful respite from the reality of war"?
- ❑ **Write.** Analyze all the images from the perspective of a soldier. What is the argument about the reality of war from this angle of vision? What kind of writing would a soldier produce to explain what these photos mean? Write out that perspective in words. Consider locating additional images and creating a photo essay.

■ *Best known for his work on the PBS series, the* NewsHour with Jim Lehrer, **Jim Lehrer** *has dedicated his life to the news, starting as a newspaperman in Dallas then eventually becoming an anchor on a local news show before moving into the national spotlight. CNN's Bernard Shaw has called him the "Dean of Moderators" because of his integral role in moderating more than ten debates by candidates in the last five presidential elections. Lehrer has won many awards for his work, including the 1999 National Humanities Medal. The selection included here is from the NewsHour Extra, a special Web site created to help students understand important cultural and political issues.*

Pros and Cons of Embedded Journalism

NewsHour Extra with Jim Lehrer

A partnership between the military and the media has changed the nature of war journalism.

Journalists are experiencing unprecedented access to the battlefield thanks to a partnership between the military and the media that has embedded journalists within specific military units. The embedded reporters have to follow several agreed upon rules as they live with the soldiers and report on their actions.

New rules in a new arrangement

The new arrangement was formed out of meetings between the heads of news organizations and the Defense Department officials aimed at allowing journalists to report on war with the least possible danger.

Before joining their battalions, the embedded journalists had to sign a contract restricting when and what they can report. The details of military actions can only be described in general terms and journalists agreed not to write at all about possible future missions or about classified weapons and information they might find.

5 In addition, the commander of an embedded journalist's unit can declare a "blackout," meaning the reporter is prohibited from filing stories via satellite connection. The blackouts are called for security reasons, as a satellite communication could tip off a unit's location to enemy forces, the Pentagon explains.

Seeing a slice of the war

At the beginning of the experiment, U.S. Secretary of Defense Donald Rumsfeld called the embedding of journalists "historic," but cautioned that the close-up view is not always complete.

"What we are seeing is not the war in Iraq; what we're seeing are slices of the war in Iraq," he said.

"We're seeing that particularized perspective that that reporter or that commentator or that television camera happens to be able to see at that moment, and it is not what's taking place. What you see is taking place, to be sure, but it is one slice, and it is the totality of that that is what this war is about."

Thus far, editors of many large papers are pleased with the quality of journalism coming from embedded journalists, according to *Editor and Publisher* magazine. Susan Stevenson of *The Atlanta Journal-Constitution* said the embedded reporters give a "sense of immediacy and humanity" that make the stories very real. "From what a blinding sandstorm feels like to reporting how one of our embeds broke his unit's coffee pot, we're giving readers a better sense of the field."

How embedding can distort

10 However there have been instances when the embedded reporters transmitted inaccurate information. On Wednesday, embedded correspondents for several news organizations reported seeing a convoy of up to 120 Iraqi tanks leaving the southern city of Basra, and most news outlets reported a large troop movement.

The next day, a spokesman for the British military said the "massive movement" was really just 14 tanks.

Additionally, some journalism professors have warned that the embedding process can distort war coverage. Syracuse University Professor Robert Thompson warns, "When you are part of the troops that you're going in with, these are your fellow human beings. You are being potentially shot at together, and I think there is a sense that you become part of that group in a way that a journalist doesn't necessarily want to be."

Final results unknown

The results of the embedding experiment will not be known for some time. Bob Steele, from the Poynter Institute, an organization for journalists, says the access "has allowed reporters and photographers to get closer to understanding (the complexities of war), to tell the stories of fear and competence, to tell the stories of skill and confusion. I think that's healthy."

But, Steele cautioned that while "closeness can breed understanding," journalists must remain objective and not write about "we" or "our," but about "they."

15 "There's nothing wrong with having respect in our hearts for the men and women who are fighting this war, or respect for the men and women who are marching in the anti-war protests. The key is to make sure those beliefs don't color reporting," Steele said.

REFLECT & WRITE

- ❑ How do the "new rules" set the contested parameters for a new form of photojournalism in war? That is, while this article might seem straightforward and informative, how does it actually offer a particular argument—the official version—on the proper form of photography for America's military engagements today?

- ❑ Looking closely at how the article uses both subheads and quotations, assess the writing in terms of both arrangement and research depth. Why do you think the author made these particular rhetorical decisions? What is the effect of these choices on you as a reader?
- ❑ For the closing line of this article, the author relies upon a quotation by Bob Steele from the Poynter Institute, in which the ideal of objectivity is advanced: "The key is to make sure those beliefs don't color reporting." How does the quotation use visual discourse? What visual choices might a reporter make in presenting "colored" reporting? What does this mean? And how does the last subtitle question the finality of that closing quotation?
- ❑ **Write.** Draft your own response to the article. Identify the central arguments made by each authority, and then compose two alternative perspectives on each argument. Include images that offer arguments for each of your own written texts, so that the visual and the verbal work in conjunction to convey your point of view for each response.

Born and raised in Detroit, **Mark Binelli** *is a contributing editor at* Men's Journal *and* Rolling Stone. *The author of* Detroit City is the Place to Be: The Afterlife of an American Metropolis *as well as the novel* Sacco and Vanzetti Must Die!, *Binelli now lives in New York City. This excerpt from Binelli's appeared in* The New York Times *magazine on November 9, 2012.*

How Detroit Became the World Capital of Staring at Abandoned Old Buildings

Mark Binelli

For decades, a succession of city officials has struggled mightily to rebrand Detroit's battered image. Their ideas have included casino gambling, an '80s festival mall, new ballparks, hosting a Formula One grand prix, hosting a Super Bowl, even commissioning (this was Mayor Coleman Young, in 1984) Berry Gordy (who fled Detroit for Los Angeles by the early 1970s, taking the entire Motown operation with him) to write a city theme modeled after Frank Sinatra's "Theme from New York, New York." Another member of the Rat Pack, Sammy Davis Jr., was conscripted to handle the vocals, but sadly, Gordy's song, "Hello, Detroit," failed to burn up the charts.

But now much of the attention being showered upon Detroit from the trendiest of quarters comes, in no small measure, thanks to the city's blight. Detroit's brand has become authenticity, a key component of which has to do with the way the city looks. Does fixing the very real problems faced by Detroiters, I began to wonder, mean inevitably robbing Detroit of some part of its essential Detroitness?

This is not exactly a question of gentrification; when your city has 70,000 abandoned buildings, it will not be gentrified anytime soon. Rather, it's one of aesthetics. And in Detroit, you can't talk aesthetics without talking ruin porn, a term that has become increasingly familiar in the city. Detroiters, understandably, can get touchy about the way descriptions and photographs of ruined buildings have become the favorite Midwestern souvenirs of visiting reporters.

Still, for all of the local complaints, outsiders are not alone in their fascination. My friend Phil has staged secret, multicourse gourmet meals, prepared by well-known chefs from local restaurants, in abandoned buildings like the old train station; John and his buddies like to play ice hockey on the frozen floors of decrepit factories. A woman who moved to Detroit from Brooklyn began to take nude photographs of herself in wrecked spaces (thrusting the concept of ruin porn to an even less metaphorical level). And Funky Sour Cream, an arts collective originally from New York, arranged an installation of little cupcake statues in the window of a long-shuttered bakery on Chene Street. A few days later, the bakery burned down. People debated whether or not this was a coincidence.

5 Meditation on ruin is a long and noble tradition. In Renaissance Italy, antiquarians like Leon Battista Alberti and Poggio Bracciolini began to promote the study and preservation of Roman ruins, which, to that point, had been unsystematically pushed aside as the city expanded. According to Alberti's biographer, Anthony Grafton, they also "made fun of those who became too depressed" about the ruins, like poor, oversensitive Cyriac of Ancona, who "seemed to mourn the fall of Rome with excessive emotion."

My grandfather, who traced our family origins back to Florence, insisted we were related to Leon Battista Alberti, also a Florentine and a prototypical Renaissance man: playwright, poet, architect, painter, astronomer, lawyer and prizewinning horseman. And thanks to the efforts of proto-preservationists like cousin Alberti, many later generations of painters and poets continued to meditate on the transitory nature of man's greatest achievements in the shadow of once-majestic edifices like the Baths of Caracalla, built in the early third century by a Roman emperor and pretty much destroyed by the sacking Ostrogoths roughly 300 years later.

Perhaps not incidentally, Michigan Central Station, the best-known Detroit ruin—a towering 18-story Beaux-Arts train station with a lavish waiting room of terrazzo floors and 50-foot ceilings, built in 1913 by the same architectural firms that designed New York's Grand Central—was modeled after the Baths of Caracalla. After the station closed in 1988, a developer talked about turning the building into a casino; the current owner, Manuel Moroun, had discussed with Mayor Kwame Kilpatrick's administration selling the station to the city as part of a plan to turn the place into police headquarters and police museum.

Mostly, though, Moroun has allowed the station to molder. Sitting nearly a mile and a half from the high-rises of downtown, Michigan Central looms like a Gothic castle over its humbler neighbors on Michigan Avenue. It's hard not to think of it as an epic-scale disaster that seems engineered to illustrate man's folly—as if the Titanic, after sinking, had washed ashore and been beached as a warning.

In the Detroit essay in "Yoga for People Who Can't Be Bothered to Do It," Geoff Dyer visits Michigan Central Station and runs into some tourists photographing the place. In a funny exchange prompted by one tourist's remarking on how bustling the train station must have been at the height of Detroit's production, Dyer disagrees, arguing:

> Ruins don't encourage you to dwell on what they were like in their heyday, before they were ruins. The Colosseum in Rome or the amphitheater at Leptis Magna have never been anything but ruins. They're eternal ruins. It's the same here. This building could never have looked more magnificent than it does now, surrounded by its own silence. Ruins don't make you think of the past, they direct you toward the future. The effect is almost prophetic. This is what the future will end up like. This is what the future has always ended up looking like.

10 It's true. While vacationing in Rome, after I had spent about a year back in Detroit, I certainly didn't find myself mentally restoring the Senate or the various temples or filling out the scene with centurions and charioteers. But the past was nonetheless on my mind, the past of Keats and Shelley, when a consumptive poet could wander among these same ruins without the security guards and throngs of German tourists—a time when the ruins were still ruins, but desolate, abandoned, free of all caretakers, not so *horribly crowded*.

But in Detroit, the tours go on, in an unofficial capacity. One afternoon at the ruins of the 3.5-million-square-foot Packard Plant, I ran into a family from Paris. The daughter said she read about the building in Lonely Planet; her father had a camcorder hanging around his neck. Another time, while conducting my own tour for a guest, a group of German college students drove up. When queried as to the appeal of Detroit, one of them gleefully exclaimed, "I came to see the end of the world!"

One evening, in a warehouse and occasional performance space in Eastern Market, I attended a talk on the ruins of Detroit. The speaker was Jim Griffioen, a 30-something white guy with a scruffy beard, dressed casually in jeans and a T-shirt. He writes the thoughtful local blog Sweet Juniper, which centers on his life as a stay-at-home dad in Detroit. Before moving back to Michigan (he grew up in Kalamazoo), he worked as a lawyer in the Bay Area, but he quit his job to write and take care of his children. His wife practices law, and on the blog, he describes his family as "just two more yuppies raising their kids in the most dangerous city in America." Close to 200 guests packed the warehouse.

On Sweet Juniper, Griffioen has posted a number of ruin shots: "feral" houses almost completely overgrown with vegetation; a decommissioned public-school book depository in which trees were growing out of the piles of rotting textbooks. But he apparently possessed a special license to publish such images, because he spent much of his talk denouncing lazy out-of-town journalists who use Detroit's ruins as a convenient recession-year symbol for the end of the American dream. (In fact, Griffioen coined the term "ruin porn," in an interview with *Vice* magazine.)

During the question-and-answer period, a stylishly dressed African-American woman in her 50s stood up to make a contrarian point: that devotees of ruined buildings should be aware of the ways in which the objects of their affection left "retinal scars" on the children of Detroit, contributing to a "significant part of the psychological trauma" inflicted on them on a daily basis. Glancing around the audience—there were four other black people—she went on: "I don't want to insult anybody. But when you talk about how 'we' need to take this city back, I look at this room, and I'm not sure what 'we' you're talking about."

15 After the talk, I introduced myself to the woman, whose name was Marsha Cusic. She grew up in Highland Park, but her father, Joe Von Battle, had been in the music business in Detroit, running a much-loved record shop on Hastings Street. She agreed to take me on a driving tour of the Detroit of her youth.

We met on a Sunday afternoon. Cusic drove us by the rough location of her father's original store, on a long-paved-over stretch of Interstate 75 that runs past Mack Avenue. Later, we passed the intersection of 12th Street and Clairmount, which was the center of the 1967 civic unrest. Cusic's father's second record store was just a few blocks south.

"Everyone likes to point to the riot as the moment everything went wrong in Detroit," Cusic told me. "But you have to understand the idea of a nodal point. It's the same way a teakettle heats up and heats up, and only at the very end does it whistle. It's easy to look at the riot as that nodal point, but really, you're ignoring all of the heat that came before."

We detoured into Highland Park, onto a handful of attractive residential streets lined with immaculate bungalows. This was where Cusic grew up. When her family moved in, she said, the area was almost entirely white, primarily automobile executives. Eventually we ended up in Corktown, the formerly Irish neighborhood adjacent to the old train station, which has become a tiny pocket of gentrification. Cusic pointed out a chicken coop in an urban farmer's backyard. "Chickens in Corktown," she said. "Some of these neighborhoods, they're turning back into what people left behind in the South."

We passed a couple of young white guys with beards standing on a corner, waiting for a light to change. "Some of the people coming here bring a sort of bacchanal spirit—like they're out on the frontier and they can do anything," Cusic said. "Detroit isn't some kind of abstract art project," she continued. "It's real for people. These are real memories. Every one of these houses has a story."

20 We stopped for lunch at a little French bistro. Cusic told me she had a grown son who moved to Los Angeles for work and a sister in Atlanta. Cusic still hadn't visited her sister and had even been reluctant to go out west to see her son. She doesn't fly, and besides, she joked sardonically, if she left she worried she wouldn't want to come back.

REFLECT & WRITE

- ❑ Binelli connects "Detroit's brand" to "the way the city looks" and attributes its tourist allure to "aesthetics". Are people drawn to images of crisis, or devastation? What differentiates Detroit from Rome? Could part of the beauty of ruins be in their survival?
- ❑ Evaluate the author's tone and make an argument about his attitude toward his former city. Use passages to support your interpretation.
- ❑ How do direct quotations function as research evidence supporting or contradicting Binelli's argument?
- ❑ **Write.** Imagine that you are organizing a "ruins of Detroit" tour. Draft the promotional text you would use to attract customers. What tone or images would be most effective?

Matthew Christopher *started photographing abandoned spaces while researching the decline of the state hospital system. He holds an MFA in Fine Art Photography and his work has been featured in gallery shows as well as in* Photographer's Forum, *the* International Journal of Arts and Humanities, *and the* United Nations Chronicle. *The website showcasing his work, abandonedamerica.us, has gained international attention. Christopher also works as a site preservation consultant.*

Abandoned America

FIGURE 14.10 Matthew Christopher's photo of an undisclosed church in a state of "elegant decay" demonstrates a crisis of faith and economics in America.

FIGURE 14.11 Christopher captures a hotel room in ruins, with only the plastic television set resisting the ravages of time and neglect.

REFLECT & WRITE

- ❑ How might Figures 14.10-14.11 function both as documentation of the "crisis" in America—economic and social decay, lowered church attendance, de-institutionalization of mental health patients—and as a tribute to the endurance of such structures?
- ❑ One viewer of Figure 14.10 posted a comment that the piano seems to be making a "last stand trying to defend the church." What argument could you make about the light fixtures in Figure 14.11? the mirror? the TV? Consider *kairos* and make an environmental argument. Consider *doxa* and generate a claim about social values.
- ❑ **Write.** Consider the author's *motive* for: "It is my hope to reach out to those who might originally have seen an abandoned site as an eyesore and encourage them to rethink their estimations and strive to foster civic pride and partnership in these vestiges of bygone eras—thus looking forward to a future where we can build on our past rather than erasing it." Create a publicity campaign, using either Figures 14.10-14.11 or your own choice of images from Christopher's website, to construct an op-ed that argues for the preservation of such spaces.

The "We Pray for Japan" wristband was designed by **Lady Gaga** *to raise funds in support of victims of the March 2011 earthquake, tsunami, and nuclear disaster in Japan. The aid campaign, publicized through Lady Gaga's Twitter account among other venues, raised over $1.5 million dollars.*

Lady Gaga's Visual Philanthropy

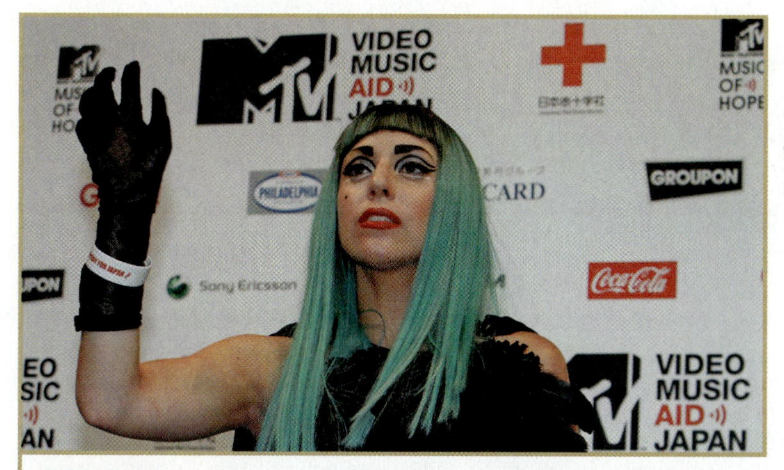

FIGURE 14.12 Lady Gaga poses with a "We pray for Japan" white wristband during a press conference to promote MTV Video Music Aid Japan in Tokyo, after the devastating earthquake and tsunami that hit the country.

REFLECT & WRITE

- ❑ Analyze the rhetorical properties of Figure 14.12. How does Lady Gaga convey her *persona* through the familiar "paw up" and the elaborate elements of her embodied rhetoric? Yet how does she simultaneously build *ethos* for herself as a philanthropist by standing before a wall showcasing visual representations of organizations also raising aid funds?
- ❑ Look up the actual wristband through a Google image search. Examine its composition: the words "Pray for Japan," the image of a storm-tossed tree, the Japanese writing, the choice of colors and font. How is both *pathos* and *doxa* at work? How do the parts work together to create one comprehensive visual argument?

- ❑ **Write**. A 2011 lawsuit charged Lady Gaga with keeping funds for herself; Lady Gaga denied wrongdoing and settled in 2012 by donating $107,500 to charities in Japan. Write a position paper on the benefits and risks of celebrity philanthropy. Does the image of the star support people in crisis and help them finds new paths towards recovery? Or does the power of the star's visual rhetoric divert media coverage from the event itself and compromise recovery efforts? Feel free to consider other celebrities, causes, and crisis situations.

ANALYZING PERSPECTIVES ON THE ISSUE

1. The situations covered in this chapter range from natural disasters—the floods in Colorado, Hurricane Sandy, the tsunami in Southeast Asia, the earthquake and nuclear meltdown in Japan—to acts of military force—the bombings in Oklahoma City and London as well as the Iraq war. In each case, within hours, photographs of the crisis swept like another tidal wave across streaming media, satellite news feeds, and newspapers worldwide. What purpose does such extensive coverage serve? Is visual rhetoric the best method for garnering support for people in crisis?
2. In his article, Daniel Okrent questions what it means to raise awareness about disaster through provocative visuals, and whether we have different standards for particular countries or communities. Drea Knufken points out the problem of media overload and viewer indifference to suffering and tragedy, while Mark Binelli suggests that people actually have a fascination with images of ruin and decay. Given these competing arguments, consider your responses to the articles and images in this chapter. What is your perspective as a contributor to this converstion?
3. Reflecting on the images taken with camera phones after the 2005 London bombings, Mark Glaser raises crucial concerns about privacy and human nature. Keeping his claims in mind, think about how the question of privacy is in fact a key issue in each of the articles in this chapter, even if the writers do not overtly mention it. Pick three articles to revisit in formulating your stance on this issue. Draft your own position paper on privacy in our age of technological innovation and ease of digital publication.
4. While discussing "Search Party," Leeson explores the different kinds of photographs possible with different technological tools—the still shot from a camera and the video. How might a series of photos or a video shape a reader's opinion differently? What is the relationship between the photographer as visual writer of moments in crisis and the visual text as one of many possible drafts? How do the words of the photographers shape our own understanding of these texts as persuasive images? How can you evaluate a photographic text to determine whether it represents crisis or resilience? Consider this question with regard to the abandoned sites of Matthew Christopher's photography as well.

FROM READING TO RESEARCH ASSIGNMENTS

1. Read Professor Paul Lester's book, *Photojournalism: An Ethical Approach* and famous critic Susan Sontag's article, "Regarding the Torture of Others." What arguments are shared between the writers? How might each one contribute to your understanding of the issues involved in photo ethics, both nationally and internationally? Using these sources as a starting point, compose a research-based argument in which you provide your own perspective on these questions. You might format your argument as a feature article modeled after Daniel Okrent's piece. Refer to Chapter 1 for strategies on developing a thesis and to Chapter 3 for guidance on incorporating multiple perspectives.

2. With regard to *embedded journalism*, do photographers remain "objective" reporters or do they somehow become part of the military mission? What happens when photographers stand aside in the face of danger—when they refuse to save a life, pick up a gun, or help those who have been protecting them? Conversely, what happens when photographers do become combatants? Locate the NPR story "War, Live," to consult various viewpoints on this question. Then, using specific quotations from PBS's *NewsHour with Jim Lehrer* as evidence for your argument about how representations of photojournalism in wartime reflect our changing attitudes about viewing—and experiencing—images of crisis, draft out your research argument.

3. Based on your reading of the articles in this chapter, how might you argue that photojournalism has changed over the years through developments in writing and communication technologies? How do new technologies—such as blogs, video footage, multimedia reports, photo essays, email, Twitter, Vine, Instagram, Vimeo, Google glass, and more—transform our understanding of the issues involved in covering events? Conduct research on this topic and compose a photo essay or Prezi to post online. Include a script for a voice-over of your argument to function as a stand-alone multimedia presentation.

4. Research and collect additional images that showcase resilience. Look, for instance, at Lalage Snow's collection "We Are The Not Dead," which features photographs and words of soliders before, during, and after their time served in Afghanistan. How does this multimedia exhibit give returning soldiers a voice and inspire others towards resiliency? Additionally, explore Liora K's photography gallery, "Feminism," where semi-naked bodies with words written on them challenge hateful social norms. How does writing on the body and photographing those posed messages function as both "an artistic response" and a "great catalyst for change"? Draft a storyboard for your own exhibition on "resilience."

CHAPTER 15

Claiming Citizenship

Surveying the social and political landscape today, it is clear that America is a place where many cultures combine and cross over one another. And yet even as we have grown accustomed to this reality, the fact of our ever-increasing diversity remains the subject of ongoing, often intense, debate. In the wake of continued demographic changes, key questions arise. In the face of competing interests, whose needs are recognized, and whose viewpoints are overlooked? What does it mean to "claim citizenship" in this country—but also in a larger global community? Questions such as these carry real power, in part, because they require us to negotiate representations of identity, ideals about belonging, and structures that often decide for us the parameters within which we live. How can we preserve the democratic principles of equality and opportunity, while confronting at the same time the many boundaries—of race and ethnicity, gender and sexuality, class and national origin—that seem to divide us? And how are these boundaries both reflected in and maintained by aspects of visual culture all around us?

FIGURE 15.1 A road sign near the U.S.-Mexico border, entitled "Caution," is caught in this Flickr photo by Penny Green.

To get started thinking about these questions, examine the photo in Figure 15.1, of a sign found on the freeway near San Diego. What do you make of the characters' shapes on the sign? Does the stance and lines of their bodies look like they are running? What might be suggested through the choice of hairstyle on the woman and the girl? How does this highway sign, located just inside the American border, speak to the tension and the trauma surrounding the borderlands of America and Mexico?

Now consider the image in Figure 15.2. How does this image challenge what we might have in our minds about who or what

FIGURE 15.2 A dynamic map reveals the history of immigration through a combination of words and images.

defines "an American"? This map, from the Library of Congress, reveals the shifting history of our country's demographics through visual rhetoric. Examine the words beneath or above the images of people who were all once considered "immigrants," crossing from one culture to another, shaping what we now consider to be "American identity" and claiming American citizenship. Both Figure 15.1 and 15.2 present a visual argument about belonging, about who has the right to live, work, be educated, and participate in America.

Throughout this chapter, you'll encounter many arguments that build upon the points raised by these two images, and you'll have a chance to explore vital issues such as the fight for equal rights, the struggle for access to land and jobs, and the movement of American culture outward, across the globe, even as new populations seek to enter and become part of this country's citizenry. In making your way through theses texts, you'll have the opportunity to reflect in critical ways on what it means to claim citizenship in a country—and a world—as diverse and in flux as our own.

From an info-graphic depicting the changes that characterize the face of contemporary American society to a meme about recent protests against gay marriage legislation, we'll move to debates about legal citizenship and immigration. Through news articles, photo essays, and a dueling set of newspaper features on what an "American Dream Team" of workers might look like, we'll explore how "paving a path to citizenship" for people from outside the USA may benefit or threaten our economy and way of life. Turning our attention outward beyond the borders of America, we'll investigate the model of national identity that gets exported through American corporations including McDonald's, Disney, and Nike. Finally, the chapter will shift from American rights and food to consider how new technologies offer the potential to extend the benefits of American education to citizens across the globe. What this means for the future of this country, and for the future of our inter-connected world, is the central focus on this chapter.

REFLECT & WRITE

- ❑ Analyze Figures 15.1 and 15.2 to determine how each one uses *pathos* or *logos* to make an argument about belonging to America's citizenry? Does either image rely on stereotypes? How do the texts confirm or refute your understanding of America's overall *ethos* as a nation?
- ❑ Revise Figure 15.2 to reflect "the changing face" of your own community. What community members are left out? What story will your images tell?
- ❑ **Write.** Compose new captions for these images that reveal your current thinking about America, citizenship, and civil rights. After working through this chapter, return to your captions and see what you would revise or keep.

■ The *Center for American Progress, based in Washington, D.C., is an independent nonpartisan educational institute dedicated to developing policy ideas and promoting those ideas through media coverage and national debate. The following infographic maps data from the 2010 Census and offers projections about future changes in the USA.*

Infographic: The New Demographics

The Center for American Progress

The New Demographics

Since 2000, U.S. communities have grown exponentially and trended toward greater ethnic and racial diversity nationwide. The release of 2010 Census data has only further illustrated a definitive decade of change in the American landscape. Progress 2050 has selected some existing facts and exciting projections from the newly released data to highlight the numerical gains communities of color have and will make in the 21st century. We believe these factoids capture the truly wide spread of change in the country.

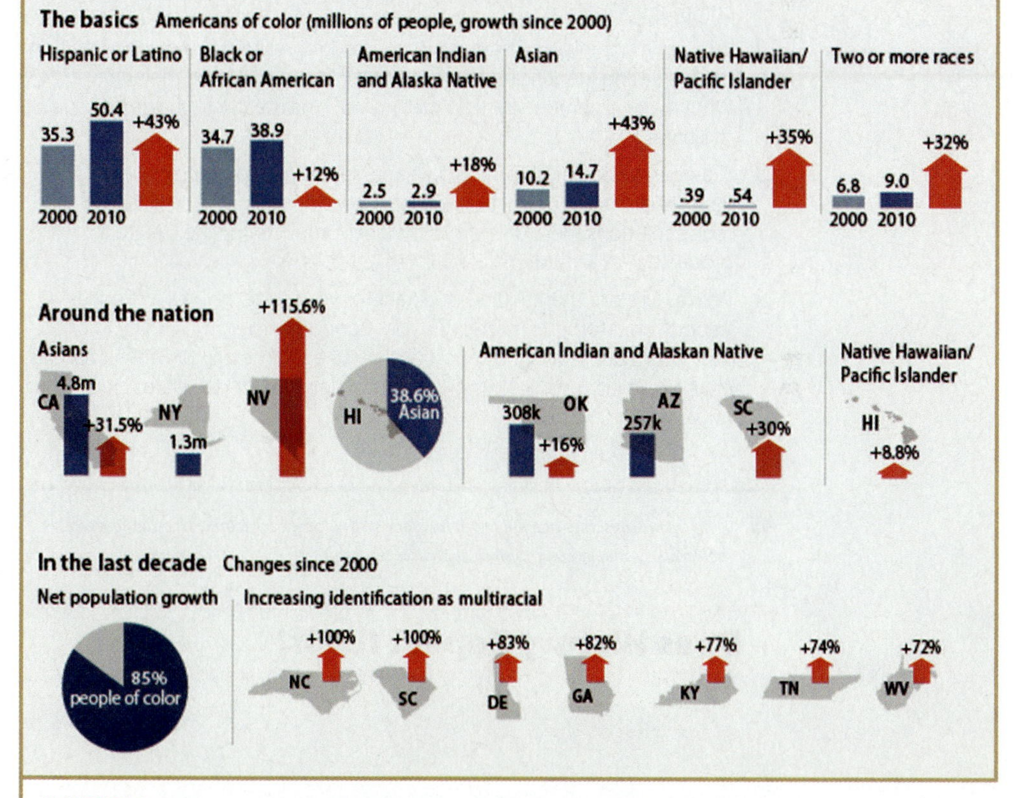

FIGURE 15.3 Focusing on racial data from the US Census, these charts demonstrate the changing face of America.

REFLECT & WRITE

- ❑ How do the visuals in Figure 15.3 shape the findings of the 2010 US census—the most extensive survey that collects data about the residential patterns, racial and ethnic backgrounds, education levels, and work experiences of all pepole in the country—into arguments about the key changes (social, cultural, demographic) in the country?
- ❑ This subset of data focuses on the changing demographics of race in America. How do the numbers and the charts compare to the demographics of your community? How would you modify the charts? What additional measures would you add? Can you construct charts to represent identity along the lines of gender, sexuality, age, etc. for your community?
- ❑ Why do you think the Center for American Progress (CAP) includes a section on "Increasing identification as multiracial"? What might be their *motive?* What larger argument are they making with the rhetorical choice to visualize this data?
- ❑ Examine the actual US census data and the many info graphics or data visualizations of it on its website. How do the charts and data representations there differ from the ones produced by the CAP as a progressive organization?
- ❑ **Write.** Explore the 2010 census data for your state, or pick a "Census Report" on a topic of interest to you. Conduct a rhetorical analysis of that data visualization or report and write a short essay on how it reveals changes in citizenship within the US as well as who can claim citizenship for your chosen focus.

■ *This meme combines two photographs, along with provocative words, in order to make a powerful argument about history and citizens's rights.*

Does History Repeat Itself?

REFLECT & WRITE

- ❑ How does this meme draw a connection between the struggle for African-American civil rights in the 1950s and 1960s and the struggle for same-sex marriage equality today? What kind of parallel between the two do these paired photos suggest? How does the argumentative strategy of *comparison-contrast* turn the parallel into a persuasive message?
- ❑ Who is the "you" being addressed in the meme's title, "Imagine how stupid you are going to look in 40 years"? How does the arrangement of the words into three separate lines help move the visual argument forward?
- ❑ How do memes function as persuasive visual texts today? While many of them rely on humor and the local knowledge of a specific community (*doxa*), how do they also convey an argument in compact form? What do you see as the difference between an op-ed and a meme?
- ❑ **Write.** Create your own meme around an issue of "claiming citizenship." Choose an image that depicts a different example of social protest or that represents an issue of concern to you. Then, add words to make a strong argument for what action needs to be taken or what message you want to send to those who may be obstructing civil rights with regard to your topic.

FIGURE 15.4 This meme compares same-sex marriage protesters to segregationists who sought to prevent interracial marriage in the 1960's.

Arthur G. Sulzberger, *following a family lineage started by* New York Times *publisher Adolph Simon Ocha, wrote this story while he served as Kansas City bureau chief. In that position, he produced quirky and insightful stories about economic and cultural issues particular to the Midwest. This story appeared in the* New York Times *on November 13, 2011.*

Hispanics Reviving Faded Towns on the Plains

A. G. Sulzberger

Change can be unsettling in a small town. But not long ago in this quiet farming community, with its familiar skyline of grain elevators and church steeples, the owner of a new restaurant decided to acknowledge the community's diversity by adding some less traditional items to her menu. Cheeseburgers. French fries. Chicken-fried steak.

"American food," the restaurant owner, Luz Gonzalez, calls it. And she signaled her move by giving her Mexican restaurant a distinctly American name: "The Down-Town Restaurant."

Such fare was all but extinct in a place where longtime residents joke—often with a barely disguised tone of frustration—that the dining options are Mexican, Mexican or Mexican. After the last white-owned restaurant serving American favorites closed this year, it fell to one of the recent Hispanic arrivals to keep the burgers-and-fries legacy alive. Ms. Gonzalez even enlisted the help of neighbors to teach her to cook more exotic dishes—like potato salad.

For generations, the story of the small rural town of the Great Plains, including the dusty tabletop landscape of western Kansas, has been one of exodus—of businesses closing, classrooms shrinking and, year after year, communities withering as fewer people arrive than leave and as fewer are born than are buried. That flight continues, but another demographic trend has breathed new life into the region.

5 Hispanics are arriving in numbers large enough to offset or even exceed the decline in the white population in many places. In the process, these new residents are reopening shuttered storefronts with Mexican groceries, filling the schools with children whose first language is Spanish and, for now at least, extending the lives of communities that seemed to be staggering toward the grave.

That demographic shift, seen in the findings of the 2010 census, has not been uniformly welcomed in places where steadiness and tradition are seen as central charms of rural life. Some longtime residents of Ulysses, where the population of 6,161 is now about half Hispanic, grumble over the cultural differences and say they feel like strangers in their hometown. But the alternative, community leaders warn, is unacceptable.

"We're either going to change or we're going to die," said Thadd Kistler, a lifelong resident who recently stepped down as mayor. "This is Ulysses now, this is the United States now, this immigration is happening and the communities that are extending a hand are going to survive."

After years in which mostly white communities throughout the region used gimmicks to lure new residents with limited success, like offering free land or lengthy tax abatements, many are wondering if this unexpected multicultural mix offers one vision of what the future of the rural Great Plains may look like.

"The face of small towns is changing dramatically as a result," said Robert Wuthnow, a Kansas-born Princeton professor who studied the Hispanic influx for his book "Remaking the Heartland: Middle America since the 1950s." "The question is: Is this going to save these small towns?"

10 There has long been a strong Hispanic presence throughout the region, which is rich with difficult work in meatpacking plants and on farms, feedlots and oil fields. But over the last decade, as their population in the rural Great Plains spiked by 54 percent—a figure comparable to gains in metro areas in the region—Hispanic residents have pushed from hubs like nearby Dodge City, Garden City and Liberal into ever smaller communities, buying property on the cheap, enticed, many say, by the opportunity to live quiet lives in communities more similar to those in which they were raised.

In the sparsely populated western half of Kansas, every county but one experienced a decline in the non-Hispanic white population, two-thirds of them by more than 10 percent.

At the same time, a vast majority experienced double-digit growth in Hispanic population, more than offsetting the declines in seven counties and many smaller cities and towns. Those places with the highest percentage of Hispanic residents tend to have the lowest average ages, the highest birth rates and the most stable school populations.

"These towns, I don't know what they would do without Mexicans," said Oscar Rivera, a Honduran immigrant who lives in a community of a few hundred people and travels through rural parts of western Kansas selling prepaid phone cards used to call overseas. "It would be like ghost towns."

One such town is Bazine, about two hours from here and little even by the standards of its neighbors. The decaying strip of downtown stores was abandoned long ago, and empty houses dotted the surrounding streets. A few years back, the high school closed and the building was sold on eBay. There was talk about shutting the elementary school as well.

15 "The decline was happening," said Patricia Showalter, the mayor, standing inside the little post office she runs. "And then the Hispanic people came."

For the first time in more than a half century, the population grew in the latest census, inching up to 334 as the Hispanic population jumped to 86 from 4. Now every house in town is occupied. A new church, La Luz del Mundo, just opened. Though there are no new businesses on Main Street, some entrepreneurial newcomers sell homemade tamales door to door.

And, most importantly to those who had watched the town become ever older, the school enrollment is growing.

In neighboring Ransom, which is almost entirely white, the student population has declined to 34 from 62 in the last eight years. Meanwhile, in Bazine, the numbers have increased to 46, up from 35. The average age in Ransom is 15 years older than in Bazine.

In Ulysses, which grew a modest 3 percent over the last decade, much appears unchanged by the years. Livelihoods are still tied to the earth, where people grow wheat and corn in the dusty soil, drill for the generous deposits of oil and gas beneath the surface and feed cows inside muddy pens that line the roads. Churches—there are more than a dozen—still play an important role, and the pace is still slower than what one usually experiences in a bigger city.

But the influx of Hispanics, a majority of whom were born in Mexico, has left an unmistakable impact.

Rachel Gallegos remembers that as a young girl she was the only Hispanic student in her class and her parents' Mexican restaurant was the first Hispanic business in town. Now, Hispanics make up two-thirds of the school population and own bakeries, clothing stores, car dealerships and computer repair shops, some catering to Hispanics and others simply filling vacant niches.

And when children become adults, a time when residents have historically headed to bigger communities seeking opportunity, her family was becoming rooted in the community—Ms. Gallegos said that of her nine siblings and their two dozen children, all but a couple remained.

Ginger Anthony, director of the Historic Adobe Museum, which chronicles the history of the onetime frontier town, discussed the changes with dismay, pausing repeatedly to reiterate that she did not want her criticism to seem "politically incorrect." She is so unnerved, particularly by illegal immigrants, that she recently started locking her door—saying that the police-beat column in the local paper disproportionately features Spanish surnames.

"This wave of new people coming into the Midwest, it's not always a good thing," she said, as a co-worker nodded in agreement. "If you talk to the average working person, a lot of them are sort of fed up. Our town isn't what it was."

But Hispanic residents here say they have been mostly well received, even if the non-Hispanics sometimes keep their distance. There are exceptions, like when students at a neighboring high school showed up to a basketball game in sombreros and tossed tortillas onto the court.

Jose Olivas, a longtime community developer with Mexican American Ministries, said that it took years of pressure to hire Hispanic employees at schools and at some businesses. Now employers are taking Spanish lessons, and expressing preference for bilingual job applicants.

"For a while you had to be careful," Mr. Olivas said. "But they've really changed their attitudes."

Mr. Kistler, the former mayor, agreed that there were culture clashes, but said they were slowly dissipating.

"At first every community, including Ulysses, was very unwelcoming, but a lot of that was because we wanted to hold on so tight to what we were," he said. "In the last five years, we've really seen that they're here, they're staying, they're part of the community. We've kind of gotten used to each other."

Part of that has been dictated by demographics.

At the hospital in town, exactly half of the 102 babies born last year were Hispanic. And in a telling sign of the future of the community, 13 babies were listed as having one white and one Hispanic parent.

REFLECT & WRITE

- ❑ What cultural stereotypes about "small town" America does the writer evoke with vivid descriptions and quotations from his field research? How does the tone of the writing and the arrangement of evidence indicate the author's stance on these stereotypes?
- ❑ Analyze the visual aspects of the language that describes the challenges confronting many rural small towns. How do word choices such as "dusty tabletop landscape[s]," or "communities withering" enhance the *pathos* appeal? How does the mention of "For generations" rely on *logos*?
- ❑ The writer concludes his article by noting the number of babies born to mixed, white/Hispanic couples. Why do you think he ends the piece this way? What final impression does this make? What larger argument might he have about "the changing face" of the Midwest?
- ❑ **Write.** Look up the images that originally accompanied the article. How do the visual texts support or complicate the portrait of small town life presented here? What larger point about racial diversity and life on America's rural plains can you glean from the images? Select the most powerful images and construct a photo essay in response to the article. Include captions and an introduction to show your stance on these social trends.

■ **Alex Webb** *is an award-winning photographer and the author of seven photography books. A graduate of Harvard, Webb also studied at the Carpenter Center for the Visual Arts. He joined Magnum Photos in 1976, around the same time he began photographing Mexico, the Caribbean, and the American South. His work has been exhibited across America and Europe. He writes of his art: "What does a street photographer do but walk and watch and wait and talk, and then watch and wait some more, trying to remain confident that the unexpected, the unknown, or the secret heart of the known awaits just around the corner." The photos here appeared as part of a Time Special Report on "The New Frontier/La Nueva Frontera."*

Life on the Border

Alex Webb

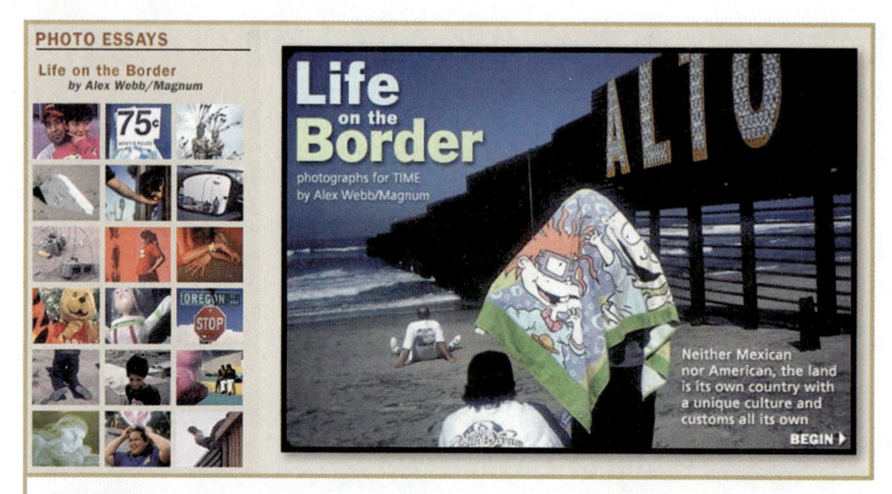

FIGURE 15.5 On the beach beside the border, a wall stretching out in the ocean, people take shelter from the heat under towels bearing the visual rhetoric of American cartoons.

FIGURE 15.6 Webb captures the man caught between two cultures, literally standing between two visual signs of American commercialism, Pepsi and Aquafina.

FIGURE 15.7 Families separated by the border reveal the deep emotional impact of immigration.

FIGURE 15.8 The visual signs of life on the borderlands reveal themselves in this photo of people kneeling for a make-shift mass.

REFLECT & WRITE

- ❑ How do the photos provide an argument about what life is like for immigrants and their families on both sides of the border?
- ❑ What appeals tell the story most powerfully? The emotions or *pathos* of the boy by the fence? The logical comparison of Pepsi and water vending machines? Or the *ethos* or character of people practicing their faith by kneeling in the dirt? What other rhetorical elements do you notice?
- ❑ Discuss in small groups how you might develop your own photo essay about cultures in your community. What images would you include? What captions would you write to tell this story?
- ❑ **Write.** Compose your own captions for these images that show what you have learned about citizenship by studying these texts. Then, write an imaginary email to the photographer, Alex Webb, sending him your new captions and explaining to the photographer what you learned from his work.

Since **Thomas L. Friedman** *joined the* New York Times *as a columnist in 1981, he has won three Pulitzer Prizes for commentary and international reporting (from Lebanon and Israel). He has authored several best-selling books including* The World Is Flat: A Brief History of the Twenty-first Century, *which won the inaugural Goldman Sachs/Financial Times Business Book of the Year award,* From Beirut to Jerusalem, *which won the National Book Award,* The Lexus and the Olive Tree, *which won the 2000 Overseas Press Club Award, and* Longitudes and Attitudes: The World in the Age of Terrorism. *Hi most recent books include* That Used To Be Us: How America Fell Behind in the World It Invented and How We Can Come Back *and* Hot, Flat, and Crowded 2.0: Why We Need a Green Revolution - And How it Can Renew America. *Friedman received a B.A. degree in Mediterranean studies from Brandeis University, a Master of Philosophy degree in modern Middle East studies from Oxford, and the honorary title, Order of the British Empire (OBE), by Queen Elizabeth II.*

America's Real Dream Team

Thomas L. Friedman

Went to a big Washington dinner last week. You know the kind: Large hall; black ties; long dresses. But this was no ordinary dinner. There were 40 guests of honor. So here's my Sunday news quiz: I'll give you the names of most of the honorees, and you tell me what dinner I was at. Ready?

Linda Zhou, Alice Wei Zhao, Lori Ying, Angela

Yu-Yun Yeung, Lynnelle Lin Ye, Kevin Young Xu, Benjamin Chang Sun, Jane Yoonhae Suh, Katheryn Cheng Shi, Sunanda Sharma, Sarine Gayaneh Shahmirian, Arjun Ranganath Puranik, Raman Venkat Nelakant, Akhil Mathew, Paul Masih Das, David Chienyun Liu, Elisa Bisi Lin, Yifan Li, Lanair Amaad Lett, Ruoyi Jiang, Otana Agape Jakpor, Peter Danming Hu, Yale Wang Fan, Yuval Yaacov Calev, Levent Alpoge, John Vincenzo Capodilupo and Namrata Anand.

No, sorry, it was not a dinner of the China-India Friendship League. Give up?

O.K. All these kids are American high school students. They were the majority of the 40 finalists in the 2010 Intel Science Talent Search, which, through a national contest, identifies and honors the top math and science high school students in America, based on their solutions to scientific problems. The awards dinner was Tuesday, and, as you can see from the above list, most finalists hailed from immigrant families, largely from Asia.

5 Indeed, if you need any more convincing about the virtues of immigration, just come to the Intel science finals. I am a pro-immigration fanatic. I think keeping a constant flow of legal immigrants into our country—whether they wear blue collars or lab coats—is the key to keeping us ahead of China. Because when you mix all of these energetic, high-aspiring people with a democratic system and free markets, magic happens. If we hope to keep that magic, we need immigration reform that guarantees that we will always attract and retain, in an orderly fashion, the world's first-round aspirational and intellectual draft choices.

This isn't complicated. In today's wired world, the most important economic competition is no longer between countries or companies. The most important economic competition is actually between you and your own imagination. Because what your kids imagine, they can now act on farther, faster, cheaper than ever before—as individuals. Today, just about everything is becoming a commodity, except imagination, except the ability to spark new ideas.

If I just have the spark of an idea now, I can get a designer in Taiwan to design it. I can get a factory in China to produce a prototype. I can get a factory in Vietnam to mass manufacture it. I can use Amazon.com to handle fulfillment. I can use freelancer.com to find someone to do my logo and manage my backroom. And I can do all this at incredibly low prices. The one thing that is not a commodity and never will be is that spark of an idea. And this Intel dinner was all about our best sparklers.

Before the dinner started, each contestant stood by a storyboard explaining their specific project. Namrata Anand, a 17-year-old from the Harker School in California, patiently explained to me her research, which used spectral analysis and other data to expose information about the chemical enrichment history of "Andromeda Galaxy." I did not understand a word she said, but I sure caught the gleam in her eye.

My favorite chat, though, was with Amanda Alonzo, a 30-year-old biology teacher at Lynbrook High School in San Jose, Calif. She had taught two of the finalists. When I asked her the secret, she said it was the resources provided by her school, extremely "supportive parents" and a grant from Intel that let her spend part of each day inspiring and preparing students to enter this contest. Then she told me this: Local San Jose realtors are running ads in newspapers in China and India telling potential immigrants to "buy a home" in her Lynbrook school district because it produced "two Intel science winners."

10 Seriously, ESPN or MTV should broadcast the Intel finals live. All of the 40 finalists are introduced, with little stories about their lives and aspirations. Then the winners of the nine best projects are announced. And finally, with great drama, the overall winner of the $100,000 award for the best project of the 40 is identified. This year it was Erika Alden DeBenedictis of New Mexico for developing a software navigation system that would enable spacecraft to more efficiently "travel through the solar system." After her name was called, she was swarmed by her fellow competitor-geeks.

Gotta say, it was the most inspiring evening I've had in D.C. in 20 years. It left me thinking, "If we can just get a few things right—immigration, education standards, bandwidth, fiscal policy—maybe we'll be O.K." It left me feeling that maybe Alice Wei Zhao of North High School in Sheboygan, Wis., chosen by her fellow finalists to be their spokeswoman, was right when she told the audience: "Don't sweat about the problems our generation will have to deal with. Believe me, our future is in good hands."

As long as we don't shut our doors.

REFLECT & WRITE

- ❑ Why might Friedman begin his article with a question? How does this engage your interest?
- ❑ Notice how he next offers an entire paragraph of names before turning to a humorous comment and another question: "No, sorry, it was not a dinner of the China-India Friendship League. Give up?" How do these opening strategies establish his *persona* as a writer?
- ❑ What is the effect of naming people such as "Namrata Anand, a 17-year-old from the Harker School in California" and "Alice Wei Zhao of North High School in Sheboygan, Wis"? How does naming people bring the writing alive to you as a reader? Does it work as a tool of persuasive writing?
- ❑ Discuss his point that "In today's wired world, the most important economic competition is no longer between countries or companies. The most important economic competition is actually between you and your own imagination." What is your response to this claim? What examples do you see from your life?
- ❑ **Write.** Develop your own perspective on this issue and write it up to send to the *New York Times* as an op-ed. Try to imitate Friedman's writing strategies, but use examples from your community and build your argument to support your own argument.

Stephen M. Steinlight *is a Senior Policy Analyst at the Center for Immigration Studies in Washington, D.C. He is also an Associate Fellow at Timothy Dwight College, Yale University. For more than six years he was the director of national affairs at the American Jewish Committee and for two years served as a senior fellow at the AJC. Steinlight is co-editor of* Fractious Nation: Unity and Division in Contemporary American Life *and* Children of Abraham.

Thomas L. Friedman: Foe of Open-Borders and 'Comprehensive Immigration Reform'?

Stephen M. Steinlight

Though Thomas Friedman's *New York Times* column "America's Real Dream Team" squandered a teachable moment, copping out by failing to offer an explicitly political condemnation of America's current immigration policies and the unending campaign for "comprehensive immigration reform," he indirectly demolished both.

That he did so while declaring himself a "pro-immigration fanatic" isn't a contradiction, nor does his deep genuflection towards immigration appear to be a sop to his publishers. His enthusiasm is authentic, but the immigration he's endorsing is of a kind that never figures in any of the tediously repetitive *Times* editorials in favor of open borders. The immigration Friedman wants—"legal," "orderly," resulting in America's attracting and retaining "the world's first-round aspirational and intellectual draft choices"—can actually be seen as consonant with the Center for Immigration Studies' advocacy of a "pro-immigrant policy of lower immigration" predicated on the national interest. In "America's Real Dream Team," Friedman reveals himself to be a passionate advocate of that vision—even while his message is substantially neutered by the role he's created for himself as the nation's leading journalistic paradigm inventor who is simultaneously naïve about, dismissive of, or simply afraid to confront the political implications of his own "future talk."

The variety of immigration over which he rhapsodizes—which he claims is key to maintaining America's world leadership—bears no resemblance to that endorsed by the president or the weird conglomeration of usual suspects and special interests: a hefty cross-section of our fiscal and financial elite, mainstream media and "newspapers of record," foundation-bankrolled cadres of immigrant activists, the Hispanic and Black Congressional Caucuses, the most exploitative employers in the corporate service sector, ethnic identity extremists, Big Religion with its posturing morally purblind post-American clerics, among others.

In fact, it's axiomatic that immigration Friedman-style is wholly antithetical to current immigration policy and "comprehensive immigration reform"—which begins with amnesty, though that's an instrumentality, not remotely an end in itself. The core component of "comprehensive immigration reform" is an exponential increase in what will become legal immigration triggered by amnesty in conjunction with extended family reunification. If passed, it won't result in a "pathway to citizenship" for a mere 11 million illegal aliens, but in the immigration of tens of millions of uneducated less-skilled foreigners, connected to the 11 million often by fraudulently alleged family ties.

5 This cataclysmic immigration will come overwhelmingly from oligarchic Latin American cultures with chasm-like divides between the rich and the poor, with oppressive, rigid class systems that give their citizenry, particularly their own poor, little access to learning or the means or motivation to pursue the life of the mind. It will result in the importation of a vast less-skilled demographic that is the inverse of Friedman's "Real Dream Team." According to data from the Pew Hispanic Center, some 30 percent of immigrants from Mexico have not finished 9th grade; some 62 percent lack high school diplomas. Conscious decisions to promote and preserve ignorance have been taken by corrupt undemocratic oligarchies to preserve their stolen wealth and power. Similarly, their complicity in illegally exporting millions of their own less-educated citizens to the United States reduces pressure on the steam cooker of potential social unrest at home, while the billions sent back by the exported poor provides just enough in a society with relatively low economic expectations to avert a potentially revolutionary situation.

Friedman wrote his paean to the benefits of immigration by the "best and brightest" as a result of having attended an award ceremony for high school kids from across the U.S., the children of legal immigrants, mostly from Asia, who were finalists in the 2010 Intel Science Talent Search. Unlike the 40 finalists, a high proportion of the children of today's legal and illegal less-skilled immigrants from Mexico and Central America have parents with very low levels of education, and the parents' education attainment is one of the best predictors of a child's success. The result is that many children from Latin American immigrant families are dropping out of school and socializing downward. While Hispanics once had the highest rate of intact families of any group, the native-born children and grandchildren of Hispanic immigrants have rates of out-of-wedlock births second only to those in the African-American community, one of the principal causes and symptoms of the crises that beset the black community. Nearly half of Hispanic immigrant families use at least one federal welfare program, and the education system is not providing a basis for upward social mobility. In our knowledge-based, post industrial society it is unlikely that the immigrants who come here from Mexico and Central America will provide many of the finalists for the Intel Talent Search for generations; meanwhile we can predict inverse outcomes: high rates of academic failure, functional illiteracy in two languages, welfare dependency, out-of-wedlock births, and disproportionate rates of incarceration.

I can already hear the accusation that Friedman is guilty of pro-Asian racialism or celebrating "model minorities," but those charges would be nonsensical. The winners weren't chosen on affirmative action bases. The finalists competed in a national contest that identifies the top U.S. high school students in science and math, and the 40 winners were selected on the basis of the quality of thinking they employed in solving scientific problems. Friedman, who believes the future belongs to democratic, free-market societies that place a high premium on the life of the mind and intellectual aspiration, came away reassured: "Gotta say, it was the most inspiring evening I've had in D.C. in 20 years. It left me thinking, 'If we can just get a few things right–immigration, education standards, bandwidth, fiscal policy—maybe we'll be O.K.' "

There's no argument these criteria are critical, even essential to maintaining American world leadership and Exceptionalism. But the Panglossian optimism, breezy confidence, and bizarre sense of relief that accompanied Friedman home from the event seem frighteningly misplaced. When he cites "getting immigration right," and "making it orderly" and adds, "This isn't complicated," one wonders whether he inhabits the same universe as 300 million other Americans.

It is astoundingly unrealistic, even oddly childish, to opine that getting immigration right is no big deal. An epic political struggle has thus far achieved nothing more than preventing America's political and fiscal elite—who have it totally wrong—from taking the nation over Niagara Falls. That we have thus far prevented America from succumbing to "comprehensive immigration reform" by defeating three legislative incarnations is our only consolation. Fighting and winning desperate rearguard actions is no minor achievement, but such actions stave off defeat rather than deliver victory. We remain on the defensive.

10 If Thomas L. Friedman chose to use his influential voice—one especially resonant among liberal Americans—to help them understand how radically different is the immigration he advocates from the sort being pushed by the cynical, greedy, or ethnically chauvinist "comprehensive reform" crowd, he might actually make a difference. But to do that he would have to descend from the mountaintop from which paradigm-creators prognosticate and enter the gritty political fray. In "Politics and the English Language" George Orwell reminds us "all issues are political issues." One would have thought Thomas Friedman would recognize that's true even of his dreams for America's future.

Seeing Connections: See Chapter 2 for a discussion of the *ad hominem* fallacy

REFLECT & WRITE

- ❑ How does Steinlight provide an *ad hominem* attack on both Friedman and the *New York Times* more generally? Do you think this is an effective rhetorical strategy?
- ❑ Notice the shifts in style in the writing, from very low or casual to quite intellectual. These shifts can be understood as levels of decorum: from low to high style. Why might the writer shift style to make certain points? Paraphrase what the writer might mean by this line: "But the Panglossian optimism, breezy confidence, and bizarre sense of relief that accompanied Friedman home from the event seem frighteningly misplaced."
- ❑ What is the value of raising a question in the title? How does the writer answer it (or not) by the end of the piece?
- ❑ **Write.** Compose a commentary in response to Steinlight, addressing the points made in Friedman's article "America's Real Dream Team," and including your own view on immigration. Decide on your own tone and choice of metaphors. When you are done, set up a class debate to share perspectives and open up even more views on this issue.

Lexington *is a regular columnist for the* Economist. *He also keeps a blog, called* Lexington's Notebook, *posting opinions about "America's political fray."*

The Hub Nation

Lexington

Immigration places America at the centre of a web of global networks. So why not make it easier?

Immigrants benefit America because they study and work hard. That is the standard argument in favour of immigration, and it is correct. Leaving your homeland is a big deal. By definition, it takes get-up-and-go to get up and go, which is why immigrants are abnormally entrepreneurial. But there is another, less obvious benefit of immigration. Because they maintain links with the places they came from, immigrants help America plug into a vast web of global networks.

Many people have observed how the networks of overseas Chinese and Indians benefit their respective motherlands. Diasporas speed the flow of information: an ethnic Chinese trader in Indonesia who spots a commercial opportunity will quickly alert his cousin who runs a factory in Guangdong. And ties of kin, clan or dialect ensure a high level of trust. This allows decisions to be made swiftly: multimillion-dollar deals can sometimes be sealed with a single phone call. America is linked to the world in a different way. It does not have much of a diaspora, since native-born Americans seldom emigrate permanently. But it has by far the world's largest stock of immigrants, including significant numbers from just about every country on earth. Most assimilate quickly, but few sever all ties with their former homelands.

Consider Andres Ruzo, an entrepreneur who describes himself as "Peruvian by birth; Texan by choice". He moved to America when he was 19. After studying engineering, he founded a telecoms firm near Dallas. It prospered, and before long he was looking to expand into Latin America. He needed a partner. He stumbled on one through a priest, who introduced him to another devout IT entrepreneur, Vladimir Vargas Esquivel, who was based in Costa Rica and looking to expand northward. It was a perfect fit. And because of the way they were introduced—by a priest they both respected—they felt they could trust each other. Their firm now operates in ten countries and generates tens of millions of dollars in annual sales. Mr Ruzo wants the firm, which is called ITS Infocom, to go global. So although he and Mr Vargas Esquivel natter to each other in Spanish, they insist that the firm's official language must be English.

Trust matters. Modern technology allows instant, cheap communication. Yet although anyone can place a long-distance call, not everyone knows whom to call, or whom to trust. Ethnic networks can address this problem. For example, Sanjaya Kumar, an Indian doctor, arrived in America in 1992. He developed an interest in software that helps to prevent

FIGURE 15.9 This illustration, accompanying Lexington's article, makes a visual argument about our changing world community.

medical errors. This is not a small problem. Perhaps 100,000 Americans die each year because of preventable medical mistakes, according to the Institute of Medicine. Dr Kumar needed cash and business advice to commercialise his ideas, so he turned to a network of ethnic Indian entrepreneurs called Tie. He met, and was backed by, an Indian-American venture capitalist, Vish Mishra. His firm, Quantros, now sells its services to 2,300 American hospitals. And it is starting to expand into India, having linked up with a software firm there which is run by an old school chum of one of Dr Kumar's Indian-American executives.

5 Ethnic networks have drawbacks. If they are a means of excluding outsiders, they can be stultifying. But they accelerate the flow of information. Nicaraguan-Americans put buyers in Miami in touch with sellers in Managua. Indian-American employees help American consulting

firms scout for talent in Bangalore. The benefits are hard to measure, but William Kerr of the Harvard Business School has found some suggestive evidence. He looked at the names on patent records, reasoning that an inventor called Wang was probably of Chinese origin, while some called Martinez was probably Hispanic. He found that foreign researchers cite American-based researchers of their own ethnicity 30-50% more often than you would expect if ethnic ties made no difference. It is not just that a Chinese boffin in Beijing reads papers written by Chinese boffins in America. A Chinese boffin in America may alert his old classmate in Beijing to cool research being done at the lab across the road.

Network effects

In Silicon Valley more than half of Chinese and Indian immigrant scientists and engineers report sharing information about technology or business opportunities with people in their home countries, according to AnnaLee Saxenian of the University of California, Berkeley. Some Americans fret that China and India are using American know-how to out-compete America. But knowledge flows both ways. As people in emerging markets innovate—which they are already doing at a prodigious clip—America will find it ever more useful to have so many citizens who can tap into the latest brainwaves from Mumbai and Shanghai. Immigrants can also help their American employers do business in their homelands. Firms that employ many ethnic Chinese scientists, for example, are more likely to invest in China and more likely to do so through a wholly owned subsidiary, rather than seeking the crutch of a joint venture, finds Mr Kerr. In other words, local knowledge reduces the cost of doing business.

Immigration provides America with legions of unofficial ambassadors, deal-brokers, recruiters and boosters. Immigrants not only bring the best ideas from around the world to American shores; they are also a conduit for spreading American ideas and ideals back to their homelands, thus increasing their adoptive country's soft power.

All of which makes the task of fixing America's cumbersome immigration rules rather urgent. Alas, Barack Obama has done little to fulfil his campaign pledge to do so. With unemployment still at nearly 10%, few politicians are brave enough to be seen encouraging foreigners to compete for American jobs.

REFLECT & WRITE

- ❑ How does the illustration in Figure 15.9 reflect and even extend the argument of the article? Can it be seen as a visual abstract for the writer's main point about immigrants as a "conduit for spreading American ideas and ideals back to their homelands"?
- ❑ Although there is only one subhead in this piece, how does it unite the two parts of the argument and propel the writer's thesis forward? What additional subheads might you compose if asked to do so? How would these new subheads influence readers?

- ❑ Assess the tone and stance by looking at word choice, sentence length, and specific examples. What passages work best for you as a reader? How would you characterize the writer's style?
- ❑ What do you make of the author's argument that "America will find it ever more useful to have so many citizens who can tap into the latest brainwaves from Mumbai and Shanghai"? Do you see America looking outward or not?
- ❑ **Write.** Draft a mock column for publication in *the Economist* describing "networks" in your own community, or observations you have had of immigration conduits. Include drawings or photos as visual rhetoric.

WRITING COLLABORATIVELY

Together with two or three peers, explore additional legal, political, economic, or even social issues concerning "citizenship" – whether that refers to native or naturalized membership in a state or nation, or more metaphorically, as a "citizen" member of a certain community or group. You might decide to focus on a legal issue, such as the controversial overturn of the Voting Rights Act of 1965, or the disputes over the "Stand Your Ground" law to protect American citizens. Alternatively, you could look into issues of national security and how government surveillance by the NSA compromises or defends the rights and privileges of citizens. Develop your project by writing a research proposal (see Chapter 4 for guidelines), and then develop a multimedia presentation (based on the lessons from Chapter 9) to present your proposed research project to the class.

Mark Rice-Oxley *is a news editor on the foreign desk of the* Guardian. *He also served as a correspondent for the* Christian Science Monitor, *where this article appeared on January 15, 2004. He writes about a wide range of topics, from finances in the Eurozone to car catchphrases and linguistic missteps to mental health issues. Rice-Oxley recently published a book on his own journey with and recovery from depression called* Underneath the Lemon Tree.

In 2,000 Years, Will the World Remember Disney or Plato?

Mark Rice-Oxley

Down in the mall, between the fast-food joint and the bagel shop, a group of young people huddles in a flurry of baggy combat pants, skateboards, and slang. They size up a woman teetering past wearing DKNY, carrying *Time* magazine in one hand and a latte in the other. She brushes past a guy in a Yankees' baseball cap who is talking on his Motorola cellphone about the Martin Scorsese film he saw last night. It's a standard American scene—only this isn't America, it's Britain. US culture is so pervasive, the scene could be played out in any one of dozens of cities. Budapest or Berlin, if not Bogota or Bordeaux. Even Manila or Moscow.

As the unrivaled global superpower, America exports its culture on an unprecedented scale. From music to media, film to fast food, language to literature and sport, the American idea is spreading inexorably, not unlike the influence of empires that preceded it. The difference is that today's technology flings culture to every corner of the globe with blinding speed. If it took two millenniums for Plato's "Republic" to reach North America, the latest hit from Justin Timberlake can be found in Greek (and Japanese) stores within days. Sometimes, US ideals get transmitted—such as individual rights, freedom of speech, and respect for women—and local cultures are enriched. At other times, materialism or worse becomes the message and local traditions get crushed. "The US has become the most powerful, significant world force in terms of cultural imperialism [and] expansion," says Ian Ralston, American studies director at Liverpool John Moores University. "The areas that particularly spring to mind are Hollywood, popular music, and even literature." But what some call "McDomination" has created a backlash in certain cultures. And it's not clear whether fast food, Disney, or rock 'n' roll will change the world the way Homer or Shakespeare has.

Cricket or basketball?

Stick a pin in a map and there you'll find an example of US influence. Hollywood rules the global movie market, with up to 90 percent of audiences in some European countries. Even in Africa, 2 of 3 films shown are American. Few countries have yet to be touched by McDonald's and Coca-Cola. Starbucks recently opened up a new front in South America, and everyone's got a Hard Rock Café T-shirt from somewhere exotic. West Indian sports enthusiasts increasingly watch basketball, not cricket. Baseball has long since taken root in Asia and Cuba. And Chinese young people are becoming more captivated by American football and basketball, some even daubing the names of NBA stars on their school sweatsuits. The NFL plans to roll out a Chinese version of its website this month. Rupert Murdoch's satellites, with their heavy traffic of US audiovisual content, saturate the Asian subcontinent. American English is the language of choice for would-be pop stars in Europe, software programmers in India, and Internet surfers everywhere.

America's preeminence is hardly surprising. Superpowers have throughout the ages sought to perpetuate their way of life: from the philosophy and mythology of the ancient Greeks to the law and language of the Romans; from the art and architecture of the Tang Dynasty and Renaissance Italy to the sports and systems of government of the British. "Most empires think their own point of view is the only correct point of view," says Robert Young, an expert in postcolonial cultural theory at Oxford University. "It's the certainty they get because of the power they have, and they expect to impose it on everyone else."

5 Detractors of cultural imperialism argue, however, that cultural domination poses a totalitarian threat to diversity. In the American case, "McDomination" poses several dangers.

First, local industries are truly at risk of extinction because of US oligopolies, such as Hollywood. For instance in 2000, the European Union handed out 1 billion euros to subsidize Europe's film industry. Even the relatively successful British movie industry has no control over distribution, which is almost entirely in the hands of the Hollywood majors.

Second, political cultures are being transformed by the personality-driven American model in countries as far-reaching as Japan and the Philippines.

Finally, US domination of technologies such as the Internet and satellite TV means that, increasingly, America monopolizes the view people get of the world. According to a recent report for the UN Conference on Trade and Development, 13 of the top 14 Internet firms are American. No. 14 is British. "You have to know English if you want to use the Internet," says Andre Kaspi, a professor at the Sorbonne in Paris.

A main problem is that culture is no longer a protected species, but subject to the inexorable drive for free trade, says Joost Smiers, a political science professor at the Utrecht School of the Arts. This means that it is increasingly difficult for countries to protect their own industries. France tries to do so with subsidies, while South Korea has tried quotas. Such "protectionist" tactics meet with considerable US muscle, Dr. Smiers says. "America's aggressive cultural policy . . . hinders national states from regulating their own cultural markets," he says. "We should take culture out of the WTO."

10 Another danger, detractors say, is the consolidation of the communications industry into a few conglomerates such as AOL-TimeWarner, Disney, and News Corporation, which means that the "infotainment" generated for global consumption nearly always comes from an Anglophone perspective. "You can't go on with just three music companies organizing and distributing 85 percent of the music in the world," says Smiers. "It's against all principles of democracy. Every emotion, every feeling, every image can be copyrighted into the hands of a few owners."

American, with a twist

A backlash is being felt in certain places. In Japan, locals have taken US ideas like hip-hop and fast food, and given them a Japanese twist, says Dominic al-Badri, editor of *Kansai Time Out.* In Germany, there is still strong resistance to aspects of US pop culture, though there is an appetite for its intellectual culture, says Gary Smith, director of the American Academy in Berlin. In France, resistance is growing partly because of frustrations over the Iraq war—but partly because Americanization is already so advanced in the country, says Mr. Kaspi.

He notes one interesting anecdotal sign of US influence—and the futility of resistance. France has repeatedly tried to mandate the use of French language in official capacities to check the advance of English. "But most of the time, the law is impossible to apply, because if you want to be understood around the world you have to speak English," Kaspi says.

In the Philippines, even the best US ideals have caused complications. "The pervasive American influence has saddled us with two legacies," notes respected local commentator Antonio C. Abaya. "American-style elections, which require the commitment of massive financial resources, which have to be recouped and rolled over many times, which is the main source of corruption in government; and American-style free press in which media feel free to attack and criticize everything that the government does or says, which adds to disunity and loss of confidence in government."

Meanwhile, for all the strength of the US movie industry, sometimes a foreign film resonates more with a local audience than a Hollywood production—and outperforms it. For instance, Japan's "Spirited Away" (2001) remains the top-grossing film in that country, surpassing global Hollywood hits like "Titanic." In addition, British TV has influenced and served up competition to US shows, spawning such hits as "Who Wants to Be a Millionaire?", "The Weakest Link," and "American Idol."

1,000 years from now

15 So how much good does American culture bring to the world? And how long will it last? Ian Ralston cautions against sweeping dismissals of US pop culture. British television may be saturated with American sitcoms and movies, but while some are poor, others are quite good, he says. "British culture has always been enriched by foreign influences. In some ways American culture and media have added to that enrichment." Others note that it is not all one-way traffic. America may feast largely on a diet of homegrown culture, but it imports modestly as well: soccer, international cuisine, Italian fashion, and, increasingly, British television.

As to the question of durability, some experts believe US domination of communication channels makes it inevitable that its messages will become far more entrenched than those of previous empires. "The main difference now in favor of American culture is the importance of technology—telephone, Internet, films, all that did not exist in ancient Greece or the Mongol empire," Kaspi says. "American influence is growing, it's so easy to get access to US culture; there are no barriers. "Disney is known worldwide now," he adds. "Plato is more and more unknown, even in Greece."

But not everyone thinks American culture will stand the test of time. "It remains to be seen whether the Monkees and Bee Gees are as durable as Plato," says Professor Young, with a dab of irony. "Let's have another look in 4,000 years' time."

REFLECT & WRITE

- ❑ Rice-Oxley immediately engages the interest of the reader with two particularly vivid opening paragraphs. Discuss the brand names and examples in those paragraphs. How many do you know? How many surprise you? How do the examples help establish the author's argument about both globalization and what Rice-Oxley calls "McDomination"?
- ❑ In asking, "how much good does American culture bring to the world?" the writer offers a critical analysis about the effects of exporting American products, expressions, and practices. In what ways does this article extend the chapter's focus on "citizenship" to a global level? What do you think constitutes a "global citizen"?
- ❑ How does the writer both construct an audience and create a unique *persona* through word choice? What word choices target a specific demographic?
- ❑ How does the article integrate quotations as research and as appeals to authority? What is the effect of this rhetorical strategy on you as a reader? What is the effect of this on the writing as a text?
- ❑ What organizational structure does this article employ? That is, how does this article itemize its arguments logically? Map out the strategies of rebuttal, concession, and qualification. What is the impact of the last paragraph?
- ❑ **Write.** Compose a *personal narrative* about how elements of diverse cultures intersect in the community around you. Include visual evidence and explore how each text shapes how you might think of yourself as participating in a "world community." What examples in your narrative strike you as having "staying power"? Be as detailed as Rice-Oxley in naming specifics. Integrate your images strategically in your personal essay, and then share your work with others.

Seeing Connections: Return to Chapter 6 to review the various strategies of arrangement.

The two pieces that follow appeared in Rutgers University's newspaper, the Daily Targum, *in October 2002. The* Targum *ran the first piece, written by 2001 Rutgers graduate* **Joseph Davicsin**, *in its October 16 edition; "Globalization or McDonaldization?" appeared in response the following day. Its author,* **Jeremy Sklarsky**, *was a first-year student at Rutgers at the time.*

The Daily Targum: Two Opinions on McDonaldization

Corporations Leave Small Business Behind

Joseph Davicsin

Three months ago, a coffee shop opened on Church Street—where the used CD store "Tunes" was—called Basic Elements. This shop offered homemade beverages and food at prices comparable to similar chain stores. I say "offered" because, as of recently, the place has flown the coop like so many boiler room scams. I later saw the proprietors at Starbucks doing espresso shots and mumbling Wicca chants at the Cranium board game. Basic Elements deserved a hell of a lot more than it was given—a crappy side street with little visibility, despite being right near the Court Tavern (which I know for a fact that you frequent because I can never get a square foot of space to stand on when I'm in there), irregular hours—which is understandable in a quality place run by two people (you can't expect Walmart)—and most of all, our apathy.

Our apathy is linked largely to globalization, which is trying to unite the planet in blanket sameness so that you can experience a thrill at the notion of shopping at a Gap in Prague and eating at a McDonalds in India. Now, something in your mind should tell you there's something wrong with going to a McDonalds in India. The idea of going abroad is to experience new things outside your microcosm. But alas, the success of these businesses in pandering their crack all over the world has gotten people comfortable with this sameness. We stick to the chains because they're familiar, convenient and plowed into our faces on a regular basis. When you get

Globalization or McDonaldization?

Jeremy Sklarsky

I am writing in response to Joseph Davicsin's commentary about international corporations conquering the world and eliminating "mom and pop" establishments. Davicsin's comments exemplify some of the most commonly held misperceptions about globalization and corporations.

Globalization is not an enemy. It is an international, socioeconomic-political system. Due to advances in information technology, the rise of a postindustrial economy and the collapse of the bipolar Cold War world, a system has arisen in which the interests of individuals and governments around the world are intertwined. The overlap of people's interests has led to increased global cooperation. It can even be argued that the motivation for acts of international terrorism like Sept. 11 is actually a categorical rejection of the globalization system. The young men who crashed airplanes into the World Trade Center were born and raised in some of the countries that are the least globalized.

Globalization is not trying to "unite the planet in blanket sameness." Actually, quite the contrary is true. Take McDonald's, a notorious symbol of globalization, for example. McDonald's was not introduced into foreign countries in order to push American cultural hegemony over the rest of the world. McDonald's was mostly imported into foreign countries by nationals of those countries that wanted to make some profit—not as a part of a master plan to make everyone American. McDonald's is just a company that wants to make money. It isn't part of a "conspiracy of American corporations to take over the world."

that taste of mocha, you're hooked and nothing else seems to matter.

Of course, if it were simply laziness and chemical brainwashing causing the underdogs to fail, it would be easier to rectify, but life is never that simple. There's also the notion of capital to think of. Corporations like Starbucks have enough money to keep their prices relatively the same no matter where you go, so there's not only uniformed coverage, but also uniformed prices. The same cannot be said of the localized stores because they have less coverage and really need the extra money to stay alive, forcing them to increase their prices to compete. This delegates them to the "fine arts" category in which only the wealthy can indulge, resulting in an even split between cheap and prevalent and expensive and exclusive, with the midways—i.e., the moderately priced Basic Elements—getting squished in the ever-shrinking gap. Our culture becomes the following: Either you go to McSystem for victuals or spend exorbitant amounts of cash on the trendier French fry.

Then, of course, there's the small matter of demand, and that's when convenience takes precedence. Anyone who still reads out there will have little hope of finding a Recto & Verso when the majority only cares about getting textbooks and spirit clothing. The alternative is Barnes and Noble. If you want a real alternative you have to walk the world over to Pyramid Books in Highland Park, which, judging by the abundance of romance novels infesting their shelves, leads me to believe that they too are trying desperately to stay afloat.

5 Countless fables tell of local pizza places rejecting the system, but are they really? Or are they just biding their time before Burger King offers pizza for breakfast? They too seem to be getting increasingly gimmicky (check out

Furthermore, a quick trip to the McDonald's Web site will put to rest anyone's fears that Ronald and friends are trying to undermine the culture of a local population. In Italy, McDonald's serves Mediterranean salads. Japanese customers can get teriyaki burgers. In Israel there are several kosher McDonald's restaurants, and in Mexico burritos are served. These are just a few examples of when McDonald's has actually changed itself to fit into the local culture. In India, the country that Davicsin used in his column as an example, consumers can get McDonald's sandwiches made with mutton and chicken instead of beef, as McDonald's recognizes the importance of the dietary laws in Indian religions and cultures. McDonald's has also initiated many community service programs. In Saudi Arabia, it was the first chain restaurant to sponsor a campaign to increase seatbelt awareness.

5 A McDonald's in every country? Sounds good to me. Thomas Friedman, columnist for *The New York Times,* recently put forth a theory—which has been proven—that states that no two countries with a McDonald's has gone to war with each other since McDonald's arrived in their countries. In Friedman's own words, people in countries that have developed an economy at the level needed for McDonald's to be successful would rather "wait in line for burgers instead of in line for gas masks."

Davicsin refers to corporations as though they are some supernatural enemy imposed upon us by some external forces. Where did they get all of their money? And why are they so successful? A chain like McDonald's or Starbucks Coffee has had so much success for one simple reason: They are just better than the "corner shop." But chances are, if a local store can make a lower-priced product of higher quality, it will thrive. Take another corporation—Pizza Hut. Pizza Hut just isn't that good. Result? There are hundreds

King's Pizza and the ultimate tax write-off that is their wide-screen TV) and streamlined (toppings ranging from tortellini to ecstasy). There are still a few locales, like Noodle Gourmet, that do solid business on their own two legs, but it's not enough. What we need to do is alternate our habits a little. Back to coffee—like Café 52? I know you do because I see you bastards flood it every Monday night for the free music, then try West End on alternate nights. Spread out! Balance the pros and cons of each place and try to find a niche in one when the other doesn't meet your needs. But above all, give newer places your undivided attention because they may not be around long enough without you. Show the smaller places that there's a need for them and that quality need not mean pricey. And don't let companies know where you're going, lest they turn that into a trend as well. Be as random as a chaos pendulum.

of individually owned pizza parlors around America. We shouldn't, however, support every local pizza place just for the sake of fighting corporations—that's just silly.

I'm not suggesting globalization or corporations are perfect—they are far from it. Many Third World countries would probably be better off if the World Bank or IMF behaved better. And corporations could probably afford to pollute a little less and pay their workers a little bit more. But that's really not the issue. The point is that globalization is not a choice. The real question is how everyone is going to act in order to benefit from its existence. If local coffee shops wish to thrive in the globalization system, they'd better be damned good, otherwise Starbucks will run them out of business—and for good reason. Consumers deserve to consume good products. If the only reason to go to a local burger joint is to prevent the domination of McDonald's, then I'll have another Big Mac.

REFLECT & WRITE

- ❑ Notice how each writer relies upon a different understanding of "globalization" and what it means to be a member of such a radically changing society. Based on this, map out the points of each argument. How does each writer use concrete examples and structure his perspective through carefully chosen rhetorical appeals?
- ❑ Davicsin emphasizes the necessity of what he calls "visibility" and small establishments. How does his language create a favorable image for local stores in contrast to his disparagement of "blanket sameness" across the globe?
- ❑ How does Sklarsky structure his rebuttal? What points does he choose to refute and do you follow the logic of his conclusion? Which piece is more persuasive to you, and why?
- ❑ **Write.** Draft a response to both pieces, advancing beyond the debate between Davicsin and Sklarsky. Be certain to quote passages from both in your own article and offer your own argument about where we stand with regard to our participation or place in a global economy. Finally, where might you publish your composition?

In this humorous essay, **Paul Feine** *discusses the fearsome aspects of the McDonald's empire but concludes that Americans both at home and abroad just cannot live without the Golden Arches. Feine is director of Innovation for the Institute for Humane Studies at George Mason University. He published this piece in* aworldconnected.org, *a project committed to promoting conversations about how to achieve a free, peaceful, and prosperous world. Feine originally posted this article on his blog,* A World Connected.

McBastards: McDonald's and Globalization

Paul Feine

On a recent trip to Paris with my family, I was standing inside a McDonald's restaurant gazing out at the street as my wife ordered Le Happy Meal for our two-year old. My son at the time was happily tugging away at my hair from his perch in his baby backpack (one of the most significant technological innovations in recent history, to my mind).

We hadn't traveled to Paris with the intention of eating at McDonald's, but we were looking for a quick fix for our hungry little boy, and McDonald's represented a cheap alternative to the more traditional cafés. Typical Paris cafés are not only far more expensive, but as previous experience made clear, they tend to be filled with Parisians who are less than charmed by the presence of toddlers.

As I pondered the differing cultural attitudes toward children and stared out onto the busy Paris street, my gaze rested on an elderly French man, whom I instantly categorized as quintessentially French, complete with black beret, long black trench coat, and a cane. The man hobbled by the entrance to McDonald's, stopped, turned to look inside, spat loudly, and sneered "bastards," or its rough equivalent in French.

I sipped my coffee, which was very good (Café Jacques Vabre, I learned later), while our son used his pommes frites as a ketchup delivery device and my wife drank from bottle Evian. We both chuckled as I shared with her image of the authentic anti-McDonald's activist I had just witnessed.

McWhipping Boy

5 As the symbol for cultural imperialism and multinational corporate greed, McDonald's takes a lot of heat. McSpotlight, the anti-McDonald's website, for instance, boasts over one million hits per month. Critics

FIGURE 15.10 This McDonald's locates itself inside a mall, inviting children to sit on the bench next to Ronald.

demonize McDonald's for its unabashed pursuit of profits, its disregard for nutritional value and the environment, and the way it panders to children.

Most recently, McDonald's has been condemned for systematically seeking to addict naïve youngsters to its fatty fare, just like its evil older brothers in the cigarette business. In fact, crusading public interest lawyer John Banzhaf (whose van sports a license plate with a shortened version of "sue the bastards") is suing McDonald's in an attempt to hold them responsible for fast food addicts' health problems.

Indeed, though this multinational giant controls 43% of the US fast food market, McDonald's avarice seems to have no bounds. As Nick Gillespie of *Reason* magazine points out, "McDonald's is so desperate for customers that it's held prices essentially constant over the past two decades, while boosting portion sizes (burgers, fries, and drinks are all bigger than they used to be), expanding its menu, and building elaborate play structures for kids while simultaneously throwing increasingly sophisticated toys at them."

As anyone with small children knows, safe and secure McDonald's Playlands can be a dream come true, especially when you're stuck inside on a rainy day with kids who desperately need to burn some energy. Tiny plastic toys are received with as much delight as any large plastic toy they might have received last Christmas and, it must be emphasized, they're free.

Maybe, just maybe, McDonald's, in its unwavering pursuit of profits, has figured out the secret to succeeding in business—you've got to give the people what they want.

McCulture?

Okay, maybe McDonald's is fine for the US. Perhaps we're too value conscious, gluttonous, and superficial to care that our landscapes are littered with gleaming arches that have already polluted our bodies and our minds. But surely the same cannot be said for other societies around the world. Isn't it true that places that still have truly authentic dining experiences should be protected from the barbaric McHordes that are clamoring at their gates?

Golden Arches East, a recent book edited by James Watson, seeks to gain a better grasp on how McDonald's is affecting Asian culture. The results of this inquiry are in many ways surprising. For instance, one essay tells the story of an unintended and unanticipated consequence of McDonald's invasion of Hong Kong—the rest rooms in the city became cleaner.

FIGURE 15.11 This photo reveals the consistent "McCulture" of each store, in terms of the trademark colors and golden arches.

Before the first McDonald's opened up in the mid-1970s, restaurant restrooms in Hong Kong were notoriously dirty. Over time, the cleanliness standards of McDonald's were replicated by other restaurants eager to out-compete the increasingly popular restaurant.

In Korea, McDonald's established the practice of lining up in an orderly fashion to order food—the traditional custom, it seems, was to mob the counter.

When the first McDonald's was opened in Moscow, it was necessary for an employee to stand outside the McDonald's with a blow horn in order to explain to those in the queue that the smiling employees were not laughing at them but, rather, were pleased to serve them.

15 Moreover, and in contradistinction to the widespread assumption that McDonald's is having an implacably homogenizing effect on global culture, *Golden Arches East* is filled with examples of the pains McDonald's takes to appeal to the unique local tastes and customs of people around the world. My own experience with the decidedly leisurely attitude of McDonald's employees in southern Spain further attests to McDonald's ability to adapt to the local culture.

Is It True That No Two Countries with McDonald's Have Ever Gone to War?

Long before I'd enjoyed the Andalucian version of McDonald's, I traveled to Belgrade, in what was then Yugoslavia, and I must admit that I was ecstatic to see a sign for a recently opened McDonald's. I'd just spent a couple of months consuming nothing but souvlaki, salad, and Ouzo in Greece, and the very thought of Quarter-Pounder and a Coke made my mouth water.

My traveling buddy and I proceeded to wait in line for more than an hour and, as I stood happily munching on a french fry that brought back sweet memories of childhood Sunday-after-church treats, I looked across a sea of dark haired Yugoslavians into the eyes of two beautiful, blonde, obviously American women (actually it turned out they were Canadian nurses, but who am I to complain?). Absurdly, we waved to each other and fought through the crowd to greet one other like dear old friends. The memory of that day in Belgrade still brings a smile to my face.

Although you often hear people say it, it's not quite true that no two countries with McDonald's have ever gone to war—both the US and Serbia, for example, had McDonald's during the conflict between the two nations. But even if McDonald's isn't a kind of multinational for-profit god of peace, McDonald's does provide cheap food, decent coffee, and free entertainment for kids, not to mention a salad-in-a-cup for health-conscious parents.

Around the world, this increasingly popular symbol (like it or not) of America is encouraging healthy competition—competition that, in many cases, is leading to improved sanitation standards and civility. And sometimes, just sometimes, McDonald's even brings people together and creates a few smiles . . . just like its commercials say it does.

20 The bastards.

REFLECT & WRITE

- ❑ Why might Feine open his article with a personal narrative? How does this writing strategy help engage his audience and construct his persona? How does it establish a humorous style for his piece?
- ❑ What role do visual stereotypes play in this piece? Notice the description of the French man, the characterization of cigarette companies, and even the playland imagery used to depict McDonald's. How do you respond to these vivid descriptions as a reader?
- ❑ What do you learn about the research that Feine conducted to write this article? What new knowledge do you now have about McDonald's?
- ❑ Notice the turn in the argument. What do you make of the sudden shift in the thesis? Do you agree with his view or not? How does his stance on McDonald's make you think about its role in shaping our contemporary world? What does it mean to be "dear old friend" in the land of the Golden Arches?
- ❑ **Write.** Compose your own blog post about encountering McDonald's—either in your community or on a recent trip away from home. Be sure to include subtitles that indicate your argument as Feine did for his piece. Include images and structure your writing around a series of scenes. Use your blog title to indicate your argument about citizens in the kingdom of McDonald's.

Colleen Walsh *is a staff writer for the* Harvard Gazette, *where the following article appeared in May 2013. The piece profiles the efforts of one now-famous entrepreneur,* Salman Khan, *who harnesses open source technologies of the Web to make college-level classroom instruction available to anyone around the globe, free of charge, through his nonprofit enterprise,* the Khan Academy.

Education Without Limits

Colleen Walsh

When he was filling out the forms to establish his new nonprofit in 2008, Salman Khan paused at the mission statement section.

The Massachusetts Institute of Technology grad, a math and computer whiz with an M.B.A. from Harvard Business School, thought for a moment, and then jotted down a powerful response: "A free world-class education for anyone anywhere."

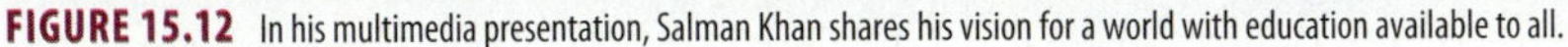
FIGURE 15.12 In his multimedia presentation, Salman Khan shares his vision for a world with education available to all.

With the academy, Khan told a crowded Radcliffe Gymnasium on Wednesday during an Askwith Forum sponsored by the Harvard Graduate School of Education, he hopes to advance a vision of education as "a fundamental human right."

He is well on his way. Khan Academy offers, at no cost, entertaining and informative videos, online lessons, and interactive software tools its founder hopes will help transform teaching and learning.

With Khan's digital tools, teachers can closely track student performance through a color-coded spreadsheet, identifying learners who are excelling and those who need help. Khan said his videos and tutorials also enable each learner to master introductory concepts at his or her own pace before moving on to harder topics.

"In a traditional academic model we group kids together usually by age . . . and then we move them all together at a set pace." Khan described the familiar process: a series of lectures and homework assignments, and then an exam to test students' knowledge and understanding.

Not all students do well on the test. Nonetheless, the entire class moves to a harder subject.

"Imagine if we applied that process to other parts of our life, say building a house," he said. If a contractor with limited time did the best job he or she could on a foundation and an inspector rated it 85 percent complete, he went on, no one would say: "Great, let's build a first floor!"

If that home topples, the first person held responsible is the contractor, much like the teacher in a classroom with struggling students. And while some teachers (and contractors) deserve the blame, more often it's the process that's at fault, said Khan. "You are artificially constraining how long someone had to work on something. And then when you inspected it and identified weaknesses, you just ignored them and moved on to the next thing, often with something that is going to build on the weaknesses that you just identified."

10 In Khan's model, struggling students receive the help they need, sometimes from peers who have mastered the material.

Early results are promising. Khan said his system is being used in a number of schools and charter networks in California. The data show students considered below average often "go on to become the best or second-best student in the class," he said.

In addition to the classroom benefits, the academy is also an effective "research tool in and of itself," Khan said.

With roughly 3 million exercises done on the site every day, Khan and his team of 40 researchers experiment with questions, adding comments, explanations, and sometimes even just an inspiring quote about the importance of flexing one's brain, in an effort to track what encourages learning.

Khan said his work also has implications for the developing world. While the nonprofit has traditionally more focused on English-speaking countries, it now has 7,000 videos in other languages, including Mandarin, Farsi, Bengali, and Portuguese, with plans to develop many more.

15 During a question-and-answer session, one listener asked Khan for his thoughts on the growing interest in online education, including Harvard's involvement with edX, a partnership with MIT that promotes Web-based, interactive study and learning.

"EdX we are very close to. Anant Agarwal [the edX president] is actually one of my former professors. So we want to coordinate with them as much as possible," he said.

The onetime financier walked the crowd through his organization's humble beginnings. In 2004 Khan was an analyst at a Boston hedge fund when he began helping his young niece with math via Internet and phone.

Word quickly spread that he was offering free tutoring. Soon he was working with a group of about 15 cousins and friends of the family. Khan started recording math tutorials in a closet in his home and posting them to YouTube.

Then his students told him they preferred the YouTube Khan to the real thing.

20 A little surprised, Khan realized their comments made perfect sense. "The first time you are learning a concept the last thing you need is someone standing right there saying 'It's easy, right?'"

Khan kept making videos, viewership spiked, and the positive reviews piled up.

"One woman wrote, 'My entire family prays for your entire family every night.' You have to put things into perspective. I was an analyst at a hedge fund. There was not a lot of prayer going on. Well, at least in that way," joked Khan.

Khan quit his job in 2009 and devoted his time to fundraising for the new project. His finances and prospects looked dire several months in, until an enthusiastic donor gave him $10,000. They met, he described his vision, and 10 minutes after they parted she wired him another $100,000.

"So that's a good day."

25 Other good days followed, including a meeting with Microsoft's Bill Gates, who became a major backer, as did Google. Today Khan's nonprofit reaches millions of students a day and is used in 30,000 classrooms around the world.

The morning assembly was also something of a recruiting session. Following the talk, Khan, who'd encouraged those interested in careers at his academy to stick around, drew a crowd.

REFLECT & WRITE

- ❑ Take a close look at Figure 15.12, the visual that accompanies this article. What does it suggest about the rhetorical strategies Salman Khan uses to make the argument that education is "a fundamental human right"? How does the solo image of the nearly naked child evoke *pathos*? How does *logos* enter through the words on the bottom of the slide? Why might Khan choose this image to go beside his company icon and how does it build his *ethos?*

- ☐ In making the case for "education without limits," Khan compares the role of the teacher to that of a contractor tasked with building a house: "If that home topples, the first person held responsible is the contractor, much like the teacher in a classroom with struggling students." In your view, does this analogy accurately reflect what the role of a teacher actually involves?
- ☐ "The Khan Academy," Walsh notes, "offers, at no cost, entertaining and informative videos, online lessons, and interactive software tools its founder hopes will help transform teaching and learning." How might this new vision of education open doors for people with less access to such resources to become members of an educated community? What can you imagine would be the benefits of such globally-expansive and technologically-based educational communities? What might be the downsides?
- ☐ **Write.** For generations, the promise of the American Dream—that anyone can be successful through education and hard work—has been compromised by real economic obstacles restricting those who can't afford higher education. But with new digital tools such as those used by the Khan Academy, as well as the emergence of MOOCs (Massive Online Open Courses), these boundaries might just be falling away. Compose two position papers in which you argue for and against the expansion of education to include all interested global citizens. Then, find common ground between these two sides using Rogerian argument, and develop a concluding position that marshalls empathy to offer a final view on this issue of "education without limits."

Seeing Connections: For guidelines on Rogerian argument, see Chapter 3.

ANALYZING PERSPECTIVES ON THE ISSUE

1. Compare how Center for American Progress infographics (Figure 15.3) and Sulzberger's *New York Times* profile of immigration and small town life make use of research. While the format of each—image versus feature article—is quite different, in many ways their arguments are complementary. What points of convergence can you discover? How does the strategic reliance on research evidence help each text make its points persuasively? Which format appeals to you most?
2. Consider the views of Thomas Friedman and Stephen Steinlight on immigration's benefit to the American economy. Which writing strategies do you admire more? How convincing is each argument? Can you read the Lexington piece as a third perspective on this issue? Now, write your own article as a fourth response to this issue. Be sure to quote from all the previous pieces and also to use evidence or case studies from your own life or community.

3. Which texts in this chapter seem to be in direct conversation with each other? What do you think Mark Rice-Oxley would say in response to the piece by Paul Feine? How does the feature on Salman Khan broaden out the very notion of "citizenship" to a more global context and how could you see his slide (Figure 15.12) as a visual response to the stereotypical image that opened the chapter with the word, "Caution" (Figure 15.1)? What can you learn from these various strategies of argument and how they work as a collection?
4. Examine the visuals throughout this chapter. How do road signs, memes, data visualizations, documentary photographs, and slideshows reveal or extend the controversies covered by the articles? What additional images would you add to this chapter to capture and convey issues of civil rights, citizenship, expanding opportunities, and changing communities?

FROM READING TO RESEARCH ASSIGNMENTS

1. Select one of the subtopics within this chapter on "Claiming Citizenship." It could be the fight for marriage equality, the battle concerning immigration, local attitudes concerning English-only or second-language signage, globalization and its effects on the American economy and American identity, or the new technology wave in education. Conduct research by looking up the subtopic through the search strategies you learned in Chapter 5. Once you have five to six additional sources on the topic, read them and take notes. Develop a thesis for your own stance, and compose a research-based argument that includes the sources you have located but emphasizes your own contribution to the conversation.
2. Review the photos by Alex Webb on immigration (Figures 15.5–15.8). Then, make a storyboard that will help you create your own visual argument about immigration. Conduct field research by interviewing members of your community. After arranging and editing your materials, create a video montage that reveals, in moving photos, your stance. You might also forge a "Director's Cut" that includes your voice-over, explaining the rationale for your images, interviews, and scenes, as well as your indebtedness to the work of Webb.
3. In what ways is America expanding beyond its borders? Consider the views on globalization and the new developments in education. How might the two intersect? What will the future of the world "look like" in terms of who works with whom and what hubs of connection bring people into shared spaces? Compose an op-ed targeted for publication in your school newspaper. Illustrate your thesis about this broader notion of "citizenship" with an accompanying drawing.

CREDITS

Images

Page 1: Reuters Photographer/Reuters
Figure 1.1: Mike Luckovich Editorial Cartoon used with the permission of Mike Luckovich and Creators Syndicate. All rights reserved.
Figure 1.2: The Advertising Archives
Figure 1.3: AF archive/Alamy
Figure 1.4: Tribune Content Agency, LLC. All Rights Reserved. Reprinted with permission.
Figure 1.7: Reynolds/Dan/CartoonStock
Figure 1.7: Clay Bennett Editorial Cartoon used with the permission of Clay Bennett, the Washington Post Writers Group and the Cartoonist Group. All rights reserved.
Figure 1.10: Cartoon by Scott McCloud - Understanding comics, with the permission of HarperCollins.
Figure 1.11: Nate Beeler/Cagle Cartoons, Inc.
Figure 1.12: Mike Thompson/Creators Syndicate
Figure 1.13: ©Copyright 2013 John Cole - All Rights Reserved./ Cagle Cartoons, Inc.
Figure 1.14: Daryl Cagle/Cagle Cartoons Inc.
Figure 1.15: Michael Ramirez/Creators Syndicate
Figure 1.16: ©Copyright 2012 John Cole - All Rights Reserved/Cagle Cartoons, Inc.
Page 34: Khalil Bendib
Figure 2.1: Christine Alfano
Figure 2.2: Anheuser-Busch/Splash/Corbis
Figure 2.3: © 2013 The LEGO Group.
Figure 2.4: Merrill Edge's IRA/Bank of America
Figure 2.6: Christine Alfano
Figure 2.6: Juan Carlos/Bloomberg via Getty Images
Figure 2.6: Natan Dvir/Polaris/Newscom
Figure 2.9: The Advertising Archives
Figure 3.1: AP Photo/Eric Gay
Figure 3.2: Margaret Bourke-White/Masters/ Time Life Pictures/Getty Images
Figure 3.3: Library of Congress Prints and Photographs Division Washington, DC
Figure 3.4: Library of Congress Prints and Photographs Division[LC-USZ62-95653]
Figure 3.5: Todd Heisler/Polaris Images
Figure 3.6: Library of Congress Prints and Photographs Division
Figure 3.7: Library of Congress Prints and Photographs Division
Figure 3.8: Library of Congress Prints and Photographs Division
Figure 3.9: Library of Congress Prints and Photographs Division
Figure 3.10: Susan Walsh/AP Images
Figure 3.11: Anchorage Daily News, with permission of PARS International Corp.
Figure 3.12: Deseret Morning News Archives
Figure 3.13: Library of Congress Prints and Photographs Division
Figure 3.14: Reuters Photographer/Reuters
Page 108: Thomas Hoepker/Magnum Photos
Page 115: Everett Collection
Figure 4.1: White House.gov
Figure 4.2: Hoover Institution Archives
Figure 4.3: National Archives and Records Administration
Figure 4.4: National Archives and Records Administration
Figure 4.5: National Archives and Records Administration
Figure 4.6: top center: National Archives and Records Administration
Figure 4.6: top right: Library of Congress Prints and Photographs Division
Figure 4.6: bottom right: Gianni Dagli Orti/The Art Archive at Art Resource, NY
Figure 4.6: bottom left: The Advertising Archives
Figure 4.7: top left: National Archives and Records Administration
Figure 4.7: top right: Library of Congress Prints and Photographs Division
Figure 4.7: bottom right: Gianni Dagli Orti/The Art Archive at Art Resource, NY
Figure 4.7: bottom left: The Advertising Archives
Figure 4.8: Library of Congress Prints and Photographs Division
Figure 4.9: Alexandra Fischer
Figure 4.10: Alexandra Fischer
Figure 4.11: Occupy Los Angeles by Lalo Alcaraz
Page 131: Library of Congress Prints and Photographs Division Washington [LC-DIG-ppmsca-02037]
Figure 5.1: Nevada Wier/Corbis
Figure 5.2: PRNewsFoto/NEWSWEEK
Figure 5.3: Steve Bronstein/Stone/Getty Images
Figure 5.4: Bonestell LLC/Paul Allen
Figure 5.6: Getty Images
Figure 5.6: Stem Cells, March 2006 cover AlphaMed Press. Reproduced with permission of Wiley, Inc.
Figure 6.1: Copyright © by Universal City Studios, Inc. Courtesy of Universal Studios Publishing Rights, a division of Universal Studios Licensing, Inc. All Rights Reserved.
Figure 6.3: top: TM & Copyright ©20th Century Fox. All rights reserved/Courtesy Everett Collection
Figure 6.3: center: Everett Collection
Figure 6.3: bottom: TM & Copyright ©20th Century Fox. All rights reserved/Courtesy Everett Collection
Figure 6.4: Sundance Selects/Everett Collection
Figure 7.1: Justin Cone
Figure 7.2: Christine Alfano
Figure 7.3: Christine Alfano
Page 246: Christine Alfano
Page 251: AP Photos/KEVORK DJANSEZIAN
Figure 8.1: Alyssa J O'Brien
Figure 8.7: The Advertising Archives
Figure 8.8: Alyssa J O'Brien
Figure 8.9: left: Alyssa J O'Brien
Figure 8.9: right: Alyssa J O'Brien
Figure 8.10: left: Alyssa J O'Brien
Figure 8.10: center: Alyssa J O'Brien
Figure 8.10: right: Alyssa J O'Brien
Figure 8.11: left: AP Photos/Farah Abdi Warsameh
Figure 8.11: top right: Ulrich Doering/Alamy
Figure 8.11: bottom right: Richard Lord/Alamy
Figure 9.1: AP Photos/KEVORK DJANSEZIAN
Page 288: left: AP Photos/Vince Bucci, Pool
Page 288: center: epa european pressphoto agency b.v./Alamy
Page 288: right: AP Photos/Brian Snyder, Pool
Figure 9.2: Stefan Wermuth/Reuters /Landov Media
Figure 9.3: AP Photos/Paul Sakuma
Figure 9.4: Pete Souza/White House/Handout/ Corbis
Figure 9.5: top: Courtesy of Professor Fred Turner
Figure 9.5: bottom: Adam Bouska, NOH8 campaign
Figure 9.11: top: Christine Alfano
Figure 9.12: Christine Alfano
Figure 9.13: Christine Alfano
Figure 9.14: Bettmann/Corbis
Figure 9.15: Topham/The Image Works
Figure 9.16: Christine Alfano
Figure 9.17: Christine Alfano
Figure 10.1: Magnolia Pictures/Everett Collection
Figure 10.2: top left: Laura Thal
Figure 10.3: top right: HaYoung Shin
Figure 10.4: bottom: Caroline M. Grant
Figure 10.10: top: Peter Menzel Photography
Figure 10.11: bottom: Peter Menzel Photography
Figure 10.12: top: Peter Menzel Photography
Figure 10.13: bottom: Peter Menzel Photography
Page 319: Peggie Peattie/The San Diego Union-Tribune/Zuma Press
Figure 11.1: Google, Inc
Figure 11.2: Mick Stevens/The New Yorker Collection/www.cartoonbank.com
Figure 11.3: all: Pearson Education
Figure 11.4a: left: Robbie Cooper
Figure 11.4b: right: Robbie Cooper
Figure 11.5a: left: Robbie Cooper
Figure 11.5b: right: Robbie Cooper
Figure 11.6a: left: Robbie Cooper
Figure 11.6b: right: Robbie Cooper
Figure 11.7: www.xkcd.com
Page 442: Evolving Ideals of Male Body Image as Seen Through Action Toys, Harrison G. Pope, Jr., Robert Olivardia, Amanda Gruber and John Borowiecki, *International Journal of Eating Disorders*, 1999 (~2484 words), John Wiley & Sons. Reproduced with permission of Wiley Inc.
Page 443: Evolving Ideals of Male Body Image as Seen Through Action Toys, Harrison G. Pope, Jr., Robert Olivardia, Amanda Gruber and John Borowiecki, *International Journal of Eating Disorders*, 1999 (~2484 words), John Wiley & Sons. Reproduced with permission of Wiley Inc.
Figure 12.1: Dana Heinemann/Shutterstock
Figure 12.2: Alyssa O'Brien
Figure 12.3: Rebecka Silvekroon
Figure 12.6: National Eating Disorders Association
Figure 12.7: Advertising Archives

Figure 12.8: Guy Cali/Fogstock/Glowimages
Figure 13.1: top: NIKE Inc.
Figure 13.2: center: NIKE Inc.
Figure 13.3: bottom: NIKE Inc.
Figure 13.4: AP Photo/Eugene Hoshiko
Figure 13.5: Tim Tadder/Corbis
Figure 13.6: Jonathan Shapiro, www.zapiro.com/ BERG + BACH B.V.
Figure 13.7: left: Bob Martin/Sports Illustrated/ Getty Images
Figure 13.8: right: Mike Powell/Sports Illustrated/Getty Images
Figure 14.1: Chris O'Brien
Figure 14.2: Chris O'Brien
Figure 14.3: AP Photo/STR
Figure 14.4: top: Samuel Rigelhaupt/Sipa USA/ AP Images
Figure 14.5: bottom: Navid Baraty
Figure 14.6: David Leeson/Dallas Morning News
Figure 14.7: top: David Leeson/Dallas Morning News
Figure 14.8: bottom: David Leeson/Dallas Morning News
Figure 14.9: David Leeson/Dallas Morning News
Figure 14.10: left: Matthew Christopher
Figure 14.11: right: Matthew Christopher
Figure 14.12: AP Photo/Shizuo Kambayashi
Page 517: Charles Porter/ZUMA Press
Page 518: Charles Porter/ZUMA Press
Figure 15.1: James Steidl/Shutterstock.com
Figure 15.2: Library of Congress
Figure 15.4a: top: Austin Jenkins, Northwest News Network
Figure 15.4b: bottom: Library of Congress Prints and Photographs Division [LC-DIG-ppmsca-19754]
Figure 15.5: top: Alex Webb/Magnum Photos
Figure 15.6: bottom: Alex Webb/Magnum Photos
Figure 15.7: top: Alex Webb/Magnum Photos
Figure 15.8: bottom: Alex Webb/Magnum Photos
Figure 15.9: Kevin Kal Kallaugher, The Economist, caltoons.com
Figure 15.10: Najlah Feanny/Corbis News/ Corbis
Figure 15.11: Ramin Talaie/Corbis News/ Corbis
Figure 15.12: Stephanie Mitchell/Harvard University Gazette

Text

Heidi Przybyla, "Giffords Shooting in Arizona May Cool U.S. Political Rhetoric, Hurt Palin," in Bloomberg.com, January 10, 2011.
Craig Schulz, "Mike Thompson, what's the point," *Detroit Free Press.*
Karl Rove, "After Four Bleak Obama Years, an Opportunity," © 2013.
Aristotle, "Rhetoric," *The History and Theory of Rhetoric.*
This paper was presented as a public lecture at Cornell University in November 1966 and at the University of Washington in April 1967. p. 4 Lloyd Bitzer.
Andrea Lunsford.
This paper was presented as a public lecture at Cornell University in November 1966 and at the University of Washington in April 1967. p. 4.
Lily Rothman, "Star Wars Fans React," *Time,* http: //entertainment.time.com/2012/10/31/star-wars-fans-react-the-best-tweets-about-disney-deal-for-lucasfilm/slide//
Quoted in Moore.
Doug Marlette, "I Was a Tool of Satan" *Columbia Journalism Review* (Nov./Dec. 2003): 52.
Political Communication 19 (2002): 251-272.
Sophie Shank.
Barbara Morrill, "Violent rhetoric and the attempted assassination of Gabrielle Giffords," *Daily Kos,* January 11, 2011, http: //www.dailykos.com/story/2011/01/10/934955/-Violent-rhetoric-and-the-attempted-assassination-of-Gabrielle-Giffords#."
Bogost, Ian, *Persuasive Games: The Expressive Power of Videogames,* pp. excerpt: 334 words, copyright 2007 Massachusetts Institute of Technology, by permission of The MIT Press.
"When your cable company keeps you on hold, you get angry…" DIRECTV.
From *Slate,* April 19, 2013, © 2013 The Slate Group. All rights reserved. Used by permission and protected by the Copyright Laws of the United States. The printing, copying, redistribution, or retransmission of this Content without express written permission is prohibited.
"Minority Presence and Protrayal in Mainstream Magazine Advertising: An Update" *Journalism and Mass Communications* © 1997, Association for Education in Journalism & Mass Communication.
Gloria Steinem, "Sex, Lies, and Advertising," *Ms. Magazine,* July 1990.
Geoffrey Dunn, "Photographic License," *San Luis Obispo Times,* © 2002.
Lindsay Funk, "Rand Paul Asks Does Foreign Aid Make Us Safer? Yes, It Does," Policymic.com, http: //www.policymic.com/articles/29625/rand-paul-asks-does-foreign-aid-make-us-safer-yes-it-does
Richard B Woodward, "One 9/11 Picture, Thousands of Words: Rorschach of Meanings," *The Wall Street Journal,* © 2006.
*Winterthur Portfolio: A Journal of American Material Culture,*University of Chicago Press.
"The Hoop Life," CNN.
Rhetoric & Public Affairs, V. 8, n. 4,University of Michigan Press.
Michael Zeligs
Bries Deerrose
Tommy Tsai
Reproduced by permission of Molly Fehr.
National Institutes of Health.
David Pinner
Amanda Johnson
Schulte, Bret. Saying it in Cinema. *U.S. News and World Report.*
Joseph Bast, "Gorgeous Propaganda Frightening Truth," *Heartland Perspectives*
Dexian Cai
Italian Neorealism and Global Cinema, Detroit: Wayne State UP, Laura E. Ruberto.
Italian Neorealism and Global Cinema, Detroit: Wayne State UP, 2007.
"How I Write Interview," Stanford Writing Center, Stanford University, 17 November 2003.
Bird by Bird: Some Instructions on Writing and Life. New York: Anchor, 1995.
Wan Jin Park
Secretary General Kofi Anan (Nielsen).
The Case of An Incovenient Truth," *Quarterly Journal of Speech* 95.1 (2009): 1–19. Communication and Mass Media Complete. EBSCO.
Wan Jin Park
Argumentation & Advocacy 44.2 (2007): 90-109. Communication and Mass Media Complete. EBSCO.
Wan Jin Park
Paramount Classics.
Quarterly Journal of Speech 95.01.
Wan Jin Park
Wan Jin Park
CNN.
Michael Rothenberg
Architectural Record.
Evaluation of Innovative Design Proposals. New York: New Visions.
Online Dialogues.
Stephanie Parker
"Why We Argue About Virtual Community" Jones.
Pew Internet and American Life Project, 12 December 2001.
Soompi. Started 1 September 2008.
Digitizing Race: Visual Cultures of the Internet. University of Minnesota Press, 2008.
Daniel Shim.
Online Interview. 25 October.http: //www.causes.com/
Alfano and O'Brien, http: //mirandarose.wix.com/march-on-washington
Dan Howell, http: //www.youtube.com/user/danisnotonfire
Power Pack being Awesome, in SuperBetter (https: //www.superbetter.com/). Used by permission.
Molly Cunningham
What's Wrong with the Body Shop?, McSpotlight, http: //www.mcspotlight.org/beyond/companies/bodyshop.html
Body Shop Mission Statement.
Quoted in 1996 Body Shop publication "Our Agenda."
Anita Roddick, speech at Academy of Management, Vancouver August 1995.
The Advertising Archives for The Body Shop
Miranda Smith
Barack Obama, 2004 Democratic National Convention Keynote Speech
Johnny Cochran.
Nicholas Spears
Morgan Springer
Natalie Farrell
Natalie Farrell
Carlos Ortiz and Jonathan Hwang
Stephen Shugart.
Kate Murphy, "First Camera, Then Fork," *The New York Times,* April 7, 2010
Michael Pollan, "How Change Is Going to Come in the Food System." Reprinted with permission from the November 14, 2005 issue of *The Nation.* For subscription information, call 1-800-333-8536. Portions of each week's *Nation* magazine can be accessed at http://www.thenation.com.

"Can Biotech Food Cure World Hunger," *The New York Times*, October 26, 2009

Delivery Let's Move Lunch, Washington, D.C., February 9, 2010 (~ 4435 words).

USDA

USDA

USDA

USDA

Courtesy of Mother Nature Network (www.mnn.com).

Taylor Clark, "Meatless Like Me," *Slate*, May 7, 2008

James McWilliams, "The Green Monster: Could Frankenfoods be Good for the Environment," *Slate*, January 28, 2009

Christine Eriksen, "The Social Psychology of the Selfie," *Mashable*, February 12, 2013.

Robbie Copper, "Profiles," Alter Ego: Avatars and their Creators, 2007.

Amanda Lenhart, et al., "Teens, Kindness and Cruelty on Social Network Sites; Part 2, Section 1," *Pew Internet*, November 9, 2011

Amanda Lenhart, et al., Figure: Mostly kind, from "Teens, Kindness and Cruelty on Social Network Sites; Part 2, Section 1," *Pew Internet*, November 9, 2011

Amanda Lenhart, et al., Figure: How peers treat one another, from "Teens, Kindness and Cruelty on Social Network Sites; Part 2, Section 1," *Pew Internet*, November 9, 2011

Amanda Lenhart, et al., Figure: Word cloud how people behave, from "Teens, Kindness and Cruelty on Social Network Sites; Part 2, Section 1," *Pew Internet*, November 9, 2011

Amanda Lenhart, et al., Figure: Word cloud how people should behave, from "Teens, Kindness and Cruelty on Social Network Sites; Part 2, Section 1," *Pew Internet*, November 9, 2011

danah boyd and Alice Marwick, "Social Privacy in Networked Publics: Teens' Attitudes, Practices, and Strategies," Paper for 2011 Symposium on the Dynamics of the Internet and Society

Clive Thompson, "I'm So Totally, Digitally Close to You," *The New York Times*, September 7, 2008

Silverblatt, Art. "Twitter as Newspeak" by Art Silverblatt, *St. Louis Journalism Review*, September/October 2009. Reprinted by permission.

Morozov, Evgeny, "Slacktivism to Activism." Copyright © 2009. Reprinted with permission of the author.

COURTESY: DANIEL TERDIMAN

Newzcrew. Screen shot from Ayiti: The Cost of Life in http:/www.ayiti.newzcrew.org/globalkids/. Used with Permission.

Breakthrough

'Reproduced from *Campaign* magazine with the permission of the copyright owner, Haymarket Media Group.'

What if Barbie Was an Actual Person? © John Riviello

What if Barbie Was an Actual Person? © John Riviello

"Distorted Images" by Susan McClelland, *Maclean's*, August 14 2000, vol 13., no.33. p. 41–42

Elino Frankel, "Should America Follow Israel's Example and Ban Too-Thin Models?," Divine Caroline, http://www.divinecaroline.com/self/should-america-follow-israels-example-and-ban-too-thin-models

Pamela Abbott & Francesca Sapsford, "Clothing the Young Female Body," from *Through the Wardrobe: Women's Relationships with Their Clothes*, Ed. Ali Guy © 2001

Evolving Ideas of Male Body Image as Seen Through Action Toys,. Harrison G. Pope Jr. et. al. 1999 in *International Journal of Eating Disorders*.

Kim Franke-Folsted, "GI Joes' Big Biceps are Not a Big Deal," *Rocky Mountain News*, May 24, 1999

"Beards of Silicon Valley," *Wired.* com, http://www.wired.com/wiredenterprise/2012/11/20-12-st_beardtaxonomy/

Beards of Silicon Valley © Kalsey Dake

Carla Filomena Silva & P. David Howe, "The (In)validity of Supercrip Representation of Paralympian Athletes," *Journal of Sport and Social Issues*, January 26, 2012

Thad Mumford, "The New Minstrel Show: Black Vaudeville with Statistics," *The New York Times*, May 2004

© 2012, *ESPN The Magazine*. Reprinted courtesy of ESPN.

Dave Zirin, "Say It Ain't So, Big Leagues." Reprinted with permission from the November 14, 2005 issue of *The Nation*. For subscription information, call 1-800-333-8536. Portions of each week's *Nation* magazine can be accessed at http://www.thenation.com.

Robert Lipsyte, "Jocks vs. Pukes." Reprinted with permission from the August 15, 2011 issue of *The Nation*. For subscription information, call 1-800-333-8536. Portions of each week's *Nation* magazine can be accessed at http://www.thenation.com.

The State of Women's Athletics, 40 Years After Title IX by Dusenber & Lee: (c) 2012, Foundation for National Progress.

Graphic 1, College Male Athletes vs. College Female Athletes from "The State of Women's Athletics, 40 Years After Title IX" by Dusenber & Lee: (c) 2012, Foundation for National Progress.

Graphic 2, Median Spending per Athlete, NCAA Div I FBS Schools from "The State of Women's Athletics, 40 Years After Title IX" by Dusenber & Lee: (c) 2012, Foundation for National Progress.

Graphic 3, % Teams Coached by Men vs % Teams Coached by Women from "The State of Women's Athletics, 40 Years After Title IX" by Dusenber & Lee: (c) 2012, Foundation for National Progress.

Graphic 4, Network Air Time Breakdown for Men's and Women's Sports Teams from "The State of Women's Athletics, 40 Years After Title IX" by Dusenber & Lee: (c) 2012, Foundation for National Progress.

Playing Unfair transcript © Media Education Foundation

Shannon Ryan, "Banking on Beauty Trying to Expand Fan Base by Marketing Its Players, the WNBA for the First Time Offers Rookies Lessons in Fashion and Makeup," *The Chicago Tribune*, May 4, 2008

The WNBA identifications reproduced herein are used with permission from WNBA Enterprises, LLC (c) 2010 WNBA Enterprises, LLC. All rights reserved.

Paul Mark Pedersen, "Examining Equity in Newspaper Photographs: A Content Analysis of the Print Media Photographic Coverage of Interscholastic Athletics." *International Review for the Sociology of Sport* December 2002 vol. 37 no. 3–4 303-318.

Copyright (c) 2006, by Daniel Okrent.

Mark Glaser, "Did London Bombings Turn Citizen Journalists into Citizen Paparazzi?," *Online Journalism Review*, July 13, 2005

David Leeson, "Visual and Verbal Reading," *Photographs and Stories*, March 2005

"Pros and Cons of Embedded Journalism," *Online NewsHour Extra*, March 27, 2003. © 2003 MacNeil/ Lehrer Productions. Reprinted with permission.

Reprinted by permission of SLL/Sterling Lord Literistic, Inc. Copyright by Mark Binelli

© James Nactwey

Porter, Charles. "Picture Power: Tragedy in Oklahoma," *BBC NEWS ONLINE*, May 9, 2005. Reprinted by permission of the author.

Strupp, Joe. "The Photo Felt Around the World," *EDiTOR & PUBLISHER*, May 1995, © Nelson Business Media, Inc. Reprinted by permission.

Drea Knufken, "Help, We're Drowning! Please Pay Attention to Our Disaster," *SALON*, September 13, 2013

AG Sulzberger, "Hispanics Reviving Faded Towns on the Plains," *The New York Times*

Print: "Infographic: The New Demographics." This material was published by the Center for American Progress. online: "Infographic: The New Demographics." This material was created by the Center for American Progress (www.americanprogress.org) in the following link http://www.americanprogress.org/issues/race/news/2011/04/04/9471/infographic-the-new-demographics/

Thomas Friedman, "America's Real Dream Team," *The New York Times*, March 21, 2010

Stephen Steinlight, "Thomas L. Friedman: Foe of Open-Borders and 'Comprehensive Immigration Reform'?" *Curious Times*, OP-ED, March 26, 2010

From Lexington, "The Hub Nation," *THE ECONOMIST*. © The Economist Newspaper Limited, London 2010. Used by permission.

By Mark Rice-Oxley. Reprinted with permission from the January 15, 2004 issue of *The Christian Science Monitor*. © 2004 The Christian Science Monitor (www.CSMonitor.com).

Joseph Daviscin, "Corporations Leave Small Business Behind," *The Daily Targum*, October 16, 2002.

Jeremy Sklarsky, " Globalization or McDonaldization?" *The Daily Targum*, October 17, 2002.

Paul Feine, "McBastards: McDonald's and Globalization," AworldConnected.org

Colleen Walsh, "Education Without Limits," *Harvard Gazette*, May 9, 2013

INDEX

A

D

E

H

I

N

Q

R

S

T

U

V

W

Y

Z